CW00829212

PLAYING THE
GREAT
GAME

PLAYING THE
GREAT GAME

BRITAIN, WAR AND POLITICS IN AFGHANISTAN SINCE 1839

Edmund Yorke

ROBERT HALE · LONDON

© Edmund Yorke 2012
First published in Great Britain 2012

ISBN 978-0-7090-9196-7

Robert Hale Limited
Clerkenwell House
Clerkenwell Green
London EC1R 0HT

www.halebooks.com

A catalogue record for this book is available from the British Library

2 4 6 8 10 9 7 5 3 1

Typeset by e-type, Liverpool
Printed in Great Britain by the MPG Books Group,
Bodmin and King's Lynn

Contents

For Louise, Madeleine and Emily

Foreword

Brigadier (Retired) Ed Butler CBE DSO

On the 31 July 2006 I noted in my brigade's monthly report back to London that there had only been three days in the preceding thirty-one when we had not hosted a senior military officer, government minister or international official in the British Task Force Headquarters. While on the one hand this was a huge drain on our already stretched helicopter fleet, we recognized the criticality (without putting it too strongly) of educating each and every one of these visitors about the complexities of the tribal tapestry we were immersed in, the ferocity of the resurgent Taliban encountering us, the excessive demands of the harsh environment on men, machines and equipment, the chameleon nature of the Afghan and the fact that we were 'red lining' on all our key equipment needs – be they helicopter hours, surveillance assets, our inappropriate vehicle fleet, shortfalls of specialist natures of ammunition right down to individual items such as pistols and tourniquets. They had many questions for my commanders and team; likewise us for them. The resource deficiencies we had highlighted back in 2005 were now coming home to roost.

However, one question none of them could answer was what success looked like for the ordinary Afghan – the Afghan we had supposedly come to help and make a difference for. The majority of these Afghans were living in almost medieval times and on a subsistence economy. When I pressed these VIPs, many of them responsible for our very strategy for being in Helmand Province, on whether we should try and bring the benefits of an agricultural, industrial, manufacturing or high-tech revolution to the Afghan farmer no one could answer. Further silence when I said that, like their western counterparts, the majority of the ordinary menfolk of Helmand were linked to the global highway (and therefore the twenty-first century) by the mobile phone. I suggested that until this fundamental question was answered we, the military, would not be able to contribute fully to the much-needed Investment Appraisal – one which detailed the political ends, ways and means to resolving this latest, intractable Great Game.

Throughout this comprehensive and knowledgeable account of Britain's four Afghan wars, Dr Yorke consistently and expertly highlights the tensions that exist between the military high command and their political masters. Clausewitz observed that 'war is the continuation of politics by other means', but as Edmund Yorke reveals again and again, in his fascinating new account of successive British engagements in Afghanistan, these military and economic means must be made available to deliver the stated political ends – and within realistic timescales. But if these political ends are never clearly articulated, and more importantly, no-one in government knows what success and failure looks like, then how can military commanders ever be expected to contribute to victory; or as we read in *Playing the Great Game*, prevent defeat?

So much of what I read in Yorke's in-depth study of British engagements in Afghanistan rang true from my time as the first Commander of British Forces in Southern Afghanistan in 2006. Foremost among these were the failures of our politicians to consider the lessons of history; be it the near defeat of the British Army at the Battle of Maiwand in 1880 (NATO forces were very close to a similar defeat on the same piece of ground in the summer of 2006) to the political misjudgements of Alexander Burnes in the First Afghan War, the lack of strategic thinking in our short engagement in the Third Afghan conflict to the present day campaign where successive Secretaries of State have failed to articulate a deliverable and sustainable end-state. Furthermore, Dr Yorke stresses the influence and role that indigenous Afghan forces have played in our exit strategy of each of these four campaigns; always a high risk approach as it has always been said that you can only ever hire an Afghan, as you will never be able to win him over.

Edmund Yorke has had access to many new, unpublished source materials on all four wars. This provides intriguing insights into the some of the key characters, the decisions they took and the vigorous debates between generals and envoys (no different from some of my heated arguments with the politicos in the long hot summer of 2006 than it was in say the 1840s between the Political Envoy William Hay MacNaghten and General Elphinstone). Yorke's use of new maps and war diaries and revised assessments of all the major battles (underpinned by our studies of the Soviet invasion and occupation) show that we have fought time and again over the same range of Afghan mountains. Interestingly, the Afghan's tactics have not changed much over the last 180 years; ours have generally been slow to adapt.

On a final note, I remember vividly an exchange I had in 2008 with a General Auschev (a retired Russian general who had spent four years commanding troops in Afghanistan, culminating in him being awarded the

Hero of Russia), where we discussed and agreed on 90 per cent of our views on the problems and solutions of Afghanistan. At the end of our meeting in Moscow, he turned to me and said: 'You and the Americans are just like we were in the 1980s – arrogant, not prepared to seek advice and thinking that we could defeat the Afghans with our superior Soviet military might. However, like us, you never listened. And now, you are making all the same mistakes!' Yorke's account of all four wars highlights these mistakes, be they military or political. If only his book had been available in 2001 and was required reading for all government ministers, officials and senior officers ... then again, knowing the history and insurmountable challenges of Afghanistan, which has been the graveyard of careers, predictions and too many men's lives, would it have made a difference?

Brigadier (Retired) Ed Butler CBE DSO
Commander British Forces Afghanistan

Preface and Acknowledgements

The danger of delegating too much of your Power to the Army must never be forgotten. If you abate of your authority over them, inconvenience and uneasiness to yourselves may not be the only consequences.

Lord Robert Clive to Calcutta Secret Committee, 17 January 1767, British Library, Oriental and India Office Collections (encl. in G. J. Bryant, Civil-Military Relations in Early British India, 1750–85, JSAHR)

War in general and the commander in any specific instance, is entitled to require that the trends and designs of policy shall not be inconsistent with these means.

M. Howard and P. Paret (eds) *Carl von Clausewitz: On War* (Princeton, 1976)

The main purpose of this book is to both discuss and analyze the political-military interface within the specific framework of Britain's four Afghan conflicts and especially in the context of the nineteenth-century diplomatic struggle between Britain and Russia commonly known as the 'Great Game'. The friction or tension generated by all these wars between the 'politicals' (the Raj diplomatic or civil service and currently, since the demise of the Raj, the London metropole) and the military establishment will, for the first time, be explored in detail. Under this structural umbrella there will be a special focus upon the causes and impact of the twin nineteenth-century disasters of Kabul (1841–2) and Maiwand (1880) as well as recent crises in the Afghan conflict of our time, notably the initial stages of the 'Herrick' campaign in Helmand in 2006. This book will seek to argue that excessive political interference or simply political negligence in regard to military operations, often resource-driven, has consistently contributed to serious, sometimes fatal failures in British policy towards Afghanistan over the past 170 years.

It will be shown that the failure of British politicians to sufficiently resource and manage the Anglo-Afghan conflicts, the first two of which were initiated and driven by the local imperial authorities, constituted a primary reason for a series of setbacks to British arms. Until recently, shortages to manpower and materials in all four wars and a failure to harness and deploy collaborators effectively were some of the most significant of many political shortfalls that became apparent and will be addressed. Above all, the consistent inability of politicians to sustain corporate intelligence, to understand the complex ethnicity of Afghanistan and thereby win hearts and minds will be highlighted. In the telling words of Lieutenant-General Aurakzai, the governor of North West Province of Pakistan, commenting in 2006 on the current Afghan conflict:

> Bring 50,000 more troops and fight for ten to fifteen years and you won't resolve it ... It is no longer an insurgency but a war of Pashtun resistance, exactly in the mould of the First Anglo-Afghan War. Then too (in 1839–42) initially there were celebrations. The British built their cantonments and brought their wives and sweethearts from Delhi and didn't realise that, in the meantime, the Afghans were getting organised to rise up. This is exactly what the Afghans are doing today and what they did against the Soviets. The British should have known better. No country in the world has a better understanding of the Afghan psyche and very little has changed there in the past couple of centuries.

He continued: 'This is the only way forward ... there will be no military solution, there has to be a political solution. How many more lives have to be lost before people realise it's a time for dialogue?'[i]

This book does not constitute a comprehensive military history of Afghanistan but, within this central civil-military theme, there will also be a revisionist interpretation of many of the key campaigns and battles of all four Anglo-Afghan wars. The deployment of new, previously unpublished source material, notably Brigadier Shelton's 1843 court martial defence notes in relation to the Kabul disaster (1841–2), will hopefully shed fresh new light upon some of these often catastrophic events.

Despite the obvious lack of indigenous oral source material, particularly for the first three Afghan conflicts, the 'Afghan voice' will not be neglected and this book will, for the first time, also shed new light upon the often vital supportive role played by Afghan collaborators, allies and trading communities in securing British success or even survival. There will be a special focus on the economic role of Afghan peasant-cultivators, traders and merchants whose activities, it will also be argued, often underpinned the resource-starved armies of the Raj during the first two Anglo-Afghan conflicts. In the post-imperial era, the current crucial political dependence of Britain and her allies upon the loyalty and support of a greatly expanded Afghan National Army and Police Force during current operations, serves as a further potent reminder of the importance of the Afghan people themselves in securing the future stability and legitimacy of a democratic Afghanistan.

The publication of this book has been greatly assisted by the support of many of my colleagues at the Royal Military Academy Sandhurst, and many more from the wider military and academic community. My first great acknowledgment must be afforded to Dr Garry Alder, retired Reader in the History Department of the University of Reading who, during the early 1970s, first introduced me, then a lowly undergraduate, to the origins of the Great Game of Central Asia and whose enthusiasm and forensic skills unravelled many of the political complexities of British policy in the region. His friendship and advice are still cherished. Professor Huw Strachan's seminal work, *The Politics of the British Army*, Dr Norris's *The First Afghan War* and Professor Yapp's *Strategies of British India* have also been key sources of inspiration to this work.

My colleagues at Sandhurst, most notably retired archivist Dr Tony Heathcote, whose book, *The Afghan Wars 1839–1919*, justifiably remains a central focus for many current students of this subject, have also provided invaluable advice in regard to source material for this book. I also wish to thank my former colleagues in the Department of International Affairs at Sandhurst for providing teaching cover for my research sabbatical during the summer term of 2008 and particularly Dr Paul Latawski, who kindly supplied technical assistance and some relevant source material for the current conflict. Of the many helpful colleagues in my new Department, the Department of War Studies, Head of Department Dr Duncan Anderson, Dr Dan Marston, Dr Chris Pugsley, Dr Stephen Walsh and Dr Greg Fremont-Barnes have been particularly supportive. Duncan Anderson has been immensely encouraging. His boundless enthusiasm and great academic expertise in this area have proved invaluable and our joint external lectures, briefings and papers on Afghanistan (largely organized by him), and the subsequent cross-fertilization of our ideas, have certainly enhanced the progress and development of this book.

My gratitude must also be extended to many military colleagues and particularly to those hundreds of cadets and captains I have tutored over the past two decades, and whose often passionate opinions on Afghan operations have always been welcomed and treasured. Tragically, several of them have been injured or killed during the current operations in Afghanistan, including Lieutenant Paul Mervis of the Rifles Regiment (a true 'philosopher soldier').

My pre-deployment lectures delivered to military units across Great Britain, such as those to the Royal Irish Regiment and The Rifles Regiment and the REME (Arborfield) have also proved invaluable in terms of feedback. My particular thanks must also be extended to Major Andrew Banks and Captain Meiklejohn, who both supplied and helped organize oral research material relating to the current conflict. My great friend and colleague, military historian Lieutenant-Colonel Ian Bennett (RCT retired) has provided wonderful support and he has proved to be a discerning critic of this work, particularly the early chapters. I also wish to thank General Graeme Lamb, head of the Field Army, Brigadier Ed Butler and Peter Millet, the British High Commissioner to Cyprus, for their great support for my first major paper on British policy towards Afghanistan, which was delivered to a 300-strong audience at the British Field Army conference on the Middle East in Episcopi military base, Cyprus, in January 2008, and to Major Jason Hurn for his sterling organization of and support for this conference. The pre-conference private dinner, hosted by Brigadier Butler and General Lamb, during which Afghan affairs were privately and indeed passionately discussed, remains a truly memorable occasion. I would also like to thank Mrs Amy Cameron for her charming hospitality, excellent support and for her skilful organization of my three National Army Museum public lectures on the Anglo-Afghan wars which I delivered to record audiences in January 2009, 2010 and 2011. Dr John Peaty of the Ministry of Defence's GEOINT Analysis Branch has also proved to be a valued correspondent on current Afghan affairs, especially regarding campaign maps and Taliban military tactics.

The archival and library staff of many research institutions across Britain have also been of enormous assistance, notably Ian Hook, Curator of the Essex Regimental Museum in Chelmsford, David Tetlow, Curator of the Green Howards' Regimental Museum in Richmond, Yorkshire and Curator Lieutenant-Colonel Cornwall (retired) and volunteer curatorial assistant, Mr McIntyre, of the Rifles' Museum, Salisbury. The curatorial staff of the Gurkha Museum in Winchester, notably Curator Major (retired) Gerald Davies and assistant curator and archivist Mr Gavin Edgerley-Harris, were also exceptionally helpful. They provided both important information on the Gurkha role in all four Afghan wars and several of the stunning images printed in this book. Two great personal friends and 'Friends of the Gurkha Museum', Mr Alan (RMP retired) and Mrs Jackie Marsh also provided invaluable advice and source material and facilitated introductions.

I also wish to thank the staffs of the National Army Museum, the British Library, the London Library, Cambridge University Library, the Bodleian

Library, Oxford University and the Imperial War Museum, London, for further invaluable assistance with this book.

At Sandhurst my great friend and colleague, Senior Librarian Andrew Orgill has been truly outstanding both in terms of advice and in securing rare books and other source material for this book. Recognition must also be afforded to his two dedicated assistants, Ken Franklin and John Pearce. In terms of technical support Mrs Maureen Everard has provided excellent word-processing support.

The Director of Studies at Sandhurst, Mr Sean McKnight, has also provided me with truly outstanding support for this project. By recently establishing a system of regular research sabbaticals he has massively enhanced the already high academic reputation of military history at the Royal Military Academy Sandhurst.

I would also like to thank the commissioning and editorial team of my original publisher, Hambledon of London, notably Dr Tony Morris and Martin Sheppard, for their patience, enthusiasm and efficiency, and particularly Alexander Stilwell, the commissioning editor of Robert Hale, who commissioned and edited this book after the tragic demise of Hambledon Books.

My close family, and particularly my dear parents, have provided great moral support for this book. Above all I must record my gratitude and deep appreciation of the exceptional love and support provided by my dear wife, Louise, and daughters Madeleine and Emily. Louise has spent countless hours word-processing documentation and interpreting my obscure memoranda. Both have somehow survived an absentee father and husband who has spent far too many hours playing the 'Great Game' in a remote garden study for over five long years.

The opinions and views expressed in this book are mine alone and do not reflect those of either the Ministry of Defence or the Royal Military Academy Sandhurst.

Dr Edmund Yorke, Senior Lecturer, War Studies Department, RMA Sandhurst

Note

i   Christina Lamb, 'Britain told: do peace deal with Taliban?; *The Sunday Times*, 26 November 2006.

1. The Lure of the Indus: the First Afghan War

It is to be hoped that the good sense of the British nation will never again permit such expeditions as the one beyond the Indus ... and that the experience acquired from [such] disasters may be made beneficial in placing the control of Indian affairs in very different hands from those who have so wilfully abused the power confided to them, and whose rashness and folly in plunging the country into wars ruinous to its reputation may yet be punished.

C. Masson, *Narrative of Various Journeys in Balochistan, Afghanistan and the Panjab*, Vol. 1, pp.xi–xii, London 1842
(repr. Munshiram Manoharlal New Delhi 1997)

The Land and its People

Afghanistan has always presented a formidable challenge to invaders whether they be Alexander the Great in 334–337 BC or the British from the early nineteenth century onwards. As a landlocked country extending 600 miles west to east and 500 miles north to south, the total area of this 'Asiatic Switzerland' comprises over 250,000 square miles, of which up to three-quarters is upland. From the south-west to the north-east it is protected from invasions by the main mountain system of the Hindu Kush. In the north the Pamirs mountain range presents a similar barrier to invasions from that direction.

As a largely arid country it is served by only four main rivers, the Amu in the north, the Kabul River in the centre, the Hari-Rud in the west and the Helmund in the south. Afghanistan is also a country of extreme temperatures, ranging from over 40 °C in the summer to below -20 °C in the winter in the higher areas. For invaders such as the British (who were obviously unable to directly deploy their vast naval power), and before the advent of substantial air-power, penetration of Afghanistan depended on securing access through several key passes, notably the Bolan, the Khojak, the Shutargardan/Kurram and, most famous of all, the Khyber Pass.

However, all could be easily dominated by fierce tribal polities who were already proven experts in mountain warfare. Of these tribal groups the Waziri groups, and especially the Mahsuds and the Orakzais represented some of the most formidable guerrilla fighters in the world. In terms of its peoples Afghanistan also represents one of the most culturally diverse nations in the world. As the late Professor Louis Dupree succinctly observed, Afghanistan is 'not a self-contained ethnic unit' and 'few of its ethnic groups are indigenous'.[1] Many Pashtun, for example (often historically and loosely termed Pathan) are by no means all Afghan citizens, with large numbers living in the tribal belt of the North West Federally Administrated Tribal Area of Pakistan. As we shall see, this ethnic diaspora has created extreme problems for the British and their coalition allies in exercising social and political control along the Iranian and Pakistani borders during the current conflict. Similarly the Baluch (or Baluchi – which usually refers to their language), whilst domiciled in the south-west corner of Afghanistan, also widely extend into north-west Pakistan and south-east Iran. In the north, the Tajik, Uzbek, Turkman and Kirghiz groups are ethnically linked with neighbouring republics of Tajikistan, Uzbekistan and Turkmanistan and Kirghizstan. Moreover, most of the people of the extreme west of Afghanistan are, geographically and culturally, an extension of the Iranian Plateau and have close and widespread family and ethnic links across the Iranian border.

Historically, in terms of broad *political* groupings, three great tribal confederations have predominated in a national population which today exceeds 30 million but which, during the first two Afghan wars, probably did not exceed a few million. First, there were the Durranis who, under Ahmad Shah, rose to power in the middle of the eighteenth century but who ceased control of Afghanistan in 1747 on the death of the Persian emperor Nadir Shah. Their heartland lies in the south-west part of Afghanistan with a significant presence around the main cities of Kabul, Jalalabad and Herat.

The 'second great division' of the Afghan people consisted of the Ghilzais who, historically, were jealous rivals of the Durranis. Their power in southern Afghanistan was initially broken by Nadir Shah in 1732 and their heartland lies in the eastern part of the country. A predominantly nomadic trading people, they spend winter in the plains and transfer their flocks in the summer to the central highlands. They comprised the major element of the so-called *Powindahs* or 'carrier peoples'.

In numerical terms the third significant political grouping are the Tajiks, who are descended from the Greco-Bactrian population established originally by Alexander the Great in the region north of the Hindu Kush.

Focused mainly in the north-east of Afghanistan, especially Kabul, they are essentially a more sedentary people with occupations ranging from farmers to shopkeepers.

Another significant political grouping are the Hazara, a predominantly Persian speaking 'mountain people' of Turkish or Mongol origin and appearance. As a distinct predominantly Shia religious grouping based in the Central Highlands, their bitter and often murderous rivalry with their Sunni Ghilzai and Duranni rivals encouraged them to become strong collaborators with the British during the first two Anglo-Afghan Wars, if only to pay off old scores.

Of the many other often numerically far smaller politico-ethnic groups, which include small pockets of Jews, Hindus and Aimaq, the predominately Shia Qizilbash (often historically termed the 'Kuzzilbash') are, politically, especially distinctive. As Persian-speaking descendants of the military and administrative personnel left behind by Persian emperor Nadir Shah in the eighteenth century, they represent a rather isolated group and their isolation also encouraged them to become close collaborators of the British during the first two Anglo-Afghan Wars. Primarily an urban group centred on Kabul, they traditionally held many important bureaucratic and professional appointments in the period up to the Soviet invasion of 1979.[2]

In purely ethnic/linguistic terms, the percentage breakdown today is as follows: the largest group are the Pashtun who, based predominantly in the south and east of the country, comprise over 40 per cent of the population. The second largest group are the Tajiks (27 per cent). The Hazaras and Uzbeks each make up 9 per cent while the remainder include small minorities such as the Baluch and Aimaq peoples.

The political structure of Afghanistan, which predominated well into the twentieth century and which perseveres in many rural areas today, often as a more perverted form of warlordism, was essentially feudal. The tribe represented the basic unit, with the chief or *sirdar* elected for life. The *sirdar*, rather than the distant Amir or ruler in Kabul, was the primary focus of loyalty of the tribesmen. However, in many cases the *sirdar* himself received grants of land or *jagirs* from the Amir, in return for which he owed the Amir service. In the words of Brian Robson:

It was in this way that the Amir could call upon very large numbers of tribesmen to assist him in time of war, quite apart from those tribesmen impelled purely by religion or xenophobic emotions to take up arms against an invader. National unity might not exist but that did not mean that an invader will not face forces of spontaneous resistance. Every rock potentially had a guerilla.[3]

In terms of character and outlook the early nineteenth-century British explorer and diplomat, Mountstuart Elphinstone, provided an interesting profile, much of which is relevant to the Afghan national character today: 'Their vices are revenge, envy, avarice, rapacity and obstinacy: on the other hand they are fond of liberty, faithful to their friends, kind to their dependents, hospitable, brave, hardy frugal, laborious and prudent.[4]

Frequently united in a common hatred of the foreign invader or *feringhee*, many citizens of this Afghan nation would, over the next nearly one and three-quarter centuries of brutal conflict, prove to be among Britain's most formidable and enduring enemies. Their defiance not only rocked the very foundations of Britain's nineteenth- and twentieth-century Central Asian Empire but, following the more recent 9/11 disaster, is again challenging the formidable power of both Britain and her NATO/Coalition allies, currently the world's most powerful military alliance.

The Origins of the 'Great Game'

Contrary to popular belief, the origins of Britain's long involvement in the 'Great Game' of central Asia were not rooted solely in terms of 'Russophobia', the fear of a Russian invasion of Britain's cherished Indian possessions. Indeed it was, initially, the threat of a French invasion of Britain's 'jewel in the crown' and, specifically, the highly aggressive militarized Bonapartist state, which first exercised the minds of British politicians in London and East India Company officials in Calcutta.

The French had never forgotten the loss of their Indian possessions during the Seven Years War (1756–63) and the main fears of a specific French invasion were triggered by Napoleon Bonaparte's invasion and occupation of Egypt in 1798. This immediately offered the French a far more viable alternative invasion route to India via the Red Sea to the Persian Gulf, and one which avoided the traditional sea route via the Cape, which was already closely guarded by British naval fleets. It was, initially, a short-lived threat. Lord Nelson's stunning naval victory at Aboukir Bay (August 1798) and the subsequent victory of the British Army in Egypt temporarily relieved British anxieties. Nevertheless this military threat inspired the local British political authorities into launching a major diplomatic offensive to safeguard their northern Indian frontier. Those crucial surrounding territories which might provide a springboard or conduit for future French invasion – notably the Sikh Kingdom, the Sind Emirate, Persia and Afghanistan – were now to be the targets of numerous diplomatic missions which were eventually extended over the next four decades.

And it was a political initiative which still rested largely in the hands of the East India Company's 'mandarins' residing in faraway Calcutta. Since Crown intervention after the Company corruption scandals of the 1780s, Indian affairs were managed jointly between Crown officials and those of the East India Company. In London the administrative framework consisted of the Secretary of State for War and the Colonies who issued instructions to the Governor-General in Calcutta, and the Board of Control, whose president, as a cabinet minister, was accountable to Parliament. But the East India Company still exercised wide local political control and still, for instance, maintained its own armies which served in conjunction with those of the Crown and were only remotely controlled by a cabinet-appointed Commander-in-Chief answerable to the War Office in London. For the first three Afghan wars, during and after the end of Company rule in 1857, political control over the military was directly exercised through the appointment of civil officers, often themselves seconded military officers, and commonly known as 'politicals'. They were given wide powers and many were selected for the often arduous and high-risk diplomatic missions to the remote territories beyond British India.

In 1800, for example, Governor-General Wellesley, on his own initiative, dispatched the experienced British diplomat John Malcolm to Teheran to secure either a Persian alliance or at least their neutrality. Armed with lavish presents, Malcolm's mission, designed 'to counteract the possible attempts of those villainous but active democrats the French'[5] resulted in two treaties, one political, the other commercial. Article 5, the key article of the political treaty, accordingly laid down that, 'should ... an army of the French ... attempt to settle ... on any islands or the shores of Persia, both Britain and Persian forces would cooperate for their expulsion and extirpation'.[6]

It was a brief respite. In 1807 the British Government at home and in India was horrified to hear the news of two successive hostile treaties, both of which directly challenged British power in India. On 4 May 1807 the Treaty of Finkenstein provided for Franco-Persian co-operation against both Russia and Britain, with Articles 8 and 12 specifically directed against the British. By Article 11 the Shah actually agreed to grant passage to French troops through his dominions. This inimical treaty was largely the product of British complacency and neglect. After their initial overtures, Britain's eye had been taken off the 'diplomatic ball' and, between 1800 and 1807, French agents had successfully penetrated the Persian Court. The second and even more formidable threat emerged from the Treaty of Tilsit of July 1807, concluded between newly allied France and Russia, which raised the worst nightmare scenario of a joint Franco-Russian invasion of northern India. Consequently, in March 1808, a panicking British Board of Control urgently considered the raising of a force of 20,000 or 25,000 British troops 'to prevent the establishment of the French on the shores of the Persian Gulf or to dislodge them if established'. This was despite the prospect of huge 'pecuniary difficulties' in deploying such a force.[7] Indeed financial parsimony was to continue to be a recurring and aggravating factor in the management of Britain's Afghan wars.

The problem was magnified by strategic changes in the power balance in the Near East. In Egypt, which experienced a significant power vacuum after the enforced departure of the French, British influence was suddenly challenged by the resurgent anti-British Pasha, the Albanian-born Muhammad Ali. After the massacre of one small British mission he actively sought to expand his power base in the Near East. This in turn encouraged further Russian ambitions in the region and it was clear that any Russian domination of the Near East, including Turkey and Persia, could have further severe repercussions for British control of India and her trade routes. As one historian succinctly observed:

> It is in the interaction of British policy towards Russia in the Near and Middle East that the explanation of much that happened in the two Afghan wars is to be found. Events in one theatre cannot therefore be understood without reference to events in the other: the Afghan wars were essentially a part of the Eastern Question.[8]

Fears of French or Russian invasion were matched by internal anxieties as, by the early 1800s and beyond to the outbreak of the First Anglo-Afghan War, British rule in India had by no means been consolidated. To the north, in the Punjab, lay the powerful Sikh kingdom secured after 1825 by the powerful armies of the redoubtable 'Lion of the North', Ranjit Singh.[9] Under his iron rule the Sikh kingdom remained fiercely independent, as did the adjoining if far less powerful Emirate of Sind. Even further to the north and also outside British power lay the unstable kingdom of Afghanistan which, as we shall see, enjoyed a fractious relationship with its Sikh and Sind neighbours to the south.

To forestall a Franco-Russian invasion, the imperative for British policymakers was therefore to secure control of these states by either force, or diplomacy, or both. Of the two threats the French were initially perceived as the more potent. Thus, for instance, on 20 June 1808, the British Governor-General of India, Lord Minto, minuted:

> If the French should be enabled to introduce their forces into Persia
> ... the first and most important step towards the invasion of India

would have been successfully taken.... But ... the hostility of the interjacent States, especially if seconded by the co-operation of the British power may yet be expected to frustrate the design or at least to reduce the invading Army to a degree of debility which will give to our troops a decided superiority in the field.[10]

Accordingly, in April 1808 a second diplomatic mission, led again by Sir John Malcolm, was dispatched to the neglected Persian Court to counteract the renewal of the French threat there. Meanwhile other British envoys were hurriedly dispatched to the key buffer states of the Sind, Punjab and Afghanistan both to establish a permanent political presence and, not least, negotiate commercial facilities. Captain David Seton, then British Resident in Muscat, was accordingly dispatched to the Sind capital Hyderabad, his colleague Charles Metcalfe to the city of Lahore in the Punjab, and Mountstuart Elphinstone to Kabul.

It was Sir John Malcolm who faced the biggest challenge, and the strength of French influence in the Persian Court soon left him dangerously isolated in the provinces. Eventually it was a Foreign Office-appointed diplomat, Sir Harford Jones who, by means of promises and lavish presents, secured, much to Malcolm's chagrin, the signing of the Anglo-Persian Treaty of 12 March 1809. This 'friendship' treaty cancelled all other Persian treaties with European states and the Shah promised to refuse permission for any European force to pass through Persia 'either towards India or towards parts of that country'.[11]

It was a fraught 'diplomat confederacy' destined to reach a climax in the years immediately preceding the First Afghan War. However, the mutual jealousies and territorial rivalries existing between all these projected satellite states made any treaty involving British aid highly problematical, so Britain was always forced to 'secure unilateral agreements with each of these states, not a multilateral entente'.[12]

By 1812, much to the relief of British officials in Calcutta and London, the French threat was dramatically reduced as Napoleon attacked his erstwhile ally, Russia, and conducted his disastrous retreat from Moscow. Three years later, on 15 June 1815, a British-led European coalition commanded by the renowned Duke of Wellington finally eliminated French power at the Battle of Waterloo. After 1815 only Russia remained the main potential threat to India but her subsequent 'alliance of necessity' with Britain after the French invasion dissipated British fears for some years. Moreover, in hindsight, even the British fears of Russia at this time might seem extreme with around two thousand miles of unknown terrain lying between Russian possessions and Britain's northern Indian border.

However, within a decade or so, renewed fears of a Russian invasion of British India, principally via Persia and Afghanistan, were suddenly revived. Once again the new scare primarily involved the integrity of the Persian state. In 1826 Russia and Persia went to war over a disputed territory between Erivan and Lake Gokcha and, after months of fighting, Persia was decisively defeated at the Battle of Tabriz. For the British the strategic implications of this war were dire. Lord Ellenborough, the newly arrived President of the Board of Control, immediately recognized the political and strategic implications of the humiliating treaty of Turkmanchai which the Russians duly imposed on the defeated Persians. Ellenborough wrote: 'What we apprehend is not the conquest of the Persian monarchy, but the establishment at the Court of Teheran of a Russian influence which would practically place the question mark of Persia at the disposal of the Court of St Petersburgh.'[13]

In June 1828, Sir Charles Metcalfe, now elevated to the prestigious position of member of the Governor-General's Supreme Council, starkly spelt out Ellenborough's fears: 'If ever Russia be in a condition to set forth an army against India, Persia most probably will be under her banners.'[14] A year later British fears were reinforced by news of the terms of the Russo-Turkish treaty of Adrianople of October 1829, which further confirmed Russian domination in the Near East and which, as historian Norris would contend, directly enhanced fears of Russian advances in Central Asia.

On the back of Russia's rapid diplomatic advances in the Near East an emerging forward-policy school in Britain was reinforced by two key publications which laid the basis for an outbreak of 'Russophobia' which was to dominate British policy-making for another century. As early as 1817 Sir Robert Wilson's tract, 'Sketch of the military and political power of Russia in the year 1817', had warned of possible Russian expansion. But it was the publication in London in 1829 of the work, 'On the Practicability of an Invasion of British India and on the Commercial and Financial Prospects and Resurgence of that Empire' by George de Lacy Evans, which most alerted both British and Indian Governments and public opinion to the potential of Russian expansion 'to secure Persia as a road to the Indus'. Evans visualized the nightmare scenario of a Russian march from the Caspian to Khiva followed by an advance as far up the Oxus River as possible, and then a march across the Hindu Kush to the Indus River. Lord Ellenborough, himself heavily influenced by this latter publication, summed up the strategic dilemma now confronting Britain in defending her Central Asian empire:

Upon the subject of the invasion of India my idea is that the thing was not only practical but easy, unless we determine to act as an Asiatic

Power. On the acquisition of Khiva by the Russians we should occupy Lahore and Cabul. It is not on the Indus that an enemy is to be met. If we do not meet him in Cabul, at the foot of the Hindu Koosh or in its Passes we had better remain on the Sutledge. If the Russians once occupy Cabul they may return there with the Indus in their front, until they have organised insurrection in our rear, and completely equipped their army.[15]

As in the 1800s, the imperative for Britain's government of India was to carry out yet another pre-emptive diplomatic strike. It was designed primarily to bolster Persia as the key buffer state and, also importantly, to collect geographical and commercial information on both her and the other key independent states in the region, notably Afghanistan, the Punjab and Sind. Any Russian commercial penetration of the Indus River would, it was hoped, be forestalled by new British commercial treaties particularly with the bordering territory, the Sind Emirate. Ultimately, the greatest prize would be to secure defensive treaties with all these satellite states. Afghanistan had now assumed greater if not equal importance to Persia in this grand strategic offensive or 'Great Game', especially in view of recent Russian backing of existing Persian territorial claims on the key western Afghan city of Herat. By 1832 reports from Henry Ellis and his successor, Sir John McNeill, the influential British agent in Teheran, confirmed nefarious Russian activities and the active support afforded by the resident Russian agent in Persia, Count Simonich, to the plans of the new Persian king, Shah Muhammed, to attack and secure this Afghan city and even Kandahar. In this way Persia would, it was believed, act as a perfect surrogate for Russian expansionist ambitions in the region. Within Afghanistan the city of Herat was now naturally perceived by the British as the strategic key for holding India. As Lord Bentinck, the Governor-General of India, postulated in 1835: 'Russia's ambition is to advance towards India via Persia and Herat. It is the interest of Russia to extend and strengthen the Persian Empire which occupies a central position between the double line of operation of the Autocrat to the eastwards and westward.'[16] Bentinck specifically focused upon Herat even submitting, as evidence, the distances from Herat to places in Persia, Afghanistan, Russia and India. By 1835 the Afghan Court had become a major focus of British diplomacy. As Sir Henry Ellis, the British Envoy to Teheran, emphasized:

If to form a connection with the chiefs of Afghanistan more intimate than has hitherto been maintained is a part of the system ... for organising the defence of the Northern frontier of India, it could ...

be ... more advantageous to effect this arrangement while Herat still separates them from this Kingdom than after the act or incorporation of that principality within Persia which we could not urge them to set aside.[17]

However, since Mountstuart Elphinstone's mission to Afghanistan in 1810, Afghan internal politics had already entered yet another turbulent and bloody phase. A year earlier, in 1809, the ruler Shah Shuja had been overthrown and had been forced to seek sanctuary at the Court of the Sikh kingdom of Ranjit Singh. Here, however, he was sternly treated and his old rival even forced him to hand over his greatest treasure, the legendary Koh-i-Noor diamond or 'mountain of light'. In 1816, therefore, he moved to the British frontier town of Ludhiana where the British afforded him a house and a small pension. Here he was politely ignored at a time when 'Russophobia' remained at a low ebb and Afghanistan's future of little direct interest. However, with renewed fears of Russian expansion in the 1820s and the 1830s, both he and his successor to the throne of Afghanistan, Dost Mohammed, became of more than a little interest to the British authorities in Calcutta.

An accelerated progress towards the outbreak of the First Anglo-Afghan War now commenced. In January 1831, as part of the new complex network of diplomatic missions representing the first rounds of the 'Great Game', a young, charming, flamboyant and highly talented diplomat, Lieutenant Alexander Burnes, was dispatched to the Sikh Court at Lahore in the Punjab. A former soldier in the East India Company, the 26-year-old 'Bokhara' Burnes had already exhibited a great flair for languages and his enterprising travels in remote areas of central Asia soon won him both public acclaim and promotion into the East India Company's Foreign and Political Department. On his return from a meeting with Ranjit Singh at Rupar, Burnes stopped at Ludhiana to meet the Afghan ruler in exile, Shah Shuja, still dreaming of a return to power. Burnes' initial impressions of Shah Shuja were, significantly, not favourable. 'From what I learnt', Burnes wrote, 'I do not believe the Shah possesses sufficient energy to seat himself on the throne of Kabul; and, that, if he did regain it, he has not the tact to discharge the duties of so difficult a situation.'[18]

By stark contrast, on a subsequent epic journey throughout Central Asia Burnes was far more deeply impressed by his first meeting in Kabul with Shah Shuja's successor, Dost Mohammed. Describing Dost Mohammed as 'the most rising man in the Cabool dominions',[19] Burnes' recommendations, delivered to the British Governor-General Lord William Bentinck, were readily accepted and a stunned and disappointed Shah Shuja was temporarily returned to his political wilderness in Ludhiana. In despair, in 1833 Shah Shuja signed a treaty with his former host and rival, Ranjit Singh. The treaty allowed for a joint expedition to try to regain his throne but Shah Shuja's subsequent tiny expedition was brushed away by Dost Mohammed's forces. Moreover, his cynical ally and benefactor, Ranjit Singh, after promising assistance, merely took the opportunity to deploy his troops to occupy the coveted Afghan border town of Peshawar. From that date Ranjit Singh's Sikh empire became the bitter foe of Dost Mohammed's Afghanistan.

Elsewhere, the British diplomatic offensive secured greater success. Under intense pressure, the rulers of Sind, whilst successfully refusing a British Resident, reluctantly conceded to Britain's main demands of commercial access to the Indus River. Although, owing largely to navigation problems, the river never realized its full commercial promise, the April 1832 Treaty with Sind was a political triumph and 'thus the first object of Britain's central Asian policy was attained within three years of the Treaty of Adrianople which prompted it'.[20]

Two events in 1836 and 1837 further propelled Britain along the path to conflict with Afghanistan. In 1836 a publication entitled the *Progress and Present Position of Russia in the East* proved, in the words of one historian, 'crucial to a proper understanding of the first Afghan war'. This book, probably authored by Britain's hawkish ambassador in Teheran, John McNeill, asserted:

> The whole Mohammedon people of Central Asia dreads the power of Russia and looks for countenance from England ... the integrity and independence of Persia is necessary to the security of India and of Europe and any attempt to subvert the one is a blow struck at the other, an unequivocal act of hostility to England.[21]

A year later, in July 1837, a single military event seemed to confirm the book's predictions when a Russian-backed Persian army commenced the long-feared attack upon the western Afghan city of Herat. As Count Simonich and his military advisers themselves appeared before Herat, it was patently obvious that Britain had lost her long diplomatic battle in Teheran. The eyes of the anxious authorities in Calcutta were now drawn by the intrepid activities of Eldred Pottinger, a young subaltern in the Bengal artillery and the erstwhile British agent in Herat. He not only provided full and alarming reports of the overt and highly provocative activity of Russian agents in the Shah's camp outside Herat, but gallantly helped organize its highly energetic defence.

News of the attack set the alarm bells ringing again in London while that summer an atmosphere of near hysteria pervaded in Calcutta. Ironically the new Governor-General of India, Lord Auckland, on his arrival in India in March 1836, had initially and for good practical reasons, been strictly non-interventionist. He asserted: 'I would abstain from interference. I would not be forward even in intercourse. I would endeavour to preserve peace ... but further than this ... unless new emergencies should arise, I would not go; India is scarcely yet recovering into strength from the exhaustion of war and conquest.'[22] In 1837, however, with news of the Persian attack on Herat, the 'new emergency' had now arisen. Herat could not be allowed to fall and Russian expansion via Persia into Afghanistan had to be forestalled. In the autumn and spring of 1837–8 a fierce political debate ensued among Auckland's advisers in Calcutta, ranging from non-interferers such as the veteran Sir Charles Metcalfe, acting Governor-General before Auckland arrived (who advised only the use of an expanded Sikh buffer state to stave off Russian expansion), to a hawkish Alexander Burnes pressing for active British intervention to support Dost Mohammed. As Professor Louis Dupree confirms: 'The reports of Russian activities in Herat, Kabul and Kandahar forced the British to make an agonising reappraisal of their policy in the area. British reaction set the course of Central Asia and Indian history for the next hundred years.'[23]

Intervention in Afghanistan was now imminent, but the eyes of Lord Auckland and several key advisers – notably Burnes' superior, William Hay MacNaghten, Head of the Foreign and Political Department of the Government of India – were focused not on Burnes' candidate, Dost Mohammed, but on Shah Shuja, the Afghan leader in exile. By 1838, from the perspective of the majority of the Auckland administration, Dost Mohammed had already forfeited his candidature when he officially accepted, in 1837, the arrival of a Russian Envoy, Lieutenant Vitkevich, a Cossack officer, to his Court in Kabul.

There was another potent strategic reason for Calcutta's rejection of Dost Mohammed. His recent territorial dispute over Peshawar with Britain's close regional ally, the Sikh kingdom under Ranjit Singh, had weighed the political scales against him: with Herat now directly imperilled the support of the powerful Sikh kingdom in the Punjab was perceived as strategically crucial for any defence of British India. Furthermore, the earlier 1833 alliance between Shah Shuja and Ranjit Singh had significantly enhanced Shah Shuja's political credibility as the main candidate for the throne of Afghanistan.

British preference for an Anglo-Sikh alliance with Shah Shuja as the primary candidate for the Afghan throne was further reinforced by the political machinations of the British diplomat Sir Claude Wade, Britain's highly influential political agent at the Sikh Court at Ludhiana.[24] It was a policy shift eagerly facilitated and manipulated by the crafty, ageing 'lion of Lahore', Ranjit Singh. He naturally welcomed the opportunity afforded to dethrone his old enemy Dost Mohammed and potentially gain even more Afghan territory. Thus, in June 1838, the British Government, Ranjit Singh and Shah Shuja signed up to the Tripartite Treaty, the major diplomatic precursor to an invasion of Afghanistan. It was agreed that the British would supply an Anglo-Indian army, money, and advisers; the Sikhs, a large contingent based on the Khyber, while Shah Shuja would be reinstalled on the Afghan throne. In reality the latter would also serve as a weak figure-head for future manipulation.

In faraway Kabul the British decision to back his deposed rival Shah Shuja understandably came as a bitter blow to Dost Mohammed. Soon after losing Peshawar to Ranjit Singh's forces and immediately after Auckland's arrival as Governor-General in 1836, Dost Mohammed had tried desperately but unsuccessfully, to court British favour and to seek their support in settling Afghan-Sikh differences. He wrote to the newly arrived Governor-General:

> The later transactions in this quarter, the conduct of reckless and misguided Sikhs, and their breach of treaty are well known to their Lordship. Communicate to me whatever may now suggest itself to your wisdom for the settlement of the affairs of this country.... Whatever directions your Lordship may be pleased to issue for the administration of this country I will act accordingly.[25]

Dost Mohammed's rejection was, initially, an equally bitter blow to Alexander Burnes, his principal British diplomatic supporter. As the Calcutta administration moved inexorably towards supporting Shah Shuja's candidature, Burnes, on his returned to Kabul in 1837, had already been ordered to remain strictly neutral. He was denied authority by his Foreign Department superior, Sir William MacNaghten, to offer Dost Mohammed any incentives to offset Russian proposals. Dost Mohammed's subsequent loss of patience and his ultimate acceptance of the presence of the Russian agent, Lieutenant Vitkevich, in his capital was therefore, perhaps, understandable.

In the final analysis, Lord Auckland's decision to go to war in 1838 was probably most immediately and decisively influenced by his close adviser, Sir William MacNaghten. The latter was himself fully supported by other influential 'hawks' on Auckland's staff, notably John Colvin and Henry Torrens. Like his junior, Burnes, MacNaghten was an ex-officer from the East India Company's army but he had soon happily exchanged the sword for the pen. Like Burnes he was also a brilliant linguist. But, unlike Burnes, MacNaghten strongly favoured the Shah Shuja candidature and with it the Sikh alliance as the solution to winning the current round of the 'Great Game'. A confirmed faceless bureaucrat who avoided the glamorous travel exploits of his colleague, 'Bokhara Burnes' he, unlike the frequently absent Burnes, was in an excellent position to directly influence Lord Auckland and outmanoeuvre any other waverers. The personal contrast between the two doomed diplomats was, as historian Edwardes observes, indeed

> profound, MacNaghten cold, delighting in intrigue for its own sake, or 'dry as an old nut' as a contemporary put it and Burnes, an almost Byronic figure, enjoying himself in native dress and with native women, seeing tragedy in the making and yet taking no action to avert it. All the two men were to have in common was the horror and futility of their deaths.[26]

This is not to say that MacNaghten did not have his admirers in the more sober atmosphere of the Calcutta political circles. Lady Eden, sister of Lord Auckland, lavishly praised MacNaghten as 'our Lord Palmerston a dry, sensible man who wears an enormous pair of blue spectacles and speaks Persian, Arabic and Hindustani rather more fluently than English'.[27]

Indeed, it was as a consequence of MacNaghten's pressure, combined with the obviously excellent prospects of political advancement resulting from any British occupation of Afghanistan, that the sudden 'conversion' of Alexander Burnes to Shah Shuja's candidature was achieved. The openly ambitious Burnes must have already seen the political writing on the wall after his superior MacNaghten had repeatedly instructed him in 1838 that not only would there be no British support for Dost Mohammed's grievances over the Sikh occupation of Peshawar but that he was specifically not to enter into any alliances with him. In June 1838, three months after his return from Kabul, a chastened but still ambitious Burnes produced a suitably ambivalent report to Lord Auckland which effectively allowed for Dost Mohammed's deposition. In his remarkable political volte-face, Burnes, whilst asserting that he still regarded Dost Mohammed as 'a man of undoubted ability and if half you do for others were done for him ... he would abandon Persia and Russia tomorrow', nevertheless conceded that if the British Government was contemplating replacing Dost Mohammed it had, 'only to send Shuja to Peshawar with an agent and two of its regiments as honorary escort and then avail to the Afghans that we have taken up his cause, to ensure his being fixed forever on the throne'.[28]

The political die was cast and in London it was left to the British Foreign Secretary and convinced 'Russophobe', Lord Palmerston, supported by Sir John Hobhouse, President of the Board of Control, to play the final if subsequently controversial role in persuading the key members of the British Cabinet to back Lord Auckland's recommendation to support the Sikh alliance and Shah Shuja's candidature. As historian Jasper Ridley observes, the decision to back Auckland's war policy was hardly democratic and 'discussed in great secrecy, not at a full meeting of the British Cabinet but only by Prime Minister Melbourne, Palmerston, Sir John Cam Hobhouse, President of the Board of Trade, Lord John Russell, Glenelg, Lansdowne and the Chancellor Lord Cottenham at a meeting at Windsor Castle on 24 October 1838'.[29] Moreover it was a decision undoubtedly secured by Auckland's promise that the finances for any expedition would be found from the coffers of Britain's allies, the unfortunate unsuspecting Emirs of Sind!

War was now imminent and, even before news of the final cabinet agreement had reached him, Lord Auckland, confident of Home Government support, had brazenly issued his infamous Simla Manifesto of 1 October 1838. It was, in the view of leading historian Norris, 'in effect a declaration of war'. A still-controversial document, the wording was predictably squeaky clean in justifying a projected British invasion of Afghanistan. To obviate Russian diplomatic sensitivities (to the end, the Russian Foreign Minister in St Petersburg, Count Nesselrode, had disavowed the actions of his agents and even recalled Count Simonich, the Russian Ambassador to Teheran), the perceived Russian threat was studiously sidelined and Dost Mohammed was predictably identified as the villain of the piece; a ruler 'urging most unreasonable pretensions' and willing to 'call in every foreign aid that he could command'. Consequently, 'the hostile policy of the latter chief showed too plainly that, so long as Caubul remained under his government we could never hope that the tranquillity of our neighbourhood would be secured, or that the interest of our Indian empire would be preserved inviolate'. Any provocations by ally Ranjit Singh's Sikh kingdom, notably the occupation of Peshawar, was carefully sanitized and even the recent and provocative construction of Sikh forts at the entrance to the Khyber Pass by his General, Hari Singh, were portrayed as innocent defensive works. Thus:

In the crisis of affairs consequent upon the retirement of our Envoy from Caubul, the Governor-General felt the importance of taking immediate measures for arresting the rapid progress of foreign intrigue and aggression towards our own territories. His attention was naturally drawn at this conjuncture to the position and claims of Shah Shooja ool Mook.[30]

For Auckland's political advisers MacNaghten and Burnes, the political rewards were, indeed, great. Any personal frictions were at least temporarily sidelined as MacNaghten was duly appointed Envoy and Minister to the Court of Shah Shuja in Kabul and his deputy, Burnes, as Envoy to the Chief of Kalat and of all other states. As preparations for war commenced both were soon to pay the ultimate price for the realization of such great political ambitions.

The March on Kabul

In the wake of the 1838 Simla Manifesto, its military executor, the grand, eloquently titled 'Army of the Indus', slowly began to assemble. In scores of cantonments scattered across northern India, officers and men received their orders to mobilize. This was the British Army's first campaign of Queen Victoria's reign and many, trapped in the tedious routine of barrack life, relished the prospect of glory, adventure, and, not least, the excellent prospects for wider promotion and plunder traversing the mysterious mountains and passes of the Hindu Kush. Lieutenant Holdsworth, attached to the Bombay column, expressed a typical emotion at the prospect of war:

What is the cause of all this bustle and war I hardly know myself.... How it will turn out I know no more than the man in the moon: a soldier is a mere machine and is moved by his superiors just as a chess man by a chess player. Should there be any scrimmaging our men are in high spirits, and, will, I think, soon make the Ameers put their pipes in their pockets. Ours is the first European army that has been on the Indus since the time of Alexander.[31]

Lieutenant William Barr of the Bengal Horse Artillery similarly expressed his pleasure on receiving a late call-up to join Colonel Wade's predominantly Sikh forces which were assembling at Lahore at the end of December 1838:

I seemed destined to pass another season at least in the 'inglorious ease' of cantonment life, instead of existing amidst the turmoil and bustle of a camp. The command that now devolved on me opened a brighter prospect, and I looked forward with intense pleasure to the time I should be traversing the rich and fertile plains of the Punjab.[32]

Over the next few months, a vast force was assembled on the banks of the Indus at the major military cantonment of Ferozepore. The initial order of battle envisaged two divisions of British troops each drawn from the Bengal and Bombay Divisions respectively. Together they amounted to around 20,000 men. This combined force was to be supplemented by around 6,000 men of Shah Shuja's own contingent. A further 10,000 Indian troops, partly belonging to Shahzada Timur, and the rest Sikhs, would operate from Peshawar. In addition, Britain's principal Sikh ally, Ranjit Singh, promised to further supply a reserve 'army of observation' of 15,000 men to be stationed on his north-western frontier. In all the force amounted to over 40,000 effectives.

Such a force was considered sufficient to initially confront five identifiable enemies or potential classes of enemies who might be encountered both along the invasion route and in Afghanistan itself. These consisted of, firstly, the Afghan rulers of Kandahar (estimated to command 4,000–5,000 men); secondly, attacks *en route* from predatory tribes (notably the Baluchis and Khyber 'robber' tribes); thirdly, the main regular Afghan Army of Dost Mohammed himself (estimated at 15,000 men, mainly cavalry but including a respectable field artillery section) and, finally, at beleaguered Herat, a possible clash with 50,000 besieging Persians and their Russian allies. Also to be considered was some initial uncertainty concerning the attitudes of the Sind Emirs, the understandably reluctant hosts and principal paymasters for this invading British Army. In addition, the authorities in Calcutta could be by no means certain of the loyalty of the increasingly recalcitrant allied Sikh contingent ruled by a clearly ailing Ranjit Singh. It represented a formidable task for a minimal force with a clear 'want all troops to guard the communications' command, but one which 'soon made itself very seriously felt'.[33] Moreover it was one which relied on the still unshaken but manifestly unproven political assumptions of the Governor-General, Lord Auckland, and his forward policy advisers that the Afghan populace would be glad to dispense with Dost Mohammed in favour of Shah Shuja and that, consequently, very little internal opposition was to be anticipated.

The Army of the Indus was drawn primarily from two of the three East India Company's great armies, those of Bengal and Bombay (the third, the Madras Army, was strategically too far south to be of use). Both combined armies were originally to be commanded overall by Lieutenant-General Sir Henry Fane, the Commander-in-Chief of Bengal and of the Queen's troops in India. Accompanying him were two Bengal divisions under Generals Sir Willoughby Cotton and Duncan respectively. The Bengal Army divisions were to act as the spearhead, marching down the Indus River as far as Sukkur, where they were scheduled to join forces with one division of the Bombay Army, marching from distant Karachi under Lieutenant-General Sir John Keane, the latter's Commander-in-Chief. However, with the sudden news (received at Ferozepore in September 1838) that the Persians had abandoned the siege of Herat, it was further decided to reduce an already minimal army by one (Bengal) division.

Fane accordingly withdrew from overall command and was subsequently replaced by Sir John Keane. Indeed, for many observers, the political *raison d'être* of the whole expedition had been duly eliminated, but Auckland and his advisers, anxious to directly secure British influence in Afghanistan and preserve existing, painstakingly constructed alliances – and seemingly oblivious to the potentially immense logistical and military problems ahead – pressed on with preparations. It was arguably – and certainly in hindsight – a major political misjudgement.

Firstly, the reconstituted new army now comprised only one division from the Bengal Army, the First Bengal Division commanded by Major-General Sir Willoughby Cotton. This incorporated three 'Bengal Brigades' commanded by Brigadiers Robert Sale, William Nott and William Dennie respectively and consisted of mixed units of British regulars and Indian troops. The First Brigade (Sale's) incorporated the 13th Foot (Somerset Light Infantry), the 16th and 48th Bengal Native Infantry. The Second Brigade (Nott's) comprised the 31st, 42nd and 43rd Bengal Native Infantry. Finally, the Third Brigade incorporated the 3rd Buffs (West Kent) and the 2nd and 27th Bengal Native Infantry. Accompanying this Bengal force was the Cavalry Brigade under Brigadier Thackwell, constituted by the 16th Lancers and the 2nd and 3rd Bengal Light Cavalry.

Secondly, from the faraway Bombay Army, the single division, (initially commanded by Lieutenant-General Sir John Keane before his subsequent replacement of Fane as Commander-in-Chief), comprised two Bombay Army Infantry Brigades and one Cavalry Brigade, led by Major-General Sir Thomas Willshire, and Brigadiers Gordon and Scott respectively. The First Infantry Brigade consisted of the 2nd Queen's Regiment, the 17th Foot and the 1st, 2nd, 5th and 19th Bombay Native Infantry. The attached Bombay Cavalry Brigade (Scott's) comprised the 14th Light Dragoons (two squadrons) and the 1st Bombay Light Cavalry with the addition of the Poona Auxiliary Horse.

The training and equipment of the British soldier during the First Anglo-Afghan War differed little from that of the great Napoleonic Wars. Until 1847 they enlisted for life. Drawn mostly from the lowest levels of society they endured extreme serving conditions with frequent punishment by flogging, poor housing, diet and pay and resultant ill-health. The main infantry weapon was the ubiquitous 1802 or India pattern 'Brown Bess' muzzle-loading smoothbore flintlock musket and 17-inch bayonet. Their uniforms comprised scarlet jackets with a cumbersome bell-shaped shako headdress, patently unsuited to the climatic extremes of Afghanistan. Their Afghan enemy, if less well-trained and equipped, was a formidable foe. The predominantly tribal irregulars were skilled mountain fighters and whilst lacking heavy artillery, possessed a formidable light weapon – the *jezail* or long-barrelled matchlock. Its long barrel gave it greater accuracy and range than the British Brown Bess and British troops could only achieve superiority in the more disciplined shorter range volley-fire tactic. The Afghan rifleman or *jezailchi* often carried several of these loaded firearms for sniping purposes while the Afghan foot soldier generally carried the curved sword or *tulwar*, a small round shield and a straight 30-inch 'Khyber knife' for close-quarter battle. Most formidable of all were the white-robed *Ghazi* – religious warriors whose fanatical or suicidal head-on tactics could easily, if not halted by sustained British volley fire, decisively turn a battle. The Afghan cavalry, while mostly levies, were excellent light horsemen. Riding nimble and rugged Afghan ponies, often clad in helmet and chain mail, and carrying either sword or lance, they could be devastating when deployed against a demoralized or broken enemy. They were of less value in set-piece battles.

The plan of campaign even before the entry into Afghanistan was, as already indicated, fraught with *political* let alone physical, difficulties. The British frontier lay on the Sutlej River (see plate section) with the furthest outpost at Ludhiana. The independent Punjab and most of the five great rivers (the Sutlej, Ravi, Chenab, Jhelum and Indus) lay between the British and the Khyber Pass while the increasingly ill-disciplined Sikh Army remained an uncertain factor along the line of communications. Ranjit Singh, Britain's ageing and unpredictable Sikh ally, was accordingly not anxious to sanction use of the northerly route, the main line of communication likely to be traversed by the invading British troops, as even he could no longer guarantee control over his armies in the northern Punjab. Numerous ground-level reports by British officers of friction between neighbouring Sikh and British military units only served to confirm this turbulent and highly unpredictable political situation which, following Ranjit Singh's death in 1839, later erupted into full-scale war between Britain and the Sikh kingdom and British annexation of the Sikh state.

Added to this there was the potentially recalcitrant attitude of the Sind Emirs, who at least were militarily much weaker than the Sikhs. In order to avoid any local political friction the British were therefore forced to adopt a far longer and surreptitious route via the Upper Sind to the crossing point on the Indus at Sukkur, a distance of 446 miles from their launch pad at the major forward base at Ferozepore. From there it would proceed to Kabul via Quetta, Kandahar and Ghazni. This alternative longer route was not wholly disadvantageous – the shorter abandoned route would have involved the forcing of successive barely penetrable passes and tumbled mountains between Peshawar and Kabul and thus had no particular attraction, while the longer alternative and politically preferred advance on Kandahar would bring the army into far easier country. It would also hopefully produce more supplies and have easier routes than the much shorter one via the Khyber Pass. Similarly, the second major column, Commander-in-Chief Keane's Bombay Division, would proceed by sea from Bombay to Karachi, traversing parallel to the Indus River and thence link up with the Bengal Division at Sukkur near Quetta for the combined drive to Kabul.

As the two great columns commenced their march, the first political obstacle, the potentially hostile attitude of the Sind Emirs, already angered about being bullied into the logistical and financial support for the campaign, soon became evident. Thus in early December 1839, Lieutenant Holdsworth dolefully informed his sister from Vikkur:

Things look now a little more warlike. The Ameers, have endeavoured to cut off everything like a supply from this part of the country, and we have to depend ... on the supplies brought by shipping. We expected 2,000 camels and 500 horses here for sale but they are not to be seen at present. News has been received that they (the Ameers) have called in their army consisting of 20,000 Belooches.[34]

War with Sind seemed imminent. As Major James Outram, 23rd Regiment Native Infantry, and later political agent to Sind, noted on 19 December 1838:

The hostile preparations of the Ameers, who, whilst they continue to profess the utmost friendship for us are levying en masse their fighting men from the age of 17 to 60, bringing their guns from Larkhana to Hyderabad ... render it imperative that the communications of our army should be maintained by a strong force stationed in Sind, even should we pass through the country without actual rupture with them: accordingly the Resident this day dispatched an express request for the Reserve Force which has previously been warned to be assembled as early as practicable at Curachee.[35]

One of the Sind Emirs the, Emir of Meerpore 'whose hostility to the English is notorious' was particularly singled out as 'amenable to punishment'. However, by mid January 1839, after a further show of *force majeure* by a section of the Bengal Army and also by the Royal Navy, Royal Marines and the Bombay Division 40th Regiment at Karachi where the Sind fort received 32-pounder broadsides delivered with 'admirable precision',[36] a delegation from the Sind capital, Hyderabad, quickly agreed to supply the British Army, and the reinforcements were dispersed. Significantly, however, this crude demonstration of British military power was carried out against the specific advice of the Envoy Sir William MacNaghten, and heralded the first of many future clashes between the military and the more politically sensitive establishment of the Government of India.

The resolution of this first operational 'political' problem did not improve the logistical crisis which was evident from day one. The Army of the Indus, so magnificent to behold, was hopelessly ill-equipped for a journey of up to 1,200 miles, far away from its main bases of supply in India and conducted in largely unknown territory. The baggage train of the army was enormous. No specific orders appear to have been issued on this matter although Sir Henry Fane had initially issued an order cautioning 'against all large tents or establishments'.[37] Clearly, little or no attention was paid to this as officers' baggage requirements reached extraordinary, even ludicrous levels. Lieutenant-Colonel Hough recalled that 'most of the officers had too many camels, too large tents and too much baggage'.[38] Captain Neill of the 40th Regiment similarly deeply lamented the 'squandering of valuable time caused by the disposal of superfluous stores kit etc. and the difficulty in procuring the requisite quantity of carriage for the transport of overgrown baggage'.[39] Sir John Lawrence later revealed how one officer (of the 16th Lancers) was accompanied by as many as forty servants and the same unit even took with them the regimental pack of foxhounds![40] It was, in short, an army still fatally 'organised on the old Mogul principle ... when the Moguls moved up and down the length and breadth of Hindustan with huge escorts' – not an army geared to endless hostile territory with every extreme of climate and terrain.[41]

The transport crisis crippled the columns at every stage of the march. Many of the camels, for instance, particularly those directly attached to the cavalry and infantry trains, were overloaded and unsuited to the rough terrain. Moreover, the hired camel men frequently deserted in large numbers taking their camels with them. Captain Abbott claimed that 'overloading ... was the main cause of the loss ... an officer of the 2nd Cavalry told me he had seen fourteen maunds [1 maund = 80 lb] taken from the back of one camel, the maximum load allowed by regulations being only five maunds'.[42] Many camels perished not just from fatigue but from feeding in the poisonous tamarisk jungle which pervaded large sections of the line of march. In his memoirs, Captain Seaton, of the 35th Bombay Native Infantry, recalled how, on the journey from Shikarpur to Rojhan in the Upper Sind Desert:

> The only forage the camels could get was the tamarisk, and, being full of turpentine, it had on them the effect of a strong purgative, that told fatally on their strength and even killed some of them.... On the third day's march the poor animals were so much affected by the heat, by the fatigue of being loaded for so many hours, and by constant feeding on the tamarisk that some of them were seen to vomit, a thing thought impossible and all were so weakened that it was pitiable to see them.[43]

The death toll amongst both the European troops and particularly their Indian sepoy comrades and many thousands of civilian followers, paralleled that of their camels and horses. Cholera and dysentery were the biggest killers but sunstroke, jaundice (hepatitis) and sheer exhaustion added to the casualties. It was soon evident that the military and strategic planners in Calcutta had grossly underestimated both climate and terrain, especially the deserts of the Upper Sind where temperatures below freezing at night competed with heat of up to 140 °F in the day. The worse stretch of the march appears to have occurred between Shikarpur and Dadur and it was the Bombay Division, outpaced by its Bengal counterpart and suffering from the lack of water and supplies already requisitioned before them, which undoubtedly suffered the most.

But the desolate Upper Sind deserts provided the graveyard for many in both the Company's armies. One sepoy of the leading Bengal column recalled that it was

> only after leaving Shikarpur that our real troubles began. The whole country was a vast sandy desert. The water in the few wells was bitter

and even firewood and water had to be transported on camels ... one valley called Dadhar was the mouth of hell ... low lying and surrounded by hills so that no air ever came there.[44]

One officer of the Queen's Regiment tersely recorded his own experience on this particular 'death march': 'The first thirty miles across a desert nearly famished for want of water, the latter part of the way under a broiling sun, whole companies falling out from the two Regiments (Queen's and the 17th Foot) ... rode the last five miles in a most exhausted state.'[45]

The experiences of Captain Thomas Seaton, in May 1839, commanding a support convoy of 4,000 camels 'laden with grain, stores of all kinds and ten lakhs of rupees [1 *lakh* = 100,000 rupees ~ £10,000] for the Army of the Indus', appear to have been infinitely worse. At Rojhan, ominously situated on the edge of the desert, the wells, presumably drained by the preceding thousands of the Bengal column, almost immediately ran dry. Despite news of dry wells at Burshoree, twenty-six miles further on, and intelligence received of the virtual destruction of an earlier 2,500-strong camel convoy, the fatal decision was taken to proceed. The decision reflected the ruthlessly logistical imperatives of the day as hundreds of miles further on, forward columns were already demanding supplies. The resultant 'march of death' was vividly recalled by the young captain. Within three days of departure:

The water in the men's brass pots was ... exhausted, for the hot wind and the dust ... created an intolerable thirst and they drank without constraint. At midnight they began to flag, then to murmur, and, shortly there was a universal cry of 'water – water' ... not a tree, bush, scrub or blade of grass was to be seen – nothing but a scene of dreary desolation; and the road over this horrible plain was distinctly marked by the skeletons of men, camels and horses abandoned by their *Kafilahs* or by the army that preceded us. Wherever a foot trod, the surface of the deposit was broken into an impalpable powder in which there was something peculiarly irritating and which the light wind carried aloft. It was this fine dust settling on the clothes and sticking on the skin that, combined with the hot wind, created the thirst that so overpowered one.[46]

Even when the column reached the first thirty-two wells at Bursharee, excavated into the bottom of a ravine 'only six contained water – one of them was poisoned by an animal which had fallen into it, and, of the others, the water was so bitter and brackish the men said it turned their lothars black'.

Within hours another 'rider of the apocalypse', cholera, reared its ugly head and it was the rearguard which suffered most from its legacy of dead and dying. On 31 May, Seaton, now in charge of the rearguard,

found several camels dead with their loads lying behind them and three poor wretched surwars (camel drivers) in the last stages of dying of cholera deserted by their comrades. I could do nothing for them ... from where we halted to Hadjee Ka Chouk the route of the column was marked by scores of men scattered along the road ill and dying from fever, cholera and sheer exhaustion.[47]

As temperatures in the tents rose to 119 °F, heatstroke killed or incapacitated dozens of men and officers. Returning from the hospital, Captain Seaton found one casualty, significantly the only European doctor, Doctor Halloran

outside my tent, rushing about, a raving maniac. As force only made him worse I got a cloth, saturated it in water and cooled it by waving it in the air folded and then applied it to the nape of his neck ... he sank into my arms as quiet as a child, and we laid him down on his bed from whence he was never moved until he was taken to his grave.[48]

The impact of the *simoom*, an infamous, scorching desert wind of the region massively increased casualties. Seaton recalled how some of the men 'sank at once as if struck by some poison air, others were brought in alive but dying fast quite shrivelled in appearance as if the hot wind had dried up all the juices in their body. The first to succumb were those who went out without their upper garments.' Returning to camp another day Captain Seaton vividly recalled the nightmare awaiting him:

The scene in Major Liptrap's tent I shall never forget – it was appalling. Beaufort, suffering all the agonies of cholera, was the colour of lead; Halloran was raving. Liptrap and Manning, both of them speechless and helpless from utter exhaustion appeared likewise as if struck by cholera. The hospital halvidar sergeant came in every few minutes to report one or two deaths ... when he had returned, with the exception of the Desert wind howling through the tents, no souls were to be heard but the groans of the dying or the wail for the dead.[49]

In this apocalyptic situation it was the overburdened sepoys and the hundreds of ill-equipped camp-followers who suffered disproportionate losses. Captain Seaton confessed:

The sepoy each with a heavy musket, sixty rounds of ammunition, clothing, haversack with necessaries, accoutrements, and his brass pot filled with water were heavy laden for such a march, the burden doubling the already unbearable oppression of their tight-fitting woollen uniforms. The condition of the men ... was pitiable and every minute their sufferings increased ... so great was the distress ... that even the all-powerful prejudices of caste were forgotten and Hindoos drank out of the leathern bags, in common with Mahomedans, water served out by a European sergeant.[50]

The accompanying Indian civilians suffered immeasurable horrors: 'the poor heavily laden camp-followers, some carrying infants, were in a pitiable condition and the children's cries were heartrending. Strong men exhausted by carrying loads were scattered on the ground moaning and beating their breasts.' Despite efforts by regimental officers in the main column to alleviate the situation, it was the rearguard which was again left to clear up the mess – the cries and entreaties of the poor wretches who, as they sank by the roadside, saw the rearguard passing and feared they would be left to die were most heartrending. 'The guard', Seaton recalled, 'behaved nobly, giving to the poor wretches every drop of water they had', but 'it was a small quantity and did not go far'.[51]

Where pestilence failed to strike, the evil hand of man was not far removed. From Shikarpur to Kodala the struggling British columns were mercilessly assailed by hordes of robbers, the dreaded *Beloochees* or *Khyberees*, whose ferocity and thirst for plunder increased the further the troops were away from their home depots. An officer of the Queen's (Bombay Division) recalled one typical brutal skirmish near Kotra: 'we lost Private Adams, No. 2 Company; fell out on the march and was murdered by the Beloochees; also brought in a man of the 17th badly wounded!'[52] Retribution was swift and often merciless. One officer routinely reported 'five Beloochees killed the same day by scouting parties or the irregular horse, commanded by Major Cunningham.'[53]

Similarly, at Quetta, 'not a day passed without fresh instances of their atrocious conduct. They used to come into camp with articles for sale, inveigle men out to their fastnesses on the pretence of selling their grain cheap and then murder them.'[54] After one incidence of firing by some *kaukers* (local bandits), 'from the loop-holes of a mud round their hut ... on the skirts on a hill', the 16th Lancers surrounded the place and

> dismounted, seized the end of the matchlocks which were pointed through the loop-holes.... Some of the Lancers mounted upon the roof, formed of branches and a layer of mud, and, getting at the enemy a deadly struggled ensued. The kaukers resisting until five of them were killed, and the sixth, unequal from his wounds to any other effort was brought into camp and, on the decision of a military tribunal, hanged the next day on a tree in front of the walls of Quetta. After another skirmish with 'Beloochees' above the mouth of the Bolan Pass in which one man and several horses and camels were killed, British marksmen, returning their fire from below, contrived to pick off a round dozen of them.[55]

Further up the Pass, the 4th Dragoons collided with a party of Beloochees and, after losing two men wounded and three horses took a terrible vengeance with 'about forty Beloochees ... destroyed' and 'Major Daly ... spearing six of them with his own hand'.[56]

The irregulars attached to the columns meted out even more severe punishment. Lieutenant William Barr, hastening to join Colonel Wade's column, witnessed the results of such retribution along the route of the march:

> As we emerged from the ravines we were considerably disgusted at observing, on our right hand, a small tree with a few forked branches connected together by means of a cord, on which was strung a number of noses, ears and hands lately cut off from thieves who had been carrying on their avocation in these parts.[57]

Near Ghazni, an officer of the Queen's Regiment saw the results of another punitive raid by the 16th Bengal Native Regiment:

> We saw some of their handiwork in a mountain pass on the march in. Heads, legs, and arms, perhaps torn asunder by dogs; one body which was nearly perfect was in a grotesque position – the arms were bent upwards, the fingers and thumbs extended and pointing to where the nose would have been, only the upper part of the skull was missing.[58]

As the intensity of the attacks increased a 'scorched earth' policy soon became the official norm. Alleged 'bandit villages' bore the brunt of the punishment. 'In our downward route from Guzhnee to the hills', one officer recalled, 'we were actively employed in revenging all the insults which we had not time to notice on the march up. Wherever an officer or batch of camp-followers had been murdered we blew up a fort or looted – *scotice* "harried" the nearest village.'[59]

But it was Shah Shuja's contingent which, early on, achieved the most notorious reputation. They perpetrated particularly brutal acts of retribution, not only against robbers or alleged robbers but even towards captured regular Afghan troops. Between Kandahar and Ghazni, for instance, a brief skirmish between British Cavalry and Horse Artillery and 'a band of Dost Mohammed's horsemen' resulted in a loss of forty enemy killed and double the number taken prisoners, 'most of whose heads were taken off the same evening by His Majesty Shah Shoojah-oo-Moolk's executioner'. Earlier at Siriusp, near Ghazni, the same horrified officer observed 'the hind-quarters of two Ghilzees, whom the Shah had caused to be blown from the mouth of a gun for attempting to steal his camels'.[60]

At Peshawar, a main staging post for the Army of the Indus, such extreme measures were equalled, perhaps surpassed, by the notorious near psychopathic allied General Avitabile, an Italian mercenary engaged in the service of Ranjit Singh as Governor of the district. He conducted a veritable reign of terror against local criminals, or merely suspected criminals. As a policy of 'instant justice by example', a gallows was permanently erected on the outskirts of the town and, daily, up to a score of corpses were left dangling. Thus Lieutenant Barr observed with morbid fascination:

> The number of gallows that it had been deemed necessary to erect in environs of the city ... constructed of a sufficient size to accommodate five or six malefactors at a time ... their bodies are allowed to marinate on the gibbets ... the number of corpses, stiffened into the attitudes they assumed when convulsed with the last agonies of death, or suspended (as some are) by the feet that are thus presented to a gaze of a stranger, renders a visit to the suburbs of Peshawar far from agreeable.[61]

Frequent deaths from accident or even suicide added to the mounting losses of the Army of the Indus. Early in their long march, the Queen's Regiment, attached to the Bombay column, were devastated by news of the deaths of three brother officers who had suddenly disappeared on a hunting expedition. It was later discovered that a forest fire near Jurruck had overwhelmed the three young Lieutenants, Sparke, Nixon and Hibbert. Their bodies were recovered and left 'lying at the quarter guard of the Light Cavalry ... there they lay, three blackened distorted corpses, their clothes burned off only to be recognised by their stature and the rings they wore on their fingers'. In one fell swoop the regiment had 'lost three of our most useful subalterns'.[62] A similar tragic accident occurred near the 'bridge of boats' laid across the Indus River at Fort Bukkur. The bridge broke as a sepoy company crossed and three boats were swept away. The boatmen were unable to stop the boats until they had gone six miles. Four sepoys were drowned.[63] In another incident near Kunduz, 'in one of the shallow torrents a little off the road', was found the 'drowned body [of] ... one of the 16th Lancers with his regimentals on, supposed to have fallen down drunk in the rear of the brigade in advance'.[64]

Yet it was by no means a universal disaster. For the many indigenous Indian and Afghan peasant and trading communities, the passage of thousands of troops of the Army of the Indus presented unrivalled opportunities for profit as well as plunder. Frequently, the British exploiters became the exploited. Lieutenant Holdsworth noted the 'great number of native merchants etc', who 'took advantage of the opportunities afforded by the passage ... of the different divisions of our Army'. Many were from the famed nomadic *Powindah* trading communities, great colourful clans of warrior merchants, including Ghilzais and Kharotis who, for hundreds of years, had seasonally brought their caravans through the passes from central Afghanistan to the Punjab plain. They occasionally paid tax to the Kabul Government and grazing tax to local officials but generally preserved their independence fiercely. There were also Jajjis, Jadrans and Mangals who travelled south to trade. Local villages probably prospered the most. As one column approached Hyderzye, across the Logar River, the villagers 'brought into camp loads of ootah [ground wheat flour] and ghee [clarified butter] for sale, but at a high rate, 5 pounds and a half for one rupee of the former and two and a half of the latter made from the Doomba sheep tails! Plenty of Doomba sheep are also procurable at two, three and four rupees each.'[65] Similarly, Lieutenant Atkinson recorded how the grain for cattle had become 'exceedingly dear, the natives raising the price to about 500%'.

Camel and horse merchants were by far the greatest profiteers, as animal mortality rates soared. They were not averse to cunning deceptions including taking payment without delivery, or departing at night with their camels before the agreed destination was reached. At Kandahar, a highly fertile region, the weary troops were besieged by scores of fruit and kebab sellers. Officers could procure countless plums, peaches, grapes and mushrooms and here, also, 'quaff bowls of sherbets which is grape juice cooled by lumps of snow which, notwithstanding the intense heat, they contrived to bring in its integrity from the neighbouring mountains'.[66] Equally valued and readily purchased were the *caubaubs* cooked at a moment's notice in the marketplace, a welcome addition to the largely biscuit and beef diet of many of the British troops. At Kandahar it was also noticed how many merchants deliberately withheld their corn stocks so as to raise prices. As one angry sepoy commented, 'a merchant will go wherever he can cheat'.[67] Nevertheless, after the horrors of the Upper Sind desert most sepoys welcomed the 'fertile country' around Kandahar, where gardens with flowers and many kinds of fruit abounded. 'We began to feel happier as none of us had ever enjoyed a good meal since leaving Shikarpur; all we had to eat was parched grain or barley, or a small quantity of flour.'[68]

Before reaching this 'Garden of Eden' around Kandahar, and, after crossing the Upper Sind deserts, both columns had to traverse the dreaded Bolan and Khojak Passes. Although these passes could not, as we shall see, be compared to the later horrors of the Khurd-Kabul, Tezeen and Jagdallak Passes, the experience of the Bombay column, again traversing over the detritus of the preceding Bengal Army, made these places to be truly dreaded. One officer described the area as 'a very counterpart of the Valley of the Shadow of Death – being full of quagmires and the road strewed with the bodies of thousands of camels, the victims of the two preceding armies; and here and there we stumbled over the corpses of men in every stage of decomposition'.[69] Sepoy Subadar Ram noted: 'The water courses were all blocked and the wells were filled with pilkwood that made the water stink so as to make one sick even when approaching the well.'[70] A Queen's officer confirmed that, 'our only beverage was facetiously termed "Dead Man's Entire" being frequently extracted from muddy ditches choked up here and there by the carcass of a Beloochee or camp follower'.[71] The less than hygienic behaviour of many of the soldiers, and especially the camp-followers, completed a deadly equation and inevitably 'caused a universal dysentery among officers and men'.[72] The Bolan Pass was also the most vulnerable part of the journey, providing good cover for *jezail* sniper fire 'by which a few hundred men judiciously placed on the heights could have prevented our forcing the Pass'.[73] While fratricidal fighting between rival tribes over opportunities for booty gave some relief to the column commanded by Major James Outram, 'distressing evidence' presented itself to the main column, 'of their previous handiwork in the bodies of upward of thirty sepoys and followers of the Bengal and Shah's columns, which were lying exposed on the road, together with the remains of carts, by burning of which others of the slain appeared to have been consumed'.[74]

The experience of this terrible journey through the Bolan Pass, in which the spectre of death was never far away, was brilliantly captured in an evocative account by Captain Seaton. He described a typical night march:

> The flanking parties on the ridge of the hills stood out clear against the sky, some looking down from the rocks overhanging the Pass; the long column of soldiers was traced by the flash of their arms glittering in the moonlight, and the gaunt figures of the camels were seen moving on with their silent unearthly pace; the parties of horsemen, with long bright matchlocks over their shoulders, or tall spears in their hands, were scattered about, some dismounted, taking a whiff of their hookah by a fire, while others moved slowly on with the camels; while crowds of camp-followers and people, all laden with burdens of one description or another, were seen crossing the stream in several places, and then vanishing in the gloomy Pass. The fitful glare of the fires tinged with red the bronze-coloured faces grouped around, or was reflected by the stream, driven up in spray by the cattle dashing through. The grand rocks forming the defile were at the same time just sufficiently lighted up to show their immensity, and to intensify the gloom beyond.[75]

The journey through this and the Khojak Pass soon finished off not only large numbers of camel transport but also many of the more finely bred cavalry horses, which were subsequently devoured by the starving camp-followers. As the columns neared Quetta a 'great number' of these cavalry horses were shot 'in consequence of being in an exhausted state from over-fatigue and deficiency of grain; and, whenever we passed the carcasses on the road left by the Column in advance, we invariably found the natives busy employed in skinning them, which they managed very dexterously. The dead camels ... were treated in the same way.'[76] Major Outram estimated that between Quetta and Khandahar about 150 of the Bombay Horse Artillery and Auxiliary horses had 'dropped on the road from exhaustion', while the Bengal Division had lost 350 – only the 'stouter Arab and Persian horses and a few Cape horses'[77] proving more resilient. By April 1839 cavalry horses were reportedly dying by the score, with the 16th Lancers even forced to dismount and goad their horses at the point of a lance.[78]

It was at Quetta in mid-April 1839 that the food supply crisis, massively exacerbated by the huge losses of transport camels and horses, came to a head. Superintending Surgeon James Atkinson noted the resultant collapse in morale:

'It was at Quetta that the state of the Army, for want of supply and of grain and oottah [flour; sometimes 'ottah'] became alarming for it was at Quetta that abundant resources were promised and expected and, when the sad reality was made known, the whole camp was filled with disappointment and dismay.'[79]

The problem was largely blamed on the 'shameful inefficiency of the Commissariat'. The Army had now gone beyond the reach of the India system of related merchants eager to sell supplies, beyond the help of 'carrier tribes' and classes and, consequently, Commissariat officers were forced to pay exorbitant prices to local merchants. It would be no exaggeration to say that at Kandahar the very survival of the grand but hopelessly maladministered Army of the Indus had depended on the logistical support of local Afghan trading communities. Not surprisingly, cash soon ran out and the British officers were themselves forced to buy provisions or replace losses with their own pay while, at the same time, their soldiers were reduced to half rations and the camp-followers to quarter rations. Lieutenant Holdsworth bitterly commented upon the injustice of this system which reduced many British officers to bankruptcy. He observed:

At Tatta each officer received a month's pay in advance, that he might purchase cattle for his baggage. This is to be deducted by three instalments, one from each of the next three issues of pay. An Ensign's pay for one month will hardly purchase sufficient conveyances ... for the loss of a camel an officer faced losing one month's pay and must leave his kit on the ground, as he has nothing wherewith to replace his loss.[80]

Several officers tried to estimate the huge human and material losses sustained by the Army of the Indus by the time it had reached Kandahar. Lieutenant Havelock, for instance, estimated that up to 27,000 rounds of ammunition and fourteen barrels of gunpowder had been lost in the transport debacle along the passes.[81] Major Outram further estimated that while at least 500 'Beluchis', 'Kakars' and Afghans had been killed between Shikarpur and Kandahar, the British had lost between thirty and forty killed in open combat, but these figures of course omitted the scores of British troops who had died from or were crippled by dysentery, cholera, accidents, fatigue and heatstroke. In addition, many more sepoys and hundreds, possibly thousands of camp-followers had died or been murdered or maimed – or even starved – in this desperate advance.[82]

Halt at Kandahar

Only at Kandahar did the Army of the Indus receive any respite, but even there it was to take three months, between April and June 1839, before the columns were again capable of moving forward. Kandahar at least provided the first opportunity for the British 'puppet' Shah Shuja to publicly celebrate his return from exile and consolidate his claim to the Afghan throne. On the morning of 24 April 1839, the King himself approached Kandahar having already outpaced even his British Army protectors. It was to be the first big test of his credibility with the Afghan people but, before he was even three miles out of the city, the signs seemed propitious as he was besieged by scores of horsemen and local *sirdars* swearing fealty. An anonymous officer vividly recalled his triumphal entry into the city of Kandahar in a column of a Bombay newspaper:

> One standard after another thus joined the King and, ere his Majesty had reached Kandahar he had been joined by about 1,500 well mounted, dressed and caparisoned horse. Mr MacNaghten and the officers of his mission with a small honorary escort were alone in attendance of the British force. On his Majesty's entry in to the city there could not be less than between 60,000 and 70,000 persons present. The balconies were crowded with women – the streets lined with men – and from all quarters a universal shout of welcome was heard. The exclamations were, 'Kandahar is gained from the Baruckzyes', 'may your power endure for ever'. 'We look to you for protection'; 'may your enemies be destroyed', 'son of Timour Shah you are welcome'.
>
> Flowers and loaves of bread were cast before his Majesty – After passing through the city the King dismounted from his horse and proceeded to the shrine containing the shirt of the prophet and offered up thanksgivings: thence he went to the tomb of his grandparents and prayed.[83]

On the surface this was indeed a triumph and may have imbued MacNaghten and his 'politicals' with a false – indeed fatal – sense of confidence at this early stage of the British occupation. Within two weeks, however, the mood had changed perceptively as hundreds more starving British troops and their followers flooded into the city, many soon to be enraged by the blatant profiteering indulged in by local merchants. In the meantime, at the grand review held in honour of the Shah on 8 May 1839 (but carefully and deliberately designed, despite the recent deprivations and losses of the march, to reveal a massive show of British force), the atmosphere remained relatively cordial. An officer of the Queen's Regiment who participated in this grand *tomasha* (ceremony) vividly recalled the colourful scenes which unfolded on a plain below the city of Kandahar:

> The troops were drawn up first in a line extending beyond where the eye could reach; the right wing comprised of the Bengal, the left of the Bombay army, and flanked by artillery, from whence we fired a double salute of twenty one guns. We then formed a column and marched past in succession at open order, all saluting and the colours of each corps lowered, a compliment only to crowned heads.[84]

It was his first glimpse of Shah Shuja:

> The Shah was seated under an unpretending canopy of red baize behind which was arranged a select portion of his own troops. His apparel, though seemingly plain, was rich; he was clad in a dark green velvet tunic girt by a cincture of emeralds and had two magnificent stones of the same quality in his cap. From the glimpse I caught of him on marching past he appeared to be a gentlemanly-looking fellow of middle age with a splendid black beard – but that indeed is no rarity in this country. He made some handsome presents of scimitars and horses to our chiefs; but as far as I can learn, the men did not profit by his liberality.[85]

Such 'liberality' did not apparently win over many of the thousands of Afghan spectators. Sepoy Sita Ram, attached to Shah Shuja's own 6,000-strong contingent, soon sensed the underlying hostility in Kandahar. 'At first the people seemed to be pleased on his return but it was said that they despised him in their hearts and only the fear of the Sirkar's (British) army kept them civil.' He recalled that the *sirdars* were particularly 'offended' that Shah Shuja had returned with a foreign army. They said that he had

> shown the English the way into their country, and that shortly they would take possession of it … it was this that enraged them … I knew the people did not care the least about them and that anger grew

when they saw that the English army was not returning to Hindustan. Instead they turned the place into a regular cantonment.[86]

Another eyewitness to the parade, Superintending Surgeon James Atkinson, concluded that the assembled Afghan crowd were more fascinated by British military might than by any love for their returned king: 'I cannot say much about the Afghan multitude ... A loud shout was raised, "May the king live forever!", but not quite in the "*vive le roi*" fashion'.... They gazed on without any emotion of any kind.'[87] Lieutenant Holdsworth similarly commented that at this grand *tomasha*, 'such ... was the unpopularity of the Shah that out of the whole population of Candahar very few persons were looking on, they the easterners are devoted sight-hunters'.[88] One officer of the Queen's Regiment was even more cynical. He ridiculed

the purest strain of humbug relying that the troops will participate in the enthusiasm expressed by all the natives of Candahar at the return of their legitimate sovereign, Soojah-ool-Moolk; the fact being that nine out of ten of the said natives would prefer the sway of Dost Mohammed, a wise and equitable monarch whom they can no longer regard as a 'usurper' since he has occupied the throne unmolested for a period of thirteen years.[89]

It was a sentiment shared, albeit for very different reasons, by their *feringhee* occupiers. Many British officers were already angered by the reneging of the Shah's earlier promise to award them presents or treasure on their arrival at Kandahar. Equally infuriating for many in the British military were the continuing conciliatory policies of the Company political agents attached to their columns, whose first and overriding priority was always to maintain social peace and not rock the financial and political boat. After the murder of one straggler and mutilation of another of the 17th Foot, one officer fully vented his feelings over the 'soft' treatment afforded to four of the captured murderers:

One of them was sworn to by the wounded 17th man as being one of the murderers and we were all in great hopes of seeing the black-guards dancing the tightrope; but, instead of that they were all brought on ... to Dadur, where they were given up to one of the polit-ical diplomatic gentlemen, who, it is said, actually let them go with five rupees to carry them home ... This was carrying the conciliation principle too far with a vengeance![90]

After the mutilation and murder of a Captain Hand of the 1st Bombay Grenadier Regiment in June 1839, Lieutenant Holdsworth again protested bitterly: 'A good number of these rascals have been since taken, and, I suppose hanged; less the conciliation principle lets these rascals off also.'[91] The same officer later criticized the unwelcome political restraint again enforced after the brutal killing and 'dreadful mutilation' of a 16th Lancer, Lieutenant Inverarty, observing: 'The Shah and Sir John (Keane) were on the point of burning down the village near which the murder occurred, but the political department would not allow it.'[92] Keane later 'begged all officers never to go out into the country unless in large parties and well armed'.[93]

At least the opportunity for action and, indeed, retribution presented itself at Ghazni, Dost Mohammed's well-defended medieval fortress which commanded the main road to the final destination of Kabul. However, before this next advance, the exhausted Army of the Indus continued to rest and recuperate for three months in the fertile region surrounding Kandahar. As Captain Seaton recalled as he belatedly joined the Army at Kandahar, 'We found ourselves in a land flowing with milk and honey', although arriving 'too late for the glory and honour we coveted'.[94] Lieutenant Holdsworth observed the 'excellent European fruit here and the gardens about the place are very large and beautiful – peaches, apricots, cherries, apples, grapes and melons. I never tasted anything more delicious than the melons here'.[95]

Nevertheless, even here, the spectre of illness and death never left the column. The huge British camp around Kandahar experienced further serious outbreaks of disease, particularly hepatitis and dysentery – a misery accentuated by incessant and murderous attacks by Ghilzai marauders. An officer of the Queen's Regiment recorded the constant boredom and ever-present fear of imminent death:

Oh the long wearisome days I have spent on my back looking at the hateful mud walls of Kandahar and beset by legions of flies against whom I have no strength to defend myself. If I fell into a broken slumber towards evening, I was generally aroused by the 'Dead March' and funeral processions burying some fresh victim by the graves in front of the quarter guard.[96]

Forced to remain for two months in the unhealthy surroundings of Kandahar, Major James Outram also noted the increasing brutality of the reprisals taken against Afghan raiders. Again the Shah's contingent exceeded the norm: 'the Shah hoping by several examples to check the evil has caused to be blown away from a gun a Ghiljee', while only two days later Major Outram witnessed the return of the 'heads of four Afghans who had been slain in an attempted raid upon his camels'.[97] Even this represented no deterrent and, on the same day as these beheadings, up to 150 camels of Her Majesty's 13th Regiment were carried off while grazing close to the camp.

One historian summed up the emasculated state of the once glorious Army of the Indus by the end of May 1839. As the force prepared to march on Ghazni the horses had been deprived of grain for twenty-six days. The Bengal Cavalry Brigade had lost 350 horses out of an establishment of 2,560, and the Bombay Cavalry 150 out of 1,950. All the British troops had been on enforced half rations for twenty-eight days and camp-followers on a very small ration for forty-eight days. By 24 April only rations for two and a half days had been left in the Commissariat for the whole force. More ominous in logistical terms was the huge loss of camels, the key means of transport. Some 20,000 camels had been lost, stolen or had died in the Bengal column alone since its departure from Ferozepore.[98] Continuing blunders by the Commissariat added to the misery. Even when a convoy of Lokhani camels carrying a total of 20,000 *maunds* (1.6 million lb) arrived on 24 June it was revealed that 'the bargain had been only to carry provisions to Kandahar and as the men could not be induced to proceed, the whole had to be left there and the force marched again on half rations'.[99] As military historian Major Helsham Jones confirmed, 'It appears to have been very fortunate for the British that no opposition was met with at Kandahar'.[100]

During the prolonged stay at Kandahar, civilian desertion also became a major problem. Countless camp-followers, until then existing only on survival rations, fled the column in a desperate dash to return to their home villages in India. For one group of over 200 the decision to leave proved fatal. Entrusting themselves to a treacherous armed bodyguard in league with local brigands, these refugee camp-followers were, on the sixth day of their march, tricked into surrendering their few arms and confined to a local fort at a place called Maroof. Superintending Surgeon James Atkinson later recorded their terrible fate:

One by one the poor wretches were brought out through the gate and savagely murdered. This dreadful slaughter had gone on for sometime when the shrieks and groans of the victims reached the ears of those still within the fort and told them of the fate that awaited them. In the agony of horror and despair, they clambered up the walls to escape; many had their limbs broken in wildly springing down outside and thus disabled, they were cut to pieces. In the frightful struggle for life, very few are understood to have got back to Kandahar to tell the horrible tale.

... it is said the murderers first deliberately made Mohammedans of the Hindoos and then cut their throats. The Mohammedans were put to death outright.[101]

The Assault on Ghazni

In the face of such adversity it was surely a huge relief when the main body finally set off to attack Ghazni on 27 June 1839. Unlike Kandahar, Ghazni had steadfastly refused to acknowledge Shah Shuja. Lying about 280 miles from Kandahar, it constituted a prestigious target as Dost Mohammed's own son, Hyder Khan, commanded the 3,000-strong garrison and its fall would open the gateway to the main prize of Kabul. (His other, eldest, son, Afzal Khan, commanded a 5,000-strong cavalry force outside the city.) Before the British arrival, however, an incredible and subsequently highly controversial tactical decision had already been taken. The four 18-pounders, the only breaching or siege guns the Army of the Indus possessed were, after having been hauled with so much trouble through the Bolan and Khojak passes, inexplicably left behind at Kandahar. At least one historian attributes this astonishing negligence to further political interference in military operations: 'This was done in consequence of the assurances of the 'politicals' that no opposition would be met with towards Kabul. Sir John Keane had been advised to proceed with a force much less than what he took.'[102]

At least the 13,000-strong British column, despite rising sickness levels, was still blessed with a sizeable force of European infantry and cavalry. The European battalions of the 13th and 17th Foot and the 2nd Queen's averaged 520 NCOs and men, while the 16th Lancers, freshly resupplied with horses, could still deploy 400 sabres. The force marched in three columns. The advance column was commanded by the Commander-in-Chief himself, Sir John Keane. The second consisted of the 6,000-strong Shah Shuja contingent and the third column was commanded by Brigadier Roberts. The British force reached the city of Ghazni in stages between 19 and 21 July. At first sight the fortress appeared impregnable. Captain Thomson, the Commanding Engineer attached to the Bengal Corps, produced an extremely pessimistic report:

When we came before it, on the morning of 21 July, we were very much surprised to find a half rampart in good repair, built on a scalpel mound about 35 ft high, flanked by numerous towers and surrounded by a 'Fausse Braje' and a wet ditch. The irregular figure of the enceinte gave a good flanking fire whilst the height of the citadel covered the interior from the commanding fire of the hills to the north. In addition to this the towers at the angles had been enlarged, screen walls had been built before the gates, the ditch cleared out and filled with water and an outwork built on the right hand of the river so as to command the bed of it.[103]

The Army of the Indus was clearly ill-equipped for a frontal assault, the works 'evidencing much stronger than we had been led to expect and such as our Army could not venture to attack in a regular manner'.[104] As a consequence of the earlier flawed political advice, 'we had no battery train, and to besiege Ghazni in force would require a much larger one than the Army ever possessed. The great command of the parapets from 60–70 feet, with a wet ditch represented insurmountable obstacles to an attack by mining or escalade.'[105]

For a brief while it seemed as if decisions by the despised 'politicals' had not just interfered with, but had fatally undermined the first major military operation of the Army of the Indus. As at Kandahar, however, fortune smiled and a combination of Afghan treachery and good engineering skills exposed a chink in the Afghan armour. An Afghan deserter approached the British camp with news of a weakened entrance to the Kabul Gate. Armed with this information, General Keane's chief engineer was now able to confirm a risky but feasible possibility of a *coup de main*: 'The road to the gate was clear, the bridge over the ditch unbroken; there were good positions for Artillery within 300 yards of the walls on both sides of the road, and we had information that the gateway had not been built up, a reinforcement from Kabul being expected.'[106] As plans were finalized, the Bengal column, including Her Majesty's 13th Light Infantry and 16th Native Infantry, assiduously prepared the ground for a full frontal attack. A concerted drive began to force the enemy out of the gardens and old buildings that surrounded the town. The stage was now set for a brief, ferocious but glorious victory for both the Army of the Indus (and the wider British Army), one which was to earn it its first campaign medal. Before the assault, however, another appalling 'war crimes' incident occurred in defiance of the view of one official historian who claimed that 'no excesses were committed'[107] during this first major set-piece action. A failed preemptive strike by 2,000 Ghilzee horseman and 1,000 Afghan infantry on the British Camp outside Ghazni was responded to with appalling savagery. As the Afghan cavalry fled, the now infamous, ill-disciplined and murderous Shah Shuja's contingent descended upon the exposed 'poor foot pads ... they were terribly mauled and a great number of prisoners taken whose heads the Shah struck off immediately'![108]

Soon afterwards the great assault on Ghazni began. Led by a storming company traditionally and appropriately entitled the 'Forlorn Hope' and, drawn from the light companies of the four European regiments – the 2nd Foot (Queen's), the 13th, the 17th Foot and the Bengal European Regiment – a major attack was conducted in the early hours of the morning of 22 July 1839. Within the spearhead company was positioned a storming party led by Colonel Dennie. Armed with 300 lb of gunpowder, its aim was to blow the vulnerable Kabul Gate to smithereens. Behind them advanced hundreds of red-coated British troops and Bengal Native Infantry. Lieutenant Holdsworth vividly recalled his pre-battle nerves:

> That day the 22nd, I shall never forget; it was a very desperate one – there was a nervous and irritability and excitement about us the whole day, constantly looking at the place through spy-glasses etc; and then fellows began to make their wills and tell each other what they wished to have done in case they fell; altogether it was not at all pleasant and everyone longed most heartily for the morrow, and to have it over. I felt as I used to do when I was a child and I knew I must take a black dose or have a tooth drawn the next morning.[109]

An officer of the Queen's Regiment, stationed amongst the first echelon, recalled the moment of the great assault as the thin red lines of 1,500 British troops and their Indian allies began their relentless advance:

> We remained ... upwards of an hour smoking our pipes and listening in to the Brigadier who chatted with us in the most affable and enlivening manner. At length ... the wistful word was passed to advance and the column moved in deep silence. As we neared the fort, the ... thunder opened from three sides simultaneously. For my own part I felt, I know not why, a most comfortable conviction that I should not be even scratched, let alone killed in the encounter; so on I marched amid showers of shot and shells whizzing, tearing up the earth and exploding in all directions. A more brilliant panorama could scarcely be conceived; for the moon was down, the day had not yet dawned and the fire of the guns and the blue lights spreading from the walls to show us the way, shed a most ghastly and truly infernal hue upon every object. Our way led up a steep ascent leading to a massive gate in one of the bastions. A few minutes before we arrived

this was blown to atoms by the action of 300 pounds of powder piled against it and the advance ... rushed in, closely followed by the column, at the head of which was the Queen's as the senior regiment.[110]

Lieutenant Holdsworth now also advancing forward, also recalled the terrifying atmosphere produced by the moonless, gusting night, eerily illuminated by the enemy's spectacular blue flares:

They pointed their Long Tom a 52 pounder at us and sent the shot over our heads and a little to our left. The ball made a terrifying row rushing over us.... The noise was fearful and the whole scene the grandest ... the most awful I ever witnessed. I caught myself once or twice trying to make myself as small as I could. As we got nearer the gate it got worse and the enemy from their own loopholes began to pepper us with matchlocks and arrows. The scene was now splendid – the enemy ... threw out blue lights in several places which looked beautiful and the flames of their and our artillery together with the smaller flashes from the matchlock men added to the roar of their big guns, the sharp crackling of the matchlocks, the whizzing of the cannonballs and ours – the singing of the bullets and the whizzing of their arrows, all combined, made up as pretty a little row as one would wish to hear.[111]

Afghan resistance was much more determined than expected and fierce fighting broke out at the breach and cascaded along the parapets. The 2nd Foot (Queen's) and the Bengal European Regiment bore the brunt of the surprisingly intense hand-to-hand fighting:

The leading and particularly the rear companies were more roughly handled – some of the men literally cut to pieces; nor would you be surprised at the gashes that were inflicted, could I show you a specimen of the arms they used – a crooked sabre, some two inches broad in the blade which I took from the first prisoner who surrendered to me.[112]

Elsewhere, as the extended companies of the 13th Foot closed up and followed the main advance body into the demolished gate, the taking of prisoners became more of a luxury. The ensuing rout added to the overkill. Lieutenant Holdsworth observed how 'the greater part were cut down by the Dragoons or spifflicated by the Lancers'.[113] Such merciless action apparently reflected British anger concerning the treacherous behaviour of Afghan snipers located *inside* the town where 'the men ... still continued to be picked off occasionally by potshots from loopholes and corners'. But it was noted that 'to every matchlock thus presented, at least a score of muskets replied.[114]

It was a great British triumph, but both sides had fought heroically. The British success was attributed not only to the Kabul Gate's weakness but to the failure of the Afghan commanders to react to this surprise attack, expecting only an escalade in daylight with apparent orders not 'to fire a shot until the heads of the British troops were above the walls, and to the fact that the blue "incendiaries" were burnt ... *on* the walls instead of throwing them over amongst the attacking troops'.[115] The casualties were relatively minor or even 'trifling' for the British – seventeen dead and eighteen officers and 147 men wounded, but severe for the 3,000 Afghan defenders who lost an estimated 1,500 captured and up to 1,000 killed. Many of the enemy, as we have seen, were killed by the ferocious mopping-up operations by the British cavalry outside the city walls. Surgeon Atkinson, who received thirty-eight wounded cases into his field hospital, confirmed the ferocity of the fighting. He observed that the bulk of the British wounds were caused by cut and slashing action: 'happily the gunshot wounds, the most dangerous, were few. All the sword cuts ... were very numerous, and many of them very deep.' The high survival rate of the British wounded was attributed by him to the shortage of rum as 'in consequence there was no inflammatory action to produce fever and to interrupt the adhesion of parts – a strong argument in favour of teetotalling'![116]

Many British officers were shocked by the carnage which confronted them in the aftermath of the battle. Lieutenant Holdsworth recalled stampeding, wounded horses still loose in the streets and evidence of ferocious fights exemplified by eight Afghans lying in one particular spot where 'a tumbril had blown up and their bodies were still burning from the effects'.[117] Major Outram noted how 'every street was strewed with the slain – no less than 500 having been killed within the walls and fifty-eight alone having fallen in the attempt to defend one fortified house against a company of Her Majesty's 17th Foot'. He also reconfirmed how numbers of the fugitives 'were cut up by the Cavalry, upwards of 50 being killed by the 1st Bombay Light Cavalry alone, with the loss of only one havildar killed and six troopers wounded'.[118] Officially supervising the burials, Surgeon Atkinson recalled the 'dreadful sight' of the incarceration of over 450 corpses in the inner fort area:

The dead bodies stripped perfectly naked ... dragged down from the ramparts to be buried in deep pits, ready prepared about fifty paces south east of the gate ... some of them in strange attitudes produced by the spasms and agonies of death; scarcely one stretched out, as in the usual position of exhausted nature but all stiff, sharp and angular as if still animated with the wild ferocious spirit which inspired their living efforts.

Fears of disease, however, led him to recommend burning the corpses but the paucity of wood led to a compromise with the three pits 'heaped well up with earth'.[119] By stark contrast to such horrors of battle, the 300 surviving wives and families of the defenders and of Mohammed Hyder Khan, Dost Mohammed's son, were carefully protected and conveyed to a place of safety.

Looting was widespread and partly compensated for the horrors of the battle, although British prize agents stationed at the gates made some of the troops refund their ill-gotten gains. The 13th and 17th Regiments of Foot fared better in the citadel itself. Five hundred thousand pounds of flour or wheat were found in the fortress, a very acceptable windfall for the hard-pressed and exhausted British Commissariat. More than one thousand 'magnificent horses' were captured as well as much-needed packhorses and camels. It was a great *strategic* triumph. One of Dost Mohammed's strongest or principal fortresses on his crucial south flank had been captured. It represented a major blow to his confidence; in the words of one military expert, 'the fall of Ghazni paralysed the defence of Kabul'.[120] The alternative for a weakened Army of the Indus had been too terrible to contemplate. 'If we had failed we should have had the whole country down upon us within a few days', wrote one relieved British officer – 'the fate of India depended on us taking this place'.[121] It was, perhaps, no surprise that Sir John Keane wept publicly on hearing the victorious cheers from his men lining the walls of Ghazni.

The road to Kabul was now relatively clear and, although sporadic attacks continued against the now combined Bombay and Bengal Army, the way forward seemed less dangerous. Captain Seaton, for instance, confirmed that his march was 'perfectly uninterrupted. The fear of us had fallen on the whole country'.[122] The force marched to Kabul in two columns, departing on the 30/31 July and completed the eighty-eight mile route by seven marches from Ghazni to Kabul. The 16th Bengal Native Infantry was left behind to garrison the city of Ghazni. Nevertheless, the column received one severe blow to its morale with the unusual and brutal murder of the extremely popular commanding officer of the 35th Native Infantry, Colonel Herring. On a sight-seeing tour with two lieutenants, a

THE LURE OF THE INDUS

thousand feet up a mountain near Hyder Khail, they were surprised by several enemy Afghans. Outnumbered, the three younger British officers fled but the older and slower Colonel Herring was soon caught and cornered. His fate symbolized the merciless and ferocious nature of the fighting in this remote part of the British Empire. As a limping Colonel Herring stumbled, one of his Afghan assailants overtook him. The Colonel turned, seized him by the throat and, bending him over one of the rocks close at hand, pounded him with his stick. At this moment, however, 'another Afghan came behind and drew his long heavy knife over the Colonel's loins and in an instant he was hacked to pieces'. By the time the rescue party had arrived, only moments too late, they were confronted with only his dismembered corpse:

> An awful sight, hacked and mangled in the most foul manner with every vestige of his clothing torn off except the wrist bands of his shirt. The body was neatly severed at the loins and there was a dreadful gash across the chest and through the ribs, exposing the cavity. There were altogether sixteen or seventeen wounds each suffice to cause death.[123]

This particular death in action and the most senior loss of the campaign so far sent shockwaves throughout the British column and challenged some of the more complacent attitudes prevailing after the Ghazni victory. Within days better news was to arrive. As Dost Mohammed and his army approached Medan to challenge his British enemies on the Kabul road, thousands of his demoralized troops promptly deserted him. This was despite his stirring address, Koran in hand, calling on them to unite against the Frankish invaders. Consequently he was forced to abandon all his artillery (twenty-three guns) and flee along the road to Bamian on the evening of 2 August 1839.

On 6 August the British finally encamped beneath the walls of Kabul. On the last few miles they had been welcomed, as at Kandahar, by numerous Afghan defectors clearly anxious to preserve their interests under the new regime. On 7 August 1839, surrounded by British bayonets, Shah Shuja formally entered his beloved Kabul, thus ending over thirty years of bitter exile.

The Occupation of Kabul

On 30 September 1839, Lieutenant-Colonel Wade's 10,000-strong, mainly Sikh, contingent also arrived in Kabul, having defeated Mohammed Akbar Khan's 2,500-strong army at Ali Masjid in the Khyber

Pass on 27 July. Despite not encountering any strong opposition, Wade's force had provided good service by distracting Dost Mohammed's attention during the advance of the main 'Army of the Indus' from Kandahar. This great British military triumph had not been achieved without serious setbacks. Within three months of the occupation of Kabul a major internal crisis erupted within the military establishment. In September 1839, the senior military authorities were astounded to receive a letter sent from Colonel Dennie of the 13th Regiment and forwarded by Brigadier Sale, which announced that their regiment, one of the 'backbones' of the Army of the Indus, was, owing to chronic sickness, no longer fit for active duty. Colonel Dennie dramatically revealed that, 'from the general condition of the corps ... there is little or no prospect of its recovery or proving serviceable under the privations, duties, and vicissitudes, it must, of necessity, be more or less liable to here'. He protested that 'its strength daily diminishes by death ... we have buried no less than forty-eight since leaving Kandahar'. Of the 416 effectives, sixty-one were in hospital and from the home depot at Karnaul, 'no adequate increase can be looked for' as there were 'only seventeen recruits and of the diseased or worn-out men left there on the regiment taking the field, very few will ever be fit for duty'.

He enclosed a damning report from his Assistant Surgeon, J. Robertson MD. Robertson confirmed that 'in addition to the mortality of 13th Infantry since taking the field amounting to fifty-nine and the number of diseased men left at Karnaul, Ferozepore and Ghazni, amounting to ninety-seven', almost the whole of the corps have 'had their health impaired by bowel complaints and intermittent fevers; and such is their present unhealthy state, that I consider them liable to relapses for the slightest exciting causes, and the worst results may be apprehended for their being subjected to the Cabool winter'. Robertson even recommended that they be returned to a 'mild equable and temperate climate, conjoined with repose, shelter, and comforts which they are not likely to find here', noting that 'every exposure to the morning cold, induces an immediate purging in a greater proportion of the regiment'. Surgeon Robertson ominously concluded that 'many of those men are subjects for invaliding' and, further, that the regiment was 'unfit for service in Afghanistan'.[124]

Their political and military superiors were incandescent with rage at what was perceived as a malicious and impertinent report. They were also clearly aghast at the potential devastating impact on the Army's discipline and morale at this crucial moment in the campaign. The loss of the 13th Regiment from active service would clearly cripple the Kabul garrison.

Both Dennie and Sale and even Brigadier Cotton were accordingly collectively and severely reprimanded. Any prospect of repatriation of the Regiment was immediately vetoed and Dennie was severely castigated for acting on 'casual communication from an irresponsible individual' and for encouraging the Assistant Surgeon 'in temporary charge of the regiment' to instantly 'report on the state of the Corps' and 'intrude on the considerations of the Commander-in-Chief, Sir John Keane'. It was considered that Dennie should have returned the report as it was 'afflicting an injury on the discipline of the regiment'; instead he had 'disseminated the mischief further' by 'addressing the present representations to Headquarters'. Brigadier Sale and Colonel Dennie were further told that, in any event, the Commander-in-Chief, Sir John Keane, had been aware of the situation as the complaints were 'unhappily too prevalent throughout the force'. It was a clear case of political interference. Dennie was effectively ordered to hush up the crisis which was 'most hurtful to discipline and to the service' and, moreover, he was ordered to use his 'best endeavours to put them down and to discourage them'.[125] It was an extraordinary clash revealing the already enervated state of one of the key regiments of the Kabul garrison and confirms Havelock's earlier fears that the 13th Regiment in particular should never have been sent on active service. It was an ominous portent for the future of the Kabul garrison as political imperatives continued to override military needs.

For the British troops and officers, the sight of the famed city of Kabul was a major revelation. Their eyewitness accounts echoed those recorded by Alexander Burnes on his first visit to the great city. Lieutenant Barr reported, from a nearby 'steep eminence, how the city of Kabul ... situated between a couple of fortified hills suddenly burst upon our sight, forming an extremely pleasing picture'. The massive British cantonment appeared to him as a

> red canopy over the green brown plain, with the three-mile road from the hill presenting an animated scene, covered as it was with innumerable tents and crowded with soldiers of every description that comprised the 'Army of the Indus'. The road ... was lined with troops from Bengal and Bombay, the several regiments presenting arms and the artillery firing royal salutes as the Shah-zada passed.[126]

For the assembled British troops some of the most popular sights proved to be the great medieval fortress/palace or Bala Hissar, the ancient 'Tomb of Babus' and the famous Kabul bazaar. All were amazed by the profusion of fruit and vegetables grown in the warm climate of the Kabul valley. 'We do not see half a dozen melons or a dozen bunches of grapes but thousands' wrote one astonished officer.[127] Quinces, damasks, plums, *rawash* (rhubarb tarts) and cherries were in abundance far exceeding those seen at Kandahar. An officer of the Queen's Regiment was further astounded by the sight of the 'magnificent bazaar, almost unrivalled in the East', a veritable 'headquarters of fruit ... our mess table has groaned under ... apples, cherries, plums, pears, mulberries, walnuts, apricots, peaches, pomegranates, nectarines and grapes of all shapes and sizes from the little stoneless kiss miss (there's a name for you) to the oblong green or purple, two of which would be a load for a Lilliputian nag,' with other stalls desporting second-rate hardware from not only cities of Russia and Persia but 'old familiar trash from London or Birmingham'.[128]

The Great Bazaar extended for up to a mile with shops three to four storeys high and many of them covered. The thousands of encamped British and Indian troops represented a splendid market opportunity for the Afghan traders: 'Today we have got the Caubul criers; men from the city hawking about camp grapes, apples, melons, silks, furs, etc and calling out most vociferously, as if determined to compel us to buy.'[129] As at Kandahar, the net result was grossly inflated prices. One nearly bankrupt officer of the Queen's Regiment, thus commented on his inability to buy any of the famous Kashmir wool: 'Woe is me! With no pay for the last two months, I could only look and die, the prices asked being from ten to one hundred tomauns, that is from twenty lakhs to two hundred lakhs prime cost!'[130]

The same officer's impression of the picturesque characters of the Great Bazaar was truly 'bizarre' and, while reflecting typical racial stereotypes, was notable for his sense of the tension and dangerous anarchy which seemed to him to pervade the bustling crowds:

> Truly they are a villainous-looking set, however regular some of their features. Here may be seen the parched countenance of a banyan, or trader, every line eloquent of fraud and lies; there a band of hill-robbers enveloped in sheep skins; their basilisk eyes glaring from under a penthouse of matted locks; any man of whom would whiz you a ball from his matchlock, or stick into your midriff the long knife he wears at his girdle, for the value of your jacket if he caught you a mile from the town unarmed. You have ample time to scrutinize these black-guards being detained in a corner by a string of some fifty camels, whose loads occupy nearly the breadth of the bazaar.[131]

As the sightseeing subsided realpolitik set in. For the British politico-military authorities the main tasks were to consolidate British rule not only in Kabul but far beyond to the outside extremes of Shah Shuja's new domain. Secondly, there was now time for campaigns of retribution against those tribal groups who had attacked the British columns on their march to Kabul. Accordingly, at the end of September 1839, a major punitive expedition was dispatched from Kabul to 'discipline' the alleged prime instigator, the Sultan of Kalat. Lord Auckland had long before targeted this particular ruler as the principal malefactor behind the murderous raids on the Company's long supply columns. In May 1839, he had written to the Court of Directors, specifically blaming the chief for instigating the incessant and murderous Baluchi raids:

> There is now strong ground to believe that ... a feeling of keen hostility to the enterprise in which we are engaged has been entertained by Mehrab Khan, the chief of Kelat, who commands the important country immediately above and below the Pass of Bolan. Mehrab Khan appears to have clandestinely employed his utmost effort to obstruct the march of the army ... the troops while at Quetta were wholly deprived of any aid from the resources and inhabitants of the country.[132]

The punitive expedition, dispatched from the newly invested Kabul garrison comprised Her Majesty's 2nd Regiment (Queen's) and the 17th Regiment of Foot, as well as sappers and contingents of the Bombay Horse, the Shah's artillery and a contingent of Bombay miners. Indian infantry support was largely supplied by the 31st Bengal Native Infantry. These were placed under the command of Major-General Sir Thomas Willshire and drawn from the Bombay column.

On 13 November 1839, Willshire duly arrived before the walls of Kalat, having been joined at Quetta by Company political officer Captain Outram, who had been engaged in parallel punitive actions against the forts of recalcitrant Ghilzai chiefs. Outram commanded irregular elements of Shah Shuja's forces. As a 'political' his relationship with Major-General Willshire was, according to one source, a 'strange position', with Outram's own memoirs suggesting that he surrendered his independent position to become ADC to his military superior.[133] It was, moreover, a small force, as Mehrab Khan had earlier been offered liberal terms for a surrender and it was known that there would be a shortage of water and forage *en route*. The bulk of the regular cavalry and nearly all the Bombay artillery were accordingly left behind in the Bolan Pass, leaving only Her Majesty's 2nd and 17th Foot and the 31st Bengal Native Infantry 'all mustering very weak'. It was a gross misapprehension: the taking of Kalat was to prove as tough as Ghazni and cost far more men. The fortress itself was described as: 'Truly an imposing sight ... some small hills in front were crowned with masses of soldiers and the towering citadel, which formed above them in their rear was completely clustered over with human beings, ladies of the harem chiefly who had assembled to witness the discomfiture of the Feringees.'[134]

It was, indeed, to be a major 'discomfiture'. The whole force ran out of supplies as it traversed across a new route, ostensibly a short-cut to Quetta from Kabul, with the 'poor sepoys and camp followers again suffering severely' in temperatures of 20 to 30 °C. Within eight miles of Kalat the lack of cavalry became evident as enemy skirmishers closed in. In the view of Lieutenant Holdsworth, Kalat was 'of rather an ugly appearance and seemed ... much more formidable than Ghaznee'.[135] As the three columns of British infantry advanced on the main redoubts, the Baluchi defence retreated in disorder. It would appear that Outram (undoubtedly exceeding his brief as a 'political'), 'rode up to us and cried out "on men and take the gate before they can all get in"'. As Holdsworth recalled, this reckless action led to a scene of great confusion as 'all order was lost and we rushed mindlessly down the hill on the flying energy more like hounds with the chase in view than disciplined soldiers'.[136] The leading British troops, however, failed to catch the fugitives before the gate was shut. Trapped beneath the walls the British were now exposed to vicious enfilading fire from the enemy matchlocks on the surrounding ramparts. Again, the lack of heavy artillery enormously complicated the situation as the few light guns could not demolish the old gate and relieve the troops massed below. Only after heavy casualties did the gates finally fall.

Inside Kalat, however, the British were, as at Ghazni, faced with a labyrinth of passageways, being fully exposed to Baluchi snipers as attempts at surrender were ignored by frustrated British troops. Only the intervention of Lieutenant Holdsworth prevented one mass slaughter as an enemy group cried out for 'aman' or 'mercy', a noble intervention which exposed him to a near-fatal wound, 'smashed to bits by a ball from a ginjall or mature wall piece'. As Holdsworth found himself, 'kicking away and coughing up globules of clotted blood at a great pace',[137] his men continued to fight their way through the numerous dark passages, in some places so narrow and low that they were forced to crawl singly on their hands and knees into the main palace area.

The stage was set for a final stand by Mehrab Khan, and other principal Baluchi chieftains. As British troops closed in, all accounts agree that Mehrab Khan himself died bravely, either sword in hand or attempting to fire his matchlock. Holdsworth recorded his dramatic end:

The others seemed inclined to surrender themselves and raised the cry of 'aman' but the Khan, springing on his feet cried 'aman nag!' equivalent to 'mercy be damned' and blew his match; but all in vain as he immediately received about three shots which completely did his business; the one that gave him the 'coup de grace' and which went through his breast being fired by a man of our regiment, named Maxwell.[138]

With him died many of the 'robber barons' and the Dadur chiefs who had so brutally attacked the British camel convoys. For the small British force it had been a pyrrhic victory, with severe losses incurred. Of 1,100 men engaged the loss was 140, about one in seven, with the Queen's Regiment burying, 'a proportion equal to that of other regiments altogether, having returned about seventy in the butcher's bill out of 280 being about one in four'.[139] An estimated 400 of the garrison fell with nearly 2,000 prisoners taken. Although one source claims quarter was given readily, another source notes that at least one section of British troops 'maddened' by some prisoners rearming and reneging their status, 'refused quarter and fired at once into whatever particular party they met without asking any questions'.[140] Burial details faced yet another gruesome task as bodies were scattered over every part of the town. The amount of the potential booty and prize money was abundant, particularly the jewelled sword of Mehrab Khan, but the acute lack of transport meant that much had to be left behind by the British victors.

As the military commenced their departure, the 'politicals' moved in, installing on the throne a British puppet, Shah Nawaz Khan. In return this new British 'puppet' transferred to Shah Shuja most of the most fertile parts of his state including 'Shal' (Quetta), 'Mastang' and Kacchi. His mulla Muhammed Hasan, the treacherous *Wazir* of the Khan, was one of the few to escape British vengeance, but he soon forfeited any claim to the throne when captured documents revealed his double-dealings with Dost Mohammed Khan.

MacNaghten's Myopia

With turbulent Baluchistan and the route from India temporarily secured, the British authorities at Kabul turned their attention to the subjugation of outlying Afghan provinces. For the ever-parsimonious Company it was to be truly an administration on a shoestring. A mere thirty-two British political officers were accordingly assigned to the often highly vulnerable outposts scattered across the provinces. The country was parcelled out into eight main political districts all under the ultimate authority of the Envoy, Sir William MacNaghten. His deputy, Sir Alexander Burnes, assumed the governorship of Kabul. Other significant appointments included Major Leech who was assigned to Kandahar and who was succeeded there in July 1840 by Major Rawlinson. More junior officers assigned to major towns included Captain MacGregor who was appointed to Jalalabad and Lieutenant Pottinger to Charikar (Kohistan). Captain Bean was posted to Shakhot (Quetta) and Lieutenant Laredy was initially appointed to the newly conquered Kalat. Each officer was protected by often ridiculously small garrisons of British or Indian troops – as much a reflection of British over-confidence as Company cost-saving strategies. It was a truly 'thin red line' of British influence stretching across thousands of miles of Afghan territory, much of which had yet to formally or fully acknowledge the suzerainty of either Shah Shuja or his British masters.

Nevertheless, by September 1839, the primary political objective of the campaign had been fulfilled. Shah Shuja was restored to the throne of his fathers and it was confidently expected in Calcutta that, in a short time, the British force might be entirely withdrawn from Afghanistan. Indeed, for the first six months of the British occupation, Afghan internal affairs appeared tranquil. Soon, however, an external crisis briefly shook the British out of their complacency as dramatic news was received of the deployment of a Russian military expedition to Khiva led by General Perovsky. The professed official Russian aim was to punish the wild slave-raiding Turkeman tribes accused of the enslavement and murder of the Tzar's subjects, but this apparent new move in the 'Great Game' of Central Asia momentarily sent shivers down the spines of the British authorities from London to Kabul. An alarmed Colonel Dennie, the newly appointed military commandant of Kabul, dramatically reported this new external crisis:

> Fifteen battalions of Russians have by this time arrived at Khiva and will reach Bokhara – fifteen or twenty marches from Kabul, before we on this side of the Hindoo-Kush can move to intercept them; we being snow or frost-bound during the winter on this side of the mountains while they, on the other side, are comparatively comfortable in a temperate climate.... We shall indeed require some more troops as we are very weak.[141]

Furthermore, the British had yet to capture the elusive Dost Mohammed who, after losing his army, had taken refuge first in Balkh and then with the Amir of Bokhara across the Oxus River. Intelligence reports flooding into Kabul revealed that he was raising yet another army beyond the Hindu Kush. To many observers, a complete evacuation of the Army of the Indus now seemed much less likely. It was a viewpoint not shared by the ruthlessly cost-conscious Company authorities in Calcutta. By October it was decided that over half of the army was to be sent home. Accordingly, on 15 October 1839, Commander-in-Chief Sir John Keane left Kabul with the remaining cavalry and artillery units of the Bengal Army. He returned to India by way of the Khyber Pass and Peshawar. On 1 January he returned to the British main base at Ferozepore, where the Army of the Indus was formally disbanded. With him he took the notable political prize Hyder Khan, Dost Mohammed's son, captured earlier at Ghazni and described as 'of a very quiet, amiable disposition'. Overall military command in January 1840 now devolved upon the distinctly less able Major-General Willoughby Cotton. Despite service in the First Anglo-Burmese War and in suppressing the slave revolt in Jamaica he lacked even the limited tactical and strategic vision of Keane (soon to be demonstrated in his disastrous arrangement of the defences of Kabul) and was himself to succumb to ill-health and relinquish command by the end of 1840.

For many officers and men of the weakened British garrison, trapped in snowbound Kabul and facing, in 1839–40, with not inconsiderable trepidation, the first of three of the notorious Afghan winters, these grand strategic issues seemed far away. The remaining British troops in Afghanistan were divided up between Brigadier Robert Sale and Major-General William Nott, their commands covering eastern and western Afghanistan respectively. Aside from the outlying garrisons, sections of the Bengal Horse Artillery and the Shah's Ghazni Regiments spent a lonely winter at Bamian. The latter's designated task was to guard the road by which Dost Mohammed might reappear. Within Kabul, the troops under the command of Lieutenant-Colonel William Dennie swiftly bedded down for the winter. The main European contingent, Brigadier Sale's 13th Foot, were quartered in the great medieval fortress-palace of the Bala Hissar alongside the main Indian infantry regiment, the 35th Native Infantry. The 13th were housed in the King's palace; the 35th consigned to the less comfortable surroundings of the royal stables. For Captain Seaton's 35th Regiment the first frosts of an Afghan winter constituted a great novelty as, in October 1839, 'the cold began to be very severe ... ice formed on the puddles by the roadside to the great amusement of the sepoys who, except when made artificially, had never seen it before'.[142] For the exposed troops departing in October 1839 from Kabul to India via the dreaded Khurd–Kabul Pass, the conditions were, by stark contrast, horrendous. As early as 21 October, the colonel of the 16th Lancers tersely recalled: 'the cold in the Pass was very severe, icicles hanging from the shaggy mane of a Turkestan pony, and from my stirrup irons ... everything that got wet was frozen; one unfortunate follower died of cold in the Pass'.[143] Worse was to follow for this ill-fated regiment. During the final stages of the return march to Meerut a terrible accident occurred in India off the banks of the swollen 400-yard wide Jhelum River. The fierce current was seriously underestimated by the staff officers and, ordered to cross in threes, the main body of the Lancers lost direction and were swept away. Captain Hilton and, with him, ten lancers and twelve horses were drowned, as well as numerous baggage camels. Other departing columns also witnessed horrific sights as they slowly traversed the desolate snowbound passes to India. After leaving Ghuznee, a Queen's Regiment officer and his men discovered at the remote village of Naunee

at the bottom of a dry well, the remains of two privates of the Queen's who had been murdered while in charge of camels on the march up. Their bodies had been shockingly mangled but, strange to say, though dead upwards of two months, many could recognise in one of the grinning mummies the features of poor 'English' of No.7. [144]

Back in Kabul, as winter closed in, one of the first tasks for the British officers was to make fireplaces, as glass windows were, 'until this time, unbeknown to the Caboolees'.[145] As the first snows fell, the men 'were furnished with sheepskin coats, warm gloves and quilts'. Each soldier and sepoy was also issued with a *neemchu* (sheepskin jacket) reaching to mid-thigh and sentries were additionally provided with a *poshteen* (sheepskin coat) reaching to the ankles. 'When the sentry was relieved he handed over his orders and his poshteen ... was thus passed on from sentry to sentry.'[146] In December 1839, Colonel Dennie wrote home: 'You would, were you to see us, never take us for British soldiers, clad in sheepskins. The mountains around are covered perpetually with snow which fills all these valleys.'[147]

This essential operational intermixing of the British 13th and Indian 35th Infantry Regiments soon developed into rare moments of racial harmony. Captain Seaton observed how the 'native sergeants frequently took command of the mixed relief party over the English corporal and the men were as steady as possible, the soldiers treating the sepoys quite as comrades'.[148]

Initially, British troops also mixed well with the local Afghans and, in December, even slides were erected on which the 'Cabolie boys ... completely took the shine off us by the wonderful antics ... they would turn round and round changing feet and would chant, go on one leg, put the toe of the other foot up to their chin and perform all sorts of manoeuvres; so shaming us that we never went on the slide again!'[149]

Christmas and January delivered the most extreme weather as the Balar Hissar moat froze over and even the Afghan crowds marvelled at British troops skating. Colonel Dennie excitedly wrote home:

> In a day or two I hope to have joined our skaters, a party of whom has just interrupted me to give an account of their perfect success with the skates made by our armourer, after a pattern of one of our ingenious mechanics. The ditch and the fortress offered them a capital field for amusement; for it is frozen solid and it is also quite safe, from being under protection of the guards and sentries on the ramparts which would not be the case if they went any distance.[150]

On Christmas Day 1839 the quick reading on the thermometer dropped 15 degrees from freezing point and the heavy 24-inch snowfalls served to 'remind us of old England'. However, the treacherous conditions made sentry duty around the two and a half miles of ramparts 'very dangerous work and took two hours to traverse'.[151] Christmas and New Year at least provided the opportunity for all of the European officers of both regiments to dine together. The 13th Foot Regimental Mess Christmas dinner was, by all accounts, a splendid affair. Colonel Dennie wrote home: 'I wish you had seen our roast beef, plum pudding and mince pies on Christmas day and you would not have pitied our *roughing it* at all.' The reaction to the New Year's dinner at the 'poorer' 35th Native Infantry mess was less salubrious as, 'our fare was plain and instead of wine we had only rations of government rum which in taste and appearance much resembled distilled leather [but] we were merry enough'.[152]

Captain Seaton recalled: 'We enjoyed the winter as thoroughly as circumstances would permit – shooting, skating, snowballing, making snow giants and picnics to the lake.'[153] Beneath the surface, however, Colonel Dennie recorded the growing heavy toll on his own men's health. On 20 January 1840, he reported on the condition of the already weakened 13th Regiment:

> Our mortality has been considerable, I regret to say. The disease of liver etc which carried off so many in India, in consequence of the intense cold has been replaced here by affectations of the chest and lungs – pneumonia, especially, and the inflammation is so great and invincible that those attacked have all gone off in a day or two ... we

have interred since we entered the fort twenty-seven of the 13th who died of this complaint. The poor private is exposed inevitably to much that his officer escapes for guards and sentries are indispensable.[154]

As the 'mercury' plunged further Dennie disconsolately wrote one month later:

Here I am as usual left in a fortress perfectly indefensible – walls and bastions all tumbling down, parapets fallen and the gates without strength.... The casualties among the soldiers and my own regiment, the 13th, have been very great and ... the 13th have scarcely 200 effective men left. The 35th Native Infantry and some black artillery, being Indians you may conclude, have suffered cruelly from the cold. All my camels are *dead*! And one of my horses, an Arab, was frozen to death the other night; many of our poor camp followers and servants have shared, I regret to say, the same fate![155]

One source attributed the defensive problems of the Bala Hissar to Shah Shuja himself who 'objected so strongly to certain works of defence which Lieutenant Durand was pushing on that Sir William MacNaghten yielded and they were peremptorily stopped'.[156] It was yet another example of political interference undermining military imperatives.

The 'indefensible' state of the Bala Hissar was matched by the generally poor tactical deployment of the British forces outside the city as the winter of 1839–40 receded. Astonishingly, the site for the main British cantonment was established *outside*, and north of the city on a piece of low, swampy ground commanded on all sides by hills and three Afghan forts! The cantonment was surrounded only by a low rampart and a narrow ditch traced on a parallelogram 1,000 yards long, north and south, and 600 east and west, with round bastions at each angle, every one of which was commanded by some fort or hill. Attached to the north face was the mission compound, which extended the whole length of it and was 500 yards wide. Half of this compound was appropriated to the residency (housing MacNaghten and his staff) and the other half crowded with buildings which entirely blinded the defence of this face and rendered it necessary to hold the compound enclosure. The mission compound was surrounded by only a simple wall.

The western face of the cantonment ran along the Kohistan Road while, nearly parallel to the eastern front, flowed the Kabul River at about a quarter of a mile off. Between the river and the cantonments – and only 150 yards from the latter – was a broad canal. Attached to the south-west angle of the enclosure was the bazaar, a mass of small houses. The fort of one of the Afghan chiefs (Muhammed Sharif) dominated this bastion at less than 150 yards. Just beyond this fort was the King's garden, a large enclosure surrounded by a high wall. At 400 yards from the north-east angle, within the effective range of the Afghan *jezail* (though significantly not the British musket!), was located another fort called the Rikabashi Fort. The distance from cantonments to the Bala Hissar – the main refuge for any crisis or defence – was nearly two miles and the road, besides running parallel to the city wall at no great distance, was commanded by the large fort of Mohammed Khan. The key element in a region of such hostile people and environment, the British Commissariat stores, were placed in a small fort 400 yards from the southern face of the cantonment towards the city, while even the magazine was placed *outside* the enclosure. Even junior officers such as Captain Seaton were appalled. He duly observed: 'Placing our stores of food in a detached fort was an outrageous violation of the first military principles.'[157]

The whole campsite had thus been denied any control of the surrounding heights. The heights of the Bemaru overlooked the whole British cantonment at a distance of 800 yards from the north-west angle. Situated under two miles from the cantonments and to the east lay, on the road to Jalalabad, the standing camp, separated from the plain in which lay the cantonments by a range of heights called the Siyah Sang Heights. Although General Elphinstone was, later, in April 1841, to construct a bridge over the Kabul River, this camp was still nearly four miles distant by a circuitous road near the city! To crown this dire tactical situation the British Army of occupation's treasury, so crucial for the purchase of local provisions and subsidies to local chiefs and collaborators, and not least for paying the troops themselves, was, instead of remaining in the far more secure Bala Hissar fortress, transferred to the private house of H. Johnson, the Paymaster, in the 'native quarter' of the city, apparently just because the ridiculously short distance 'gave him and his clerks some additional trouble'![158]

It was a clear recipe for future disaster if ever the Army of the Indus became either isolated or overstretched. Critics of this militarily insane deployment were abundant both during and before the crisis. Victorian historian, J. W. Kaye, later wrote scathingly of these 'sheepfolds in the plain' where 'human folly seemed to have reached its height in the construction of these works'. He continued:

There stood those great indefensible cantonments, overawed on every site, a mountain of madness which prudence for its own ends had permitted to cloud and bewilder the intelligence of the 'greatest military nation of the world'. There it stood, a humiliating spectacle; but except by newcomers, who stood in amazement before the great folly little account was taken of it. Men's eyes had become accustomed to the blot.[159]

'One man's eyes' were particularly critical. Brigadier Roberts conducted a furious running battle with fellow officers and, in particular, with chief 'political' Sir William MacNaghten throughout the summer of 1840 on this very issue. In a significant memorandum addressed to the senior engineer officer, Lieutenant Sturt, Brigadier Roberts noted that 'soon after his arrival in Cabul', in May 1840, 'I looked at the ground selection by the engineer for barracks; and considering his plan most objectionable ... for a country where the cold in winter was intense and where no person considered life secure outside of a fort.' He recommended 'amalgamation of all the separate buildings and squares for wings or regiments, which would have the tactical advantage of much less ground to defend with one quarter of the sentries required'. Moreover, this consolidation of defence would be far more convenient for both communications and health, as the men would be 'sheltered from the piercing cold'. Roberts felt 'obliged' to comment as 'many of the 13th Foot had died out of Caubul during the winter from complaints of the lungs' as the 'snow remains on the ground for a considerable time'. Moreover, the 'natives' were 'expert thieves and assassins and the ranges of barracks would require at least sixty sentries. The Europeans will ramble and no man was safe beyond the limits of the cantonments'. Furthermore, Roberts considered the site 'very objectionable ... a small river running between it and the Bala Hazaar and it was ... commanded in two places'.[160]

He received an abrupt reply from a frustrated Sturt who told him: 'Your recommendation ... has come too late, for I have laid the foundation of one half ... I know little about what is convenient or not'. He confirmed that he had 'substituted a plan to Sir William MacNaghten whether it went further than his military councils I cannot say; but, as I heard no more about it I took silence for consent and worked away ... it is useless to question the expeditiousness or otherwise now of any plan'.[161]

Roberts was considerably put out by this disrespectful reply 'more especially from an officer who belongs to the force under my command'. His appeal to Captain Douglas, the Assistant Adjutant-General, produced further 'sloping shoulders'. Douglas wrote to Roberts: 'Sir Willoughby (Cotton) saw and approved of the new cantonments; if therefore you have any objection to the progress of the work, you have only to state them to the Envoy.'[162] After duly consulting the Envoy, Roberts felt again deeply 'dispirited', concluding, 'By some it was considered that I was interfering with what did not concern me; but it was afterwards proved, to a sad degree, how badly the plan was suited to the country.'[163]

Although Brigadier-General Cotton enjoyed overall responsibility, it cannot be denied that any blame for the clear inadequacy of the Kabul defences must at this stage be shared equally by the senior 'politicals'. The extremely able British engineer, Lieutenant Sturt, had already been over-ruled by MacNaghten in regard to his earlier 1839 and 1840 defensive plans for both the Bala Hissar and the cantonments. Hence his deferential reference to higher authority in his reply to Roberts. The pattern of polit-ical interference, so evident during the march of the Army of the Indus, was now becoming further consolidated. A last initiative by Brigadier Roberts revealed how far military concerns were being undermined by political imperatives. 'As the country became in a very unsettled state and the town of Caubul full of armed men ripe for mischief', he further warned MacNaghten that he considered the location of the army's 'trea-sure' was 'very unsafe'.[164] After MacNaghten's reluctant initial consent to move the treasure to the safety of the Bala Hissar, however, the matter was suddenly reversed by a joint decision of both 'political mandarins', Burnes and MacNaghten. Captain Johnson subsequently argued that, 'Burnes is of opinion that the treasure be returned to the town – a very great conven-ience to me for I am now considerably bothered having to send up to the Bala Hissar for coin requisition'. MacNaghten, now siding with Burnes, concurred: 'Johnson may ... put his treasure where he deems it most safe and convenient.' Johnson was then glibly able to inform a frustrated Roberts: 'MacNaghten has allowed me to have the whole of the treasure at my house in the town. It amounts to close upon seven lacs. Will you kindly allow me whatever you may consider a sufficient guard to come tomorrow?'[165]

A 'surprised' and 'annoyed' Roberts recorded that: 'I stated that there was a great risk and that the treasure was removed from the Bala Hissar entirely against the opinion of Brigadier-Major Troup and myself; but I was considered an alarmist and my opinion had no weight with the Envoy, who could not be persuaded that there was "any necessity for the precau-tion".'[166] Thus, by May 1840, in the space of nine months two major military critics – Brigadiers Dennie and Roberts – had been effectively silenced by the political authorities, leaving a weakened fortification and a severely undermanned British garrison to face both growing political discontent and the rigours of yet another Afghan winter.

The Gathering Storm

As rows over the security of the Kabul garrison raged on, the first small – if not yet decisive – signs of overstretch duly appeared. The first of several significant military setbacks occurred in January and April of 1840. In January, in the middle of winter, in the Kunar Valley, located forty-five miles north-east of Jalalabad, a small force led by Lieutenant-Colonel Orchard (consisting of about 800 infantry with nine guns and about 700 of the Shah's cavalry) was sent to take the rebel Afghan fort of Pashut. On 18 January, Orchard made two futile and disastrous attempts to capture it by blowing in the gate with powder but the attempt failed owing to heavy rain and the powder being damp. The resultant British losses were heavy, as was the damage to British prestige. One officer, Colonel Abbott, remembered the subsequent disastrous siege tactics adopted as the troops 'after making three trips forward and the same back again, were exposed to the fire of eighty rifles at fifty or sixty paces each time'. In fact the troops were recalled only after he personally intervened and 'succeeded in dissuading Colonel Orchard from an idle exposure of his men ... the troops having being five hours under very heavy rain and sleet with all their firearms totally useless'. Nineteen British troops were killed on the spot and forty-eight wounded. Several later died from their wounds As Abbott bitterly recalled: 'This dirty little expedition has cost us thirty lives of fighting men, about a dozen camp followers drowned or frozen to death and about 120 camels.'[167]

In April 1840, a much more serious blow to British prestige occurred nearer home in turbulent Baluchistan when the British garrison at Kahan, the chief town of the troublesome Marri tribe, was attacked. Commanded by Captain Lewis Brown, the 300 men of the 3rd Bombay Native Infantry faced an attack by overwhelming numbers of Marris. Brown made a fatal tactical error in dividing his forces without precise knowledge of the enemy when, in May, his subordinate, Lieutenant Walpole Clarke, was detached to bring back 600 camels from the British post at Pulaji. Clarke and his force of 50 horse and 150 infantry were surrounded and annihilated except for one havildar and eleven sepoys, while his *sowars* simply fled. This left Brown with only 140 bayonets and one gun. Brown soon made up for his tactical error by brilliantly reorganizing the defences of Kahan and arming even his camp-followers, but the force was only relieved by evacuation in September 1840, and then only after a further terrible disaster which occurred in the preceding months. A relief force led by Major Clibborn was brutally repulsed on the way from Pulaji in the drought-ridden Naffusk

Pass on 12 April: 'A most painful and calamitous event evidencing ... gross ignorance of the country or a recklessness utterly indefensible in sending a detachment on a most difficult service by a route almost impracticable.'[168] Clibborn lost four European and two native officers amongst 179 men killed and 92 wounded from a force totalling 700. This included a large number of men who died of thirst in the retreat. A humiliated and now isolated Brown was subsequently forced to sue for peace with the Baluchi besiegers. He subsequently evacuated the fort on 29 September 1840, and only then returned safely to Pulaji.

Despite these serious military setbacks the political authorities in Kabul continued to portray the political situation in Afghanistan as eminently calm. Both MacNaghten and Burnes exuded confidence and the former even indulged in wild military schemes to confront an already much reduced Russian threat. In April 1840 MacNaghten (for whom one source causti-cally comments, 'no enterprise seems to have been too adventurous'[169]), even proposed sending a British force hundreds of miles beyond the Hindu Kush to Bokhara! The designated force of one brigade and a due proportion of artillery was only stood down on news of Clarke's disaster at Kohan.

Equally dire was the news from recently conquered Kalat. In August 1840, the Brahaimi elite rebelled against the disastrous rule of Shah Nawaz Khan, universally despised as a British puppet. He was deposed in favour of Nuseer Khan, the heir of Mehrab Khan. A major blow to British pres-tige then occurred as the British political agent in Kalat, Lieutenant Loveday, was captured, imprisoned and brutally tortured 'with the greatest barbarity' after surviving a brief siege with his tiny escort of only forty of Shah Shuja's sepoys. As a force under Major-General William Nott moved to recapture Kalat, Loveday's fate was tragically sealed and his body was discovered with his throat cut before the final rescue could be achieved. One eyewitness graphically recorded the horrors of his incarceration:

Loveday was ... carried about in a *kajavah* (a sort of chair, placed like a pannier on either side of a camel), to which he was chained, exposed to the burning heat of the climate, and almost divested of clothing. When he was found, his head was nearly severed from the trunk, which was yet warm, and the galling chain had struck into, and grated on his weak and emaciated body.[170]

Only a month before this, another political agent, Captain Bean, was besieged at the Fort of Shalkot. Nevertheless, such brutal indications of the precarious nature of British control in large parts of Afghanistan remained ignored by the Kabul authorities.

At least the autumn of 1840 produced one last 'political victory' for the Company's armies in Afghanistan as Dost Mohammed was finally cornered, brought to battle and captured. After fleeing from Argandeh in August 1839, following the desertion of his army, Dost Mohammed had taken refuge with the Nasir Ullah Khan, the renowned, brutal ruler of Bokhara who later, in June 1842, tortured and beheaded two British Envoys, Captain Arthur Connolly and Colonel Charles Stoddart. Imprisonment and similar veiled threats on his life led Dost Mohammed to flee to Khulm where, conversely, he was well received by the loyal *Wali* of Khulm. Here, at last, he was able to rebuild his military power, raise an army of 6,000 Uzbeg Lancers and prepare again to challenge British authority.

His reappearance certainly caused panic initially within local British garrisons. Colonel Dennie recalled that: 'In consequence of this alarming intelligence, letters have been sent to all the outposts stating, that the game being up, nothing was left but to fall back upon Cabool; advising that all the outposts should be withdrawn, the 48th called up from Jellalabad and the whole force concentrated in and around the Bala-Hissar.'[171]

One British outpost was immediately abandoned at Syghan, resulting in 'shocking disorder, the loss of arms and military stores etc' and the supposedly loyal Afghan levies, 'hearing of the approach of their ancient master ... comported themselves between fear and old affection' and 'plundered their officers and behaved in a most mutinous and shameful manner'.[172] The remainder of the garrison was forced to fall back to Bamian, where it was finally relieved by Colonel Dennie, who had arrived 'after desperate marches ... across the mountains' to disarm the Afghan mutineers. However, after being mistakenly assured by Dr Lord, the political agent at Bamien, that he was confronting only light forces, Colonel Dennie advanced on 18 September 1841, with only one-third of the rescued garrison. To his dismay he found he was facing, 'an army with the Dost and Wali in person'. Dennie opted for a bold, costly frontal attack in which he recalled, 'I am sorry to say, the Ghookha has suffered', but 'after three or four volleys, seeing our steady and rapid advance', Dost Mohammed's forces 'lost heart and fled in a great mass to the gorge of the Pass; and I then let slip all our cavalry on them ... I do not believe an Usbec among them all will stop until he gets to the Oxus'.[173] This resounding British victory, was, however, soon to be followed by another minor but significant disaster before Dost Mohammed finally surrendered and which again revealed how volatile and unpredictable British control remained in this region.

For several weeks Dost Mohammed eluded the hot pursuit conducted by Brigadier Sale's troops and accompanying British political agents. On 2 November 1840, he was finally trapped and brought to battle in the valley of Parwandara situated about fifty miles from Kabul. On this day, a day which, in the dramatic words of Victorian historian Kaye, 'has obtained a melancholy celebrity in the annals of the English in Afghanistan',[174] the British experienced another serious reverse to their arms. Again it would appear that the reckless actions of a political agent partially accounted for the disaster as, at the signal of political agent Dr Lord, the British cavalry were foolishly moved forward to outflank a frontal attack by 200 Afghan horse. Unfortunately for the British, at this crucial moment, two squadrons of the Bengal Light Cavalry took fright and, as one veteran recalled, there occurred an extremely rare case of desertion in the face of the enemy by Britain's Indian allies:

The two squadrons of the 2nd Cavalry were detached ... they moved up at a slow trot but when Captain Fraser, commanding officer, called upon them to charge their pace was not quickened and the urgent repetition of 'charge', 'charge' from the other officers had no better effect. On approaching the enemy they turned round and leaving the officers surrounded and attacked, basely galloped back to the rear and only stopped at Abbott's Battery which, when their flight commenced, was advancing to support.[175]

Two officers, Fraser and Ponsonby, were severely wounded while Lieutenants Broadfoot, Aires and Adjutant Crispin of the 2nd Cavalry were killed on the spot. Dr Lord paid for his recklessness with his life, knocked from his horse and slashed to death by Afghan knives. Dr Heathcote provides a fitting epitaph for this somewhat reckless if gallant individual: 'Among the dead was Assistant Surgeon Percival Lord ... his restless spirit and thirst for adventure had put him in the forefront of a cavalry battle where neither his medical profession nor diplomatic calling required him to be.'[176]

In punishment for their 'dastardly conduct', the 2nd Regiment was by general orders of the Governor-General in Council of 10 February 1841, 'struck off the list of the Bengal army'. The two rogue squadrons were dismissed with ignominy after returning to Kurnaul, India, while the remaining native commissioned and non-commissioned officers and troopers of the rest of the corps were drafted into the other regiments.

But political damage had been done. Although not a crucial military setback, the news of the British defeat on the evening of 2 November had caused a second major panic in Kabul and the long-term political consequences were arguably much more severe. On the back of his small but significant victory, Dost Mohammed now felt able to surrender with honour: his military reputation had been restored and it was to be an ominous precedent for the future of British rule. The surrender itself was tinged with drama, with the former Afghan ruler allowing himself to be personally 'captured' by the British Envoy himself. Thus returning from his daily ride on the outskirts of Kabul, and within fifty yards of his residence, Envoy MacNaghten was astonished to be confronted by his arch enemy. One eyewitness recalled the scene as follows:

> A horseman, passing his escort rode directly up to him and said: 'Are you the Envoy?' 'Yes I am the Envoy.' Then, rejoined the horseman 'here is the Ameer.' 'What Ameer?' 'Where is he?' 'Dost Muhammed Khan' was the reply. The surprise and the amazement of Sir William MacNaghten at this announcement may be readily conceived and, in the instant afterwards, he beheld the very ex-chief himself alighting from his horse and claiming his protection. The whole scene was truly electrical. The Dost was requested to remount and ride onto the gateway where both alighted. The Envoy then took his arm and led him through the garden up to the house saying, 'Why have you persevered so long in opposing our views and subjecting yourself to so much vexation and anxiety aware as you must be of the good faith and liberality of the British government as well of its power?' His only reply was in the true Asiatic spirit – 'that it was his fate he could not control destiny!' Arriving at the house and seated in the very room where, a year before, he was 'monarch of all he surveyed' the voluntary prisoner delivered up his sword into the hands of the Envoy, observing that he had no further 'use for it'; but the Envoy, with becoming generosity, begged him to keep it.'[177]

Politically it was, however, a pyrrhic victory for the British. Having surrendered with his military reputation intact, Dost Mohammed remained a potent symbol of resistance for his people and a significant threat for the future. The pleas of his old rival, Shah Shuja, for him to be 'hanged like a dog' were ignored and he was soon reunited with his family and dispatched to a comfortable exile in India. In overall military terms also, his surrender had been a wise tactical move – in the short term his reduced and weakened forces were clearly no match for the British, and Brigadier Robert Sale's forces had already scored several tactical successes against his forts and allies in the course of the punitive expeditions of September and October 1840. Now, as a captive, Dost Mohammed would retain his potent political image as a 'leader in exile' while his most able son, Akbar Khan, still remained at large somewhere in the Hindu Kush.

Outside Afghanistan, the New Year of 1841 heralded a new, if short-lived, era of stability. Aside from Dost Mohammed's capture, Kalat had already been swiftly retaken by General Nott on 13 November 1840 with no defence offered. Nott left Colonel Stacey with the 42nd Native Infantry and fifty horse to hold the town and the Shah's 2nd Regiment and fifty horse to garrison Mastung. The Shah's 1st Regiment and 6th Horse Artillery and a party of cavalry were also left to aid in the defence of Shalkot. Nott himself returned to Kandahar on 14 December 1840, with the 43rd Native Infantry. Further south, affairs in the turbulent Sikh state in the Punjab also seemed to be more stable despite news of the death of the 'Lion of the North', Britain's wily ally, Ranjit Singh. Kurruck Singh and his mutinous son were dead – the latter being killed by accident on returning from his father's funeral. The Sikh Government now devolved upon Shere Singh, who, despite his alleged 'depraved and sensual habits' soon concluded a treaty of friendship with the British and thus helped to secure their long line of communication from India.

In Afghanistan, however, despite Burnes' and MacNaghten's continuing optimistic reports, affairs remained deeply unsettled. By early 1841, the main focus of discontent had spread to the Durrani country near Kandahar. Durrani grievances reflected the still-chaotic political administration imposed by Shah Shuja and his British protectors. When Shah Shuja had 'liberated' Kandahar in April 1839, the Durrani clan had welcomed his return as it initially promised greater freedom from the oppressive rule of the Barakzai supporters of Dost Mohammed. Shah Shuja had then made promises of tax reduction but soon afterwards he made the fatal error of entrusting the execution of these popular reformist measures to the old, deeply unpopular tax agency, the 'Parmesan' revenue-collectors, who had earlier oppressed the Durrani tribes.

As a direct consequence, in December 1840, a major rebellion exploded in the Zamindawar district, north-west of Kandahar. Yet another British punitive expedition under Captain Farrington had to be dispatched. He defeated and dispersed the main body of rebels near Shahrak, about ten miles north-west of Kandahar, temporarily checking this ominous challenge to British authority. Historians Kaye and Ferrier have, however, pinpointed this rebellion as the first sign of a double intrigue by Shah Shuja himself, who, after Dost Mohammed's removal to India, was showing signs of an ambivalent attitude towards the British. Kaye argues 'it was said by many that Shah Shuja had secretly fermented the rebellion of the Durranis'.[178] If these authorities are to be believed, then British political authority was already being deeply compromised by abject betrayal by their own principal collaborator.

Further south, in January 1841, along the crucial line of communications to British India, British forces suffered another serious reverse. A small force, under Colonel Wilson of the Bombay Cavalry, was sent to subjugate the recalcitrant Kakar tribes at Kajak, about thirty miles northeast of Dadar. The force was ambushed in the narrow streets of the town, having complacently 'marched into the body of the town without taking possession of the houses right and left'. The enemy waited until they had entered and then poured in a murderous level of fire, killing Colonel Wilson himself and Lieutenant Creed who had gallantly launched a second attack with dismounted artillery men.[179] Only a show of force by Brigadier Valiant's Brigade from nearby Sakkar saved the day and, as punishment, the town was subsequently destroyed.

Elsewhere in Afghanistan, the outbreak of other equally serious disturbances in early 1841 put further pressure on the British authorities. In February 1841, near Jalalabad, Brigadier Shelton, commanding the newly arrived, ill-fated 44th Regiment of Foot, was compelled to conduct arduous punitive operations in the Nazian Valley, where he destroyed a number of rebel forts. The operation was also notable for the loss of two key ordnance officers – Captain Douglas and Lieutenant Pigou of the Engineers, the latter blown up by a short-fused powder bag.

Just as this revolt was suppressed, British troops raced to crush further rebellions in the Zamindawar and Kaddur districts. The whole country began to resemble a tinderbox – as one force put a fire out another reappeared. By 1 March 1841, a worried Major-General Nott was forced to order up further reinforcements from India to the Kandahar region, with seven regiments of infantry, one of cavalry, two troops of horse artillery and one company of foot artillery, put at his immediate disposal.

Military overstretch was matched by political overstretch. A combination of poor decision-making by over-zealous, often inexperienced political officers and further blunders by Shah Shuja's advisers added to a sense of mounting crisis. Thus one political officer, Major Leech, on the basis of an alleged 'insult', sent a ridiculously over-large force of two corps of infantry and around 300 cavalry and four guns against the 'inhabitants of a small but strong fort near Kalat-i-Ghilzai'. While the fort was captured and the chief killed, the resultant Ghilzai anger led to a full-scale uprising and his outnumbered force was rapidly surrounded.

When a 400-strong relief force was dispatched from Kandahar under Lieutenant Wymer it was also attacked on 29 May 1841, by 5,000 Ghilzais! Only a protracted five-hour battle narrowly retrieved the situation for the British.

In Kabul itself, however, during the spring and summer of 1841, an observer would be hard put to find any overt sense of impending crisis. After the milder winter of 1840/1, British troops had firmly settled down to peacetime activities in their spacious if highly vulnerable cantonments. Polo and cricket pitches had been constructed and, with the arrival of officers' wives from India (notably Ladies Sale and MacNaghten), garrison life consisted of parties, band concerts, dog shows and even picnics conducted in the luxuriant orchards outside Kabul. Captain Seaton's own memories of this deceptively peaceful period epitomized the pervading complacency of the British occupiers. He rhapsodized over the marvellous gardens located west of Kabul beside the tomb of the Emperor Babur:

> Filled with flowering trees and shrubs ... this spot was the scene of many a picnic during my time. A complete view was obtained of the whole valley and the Lughman Hills beyond. It was delightful to sit under the shade of these grand old trees and let the eye range over the valley, studded with forts and villages and filled with gardens, fields, orchards and vineyards.

Any danger was dismissed, although Seaton, almost in passing, recalled that on 'one or two occasions our picnics were disagreeably interrupted by a shot from the city hill, fired by some fanatic Mohammadon, to show his hatred of the infidels. As no damage, however, was done, we did not much mind it'.[180]

Equally popular with the British troops and local 'Cabolee' families were the 'royal apple orchards' also located a short distance from the city and 'many acres in extent'. On Fridays and Sundays in the summers of 1840 and 1841 large fairs took place and in this garden resort congregated

> cooks and sweetmeat sellers, men with dried fruits, with milk, cream and curds; vendors of sherbet and ices ... in all directions cababs are frizzling, meats are cooking, and men are calling out nan (bread), nan-i-wurduk (wurduk bread), nan-i-sheeren (sweet cake), ab (water) and also abi-i-koonuk (cold water) – nor are toys for the children forgotten. In fact, it is a regular fair, and altogether a very pretty and curious sight.[181]

However, other 'delights' actively pursued by the British in Kabul were far less acceptable, caused great offence to local Afghan Muslim society and became an immense source of political tension for the future. Hundreds of miles from home and with so few European women available, sexual liaisons between local Muslim women and British troops soon became common. Particularly damaging were the sometimes brazenly open affairs conducted between British officers and the aristocratic wives of leading Afghan *sirdars*. In the words of one sepoy eyewitness:

> High-born Afghan ladies used to visit the sahibs secretly.... The women liked the foreigners because they were fair.... These proceedings gave rise to great jealousies, and more than one officer was stabbed or fired at.... It was a matter of wonder to us how this could go on when the foreigners were regarded by the whole population in the bazaars with great contempt, and referred to as 'cursed kaffirs'.[182]

As historian James Lunt confirms: 'So many eyewitnesses have referred to affairs ... that there must have been many of them.'[183] 'The politicals were not exempt from such licentious behaviour; Sir Alexander Burnes ... undoubtedly conducted intrigues with Afghan women',[184] writes Lunt; although his far more politically correct and married superior, MacNaghten, apparently behaved in exemplary fashion.

In the face of such social delights security was demonstrably relaxed. Thus Ensign Stapylton recalled the cavalier attitude to security adopted by military and political figures alike. Officers, soldiers and civilians roamed the Kabul streets often without escort. On 16 May 1841, for instance, he scribbled in his diary: 'Sir Alexander Burnes lives in the city and anybody who wishes to see him goes to breakfast with him, he is a very good fellow.'[185] Such idyllic scenes belied the horrors to come: it was indeed a veritable calm before a storm.

It was a growing crisis which reflected not only the initially, deeply flawed *casus belli* and a chronic military and political overstretch, but a clear lack of intelligence and civil-military co-ordination, exemplified by the debacle over the Kabul defences and a fundamental inability or unwillingness to understand or grasp the political or ethnic complexities of this faraway country. It was also a campaign and occupation already seriously under-resourced in both men and materials, again the direct result of political decision-making not only to withdraw nearly half the invading army, but which had underpinned a series of disasters. The belated capture and exile of Dost Mohammed and one of his sons would

do little to compensate for these fundamental errors of policy and judgement. It was a classic situation of mission creep. In the retrospective but
wise words of the leading diplomat/soldier, Sir Richmond Shakespear:

> The policy which dictated the invasion of Afghanistan has long since
> been acknowledged to have been defective.... Dreading a supposed
> friendship for a rival power, we invaded this country, where we had
> been rather popular than otherwise, and in the course of four years
> we have managed to have a blood feud with each tribe, and to make
> an individual enemy of each of the inhabitants. Surely history ought
> to have taught us that such would be the necessary consequence of
> supporting a king by foreign bayonets.[186]

The consequences of this abject failure to learn such key lessons were
now soon to be horribly realized and, astonishingly, as we shall see, to be
repeated in future wars.

Notes

1   L. Dupree, *Afghanistan* (Princeton University Press, Princeton, 1980),
    p.57. He provides an excellent description and analysis of all the key
    ethnic groups in Afghanistan.
2   For a detailed, valuable perspective on the Qizilbash community in the
    late nineteenth century see H. Hensman, *The Afghan War, 1879–80* (W.
    H. Allen, London, 1882), pp.413–5.
3   B. Robson, *Road to Kabul* (Spellmount, 2003), pp.23–34.
4   M. Elphinstone, *An Account of the Kingdom of Caubul and its
    Dependencies* (repr. New Delhi, 1998), p.253.
5   A. Majumdar, 'Lord Minto's Administration in India (1807–13) with
    special reference to his Foreign Policy', (D Phil., Oxford, 1962–63), p.31.
    For the best, classic study of British policies during the early phase of the
    'Great Game', see M.E. Yapp, *Strategies of British India: Britain, Iran, and
    Afghanistan, 1798–1850* (Clarendon Press, Oxford, 1980).
6   C.U. Aitchison, 'Collection of Treaties' (1933) vol 13, p.69, Reading
    University Library Collection (RULC).
7   RULC, Governor-General to Secret Committee, 31 March 1808.
8   P. Spear (ed), *Oxford History of India* (OUP, Oxford, 1958), p.601. See
    also J.A. Norris *The First Afghan War, 1838–42* (CUP, Cambridge, 1967),
    passim. Norris's erudite thesis reassesses the origins of the First Anglo-
    Afghan War by relating it far more directly to the Eastern Question as part

of a Whig plan for the containment of Russian ambitions in Asia as a whole.

9 For studies of the rise to power of the Sikh Kingdom, see, especially, J.D. Cunningham, *History of the Sikhs* (Calcutta,1904), and B.J. Hasrat, *Anglo-Sikh Relations,1799–1849*, (Hoshiapur,1970) and M.E. Yapp, *Strategies of British India,1798–1850* (Clarendon Press, Oxford, 1980), esp. Chapter 5.

10 RULC, Minute by Lord Minto, 17 June 1808 (encl. in Bengal Secret and Separate Consultations 207, No.2, 20 June 1808).

11 Norris, *First Afghan War*, p.13.

12 Majumdar, *Lord Minto's Administration*, p.50.

13 Secret Committee, to Governor of Bengal, 2 December 1828 (encl. in Norris, *First Afghan War*, p.22).

14 Sir J. W. Kaye, *The Life of Sir Charles Metcalfe* (3 vols), vol 2, p.197.

15 Lord Ellenborough, 'Political Diary' 30 October 1829 (encl. in Norris, *First Afghan War*, p.30).

16 D.C. Boulger, *Lord William Bentinck* (Oxford, 1892), p.181.

17 Norris, *First Afghan War*, p.87.

18 M. Edwardes, 'North West Frontier', *The British Empire*, vol 2 (BBC/Time Life, London), p.507.

19 Sir A. Burnes, *Travels into Bokhara* (London, 1834), (3 vols), vol 2, p.334.

20 Norris, *First Afghan War*, p.54.

21 Ibid, p.85.

22 Ibid, p.86.

23 Dupree, *Afghanistan*, p.372.

24 For a detailed study of this key influential diplomat see, especially E.R. Kapadia, 'The Diplomatic Career of Sir Claude Wade', (MA thesis, University of London, 1938), especially chapters 5 to 7.

25 Norris, *First Afghan War*, p.92. For a political portrait of Lord Auckland, see L.J. Trotter, *Rulers of India: The Earl of Auckland*, pp.16–7, who notes that while he was seen by some as 'by far the ablest member of his party, the weak point in his character was a certain diffidence in his own judgement, a diffidence which was soon to lead him, his party, and his country, into disaster.'

26 Edwardes, *North West Frontier*, p.508.

27 Hon E. Eden, *Up the Country: Letters written to her sister* (London, 1866), p.300.

28 Dupree, *Afghanistan*, p.376.

29 J. Ridley, *Lord Palmerston* (London, 1972), p.335. Palmerston later wrote in February 1840 to Hobhouse, President of the Board of Control observing that it was inevitable that Britain and Russia – 'the man from

the Baltic and he from the British Islands' – should meet in the centre of Asia, and that his job was to see that this clash occurred as far as possible from the frontiers of India. ibid p.332.

30 Norris, *First Afghan War*, pp.234–5.
31 Holdsworth, to father, 27 November 1838, A.H. Holdsworth, *Campaign of the Indus* (Private Print, 1840).
32 W. Barr, *Journal of a March from Delhi to Peshawar and thence to Cabul* (repr. Munshiram Manoharlal, Delhi, 2003), p.1.
33 H. Helsham Jones, *The History and Geography of Afghanistan and the Afghan Campaigns of 1838–9 and 1842*, (RMAS Staff College, 1878), pp.117–8.
34 Holdsworth, *Campaign*, pp.6–7.
35 J. Outram, *Rough Notes of the Campaign in Scinde and Afghanistan in 1838-9* (repr. Naval and Military Press, Uckfield, 2003), p.12.
36 J.D. Neill, *Four Years Service in the East with H M Fortieth Regiment* (London, 1845), p.19.
37 Helsham Jones, *History and Geography*, p.120.
38 Ibid.
39 Neill, *Four Years Service,* pp.3–4.
40 Helsham Jones, *History and Geography*, p.120.
41 Lt. General Sir George MacMunn, *The Lure of the Indus* (Jarrolds, London, 1934), p.47.
42 NAM, Abbott Diary, pp.73–4.
43 T. Seaton, *From Cadet to Colonel* (Routledge & Son London, 1866), p.82.
44 J. Lunt (ed), *From Sepoy to Subedar* (London, 1970), p.88.
45 Anon 'The Campaign of Affghanistan' in a series of letters by an officer of the Queen's Regiment, United Services Journal (USJ, 1–2 June 1840).
46 Seaton, *From Cadet to Colonel*, p.86.
47 Ibid, p.88.
48 Ibid, p.91.
49 Ibid.
50 Ibid, p.84.
51 Ibid, p.88.
52 'Campaign of Affghanistan' (USJ, 1–2 June, 1840), p.167.
53 Ibid.
54 J. Atkinson, *The Expedition into Affghanistan* (repr. Naval and Military Press, 2003), pp.132–3.
55 Ibid, p.133.
56 'Campaign of Affghanistan' (USJ, 1–2 June, 1840), p.167.
57 Barr, *Journal of a March*, p.105.
58 'Campaign of Affghanistan', p.329.

59 Ibid, p.331.
60 Ibid p.171.
61 Barr, *Journal of a March*, pp.164–5.
62 'Campaign of Affghanistan' (USJ, 1–2 June, 1840), p.165. See also Holdsworth to his father, 31 January, 1839 for details of the same tragic incident: Holdsworth *Campaign of the Indus*, pp.26–7.
63 Outram, *Rough Notes*, p.51.
64 Atkinson, *Expedition into Affghanistan*, p.113.
65 Atkinson, *Expedition into Affghanistan*, p.137.
66 'Campaign of Affghanistan' (USJ, 1–2 June, 1840), p.169.
67 Lunt, *Sepoy to Subedar*, p.91.
68 Ibid. Profiteering, however, could be ruthlessly exploited: 'At Quetta', one Queen's officer wrote 'we found some adventurous Parsees who sold us liquor, cheroots and European articles at 150% –"Master never ask price – write name – plenty make out of prize money, by and bye". So as there was nothing to be paid at present, we fell upon their goods, just like a priest, a shark, an older man or pike.' (USJ, 1–2 July, 1840), p.331.
69 'Campaign of Affghanistan' (USJ, 1–2 June, 1840), p.168.
70 Lunt, *Sepoy to Subedar*, p.90.
71 'Campaign of Affghanistan' (USJ, 1–2 June, 1840), p.168.
72 Ibid.
73 Ibid.
74 Outram, *Rough Notes*, p.72.
75 Seaton, *Cadet to Colonel*, pp.100–1.
76 *Expedition into Afghanistan,* pp.139–40.
77 Outram, *Rough Notes*, p.89. Lieutenant Thomas Gaisford recalled that Bombay camp-followers 'were to be seen gorging carrion from the excrement of animals ... I saw one day the body of a man who died by the wayside in the act of gnawing the gristle from the carcass of a dead bullock.' (Gaisford Diary, NAM, 83311-28).
78 Helsham Jones, *History and Geography*, p.128.
79 Atkinson, *Expedition into Affghanistan*, p.127.
80 Holdsworth to father, 6 March 1839, *Campaign of the Indus*, pp.49–50.
81 H. Havelock, *Narrative of the War* (London, 1840).
82 Outram, *Rough Notes*, p.89.
83 Ibid, p.91.
84 'Campaign of Affghanistan' (Army Quarterly (AQ), June 1840).
85 Ibid.
86 Lunt, *Sepoy to Subedar*, p.91.
87 Atkinson, *Expedition into Affghanistan*, p.168.

88 Holdsworth to father, 8 June 1839, *Campaign of the Indus*, p.73.

89 'Campaign of Affghanistan' (USJ, 1–2 June, 1840).

90 Holdsworth to father, 8 June 1839, *Campaign of the Indus*, p.60.

91 Ibid, p.75.

92 Ibid.

93 Ibid.

94 Seaton, *Cadet to Colonel*, p.106.

95 Holdsworth to father, 8 June 1839, *Campaign of the Indus,* p.79.

96 'Campaign of Affghanistan' (USJ, 1–2 June 1840), p170.

97 Outram, *Rough Notes*, p.96.

98 Helsham Jones, *History and Geography of Afghanistan,* p.129.

99 Ibid.

100 Ibid.

101 Atkinson, *Expedition into Affghanistan*, p.175.

102 Helsham Jones, *History and Geography of Afghanistan*, p.130.

103 Ibid, p.132.

104 Ibid.

105 Ibid.

106 Helsham Jones, *History and Geography of Afghanistan*, p.134 and Holdsworth to father, 24 July 1839, *Campaign of the Indus*, p.89.

107 Helsham Jones, *History and Geography of Afghanistan*, p.134.

108 'Campaign of Affghanistan' (USJ, 1–2 June, 1840), p.172.

109 Holdsworth to father, 24 July 1839, *Campaign of the Indus*, p.92.

110 'Campaign of Affghanistan' (USJ, 1–2 June, 1840), p.172.

111 Holdsworth to father, 24 July 1839, *Campaign of the Indus* p.92.

112 'Campaign of Affghanistan' (USJ, 1–2 June, 1840), p.173.

113 Ibid.

114 'Campaign of Affghanistan' (USJ, 1–2 June, 1840), p.175.

115 Helsham Jones, *History and Geography of Afghanistan*, p.134.

116 Atkinson, *Expedition into Affghanistan*, p.209.

117 Holdsworth to father, 24 July 1839, *Campaign of the Indus*, p.95.

118 Outram, *Rough Notes*.

119 Atkinson, *Expedition to Affghanistan*, pp.213–4.

120 Helsham Jones, *History and Geography of Afghanistan*, p.135.

121 Ibid.

122 Seaton, *Cadet to Colonel*, pp.107–8.

123 Ibid, p.109.

124 Dennie, *Personal Narrative of the Campaigns in Affghanistan* (William Curry Jim and Company, Dublin, 1843), pp.174–5.

125 Ibid, pp.176–8.

126 Barr, *Journal of a March*, p.369.

127 Atkinson, *Expedition into Affghanistan*, p.271.

128 'Campaign of Affghanistan' (USJ 25 August, 1839), pp.326–7.

129 Barr, *Journal of a March*, p.213.

130 'Campaign of Affghanistan' (USJ, 1–2 June, 1840), p.327.

131 Ibid.

132 RULC, Parliamentary Accounts and Papers (Blue Books, 1839) Auckland to Secret Committee, 9 May 1839.

133 Outram, *Rough Notes*, p.160.

134 Ibid, p.162.

135 Holdsworth to father, 8 December 1839, *Campaign of the Indus*, p.114.

136 Ibid.

137 Ibid.

138 Ibid, p.126.

139 Ibid.

140 Dennie, *Personal Narrative*, pp.98–9.

141 Ibid.

142 Seaton, *Cadet to Colonel*, p.116.

143 H.C. Wylly, *The Military Memoirs of Lieutenant-General Sir Joseph Thackwell* (London, 1908), p.151.

144 'Campaign of Affghanistan' (July, 1840, USJ), p.330. 145 Seaton, *Cadet to Colonel*, p.118.

146 Ibid, p.118.

147 Dennie, *Personal Narrative*, p.98.

148 Seaton, *Cadet to* Colonel, pp.118–9.

149 Ibid, p.119.

150 Dennie, *Personal Narrative*, pp.98–9.

151 Ibid, p.164.

152 Seaton, *Cadet to Colonel*, p.120.

153 Ibid, p.121.

154 Dennie, *Personal Narrative*, p.103.

155 Ibid, pp.107–8.

156 Helsham Jones, *History and Geography of Afghanistan*, p.142.

157 Seaton, *Cadet to Colonel*, p.135.

158 J.W. Kaye, *History of the War in Afghanistan* (repr. Elibron, Classics), (3 vols), vol 1 Appendix, p.403.

159 Ibid, pp.141–2.

160 A. Roberts to Sturt, 9 May 1840, ibid, pp.400–1.

161 J. Sturt to Roberts, 10 May 1840, ibid, p.402.

162 J. Douglas to Roberts, 11 May 1840, ibid, p.402.

163 Ibid, p.402.

164 Ibid, p.403.

165 Memo. W.H. MacNaghten to Roberts, and Johnson to Roberts (undated) ibid, p.404.

166 Kaye, *History of the War*, vol 2, p.404.

167 C.R. Low (ed), 'The Afghan War, 1838-42' from the Journal and Correspondence of the late Major-General Augustus Abbott (London, 1879), p.145.

168 Neill, *Four Years Service*, p.71.

169 Helsham Jones, *History and Geography*, pp.144–5.

170 Neill, *Four Years Service*, p.75.

171 Dennie, *Personal Narrative*, p.121.

172 Ibid, p.124.

173 Dennie to Cotton, 18 September 1840, Dennie, *Personal Narrative* pp.126–7.

174 Kaye, *History of the War*, vol 2, p.93.

175 Atkinson, *Expedition*, p.353.

176 T.A. Heathcote, *The Afghan Wars 1839–1919* (Osprey, London, 1980), p.50.

177 Atkinson, *Expedition* p.355.

178 Kaye, *History of the War*, vol 2, p.106 and J.P. Ferrier, *History of the Afghans* (John Murray, London, 1856), pp.341–3.

179 Helsham Jones, *History and Geography*, p.152.

180 Seaton, *Cadet to Colonel*, pp.114–5.

181 Ibid, p.115.

182 Lunt, *Sepoy to Subedar*, p.103.

183 Ibid.

184 Ibid. French writer, Ferrier, even claims that some Afghan women: 'gave themselves up to the English for money, even with the knowledge of their husbands', and 'fathers and brothers sold their daughters and sisters', while, 'many officers were legally married to Afghan women'. In any event these liaisons, illegal or legal, aroused considerable outrage and 'the Mollahs did not omit to rouse the anger of the faithful'. (F.P. Ferrier, *The Afghans* (John Murray, London, 1858), p.335.) The narrative of Shaik Ghaussie, the 44th Regiment Kotwaal, provides more precise damning evidence of Burnes' outrageous behaviour. He testified that, 'some months previous to the general rising of the people of Cabool ... it was generally believed that Sir Alexander Burnes ... had sent for and taken by force a very beautiful young Cashmeer girl from the house of Sirdar Abdoolah Khan Echukzai, who had intended her to be the wife of his son, and ... that the Sirdar complained of his conduct to the King Shah Soojah, who made a remonstrance on the matter with ... MacNaghten, but the girl was never restored to the Sirdar's house ...

This ... seems to have contributed much to fan the flame of the insurrection which followed.' [ERM, Narrative of Shaik Ghaussie].

185 Chetwynd Stapylton (ed), *The First Afghan War; An Ensign's Account* (Worthy Down, 2006).

186 Sir R. Shakespear to Major Outram, 4 May 1842 (enclosed in Stocqueler, *Nott,* vol 1 p. 480).

2. Elphinstone's Blunder

I am at the present moment engaged in effecting reductions which will have the double effect of breaking the power of the chiefs and diminishing the expense of the Government.

MacNaghten to Secretary Governor-General of India,
17 June 1841 (PRO, 30/12/33/4)

I deeply regret that I have to give you a history of lamentable disaster … a deep-rooted offence had been taken by some of the Chiefs at measures affecting their interests and dignity and this offence was probably among the leading and more immediate causes which induced them to declare against us.

Lord Auckland to Lord Ellenborough,
28 January, 1842 (PRO, 30/12/31/11)

The Affghans are certainly cowardly, the Cabool tragedy must have been Elphinstone's own doing. MacNaghten indeed! Why did he not put him in the quarter guard with a sentry over him!

Lt.-General Sir W. Napier, *The Life and Opinions of General Sir Charles James Napier*, (John Murray, London, 1857), (4 vols), vol 2, p.226

It must always be understood that the General was the responsible person.

W. Haigh, *A Review of the Operations of the British Force at Cabool* (Calcutta, 1849), p.1

One of the first real signs of impending crisis can be traced back to the radical change of military leadership which occurred in the autumn of 1840 and spring of 1841. Supreme command of the British troops in Afghanistan was handed over by Major-General Cotton to the ailing, aged and virtually senile Major-General William Elphinstone (1782–1842). His past military record was impressive – he was Commander of the 33rd Foot at Waterloo, promoted to Colonel in 1825, assigned as ADC to George IV and, finally, promoted to Major-General in 1837. But although, on paper, as historian Kaye points out, his formal credentials for the post were impeccable: 'an old officer of good repute, gentle manners and outstanding connections', he significantly, 'had no Indian experience of any kind and he was pressed down by physical infirmities'.[1] This, as we shall see, was to severely undermine his capacity for decision-making. Signs of his physical frailty were noted as early as February 1840 by no less than Lady Eden, the sister of the Governor-General, Lord Auckland. She recalled a meeting with General Elphinstone whilst on her travels in India. She portrayed a man clearly crippled by pain, a condition matched by his bouts of homesickness and deep depression: 'He is in a shocking state of gout poor man – one arm in a sling and very lame ... he hates being here, and is in all of the first struggles "of a real ancient Briton".' His social naivety, failure to assimilate to Indian culture and conditions and his overall low morale were clearly evident to her. 'He is wretched because nobody understands his London topics or knows his London people', she asserted. Physically comparing him to a 'remnant of faded yellow gingham', she continued, 'he cannot of course speak a word of Hindostannee', referring to Indians as 'negroes', he being what an artful dodger in *Oliver Twist* would have called 'jolly green'[2]. He was clearly no replacement even for the far more 'Indian-experienced' and physically active, if still flawed, predecessor, Sir Willoughby Cotton and, moreover, his appointment undoubtedly helped the Company authorities to politically dominate the military chain of command. The damage at ground level was soon evident by the balmy summer of 1841. Ensign Stapylton recalled the impact of Elphinstone's infirmities on basic military training: 'It is warm in the middle of the day but the evenings are pleasant. Our half yearly inspection by General Elphinstone took place a short time ago but he was taken ill before he could see us at light infantry drill.'[3]

Two other officers were appointed to be next in command to General Elphinstone. These were Major-General Sir Robert Sale (13th Light Infantry) and Brigadier John Shelton (44th Foot). While both were noted for their personal courage, neither had reputations for political judgement. Another extremely brave officer, Brigadier Anquetil, soon to achieve posthumous glory in the desperate retreat from Kabul, was appointed to replace Brigadier Roberts as Commander of the Shah's troops. Again these appointments probably reflected a 'hidden Company hand'. Roberts had been, as we have seen, an unrelenting critic of the Company's administration of Afghanistan and his successor Brigadier Anquetil, a strictly 'military man', was much less likely to be such an alarmist. Two potentially more effective leaders but well-known critics were significantly bypassed. Brigadier Dennie, who had earlier clashed with the Company authorities over the 13th Regiment's fitness for occupational duty, and who remained bitterly angry over the lack of honours accorded for his prominent role at Ghazni, had already been brutally stripped of his command in the middle of a freezing Kabul winter. The continuing deep anger of the sick, humiliated Dennie clearly emerged in his letter of 1 March 1841. 'I was forced to vacate the dwelling or shelter I had at so much cost and trouble constructed in the Bala Hissar, and repaired to the lines of my corps, where a wet mud hovel was my only abode, to which I owe no doubt, a great part of my present ailments.' In May 1841, he reiterated, 'how despicably and ungratefully they took my brigade from me last January ... the ... only reason that can be assigned ... consists of my having declined the second class Doorannee order for Bamean, the which I had been entitled to at Ghuznee ... it is difficult to account in any other matter for such unprovoked injustice and injury.'[4]

The neglect or demotion of these two prominent Brigadiers was matched by the bypassing of yet another dedicated, proven and capable senior officer, Major-General William Nott, the redoubtable commander of Kandahar garrison. His 'crime' had been to also challenge both MacNaghten's and Shah Shuja's authority and, as we have already seen, to call attention to the defects and weaknesses of the Company military garrisons in the west around Kandahar.[5] In September 1840 Nott had already been severely reprimanded for daring to punish, by flogging, some servants of Prince Timur, Shah Shuja's son, for oppressing and plundering Afghan refugee camps around Kandahar without political authorization from Kabul. Even Major-Generals were not permitted to rock the political boat. Nott was clearly no diplomat but he remained angry and defiant. In a letter home to his family, dispatched in late September 1840, he provided a truly damning indictment of the state of Company rule in Afghanistan and particularly the role of the 'politicals':

> The authorities are never right, even by chance, and, although most of them are stupid in the extreme, they fancy themselves great men and even possessors of abilities and talents.... They drink their claret, draw large salaries, go with a numerous rabble at their heels – all well paid by John Bull [or, rather by the oppressed cultivators of land in Hindustan] – the Calcutta treasury is drained of its rupees and good-natured Lord Auckland approves and confirms all. In the meantime all goes wrong here. We are become hated by the people and the English name and character, which, two years ago, stood so high and fair, has become a bye-word. Thus it is to employ men selected by intrigue and patronage! The conduct of 10,001 politicals has ruined

our cause and bared the throat of every European in this country to the sword and knife of the revengeful Affghan and bloody Belooch and, when several regiments be quickly sent, not a man will be left to note the fall of his comrades. Nothing but force will ever make them submit to the hated Shah Shooja who is most certainly as great a scoundrel as ever lived.[6]

There was also a significant regimental changeover which, as we shall see, may have had grave implications for future Anglo-Afghan relations. The experienced 13th Light Infantry, crippled by illness, was finally scheduled to return to India and it would appear that, as Captain Seaton and others confirm, the regiment had integrated well, not only with its companion regiment the 35th Native Infantry but also with the local Kabul populace. Its replacement, the 44th Regiment of Foot (Essex Regiment), led by Brigadier Shelton was, by all accounts, a far more exclusive and less racially integrated regiment and this arguably bode ill for future political harmony in the city. During its march up to Afghanistan the regiment had already lost two senior and experienced officers, and Shelton's well-documented difficult and martinet temperament, which some accounts claim (and as we shall see), made him loathed by many of his own men, may well have accounted for its later lack of fighting cohesion. Lieutenant MacKenzie probably remembered his notorious brittle personality when he met Brigadier Shelton at Ferozepore, India, as they crossed paths on their way to relief duty at Kabul, when he concluded, 'he has been very civil; but I shall not join his brigade'.[7]

The central political leadership was also showing distinct signs of decay by the summer of 1841. Despite growing reports of unrest, both MacNaghten and Burnes continued to adopt an unrealistic and over-optimistic posture. On 20 July 1841, for instance, as the weary Kandahar garrison suppressed yet another Durrani revolt, MacNaghten famously reported from Kabul that the whole country was 'quiet from Dan to Beersheba'! Both MacNaghten and Burnes had other, more personal reasons for their complacency. In historian Kaye's well-chosen words, MacNaghten was, 'preparing to shake the dust of Afghanistan from his feet forever'.[8]

He had been offered promotion to the highly prestigious post of Governor of Bombay and, clearly, it was not in his interest to 'rock the Afghan boat'. Similarly, for Burnes, the prize post of Envoy in Kabul, as successor to MacNaghten, now beckoned. This probably accounts for his pronounced deferential attitude to MacNaghten and, despite his former proclivity for Dost Mohammed, his sudden enthusiasm for Shah Shuja's candidature. Like MacNaghten, his personal ambitions undoubtedly challenged or even overrode his political judgement at a crucial time for the safety and survival of the British garrison in Kabul and for British rule in general.

But neither political nor military neglect, rivalry and backbiting can, by themselves, solely account for the rapid descent into crisis in the late summer and autumn of 1841. It was the familiar overriding imperative of financial economy, one so consistently pursued throughout the British Empire, which now played a key role in the collapse of British political authority in Afghanistan. Sir Robert Peel's new Tory administration, which replaced the Whig Government headed by Lord Melbourne in August 1841, was one unusually wedded to the principle of financial retrenchment and the 'Afghan adventure' was proving hideously expensive. It was a sentiment shared by the Company authorities in Calcutta. In a series of damning entries in his journal, Sir Jasper Nicholls recorded his horror over the spiralling deficit. As early as 12 May 1841, he scribbled:

> We cannot afford the heavy yet increasing drain upon us. Nine thousand troops between Quettah and Kurachee; as least 16,000 of our army and the Shah's to the north of Quettah. The King's expenses to bear in part – 28 political officers to pay, besides MacNaghten – Dost Muhammed's allowance – barracks – a fort or two to build – loss by exchange.... To me it is alarming. The silver does not return and it is becoming scarce.[9]

Eight days later, on 20 May, he recorded far more damning observations about the deteriorating situation:

> Here is a very untoward account of the Afghan finances. It will never do to have India drained annually for a rocky frontier requiring about 25,000 men and expensive establishments to hold it even by threats, as at present. The specie too, is drawn away not to return. Little comes from China. How is it to end? Money is not rapidly subscribed to the loan, because it gains 12 to 18 per cent for short periods elsewhere – amongst natives, 24 per cent or more. Unless a large access of Punjab territory comes in to connect us safely with Caubul, and to aid our heavy expenses, *we must withdraw*.[10]

In the less dramatic, but equally cynical view of historian, Ferrier, 'the Directors of the East India Company, who have a habit of judging of the value of the conquest only by the revenue it produces were more disappointed than can be described at the deficit which the expedition of Afghanistan had occasioned in their treasury.[11] Acquisition of the Punjab and the revenue of its taxpayers was not then militarily feasible. Neither was the further squeezing of the Indian taxpayer politically acceptable. Overall, the East India Company revenue was a quarter of a million pounds in deficit by 1841 and their Afghan commitments, including the expense of keeping up a flotilla of steam boats on the Indus River, was costing another one and a quarter *crore* of rupees per annum (one million pounds at the current exchange rate).

At the heart of the problem lay the huge and expanding wastefulness and corruption of the Shah's Court. The Shah's administration was propped up not only by scores of corrupt, highly unpopular tax and revenue collectors, but by an exorbitant court and military establishment including over 800 attendants and 2,000 'household troops' largely subsidized, to the surprise and growing anger and frustration of senior Company officials, by the Calcutta Treasury. From early 1841 McNaghten was accordingly bombarded by letters from Calcutta requesting explanation for the spiralling deficit. While claiming to be 'deeply sensible of the most rigid economy' he admitted in reply to the collection of 'objectionable taxes' and that the Shah's Vizier, (or Prime Minister), Nizam oo Dowla, had 'let out' tax farming posts to 'inferior contractors', admitting that, 'nor can it be imagined that such a system is not liable to serious abuse'.[12] MacNaghten made little headway in his belated attempts to reform the system despite claiming the removal of the 'obnoxious revenue managers' which, as subsequent events showed, he also falsely claimed 'has proved a most salutary measure and tranquillity and contentment are now … prevailing throughout the Candahar territories'.[13] Even the infuriated Shah himself protested: 'It is indispensable that I should have this number of Horse and Foot to attend to my possessions and keep guard … what is to be done for my personal expenses?… The guns cannot be filled with wind – so with everything else.'[14] In August 1841 the Calcutta authorities finally lost patience and MacNaghten was given a virtual ultimatum: 'It is painful to the Government to be under the constant necessity of observing a tendency to increase expenditure in a quarter where the strictest economy is so indispensably called for … the retrenchment of our expenses of every description in Affghanistan has become a duty no longer to be neglected.'[15]

Something had to give and, in October 1841, the financial axe duly and fatally fell on two key administration areas in Afghanistan. One was to result in a total undermining of the British position. The first 'axe' fell on the expenses of the Shah's Court and army and the second, mainly disproportionately and politically most crucially, on the subsidies paid to the

Afghan chiefs and particularly the Eastern Ghilzai chiefs who controlled most of the key passes to India. Astonishingly, and without any attempt at negotiation, dozens of predominantly Ghilzai chiefs were summarily informed by MacNaghten that they must submit to a huge reduction of 40,000 rupees from their subsidies. Dozens of outraged chiefs immediately descended upon Kabul to protest. Here they were callously stonewalled by MacNaghten and his administrators and even cynically referred to the virtually bankrupt Shah's Court for recompense! The Shah, wholly dependent upon British bayonets and their diminishing gold, could offer nothing. The result was wholly predictable – the furious Ghilzai *sirdars* returned to their homes, raised their tribal levies and, in hours, cut off all communications. All the passes around Kabul were immediately closed. The Kabul authorities, instead of renegotiating the situation, merely responded with coercion, dispatching yet another military expedition to enforce obedience in the region. It was left to Brigadier 'Fighting Bob' Sale and his weary '13th', their orders to return to India perfunctorily cancelled, to conduct these punitive operations. At ground level many British military officers were appalled by this incompetence, again widely blamed on the 'politicals'. Thus Captain Seaton bitterly recalled:

Sir William MacNaghten most unwisely stirred up the wrath of the Ghilzaee chiefs by diminishing the subsidies paid to them for keeping the passes open.... He had interfered so much with the Shah's mode of governing the country that the system of administration had become a compound of Affghan severity and MacNaghten's milk and water philanthropy, a mixture of iron and clay, as, in the image of the Chaldean King's dream, utterly unsuited to the fierce tribes of the country who soon detected the weakness of their rulers.[16]

His words were echoed in the diary of Ensign Stapylton. On 4 November 1841, he also protested:

The origins of the whole business was an attempt by the Envoy to reduce the expenditure of the country, which experiment he unfortunately tried by cutting by 40,000 rupees the allowance of the chiefs on these mountains. The chiefs would not stand for this and the consequence was that we were sent with a large train of baggage and other encumbrances to fight these men who are accustomed to the mountains from their birth and had every advantage over us, for it was as much as we could do to mount the hills, much less to fight at the top.[17]

On 12 October 1841, as Brigadier Sale moved his column from Bhutak into the Khurd-Kabul Pass, his troops were confronted by the full fury of Ghilzai marauders. Brigadier Dennie brilliantly evoked the dark, ominous scene confronting the 13th Light Infantry and the 35th Native Infantry as they entered the pass: 'The heights around were crowned by these infuriated bands, and numbers, screening themselves behind a breast-work in the centre of the valley directly to their front, showed to our brigade the work they had before them.'[18]

The terrain itself presented enormous obstacles. Captain Seaton supplies a vivid, accurate account of the dangers awaiting his force in this infamous pass, soon destined to be the graveyard of many of the 16,000-strong Kabul garrison. It was, he observed

one of the most formidable-looking defiles I ever saw and, to an enemy either weak in numbers, poorly armed, badly commanded, or, wanting in 'pluck', an impassable barrier. A little river runs between the two ranges of hills – the eastern range at a point where it approaches close to the stream, towering directly over it to the height of 1,000 feet. The western range is half that height and the spurs of both so interlace each other that the stream is turned alternatively to the right and left twenty times in the course of about 3,000 yards. Not more than 140 or 150 yards of the stream can be seen at one time, and every inch of it is completely commanded by these natural breast-works and by the peaks above them.[19]

He further noted:

In winter this little river becomes a foaming torrent which brings down vast quantities of shingle and large boulders that block the bed of the stream and fill the bends. The only road through the pass is by the bed of the river.... No body of men, however well armed and commanded, could hope to get through it without a sharp and possibly a desperate struggle.[20]

The column nevertheless plodded on through. *Jezail* matchlock balls, fired by countless Afghan snipers, caused terrible head wounds as the British troops were constantly exposed to fire above them. Lieutenant Mein of the 13th Light Infantry, for instance, 'was hit on the head' and 'his life was despaired of for several days as half the ball penetrated the brain whilst the other was above and held by the skull'.[21] It was classic ambush country. Stapylton recalled one dramatic incident in which the Major-General himself was hit: 'They allowed our advance guard to almost reach them before they showed themselves. Suddenly a tremendous fire opened on the head of the main column by which General Sale was wounded severely in the ankle.'[22] Under such relentless fire the pass was only forced by crowning the heights at the cost of numerous casualties, which amounted to six killed and thirty-three wounded amongst the 13th Light Infantry alone. A further six-day delay in Butkhak Pass increased the losses. On 23 October 1841 the harassed force finally struggled into Tezin, but only after a sharp action in which part of the British ammunition and stores were cut off by the enemy, 'in consequence of too greater an interval which occurred between the rear guard and the main body'.[23] Ensign Stapylton duly recorded the scale of material losses in his campaign diary: 'We lost an immense deal of baggage on the way to Tezin as the rear guard was attacked and every camel that dropped we were obliged to shoot and destroy the load. 32,000 rounds of ammunition were obliged to be destroyed that day from want of carriage.'[24]

Yet again, the British troops were made distinctly aware of the inferiority of their Brown Bess muskets at long range. Ensign Stapylton dolefully recorded: 'The long rifles of the natives carry much farther than our musket which gives them great confidence.'[25] Captain Seaton was personally and deeply unnerved by the incessant and eerie echoes of the enemy *jezails* being loaded in the heights and caves above. He explained:

The juzzail ... is a long heavy rifle generally carrying an ounce ball ... the ball is put into the rifle naked, and requires to be hammered a good deal with an iron ramrod to get it home. The hammering makes a loud singing noise that can be heard at a considerable distance; so unmistakable in its character that it can never be forgotten by those whose ears have once been startled by the unfamiliar sound.[26]

The column was soon joined by the energetic young political agent, Captain G.H. MacGregor of the Horse Artillery on 15 October. The subsequent behaviour of his escort, a party of Duranni horsemen, significantly selected by the Shah's own prime minister, gave the first tangible clues to Sale's force that they were facing a much wider conspiracy involving their own protégés in Shah Shuja's Government. The writer and commentator Ferrier even contends that Shah Shuja himself, already deeply humiliated by enforced economies and his dependence on his British masters, had already been negotiating with the rebel Ghilzai chiefs (notably Abdullah Khan) earlier in September, even before the 'subsidy crisis' erupted.[27] The subsequent actions of these Duranni horsemen arriving fresh from Kabul in

October gives some credence to this conspiracy theory. Thus Captain Seaton records a notable incidence of treachery as the same Duranni cavalry unit lit signal fires facilitating a ferocious surprise attack on his camp by the Tezin chiefs, in which Captain Jenkins and twenty of his Grenadier Company were shot down and the Commissariat treasure chest seized.[28]

The column, increasingly encumbered with wounded men and the usual, unnecessarily large amounts of baggage, struggled on to Jagdalak although managing to temporarily, but brilliantly, deceive the enemy by taking an alternative longer route there which avoided the shorter Peri Pass which was packed with Afghan rebels. However, between Seh Baba and Kuttar Sung, the descending British rearguard faced a ferocious attack on 29 October by an overwhelming number of the enemy, who rushed down the road through several small ravines. Both sides suffered heavy losses. The British loss that day was terrible: three officers and thirty-seven men killed and four officers and eighty-seven men wounded. Captain Seaton recalled this particular attack by hundreds of Ghilzai tribesmen. It had been a desperate affair in which the rearguard, 'with much baggage entangled in the gully' and 'cooped up in a narrow place, not thirty feet wide' where 'discipline was of little use' were reduced to 'great confusion, for the men were fired into both from the gully and from the rocks above'. A great loss to the regiment was 'poor Captain Wyndham, who, seeing a soldier of the 13th badly wounded, dismounted from his pony and placed the disabled soldier upon it. As the Captain was himself lame, he could not keep pace with the men who were hurrying up the steep and stony gully and, to our great regret, was killed and could not be brought off.'[29]

Revenge for this near disaster, and particularly the killing of Captain Wyndham, was fully exacted at the village of Futtehabad, further along the route to Jalalabad. After an artillery action by the newly reformed rear-guard, including Lieutenant Broadfoot's sappers, a full-scale cavalry charge exacted terrible retribution. The Ghilzai foot soldiers, caught in the open valley, were soon routed and a full-scale massacre ensued. Captain Seaton recalled how:

Their triumphant taunting cries turned into shouts of terror and yells of agony. Swords, juzzails, turbans and clothing were all cast away to facilitate flight; but it was too late; the cavalry were amongst them with vengeful hearts and remorseless swords, our skirmishers at the same time playing their parts, firing into groups of fugitives with steady and successful aim, and picking off numbers as they laboured up the slope of the hills.[30]

It would appear that there was a complete loss of command and control as the 'blood lust' increased. Brigadier Dennie, Seaton remembered, 'was obliged to let us have our way and our revenge'. As desperate groups of the enemy concealed themselves in numerous stacks of fodder in the field on the Jalalabad side of Futtehabad, the revenge cycle was cruelly completed. Seaton recalled one horrific incident:

> Some of the men roaming about observed a pair of shoes sticking out of one; and, upon inspection, a pair of feet was found in the shoes. The owner was instantly pulled out, and as he was found to be one of the fugitive enemy, he was at once cut down. In revenge ... as quick as thought, every stack was fired. They were filled with the enemy many of whom were miserably burnt.[31]

Others were 'pulled out of riverbed reeds' and, 'were put to death before we could interfere.' As officers lost control, the incensed infantry joined their cavalry colleagues in the massacre. As Captain Seaton explained, 'the soldiers could not forget and would not forgive the iniquities shown to the body of our poor comrade at Jugdulluck. The Afghans had cut off the head and set it up for a mark to throw stones at!'[32]

At Gandamak, Sale's troops received their first hard evidence of the scale of the crisis now facing British rule in Afghanistan. Rumours of a major uprising in Kabul were confirmed as truth. More fascinating was further evidence of a possible conspiracy organized by either the Shah or leading members of his ministry for, as news flooded in, a major mutiny erupted amongst the Shah's troops stationed in the Gandamak garrison. Thus, a shocked Ensign Stapylton scribbled in his diary on 11 November 1841:

> In the course of the day the Cavalry Corps, which formed part of the Shah's troops at Gandamak, went over to the enemy and the European officers and the Jezailchis and some of the Khyberees who remained faithful were obliged to follow us and joined us during the night. The cantonment and all the baggage was burned by the enemy immediately after it was deserted.[33]

At Gandamak, Brigadier Sale faced a crucial test of his own decision-making and one which was to play a prominent role in the fate of the Kabul garrison – whether to retreat back down the perilous passes in the heights of an Afghan winter to relieve the Kabul garrison, or to proceed further and garrison Jalalabad in the hope of further relief from India in the spring. He chose the latter and, in view of his earlier heavy casualties sustained in the passes and in light of the most recent (again over-optimistic) intelligence sent to him by MacNaghten via political envoy Captain MacGregor that he, 'hoped the business last reported was the expiry effort of the rebels', it can probably be justified. Other critics have been less kind, but it was probably the right tactical choice. There was a possible third option. One critic opined whether 'he should not have remained at Gandamak and fortified himself there – a place which is represented as fertile and well supplied – seems an open question'.[34] Again, with the ongoing mutiny at that place it was clearly less viable. Above all, Jalalabad offered far more prospect of relief from India. In the event his column marched on to the great walled town of Jalalabad where, on 12 November 1841, he faced the awesome task of holding 2,100 yards of largely ruined buttresses and bastions against an expected mass attack from thousands of fanatical Ghilzai tribesmen. The circumstances were not propitious. Captain Abbott wrote despairingly in his journal:

Our prospects are rather dismal. The defences of Jalalabad are in a miserable state and there is cover for an enemy within pistol shot of the walls and in every direction. We have no supplies of food except a small store of barley intended for the horses; we have about 2,000 men to hold a mile and a half of dilapidated ramparts and the number of sick and wounded are so great as to render any movement or retreat through the Khyber impossible.'[35]

Meanwhile, in Kabul, even during the few weeks before Sale's expedition, MacNaghten had retained his highly optimistic view of the political situation. In a letter of 25 September 1841, addressed to the Governor of Agra, India, for instance, he reported: 'The progress we have made towards pacifying or rather subjugating (for remember the Douranees nor the Ghilzyes were ever before subject to a monarchy) is perfectly wonderful.... Now the whole country is as quiet as one of our Indian chiefships'. He dismissed, in rather cavalier fashion, the burgeoning financial crisis. 'A million and a quarter per annum is certainly an awful outlay; but if the items were examined, you would find that a full moiety of this is to be laid to the account of Mr Bell's procession in Upper Sindh where they have had an army, *cui bono* larger than the Army of the Indus.'[36]

At this time at least one Company official, Major Pottinger, formerly political agent at Herat, desperately tried to inject a note of realism into the thinking of the British authorities in Kabul. On the evidence of the Kohistani disturbances of early September 1841, he impressed on MacNaghten the urgent necessity for strong measures of deterrence. Under such pressure, MacNaghten, to his credit, finally if belatedly, partially responded to this one desperate warning and 200 men of Her Majesty's 44th Foot were sent to punish local rebels in the Zurmat Valley. Dispatched with them were elements of the 5th Native Infantry, 6th Regiment Shah's subsidiary force, four guns of Abbott's Battery, two iron 9-pounders from the Mountain Train, two companies of the Shah's sappers and two squadrons of Anderson's Horse. All were placed under the command of Lieutenant-Colonel Oliver. Confronted by this force the rebels soon fled and, after destroying their principal stronghold with powder, the British force returned to Kabul.

Insurrection

However, in the light of the financial crisis and such ferocious cutbacks it was not enough. A military crisis now materialized to ring the death knell of the depleted 'Army of the Indus'. On 2 November 1841, the thunderclap duly arrived. The imagined security of the Kabul authorities was suddenly and, as it proved, fatally challenged from within. Lady Florentina Sale, indomitable wife of the absent Brigadier Sale and the most famous and assiduous chronicler of events in Kabul over the next few months, unknowingly recorded the first signs of an uprising. On the previous day, 1 November, as rebels flooded into the city she noted in her journal: 'Last night a party of Kohistanees entered the city; a large body of horsemen were also seen proceeding towards the city from the road that leads by the Shah's camp behind Siah Sung.'[37]

Her initial fears were soon horribly realized. In the early hours of 2 November 1841, some time between 8 and 9 a.m., a ferocious attack was launched upon the political residence of Deputy Envoy Sir Alexander Burnes by an incensed, estimated 300-strong mob. Historian Ferrier estimates 130 rebels as the hardcore 'nucleus of the mob'. Burnes had been warned days before of the impending attack, and Abdullah Khan, effective head of the conspiracy in Kabul, whilst confirming a *jihad*, had declared 'openly that he would kill Burnes before eight days were over'. Until the last moment, however, a persistently complacent Burnes had chosen to ignore these threats. It was only early in the morning of that fateful day that he had even requested that the rebel chief meet him for negotiations. In the event his messenger was brutally murdered and the mob duly arrived, headed by Abdullah Khan and other leading conspirators. These included Seidal Khan, Sikander Khan, Mohammed Akbar Khan, Abdul Selam Khan and Emir Ullah Khan. Any unsuspecting Europeans who inadvertently crossed their path that night were mercilessly killed. It was only news filtering in of these deaths which finally spurred Burnes into action. At 8 a.m. on 2 November he sent his last hurried note to Envoy MacNaghten, reporting the commotion 'excited by some mischievous reports'. Other notes followed to the British headquarters requesting a battalion of infantry and two pieces of artillery and support. It was all too late. By 2 p.m. that day Burnes was dead. Ferrier provides a vivid account of the last moment of Burnes and his twenty-two-man 'garrison'. At the heart of the mob that besieged his residence were the *badmashes*, or 'the dregs of the people' so clearly identified by nervous British officers in their first entry into Kabul. These, however, who were soon joined by more respectable city shop-keepers and workmen testifying to widespread class disaffection. Undoubtedly, many of the latter had been incensed by the tax increases so recently imposed to help pay for the British occupation, but all were no doubt also lured by the prospect of plunder. In Kaye's words, 'the Treasury of the Shah's paymaster was before them'.[38]

It was a desperate but doomed struggle for survival. Burnes apparently made a futile attempt to placate the mob, only to be met by enraged cries of defiance from the crowd, many calling for the death of all English offi-cers. There were other more personal scores to settle: Burnes' role as Governor of the city had frequently obliged him to administer stern justice to criminal groups, and his public dalliances with the wives of Afghan nota-bles had made him many influential enemies. A gallant resistance ensued as the besieged, including several British officers and ten sepoys, frantically plugged the holes in the walls and coolly shot individual attackers as they attempted to infiltrate the building. The hollow sounds of the attackers' frenzied blows against the walls at least provided evidence of the next incursion and, in this way, the defence was prolonged from eight in the morning until two in the afternoon.

By midday most of the British officers had been killed and the ammuni-tion had virtually run out. The final blow was the firing of the roof which literally 'smoked' the defenders out into the open. Lieutenant William Broadfoot of the 1st Bengal Europeans was one of the first to be shot, apparently after personally killing five or six men. Burnes was one of the last. Accounts differ of the manner of Burnes' death; one, that of Kaye, suggests he was lured out by a 'Mussulman Cashmerian', who promised to convey Burnes to the loyal Qizilbash Fort in native disguise in return for a ceasefire. Once exposed in the open garden, however, Burnes' erstwhile saviour allegedly betrayed him to the mob with the fateful words: 'This is sekunder Burnes'. An enraged mullah (religious teacher) dealt the first blow and the frenzied crowd soon cut him to pieces with their deadly Afghan knives.[39] A second alternative account, by Ferrier, records that Burnes received a pistol ball in the eye at point blank range and 'died instantly ... his body was then hacked to pieces with repeated sabre cuts and, horribly mutilated, thrown into the garden of his own house'.[40] What we do know is that the head and trunk of his dismembered body were, hours later, displayed in the centre of the *chouk*, or Great Bazaar of Kabul.

The next predictable target of the mob was the 'jewel on the crown' of the British occupation, the now terribly exposed and highly vulnerable 'treasury house' protected only by Paymaster Trevor and a ridiculously small guard. An eyewitness account by Lieutenant MacKenzie, stationed in the nearby fort of Nishan Khan which housed the Shah's Commissariat, recalled his own desperate struggle to save himself and his miraculous escape alongside Trevor and his family. The first hint of danger materialized on the morning of 2 November when, Mackenzie recalled: 'Suddenly a naked man stood before me covered with blood from two deep sabre cuts in the head and five musket shots in the arm and body.'[41] This man was a messenger sent by MacNaghten, who had also tried to reach the house of Captain Trevor nearby. 'This being rather a strong hint as to how matters were going', inspired Mackenzie to promptly close the fort gates and stand his men to arms. The first signs of British paralysis now occurred as, within the British cantonment, a frustrated Captain George Lawrence, the Military Secretary, offered to go to Mackenzie's rescue with a supporting detachment, but he was 'refused permission'[42] ostensibly by Elphinstone himself. The British force remained frozen and inactive.

As a result both Mackenzie and Trevor were left to literally save themselves. On the morning of 3 November, a stunned Mackenzie witnessed the Afghan rebels 'swarming into Treasury House'. Mackenzie himself, encouraged by the loyalty of his Afghan *jezailchees* (musket men), held out for another forty-eight hours until his ammunition was exhausted. On the night of 5 November, soon after Trevor and his family had escaped, Mackenzie also made his own desperate run for the safety of the main British cantonment. Surrounded in the process of escape, he managed to sever the grasping arm of one of his attackers but a blow to the back of his head knocked him from his saddle. Amazingly, he still managed to continue his fighting retreat and stagger to the safety of the cantonment lines. He had been literally seconds from death. As he recalled: 'the idea passed through my mind – well this is the end of my career, and a miserable end it is in a night skirmish with the Afghans'.[43]

On the same day the Shah's treasury, weakly protected by a small guard under Captain Johnson, proved an additional and predictably irresistible target for the mob. It was again an indiscriminate and massive attack.

'Thirsty for gold and thirsty for blood, the insurgents undermined the walls and burnt the gateway of the house; then falling like wild beasts on all whom they met and slaughtering guards and several men, women and children alike they glutted themselves with treasure.' Other, ulterior motives for the attack were soon revealed as the mob also took care to burn all the Shah's tax records kept in the office – another striking indication of the widespread hatred of the Shah's taxation regime. Lady Sale recorded the grim toll exacted with forty of the treasury guard massacred, the mob looting one *lakh* and 700 rupees of public property and Johnson (who luckily escaped with his life) losing 10,000 rupees of his own finances.[44]

It had indeed been a horrendous day for the British authorities, with brutal murders of Europeans continuing in the streets of Kabul and shops and businesses ransacked. In Lady Sale's words, 'all was in commotion in Cabool'.[45] Evidence of wider conspiracy from within the Shah's Court again emerged in the allegations of one officer, Lieutenant John Sturt, who barely survived an assassination attempt in the precincts of the Shah's palace, being 'stabbed in three places by a young man well dressed, who escaped into a building close by where he was protected by the gates being shut'. Rescued by the indefatigable Captain Lawrence, himself the victim of an earlier assassination attempt, Sturt was tended by a distressed Lady Sale. She recalled his terrible wounds:

> He had been stabbed deeply in the shoulder and side, and on the face
> ... he was covered with blood issuing from his mouth and was unable
> to articulate. From the wounds in the face and shoulder, the nerves
> were affected; the mouth would not open, the tongue was swollen
> and paralysed and he was ghastly and faint from loss of blood.[46]

As the British authorities reeled from this bloodthirsty outburst, more signs emerged of a creeping and ultimately fatal paralysis. Having failed to relieve Burnes, Johnson and Mackenzie, the still-powerful 5,500-strong British garrison continued to lie inactive. Elphinstone stubbornly refused to act. On 2 November, that fateful first day, he lamely informed MacNaghten: 'We must see what the morning brings, and then think what can be done.' At this moment of crisis, when a firm military reaction was required, it was again the 'politicals' who took full control. A horrified MacNaghten stepped in and insisted that the increasingly indecisive General Elphinstone garrison the Bala Hissar. Accordingly Brigadier Shelton, the 44th Regiment Commander, was sent from the Siah Sung Camp to the fortress with one company of the 44th, a wing of the 54th Native Infantry, the 6th Shah's Infantry and four Horse Artillery guns.

Similarly, the remainder of the troops scattered around in camp on the plain were hurriedly brought into the cantonment and the 37th Native Infantry and the mountain guns were called in from guard duty at the mouth of the Khurd-Kabul Pass.

Apart from this consolidation of their defences, the garrison still remained in a dangerously defensive posture, with British forces ominously failing to penetrate the city itself. Indeed, only on 3 November was Brigadier Shelton finally permitted to open fire on the city and to endeavour to force it by means of shell and shot; a belated indiscriminate action which probably only served to further exacerbate the fury of the mobs inside rather than to quell them. Military paralysis was paralleled by a dangerously symbolic 'political retreat' as MacNaghten and his wife and other officials fled the city to the safety of the British cantonment outside. The hurried evacuation of his residence before 11 a.m. on 3 November was, in the words of Lady Sale: 'a circumstance ... no doubt soon known to the insurgents and must have given them the idea that we greatly dreaded an attack from them'.[47]

Ironically, during that crucial first forty-eight hours, it was only loyal elements of the Shah's troops who put up a brave, if futile, attempt to restore order within the city. As news reached the Shah of the rapid spread of the insurrection, he dispatched from the Bala Hissar 200 Hindustani troops of his personal guard under Captain Campbell with two guns. With no British troops in support, however, the outnumbered men were soon ambushed and driven back with great slaughter. Only at the Bala Hissar gate were Shelton's 44th regulars finally able to provide covering fire. For Shelton at least this disproved earlier suspicions of the Shah's role in any conspiracy. He later directly cited the incident as politically significant 'because it was said his Majesty was implicated in exciting the rebellion – for in such case he never would have made so noble an effort and the only one that was made to strike at the root'.[48]

Lady Sale also indirectly reinforced his view, recording in her diary the Shah's public threats to 'burn the city' in retaliation for the attacks and his declaration that Meer Akber (who protected Sturt's attackers) would be hanged if he failed to deliver up the felons. She instead pointed the finger of blame firmly at the Shah's Prime Minister, 'the Wuzeer who is strongly suspected of having instigated the conspiracy', noting that the supposed letters calling on all true 'Musselmans' to rise against the 'Kaffirs' (English unbelievers) bearing the King's signature, were in fact forgeries. MacNaghten also apparently supported Sale's and Shelton's views; he had 'always insisted that they were forgeries of a very peculiar description and that papers bearing the veracious signatures had had their contents washed out and these seditious writings inserted'.[49]

In terms of military power his role was irrelevant, as only Shah Shuja's British masters now had the force to intervene decisively. But, 'on that day nothing was done.... General Elphinstone had been talking about tomorrow when he should have been acting today'.[50] As William Hough observed: 'There could be no security for the force if the insurrection could not be put down.'[51] Lieutenant Eyre provided a damning summary of the disastrous political and military implications of that first day:

The day was suffered to pass without anything being done demonstrative of British energy and power. The murder of our countrymen and spoliation of public and private property was perpetrated with impunity within a mile of our cantonments and under the very walls of the Bala Hissar. Such an exhibition of weakness on our part taught the enemy their strength – confirmed against us those, who, however disposed to join in the rebellion, had hitherto kept aloof for prudential motives.[52]

Lady Sale fully concurred:

No military steps have been taken to suppress the insurrection, nor even to protect our only means of subsistence in the event of a siege. The King, envoy and general appear perfectly paralysed by this sudden outbreak; the former is deserted by all his courtiers, by even his most confidential servants except the Wuzeer who is strongly suspected of having instigated the conspiracy suspicion attached to his majesty again.[53]

While the 'politicals' had laid much of the ground for future disaster, it was to become, in essence, 'Elphinstone's blunder'. After the insurrection of 2 November the 'politicals' were fatally compromised and it was only the British military that could ultimately solve the crisis and this patently sick, ineffective British general was clearly no man to do it. Over the next few weeks a series of military blunders, mainly reflecting his continued indecision, served only to confirm that the Kabul garrison was doomed.

Within two days of Burnes' murder, another equally serious military disaster occurred with the loss of the woefully ill-placed and vulnerable Commissariat fort. Its defence was now to be paralyzed by further prevarication by Elphinstone. As early as 2 November Lady Sale had, with remarkable foresight, already noted the serious implications of its loss: 'We have only three days' provisions in cantonment: should the commissariat be captured, we shall not only lose all our provisions but our communications with the city will be cut off.'[54]

The fort, in Sale's words, while only 'an old crazy one undermined by rats' nevertheless contained the *whole* of the Bengal Army Commissariat stores, valued at four *lakhs* of rupees and including about 12,000 *maunds* of *ottah,* wheat and barley as well as all the medical stores. The initial rapid capture of Mohammed Sharif's fort had soon decisively outflanked the Commissariat stores and, by 4 November, spelt the end of this crucial asset. The Commissariat garrison of a hundred-odd men led by Ensign Warren of the 5th Native Infantry was soon besieged. Again, General Elphinstone made another fatal tactical error, initially giving extraordinary instructions to Captain Swayne and the 44th Foot not to relieve the fort at all costs but to 'proceed immediately to bring off Ensign Warren and his garrison to the cantonment',[55] thus abandoning the fort to the enemy! But even after Elphinstone suddenly reversed this decision, the two belated attempts to relieve the fort proved disastrous. The first one comprising Ensign Gordon and a company of 37th Native Infantry and eleven ammunition camels was driven back and Gordon killed. Captain Swayne's second attempt with the belatedly dispatched 44th contingent was soon repulsed by fire from Mohammed Sharif's force, with both Swayne and Captain Robinson of the 44th eventually killed and Lieutenants Hallam, Evans and Fortye wounded. A third final and desperate attempt, by a party of 5th Light Cavalry, was repulsed with the loss of eight troops killed and fourteen badly wounded. The extremely high officer-casualty rate was set to continue and, as we shall see later, to greatly exacerbate the military crisis.

Moreover, the subsequent hours of tactical chaos that succeeded these failed attacks revealed again the extent of Elphinstone's unfitness for command. Only an intervention by Captain Boyle, the Assistant Commissary General, to 'lay before him the disastrous consequences', had led Elphinstone to reverse his previous command and to send orders to Ensign Warren to hold out the fort 'to the last extremity'.[56] At 9 p.m. on 4 November an assembly of staff at Elphinstone's headquarters met and the Envoy himself reluctantly took the initiative, 'furiously arguing' that Mohammed Sharif's fort be retaken that night or the Commissariat fort would be lost. The ever-hesitant, ailing Elphinstone merely consented to a 'reconnaissance', only delaying action further. On his return the debate was resumed but again, 'the General could not make up his mind'.[57] Only Lieutenant Sturt, still recovering from his wounds, finally swayed the gathering, deferring the assault to the early morning. Eyre commented: 'this decided the General, although not before several hours had slipped away in fruitless discussion'.[58]

By the time Captain Bellew, Deputy Assistant Quartermaster-General, and a party of Her Majesty's 44th, were marshalled to 'blow the gate' their nightmare fears were abruptly realized as an understandably demoralized Ensign Warren precipitately evacuated himself, without orders, from the Commissariat fort via a hastily prepared hole in the wall. In his later defence to the Assistant Adjutant-General, Warren claimed he saw no prospect of reinforcement and also claimed he had not received Elphinstone's note to hold at all costs. He even volunteered himself for a court of inquiry! Predictably, no investigation followed, adding to the blow to morale already sustained by the loss of the forts to the enemy, and significantly further undermining the overall fighting spirit of the garrison. Lady Sale firmly sided with Warren: 'no blame can attach to him but much to those who withheld aid'.[59]

It was this event on 4 November 1841, rather than the insurrection of 2 November, which provided the decisive turning point in the fortunes of the British garrison. The loss of the Commissariat fort not only massively increased the confidence of the enemy forces and crippled British food supplies, but struck a severe blow to the morale of the garrison as the Afghan winter mercilessly closed in. Indeed, it must have been a deeply frustrating and humiliating spectacle, as 'the enemy were busied in hundreds all day carrying off our stores all of which we plainly saw from the cantonments'.[60] The old adage that an army marches on its stomach could not have been more true at this crucial moment. Moreover, this particular military debacle had catastrophic political implications for Britain's relationship with the Quisilbash, her main Afghan allies in the Kabul region. In Lieutenant Eyre's words:

> It is beyond a doubt that our feeble and inefficient defence of this fort and the valuable booty it yielded was the first *fatal* blow to our supremacy at Kabul, and at once determined those chiefs and more particularly the Kazilbashes – who had hitherto remained neutral, to join in the general combination to drive us from the country.[61]

Furthermore, the abject failure to secure or reinforce the strategic significantly 'Trevor Tower' commanding the heights of the city not only placed the British military on a 'back foot' from which they never really recovered, but destroyed the confidence of Britain's potential Qizilbash allies.[62] The sapping of troop morale over this failure and others is clearly evident elsewhere in Lady Sale's diary; when, for instance, the 44th retreated from Mohammed Sharif's fort 'all were in amazement; the 35th asked leave to go and take it but were not permitted to do so'.[63] The resultant ration cuts were disproportionately applied to auxiliary units. The siphahees (sepoys), for instance, were reported as, 'grumbling at short allowances and not being able to do anything'.[64] At times, military decision-making reached farcical proportions. On 7 November, for instance, Elphinstone indulged in a fruitless, 'frivolous' tactical debate over whether the trees in the garden next to the Commissariat fort were planted in lines parallel to the wall or not; he apparently being unable to comprehend that, 'even if a tree intervened a shot would destroy it from a heavy nine pounder'![65] His frequent meanderings were reflected in numerous other plans which never achieved fruition.

Two companies under Captain Corr of the 54th were also 'warned for service' to enter the city at last but 'it was as usual only one of the theoretical plans so often talked of and so little practised'.[66] A succession of frustrated British officers, even the most junior officers, constantly visited the General but probably only further complicated Elpinstone's already flawed decision-making. In the words of contemporary critic William Hough:

> There were many young officers allowed to join a very extensive Council of War and to give their opinions often unasked: so that the opinions of Brigadier Shelton and other older officers were set aside. Under the peculiar circumstances at Cabool the General would have acted wisely to have adhered to the advice of senior officers and never to have asked the opinion of young officers who had no experience or official position to warrant their giving any advice, as the result proved.[67]

In the meantime the British troops continued to engage in somewhat fruitless artillery duels with the enemy: this served only to waste valuable ammunition.

Aside from the loss of the bulk of the food supply, for the first time Afghan rebel military superiority was rapidly coming to the fore, not only in terms of their ever-increasing numbers but in tactics and equipment as they progressively took the initiative from the static cantonment and Bala Hissar garrisons. In despair, Lady Sale recorded the emerging shortcomings of the British artillery units, noting how as 'the enemy continued to crown the heights; our guns were out of range and the shot fell short'.[68] The artillery problems were exemplified by two other factors, one being the direct consequence of earlier Company economies. There was a profound shortage of heavy-calibre shells. Moreover, the two guns lost earlier in the city were turned on the British with a vengeance; the British cannon balls ingeniously honed by Afghan blacksmiths into an egg shape for more lethal effect. Captain Abbott's artillery contingent also felt the impact of Company's prevailing parsimony; having previously requested three 18-pounders, the military barracks 'made it a case for arithmetic' and sent 'six nines'! The one 5½-inch mortar had 'little more effect than a pop gun of large calibre'.[69] Lady Sale observed other emerging inequalities in tactics and equipment between the two sides, so evident in officer's memoirs during the march into Afghanistan:

> The Affghans have many advantages over our troops; one consists in dropping their men fresh for combat; each horseman takes a foot soldier up behind him and drops him when he is arrived at the spot he is required to fire from … their baggage ponies can manage the hills much better than our cavalry. As regards pistols we are on a par … but their juzails carry much further than our muskets and, whilst they are out of range of our fire, theirs tell murderously upon us.[70]

Nevertheless, at this early stage of the siege, the British cause, although deeply compromised, was not yet totally lost. On 6 November, for instance, the garrison at last made a brave, if limited, attempt to storm Mohammed Sharif's fort by regular breach and assault. They deployed two howitzers and three iron 9-pounder guns but, even when Lieutenant Sturt had positioned those guns, Major Thain 'was sent to him to desire that he would be careful not to expend ammunition as powder was scarce, there being at the time a sufficiency for a twelve month siege'![71] Nevertheless the attack proceeded and Major Griffiths led storming parties comprising one company of H.M. 44th under Ensign Raban, one company of 37th under Lieutenant Steer and one company of the 5th Native Infantry under Lieutenant Deas. These speedily carried the fort. However, the strategically important Shah Bagh or 'King's Garden' was neglected and much of the tactical gain was lost. Furthermore the undoubted hero of this attack, Lieutenant Raban, was shot through the heart 'when conspicuously waving a flag on the summit of the breach'[72] – a tragic loss of yet another courageous 44th officer. His death was only partially compensated for by the killing of an estimated one hundred of the enemy and the slaying of the brother-in-law of Abdullah Khan by a Captain Anderson. Lady Sale was an eyewitness to the follow-up attack on the hill where a very 'severe and indecisive encounter' occurred between the 5th Cavalry and two to three hundred Afghan horsemen: 'From the top of our house we saw everything distinctly; the gleaming of their swords in the sun and the fire of their pistols and matchlocks.'[73]

However, this minor success was not enough – by 10 November a full military and political crisis that could only deteriorate had begun. The crisis expressed itself in three key areas – increasing shortages of food and ammunition and continuing political confusion.

On 8 November the first major food crisis erupted as the 'want of provisions' was felt and MacNaghten 'could only obtain them by large bribes from the village of Bemaru and even then there was a scanty supply'. This undoubtedly served to further undermine the credibility of British power. As Lieutenant Eyre confirmed, 'our chief cause of anxiety now was the empty state of our granary' and 'the object of the enemy undoubtedly was to starve us out; to effect which, the chiefs exerted their whole influence to prevent our being supplied from any of the neighbouring forts'.[74] He added, ominously, 'their game was a sure one; as so long as they held firmly together, it could not fail to be sooner or later successful'. The result was an acute over-reliance by the cantonment troops on the dwindling food supplies from the Bala Hissar, but this had severe knock-on consequences. As early as 7 November, the Bala Hissar garrison were themselves put on half rations, 'in consequence of the large supplies of ottah required to be sent to the cantonments'.[75]

Ammunition for the heavy guns was also reaching a critical point. Earlier, on 5 November, Elphinstone had cancelled one attempt to retake Mohammed Sharif's fort, partly on the grounds that 'gun ammunition was running short'.[76] The daily continued bombardment of Afghan forts only served to exacerbate this shortage.

Much more serious though was the continuing paralysis of military and political decision-making. On 9 November, soon after midnight, as enemy forces amassed for fresh offensives, a desperate MacNaghten, clearly dismayed by Elphinstone's physical and mental paralysis, took a momentous decision to, 'relieve him of the command of the garrison and summoned Brigadier Shelton from the Bala Hissar to replace him'.[77] Shelton accordingly arrived at 4 a.m. on the morning of 9 November with a company of the 44th, two guns and the Shah's 6th Infantry. According to Eyre, this was done 'in the hope that by heartily co-operating with the Envoy and the General, he would raise the sinking confidence of the troops'.[78] In fact Shelton never formally took control, although in many respects the burden of military decision-making had now, *de facto*, fallen squarely on his shoulders. As Lady Sale confirmed, 'the people in cantonments expect wonders from his prowess in judgement'. By contrast, 'Elphinstone vacillates on every point. His own judgement appears to be good but he is swayed by the last speaker'.[79]

Shelton quickly took some welcome, much-needed initiatives. On 10

November he led the 44th and 37th Foot and 6th Shah's Infantry out in action against the enemy-occupied Rikabashi Fort. Even then, considerable delay took place and it was only after the Envoy had assured the General that he would take the responsibility of the act on himself that the troops were sent out at all. It was a courageous move but effectively ended as a pyrrhic victory. The fort was taken but with severe losses – 200 killed and wounded. Three more key officers were killed, notably Colonel McCrea commanding the 44th. It was 'a near run thing' as a charge by Afghan horsemen briefly turned both the 44th and their sepoy comrades and the day had only been saved by a heroic rally led by Brigadier Shelton himself. The 44th's colonel was cut up 'dreadfully' by the Afghan cavalry – 'wounded in both legs with three cuts to the back, two toes cut off and three or four cuts on the arm which was amputated immediately after'.[80] The other officers met a similar, terrible fate. Nevertheless, some soldiers demonstrated commendable fighting spirit; one sepoy and a British officer managed to barricade themselves in a stable and killed thirty of the enemy before being rescued! Hitherto Brigadier Shelton had been unpopular with his men but this bold action at least partially rehabilitated him. Lady Sale noted that his heroic initiative: 'has excited so much astonishment that the men of the 44th were all inquiring after the "little brig" as they called him. They say they are ready to be led to any work there may be for them to do'.[81] The action had temporarily restored British prestige with at least one Afghan chief sending his 'salaam' to Envoy MacNaghten. It could not, however, last long: Brigadier Shelton's military triumph was to be short-lived.

Soon afterwards, the military command structure further dissolved into competing individuals and factions. As early as 6 November, as a bed-ridden Elphinstone remained largely marginalized, small groups of more active officers, appalled by his inactivity, had begun to organize their own councils, paralleling, if not undermining, his overall command structure. Lieutenants Sturt, Patten and Bellou, for instance, regularly met at Lady Sale's house, 'at nine most evenings' to discuss future tactics.[82] Indeed Sturt, supported by the Envoy, now pushed for a more active but consolidated defence based solely on the Bala Hissar, with a night evacuation of all personnel from the vulnerable cantonments. In stark contrast Brigadier Shelton, now flushed with this minor victory but acutely aware of British long-term logistical weaknesses, pressed for retreat to Jalalabad before the winter snows fell. Shelton's option was itself considered briefly on 10 November by Elphinstone, but he was quickly overruled by MacNaghten: 'The General asked the Envoy if he was prepared to retreat to Jalalabad as of tonight; Sir William replied that he would do his duty and never desert the King; and, if the army left him, would die at his post.'[83] It was the start of a titanic struggle of wills which could only result in further fatal delays and indecision over the next eight weeks. Again MacNaghten's continuing stubbornness on this issue at least partially reflected his personal fears of the loss of his promised political advancement if such a drastic strategy, effectively spelling the failure of his Afghan mission, was pursued.

The Kabul Brigade was to enjoy only one more successful military action and even this was marred by a brief but significant collapse of morale by the 44th Foot, the European backbone of the garrison. On 13 November 1841, a major enemy force appeared on the western Bemaru heights where they positioned two guns and proceeded to fire into the British canton-ments with 'considerable precision'. Lady Sale recorded yet another crisis in political and military decision-making: 'The General again (as in the late attack on the Kizalbashi Fort) asked the Envoy if he would take the respon-sibility of sending out the troops on himself; and, on his conceding, the force was sent.' She added: 'The Envoy also had much angry discussions on this point with Brigadier Shelton.'[84] Again it was the 'politicals' who had taken charge over a moribund military leadership and it was only the 'earnest entry' of MacNaghten that spurred the General into offensive action. Brigadier Shelton was accordingly sent out with four squadrons of cavalry, two guns and sixteen companies to dislodge the enemy forces. The day started well but ended in near disaster. Because of the procrastination 'it was late (4–5pm) before the troops were ready'. The three British columns (the 37th leading the 44th in the centre and the Shah's 6th in reserve) advanced rapidly, probably too rapidly 'at so brisk a pace that it seemed a race which should arrive at the scene of action'. Almost immedi-ately, it provoked a furious headlong charge down the hill by Afghan horsemen. Inexplicably, the British infantry columns panicked, dissolved into chaos and, momentarily, all tactical control and discipline broke down. Lady Sale observed the horrifying scene from the cantonments: 'No square or bulls were formed to receive them. All was a regular confusion; my very heart felt as if it leapt to my teeth when I saw the Afghans ride clean through them. The onset was fearful. It looked like a great cluster of bees but we beat them and drove them up again.'[85]

In fact, only heroic intervention by the 120-strong section of the 5th Cavalry under Captain Andrew, supported by Lieutenant Eyre's artillery section, saved the infantry and enabled the 44th under Major Thain to recover and take the summit of the ridge. Even here the enemy 'resolutely stood their ground on the summit of the ridge and unflinchingly received the discharge by musketry, which, strange to say, even at the short range of ten or twelve yards, seemed to do little execution'.[86] Under the onslaught of several rounds of grapeshot and shrapnel, however, the enemy broke, pursued by Anderson's Horse, with a lone Horse Artillery gun playing on the reserve body of Afghan horsemen in the plains below. The opportunity was then taken to try to capture the two enemy 4-pounder guns. However even the removal, under hot fire, of one of these Afghan guns, for the first time revealed a crisis of morale amongst the 44th Regiment. The gun suddenly had to be spiked and abandoned, 'as the men of the 44th, under constant jezail fire and in spite of the appeals of their commanding officer and Major Scott, would not drag it in'.[87] Their bad example was followed by the sepoys. The second gun was only retrieved with great difficulty, owing to the steepness of the hill and numerous water cuts, and by deploying a company of the Shah's 6th Infantry under the zealous Lieutenant McCartney. The force arrived back in disarray.

It was an untidy and ominous finish to an initially successful action, the whole affair blighted by the fact that, 'No temporary success of our troops over those of the enemy could be followed up nor even possession of the ground gained by us at the point of the bayonet, owing to the necessity of withdrawing our men into their quarters at night.'[88] Lady Sale placed the blame squarely on Brigadier Shelton, who 'deferred his return to cantonments until the shades of the evening had closed over the troops; and, it being impossible to distinguish friend from foe, we could not assist with our guns from the cantonments which in daylight would have swept the plain and had prevented the enemy from following up our return'.[89] But the disarray was probably more reflective of the significantly high losses of more junior officers experienced in earlier actions. Worse still, the disaffection on the battlefield seems to have spread into the cantonment. Lieutenant Eyre spoke of scenes of panic as exhausted troops retreated through the cantonment gates: 'We found the garrison in a state of considerable alarm and a continued blaze of musketry illuminating the whole line of ramparts ... it was long ere quiet could be restored, the men continuing to discharge their pieces at they knew not what.'[90] Lady Sale also observed the demoralization in camp as Shelton brought in the rearguard at around 8 p.m.: 'When the men of the 37th were upbraided for turning they replied, "We only retreated when we saw the Europeans run and we knew we should not be supported".'[91] Both morale and ammunition supply had been fatally dented by this successful but ultimately inconclusive and frustrating action.

All contemporary and later sources agree that this was a watershed in British military fortunes. While the 2 November rising had proved a political turning point, and the events of 4 November a logistical disaster, the costly inconclusive action of 13 November heralded a steady slide into military disintegration. In the words of Helsham Jones: 'This was the last success achieved, and afterwards, until the final destruction of the brigade, there is nothing but a sad list of blunders and disasters to record.'[92] Lieutenant Eyre lamented: 'Henceforward it becomes my weary task to relate a catalogue of misfortunes and difficulties which following close upon each other, disheartened our officers and men, and, finally, sunk us into irretrievable ruin, as though heaven itself, for its own inscrutable purposes, had doomed our downfall.'[93]

Only one major and failed offensive action took place between 13 November and the great retreat of 6 January 1842. The clear defeat occurred on 23 November, and it was one that revealed the full extent of demoralization and paralysis of the Kabul garrison. In the days before this defeat and, indeed after 23 November, the British military leadership continued to engage in continuous, sometimes furious, but ultimately deleterious unresolved discussions over the best course of action. On the one side remained the 'retreat to Jalalabad' group led by Brigadier Shelton. On the other were the 'stand and fight' group led by Lieutenant Sturt amongst others and still strongly favoured by Envoy MacNaghten. Soon a furious debate erupted even over the prospect of a compromise between the two, namely a partial or limited retreat from the exposed cantonment into the Bala Hissar fortifications. Lieutenant Eyre recorded in his account the series of objections which were raised against even this limited proposal. These included the difficulty of conveying the sick and wounded; the lack of firewood in Bala Hissar and access to forage from the country; the risk of a defeat on the road, and, above all, the detrimental effect on morale of abandoning the cantonments and giving a triumph to the enemy.[94]

The counter-arguments of 'Sturt's camp' included arguments that conveyance of the sick, though difficult, was not impracticable; that there was sufficient wood for cooking and that the horses would or could be shot, as cavalry would not be wanted in a static garrison. The supposed enemy triumph would also be short-lived as everything not removed from the cantonment would be destroyed in a 'scorch and burn' policy. Finally, it was argued that the distance travelled in the evacuation would be merely two miles, one half of the distance being protected by the guns of the Bala Hissar. Also a pre-emptive occupation of the Sujah Sang Heights would, it was argued, prevent the enemy impeding any British movement to the Bala Hissar.

Over these crucial days and weeks the arguments raged back and forth, with Shelton's camp refusing to concede and demanding a retreat to

Jalalabad. Shelton, himself, often feeling marginalized from central decision-making, and frequently overruled by opinions from junior officers, steadily retreated into sullen silence. This merely compounded the awful paralysis of command and control. Towards the end of November, Elphinstone had become even more marginalized, almost a spectator to the events, and unable to make headway with any of the contending groups. Lady Sale confirmed: 'Captain Grant's cold cautiousness and Captain Bellew's doubts on every subject induces our chief to alter his opinions and plans every moment.'[95]

During this time of fruitless debate, supplies rapidly dwindled and the weather ominously closed in. At one point on 10 November, the garrison's provisions were discovered to be reduced to a two-day supply. Only the payment of exorbitant prices for food, mostly obtained from nearby Bemaru village, alleviated this crisis. As early as 6 November Lady Sale had reported the first arrival of the dreaded Afghan winter: 'We had rain here later in the evening and at night and this morning I saw a great increase in the snow on the hills.'[96] Britain's ill-equipped native troops proved particularly vulnerable. As Lady Sale again observed, 'The Sipahees complain bitterly of the severity of the weather, particularly at night and above sixty men are in the hospital at Bala Hissar; already, beside the wounded they are attacked with pneumonia which carries them off in the course of a couple of days.'[97]

By 23 November, three weeks after the first day of insurrection and on the day of the last significant military offensive, the extent of demoralization amongst *both* officers and men had become patently clear. Lady Sale reported more furious rows between Shelton and Elphinstone, with officers beginning to neglect essential duties and even civilians entering the military decision-making cycle. Mutiny was in the air. On 22 November Lady Sale scribbled in her diary:

> Grand dissension in military councils. High and very plain language has been this day used by Brigadier Shelton to General Elphinstone; and people do not hesitate to say that our chief shall be set aside – a mode of proceedings recommended a fortnight ago by Mr Baness, the merchant....
>
> The poor General's mind is distracted by the diversity of opinions offered; and the great bodily ailments he sustains are daily enfeebling the powers of his mind. He has lost two of his best advisers in Patten and Thain; the former confined by his wound, the latter declining to offer advice from disgust at it being generally overruled by the counsel of the last speaker being acted on!'[98]

The morale of the surviving junior officers was noticeably deteriorating. One observer wrote:

> There is much reprehensible croaking going on; talk of retreat, and consequent desertion of our Musselman troops and the confusion likely to take place consequently thereon. All this makes a bad impression on the men. Our soldiers like to see the officers bear their part in privation; it makes them more cheerful; but in going the rounds at night, officers are seldom found with the men'.[99]

Even one senior officer, Colonel Oliver of the 5th Native Infantry, achieved widespread notoriety for his 'croaking'. On being told by the same men of his corps with great glee that a certain quantity of grain had been brought in, he replied 'it was needless for they would never live to eat it'![100]

The crisis of morale reached a dreadful climax on 23 November as the Kabul force launched their last desperate offensive action. A failed attempt to occupy the village of Bemaru (apparently by the same officer who failed to take Sharif's fort on 5 November), crucial to the cantonment supplies and now infiltrated by the enemy, set the scene for the ensuing disaster. The construction of *sangars* (breastworks) on the Bemaru Heights and the commencement of serious shelling of both the Bala Hissar and the cantonment by the insurgents now reluctantly forced the British hand. At 2 a.m. on 23 November 1841, Brigadier Shelton, having opposed the action on the grounds of the fatigued and half-starved state of his troops, silently marched out of the cantonment via the Kohistan Gate with seventeen companies of troops including men from the 44th Foot, the 5th and 37th Native Infantry and the Shah's 6th. The British aim was to conduct a surprise attack, to destroy the Afghan gun positions and drive them from the heights. Most of the British infantry companies were, however, significantly undermanned (often mustering below forty men), a testament to the scale of earlier losses and growing illness. Accompanying them was one squadron of regular cavalry and two detachments of irregular horse as well as one hundred sappers and miners (required to raise breastworks of the heights when captured), but only one 6-pounder gun. Moreover, of the approximate number of 1,350 men deployed, only 900 were infantry.[101] The enemy were, initially, completely surprised as the British swiftly occupied the Heights and opened up on them with grapeshot as they slept in the occupied village of Bemaru. From then on, however, the initiative was lost. The chance of assault on the village itself was missed (allegedly owing to indecision by Brigadier Shelton) and the British infantry were left hopelessly exposed to enemy *jezail* fire from behind the walls of the village. A prolonged fire-fight broke out. With surprise gone and daylight arriving, the situation soon deteriorated. A belated futile attempt by Major Swain of the 5th to capture Bemaru village led only to him being trapped and forced to retreat with several men killed and wounded. The now-vulnerable British force remained on the hill until the afternoon as thousands of the enemy progressively surrounded them. Despite pleas for reinforcements and for another gun by Brigadier Shelton neither was sent. It was a situation which again revealed Elphinstone's profound lack of command and control. From her favourite observation point behind the chimney of her house in the cantonment, 'where I had a fine view of the hill', Lady Sale noted with trepidation the escalating crisis. By midday she estimated the number of Afghan foot-soldiers to have increased to 10,000, with some three to four thousand Afghan cavalry besieging the two diminutive squares of British infantry. Casualties soon mounted, with marauding Ghilzai tribesmen even cheekily planting three red, yellow and green standards on the brow of the hill. Morale soon plummeted. Lady Sale actually witnessed the start of a collapse as, when the enemy 'fairly appeared above ground it was very evident that our men were not inclined to meet them'. The officers of the 44th, in desperation and 'to encourage the men' even 'pelted the Ghazees with stones as they climbed the hill' but 'nothing would do and the men would not advance'. The first square then collapsed; 'the enemy rushed in and drove our men very like a flock of sheep with a wolf at their heels'.[102] Only the British artillery section put up a desperate fight, most being killed or wounded as the gun was captured.

The second British square lasted longer as, joined by remnants of the first, it drove off a prolonged insurgent attack. The lost gun was retaken. But again the chance was lost to pursue the fleeing Ghilzai as Elphinstone refused the Envoy's request to pursue them into the city. By 12.30 p.m. the still inexplicably static force was subjected to galling fire 'so severe that our men in square could scarcely fill up the gaps as their comrades fell'.[103] Chronically short of water and ammunition, the whole force was finally 'driven down the hill' and the gun recaptured again by the enemy.

Only rapid supportive action by forces in the mission compound (Shah's 6th and Mackenzie's Juzailchees) nearby and a charge by the cavalry of the 5th saved the force from complete destruction. Fortunately for the British, the enemy commander, Osman Khan, decided not to follow up his victory. Major-General Elphinstone, finally stepping outside the cantonment gate, could now see for himself the extent of demoralization and a profound loss of confidence in his leadership. As the bedraggled force limped in he complained to MacNaghten, 'Why lord, sir, when I said to them "Eyes right" they all looked the other way.'[104] It must have been a traumatic moment for the General – while retaining formal command, he was never again to appear in front of his men until the first day of the retreat.

It was fitting epitaph to a disastrous day for British arms. The losses were terrible: 178 killed and 55 wounded with unknown casualties occurring amongst the 5th Native Infantry and 'after this there was no more attempt at military operations'. Lieutenant Eyre recalled this final deadly blow to military *esprit de corps*:

> Our troops had now lost all confidence; and even such of the officers as had hitherto indulged the hope of a favourable turn in our affairs began at last to entertain gloomy foreboding at to our future fate. Our force resembled a ship in danger of wrecking among rocks and shoals for want of an able pilot to guide it safely through them ... it seemed as if we were under the ban of Heaven.'[105]

The fate of the military now lay firmly in the hands of MacNaghten and his advisers. The stage was set for the inexorable, final, political tragedy. Since the outbreak of the insurrection on 2 November, MacNaghten had pursued clandestine negotiations with the insurgent Afghan chiefs, adopting a classic but extremely risky policy of 'divide and rule'. Such a strategy had certainly succeeded in the circumstances of overwhelming British force as had pre-existed in 1839–40 but, with British power now clearly deeply compromised, it was a strategy to cost him not only his life but those of thousands of his countrymen and allies.[106] His aim was simple – in the words of historian Durand: 'to create discord amongst the rebels and thus break up the league against Shah Shooja and his allies'. Unfortunately, much of this was to be done in secrecy, with even Elphinstone and leading military counsellors left in ignorance. The intermediary was Mohan Lal, a key British collaborator He had earlier miraculously escaped the Burnes massacre on 2 November, ultimately finding asylum in the house of a Qizilbash chief, Khan Sheereen Khan, in the Persian quarter of the city. He was therefore, considered to be ideally suited to carry on negotiations, or intrigues, with those and other chiefs willing to work for MacNaghten. Working alongside Lieutenant John Connolly, the Envoy's political assistant, he commenced negotiations in early November with the Qizilbash chiefs, the ethnic group most likely to be loyal to the British cause and who had continued to remain relatively neutral since the disturbances began. Thus, on November 6, Lady Sale remarked in her diary: 'Sir William has given one of the Kuzzilbash chiefs fifty thousand rupees to raise a diversion in our favour and has promised him two lakhs more if he succeeds.'[107]

Up until 13 November, at least some limited success had been achieved with this strategy when, for instance, the Khojeh Meer of Bimaru 'sent his salaam to know our pleasure'. But this only reflected the limited military success against nearby forts on 10 November. As the military slowly lost ground and Qizilbash support slowly evaporated, MacNaghten's strategy (either deliberately or by default) changed from negotiation to a far more high-risk policy which included even the assassination of selected rebel chiefs. MacNaghten's role in this latter policy remains in dispute; he later vehemently denied any part in a policy of assassination and it may simply have been a misreading of his aims by Mohan Lal or other Afghan collaborators. At the very least he may have turned a Nelsonian blind eye to Mohan Lal's advance of 9,000 rupees to be paid for the deaths of the leading rebels, Meer Musjidi and Abdullah Khan, and a balance of 12,000 rupees for their 'heads'. In any event, two men, Abdul Azeez and Mohammed Odah, were enlisted as the potential assassins and both rebel leaders 'were soon killed' – the former died suddenly and Abdullah Khan was himself mortally wounded during the Bemaru battle of 23 November. Whether the latter died by a British musket ball or (equally likely) by a musket ball from one assassin, Abdul Azeez (allegedly firing from behind a nearby wall) remains an open question. In the event, MacNaghten's agent, Mohan Lal, chose not to pay either of their fees as their deaths remained unattributed and no physical evidence was supplied. It was a fatal tactic – from then on, whether by intent or accident, or both, MacNaghten (and his agents) were linked with treachery and assassination rather than the more traditional methods of bribery and intrigue.

MacNaghten was rapidly losing the moral high ground and effectively signing his own death warrant. Trust between the two rival sides certainly deteriorated after mid-November 1841 and MacNaghten's negotiations became significantly tenser, with frequent allegations of his betrayal by rebel chiefs. By 14 November, for instance, the day after the inconclusive 13 November battle, enraged Ghilzai chiefs had already 'complained that we broke faith with them yesterday in attacking them when they had expressed a wish to treat'.[108]

MacNaghten's own obsessively secret diplomatic tactics did not help the deteriorating political situation. Elphinstone, Shelton and Shah Shuja himself were kept in the dark in regard to his diplomatic manoeuvring. On 27 November, for instance, Lady Sale reported the King as 'in an awful state of alarm … believing us to have abandoned him'.[109] She later acidly commented on the rumours which inevitably spread; 'whenever the political horizon clears a little, mystery becomes the order of the day'. On 30 November, Lady Sale again commented: 'the politicals are again very mysterious and deny that any negotiations are going on ... but letters come in constantly and we know they are treating with the Ghilzyes'.[110] Meanwhile, as MacNaghten took false confidence from the death of two of his two rebel opponents, his refusal to contemplate retreat (as advocated by Brigadier Shelton) significantly strengthened. The arrival in Kabul of Mohammed Akbar Khan, the vengeful son of exiled Dost Mohammed, on 22 November, further stacked the political cards against the Envoy. News of the disasters outside Kabul (notably at Charikar, where a British-led Gurkha garrison was virtually annihilated[111]), the 23 November debacle at Bimaru, and news of the near exhaustion of supplies, triggered off the last desperate round of negotiations. The first significant enemy demands appeared on 27 November. The rebel chiefs required, in addition to giving up the King and his family, that all guns and ammunition, muskets and bayonets, pistols and swords were to be surrendered, and married men, women and children were to be handed over as hostages. Then, as Lady Sale cynically observed, 'we are to trust to their generosity'. A depressed but now infuriated Envoy haughtily replied to insurgent chiefs that 'death was preferable to dishonour – that we put our trust in the God of battles and in His name bade them come on'.[112]

On 11 December 1841, MacNaghten, accompanied by his political secretary, Lawrence, and by Captains Mackenzie and Trevor, arranged the penultimate public conference with the assembled rebel leaders on the plain near Siah Sung Hill. Of the threats now facing MacNaghten the 'food supply crisis' was the most pressing. On 3 December the main Afghan supplier to the garrison, Khojeh Meer, had dramatically announced that he had no more grain and only fifty *maunds* were delivered that day. His explanation revealed the success of the rebel strategy of starving out the garrison. Meer revealed that 'the moolahs had been to all the villages and laid the people under ban not to assist the English and that, consequently, the Mussellman population are as one man against us'. He also claimed to be in fear of his life, as he had been identified as the principal collaborator with the British. Lady Sale theorized, however, that the problem may equally have been generated by British greed as, 'much more grain might have been procured had we not foolishly tried to drive hard bargains'.[113] Khojeh Meer subsequently informed the British authorities that the villages to the rear (from where the grain was brought to the depot at Bimaru) were now occupied and the only village capable of providing six months' supply was Kojah Rewash, unfortunately also occupied by Sekundur Khan and 500 rebels. The stranglehold over the British garrison was virtually complete.

At this same 11 December conference the extent of distrust on the part of the chiefs was immediately evident in their demand to take Captain Trevor as hostage; clear evidence of their 'thorough want of confidence in the Envoy's sincerity'.[114] The weakness of the British position was further manifested in the new treaty proposals. The unmolested withdrawal, not only of the Kabul garrison, but of *all* British troops in Afghanistan; their supply with food, fodder and means of transport; the return from India of Dost Mohammed and every Afghan in exile; that Shah Shuja was to be given the option of remaining at Kabul or accompanying the British Army to India; an amnesty for all political opponents and the partisans of the Shah and that no British force should again be sent into Afghanistan unless called for by the Afghan Government, comprised the main features of the proposed, significantly harsher treaty. More ominous was the hard-line attitude of the newly arrived rebel chief, Mohammed Akbar, who tried but failed to oppose the amnesty for 'collaborators', but who succeeded in his refusal to allow the garrison to be supplied with provisions *until it had quit the cantonments.*

There was one final political act. The hated MacNaghten was now himself to be enticed into a fatal encounter with his principal opponent, Mohammed Akbar Khan. Since his arrival, Akbar Khan had been fully informed of MacNaghten's previous duplicitous negotiations and the official or unofficial policy of assassination by hired henchmen. Profound existing distrust over this was compounded by a deep personal motive; the British failure to honour their earlier understanding to release Akbar Khan's father, Dost Mohammed, from exile in India. The latter issue probably proved to be the final straw. Over the next two weeks, MacNaghten was slowly inveigled into a plot which would cost him his life.

During this last month of frantic negotiation there were further signs of military disintegration within the British cantonment. As temperatures plunged, the standards of discipline visibly deteriorated. Little attention was now being paid to orders. By now Brigadier Shelton had totally retreated from the decision-making process, apparently spending his time in Elphinstone's War Councils either pretending to be asleep or whittling away pieces of wood, to the intense annoyance of the now deeply stressed MacNaghten. Two other incidents in December revealed the true state of deterioration of morale amongst officers and men. In the mud fort guarding the canal bridge – a potential future escape route for the garrison – the guard of 100 men under a Lieutenant Hawtrey (forty 44th Foot and sixty sepoys) were surprised by Afghan rebels equipped with scaling ladders. The troops panicked and ran, leaving only the brave Hawtrey and one brave 44th soldier to defend the breach with hand grenades. The latter was soon shot dead. The 44th subsequently claimed that the 37th Native

Infantry ran first and, as they were too few, they fled too. Hawtrey was blunter, describing his men as 'all cowards alike'.[115] Faced with this crisis, even Brigadier Shelton briefly raised himself from his stupor to try to reorganize the deserters and retake the fort. Unfortunately, the men were kept on muster until 3 or 4 a.m. with snow lying on the ground, only to be dismissed without any action. It was a devastating further indictment of the command and control situation.

On 9 December some officers of the 44th even asked for a court of inquiry to 'clear their name' but, as Lady Sale cryptically observed, 'there is too much evidence to prove that the Europeans were the first to run away from the captured fort',[116] while the rest of the disgusted 44th voted with their feet by ostracizing the company involved in the flight. Dissension was now rife even within the regiments themselves.

Another incident arose from the treaty terms of 11 December when Elphinstone, as a result of the imminent handover of the army's magazine, foolishly allowed the muskets and other arms to be left piled under a tree in the cantonment orchard, guarded by only a few soldiers. Confusion reigned as a rush of camp-followers overwhelmed the guard, all imagining that a licence had been given to take whatever they pleased. Order was eventually restored but a portion of the stolen armament was never recovered.

As military chaos reigned, MacNaghten was quickly drawn into Akbar Khan's web of deception. On 22 December Captain Skinner, acting as an intermediary for Akbar, presented the Envoy with a plan by which Akbar would seize Ameer Oollah, another rebel chief, and deliver his head to the Envoy. In return, it was proposed that MacNaghten would arrange for Akbar to be *Wazir* to Shah Shuja, whose throne would then be guaranteed. Furthermore the Bala Hissar, and Mohammed Khan's fort would be retained by the British ready for evacuation in the spring. The proposals were clearly too good to be true, but MacNaghten fell for the plot hook, line and sinker. As Durand observed: 'the deliberate faithfulness which led the Envoy to accept Mohammed Akbar's proposal sealed his doom'.[117] The worst suspicions of Mohammed Akbar and his fellow rebel chiefs about British perfidy were confirmed by this act. It was the final nail in the coffin for both MacNaghten and his ill-fated mission.

After a preliminary meeting on 21 December, in which the chiefs significantly insisted on the handing over of *four* hostages (Trevor, Drummond, Connolly and Airey), the Envoy rode out for his final fateful meeting with the assembled senior rebel chiefs. From the start the signs were not auspicious. Lieutenant Sturt, now aware that the Bala Hissar was to be abandoned, was already proposing to break off the treaty with an open retreat to Jalalabad (in line with Shelton's original proposal). MacNaghten's immediate colleagues warned him of the dangers of the meeting and of the 'perfidious' character of Mohammed Akbar. Eyre and Durand faithfully record his final words in reply, a reply revealing a truly desperate man and a man clearly paralyzed by nervous exhaustion:

> Dangerous it is; but if it succeeds, it is worth all risks: the rebels have not fulfilled even one article of the treaty, and I have no confidence in them; and if by it we can only save our honour, all will be well; at any rate I would rather suffer a hundred deaths than live the last six weeks over again.[118]

Two accounts record the melancholy story of his final hours. These were written by Captain Colin Mackenzie and Captain George Lawrence, MacNaghten's Political Secretary, his companions on that fateful day. Mackenzie's own personal warning of the dangers of the meeting that day and of a plot against him were hastily rebuffed by MacNaghten. 'A plot! Let me alone for that, trust me for that!' was MacNaghten's distraught reply. As the mission left the cantonment gates and approached the Siah Sung ridge, MacNaghten immediately noticed that, despite his request, General Elphinstone's proposed escort, comprising the 54th Regiment under Major Ewart and the Shah's 6th Infantry, had not turned up. In Mackenzie's words this 'betrays the unhappy vacillation of poor Elphinstone',[119] who had sent a last-minute letter approving their departure which in the event never reached the Envoy. The non-arrival of the escort apparently caused MacNaghten 'much vexation' and his state of mind was such that he even forgot the horse he had acquired as a present for Akbar and duly sent Mackenzie back for it. When Mackenzie later rejoined him he found that the escort had shrunk further and, astonishingly, that the bodyguard had also been ordered to halt. MacNaghten, Trevor and Lawrence had by now advanced well in the direction of Mohammed Khan's fort, 500 or 600 yards from the eastern rampart. There they awaited the arrival of Mohammed Akbar and his party of rebel chiefs.

MacNaghten and his diminished escort were directed to a small hillock, chosen they were told, 'as being free from snow' but a spot, which Lawrence significantly noted, 'partially concealed us from the cantonments'.[120] Mackenzie was the first to become openly suspicious: 'Men talk of presentiment; I suppose it was something of the kind which came over me, for I could scarcely prevail upon myself to quit my horse.'[121]

Lawrence named the chiefs present besides Akbar Khan. Their ethnic background was immensely significant. Most were Ghilzai chiefs representing the tribal group most hostile to the British, and who had been most severely affected by the subsidy cuts, namely Mohammed Shah Khan, Dost Mohammed Khan, Khuda Baksh Khan and Azad Khan. After the usual salutations the Envoy presented the horse and Akbar expressed thanks for the handsome brace of double-barrelled pistols sent to him by the Envoy the day before. Next, a carpet or horsecloth was spread on the hillock and the Envoy, 'threw himself on the bank' with Akbar, Trevor and Mackenzie. Akbar then commenced business by asking the fateful question as to whether the Envoy was 'perfectly ready to carry into effect the proposition of the preceding night'. MacNaghten's answer, 'Why not?' sealed the trap.

Events now moved quickly. Lawrence noticed the rapid approach of armed retainers around the Envoy. 'I stood behind Sir William until pressed by Dost Mohammed Khan, I knelt on one knee, having first called the Envoy's attention to the number of Afghans around us, saying that if the subject of the conference was of that secret nature I believed it to be they had better be moved.'[122] MacNaghten then spoke to Akbar about this, and he replied, 'No, they are all in the great secret'. His game up, Akbar Khan then gave the signal for the attack. Mackenzie recorded the next few horrific seconds:

> I heard Muhammed Akbar call out 'Bigir, Bigir' (seize! seize!) and, turning around, I saw him grasp the Envoy's left hand with an expression in his face of the most diabolical ferocity. I think it was Sultan Jan who laid hold of the Envoy's right hand. They dragged him in a stooping posture down the hillock, the only words I heard poor Sir William utter being 'Az barai Khuda' [for God's sake!]. I saw his face however and it was full of horror and astonishment.[123]

Lawrence also glimpsed MacNaghten's last terrible moments. 'I turned and saw the Envoy, lying where his heels had been and his hands locked in Muhammed Akbar's, consternation and horror depicted in his countenance.'[124] MacNaghten's 'hundred deaths' now commenced. A pistol shot either killed or wounded him and his body was then decapitated and hacked to pieces by the hordes of predominantly Ghilzai warriors, who closed in for the kill.

Poor Captain Trevor met a similar fate – dragged from his horse to the ground and hacked to pieces. Both Mackenzie and Lawrence, however, were mercifully saved from the 'butcher's yard' as other members of the wider escort were struck down. Mackenzie, in fact, owed his life to the efforts of an Afghan friend, Ghulam Muyan-ud-Din, former chief of the

Kabul police, who had earlier distracted him to the extent of raising him from his recumbent posture ready for escape. Like Lawrence, however, Mackenzie had become aware that 'a number of men, armed to the teeth had gradually approached to the scene of conference and were drawing around in a sort of circle'. As the attack was launched on the Envoy, Mackenzie's view of the end of both Trevor or MacNaghten was rapidly obscured as he himself was 'surrounded by a circle of Ghilzais with drawn swords and cocked juzails'. His right arm was gripped and a pistol held to his temple as his Afghan saviour dragged him through the snow to his horse. He was still by no means safe:

> As I mounted behind my captor, now my energetic defender, the crowd increased around us, the cries of 'kill the kafir' became more vehement and, although we hurried on at a fast canter it was with the utmost difficulty; Gulam Muyan-ud-Din although assisted by one or two friends or followers could ward off and avoid the sword cuts aimed at me, the rascals being afraid to fire lest they should kill my conductor.[125]

Despite a severe blow to the head, an attempted strangulation by one enraged 'fanatic' and a fall from his horse, Mackenzie reached the relative security of Muhammed Khan's fort, where Mohammed Akbar, after receiving the congratulations of the multitude, protected him with the use of his sword. Akbar's own deep sense of anger and betrayal was soon revealed, however, as he yelled at Mackenzie 'in a tone of triumphant derision, 'Shuma mulk-i-ma me-gired!' (You'll seize my country will you!). After surviving further attacks from Mulla Mumin and his followers, and being rescued by Muhammed Shah Khan, he was bundled into a dungeon with his erstwhile companion, Captain Lawrence.

It was the same Mohammed Shah Khan who, earlier, had also saved Lawrence's life by pulling him onto his horse. The chief's several armed retainers beat off 'a crowd of Ghilzais who sprang up on every side cutting at me with their swords and knives and poking me in the ribs with their guns'. Again, fortunately, 'they were afraid to fire unless they injured their chief'.[126]

The British captives endured a night of extreme tension, protected only by a few soldiers from a howling mob 'execrating and spitting at us'. At one horrendous moment 'one assailant produced a hand (European) which appeared to have been recently cut off'. Mackenzie later confirmed that it was the hand of MacNaghten. Both men were then subjected to further threats from another rebel chief, Amanulla Khan, who 'said that we either should be or deserved to be blown away from a gun'. Significantly it was this chief who had been the target of Akbar's false plot.

Finally evacuated to safety in Mohammed Akbar's abode, the two British officers were violently harangued at a meeting of the Council of the Khans: 'we were vehemently accused of treachery and everything that was bad and told that the whole of the transaction of the night previous had been a trick of Mohammed Akbar and Amin-ullah to ascertain the Envoy's sincerity'.[127] Captain Connolly, one of the earlier hostages from the 11 December negotiations, also confirmed to the two men that, on the preceding day, 'the Envoy's head had been paraded alone in the courtyard; that his and Trevor's bodies had been hung up in the public bazaar or *chouk*; and that it was with the greatest difficulty that the old Nawab, Zaman Khan, had saved him and Airey from being murdered by a body of fanatics'.[128]

It had been a calamitous day for the British garrison. Only a few hundred yards away, British troops had witnessed MacNaghten's departure but, in the ensuing chaos, had not seen the eventual fate of the Envoy and his escort. As the plain was 'covered with people', it was twenty-four hours before news of the murders was confirmed within the cantonment. Lady Sale glimpsed only 'a body which the Affghans were seen to strip; it was evidently that of a European' but, she tellingly remarked, 'strange to say no endeavour was made to recover it which might easily have been done by sending our cavalry'. On Christmas Eve 1841 it was Lady Sale herself who had the 'sad office imposed on me' of informing both Lady MacNaghten and Mrs Trevor of their husbands' assassinations – 'over such scenes I draw a veil. It was a most painful meeting to us all'.[129]

It was a military officer, Major Eldred Pottinger, who had only recently and narrowly escaped from the almost simultaneous disaster in nearby Charikar, who now, at the behest of the totally demoralized Elphinstone, hurriedly occupied the murdered Envoy's post. The British now re-engaged in frantic negotiations. British decision-making, in the succinct words of historian Louis Dupree, had now rapidly 'simmered down from whether to negotiate to *how* to negotiate'.[130] The rebel chiefs now took the initiative as British food, water, medical supplies and morale dwindled. At a conference at the house of rebel leader Nawab Zaman Khan, the late Envoy's treacherous conduct was 'severely commented on' and a revised treaty was discussed. After further alterations and additions the treaty was sent back to Elphinstone 'with an explanation of the breach of faith which cost the Envoy his life'. The additional clauses provided that the British should leave behind *all* their guns except six and, secondly, that they should *immediately* give up *all* their 'treasures'. Finally, it reaffirmed that the hostages should be exchanged for married men with their wives and families.

Christmas Day 1841, was spent by the General and his advisers considering this virtual ultimatum. Lieutenant Eyre recalled that: 'A more cheerless Xmas day never dawned upon British soldiers in a strange land the few whom the force of habit urged to exchange the customary greetings of the season, did so in countenance and in tones indicative of anything but merriment.' At least, on that sacred day, there was no fighting: 'At night there was an alarm and the drums beat to arms, but nothing occurred of any consequence.'[131]

On 26 December 1841, the final War Council took place, convened by a deeply depressed General Elphinstone. Those present were Envoy Major Eldred Pottinger, Brigadiers Shelton and Anquetil, Colonel Chambers, Captain Bellew and Captain Grant. At the Council, Pottinger made a last desperate plea for military action, arguing that no confidence could now be placed in the rebel chiefs. He advocated that it would be dishonourable to bind the hands of the Government by agreeing to evacuate the country and to restore the deposed Amir. In his view, the only 'honourable course' would be to hold out to the last in Kabul, specifically by retaking the Bala Hissar, or force an *immediate* retreat to Jalalabad. His pleas fell on deaf ears; the rest of the Council arguing that logistics, the lack of provisions, as well as the loss of surrounding forts and the awfulness of the road, would render immediate retreat impracticable. The Council's conclusion was to delay action, adhere to the treaty and to pay the sums to the chiefs. Captain Bellew later claimed, in conversation with Lady Sale, that other wilder schemes raised had included a plan to erect a battery on Siah Sung Hill or force British troops into the Bala Hissar, but with no idea how to transport the powder or ammunition or protect the men in the battery. Lady Sale thought him to be joking as 'the time for action is long passed'.[132]

The demand to hand over married British officers and their families proved a major cause of dissension, with only Lieutenant Eyre reluctantly agreeing, under orders, to the proposal. An incensed Captain Anderson, by contrast, threatened to put a pistol to his wife's head and shoot her, while Lieutenant Sturt claimed that his wife and mother should only be taken at the point of a bayonet! In the meantime, Captain Lawrence was released by the rebels to arrange the payments to the chiefs as under the treaty. The British sick were slowly transferred into the city of Kabul during 29 and 30 December, the medical officers apparently drawing lots on who were to stay with them. On 30 December, however, military pressures suddenly intensified with 'five hundred Ghazees making a rush at the rear gate of the cantonment' but retreating when faced with a port gun loaded with grape shot'. Easier targets comprising the camel drivers and *doolie* bearers who conveyed the British sick were not so lucky. On their return to the city from the cantonment on the 30 December, they were 'brutally attacked and plundered; the men were stripped and had to run for their lives without any clothing, their black bodies conspicuous as they ran over the snow'. The *doolies* and camels, it was reported, 'were carried off'.[133]

The now complete loss of control of the communications with the city appears to have speeded up plans for evacuation, especially when, on 31 December, the insurgent chiefs reported that they no longer had, 'control over the Ghazees'. Captain Lawrence's report of the fate of MacNaghten's and Burnes' bodies only served to increase the gloom pervading the half-starved garrison, with Burnes' body reportedly cut into many pieces and still hanging on the trees of Naib Shureef's garden, and the Envoy's head 'kept in a bhoosa [chaff] bag on the chouk [bazaar] apparently accompanied by a promise by Akbar that he would send it to the brutal ruler of Bokhara as proof of how he had seized the Feringhees and what he means to do with them'.[134]

As the British heavy guns were handed over in accordance with the treaty, the engineers, led by Lieutenant Sturt, commenced frantic preparations for the retreat. These included the collection of some 250 planks to cross the Kabul River and to carry on to the Loghur River in case the bridge there was destroyed by the enemy. More immediately Sturt, assisted by fifty Afghan workmen, was sent to work on the banks of the canal located by the cantonment to make it more fordable. The General's earlier projected departure date, under the promised escort of the chiefs, was Tuesday 4 January 1842. Again, the transport needed for the timber – 125 camels carrying two planks each – would clearly deprive the column of ammunition capacity and many questioned whether they were essential to cross frozen streams, often only a few inches deep. Soon the initial breaches in the canal banks were prepared for evacuation. Delays continued, however, as the rebel escort for the retreat, promised under the treaty terms, failed to materialize. An ever-more cynical Lady Sale confirmed: 'The forty thousand rupees given by us to the Chiefs to raise two thousand men at twenty rupees each to protect us to Jalalabad, have not succeeded. They have kept the money of course.'[135] However, she conceded that finding such men in mid-winter was, in any event, unlikely and would weaken the chiefs' own power.

Annihilation: the Death March to Jalalabad

On Wednesday 5 January 1842, a desperate Elphinstone gave his final, fateful command to commence the retreat and orders were issued to that effect 'for 7 and 8 o'clock am' on Thursday 6 January. Astonishingly,

Brigadier Shelton, as second-in-command, had been one of the last to know, a testament perhaps to the degree to which he had been left isolated from the command cycle. He later claimed, 'I knew nothing of the arrangements for the retreat till they were published the night before.' When at 8 a.m. the next day he desperately tried to get permission from Elphinstone to release the gun-carriages in order to make a footbridge over the Kabul River for the infantry he 'got offended for his trouble' by the former, who was 'just sitting down to his breakfast'![136] Not only was this a testament to the breakdown of personal relations between the two men, but it resulted in the construction being delayed until 'past twelve'. This served to exacerbate what was already a militarily disastrous decision. In the words of Hough, 'to retreat through the frost and the snow was the most hazardous of all the measures adopted, the troops having to contend against the frost as well as the enemy and it was especially "fatal" to the less protected and acclimatized Native troops who comprised five sixths of the force'. He tellingly added: 'Before the snow fell i.e. before the 18th of December a retreat was practicable.'[137]

'General January' struck the first vengeful blow. Captain Souter, 44th Foot, one of the few European survivors of this great retreat, commented: 'The weather was remarkably and intensely cold and the snow fell to a great depth.'[138] Snow had been falling and indeed settling consistently since 18 December, reaching up to four feet in depth in places. Lieutenant Eyre also recalled the desolate landscape confronting the weary garrison as it commenced its ninety-mile winter march to Jalalabad in initial temperatures plummeting to -20 °C: 'Dreary was the scene, over which, with drooping spirits and dismal foreboding we had to bend our unwilling steps. Deep snow covered every inch of mountain and plain with one unspotted sheet of dazzling white and so intensely bitter was the cold, as to penetrate and defy the defences of the warmest clothing.'[139]

His deep foreboding was shared by Lady Sale. The night before the retreat, as she assisted Lieutenant Sturt in sorting and reading through some valuable books ready for safe-keeping by an Afghan friend, she stumbled across a most appropriate verse taken from 'Campbell's Poems':

> *Few, shall part where many meet*
> *The snow shall be their winding sheet*
> *And every turf beneath their feet*
> *Should be a soldier's sepulchre.*

It was a verse 'never absent'[140] from her thoughts during the terrible days ahead.

The retreat began and ended in shambles. No signs of the promised escort appeared and, at an early hour, on 6 January 1842, preparations commenced with a final cut made through the already breached eastern rampart and a rear gate. Logistical planning was already dangerously flawed, with every available camel and *yaboo* (Afghan pony) – approximately 2,000 pack animals in all – laden with military stores and Commissariat supplies, but with only a minimum of camp equipage included – an inexplicable oversight in a climate of such severity.

The force that departed Kabul on that fateful January day comprised about 4,500 British and Indian troops and 12,000 followers The main combat units of the advance party, initially led by Brigadier Anquetil, comprised the already severely depleted Her Majesty's 44th – nineteen officers and 438 fighting men – 'in which numbers were included Brigadier Shelton, twelve boys and thirty-four sick'.[141] This key element was supported by a couple of dozen sappers and miners, one squadron of irregular horse and three mountain train guns.

The main or centre column under Brigadier Shelton comprised the 37th and 5th Native Infantry (totalling around 1,250 fighting effectives), Captain Anderson's Irregular Horse and two Horse Artillery guns. This column also provided the escort for the ladies, invalids and sick, although the redoubtable Lady Sale herself preferred to take her chances in the more vulnerable advance column.

The more numerous but arguably weaker rearguard under Colonel Chambers included the 54th Native Infantry (around 650 effectives), the significantly less-disciplined 6th Shah's Infantry (also around 600 effectives), the 700-strong 5th Light (Native) Cavalry and four Horse Artillery guns. In all, it totalled around 2,000 men or half the combat force.

By around 8 a.m. 'a great part of the baggage was deposited outside the cantonments' but with further delays the advance did not actively commence until 9 a.m. (9.30 a.m. by Lady Sale's calculations). Further delays occurred, however, following a message from rebel chief Nawab Jabar Khan, requesting a halt for another day 'as his escort was not ready to accompany us'.[142]

In any event, the slow momentum of this truly 'elephantine' force probably could not be stopped, particularly as the advance party had already disappeared into the snowy wilderness meeting, initially, little resistance. Despite Lieutenant Sturt's overnight courageous efforts, working waist-deep in a freezing river to make a bridge with gun-carriages across the icy, eighteen-foot broad but deep Kabul River, it proved unsuitable for even the weight of the advance column of infantry cavalry and guns. Another hour's delay for strengthening resulted; it had taken two and a half hours to traverse just one mile.

By then, the rearguard and the rear of the main centre column were already in deep trouble. Afghan looters from nearby Bemaru village had already forced their way into the deserted northern cantonment or mission compound, mistakenly evacuated too early by the less reliable and ill-disciplined men of the Shah's 6th Infantry. These looters were soon 'busily engaged in their work of pillage and destruction'.[143]

As elements of the British rearguard fought a desperate holding action within the cantonment, the ponderous main body proceeded until early evening to pour out of the gate. By this time, thousands of Afghan rebels, 'the majority of whom were fanatical Ghazis', occupied key areas of the cantonment, 'rending the air with exalting cries and committing every kind of atrocity'.[144] Step by step the British rearguard retreated through the rest of the cantonment, each vacated area being 'immediately filled with rebels'. The problems of the rearguard in fending off the incessant attacks may have been as much political as military. The survivor, Sergeant-Major Lissant of the 37th Native Infantry, later claimed he overheard Lieutenant Hawtrey say that: 'Much of the baggage was still in the cantonment when the enemy broke in over the ramparts on every side and that the troops left behind to protect this were ordered not to fire but to get together as quickly as possible and get away from the cantonments.'[145] Again, such passive behaviour, designed to conform with an already violated treaty, could only have boosted the confidence of the insurgent Afghan chiefs and their troops.

Finally, the rearguard was forced out of the cantonment onto the exposed but militarily more practical defensive position on the plain. Here, however, it collided with the now virtually static centre column, which was still held up by the 'great quantity of baggage'. The latter had been brought to a standstill at the canal within 150 yards of the gate. The waterway's slippery sides afforded 'no safe footing for the beasts of burden'. Increasingly exposed outside the cantonment, both the rearguard and much of the main body became easy targets for the Afghan snipers now occupying the captured British ramparts behind them. With increasingly severe losses the two Horse Artillery guns had to spiked and abandoned, seriously undermining the firepower of this section of the force. Widespread panic soon broke out amongst the unarmed camp-followers, servants and bearers who, understandably, abandoned their loads under such intense fire. Apart from the human losses it was a mortal blow to the logistical credibility of the British force as vast quantities of food and tentage were now lost to the enemy. In the heart-rending words of the indefatigable Lady Sale: 'Private baggage, commissariat and ammunition were nearly annihilated in one fell swoop. The whole road was covered with men, women and children lying down in the snow to die.'[146]

As during the original invasion march to Kabul, it was the ill-equipped, predominantly Indian, camp-followers who paid the ultimate price, even during these first hours. As scores froze to death in the snow, others predictably fled from the long knives of the pursuing Afghan marauders into the main column. This caused further massive disruption. In Lieutenants Eyre's words:

> The order of march in which the troops started was soon lost and the camp followers with the public and private baggage, once out of the cantonments, could not be prevented from mixing themselves up with the troops to the utter confusion of the whole column ... these proved from the very first minute a serious clog upon our movements and, were, indeed, the main cause of our subsequent misfortunes.[147]

By contrast, the advance guard, after the initial delays in crossing the Kabul River, had by early evening managed to reach a point a mile further than Begram, the first designated halting place. This bivouac was reached about 4 p.m. Nevertheless, even these first elements of the British force had only covered six miles in seven hours, with over eighty miles in below freezing temperatures still to endure. Some delay had even been caused to the advance column by the slow-moving bullocks dragging the planks in case the Loghar Bridge was destroyed. The lack of tentage, either already lost or located far behind with the struggling main body, became immediately evident. As Lady Sale observed: 'There were no tents save two or three small palls that arrived. All scraped away the snow as best they might to make a place to lie down.'[148] A shortage of food was also evident. 'The evening and night were intensely cold; no food for man or beast procurable, except a few handfuls of bhoosa for which we paid from five to ten rupees.'[149]

For the more harassed centre column on that horrendous first day it was a story of untold misery. Sergeant Major Lissant recalled:

> The snow was eight or ten inches deep and we were from six in the morning until ten or eleven that night (the 6th), before we reached the opposite side of the Logar river where we were to sleep.... I can safely say that not one camel out of twenty that left the cantonment reached the Logar river.'[150]

As the centre column, having lost most of its transport to Afghan marauders between the cantonment and the Siah Sung Hill, belatedly linked up with the advance party camp at Begram, the loss of baggage, especially tentage, caused even greater problems. Even their commander, Brigadier Shelton, had 'no tent' and for six days and nights was 'exposed on a bed of snow' – a tribute to his personal courage and hardy constitution.

As the freezing Afghan winter night closed in, the rearguard, still several miles away, was still being reduced by a deadly combination of weather exposure and *jezail* fire. Before it had even commenced its march from outside the cantonments, it was reported that 'Lieutenant Hardyman of the 5th Light Cavalry, with 50 rank and file were stretched lifeless in the snow'.[151] Most of their baggage was plundered on the road to Begram. As the rearguard finally pulled away, the jubilant Afghan rebels set fire to the cantonment, the conflagration illuminating the surrounding country for several miles. As abandoned gun-carriages and ramparts were indiscriminately burnt by the enemy, the former apparently in order to secure the much prized iron, Lieutenant Eyre considered that this was at least a bonus as it would paralyze their heavy artillery capability. The less well-equipped Indian troops and those camp-followers abandoned by the rearguard again bore the brunt of the suffering. Lieutenant Eyre recalled how even on that first day, 'scores of worn out sepoys and camp followers lined the way, having sat down in despair to perish in the snow'.[152] Dr Brydon, another survivor of the retreat, confirmed 'though this march is not more than five miles a great number of women and children perished in the snow which is about six inches deep'.[153] It wasn't until as late as 2 a.m. on the morning of 7 January before the exhausted, frozen rearguard finally reached the camp at Begram. Lady Sale, woken by the noise, witnessed chaotic scenes as they arrived: 'As stragglers came up we heard them shouting out to know where their corps were; and the general reply – that no one knew anything about it.'[154]

Such disorganization was reflected in the complete collapse of disciplined camp organization – fatal in such an extreme and unrelenting climate. Even amongst the centre and rear columns, where tentage was more available, other basic essential duties of preparing food and lighting fires were widely neglected by the exhausted troops. As Lieutenant Eyre observed:

The tents had been pitched without the slightest regard to regularity, those of different regiments being huddled together in one intricate mess mixed up with baggage, camp followers, camels and horses in a way which beggars description. The flimsy canvas of the soldiers' tents was but a poor protection from the cold, which, towards morning, became more and more intense, and thousands of poor wretched creatures were obliged to lie down on the bare snow without shelter, fire or food. Several died during the night; amongst whom was a European conductor of ordnance.[155]

The impact of such extreme adversity on the morale of the troops was already evident. Even on this first night the favourite 'strategy for survival' was clearly desertion. During the early hours, scores of frozen, demoralized sepoys abandoned their units. Lady Sale reported that nearly all of Hopkins' sepoy corps and most of the Shah's 6th Regiment deserted from the Begram camp overnight, as did the Shah's sappers and miners, 250 in total. Lieutenant Eyre also confirmed that next morning, the Shah's 6th Infantry was 'nowhere to be found: only a few struggling files were perceptible here and there; and it was generally believed that the majority of the rest had absconded during the night to Kabul'.[156] The rearguard, from whom most of these soldiers originated, was severely weakened. Scarcely one half of its sepoys were left present or fit for duty.

By the second day, Friday 7 January, such early losses by death or desertion to the rearguard forced Elphinstone and his senior commanders to radically reorganize the force. The advance guard, primarily the 44th Foot, was now hastily redeployed to occupy the rearguard position. Such 'reverse order' could not solve the continuing problems of maintaining cohesion and discipline. At 7.30 a.m. that Friday the reformed advance guard, comprising mainly the 54th Native Infantry, moved off amidst continuing chaos. Lady Sale noted the erosion of basic discipline even at this early stage: 'no order was given – no bugle sounded'.[157] The baggage and camp-followers were now fully mixed with the soldiers and even the advance guard had to force its way through the panicking mass of people, many of whom had started off at first light. On this second day, 7 January, the columns started for Butkhak, a distance of five miles but 'had not proceeded far when a sharp fire was opened on us and the road from Kabul covered with Afghans following hard on us'. As the 44th Regiment gallantly brought up the rear, Dr Brydon vividly recalled the still 'dense mass of people' sprawled along the whole road, with the loss of property reportedly as immense as the previous day.[158] Sporadic Afghan attacks continued. At one point, as the mountain guns were forced to make a detour to avoid a watercourse, an intrepid party of Afghans suddenly sallied from a nearby fort and captured them. Although the guns were soon recaptured, another worrying collapse of morale by a section of the 44th was recorded by Lady Sale, who noted that, during the attempted rescue, the 44th escort suddenly 'made themselves scarce'. The situation was only partially restored by their officers when the courageous Brigadier Anquetil and Lieutenant Green themselves rushed forward and 'spiked the guns with their own hands amid the gleaming sabres of the enemy'.[159] Lieutenant Green was severely wounded as a consequence of his action.

Soon afterwards, two more of the Horse Artillery guns had to be spiked and abandoned as the horses were found incapable of dragging them any further through the deep snow.[160] By midday, the extreme vulnerability of the British column was made clear as Afghan attackers closed in, clearly benefiting from the collapse of column cohesion which increasingly precluded any movement of reinforcements from front to rear. Sergeant-Major Lissant confirmed that 'no parties were thrown out' and Lieutenant Eyre agrees that even when Brigadier Anquetil was 'sent to the front for reinforcements ... it was found impractical to refurnish from the crowded state of the road'.[161] By the afternoon it had become possible for their increasingly aggressive Afghan enemy to penetrate even the central sections of the main column: 'The Afghan horse shortly after this charged into the very midst of the column and carried off large quantities of plunder creating the greatest confusion and dismay.'[162] Desperate delaying strategies were now deployed by the British to reduce such murderous attacks. As survivor Sergeant-Major Lissant recalled: 'From time to time some portion of baggage was left behind to give us a start but, in a short time, they would be at us again like hungry wolves.'[163]

The arrival at Butkhak gave the column a brief respite and the opportunity for some tactical repositioning. Her Majesty's 44th Regiment, as always the strongest and most cohesive military unit, was detached to drive the enemy off the hills 'which they effected and maintained the post until night when they were called in'. Lieutenant Eyre recalled how Shelton with his loyal 44th 'kept the enemy in check for upwards of an hour'.[164] Even Elphinstone, informed that the rear was in danger of being entirely cut off, briefly rose from his sickbed and sent back all the troops that could be spared, together with the two remaining guns to drive off the enemy. Some semblance of order was temporarily restored to this camp – 'regiments forming a kind of square facing outwards and all the cattle and what was left of the baggage in the centre'[165] – a great contrast to the chaos of the first night. There were other glimmers of hope. Captain Skinner managed to restart negotiations with Mohammed Akbar Khan, who insisted the force halt at Butkhak until the following morning so as to enable him to provide protection as under the treaty. He further claimed that the column had only been attacked in consequence in having marched 'contrary to their wishes'. There was indeed a temporary ceasefire as the British force awaited the delivery of promised food, forage and firewood and Mohammed Akbar's men were seen to move ahead, ostensibly to clear the pass.

Nevertheless, Lady Sale remained extremely sceptical of such negotiations: 'So bigoted are our rulers that we are still told that the sirdars are faithful and that Mohammed Akbar Khan is our friend!' [166]

The freezing night of 7–8 January exacted a far greater toll on the already weakened force. Lieutenant Eyre described the ordeal endured by thousands of men and camp-followers 'closely joined together in one monstrous, unmanageable mass'. Frostbite carried off scores more of the starving, exhausted sepoys: 'Of all the deaths, I can imagine none more agonizing than that where a nipping frost tortures every sensitive limb, until the tenacious spirit itself sinks under the extreme of human suffering.'[167] Most of the five-and-a-half-day rations, designed to sustain the force from Kabul to Jalalabad, were now exhausted and the snow was now more than a foot deep. Lady Sale and her dozen other female companions and their children probably only survived through the kindness of their military colleagues, who provided both a small tent and a few 'Cabul cakes' and some tea. Most of the force, however, simply lay down in the snow without any form of shelter. For the first time, water also became a problem with men reported being constantly fired on by Afghan snipers as they fetched it from a nearby stream.

As the third day of the retreat, Saturday 8 January 1842, dawned, all hopes were shattered as the column moved off into the dreaded Khurd-Kabul Pass. Sergeant-Major Lissant recorded what appeared to the British to be an act of gross treachery by Akbar Khan but which may, in hindsight, have simply reflected his now total loss of control of his own troops. 'We were no sooner in motion than the enemy again opened a terrible fire on us and the party left by Akbar Khan to protect and bring up the rear were most busy in plundering and murdering all they could lay hands on.'[168] The result was renewed panic and confusion, particularly amongst the now totally demoralized camp-followers and sepoys, a crisis deepened by the lack of any clear orders to march. At sunrise Lady Sale provided yet another devastating eyewitness account of the terrible scenes as the bedraggled column moved off. She and others witnessed a total political and military collapse marked by ill-disciplined and drunken behaviour, even amongst many of the hitherto-steady European troops:

The force was perfectly disorganized, nearly every man paralysed with cold so as to be scarcely able to hold his musket or more. Many frozen corpses lay on the ground. The Siphahees burnt their caps, accoutrements and clothes to keep themselves warm. Some of the enemy appearing in rear of our position, the whole of the camp followers rushed to the front; every man, woman and child seizing all the cattle that fell in their way, whether public or private. The ground was strewn with boxes of ammunition, plate and property of various kinds. A cask of spirits on the ground was broached by the Artillery men and no doubt by other Europeans. Had the whole been distributed for the men, it would have done them good: as it was they became too much excited.[169]

Only the 44th remained a cohesive fighting unit. The clearly demoralized drunken European artillery men were only finally brought to order by a mixture of admonishment by their commander Captain Nicholl and persuasion by the more respected Lieutenant Sturt. Led by Major Thain, the 44th Foot halted the chaos, mounting a gallant bayonet charge to disperse the Afghan marauders closing in for the kill. As order was restored the 'rescued' alcohol at least restored the spirits and constitution of the frozen Lady Sale and her companions. Cups full of sherry were gallantly supplied to both them and surviving European children, some as young as three or four years old.

Such brave deeds could not alleviate the bleak military picture. In two days the British column had only marched ten miles from the Kabul cantonment. As the force moved into the pass that third day, a notable and fatal tactical error was committed as a result of either paralysis of command, or exhaustion, or both. Dr Brydon confirmed that, for the first time 'our troops did not attempt to crown the heights'.[170] The results were predictable and horrendous as the column was now totally dominated and subjected to merciless enfilading fire from caves and mountain-tops. Dr Brydon remembered how 'the heights were in possession of the enemy who poured down an incessant fire upon our column'.[171] One sepoy survivor, Sita Ram, dramatically recalled: 'They fired into us from the hills and we were as helpless as a handcuffed prisoner.'[172] Again, the ragged 'Brown Bess' volleys fired from frozen hands were no match for the longer-range *jezails*. Some of the best and most senior British officers, easily targeted by the Afghan snipers in the heights, fell on this tortuous march through the five-mile Khurd-Kabul Pass. On each side the troops were hemmed in by a familiar line of lofty hills, narrowing to a few feet in places. Amongst the estimated 3,000 civilian and military personnel who perished at this point were Captain Payton, Assistant Quartermaster-General, Lieutenants Scott and Throup of the 44th and also a Brigadier-Major of the Shah's force. Possibly the greatest loss, however, was represented by the death of the brave and ever-resourceful Lieutenant Sturt. He was killed by a shot to the groin after nearly clearing the defile, despite a heroic rescue attempt by Lieutenant Mein of Her Majesty's 13th Light Infantry.

The hazards of the five-mile journey were magnified by the same fero-cious mountain stream earlier encountered by Major-General Sale's Brigade on their march to Jalalabad. The delay afforded to the column was vividly recalled by Lieutenant Eyre:

> Down the centre dashed a mountain torrent whose impetuous course the frost in vain attempted to arrest, though it succeeded in lining the edges with thick layers of ice over which the snow lay consolidated in slippery masses, affording no very easy footing for our jaded animals. This stream we had to cross and re-cross about eight and twenty times.[173]

A barrier erected by the enemy at one narrow point near the end of the Khurd-Kabul pass accentuated the confusion. Lissant recalled: 'The crush was tremendous, the baggage, camp followers and soldiers were all inter-mixed and, of course, great slaughter ensued. From the barrier to the end of the Pass there was no order or regularity among the troops and hundreds must have fallen.' In the mêlée another of the valuable Horse Artillery guns was abandoned and captured and 'every man' who tried to defend it, 'was cut down at his post'.[174]

Even the precious European wives and children could no longer be protected under such relentless fire. At least two children, Captain Anderson's eldest girl and Captain Boyd's youngest boy, were snatched from their by parents by the ever-bolder Afghan enemy. Mrs Sturt's pony was wounded in the ear and neck and, at fifty yards range, three shots passed through Lady Sale's *poshteen*, one ball passing through her arm. To their credit, rebel Afghan chiefs did try to intervene to protect the European women and children, apparently shouting to their men on the heights not to fire. The response from Lady Sale was, however, less than forgiving: 'These chiefs certainly ran the same risk we did; but I verily believe many of these persons would individually sacrifice themselves to rid their country of us.'[175]

That day, 8 January, also witnessed the last effective stand of the main sepoy units; those who had not deserted were now literally too frozen to fight. Several sources record their dramatic collapse, particularly those of the 37th Native Infantry, which had remained relatively cohesive until that day. Their commanding officer, Major Griffiths, appalled at 'seeing so few of the corps at Khurd Kabul', ordered Sergeant-Major Lissant to conduct a roll-call that evening. The results were devastating – out of 600-odd men who started at Kabul the return was only 23 *halvidars*, 17 *naicks* and 207 sepoys but only 'one hundred were as many as I could call fit for duty having had nothing to eat or cover them since leaving Kabul'.[176] Similarly, one Light Company of the 54th Native Infantry, which had left Kabul thirty-six hours previously, was reduced to a mere eighteen files. Scores of sepoys lay down unable to proceed, 'their feet like burnt pieces of wood and their hands so dreadfully swollen and cracked that they could not hold or much less use their muskets'.[177] Lady Sale also witnessed the death-throes of the sepoy regiments on that third day in the pass as they 'continued to slowly move on without firing a shot; being paralysed with cold with such a degree that no persuasion of their officers could induce them to make any effort to dislodge the enemy, who took from them not only their firelocks but even the clothes of their persons'.[178]

Saturday, 8 January was also the first day of significant ammunition shortages, no doubt exacerbated by the prolonged, heavy and often static exchanges of fire which occurred along the Khurd-Kabul Pass. For the gallant, constantly engaged 44th rearguard, ammunition was so low that several of them were forced to supply themselves from the pouches of frozen or dead sepoys. At least one gallant attempt to supply the rear eche-lons was made by Lieutenant Steer of the 37th Native Infantry by means of a *yaboo* loaded with ammunition, but before a few rounds were extracted from the boxes the party was overwhelmed by their Afghan enemy. The ammunition of the *siphahees* was also chronically low. Each had appar-ently started with about forty rounds in their pouches but, with only three supporting camel-loads of ammunition, many of them were left with none.

In this desperate, close-quarter fighting, many stragglers were killed by indiscriminate friendly *British* fire as the enemy constantly intermingled with the rearguard. Sergeant-Major Lissant witnessed tragic scenes unfold as the often-harassed 44th regulars, attempting volley fire, were 'ordered not to fire on the people in our rear as they were our friends; the men forbore as long as possible but when they saw so many of their comrades falling around them they opened fire on all sides'.[179]

Near the end of the day, another small ray of hope was provided by Captain Skinner, who again went to negotiate with the rebel leader Akbar Khan. The latter, in return for a ceasefire, demanded that Major Pottinger and Captains Lawrence and Mackenzie be kept as hostages and a further 15,000 rupees handed over. Lady Sale roundly condemned how 'these disgraceful propositions were readily assented to', but it was clear by now that the British command and its crippled force had no further room to negotiate.[180]

As the depleted British force finally reached the village of Khurd-Kabul, two miles from the end of the pass, on the evening of 8 January, a tempo-rary lull in the fighting was replaced by further setbacks at the hands of the weather. Heavy snowfalls led to another night of abject misery for the surviving soldiery and camp-followers. The British force now experienced the lowest temperatures so far as they had *ascended* out of the pass. Virtually no tentage had survived the day's fighting. In his recollection, Lieutenant Eyre marvelled how anyone survived that third night in the open, as the force was now 'without tents, firewood or food: the snow was the only bed for all and of many, ere morning, it proved the winding sheet'.[181] Lieutenant Eyre was not quite correct. Four small tents had, in fact survived, one assigned to the ailing General Elphinstone, two to the ladies and children and one to the sick.

Desperate scenes were repeated as temperatures plunged to well below zero. Lady Sale, taking refuge in her half of a *siphahee* tent with the other ladies and their husbands ('nearly thirty of us packed together without room to turn'), was horrified as, in the middle of the freezing night, 'the siphahees and camp followers, half frozen, tried to force their way not only into the tent but actually into our beds if such resting places can be called – a poshteen (or pelisse of sheepskin) half spread on the snow and the other half wrapped over me!' She confirmed; 'many poor wretches died around the tent in the night'.[182]

On 9 January, the fourth day of the march, the crippled force commenced its progress to the next projected campsite at Tezin. In chaotic scenes a large section of the troops left without orders at around 8 a.m., but little progress was made as, suddenly, around mid-morning, the General gave the order to halt. The halt was in fact a response to a proposal from Akbar Khan, communicated again by Captain Skinner, to take the ladies and married families under his protection. Only after Captain Skinner's recommendations did the hopelessly indecisive Elphinstone give his consent. The European women, mainly officers' wives, and children were duly handed over at around midday, escorted by some rebel chiefs to a fort two miles distant where Mohammed Akbar Khan had made his headquarters. Significantly, Lady Sale's own initial reluctance to desert the force was firmly overruled by the senior officers in the column. The halt was catastrophic for many who had barely survived the previous night, as 'the intense cold at this elevated spot again proved exceedingly destructive to the lesser acclimatized sepoys and camp followers'.[183]

Such wasteful delays, and the demoralizing sight of these European hostages departing the column, inspired the first outbreak of dissent amongst the hitherto-loyal remnants of the sepoy contingents. Mutinous attitudes were quickly replaced by desertion and the few survivors of the Shah's Cavalry were the first to slip away. It was wholly understandable. Sergeant-Major Lissant, recalled to the camp from the halted column, thus 'witnessed the effects of the cold and snow on all classes of the natives. They lay in the snow dead and dying in scores and it was truly heart-rending to see the supplicating looks of the poor sepoys who are unable in any other way to ask for assistance'.[184] The halt was called for another reason unknown to the men. Sergeant-Major Lissant overheard Captain Skinner tell Lieutenant Carlyon 'that the reason for our not moving on was that about 8,000 of the enemy had assembled in the Pass of Tezin, deter-mined to deter our march and it was necessary for Akbar Khan to proceed ahead and settle affairs there'.[185] In hindsight it was probably a good thing that such a devastating piece of news was kept from the men.

On the afternoon of January 9, the camp was called to parade to confront a menacing large body of Afghan horse. A final recorded roll-call held here starkly revealed the weaknesses of the British force. The 44th Foot, the key surviving unit, was reduced in strength by three-quarters to barely a hundred files; the Native Infantry regiments on average to about sixty files each. Of the Irregular Horse only about one hundred effective troopers remained and the most reliable cavalry unit, the 5th Light Cavalry, was down to only seventy 'fighting men'. Significantly, at this crucial time, the paraded troops were formally warned that future desertion would be punishable by death. An example was then made of a 'chauprassi of the Mission', who, 'being caught in the act was instantly shot by order of the General'.[186] Such drastic measures testified to the devastating impact of desertion over the previous three days.

On the next day, Sunday 10 January, the fifth day of the retreat, the bedraggled force struggled onto Tezin amidst the now-normal confusion, with troops and camp-followers 'crowding promiscuously to the front ... everyone dreading ... to be left in the rear'.[187] In terms of the cohesion of the whole force it was perhaps the most decisive day. As the temporary truce rapidly expired, Sergeant-Major Lissant recalled the difficulties of even establishing formations of recognizable units, many being paralyzed by the previous day's delay in the snow:

We started ... under a sharp fire. Her Majesty's 44th with two guns and some cavalry forming the advance guard. The 37th Native Infantry (who had charge of the treasure of 13,000 rupees) followed next. How other regiments formed that morning I cannot positively say but I believe that the 5th Native Infantry followed the 37th and 54th Native Infantry and the Shah's 6th forming the rear guard.[188]

Military historian Carter has described the 'native force' as 'reduced to a shadow and the few sepoys who remained faithful to their corps were quite disabled by the cold'.[189] In truth, the four Native Infantry units – the 37th, 5th, 54th and 6th – were mere skeleton formations comprising a few dozen men each. As Eyre confirmed:

> The European soldiers were now almost the only efficient men left, the Hindustanis having all suffered more or less from the effects of frost in their hands and feet; few were able even to hold a musket, much less pull a trigger; in fact the prolonged day in the snow had paralysed the mental and bodily powers of the strongest men, rendering them incapable of any useful exertion.[190]

It was a decisive day in other respects. Any sense of unified defensive tactics had now descended into a struggle for survival and, at times, a naked internecine conflict in which the strongest invariably turned on the weak. In the narrow ascent of Khak-i-Jabar, on the way to Tezin, facing a murderous enfilading fire from the Afghan warriors perched on the heights above, brother began to turn on brother. Sergeant-Major Lissant accordingly witnessed horrific scenes which finally confirmed the disintegration of the British force:

> When the ascent began to Khak-i-Jabar – a terrible fire was commenced on us and the followers were so mixed with the column that all order was lost. I saw several of the followers bayoneted and shot, but nothing could keep them out of the column and here commenced the slaughter that destroyed the native regiments, for both horse and foot rushed amongst the crowd and cut down sepoys and followers without opposition. Numbers they were content with stripping and driving back to Kabul. Many sepoys in despair abandoned their weapons and fled for their lives alongside the camp followers.[191]

Here also 44th Foot survivor Captain Souter recalled how many of the 'native cavalry refused to follow their officers against the enemy, clung to the infantry and embarrassed their movements'.[192] Lieutenant Eyre also confirms that, on this tortuous ascent, 'the last small remnant of the Native Infantry regiments were here scattered and destroyed; and the public treasure with all the remaining baggage fell into the hands of the enemy'.[193]

Five miles from the bottom of the Khak-i-Jabar Pass a halt was called by the advance body, now led by the 44th, to await stragglers. As only tiny numbers struggled in 'the astounding truth' dawned that 'they were almost the sole survivors; nearly the whole of the main and rear columns having being cut off and destroyed'.[194] Of the 4,500 fighting effectives out of the 16,000 force that left Kabul five days earlier, only approximately seventy 44th Foot and fifty Horse Artillery men, together with around 150 cavalry (mainly 5th Light Cavalry) were left – although, astonishingly, several score of the 12,000 camp-followers miraculously survived, still clinging to the tiny band of soldiers for protection.

At this crucial moment Akbar Khan again appeared to offer what proved to be impossible terms. Whilst still expressing 'regret' at their losses, he offered 'as a last recourse' that the troops lay down their arms and place themselves under his protection for escort to Jalalabad. The terms made it clear, however, that the surviving camp-followers would be left to their fate. Horrified at this proposal and mindful of the collapse of previous cease-fires, Elphinstone declined the offer and the force, again under hot fire, descended into the valley of Tezin, reaching it at about 4 p.m. Already, however, many of the enemy had overtaken the tiny force and were preparing further ambushes ahead. Brigadier Shelton now assumed control of the 44th rearguard. In the valley of the Tezin, thankfully free of snow, the force battled for another four hours between about 4 and 8 p.m., during which time the last British gun, a 12-pounder howitzer, had to be spiked and destroyed. This now enabled Captain Nicholl's troop of Horse Artillery to revert to a purely cavalry role.

The desperate plight of the force was now revealed by its decision not to risk a further night in the open. There was to be an all-out dash for Jalalabad. A night march was resumed, but amidst further chaos as terrified camp-followers clung to the column for protection. According to Dr Brydon the remnants of the cavalry now moved up to form the advance guard. Despite the darkness, the diminished British force was 'fired upon ... from the heights during the whole time'.[195] One astonishing sight greeted the column as they traversed the Tezin Valley towards Kuttar Sung. At about 11 p.m. the valley ahead was seen to be full of fires. Instead of the dreaded enemy, however, the men warming themselves by fire turned out to be sepoy deserters who had earlier fled and, by a short-cut, had arrived ahead of the column! To the dismay of the column, however, 'not one attempted to move or offered to proceed with the troops', a clear testament to the total collapse of morale amongst Britain's Indian auxiliaries.[196]

This night march was notable for the survival of some fighting spirit, albeit only amongst the much-reduced, frozen band of European soldiery. Brigadier Shelton again displayed his qualities as a 'leader of men', repeatedly organizing the firing of volleys into their attackers, a tactic helped by the 'figures of the enemy being distinctly visible against the now lightening sky as dawn approached'.[197] Only one major skirmish occurred during the night, at Barikab, where heavy enemy fire from nearby caves created fresh disorder. This continued all the way along the Kuttar Sung, where the rear-guard under Shelton finally caught up with the main band at 8 a.m. on Tuesday 11 January.

The morning of that day, the sixth day of the retreat, exposed the force to renewed, heavy losses occasioned by more relentless enemy fire from the surrounding heights. A running fight commenced along the ten-mile route to Jagdalak. Brigadier Shelton again kept up morale by his refusal to abandon any wounded 'always keeping some of the 5th Cavalry nearby to pick up everyone who was hit and still able to be moved. Those left dead were cut up with the large knives of their relentless adversaries'.[198]

Another halt took place at Kuttar Sung but, after failing to find water, the march was resumed for about three miles, with another fruitless halt which again yielded no water for the troops. As Captain Souter recalled: 'hourly the column became diminished in numbers'.[199] Lieutenant Eyre remembered that now 'no efforts could avail to ward off the withering fire of jazails, which, from all sides, assailed the crowded column, lining the road with bleeding carcasses'.[200] The column had become a virtual sitting target. Brief respite was, however, provided by an old ruined fort situated just before Jagdalak, and here Elphinstone's advance party pitched camp with a motley band of the remaining artillery men, 5th Light Cavalry and the surviving camp-followers. As they awaited Shelton's rearguard, mostly 44th men, the beleaguered fort contingent was forced to resort to pathetic, purely symbolic acts of defiance, the surviving European officers 'extending themselves in line' in order 'to show an imposing front to the now over-whelming numbers of the enemy'. Brigadier Shelton himself was nearly captured as they fought at close quarters and with fierce tenacity against the enemy, their comrades from the fort frantically cheering the last yards of their approach. Soon, however, the fort itself was outflanked as Afghan foot-soldiers rapidly occupied the heights above. Sepoy Sita Ram recalled this nightmare: 'We went on fighting and losing men at every step of the road. We were attacked in front, in the rear and from the tops of the hills. In truth it was hell itself. I cannot describe the horrors.'[201]

Thirst and hunger after six days and five nights in the snow had reduced the survivors of the Kabul force to a pitiful condition. The raw flesh of several bullocks, 'requisitioned' from the remnants of the camp-followers briefly assuaged the ravenous hunger of the 44th Foot regulars. In the midst of their 'meal break', however, as Captain Skinner was called forward by Akbar Khan for further negotiations, the Afghan enemy renewed their onslaught. Despite their chronic fatigue, the 44th rushed to arms, although lack of ammunition now forced them to hold back their shots except in moments of extreme necessity. In fact it was only a desperate bayonet charge by a mere fifteen European soldiers which temporarily drove the enemy from the heights and probably saved the force from immediate annihilation.

Captain Skinner's return from Mohammed Akbar's headquarters renewed hopes of a negotiated ceasefire. The presence of the General and of two hostages, Captain Johnson and Brigadier Shelton, was now demanded and, under escort, these three officers were taken to Akbar Khan's nearby headquarters and detained overnight. As their virtually leaderless men rested in the frozen wilderness, all three officers enjoyed their first square meal and proper night's sleep since leaving Kabul, although such hospitality was accepted only after being assured that food would be given to their starving troops, and also safe escort to Jalalabad (neither materialized).

On the following day, 12 January, the seventh day of the retreat, negotiations dragged on as Akbar Khan held a simultaneous conference with numerous other local Ghilzai chiefs. Most of these, however, predictably adopted a hard-line approach and the offer of two *lakhs* of rupees only partially appeased their bloodlust and calls for further revenge against the hated, helpless *feringhee*. Whether sincere or not, the strength of their opposition almost certainly precluded any chance of Akbar's earlier promises being fulfilled. Meanwhile, an impotent Elphinstone, Shelton and the other officers were further detained and, to their deep dismay, prevented from even rejoining their troops. The issue was, in effect, resolved by the officers and men of the column who, by darkness, lacking orders and fearing the worst, resumed their frantic retreat to Jalalabad and safety. The die was now cast. Regarding this last pitiful night march commencing at 8 p.m., survivor Captain Souter disclosed the tiny numbers of survivors. The once glorious 44th Foot were now reduced to between seventy and eighty men 'capable of carrying arms', with a few European artillery men and Indian 5th Cavalry although, amazingly, there was still an 'encumbrance of camp followers'.[202] The absence of their Commander-in Chief, Elphinstone, and particularly the redoubtable Brigadier Shelton, undoubtedly destroyed the morale of the remaining British sepoys, if not that of the British regulars themselves. Sepoy Sita Ram remembered the impact upon his compatriots of the loss of so many senior British officers to capture or death: 'Once the enemy had the officers in their power our army was deprived of leaders. Every sahib taken away was as bad as 200 men lost ... when the General sahib left all discipline fell away.'[203]

Despite continued sallies by the 44th Foot, now led by Major Thain, Captain Bygraves and Lieutenants Wade and McCartney, these were no substitute for Shelton's dogged leadership. Now even the sick and wounded were abandoned to their fate as the remaining men made one last dash for Jalalabad. Before them, however, was one last great obstacle, the two-mile excessively narrow valley of Jagdalak. It was here that Brigadier Sale's troops had earlier, in the autumn of 1841, taken terrible punishment. After a descent, the struggling force had to move steeply upwards. Here the horrified, exhausted men faced two formidable barriers erected by their enemy, comprising heavy stones and branches of prickly hollyoak. A long furious, struggle ensued to surmount this formidable obstacle as, all around, fanatical Ghilzai foot and horse closed in. It was the penultimate struggle for survival for the doomed party, in which extreme heroism was matched, as we shall see, by desperate, sometimes less-than-honourable tactics by some officers. In the ensuing massacre – exceeding in ferocity even that of Khurd-Kabul – the vast majority of European officers and men fell and most of the few remaining camp-followers and sepoys were probably eliminated. Twelve officers of the 44th Foot were killed, notably Lieutenants Dodgin, Wade, Paymaster Bourke, Quartermaster Hallahan and Surgeon Harcourt. The body of Bourke, a 40-year-old veteran, was later found sprawled amongst enemy dead and recognized only by a small part of his silvery grey hair still adhering to his skull! Quartermaster Hallahan, his face 'black with powder', known to be physically the most powerful man in the 44th Regiment, and already renowned for dispatching many of the enemy in the retreat, also undoubtedly took many insurgents with him as he perished at the barricade. Sepoy Sita Ram dramatically remembered how 'The men fought like gods, not men but numbers prevailed against them.'[204] Perhaps the greatest loss to the force was the one remaining and deeply respected senior officer, Brigadier Anquetil. Having first successfully cleared the *abattis* (a defence work of sharpened branches), and nobly and coura-geously returning to rescue his wounded men, he was also killed at the barricade. Most of the weakened and wounded men soon fell under the Afghan knives as the yelling Ghilzais closed in for the kill.

Less honourably than Anquetil, but perhaps understandably, as men struggled no longer for Queen, Country or even for their comrades, several officers opted to flee. Sources confirm that some British soldiers even attacked their own officers as several mounted officers jumped the barri-cades and fled. Seaton attributes the breakdown directly to Anquetil's loss: 'On being missed the 44th called out "Where's our Brigadier? Where's our Brigadier?" and as no answer was returned to this importunate cry, all subordination was at an end; the men selected their own officers and the wildest confusion ensued.[205] Dr Brydon confirmed that: 'The confusion was now terrible; all discipline was at an end and the shouts of "halt" and "keep back the cavalry" were incessant.' Beyond the barricades, Dr Brydon

> found a large body of men and officers who, finding it was perfectly hopeless to remain with men in such a state, had gone ahead to form a kind of Advance Guard, but, as we moved steadily on whilst the main body was halting every second, by the time that day dawned we had lost all trace of those in our rear.[206]

Subaltern Cumming's diary is blunter. He strikingly confirms the terrible scenes as elements of the hitherto-loyal 44th Infantry turned on their officers as the latter struggled to escape: 'The men, fearful that their officers would desert them, kept them back with their firelocks and otherwise ill-treated them; in fact became beyond all control. A fearful state of confusion ensued – the men in disorder were soon cut up by the enemy.' All vestiges of command and control had clearly broken down. An appalled Subaltern Cummings continued, 'this has been a *shameful business*, from first to last and calls for a *rigid investigation*'. It was now truly *sauve qui peut*.[207]

Even the escaping Captain Souter was himself unhorsed by 'a trooper of the 5th Cavalry who, in trying to pass me, pushed me down the side of the hill; the horse from weakness (having been hit by two balls and having eaten scarcely anything for days) lay unable to rise and I was unable to rise either until two men raised the horse a little and I extricated myself'.[208]

The force had now disintegrated into several tiny, struggling parties totalling less than a hundred men, with the mounted groups of mainly officers and civilians well ahead of the struggling pockets of infantry. The more open country certainly helped their chances of survival, but it was now clearly a matter of hours, not days, before these last remnants would be overtaken and finished off. At the Surkab River, yet another hot skirmish reduced numbers further. Here, Lieutenant Cadett of Her Majesty's 44th was killed, along with several more private soldiers of the 44th.

The eighth day, 13 January 1842, was destined to be the final day of the retreat of the Kabul garrison. The surviving fifty-odd European infantry, mainly 44th Foot, blocked by numerous Afghan horse and foot, were forced to retreat up a nearby conical hill near the village of Gandamak. For the vast majority, this hill was destined to be their final resting place. Even in these last moments there seemed a glimmer of hope of negotiation as one British soldier waved a white handkerchief at a group of Afghan horsemen and thereby achieved a parley. For a few precious moments hostilities were suspended as Major Griffiths, the surviving senior officer, accompanied by a civilian, Mr Blewitt, were invited to descend the hill 'to negotiate with a neighbouring chief for a certain sum of money to let us proceed to Jalalabad'.[209]

The ceasefire was short-lived. The mood soon changed as several, ostensibly friendly Afghans, professing to offer bread for sale, climbed the hill and began a conversation but then suddenly commenced, 'snatching swords and pistols from the officers'. With this clearly unacceptable action, trust rapidly broke down. As Captain Souter put it, 'this we could not stand, but drove them from the hill and the fight commenced again'.[210]

Astoundingly, this sad, tiny remnant of the once-mighty Kabul Brigade fought on for up to two hours. Most were steadily and easily picked off by Afghan snipers from below, with only sporadic hand-to-hand encounters. Eventually, however, with most men wounded or dead and barely twenty standing, Captain Souter recalled how the 'enemy suddenly rushed upon us with their knives and an awful scene took place and ended in the massacre of all except myself, Sergeant Fair (our mess sergeant) and seven men that the more than usual humanity displayed by the Afghans were induced to spare'.[211]

So ended, in horrible carnage, the last stand of the 44th Foot and other pitiful remnants of the Kabul brigade. Barely fifty Europeans survived, a notable survivor being Dr Brydon. No more than a few hundred sepoys and camp-followers, who had earlier either deserted or been captured, had also lived to tell the tale. Thousands of sepoys and camp-followers had perished.

Strategies of Survival

One question arises, however, as to how *anyone* could have survived so long in such terrible conditions, conditions which can be likened in experience, if not in scale and duration, to two of the great retreats of recent history, notably Napoleon's disastrous march home from Moscow in 1812, and the retreat of the Nazi Wehrmacht from the USSR in 1943–5. Aside from 'luck' some of the European and Indian survivors exhibited enormous resilience and consummate skill in combating the extreme weather conditions. Lieutenant Eyre, for instance, noticed the excellent survival strategies adopted by one twenty-strong group of loyal *jazailchis* (Afghan riflemen) early on in the retreat:

Their first step on reaching the (camping) ground was to clear a small space from the snow, where they then laid themselves down in a circle, closely packed together, with their feet meeting in the centre; all the warm clothing they could muster upon them being spread equally over the whole. By these simple means suffice enough warmth was generated to preserve them from being frost-bitten; and Captain Mackenzie, who himself shared their homely bed, declared that he had felt scarcely any inconvenience from the cold.[212]

By contrast, the predominantly Indian and unarmed, chronically ill-provisioned camp-followers, normally domiciled in the warmer north Indian plains, stood little or no chance of survival in the extreme conditions.

Some European officers also learnt how to survive. Captain Souter, in a letter to his wife from captivity, revealed his own survival strategy: 'Though a great many of the officers and men were severe sufferers from frost and from lying on the snow, I escaped by always taking the precaution to wrap the sheepskin that I had upon the saddle round my feet when I lay down, but I have suffered from rheumatism and have it still about me.'[213]

Being European was clearly a distinct advantage. Primary access to food and ammunition supplies was afforded to the European civilians, officers and their men. Gender and married status also proved crucial factors for the survival of some. Lady Sale and her female colleagues, under the code of chivalry of that era, had already enjoyed the use of tents and the provision of hot meals before being taken into captivity, while their European husbands also clearly benefited from the negotiations of 9 January for their transfer to Akbar Khan's protection, thus escaping further ordeals of the march.

However, not all the European women were so fortunate. Mary Anderson was carried off in the confusion and massacre in the Tezin Pass, where Mrs Mainwaring and her 3-month-old child were also captured but then abandoned by an Afghan horseman, 'who ... snatched her shawl off her shoulders and left her to her fate'. She barely survived in the snow, having

to walk a considerable distance with her child in her arms through the deep snow [and] pick her way over the bodies of the dead, dying and wounded both men and cattle, and constantly to cross the streams of water, wet up to the knees pushed and shoved about by men and animals, the enemy keeping up a sharp fire and several persons killed close to her.[214]

Mrs Bailey was cruelly separated from her child, who was 'carried off by the Afghans'. European women of lower status were also subject to similar ordeals, with 'Mrs Bourke, Little Seymour Stoke and his mother, and Mrs

Cunningham, all soldiers' wives and the child of a man of the 13th' being 'carried off' by Afghan rebel horsemen.[215]

For the sepoy regiments, it was purely a question of *sauve qui peut*. Many deserted early in the retreat; other demoralized groups fled after the European hostages were delivered to Akbar Khan on 9 January. Some survived longer by attaching themselves to the better-equipped and provisioned European artillery or 44th Foot regiments. Survivor Sita Ram chose the latter. He recalled that after his regiment 'had disappeared and I attached myself to the remnant of a European regiment I thought by sticking to them I might have some chance of getting away from that detestable country'.[216] Others merely surrendered and accepted captivity or slavery, some even converting to the Muslim religion and joining their Afghan enemies against the British. Hindustani servants were certainly valued. As Sita Ram confirmed, 'a number of sepoys and followers went over to the enemy in an effort to save their lives'.[217] Still others chose to detach themselves from the main column and survive in isolated groups – as witnessed by the discovery of one group of sepoy deserters by the main column near Jagdalak, calmly warming themselves by fires.

Whether 'native' or 'European', being mounted was clearly a distinct advantage in the struggle for survival. It was significant that the predominantly Indian 5th Light Cavalry survived longer and in much greater numbers than their infantry counterparts, and it was a dozen *mounted* Europeans who survived until the last stages of the retreat, although nearly all of them were eventually overtaken and cut down by Afghan cavalry.

Theft from both the living and the dead played a key role in many survivors' stories. As we have seen, the artillery men plundered the liquor stocks, and probably the food stores as well, and the 44th Foot frequently 'borrowed' ammunition from the pouches of dead sepoys, thus prolonging their survival in action. Before the final stand at Gandamak it was the 44th who ruthlessly plundered the remaining meat supplies of the camp-followers, killing and devouring several bullocks raw.

Luck inevitably played an enormous part. Sepoy Sita Ram, apparently struck unconscious at the barrier by a *jezail* musket ball in the head, awoke to find himself 'rescued' albeit into slavery by an Afghan cavalryman. He was returned to Kabul 'tied to a camel panier ... clothed in Afghan garments and sold in the marketplace as a slave. "I was a fine looking strong man and I fetched two hundred and forty rupees", he remembered. Before that he had to endure a return journey along the whole route of the retreat. "What dreadful carnage I saw along the road – legs and arms protruding from the snow, Europeans and Hindustanis half buried, horses and camels all dead! It was a sight I shall never forget as long as I live!"[218] This was a route earlier retraced by Lady Sale and her colleagues as they were led into captivity on 8 January. She also recalled the 'dreadful scenes' that awaited them as, on 11 January, they were escorted by foot along the road to Tezin Fort:

> The road [was] covered with awfully mangled bodies, all naked. Fifty-eight Europeans were counted on the Tunghee and dip of the mullah; the natives innumerable. Numbers of camp followers, still alive, frost bitten and starving; some perfectly out of their senses and idiotic – the sight was dreadful; the smell of blood sickening and the corpses lay so thick it was impossible to look for them; as it required care to guide my horse so as not to tread upon the bodies.[219]

Three days later, on 14 January, at the start of a defile near the Adrak–Budrak Pass, Lady Sale's captive party stumbled across far more horrifying scenes of cannibalism. They passed two to three hundred 'of our miserable Hindostanees who had escaped up the unfrequented road from the massacre of the 12th, who 'all naked ... wounded and starving ... had set fire to the bushes and grasses and huddled all together to impart warmth to each other'. She subsequently heard that 'scarcely any ... had escaped ... and that driven to the extreme of hunger they had sustained life by feeding on their dead comrades'.[220]

Others survived through amazing good fortune. It was luck which undoubtedly saved Captain Souter's life during the final stand at Gandamak Hill. Entrusted with the 44th's colours (the Queen's colours had already been lost), which he wrapped around his waist, he was severely wounded by a cut from an Afghan knife to his right shoulder, penetrating 'a long way down my blade bone'. Since the blow had cut through his sheepskin *poshteen*, the *poshteen* flew open and exposed the colours. He recalled: 'Thinking I was some great man from looking so flash I was seized by two fellows (after my sword dropped from my hand ... and my pistol missing fire) who hurried me from this spot ... to a village.'[221] The prospect of ransom had saved him and also played a key part in saving the lives of his seven surviving colleagues from the 44th Foot.

For the European infantry, the example of leadership exhibited during the final stages of the retreat after Jagdalak was certainly a key factor in their prolonged survival. Three officers excelled in the retreat: Brigadier Anquetil constantly rallied his men and, as we have seen, died trying to save them, and Brigadier Shelton's outstandingly gallant and disciplined rear-guard actions clearly sustained the cohesion of the 44th Foot until his loss to captivity on 12 January. Indeed, his departure and the death in action of

Brigadier Anquetil at Jagdalak Pass undoubtedly dealt a mortal blow to morale of the few survivors as they struggled on to the final stand at Gandamak Hill. Lieutenant Sturt's brilliant engineering skills securing the departure of the column and his leadership qualities were also a key advantage until his tragic death in Khurd-Kabul Pass.

The Reckoning

The second key question arising from this great British disaster is that of culpability. The siege and disastrous retreat from Kabul represented one of the two greatest military disasters for British arms during Queen Victoria's reign. Only the annihilation of General Lord Chelmsford's garrison at Isandlwana during the 1879 Anglo-Zulu War, matched the percentage of losses (over 75 per cent killed). Later, Field-Marshal Gerald Templar described the Kabul retreat as, 'the most disgraceful and humbling episode in our history of war as any against an Asian enemy up to that time'.[222] The editors and correspondents of *The Times* were quick to blame most of the political and military senior commanders but, singled out Lord Auckland and his 'politicals' as primary instigators of the disaster. *The Times* thundered:

> It makes one believe that there is a fatality attending our present efforts in India to hear of such madness. Except cowardice, almost every fault of which men in command could be guilty has already been committed. The adoption of the cruel and contemptible Shah Shoojah instead of an alliance with the popular Dost Mohammed whom the address of Sir Alexander Burnes had conciliated, the haughty and ill-judged behaviour ... of the late Envoy – the reckless massacre at Khelat-i-Ghizie – the neglect of the warning given to Sir Alexander Burnes ... of the intended rising ... the unfortunate departure of General Sales' brigade from Cabul at the very moment when his presence was most required – the neglect to secure the magazine or provisions which fell prey to the first rising of the insurgents and which would else, after other mistakes have been made, have saved our troops – crime – negligence – miscalculation – one upon another – ending in the terrible catastrophe.[223]

Such enormous military casualties but, especially, the loss to the enemy of British female captives, traumatized Victorian England:

> We cannot ... believe the account which is put forward. It is too terrible. It seems not an event of the English Empire in the 19th century but a hideous dream, a horrible tale, when we read of 6,000 men massacred almost in cold blood, a British Envoy treacherously murdered and ten of our countrywomen ... carried off by an army of savage enemies with sickening details of which we could barely give space to write.[224]

The political establishment in India certainly deserved a high proportion of the blame. Lord Auckland's 'forward policy' had been tainted in several ways long before the Army of the Indus began its fateful intervention into Afghan affairs. Burnes' initial support for Dost Mohammed, clearly the more popular of the two candidates for the Afghan throne, had been too easily discarded by the Governor-General. The lifting of the Russian-backed Persian siege of Herat in November 1838 had, as many critics observed at the time, at least partially, if not wholly, compromised the whole *raison d'être* of the expedition before it had even started. Furthermore, the Company's central authorities had failed to assess the dangers of the invasion route, particularly in terms of terrain and climate, with a resultant heavy loss of men, animals and materials. Once committed to a policy of occupation, Lord Auckland and his advisers, under pressure from the British Government, had sacrificed military imperatives for the sake of financial economy by committing the military to an indefinite occupation with only half the military assets needed to police such an intractable country. Above all, the decision of the Governor-General and his Treasury officials in Calcutta to cut subsidy payments had clearly dealt a mortal blow to the collaboration of key chiefs along the lines of communications, and on whose loyalty the British presence had largely depended. The Kabul garrison had truly paid the full blood price for such policy failures. As the supreme executor in India of this disastrous enterprise, Lord Auckland must alone shoulder the ultimate political blame, not only for his aforementioned weak policy decisions but for his appalling man-management. He had been too easily swayed or dominated by MacNaghten and other 'hawks' and he was the man directly responsible for the appointment of the reluctant and clearly ailing Major-General Elphinstone to the Kabul command. As one officer aptly put it:

> That General Elphinstone's imbecility was the immediate cause of this disgrace and of these terrible disasters, is beyond all doubt; but the real author was he who selected for a Post of such difficulty and responsibility a man crippled by gout in his hands and feet, whose

nerves had succumbed to bodily suffering, and who was in no way remarkable for capacity.[225]

In the damning, more brutally succinct, words of Field-Marshal Templer, Auckland was indeed 'a bad picker of men'.[226]

On the ground in Afghanistan, MacNaghten, Burnes and many of their thirty-odd political agents running their 'fiefdoms' scattered around the country, had frequently interfered with military and security requirements. As we have seen, along the army's invasion route, military decisions were frequently undermined (often to the fury of the military), by local political agents either too anxious to placate chiefs guilty of outrageous attacks on the British supply lines or, conversely, on at least two occasions, over-reacting to minor infringements of British authority by launching major punitive expeditions. These decisions testified to the inexperience of many of these often-young military officers, so rapidly promoted or seconded to political work. Certainly, the siege and brutal sacking of Kalat, as the editorial in *The Times* indicated, may also be considered a major over-reaction to perceived insults. As General Napier scathingly asserted in correspondence with the newly arrived Lord Ellenborough in early 1842: 'I told him that the chief causes of our disasters was fancying that when a smart lad could speak Hindostanee and Persian he was a statesman and a general and was therefore made a political agent.' [227]

Two individuals, Envoys MacNaghten and Burnes, although clearly men of physical and moral courage, bear significant responsibility for the débâcle. Both were ambitious, their imminent promotion to higher political posts in the autumn of 1841 clearly distracting them from the urgent needs of political administration and clouding their judgement of the emerging crisis. Burnes had already committed a volte-face, suddenly switching his support from Dost Mohammed in order to encourage MacNaghten's support for his promotion, and the Envoy's imminent departure for the prize post of Governor-General of Bombay had clearly contributed to his complacency. Moreover, the recorded social indiscretions of Alexander Burnes with the wives of the local Afghan nobility probably paid a key part in the swift and brutal nature of his death and the resultant blow to British authority.

Above all, a hitherto-neglected piece of evidence reveals that Burnes had been grossly negligent in the immediate period before the November crisis, which arguably raises his level of culpability to equal if not surpass that of his superior, MacNaghten. Only days before the insurrection, a Captain Gray of the 44th Foot, significantly escorted by a score of loyal Qizilbash horsemen, had been dispatched to conduct an extremely hazardous intelligence-gathering mission along the Eastern Ghilzai passes towards Gandamak. Here, friendly chiefs confirmed the existence of a widespread conspiracy 'to drive out and murder every Feringhee in the country ... and that the country round about and Cabul itself was ready to break out'. On 7 October 1841, Gray wrote to Burnes 'an official letter acquainting him ... that treachery was at the very threshold of their doors and also informing him of the attack upon us at Tezeen'. Gray further confirmed: 'The letter was taken and delivered to Sir A. Burnes and the bearer brought a letter ... acknowledging its receipt.... But I never heard a line from Sir A.B.' Gray angrily asserted:

> This can be easily accounted for – the idea of my writing and telling such big-wigs that treachery was on foot! Had I been a little 'Political' they might have given ear to it! What has been the consequence.... Why he, his brother, Swayne, Robinson and Raban of ours, and several others were murdered at his house!... As it was official, Burnes ought to have laid it before Sir William MacNaghten and the General.[228]

Of the two men, MacNaghten, as Burnes' senior, must nevertheless take the primary local political responsibility for failing or refusing to recognize the clear signs of crisis from as early as May 1841, and particularly the September and October crises as British forces and outposts were progressively beleaguered by recalcitrant chiefs.

MacNaghten's failure to influence or even reform Shah Shuja's Government, especially in the areas of expenditure and taxation (the latter a major source of grievance in the Kandahar disturbances of late 1841), which were reflected in his complacent or exaggerated reports of continued stability to the Calcutta authorities, was a major misjudgement – if not deceit. His cutting of the subsidies to key Afghan chiefs was an unforgivable error of judgement and the key political cause of the ensuing crisis and disaster. To his credit, however, he made herculean efforts to recover the political crisis after 2 November 1841, but soon lost the moral high ground in negotiations by eventually resorting to less-reliable Afghan intermediaries rather than established agents. Many of the former could clearly not be controlled or even trusted and probably led MacNaghten (perhaps unknowingly, as he later claimed), into the highly dangerous policy of selective assassination of rebel chiefs. This, in turn, destroyed all existing trust between him and the rebel leaders, notably Akbar Khan. In short, MacNaghten's bid to 'out-Afghan' the Afghans led to a complete loss of trust in his integrity, already evident in his tense meetings and communications with the rebel chiefs before his horrible demise on 23 December 1841.

At the same time, his failure to get to grips with a clearly ailing Elphinstone (arguably unfit to command after the 9 November 'command crisis' – if not well before) and replace him with the more robust Shelton, or even Anquetil, contributed to the military collapse. Moreover, he worsened an already deteriorating command and control situation by continuing to conduct negotiations with the enemy in an obsessive, secretive way. His abject failure to notify Elphinstone's War Council of the process of negotiation was a particular error of judgement, which ensured that the political and military arms were never co-ordinated at this critical time and soon collapsed after his murder on 23 December 1841. General Sir Jasper Nicholls, Commander-in-Chief, India, who was a particular critic of MacNaghten's performance wrote: 'I admit that blind confidence in persons around the Envoy – a total want of forethought and foresight on his part – unaccountable indecision at first followed by sessions which day to day rendered our force into more helpless, inactivity, perhaps, on some occasions – have led to these reverses.'[229] Major-General Nott, so frequently the focus of MacNaghten's rebukes had, on news of his murder, been even more scathing:

> His end was like the rest of his proceedings from the day we entered the country. He ought *not* to have trusted those wretched half-savage people; but his system was always wrong. It has always appeared wonderful to me how Government could have employed so very weak a man. I fear his three years' doings cannot be retrieved, and that our blood must flow for it.[230]

At home, the 'Iron Duke' himself was also a stern critic of MacNaghten's political judgement and overall management. Responding to one of MacNaghten's last letters from Kabul before the crisis broke, in which MacNaghten complained bitterly of libellous complaints against his government, he lambasted the Envoy for initially appointing Humza Khan, the Governor of Kabul, and other persons to command the key posts or *thanahs* between Kabul and Gandamak, 'who were the very men who were the leaders of the rebellion, in the attack, and destruction and murder of the East India Company's officers and troops'. The Duke of Wellington added scathingly: 'No libels can state facts against the Afghan Government stronger than these.' On MacNaghten's failing security policies, Wellington was equally scathing, particularly of his policy of relying upon cheap, ill-equipped and unreliable Afghan mercenaries. 'It will not do', the great man thundered, 'to raise pay and discipline matchlock men in order to protect the British troops and their communications, discovered by Mr MacNaghten to be no longer able to protect themselves.' In response to the Envoy's complaints that the Company's troops were not 'sufficiently active personally', or 'sufficiently well-armed for the warfare in Afghanistan', Wellington drew upon his vast Indian and Peninsula campaign experience to flatten MacNaghten's argument:

> We have carried on war in hill countries, as well in Hindostan and the Deccan as in the Spanish Peninsula; and I never heard that our troops were not equal, as well in personal activity as by their arms, to contend with and overcome any natives of hills whatever. Mr Macnaghten ought to have learnt by this time that hill countries are not conquered, and their inhabitants kept in subjection, solely by running up the hills and firing at long distances. The whole of a hill country of which it is necessary to keep possession, particularly for the communications of the army, should be occupied by sufficient bodies of troops, well supplied, and capable of maintaining themselves; and not only not a Ghilzye or insurgent should be able to run up and down hills, but not a cat or a goat, except under the fire of those occupying the hills. This is the mode of carrying on the war.[231]

In mitigation, MacNaghten was always severely constrained in his policy-making by the Calcutta Treasury and, for all his political blunders, he faced his final fatal meeting with Akbar Khan with great courage, persevering with negotiations even in the face of the loss of his escort. This stunning overall political neglect or myopia in regard to the massive threat posed by *jihadism* in 1841 will, as we shall see, be repeated in the context of both the Second and Third Anglo-Afghan Wars and, latterly, in the post-Cold War neglect of the rise of Al Qaeda and the Taliban.

The military authorities must also share much of the blame. Initially, they bear and share some culpability for the failure to fully reconnoitre the invasion route, and for the consequent serious losses in manpower and equipment. Although the military, as mentioned, were also the undoubted victims of ruthless Company economies, the initial commander, Brigadier Sir Willoughby Cotton, must be made partially accountable for the poor state of the Kabul defences and the weaknesses of the outlying garrisons such as Charikar, the latter so easily overrun in the first days of the great insurrection. Much evidence has already been cited of the failure to address critical reports submitted by Brigadier Roberts and others on the vulnerability of the cantonment defences and the isolation of the main force from the Treasury and the Commissariat. Ultimately, however, it must be reiterated that it was Major-General Elphinstone's blunder, as he retained command throughout the crisis period of 2 November 1841 right up to the virtual annihilation of his brigade in January 1842. Despite MacNaghten's and Burnes' earlier terrible political misjudgements, which undoubtedly precipitated this crisis, Elphinstone, by deploying his significant combat power (a full brigade of troops at his disposal and with the experienced 44th Foot as a spearhead), could – and within the first few crucial hours, should – have nipped the rebellion in the bud.

Elphinstone's chronic indecisiveness and vacillation on numerous occasions (notably the crisis days of 2, 9 and 23 November, dates when firm offensive action might have broken the back of the rebellion), sapped and indeed ultimately destroyed the morale of his officers and men. In the opinion of the veteran General Napier: 'I know not why ... he did not at once give battle, and he had no right to negotiate with rebels. Had General Elphinstone made a vigorous attack he would probably have now worn well-earned laurels, instead of chains!'[232] His personal failure even to control War Council meetings allowed junior and often much less experienced officers to hold sway and, eventually, even isolate more senior officers such as Shelton. Numerous contemporary observers stressed how a simple decision to take the offensive during the early days of the crisis would have probably defused the rebellion, and a concentration of all the forces in the more defensible Bala Hissar, along with consolidated ammunition and food supplies, might have been more productive. Alternatively, there was the 'Shelton option' to retreat immediately to Jalalabad and return to the offensive in the spring. Instead, the garrison relapsed into passivity; a decisive show of force was never achieved. Moreover, during the retreat, Elphinstone remained almost wholly inactive, with his junior officers, notably Shelton and Anquetil, being forced to assume command to repel the incessant attacks.

In mitigation, Elphinstone was a very sick man (according to Lady Sale he did try on two occasions to resign on the grounds of ill-health[233]) but, in the early stages of the crisis, when he was still *compos mentis*, there was ample opportunity to hand over command to more able subordinates. On his arrival in Kabul in November 1840, he did inherit from his predecessor a very poor defensive organization around Kabul, but there was still time at this stage to redress this and, even in the midst of crisis in November 1841, the option existed of retreating to the more defensible Bala Hissar. As one *Times* correspondent protested:

The disasters in Afghanistan have arisen in the paucity of troops employed and in a suicidal economy in omitting to repair and consolidate the defences of the Bala Hissar fort in Kabul, provision it and by the aid of an efficient artillery behind its walls render it impregnable against any amount of the fire.... There is a military adage to this effect, that troops well provisioned, ammunitioned and placed behind parapets are invincible to a force without a battery train (the case with the Afghans before we made them a present of our guns at the 'Convention of Cabul').[234]

The Company authorities were certainly quick to absolve themselves and to blame General Elphinstone for the disaster. In January 1842, the Governor-General, Lord Auckland, wrote to Commander-in-Chief Sir Jasper Nicholls asserting that, 'on our present information, we are disposed to view the conduct of Major-General Elphinstone in command of the force there with the most severe displeasure and indignation'. A full military inquiry into all the circumstances connected with the direction and conduct of the troops at Kabul was demanded. In the meantime, it was directed that Elphinstone 'should not retain control of troops to the west of the Indus',[235] control there to be handed over to General Pollock.

News of the death in captivity of General Elphinstone (in April 1842), however, ensured that the one surviving senior officer of the retreat, Brigadier Shelton, released alive from captivity in September 1842, bore the brunt of blame for this disaster. Burnes, MacNaghten and Elphinstone were dead – Brigadier Shelton was to be made the scapegoat. Within a year, he was subjected to a court martial.

His hitherto-unpublished court defence notes shed new light, not only on the shambolic conduct of the Kabul siege, in which he was by no means the chief culprit, but also on the neglect of Afghan affairs by the political authorities during the preceding six months before the insurrection broke out. Indeed, Shelton laid the primary blame for the crisis and disaster squarely on the shoulders of the Envoy, particularly for his wholesale suppression of the many negative reports which arrived on his desk long before the insurrection actually broke out on 2 November 1841. His defence of his actions is worth examining in detail.

Beginning by saying that: 'The inexplicable infatuation and confiding security of the Political Ambassador ... in the face of an overt Rebellion is a source of regret', Shelton cited the warning signs of rebellion and argued that the situation in

the districts in Kelat-i-Ghilzie country in July and August, the necessity to send a large detachment to the Laughan district in September, the actual hostile progression and blocking up of the Khurd-Kabul

Pass in October, the attack upon the camp there as well as the two regiments the whole way to Kandahar, all failed to impress the belief of discontent or inimical feeling.

He went on to say that, even when Captain Trevor's 200 Afghan *sowars* deserted and joined in a night attack on the 35th Native Infantry, leading to the 'annihilation of nearly a whole company', and even when 'rebellious mullahs', sent in as 'abettors' by the Military Authority 'with indefinite proof' of their 'conspiracy' were 'declared to be peaceable and well meaning and set at liberty; nothing was believed that implied a rebelling spirit'. Shelton then cited Captain Gray's well-publicized letter to Alexander Burnes from Laughan which while 'communicating unequivocal proofs not only of the disturbed state of the country ... was perceived with the same unsuspecting confidence and, I heard, treated with indifference as the effusion of a mind teaming with imaginary evils that had existence save in creation of a writer's fancy'.

Shelton also cited the threats on the life of the Envoy himself, resulting in his being warned 'not to go out or venture on his usual rides'. Shelton continued:

> Such numerous instances in proof of discontent in the minds of general and extensive dissatisfaction, might have awakened arousal, alarmed the most suspicious minds and dictated the presence of pre-preparatory prevention measures to meet such threatening dangers, instead of facilitating or encouraging the wide spreading infection by a misplaced and ill-timed self-confiding security when so much was at stake.

On the specific subject of the insurrection, after 2 November 1841, Brigadier Shelton delivered a bitter broadside against the continued complacency of the 'politicals'. Answering the charge that he had advocated retreat (presumably with the intimation of cowardice), he presented new evidence, in the form of General Elphinstone's letter of 5 November 1841, 'as further proof that the subject of retreat had been in agitation even before I entered cantonments'. Before his entry into the cantonments from the Bala Hissar on 9 November, Shelton also revealed that he had, 'frequent conversations with the Envoy and Sir Alexander Burnes regarding the extent to which the disaffection might have spread and was anxious in my enquiries as to the state of the feeling in the City'. 'They', he points out, 'assured me, particularly the latter, of their conviction that the disturbances were merely caused by some Ghilzies and that the disaffection was not widely disseminated and did not extend to Cabool.'

On the issue of the supply crisis and the proposed retreat to the Bala Hissar, which he vehemently opposed in favour of an immediate retreat to Jalalabad, Shelton argued that, 'once ensconced in the Bala Hizar, the loss of horses and cattle (and the changes involved) would have involved much, not only of sending out foraging parties but have effectively deprived us of the means of retreat in the discovery that supplies were not procurable'. He further claimed: 'It has been argued that once in the Bala Hissar, larger bodies would be disposable to send on foraging parties', but, he argued:

Such parties would have to make distant expeditions to fight their way out to attack forts and collect provisions, defend the convoys, fight their way back, exposed to intense cold over a country intercepted with difficulties in the form of an enemy inured to the climate and unerring shots and skilled in the art of taking advantage of every natural objective that favoured their desultory system of warfare – a force … thus reduced to the necessity of procuring daily supplies and in such inclement regions … having to wade through an invidious population up in arms and burning with revenge, each day's expedition more distant and, consequently, more trying and difficult than the preceding one, must inevitably further erode away in strength and numerical force by continually occurring casualties in killed and wounded.

Moreover, he explained:

In the course of a series of such hazardous and perilous enterprises – the enemy movements, having conceived the idea of starving the force out, would have thwarted all attempts to forage by causing all the grain in the … vicinity to be removed leaving every fort within reach empty, the removal to the Bala Hissar would have involved the destruction of the greater part of the cavalry horses and carriage cattle without which forage parties would not have been practicable.

On the argument that refuge in Bala Hissar would have enabled the force to control the outbreak and link up with 'Afghan allies' in the city, Shelton remained brutally dismissive. He described it as a further example of, 'delusive subterfuge' by the 'politicals', 'to cover their mistaken policy and having neglected all preventive measures', notably, 'by placing well stored magazines in places of safety in a country where every beggar lays in his winter stock'.

Shelton further castigated the Envoy's paralysis at the start of the insurrection, his failure 'to suppress it in its infancy ... when notice was brought early in the morning of the 2nd of the revolts and plunder of the Treasury', and that, 'instead of going over immediately to consult with the King and ascertain the nature of the disturbances, remained quiet at home listening to reports and indulging in these delusive expressions'. In a tone of bitter irony, Shelton concluded:

> Is it natural or consistent that these Politicals should stand forward boldly in the face of these events to cover the impolitic measures by the assurance that the removal from one location to another should secure our friends and protection, or, is it feasible to suppose that the chiefs had thus all compromised themselves by the plunder of the Treasury – the distribution of all of our property and the murder of the senior Political and assistants together with his brother and Captain Broadfoot, and would trust themselves to our mercy after such acts of cruelty?'

To expect any supplies from the city to be furnished to the Bala Hissar was, he contended, an 'absurd pretension'. 'I', Shelton exclaimed, 'will demonstrate to the satisfaction of the court the impracticability of going to the Bala Hissar...for had the enterprise, dangerous, hazardous and impracticable as I have shown it to be, failed, the force was beyond redemption.' Alternatively, had his option 'retreat upon Jalalabad', if well managed and conducted, been adopted, 'the force would then have quit the cantonments at once which would have been effected without any of the risk attending the former operation ... and so placed us in a situation to resume active operations in the spring.' In summary, he maintained that it was 'evident to every reasonable person, especially to every military man, that any pretensions to that knowledge of his profession which you Gentlemen all profess, that, for a force without a magazine or provisions, or a prospect of getting any, early retreat was the only wise plan to adopt'.

Brigadier Shelton proceeded to destroy MacNaghten's reputation further in regard to his personal conduct during the actual Siege: 'We sacrificed the Force', he claimed, 'by indulging a mistaken policy in the delusive hope of enforcing the Affghans to order by diplomatic intrigue of which the melancholy catastrophe of the Envoy's murder was the unhappy result.' Shelton ended his arguments with a dramatic appeal to the court martial board for having advocated the course

> which the enlightened Court will, I am sure, in pronouncing as the only one which wisdom could justify ... there is no dishonour in

retreat and that, according to the rule of war, where rendered necessary for adverse circumstances was preferable to a disadvantageous
victory, as to allow attacks from cantonments were merely defensive
measures without leading to any ulterior beneficial results as regard
to the suppression of the rebellions, and productive of more evil than
good by diminishing our force in killed and augmenting our encumbrance in wounded.

As a 'military man', Shelton's defence inevitably included a less overt
attack upon the conduct of his immediate commander, General Elphinstone,
during the siege period, highlighting rather the general policy of

remaining to fritter away our force, increase our wounded and
augment our encumbrances and futile encounters, our troops without
food, horses without forage and no prospect of being able to procure
any, instead of availing ourselves of the favourable season to retreat
upon Jalalabad while a few days of provisions yet remained.

Again, the Envoy's unrelenting belief that provisions were procurable
was castigated:

I simply appeal to the common sense of every military man ... how
far it was possible or to be expected that a force as circumstanced as
the troops were, in a weak ... extensive cantonment with defenceless
parapets required to be manned night and day ... could hope to
struggle through a severe winter in the inclement region of snow with
a temperature below zero?

It was, in Shelton's view, a serious political as much as a logistical error
and he stunningly recounted how, during the siege, MacNaghten:

In the presence of General Elphinstone, reminded him that the
country was lost for the time ... that the troops by staying under such
existing circumstances must be inevitably sacrificed and that their
destruction would be a more serious blow to our moral influence in
India than the loss of the country.

However, as Shelton reiterated, 'by remaining we compounded both,
whereas, by a timely well-managed retreat on Jelalabad, the army might
not only be saved but be in a position to resume active operations in
spring'. Shelton also damningly recalled challenging MacNaghten head-on

about his 'obsession' that provisions 'can easily be obtained'. He asked what MacNaghten had done towards procuring any, to which MacNaghten had, allegedly, bluntly replied, 'I am not a commissary.' Shelton equally bluntly countered this with: 'If your influence is gone ... I much fear the idea you cherish in so readily getting supplies is very fallacious; you will I trust, duly appreciate the dangers of both delaying until the provisions are exhausted and the troops are reduced to the last days.'

It was a terrible indictment of MacNaghten's and Elphinstone's performance in the siege. In effect it had been due to them, but primarily MacNaghten, 'that all objects of such vital importance were so fatally disregarded and must ever be deplored'.

In his defence summary, Shelton reserved some of his greatest venom for the invidious behaviour of the 'politicals'. Their culpability for the 'later misfortune', he hoped, would have 'impressed the Government with a due sense of the impolicy of placing their foreign affairs ... in the hands of civil servants'. He expressed his gratitude to the new Governor-General, Lord Ellenborough (who replaced Auckland in 1842), for his new policy

of relieving officers of the highest rank from the thraldom of subjecting themselves to the disastrous and degrading control of young officers in the capacity of Political appointments whose offensive consequences in dictating, had challenged the wisdom of old and intelligent officers, whose experience entitles the confidence of the Government in the conduct of military affairs in which they were so much overruled during the operations in Afghanistan.

Shelton completed his defence with a passionate personal plea for justice in the face of such 'lamentable events', which 'have become the subject of public interest' and 'awakened the sympathy of all Europe', and the 'contending opinions of the origins and consequences'. To the court, he outlined a situation over the past fifteen months since the disaster in which 'slander has been busy with the many-tongued' and he had been 'made to bear the brunt of faults and errors that have originated in others'. Shelton stressed his unfair predicament as 'the senior survivor of the lamentable catastrophe which has sent to an early grave so many brave officers and soldiers, many of whom had they lived would have been an ornament and a credit to their country'. He was now 'assailed with the insidious suspicions and made a subject of public tribunal to stigmatise his character'. He took pains to cite his excellent military record, 'unscathed for a period of thirty-seven years ... through the most arduous campaigns of the Duke of Wellington – who was present at every action and siege in the Peninsula, who has fought in every quarter of the Globe and lost an arm in the service of his country, though not decorated'. He pointed out the lack of any witnesses for his defence: 'All those who could directly refute them in full were sacrificed to the ... late disasters in Afghanistan and whose bones are even now bleaching on the bleak mountains of these inclement regions.' Shelton again protested at having his character 'analysed ... for not agreeing an operation with officers who have not attained even the regimental rank of captain' (a clear swipe at Lieutenant Sturt and others who had favoured the Bala Hissar tactical option!). He claimed an 'indisputable refutation of the soundness of their judgement in the opinion now produced both of General Elphinstone and the Envoy, chief political and military authorities'.[236]

The veracity of Shelton's defence clearly struck a chord with the court martial board. Shelton was only reprimanded and resumed his military service within the army, but his robust defence, so clearly detailed here, casts more shadows on the reputation of MacNaghten, so clearly evidenced by the surviving Elphinstone letters submitted by Shelton in his defence of his actions.

The role or culpability of Shah Shuja and the alleged villain of the disaster, Mohammed Akbar Khan, remain controversial and shrouded in mystery. As we have seen, Shelton and Lady Sale remained convinced of Shah Shuja's innocence and his initial robust responses to the crisis seem to verify their views. Nevertheless, like many of the Afghan chiefs, he was angered by the proposed cuts in his subsidy and allowances and frustrated by MacNaghten's domineering attitude. This may have swayed him to, at least tacitly, support the conspiracy. It is more likely, however, that members of his court, notably his vizier or prime minister (as Lady Sale firmly believed), were more directly involved and he was merely the stooge for their ambitions. Akbar Khan's role was obvious as the key rebel leader, but he had understandable grievances against the British, notably the alleged perfidious treatment of his father and, not least, from a patriotic perspective, the brutal occupation of his country. His culpability for the murder of MacNaghten was clear (but not without considerable provocation), and that for the subsequent massacre of the retreating British garrison was high. The latter must, however be weighed against the immense difficulties of controlling his vengeful fellow warlords and his later recorded acts of kindness towards the British captives.

The 'blame game' continues today and it will surely be an eternal debate in the face of such a complete and disastrous defeat for British arms. The political controversy raged for decades after the events, with allegations of the doctoring of the official documents of the lead-up to the disaster as represented in the Parliamentary *Blue Books* of 1839, an issue which still provokes intense discussion today.[237] Arguably, Shelton's fierce attack on the 'politicals' still does not absolve his superior, Elphinstone from ultimate responsibility for what was essentially a military disaster. But, if there were villains of this 'signal catastrophe' there were, as assuredly, many heroes.

The heroism of Brigadier Anquetil and Lieutenant Sturt has already been alluded to. Two other heroes must be included, namely Major Pottinger and Captain Skinner. It was Major Pottinger who first warned of the coming outbreak and who took full political responsibility for the fate of the army after MacNaghten's untimely death. He made heroic efforts to retrieve the situation in the days preceding the retreat. Skinner also played a courageous part in maintaining political negotiations with Mohammed Akbar Khan during the retreat itself. Above all, the much-maligned Brigadier Shelton, despite his controversial role during the siege negotiations and his sometimes petulant behaviour in regard to command and control situations, emerged as a fearless leader of men in battle during both the two siege offensives and the final stages of the retreat. Of course, Shelton was by no means blameless. His cantankerous temperament clearly did not suit him for diplomacy or for higher military office, or always endear him to his colleagues and men, as demonstrated by his frequent recorded (if often justified) tantrums which took place during Elphinstone's frustrating War Council meetings. But as an extremely brave 'fighting soldier', it is hard to criticize him. When he occasionally failed militarily it was usually as a consequence of the lack of logistical or political support from his superiors. Sir John Fortescue, the great nineteenth-century British military historian, probably got the balance right in his stirring epitaph of Shelton:

It was characteristic that he was the one individual who was not softened by the mental and bodily distress of Elphinstone.... He quarrelled with every one of his fellow captains save Colin Mackenzie.... He met his end through a fall from his horse in the barrack square in Dublin ... and it was said that the regiment turned out and gave three cheers. Yet the brightest figure in the retreat from Kabul is that of the little cantankerous man with his right sleeve empty, ever at the point of greatest danger, watching every movement with untiring vigilance, securing every point of vantage, husbanding the strength of every man, inspiring every soul of the rear guard with his own calm heroism.... To so gallant a spirit much may be forgiven.[238]

Lady Sale, despite her occasional unjustified personal prejudices, emerges as the great heroine of both the siege and particularly the retreat. Her elevated status prolonged her chances of survival but she selflessly shared the rigours of the retreat, even attaching herself to the vulnerable advance guard. Despite her wounds and privations she remained an inspiring figure during the long period of captivity, before, as we shall see, her rescue by Nott's and Pollock's avenging armies.

The erratic conduct of the 44th Regiment, both during the latter period of the siege of Kabul and, at times, in the retreat, has come under some scrutiny. The alleged lack of fighting spirit among some units of this regiment, so clearly evident during the actions of 13 and 23 November, can, however, be partly explained by the high level of casualties they sustained daily. At the forefront of the defences and bearing the brunt of the often fruitless offensive actions, they saw many veterans and most of the senior and middle-ranking officers of the regiment killed early on in the siege, including their commander, Lieutenant-Colonel Mackrell, Major Scott and Captains Robinson and McCray, with many lieutenants and subalterns wounded. Elphinstone's continued indecision and procrastination clearly also served to severely undermine the morale of this key regiment. At least two experienced commentators have also claimed that the regiment's campaign inexperience and unfitness for duty may have contributed to their initially indifferent military performance. Historian James Lunt notes that the regiment 'had suffered severely from sickness in the Arakan before coming to Afghanistan and their morale was poor', while Lieutenant-General Sir George MacMunn, a veteran Indian military historian, has commented less sympathetically on the deleterious implications of the changeover of troops in late 1840:

> A further misfortune was that the troops in Kabul were due for relief. The 13th Light Infantry who were *au fait* with every inch of the country and whose relationship with their comrades, black and white, of the Indian Army had always been most cordial, were due for Europe. The experienced 35th Native Infantry ... with effective commandants were also to go. The 13th had been relieved by the 44th Foot whose conduct in India had been entirely opposite and had been marked by a disinclination to fraternize with the Indian Army and who were disliked in consequence, which bore its ill fruit in times of danger.[239]

Captain Seaton's earlier evidence of the close bonds existing between his 35th Native Infantry and the 13th Light Infantry bears some testimony to this view, as do the 44th's record of poor performance when positioned alongside 'native regiments', both during the siege and even along the routes of march. Nevertheless, the regiment ultimately performed extremely well during the retreat, especially under the inspired leadership of Shelton. Their gallant, 'last stand' at Gandamak truly deserves its elevated position in the annals of British military history.

It remained for General Sir Jasper Nicholls, Commander-in-Chief of India, to succinctly summarize the causes of the Afghan 'failure'. At a logistical level, he identified the causes as, first: 'Making war with a peace establishment, making war without a safe base of operations, carrying our native army out of India into a strange and cold climate where they and we were foreigners and both considered as infidels. Invading a poor country and one unequal to supply our wants, especially our large establishment of cattle.' On a political level, he roundly condemned: 'Giving undue power to political agents, want of forethought and undue confidence in the Afghans on the part of Sir William MacNaghten and, finally placing our magazines, even our Treasure, in indefensible places and the overall great military neglect and mismanagement after the outbreak.'[240]

The lessons of this appalling disaster to British arms were clear and unequivocal. The British forces in Afghanistan have been scandalously under-resourced in both manpower and materials, and subjected to severe overstretch. But, at the heart of the problem, lay the misjudgements and myopia of leading politicians, notably Lord Auckland, who had launched and conducted this flawed enterprise, and in particular the acute breakdown in relations between the local political and military establishment. Nowhere had this been more evident than in the catastrophic collapse in relations between British Envoys MacNaghten and Burnes and their leading military critics, notably Major-General Nott, Brigadier Roberts and ultimately Elphinstone himself. Such follies were, as we shall see, to have a deep resonance in the conduct of future British wars in Afghanistan, not least in the early stages of the current Herrick Campaign in Afghanistan, where such fundamental lessons have still not been fully absorbed by politicians at both the strategic and tactical level.

But it was by no means a *total* disaster. The Kabul Brigade represented only one, albeit significant, element of British power in Afghanistan. The British forces in southern and western Afghanistan, under the redoubtable General Nott, remained intact and, moreover, in a state of high morale. Rejoined by McClaren's Brigade, earlier forced to turn back from relieving Kabul by the severe weather in November 1841, his overall command represented a powerful force for any policy of retribution. And retribution – indeed dark bloody revenge – was clearly in the air in the spring of 1842 as two British columns, under Major-Generals Nott and Pollock, were poised to return, to wreak a terrible retribution upon the Afghan people.

Notes

1 Kaye, *History of the War*, vol 2, p.138.
2 Eden, *Up the Country*, pp.389–90.
3 Chetwynd Stapylton, Stapylton, Letters/Diary, 16 May 1841, p.8.
4 Dennie, *Personal Narrative*, p.141–2.
5 For Nott's acidic comments upon the misrule of the Company authorities in India and Afghanistan see, for instance, J.S. Stocqueler, *Memoirs and Correspondence of Sir William Nott* (London, Hurst and Blackett, 1854), (2 vols), vol 1, pp.254–5.
6 Nott to Family, 29 Sept 1840, Stocqueler, *Nott Memoirs*, vol 1, p.256.
7 Mackenzie (encl. in Pottinger).
8 Kaye, *History of the War*, vol 2, p.136.
9 Sir J. Nicholls, Journal, 29 March 1841 (encl. in Kaye, *History of the War*, vol 2, p.149).
10 Ibid.
11 Ferrier, *The Afghans*, p.343.
12 Public Records Office, Kew (hereafter PRO) 30/12/33/4, MacNaghten to Secretary, Government of India, 17 June 1841.
13 Ibid, MacNaghten to Maddock, 8 April 1841.
14 Ibid.
15 Ibid, Secretary, Government of India to MacNaghten, 9 August 1841.
16 Seaton, *Cadet to Colonel*, pp.136–7.
17 Chetwynd Stapylton, Stapylton, Letters/Diary, 4 November 1841, pp.10–11.
18 Dennie, *Personal Narrative*, p.144.
19 Seaton, *Cadet to Colonel*, p.141.
20 Ibid.
21 Chetwynd Stapylton, Stapylton, Letters/Diary, 20 October 1841, p.9.
22 Ibid, p.8.
23 Ibid, p.11.
24 Chetwynd Stapylton, Stapylton, Letters/Diary, 4 November 1841, p.11.
25 Ibid.
26 Seaton, *Cadet to Colonel*, pp.137–8.
27 Ferrier, *The Afghans*, p.343.
28 Seaton, *Cadet to Colonel*, pp.137–8.
29 Ibid, pp.155–6.

30 Ibid.
31 Ibid.
32 Ibid.
33 Cheytwynd Stapylton, Stapylton, Letters/Diary, 11 November 1841, p.12.
34 Helsham Jones, *History and Geography of Afghanistan*, p.156.
35 Low, *Abbott, Journal*, p.225.
36 MacNaghten to Governor of Agra, 25 September 1841 (enc. in Kaye, vol 2 p.151).
37 Lady F. Sale, *A Journal of the Disasters in Affghanistan 1841–2* (John Murray, London, 1843), p.31.
38 Kaye, *History*, vol 2, p.171.
39 Ibid.
40 Ferrier, *The Afghans*, p.348.
41 G. Pottinger, *Mackenzie*, p.344.
42 Ibid, p.345.
43 Ibid.
44 Sale, *Journal*, p.35.
45 Ibid, p.31.
46 Ibid, pp.33–4.
47 Ibid, p.42.
48 Kaye, *History*, vol 2, p.177.
49 Sale, *Journal*, p.46.
50 Kaye, *History*, vol 2, p.177.
51 W. Hough, *A Review of the Operations of the British Force at Cabool*, (Calcutta, 1849), p.3.
52 Major General Sir Vincent Eyre, *The Kabul Insurrection of 1841–2*, (revised, W.H. Allen, London, 1879), p.87.
53 Sale, *Journal*, pp.45–6.
54 Ibid.
55 Eyre, *Kabul Insurrection*, p.101.
56 Ibid, p.103.
57 Ibid, p.104.
58 Ibid.
59 Sale, *Journal*, p.59.
60 Ibid, p.60.
61 Eyre, *Kabul Insurrection*, p.105
62 Sale, *Journal*, p.54. Lady Sale considered the capture and burning of Trevor's Tower was the crucial turning point for the 'Kuzzilbashes'. 'Had reinforcements arrived to save the Tower', she asserted, 'the Kuzzilbashes would have discharged openly in our favour with Khan Shireen Khan at their head.'

63   Sale, *Journal*, p.60.
64   Ibid.
65   Ibid, pp.76–7.
66   Ibid, p.58.
67   Hough, *A Review of the Operations*, p.3.
68   Sale, *Journal*, p.58.
69   Ibid, p.55 and 77.
70   Ibid, p.64.
71   Ibid, p.62.
72   Eyre, *Kabul Insurrection*, p.108.
73   Sale, *Journal*, p.64.
74   Eyre, *Kabul Insurrection*, p.12.
75   Sale, *Journal*, p.85.
76   Ibid.
77   Eyre, *Kabul Insurrection*, p.113.
78   Ibid.
79   Sale, *Journal*, p.83. On his arrival, Shelton was himself appalled by the command chaos and crisis of morale which pervaded the over-extended cantonment. He read 'anxiety in every countenance' and 'serious defects' with 'so many troops ... necessary for the actual defence ... that only a few could be spared for external operations. I was put in order to command cantonments ... this however Elphinstone soon corrected, by reminding me that he commanded not I'. Statement of Brigadier Shelton, Kaye, *History of the War*, vol 2, p.208.
80   Sale, *Journal*, p.89.
81   Ibid, p.92.
82   Ibid, p.67.
83   Ibid, pp.42–3.
84   Ibid, pp.98–9.
85   Ibid.
86   Eyre, *Kabul Insurrection*, p.127.
87   A. Forbes, *The Afghan Wars* (Seely and Co. Ltd, London, 1892), p.80.
88   Eyre, *Kabul Insurrection*, p.129.
89   Sale, *Journal*, p.99.
90   Eyre, *Kabul Insurrection*, p.129–30.
91   Sale, *Journal*, p.100.
92   Helsham Jones, *History and Geography*, p.160.
93   Eyre, *Kabul Insurrection*, p.131.
94   Ibid.
95   Sale, *Journal*, p.83.
96   Ibid, p.72.

97 Ibid, p.73.

98 Ibid, p.120.

99 Ibid.

100 Ibid, p.121.

101 T. Carter, *Historical Records of the 44th or the East Essex Regiment* (repr. Naval and Military Books) p.112.

102 Sale, *Journal*, pp.124–6.

103 Ibid, p.128.

104 Ibid, p.129.

105 Eyre, *Kabul Insurrection*, p.174.

106 Sir Henry Durand, *The First Afghan War and its Causes* (repr. Bhavansa Prints, New Delhi, 2000), p.363.

107 Sale, *Journal*, p.66.

108 Ibid, p.101.

109 Ibid, p.142.

110 Ibid, p.145.

111 For a detailed contemporary narrative of the Charikar disaster see Colonel Haughton, *Char-ee-kar* (London, 1880) *passim*.

112 Sale, *Journal*, p.142.

113 Ibid, pp.149–50.

114 Durand, *First Afghan War*, p.169.

115 Sale, *Journal*, p.158.

116 Ibid.

117 Durand, *First Afghan War*, p.374.

118 Durand, *First Afghan War*, p.374, and Eyre, *Kabul Insurrection*, p.217.

119 Mackenzie to Eyre, 29 July 1842, enc. in Eyre, *Kabul Insurrection*, p.225.

120 Lawrence to Pottinger, 10 May 1842, enc. in Eyre, *Kabul Insurrection*, p.237.

121 Mackenzie to Eyre, 29 July 1842, enc. in Eyre, *Kabul Insurrection*, p.227.

122 Lawrence to Pottinger, 10 May 1842, enc. in Eyre, *Kabul Insurrection*, p.236.

123 Mackenzie to Eyre, 29 July 1842, enc. in Eyre, *Kabul Insurrection*, p.227.

124 Lawrence to Pottinger, 10 May 1842, enc. in Eyre, *Kabul Insurrection*, p.237.

125 Mackenzie to Eyre, 29 July 1842, enc. in Eyre, *Kabul Insurrection*, pp.227–8.

126 Ibid, p.237.

127 Ibid, p.239.

128 Ibid.

129 Sale, *Journal*, pp.197–8.

130 Dupree, *History of Afghanistan*, p.386.

131 Eyre, *Kabul Insurrection*, p.243.
132 Sale, *Journal*, p.217.
133 Ibid, pp.208–9.
134 Lawrence to Pottinger, 10 May 1842, enc. In Eyre, *Kabul Insurrection*, p.236.
135 Sale, *Journal*, p.216.
136 Statement of Brigadier Shelton, Kaye, *History*, vol 2, p.363.
137 Hough, *A Review of Operations*, p.4.
138 ERM, Souter to wife, 2 April 1842.
139 Eyre, *Kabul Insurrection*, p.255.
140 Sale, *Journal*, p.227.
141 Carter, *Historical Records*, p.115.
142 Sale, *Journal*, pp.221–2.
143 Eyre, *Kabul Insurrection*, pp.258–9.
144 Ibid.
145 Essex Regimental Museum archives (hereafter ERM), 'Letters concerning the 44th Regiment during the retreat from Cabul during the First Afghan War', Journal of Sergeant Major Lissant, 6 January 1842.
146 Sale, *Journal*, p.225.
147 Eyre, *Kabul Insurrection*, p.258.
148 Sale, *Journal*, p.226.
149 Ibid.
150 ERM, Lissant Journal, January 1842.
151 Eyre, *Kabul Insurrection*, p.259.
152 Ibid.
153 Brydon.
154 Sale, *Journal*, pp.227–8.
155 Eyre, *Kabul Insurrection*, p.260.
156 Sale, *Journal*, p.227 and Eyre, *Kabul Insurrection*, p.261.
157 Sale, *Journal*, p.229.
158 Brydon.
159 Sale, *Journal*, pp.229–30.
160 Eyre, *Kabul Insurrection*, p.263.
161 ERM, Lissant Journal, 7 January 1842, and Eyre, *Kabul Insurrection*, pp.262–3.
162 Eyre, *Kabul Insurrection*, p.263.
163 ERM, Lissant Journal, 7 January 1842.
164 Eyre, *Kabul Insurrection*, p.263.
165 ERM, Lissant Journal, 7 January 1842.
166 Sale, *Journal*, p.231.
167 Eyre, *Kabul Insurrection*, p.264.

168 ERM, Lissant Journal, 8 January 1842.
169 Sale, *Journal*, p.232.
170 ERM, Brydon Account, and P. Macrory (ed), *Lady Sale*, pp.164–5.
171 Ibid.
172 Lunt, *From Sepoy to Subedar*, p.114.
173 Eyre, *Kabul Insurrection*, p.268.
174 ERM, Lissant Journal, 8 January 1842, and Eyre, *Kabul Insurrection*, p.270.
175 Sale, *Journal*, p.237.
176 ERM, Lissant Journal.
177 ERM, Lissant Journal, 9 January 1842.
178 Sale, *Journal*, p.240.
179 ERM, Lissant Journal, 8 January 1842.
180 Sale, *Journal*, p.236.
181 Eyre, *Kabul Insurrection*, p.271.
182 Sale, *Journal*, pp.242–3.
183 Eyre, *Kabul Insurrection*, p.271.
184 ERM, Lissant Journal, 9 January 1842.
185 Ibid.
186 Eyre, *Kabul Insurrection*, p.277.
187 Ibid.
188 ERM, Lissant Journal, 7 Jan 1842
189 Carter, *Historical Records,* p.119.
190 Eyre, *Kabul Insurrection*, p.277.
191 ERM Lissant Journal, 9 January 1842.
192 ERM, Souter to wife, 21 April 1842, and NAM 6912/6.
193 Eyre, *Kabul Insurrection*, p.278.
194 Ibid, p.279.
195 ERM, Brydon Account, and Macrory, *Lady Sale*, p.166.
196 Carter. *Historical Records*, pp.121–2.
197 Ibid.
198 Ibid.
199 ERM, Souter to wife, 21 April 1842, and NAM 6912/6.
200 Eyre, *Kabul Insurrection*, p.283.
201 Lunt, *From Sepoy to Subedar*, pp.114–5.
202 ERM, Souter to wife, 21 April 1842, and NAM 6912/6.
203 Lunt, *From Sepoy to Subedar*, pp.114–5.
204 Ibid.
205 Seaton, *From Cadet to Colonel*, p.180.
206 ERM, Brydon Account.
207 J.S. Cumming, *A Six Years Diary*, (Martin and Hood, London, 1847), and NAM 92 CUM. 28141.

208 ERM, Souter to wife, 21 April 1842, and NAM 6912/6.

209 Ibid.

210 Ibid.

211 Ibid.

212 Eyre, *Kabul Insurrection*, p.260.

213 ERM, Souter to wife, 21 April 1842, and NAM 6912/6.

214 Sale, *Journal*, pp.238–9.

215 Ibid.

216 Lunt, *From Sepoy to Subedar*, p.114.

217 Ibid.

218 Lunt, *From Sepoy to Subedar*, p.115.

219 Sale, *Journal*, p.249.

220 Ibid, p.281.

221 ERM, Souter to wife, 21 April 1842, and NAM 6912/6.

222 P. Macrory, *Kabul Catastrophe*, Foreword by Sir G Templar, p.1.

223 *The London Times*, 10 March 1842.

224 Ibid.

225 Seaton, *From Cadet to Colonel*, p.190.

226 P. Macrory, *Kabul Catastrophe*, p.1.

227 S.W. Napier, *The Life and Opinions of General Sir Charles Napier* (John Murray, London, 1857), vol 2, p.183.

228 'Narrative of Captain Gray's escape from the Ghilzies' (encl. in Stocqueler, *Memorials of Afghanistan*, Appendix iv, pp.xii–xiii.).

229 Sir Jasper Nicholls to Ellenborough, PRO 30/12/31.

230 Stocqueler, *Nott Memoirs*, vol 2.

231 Memorandum by Duke of Wellington on Sir W.H. MacNaghten's letter of 26 Oct. 1841, dated 29 Jan. 1842. Kaye, vol 2, Appendix, pp.404–6.

232 S.W. Napier, *Life and Opinions*, vol 2, p.163.

233 Sale, *Journal*, p.79.

234 *The Times*, 10 March 1842.

235 NAM 6502-124, Governor-General Lord Auckland to Nicholls, 12 January 1842, Nicholls Papers/Diary.

236 NAM 6807/417, 'The Court Martial defence notes of Brigadier Shelton'.

237 For an excellent and erudite discussion of the controversy surrounding the alleged garbling of the Afghan war parliamentary 'Blue Books' of 1839 see, G.J. Alder 'The "Garbled" Blue Books of 1839 – Myth or Reality?,' The Historical Journal, 15, 2 (1972) pp.229–59. For two other contending views see Kaye, *History of the War* vol 1, pp.204–5, and Norris, *First Afghan War*, pp.224 and 423.

238 Sir John Fortescue, *A History of the British Army* (Macmillan, London, 1899), vol 12, p.245. Shelton's immediate contemporary, General Napier,

was far less forgiving. He considered that, for Shelton's truculent behaviour, he ought to have been shot – this man was the 'evil spirit' of the force; to Shelton may be traced the whole misfortune of this army – see Norris, *First Afghan War*, p.449.

239 MacMunn, *Lure of the Indus*, p.73 and J. Lunt, *Sepoy to Subedar*, p.110. Lt-General Colin Mackenzie, observing earlier the march of Shelton's Brigade up to Afghanistan also recorded: 'A bad feeling ... exists between the Queen's 44th Regiment and the native troops. Swords and bayonets have been drawn between them'. Lt.-General C. Mackenzie, *Storms and Sunshine of a Soldier's Life* (David Douglas, Edinburgh, 1884), p.140.

240 Memo by Sir Jasper Nicholls, undated (encl. in MacMunn, *Lure of the Indus*, p.91).

3. Retribution, Fire and Sword

The war was ... not conducted with the magnanimity and compassion hoped for.... A revengeful spirit was evinced ... and with savage fierceness: the destruction of the bazaar of Cabool, in itself a vindictive Vandalism, was accompanied with very terrible excesses.

Lieutenant-General Sir W. Napier, *The Life and Opinions of General Sir Charles James Napier* (John Murray, London, 1857), vol 2, p.166

War ... is a terrible thing ... on the last day the troops broke loose. The Hindu sepoys being naturally most bitter against the Afghans, and maddened by the ... sight of the spoil of their unfortunate comrades, plundered the greater part of Kabul.

Lieutenant-General Colin Mackenzie, *Storms and Sunshine of a Soldier's Life* (David Douglas, Edinburgh, 1884), pp.370–1

Great atrocities were committed by the seapoys and neither infancy nor age were spared.... I saw one little child, not more than three months old, shot through both thighs and still alive and lying by its mother who had received the same bullet in the body.

NAM 6807–319, Journal of Lt. Yerbury, 3rd Light Dragoons, Istalif, 29 Sept 1842

Over the next days, news of the terrible disaster at Kabul spread like wildfire across India and, within weeks, thousands of miles across the oceans to Britain and Europe. Almost to a man, the British demanded bloody and, in many cases, indiscriminate revenge. Even before news of the disaster arrived, a distressed Captain Pearson scribbled in his diary:

I am sorely grieved at the disastrous aspect of affairs in Afghanistan ... much do I feel for the men sent in amongst a race of blood thirsty heathens ... dulce et decorum est, but, to be slaughtered in cold blood should necessity oblige our gallant fellows and friends, is dreadful to think ... I mourn over the situation of our troops but sooner than England should be insulted with impunity or arms be dishonoured by a degrading treaty.[1]

The first response of the deeply traumatized Auckland administration in Calcutta, on receiving the harrowing news of the disaster on 30 January 1842, closely matched these sentiments:

A faithless enemy, stained by the foul crime of assassination has, through a failure of supplies followed by consummate treachery been able to overcome a body of the British troops, in a country removed by distance and difficulty of season from possibility of succour. But the Governor-General-in-Council, while he most deeply laments the loss of brave officers and men, regards this partial reverse as a new occasion for displaying the stability and vigour of the British power and the admirable spirit and valour of the British Indian Army.[2]

As in 1838, a renewed call to arms echoed across northern and central India. From within his temporary cantonment at Meerut, Lieutenant John Greenwood recalled the sudden frenzy of activity and a mood of grim determination, spurred on by the palpable grief of the relatives of the massacred troops:

Such a bustle, perhaps, was never seen at Meerut before. The officers had just got settled in their bungalows when the orders arrived, and at every turn we met men hurrying about in search of pony trunks.... Our men were in the highest spirits, although the lamentations of their spouses were loud enough. We had heard of the appeal made by the widows of the 44th to the regiments ordered to Afghanistan. They called on them to revenge their slaughtered husbands, and every heart responded to the call.[3]

Two experienced and deeply respected 'Indian' commanders, Major-Generals Nott and Pollock, were rapidly assigned the arduous task of retribution. William Nott, the former Company pariah, but now vindicated after saving Kandahar, relished the task before him and the prospect of fresh glories. The more venerable and senior of the two, George Pollock, a veteran of the 1824 Burma War, had served in India since 1803 but shared none of Elphinstone's physical or mental infirmities. He was renowned for his calmness and discipline under pressure. Their appointment coincided with a major volte-face in terms of political-military operational control. In a momentous dispatch, all political authority in Afghanistan was suddenly transferred into the hands of these two avenging Generals:

> In the conduct of military operations at the present crisis in Affghanistan it appears to the Governor-General-in-Council ... essential to attend to the expedience, the safety and the necessity of military movements with reference to military considerations in the first place.... His Lordship in Council has come to this resolution, in no mistrust of our political officers in that quarter ... but, in the present circumstances of great difficulty, and, in the absence of all means of receiving orders from Sir William MacNaghten, the constitutional representative of government in that country, his Lordship-in-Council would throw upon each military commander a more than usual discretion in whatever may regard military movements or the safety of the troops, or the defence or abandonment of the positions occupied by our forces ... the political officers ... will consider themselves under the direction of military commandants and will address to them all those communications which would formally have been addressed to the Envoy and Minister.[4]

The statement represented an astonishing public acknowledgment of the failures of political authority at ground level in Afghanistan; the gloves were now off in what was to become a total war of revenge, with severe implications for the fate of Afghan villages lying in the path of the two 'armies of retribution', and especially for the city of Kabul. The suppression of the hated 'politicals' was welcomed by many of all ranks in the military. Captain Neill applauded Ellenborough's act:

> Of the wisdom of this bold step the strongest proof ... is the new and better spirit which distinguished our operations after the power of acting for themselves had been conferred on the Generals. No longer were the proceedings of these distinguished men cramped by the interference of juniors who, however talented ... were frequently too deficient in experience to understand aright the responsibility of, or to wield circumspectly, the power which their false position gave them.[5]

In faraway Sind, General Napier agreed:

> Lord Ellenborough says that all 'politicals' are to be placed under my orders; I ... was resolved not to be under them ... I never quarrel with

such people if they behave well, and I think them useful in their place; but that place is not as councillors to a general officer, he should have none but his pillow and his courage.[6]

The Siege and Defence of Jalalabad: November 1841 to April 1842

For Major-General Pollock, the primary objective was to relieve the ongoing siege at the key, heroically defended town of Jalalabad. Since his arrival there from Kabul in November 1841, Major-General 'Fighting Bob' Sale had been confronting a large force of several thousand rebels. These were soon massively reinforced by 5,000 levies under Akbar Khan himself, fresh from completing the annihilation of the reteating Kabul garrison. Against these enemy forces Sale could only deploy approximately 1,500 men, comprising around 500 men of the 13th Somerset Light Infantry, 300 sappers, 500 of the 35th Native Infantry and around 120 cavalry. His provisions were initially so low that his men were immediately put on half rations and camp-followers on quarter rations. Available ball ammunition amounted to only 120 rounds per man.[7] As previously explained, the initial state of defences of Jalalabad, as in Kabul, was also truly precarious, with only a few hundred yards of parapet reaching not more than two feet high and only partially enclosing a huge perimeter of 2,300 yards. After their desperate march through the Khurd-Kabul and Tezeen Passes, Sale's Brigade had provisions for less than two days left.

The gallant defence of Jalalabad has been fully examined by many other sources,[8] but it merits further investigation, if only as an example of how the much-larger Kabul garrison could and might have survived. In terms of command and control, from the outset, Major-General Sale, by stark contrast to General Elphinstone, established a highly effective and energetic 'committee of officers', 'of which Captains James Abbott and George Broadfoot were the leading spirits'. Abbott, already famed for his artillery expertise during the numerous punitive expeditions of 1840–1, was appointed Commander of Ordnance. He received 'cheerful and able assistance' from Captain Backhouse of the Shah's Artillery and, from his subaltern, Lieutenant Michael Dawes. With no senior engineer officers present with the Brigade, the duty was assumed by Captain George Broadfoot of the Madras Infantry (also attached to the Shah's Artillery), of whom Captain Henry Havelock said he 'possessed an uncommon genius for war'.[9]

The infantry commanders were of similarly high calibre. Both Colonel Monteith of the 35th Native Infantry and the (albeit still resentful) Colonel Dennie were to prove outstanding, energetic officers. Unlike Kabul, the garrison was also blessed with the absence of any political interference with operations. The resident political officer, Captain MacGregor, wisely abandoned his political duties to undertake the highly successful role of Commissariat Officer. The presence of Havelock, soon to win glory in the Anglo-Sikh wars of the 1840s and the 1857 Indian Mutiny, complemented the veritable array of talent supporting their brave if, at times, somewhat pedantic commander, Sir Robert Sale.

Indeed, it was one of those talented subordinates, the ever-zealous Captain George Broadfoot, who, in only a few days, miraculously transferred the fragile defences of Jalalabad. The sentries were given shelter by the ingenious method of ranging 'hundreds of camel saddles ... two deep high ... forming a tolerable protection for the guards lying behind them'.[10] Ditches were dug, existing walls reinforced and food supplies consolidated.

Again, unlike in Kabul, the Jalalabad 'Council of War' immediately decided on a policy of active defence, designed both to keep the enemy guessing their tactics and to sustain garrison morale and, if the opportunity arose, secure provisions. Moreover, as Afghan incendiaries burnt down the cantonments outside the walls, the sentries recalling them 'dancing around each conflagration like demons',[11] it was decided to retain control of the city walls as well as the central bastion so as to deny the enemy a dominating firing position on the walls. Led principally by Colonel Montieth of the 35th Native Infantry and Colonel Dennie of the 13th Foot, numerous forays were also launched against the enemy. For instance, as early as 1 December 1841, in one of many surprise expeditions designed to crush the advancing enemy parties of 4,000 attackers who had brazenly closed to within twenty yards of the defences, even firing 'through our loopholes', Colonel Dennie led 800 British infantry, followed by 200 cavalry and two guns in a gallant dash from the Kabul Gate. The totally surprised rebels fled in panic with the British cavalry killing 'almost 100 on the plain'. Concerted and skilful fire from Abbott's mobile guns drove the massed remnants into the river, where many more were killed or drowned. Captain Abbott even theorized that 'had the infantry pushed on, the greater part of Akbar Khan's force would have been destroyed' but, he added disappointedly, 'Sale halted them'.[12] Such robust and active defence impressed the local valley tribes so much that, under pressure from MacGregor and, 'seeing we were too dangerous to be trifled with', men 'came in daily with donkey-loads of flour, wheat ... which alone were a supply for the whole garrison for 15 days, at full rations'.[13] It was a stark contrast to the failed provision strategy of the Kabul garrison.

One of the most daring forays to secure supplies occurred on 24 March 1842. On this occasion, Mohammed Akbar had driven sheep herds to feed near the walls to deny the garrison forage for their own declining flocks, as well as murdering the garrison's grass-cutters. Inspired by another energetic young officer, Lieutenant Plowden of the 5th Cavalry, Sale permitted a sudden sally of the cavalry supported by 650 infantry, who together secured three flocks totalling 520 sheep! The garrison were understandably 'jubilant at this great success'.[14] Again it provided a stark contrast to the earlier disastrous conduct of the Kabul siege, where many such ventures were vetoed by the indecisiveness of Elphinstone or his divided councils.

The defences were streamlined in other innovative ways never deployed in the Kabul siege. In a ruthless but, perhaps, militarily justifiable move, suspected malcontents amongst the Afghan auxiliaries attached to the garrison were promptly expelled. Abbott wrote in mid-July: 'We shall have hard work to defend our position with so few troops. I have sent out all our Afghans even including the Jezailchees, who have hitherto fought well but some of whom have been tampered with by the enemy.'[15] Conversely, manpower resources were significantly increased by the clever decision to arm many of the garrison's Indian camp-followers with a variety of crude weapons. These at least could be deployed to relieve the exhausted regulars on the parapets. Abbott recorded on 20 January 1841: 'We are endeavouring to form a corps of armed camp followers.... I have one hundred good stout men who I am arming with pikes, a really formidable weapon anywhere, having a staff six foot long with eight inches of iron head, as sharp as a needle. My forge and carpenters make up twenty per diem.'[16]

The ammunition shortage was similarly remedied by the collection and widespread use of expended Afghan musket balls and artillery shells. To protect against mining, Sale ordered a fourteen-foot wide, ten-foot deep trench to be dug all over the town, while an enormous well was sunk to provide an unlimited supply of water to the garrison. Alongside these measures, the transparency of command decision-making and spirit of teamwork enabled the garrison to survive a series of crises of morale. The news, from Pottinger on 3 January 1842, of the murder of Envoy MacNaghten was the first major blow, soon followed, on 9 January, by a letter from his superior, the doomed Major-General Elphinstone, directing the garrison to retreat to Peshawar in order to fulfil his December treaty with the rebels at Kabul. Sale deliberately disobeyed the order, apparently in the vain hope that this would discourage the General from also conducting a hundred-mile retreat in the middle of winter. In this he was staunchly supported by all of his officers and men. Captain Seaton, tellingly recalled: 'I don't know in what words Sale penned his reply but the universal answer of the garrison was short and energetic, in the words of that celebrated character, Mr Sam Weller "they would see Mr Akbar Khan – something unpleasant – first!".'[17]

Three other psychological hammer blows were delivered to the Jalalabad garrison during the next two months of 1842. One event, the arrival, in mid-January 1842, of the first bedraggled survivors of the Kabul retreat, seemed to fulfil Colonel Dennie's earlier and oft-repeated prophecy of doom: 'You'll see. Not a soul will escape from Cabul except one man; and he will come to tell us that the rest were destroyed.'[18] Captain Seaton accordingly recorded the dismal news of Dr Brydon's lone arrival:

On the 13 January I was on guard at the south gate, when a little after 12 o'clock someone came rushing along the passage leading to my guard-room. The door was burst open and a Lieutenant of my regiment threw himself into my arms exclaiming: 'My God, Seaton, the whole of the Cabool army has been destroyed.'[19]

Captain Abbott also recalled the blow delivered to garrison morale by the news of the 'greatest calamity that has ever befallen a British force in India where the catastrophe will cause a greater sensation than it has amongst us, as the men, accustomed as we have been to horrors of all sorts, are not easily excited'.[20]

The impact was, nevertheless, devastating. In a desperate attempt to alert more survivors, the garrison flag was hoisted and, that night, lanterns were hung out above the 'Cabul Gate', with two buglers stationed in the south-west bastion to sound the advance every quarter of an hour. Seaton remarked: 'The terrible wailing sounds of those bugles I shall never forget. It was a dirge for our slaughtered soldiers and heard all through the night, it had an inexpressibly mournful and depressing effect.'[21]

The search conducted next day by a garrison cavalry patrol four miles along the Kabul road only discovered the horribly mangled remains of Doctor Harper, Captain Hopkins and Lieutenant Collyer, whose features 'could not be distinguished'.[22] While a few other survivors, including Sergeant Major Lissant, did arrive later, it did little to reduce the shock of the catastrophe.

The second setback occurred on 25 January 1842, with news of the disaster sustained by Brigadier Wild at Ali Masjid. This destroyed any hopes of immediate relief from India. A deeply frustrated Abbott was scathing in his appraisal of this mini-disaster:

The repulse was owing partly to the vile Sikh guns which broke down at the first round, partly to the viler Sikh regiments which ran away without firing at all, and partly to the want of spirit in our own troops. The moral effect of this will be so bad for us, both as encouraging our enemies and alarming our troops, that I do not think that General Pollock ought to advance with less than 10,000 men to force the Khyber.[23]

The third blow was delivered by a natural catastrophe, this time an event far beyond the control of the garrison. At around 11 a.m. on 19 February 1842, a cold, windy day, the area experienced a massive earthquake which overnight virtually destroyed the carefully constructed defences of Jalalabad. Captain Seaton witnessed the ensuing terrifying scenes:

> The ground heaved and set like the sea and the whole plain appeared rolling in waves towards us ... my eyes being attracted towards the fort, I saw that the houses, the walls, and the bastions were rocking and reeling in a most horrific manner and falling into complete ruin ... the whole fort was enveloped in one immense impenetrable cloud of dust, out of which came cries of alarm and terror from the hundreds within ... the men were absolutely green with fear.[24]

Scores were buried alive. In historian Gleig's words, 'the earthquake of 19 February ended in an hour all that it had taken the Jalalabad garrison three months to accomplish'.[25] The highly respected and beloved Colonel Monteith, commander of the 35th Native Infantry, was buried but speedily dug out alive by his men. Amazingly, only three men were crushed to death in the cavalry hospital while, equally fortuitously, the quake paralyzed the enemy: 'Akbar Khan and his army who had removed to Amukail, within seven miles of the town, were too much horror struck at the calamity, which levelled their forts and dwellings, to take advantage of the helpless state to which the Jalalabad garrison was reduced.'[26] By herculean efforts, all the officers and men, again ably directed by Captains Abbott and Backhouse, entirely restored and retrenched the parapets by the end of the month. Again, such energy and dedication to duty proved a stark contrast to the lethargic performance of their compatriots in the doomed Kabul garrison, barely a few months earlier.

As the siege tightened in March and April 1842, other ingenious methods were employed to replenish the dwindling ammunition supply. Captain Seaton recalled one humorous but extremely effective ploy:

Lead for the rifles was in great request so some of the officers of the 13th hit upon a comical but effectual method of procuring it. They dressed up a figure and put it on a short pole – cocked hat, red coat, painted face, not unlike a better sort of 'Guy'. Hoisted up the ramparts and, managed adroitly, it created no end of fun. It was laughable to see how eagerly the Affghans fired at it and to hear the thousands of bullets sent over our heads ... in the evening with the enemy retired or in the early morning we used to go and pick up the bullets.[27]

Ensign Stapylton's journal also reveals how pewter basins, mugs and everything that could be brought into play was melted down for bullets. Sniper parties were particularly effectively used to further demoralize the enemy:

Amongst the officers there was upwards of thirty double-barrelled guns and rifles and we formed ourselves into amateur corps, posting ourselves on the most favourable places around the fort and picking off ... the enemy ... a good deal of execution was done. Some of the more adventurous used to skirmish outside the walls but this was put a stop to on orders.[28]

On the basis of what proved to be false news of Pollock's defeat in the Khyber Pass and, 'as our only chance of deliverance', Sale, after heated argument, was persuaded by Abbott, Oldfield and other 'fiery spirits' to mount a final offensive to break the siege. It proved to be the decisive action of the 'illustrious garrison'. At daylight, on 7 April 1842, three columns of British troops sallied forth from Jalalabad. In the centre was the 500-strong 13th Regiment under Colonel Dennie. On the left wing, Sale deployed the 35th Native Infantry under Colonel Monteith and, on the right, 360 bayonets of the sappers and further single companies of the 35th and 13th. The whole column was supported by Abbott's guns and a handful of cavalry led by Captain Oldfield and Lieutenant Moye. Mohammed Akbar had drawn up his force, totalling nearly 6,000, in strict order of battle. The Jalalabad force was, however, initially and near-fatally separated as the 13th, under hot fire, struggled to capture a key small fort, but it was again the British artillery which provided the decisive turning point. They broke the rebel forces and, as they followed through at a quick pace, the 13th forced the rebels into the river 'which swollen and rapid, destroyed the greatest part of them'.

It had been a resounding victory. 'The whole of Akbar's camp fell into our hands', wrote Seaton: 'His guns, ammunition, standards and plunder – everything he had with him ... I was detached from the party to fire the tents and huts made of boughs and reeds. They were very numerous and the smoke proclaimed our victory to the whole valley.'[29] British leadership, discipline and the effective use of artillery – frequently a decisive factor in Britain's Afghan victories – had again won the day. The British sustained losses of only thirteen killed and seventy-one wounded, but suffered one grievous loss with the death of the 13th's commanding officer, Colonel Dennie, who was shot dead leading the assault on the fort.

The earlier arming of the garrison camp-followers had proved to be an excellent tactic, as their temporary guarding of the ramparts defences allowed most of the regular troops to take part in the offensive. The news of the victory was received with jubilation. Hundreds of miles south, on 30 April General Napier wrote: 'That noble fellow Sale has given Acbar Khan a thrashing at Jellalabad; it is one of the most brilliant things ever read of: with fourteen hundred men he attacked the 6,000 besieging him and totally defeated them.'[30] Nine days later, General Pollock's avenging army finally arrived to lift the siege. The joyful but frustrated mood of the besieged – who, in the end, had effectively saved themselves, was appropriately expressed with 'a sly bit of sarcasm' in the choice of tune to which the band of the 13th played in the 'relief': 'Yere O'er Lang A'coming'![31]

In fact, General Pollock's considerable delay had been largely unavoidable. Lieutenant Cummings of the 9th Foot recalled the good reasons for the delay in the relief of Jalalabad. Early on in the preparations, there had been deep fears of imminent mutiny. Following reports that the recently defeated Sikh regiments of Brigadier Wild's Brigade were resolved on refusing to proceed to Kabul, and were 'conferring' with elements of the recently arrived 33rd Native Infantry, General Pollock called a crisis meeting with the commanding officers of the regiments involved. When each officer staked their commission on their regiment's loyalty, Pollock's fears subsided. It had been a close-run thing. As Cummings put it: 'How precarious is the state of affairs when a spirit so deucedly is evinced?'[32]

Pollock had, in fact, only reached Peshawar on 5 February 1842, where he had to face the task of rebuilding the morale of Brigadier Wild's Brigade which had been literally prostrated by its recent setback and appalling levels of sickness. Forced to wait for reinforcements of cavalry and artillery, Pollock was unable to move for a further two months. This was despite the welcome arrival in support of Brigadier McCaskill's force, comprising the 9th Foot, the 26th Native Infantry, the 10th Bengal Cavalry and three guns.

Major-General Pollock's Campaign of Retribution

Major-General Pollock finally left Peshawar on 5 April 1842, and his march of twelve days was largely unopposed. Pollock's tactics were exemplary. He used three columns, deploying the right and left ahead, and the centre or main column only advanced against the enemy breastworks at the entrance of the Khyber Pass when the breastworks had been turned by the two flanking columns. 'The Khaibaris were beaten in every direction' and the fighting, fuelled by revenge, achieved unparalleled levels of savagery. Lieutenant Greenwood of the 31st Foot recalled how one group of 'Khyberee' raiders were shot 'and soon decapitated and the sepoys carried their heads into camp in triumph stuck on the points of their bayonets'. Among the headless corpses was a woman and, when Lieutenant Greenwood protested, a sepoy calmly replied, 'Sahib ... she must have been killed by mistake, but as for males, I have lost twelve brethren in this cursed Pass and I would bayonet a kyberee if a month old at his mother's breast!'[33]

Such actions set the tone for the savage and indiscriminate nature of the campaign which was to follow. A further two-month delay occurred at liberated Jalalabad, in part because of the continuing logistical and manpower crisis, but also because scores of Pollock's men had succumbed to dysentery in the searing heat of an Afghan summer in a camp besieged by myriads of flies. So severe was the epidemic that Sale's Brigade was evacuated to the cleaner air of Futtehabad, seventeen miles away. But it was, ultimately a 'camel crisis' which paralyzed Pollock's force. On 18 May Abbott wrote in his journal: 'We cannot advance because 9,000 camels are wanting and, far from getting any addition to our present stock, we are daily losing from ten to twelve by death.'[34] During July and August 1842, amidst the frustration caused by such delays, punitive expeditions, drawn from both Sale's Brigade and Pollock's units, were ordered out of disease-ridden Jalalabad to begin a cycle of revenge which remains controversial today. The aim was not just a short-term campaign of 'butcher and bolt' but a veritable scorched-earth policy, officially designed to cause maximum long-term damage to the economy of the region.

The Shinwari tribe were notorious tax defaulters under the failed Shah Shuja regime and leading participators in the attacks on Company forces during the occupation. Moreover, their chief, Sekunder Khan, had been one of the leading conspirators in the Kabul insurrection and was himself a close friend of the rebel paramount, Akbar Khan. This tribe's country bore the brunt of the British incursions. Three villages, Ali Bogan, Pesh Bolak and Goulai, were particularly identified for 'special treatment'. For six weeks the area was subjected to ferocious attacks by a column of 2,300 men 'exclusively drawn from the newly arrived troops' and led by Brigadier Monteith. At Ali Bogan, for instance, British troops, incensed by the discovery of plundered items from Elphinstone's destroyed column (notably parts of the 44th Regiment's uniforms), briefly ran amok. 'At Ali Boghan', confirmed one observer, 'our troops, infuriated by the sight of some plundered property, began to set fire to the village'.[35] The village was then, effectively put to the sword.

The scale of destruction reached the ears of the newly arrived Governor-General, Lord Ellenborough. His subsequent concerned inquiries engendered a rather belated, lame excuse from the vengeful Pollock. Whilst denying the charge of excesses he 'regretted' that the village was burnt. 'The destruction of Ali Boghan' Pollock claimed, 'was caused by one of those sudden outbursts of feeling against which, being wholly unexpected, no precautions were taken'. He claimed that the Brigadier concerned 'immediately took steps to prevent the occurrence of such scenes' and 'I heard of no more excesses'.[36]

In fact the accounts of eyewitnesses and the fate of other Afghan villages throw some doubt on Pollock's defence, although it was quite possible that he was out of touch with the ground-level activities of some of his commanders. Lieutenant Greenwood's account does, however, shed more light, not only on the scale of retribution but suggests that it was a common practice with tacit approval from above. His description of the fate of the village of Goulai, three miles from Pesh Bolak, alleged to have stolen most of Elphinstone's treasure, is revealing:

The people of that place were very penitent for their misconduct and, I believe, gave a sum of money to be let off. The tribes about Goulai, however, had all absconded leaving numberless forts and villages at our mercy. These we pulled down and utterly destroyed. Their wells ... were blown up with gunpowder and rendered useless. These people lived in great measure on dried mulberries, as the land would not produce sufficient corn for their consumption. There were beautiful 'topes' (woods) of mulberry trees around the forts. Every morning and evening two companies from each regiment were sent to cut them down. We found that by cutting rings through the bark into the heart of the tree it was as effectively destroyed as if cut down ... we became quite adept in the work of destruction and a greater scene of devastation was perhaps never beheld.[37]

He continued: 'The Goolai people had however, richly deserved it all.

They could expect no better treatment when the game was again in our hands.'

In his report, even 'political' Captain MacGregor accepted the scale of destruction of this 'flourishing little settlement', deliberately carried out when the 'summer harvest had just been collected ... three or four days delay would have enabled them to carry off their grain'. The aim was clearly a long-term collapse of the region's economy and, above all, it was portrayed as an example to other hostiles. 'The Goolai people', he asserted, 'were deserving of no mercy'. The amount of treasure they had plundered, 'viz 18,000 to 20,000 rupees was considerable. They had been very pertinacious in attacking Captain Ferris's cantonment ... and our troops at Jellalabad'.[38]

This work of destruction in the Shinwari Valley was prosecuted for some days and, on one momentous day, thirty-five forts were set ablaze. On 10 July 1842, Captain Abbott reported that in the valley of Kote: 'We have commenced un-roofing a few villages, and the sixteen day operation could, albeit on a far smaller scale, be likened to Sherman's famous "March through Georgia" during the American Civil War.' It was, MacGregor concluded, 'highly beneficial to British interest', especially as 'both men and cattle had entirely subsisted on the resources of the country'.[39]

Significantly, although Sekunder Khan was absent in Kabul, the whole of his family was systematically either dispersed or eliminated during the process of these operations. Not surprisingly, submission rapidly followed, with deputies sent to the British camp to beg for mercy. For the many dispossessed in the Shinwari Valley, the only prospect was now one of slow starvation or death from cold with the notorious Afghan winter less than three months away.

The policy of terror was not wholly indiscriminate – the poorer, considerably more loyal, Tajik villages were significantly spared *en route*, but the overall message was clear: future acts of defiance would be met by such terror tactics, amounting to total war. Major-General Pollock's own later dispatches show that he was more than aware of the scale of destruction and, by the end of July 1842, he duly reported to the Company authorities that, as a result of Brigadier Monteith's 'attack on the enemy in the Shinwarree Valley ... the loss sustained by the enemy must be considerable ... they were still burying their dead. The effect in the whole valley by such a complete defeat ... and the destruction of so many of their forts will be productive of the most beneficial effects'.[40] It was, indeed total war '*pour encourager les autres*'.

The bloodlust was only temporarily sated and Pollock's column finally left Jalalabad on 20 August 1842 to commence their tortuous march to Kabul, during which even greater acts of vengeance were to follow.

The retribution policy was not without its critics. Historian Gleig, reviewing one ferocious punitive operation launched by Captain Broadfoot and 300 men of the 35th Native Infantry against Akbar Khan's fort near Futtehabad, which resulted in its surrender and complete destruction, wrote:

> There followed a course of devastation, of which, though it may have been necessary for the purpose of striking terror elsewhere, we cannot, now that all angry feeling has subsided, read without regret ... every house was destroyed, every tree barked or cut down; after which, the detachment having collected a considerable spoil of bullocks, sheep and goats marched back to camp.[41]

But such protests were often recorded as much for reasons of practicality as morality. As Captain Backhouse observed:

> Punishment for the 'children of the sword' is a thing now only thought of but how is it to be effected? We are entirely dependent on the country for supplies and if the ryots [peasant villagers] bolt to the mountains we starve ... discipline will soon be at an end if anything like the slaughter of Affghans is permitted even for the shortest time. We hear that the troops coming up have already committed lots of murder and that no Affghan can come near to camp and that their discipline is suffering; some prisoners appear to have been butchered before the General's eyes, he having tried in vain to save them; but this is no doubt soon to be stopped. We must in great measure 'Bear and Forbear', not only for our character as a nation but for our safety as an Army. There is no need of discrimination between Guilty and Not Guilty; every man and perhaps most women and children are stained with our blood upon their heads.[42]

Nevertheless, while arguing for 'forbearance' to secure supplies and to allow the rebels time to 'bring in the offending chiefs', so as to 'let them know we are not blood thirsty but will not go unsatisfied', he further asserted, that any refusal would still justify an 'iron fist'. In such cases, Backhouse concluded the British should 'wait till the crops are ready for reaping, then suddenly, upon them and let loose the fire and the sword at the villages and forts'.[43]

As Pollock's forces, already weakened by sickness, evacuated Jalalabad on 20 August 1842, entering the grim passes still littered with the bones of their fallen comrades of the Kabul Brigade, any 'forbearance' was unlikely to prevail. On 3 September the advance party of the 1st Division arrived at Gandamak to be greeted by the grim detritus of the last stand of the 44th Foot. Captain Seaton was one of the first to climb the 'little conical hill of death'. He recalled:

> Some of the bodies were still recognisable and we found and buried that of an officer of my regiment who had been left behind at Cabool ... it was one of the most harrowing spectacles I ever beheld in my life; about sixty skeletons scattered on the hill, the officers plainly distinguishable by the long hair which still remained attached to their skulls.[44]

Lieutenant Greenwood's experience at Gandamak was even more heart-rending. As the British guns remained temporarily stuck below the hill he took the opportunity to climb to the summit. Here he recalled:

> The hill was very steep, covered with large masses of stone and diffi-cult of ascent. Had they possessed ammunition, they might have made a stand for some time on it. The top of the hill was thickly strewn with the bodies of the slain. Some were mere skeletons, while others were in better preservation. The hair was on their heads and their features were perfect, although discoloured. Their eyes had evidently been picked out by the birds of prey, which, wheeling in endless gyra-tions above my head, seemed to consider me an intruder on their domain. On turning the corner of a large rock where five or six bodies were lying in a heap together, the vulture, which had been banqueting upon them hopped carelessly away to a little distance, lazily flapping his huge wings, but too indolent to fly. He was evidently gorged with this horrid meal, and, as the foul bird gazed deliciously at me, I almost fancied him the genius of destruction gloating over his prey. I turned from the sickening sight with a sad heart but a stern determination to lend my best efforts to paying the Affghans the debt of revenge we owed them.[45]

Despite his earlier protestations, Major-General Pollock himself appears to have abandoned all restraint in a campaign of retribution now aimed specifi-cally at the 'treacherous' villages near the site of the Gandamak massacre. 'Koodee Khail has been destroyed by fire', he calmly informed Major-General Lumley, Adjutant-General of the Army. 'The fort and village of Mammoo Khail has also been destroyed by fire, and, before I quit this place, the trees to which much value and importance are attached will be cut down.'[46]

Dark revenge was again evident in the increasingly savage and barbarous nature of the fighting after Gandamak. On both sides, the principle of taking prisoners was now almost entirely ignored: bodies of both sexes, alive or dead, were mutilated, especially by the British sepoy regiments, enraged at the sight of the corpses of their own massacred colleagues littering the passes to Kabul. One morbid discovery by Captain Seaton at Seibaba Tower, on the road between Jugduluck and Kuttar Sung, 'the horror of which I shall never forget', apparently excited a new wave of revenge. Seaton described the horrific scene:

> A mile beyond our camp was a small round tower about thirty feet high and twenty feet in diameter. The entrance to one room in the tower was by a doorway ten feet above the ground, with earthen steps up to it. The whole of the room was filled with skeletons and decaying bodies, up to the very roof, and there was a mound of them outside, halfway up the door, extending to a distance of twenty six or twenty five feet from the wall, and completely covering the steps. It was a ghastly sight. These were the remains of the poor fugitives ... stripped naked by the Affghans and left to perish in the bitter cold. They appeared to have crept in here for shelter, the last comers treading under and suffocating those who had preceded them, and, then, throwing out their bodies only to be themselves served in the same way, trampled upon, suffocated and thrown out by those that followed.[47]

Further retribution was soon forthcoming The British sepoys relished taking a special form of revenge when encountering the bodies of Afghan insurgents: 'They would invariably (if not prevented) put a little grass on the breast and set it on fire, so as to scorch the body, mahomedans believing that the souls of men whose bodies are burnt descend to hell – "Son of a burnt father", is a well known common term of abuse.'[48] As Pollock's column proceeded via Sourkab to the Jagdalak Pass, numerous caves were encountered which 'contained the bodies of Hindoostani people recently murdered ... suffice to say, we passed skeletons thrown into heaps of eighty and a hundred'. The scale of savage reprisal mounted proportionally as each new horror was discovered and the 'cruelties practised on the wounded' as well as the 'insults heaped on the dead', led both sides to take extraordinary protective measures. The British now regularly buried their dead at night inside their tents and used horses to trample the ground to prevent discovery and mutilation of the corpses, while the Afghans themselves made 'strenuous and persevering efforts to carry off their dead and wounded'.[49] Even Afghan children were not spared in the frenzied bloodlust which characterized Pollock's advance on Kabul. Lieutenant Greenwood recalled one incident which convinced him of the existence of 'a ferocity about the Affghans which they seem to imbibe with their mothers' milk'. He recounted the experience of one comrade in the 9th Foot:

> In storming one of the heights, a colour sergeant was killed, and for some cause or other his body was left where it fell. A soldier of the same corps, happening to pass by the spot some time after, saw a Khyberee boy apparently about six years of age with a large knife, which his puny arm had scarcely sufficient strength to wield, engaged in an attempt to hack off the head of the dead sergeant. The young urchin was so completely absorbed in his savage task, that he heeded not the approach of the soldier, who coolly took him up on his bayonet, and threw him over the cliff.[50]

As they fought their way through the Khurd-Kabul Pass, Pollock's troops faced a fresh ordeal. The bodies of an estimated 3,000 members of Elphinstone's doomed force, 'lay in heaps of fifties and hundreds' with 'our gun wheels passing over and crushing the skulls and other bones of our late comrades at almost every yard for three, four or five miles'.[51] Lieutenant Greenwood again remembered this part of the march with special horror: 'Elphinstone's army had suffered most dreadfully here and the dead lay in heaps. They seemed, indeed, in some places to have been mowed down by whole battalions. They have been preserved in the snow and their ghastly faces, often apparently turned towards us, seem to call upon their fellow countrymen to revenge their fate.'[52]

After numerous murderous skirmishes in which the 'little Ghourkees' distinguished themselves, the final showdown with Akbar Khan's 16,000-strong army took place at Huft Kotal. The rebel forces, after attacking the British rearguard in the Tezin Valley and blocking the British advance by stone *sangars*, tried to cut their main body in two. Pollock, however, countered by breaking his force into small bodies, driving the Afghan rebels through the heights and into the waiting arms of the British Dragoons, while his artillery pounded the stone barriers to pieces. The battle soon turned into a complete rout, the 'Ghookchas and sepoys, infuriated by earlier memories of the massacre site', mercilessly driving and bayoneting their Ghilzai assailants 'from crag to crag' right up to the 8,000-foot high summits of Huft Kotal while the British cavalry mercilessly cut down the fugitives in the valley below.[53] No quarter had been given. Akbar Khan fled the field towards Kohistan. The British had lost a mere 32 killed; the Afghans over 1,000 dead.

After this crushing victory, the column passed through, largely unmolested, to Butkhak and on 16 September 1842 – a momentous day – encamped on the old British racecourse before Kabul. On the evening of that day, after receiving the submission of numerous Afghan chiefs and notables, General Pollock, accompanied by a strong escort, proceeded into the city 'and the British flag, from which all stains of dishonour had been washed out by this brilliant campaign, was once more hoisted on the Bala Hissar, amid the cheers of the troops and under a royal salute'.[54]

Major-General Nott's Campaign of Retribution

For the other main 'avenging army', commanded by Major-General Nott, the march to Kabul from his base in Kandahar had also been fraught with difficulty. He, like Pollock, faced political interference from above as the initially cautious new Governor-General, Lord Ellenborough opted for an immediate retreat back to Peshawar. Like Pollock, Nott vehemently opposed such a defeatist strategy. He had a track record in this respect. As we have seen, since his arrival in Afghanistan in 1839, he had sternly opposed any interference by the 'politicals' in military matters, a policy which undoubtedly had cost him promotion during the changeover of command in November 1840. As the crisis in Kabul reached a climax in December 1841, he had continued to ignore urgent letters from Elphinstone and Pottinger (successor to the murdered MacNaghten), to retire as laid down under the ill-fated treaty terms. Thus on 25 February 1842, for instance, General Nott informed the Indian Government:

> The lamented disasters which have occurred at Caubul, the murder of the British Envoy and Minister and the reported fate of the force under Major General Elphinstone retiring under the supposed safeguard of a debated and sacred convention, are so unheard of and atrocious in nature, as to induce me to conceive that the instructions of the government are no longer applicable ... I shall not therefore think of acting upon them.[55]

Meanwhile, Nott had faced equally severe military challenges on his own doorstep in Kandahar. In the words of one Bengal officer: 'The neighbouring chiefs were only awaiting a favourable opportunity of following the example of their northern allies and it soon became evident that the

Candahar force would have to struggle for its existence against innumerable foes.'[56] In February 1842, Nott confessed to having only five months' reserve supply of grain, and lamented his ability to hold out with only 'a little aid from Scinde ... at present we are in want of Cavalry, the Candahar Treasury is exhausted, and the troops are three months in arrears; we have but a small quantity of musket ammunition and scarcely any medicine for the sick'.[57] Nott's first major challenge at Kandahar was a mutiny among the hitherto loyal *Jaubal* or Afghan cavalrymen in the pay of Shah Shuja. It was an ominous repeat of the Gandamak mutiny, which had erupted during Brigadier Sale's advance to Jalalabad in November 1841. Fortunately, the loyalty of these troops had already been suspected and, in December 1841, the whole unit had been moved from Kandahar garrison to Girishk, where it was hoped it would do less mischief. Within hours, however, the unit duly mutinied, murdered its commander, Lieutenant Golding and mortally wounded Lieutenant Patten, the assistant political agent. The mutineers promptly fled to join the insurgents. Nott's response was decisive and ferocious. Captain Christie's Horse were immediately dispatched from Kandahar and, after a ten-mile pursuit, overtook the mutineers. After a desperate skirmish the mutineers were crushed, with the head of the ringleader, Keunder Khan, brought back in triumph.

Militarily, however, this represented a drop in the ocean. Within days, Prince Sufter Jang (third son of Shah Shuja) had defected from Kandahar and joined the Durrani rebels now amassing in the countryside. Nott took the offensive, again in stark contrast to his compatriots in the Kabul garrison, and, on 12 January 1842, met and dispersed the rebel forces at a village called Kaleshukh. It was a short-lived victory. There followed a series of skirmishes as the outnumbered Nott was steadily surrounded in Kandahar. By the start of March 1842, the increasing boldness of the enemy impelled Nott to take some offensive action. However, before departing Kandahar with 7,000 troops, he took the precaution to round up 1,000 suspected Afghan townspeople, a task in which he was ably assisted by the political agent Major Rawlinson, which again illustrated the new co-operation between 'politicals' and the military. Drawn out up to fifty miles from the garrison, however, Nott's force was briefly outflanked by the rebels, who launched a ferocious attack on Kandahar to his rear. The weakened 2,000-strong garrison of Kandahar, valiantly led by Major Lane, now faced a relentless assault and the old wooden Herat Gate was soon set alight. A Bengal Army officer recalled the desperate fight that ensued as both sides fought heroically: 'The enemy rushed forward with frantic violence yelling in a most horrific manner and, regardless of the galling fire from the ramparts ... tore down the burning fragments of the gate, scrambling over a barrier and grain bags piled inside; and several of the boldest actually gained an entrance, but were instantly shot.'[58]

After a struggle lasting several hours the enemy retreated, leaving fifty dead in or near the gateway.

A thwarted and outflanked Nott again revealed the ruthless, uncompromising side of his character when he returned to Kandahar only to reprimand his heroic garrison for 'want of vigilance'. This ungenerous and incredible response was 'loudly condemned by the whole force' and, one horrified one officer postulated, 'will ever remain a blot on the military reputation of General Nott'.[59] But it was a ruthlessness sorely needed as Nott's command faced further severe military challenges. In March 1842, a major setback occurred as the key British outpost at Ghazni finally surrendered. Held by the 450-man garrison of the 27th Native Infantry under Colonel Palmer, the city's defences had, however, been left in considerable disorder after its glorious capture in 1839. With insufficient supplies of water and no artillery support the over-extended town defences had been overwhelmed on 20 November 1841, forcing the garrison to retreat to the main fortress. Here, the under-equipped sepoys were progressively crippled by frostbite and lack of food and, by mid-January 1842, a truce had been arranged by Colonel Palmer. The surrender was delayed until 6 March 1842 and, as with their compatriots in Kabul, the day soon turned into a partial massacre. The garrison was tricked into leaving the citadel for nearby defenceless dwellings where, during a meal break, it was apparently treacherously and ferociously attacked by fanatical *Ghazis*. Only a few escaped and ten surviving British officers were held as hostages.[60]

The shock of this loss was matched by another setback which occurred to Nott's projected reinforcements advancing along the road from Quetta to Kandahar. Major-General England's relief force, comprising elements of Her Majesty's 41st Regiment, the 6th, 20th and 25th Bombay Native Infantry and several batteries of horse artillery, left Quetta at less than full strength, ostensibly to secure the country for forage. It was, arguably, a high-risk strategy. Thirty-one miles east of Quetta, England's force was repulsed at Haikalzai by the enemy and, on 28 March 1842, with the loss of one hundred killed and wounded, England scuttled back to Quetta declaring it almost impracticable to force the Khojak Pass. Blame was subsequently laid and, on this occasion, probably unfairly, on the local 'political', a certain Lieutenant Hamersly for not warning Major-General England of enemy fortifications 'which had been worked at for two months'.[61] In the ensuing row Major Outram, another more senior 'political', was sacked by Governor-General Ellenborough for defending Hamersly, although it is likely this represented yet another opportunity to further dismantle Auckland's now deeply discredited political system. An already sick Hamersly died soon afterwards, his doctors opining that 'he was killed by the bad treatment received'. He was, seemingly, a tragic scapegoat and even General Napier – no great friend of the' politicals' – recognized it as simply a matter of military incompetence. He observed:

> General England, knowing he was to be encountered, quitted a fortified town when nothing called on him to do so, and, when a part of his force was defeated, did not bring the whole into action.... He marched out with half his force, he attacked with half of that half force and did not bring up the remainder in support: this was terrible work.[62]

General Nott agreed and, in contrast to Elphinstone, showed his decisiveness and mettle by ordering England to immediately restart from Quetta whilst adding, sarcastically that, 'in all military operations difficulties were to be expected which it was the duty of a commander to overcome'.[63] On a second attempt, the passage was effected by England's subordinate, Colonel Wymer, commanding the 2nd, 16th and 38th Native Infantry and a troop of horse artillery and some cavalry: The final assault on the heights proved so steep that the sepoys were even forced to change from their European pantaloons to traditional *dhotis*. Once they had linked up with a chastened England's forces, the combined brigades reached Kandahar on 10 May, thereby placing nearly 12,000 extra men, together with essential treasure, ammunition and carriage, at the disposal of General Nott. These valuable reinforcements now allowed Nott to undertake a major offensive to relieve the beleaguered British garrison of Kalat-i-Ghilzai, which comprised detachments of the 43rd Native Infantry, the Shah's 3rd Infantry and forty European artillerymen, all commanded by Captain Craigie. Colonel Wymer's Brigade was again dispatched and successfully relieved the outnumbered garrison on 26 May 1842, just after it had survived a massive three-pronged Ghilzai attack on 20 May. The defences were razed and the garrison safely evacuated back to Kandahar, where it arrived on 7 June 1842.

In Wymer's absence, and with these substantial reinforcements, Nott was also now in a position to take the offensive again. On 29 May 1842 he left Kandahar with barely 2,000 men and inflicted an easy, decisive defeat on the besieging 10,000-strong Durrani Army. His triumphant dispatch home revealed his renewed determination to follow it up with a drive on Kabul: 'How I should like to go to Caubul! It is wonderful that the people in Hindostan should be so panic-struck; and they seem to believe that our sepoys cannot stand the Afghans. Now, I am quite sure, I should like to try it tomorrow, that 5,000 Bengal sepoys would lick 25,000 Afghans![64]

The political tide was also turning; defector Shuja's son, Prince Sufter Jang, on hearing news of the British victory of 29 May, swiftly changed sides again and, on 18 June 1842, Nott, on the advice of his 'political', Major Rawlinson, reluctantly accepted the prince's submission. Submission of other Durrani rebel chiefs soon followed.

At higher levels, the political tide had also been turning since February 1842. In his 'retreat policy' the new Governor-General, Lord Ellenborough, had become increasingly isolated and frustrated. From March to July 1842 his orders were not only, as we have seen, stonewalled by his two recalcitrant Major-Generals, Nott and Pollock, but openly challenged by leading politicians and military figures at home. The foremost if somewhat benign critic was the ageing former Sepoy-General Lord Wellington himself. On 31 March 1842, for instance, he firmly reminded Lord Ellenborough that British prestige had received a serious reverse and that severe retribution, if only short-term, was essential as:

From the effect of the Kabul disaster, we shall not recover for some time. There is not a Moslem heart from Pekin to Constantinople which will not vibrate when reflecting upon the fact that European ladies and other females attached to the troops of Cabul were made over to the tender mercies of the Moslem chief, who had with his own hand, murdered Sir William MacNaghten, the representative of the British government at the Court of the Sovereign of Afghanistan. It is impossible that that fact should not produce a moral effect injurious to British influence and power throughout ... Asia, and particularly among the Moslem population of the British dominions in the Peninsula of India and the Dependences thereof.... it is impossible to impress upon you too strongly the notion of the importance of the restoration of our reputation in the East. Our enemies in France, the United States, and wherever found are now rejoicing in Triumph upon our Disasters and Degradation ... you will teach them that their triumph is premature.[65]

Ellenborough's 'retribution and retreat' dispatch, sent to both Nott and Pollock on 23 July 1842, confirmed his effective volte-face, although one still cleverly disguised to reflect his original policy of withdrawal:

The object of the combined march of your army and Major General Nott's upon Caboul will be to exhibit our strength there where we suffered defeat to inflict just, but not vindictive retribution upon the Affghans and to recover the guns and colours as well as the prisoners lost by our army ... giving every proof of British power which is not inconsistent with the usages of war and the dictates of British humanity. But you will never forget that after exhibiting that power you are ... to obey the positive orders of your government and to withdraw your army from Afghanistan.[66]

It was indeed a pragmatic reversal of policy but probably not, in the words of the more prejudiced historian Kaye, a 'masterpiece of Jesuitical cunning'.[67] Nott's advance was to more than reflect its guiding *modus operandi*. As with Pollock, however, his tactics, officially or unofficially, were soon to be tainted with inconsistency with Ellenborough's dictum of observing both the 'usages of war and dictates of British humanity'. Nott left Kandahar on 8 August 1842 amidst a veil of secrecy and in conditions of extreme heat, ranging from '111 to 116 degrees in our tents'. For logistical reasons, he split his force into two, with Brigadier England's column of native artillery and horse sent back to Sind with orders to withdraw the garrisons of Shalkot and Kala Abdullah on his way. It was indeed to be a 'lean and mean' expedition with the minimum of baggage, and fortified by his finest Indian sepoy regiments – the 2nd, 16th, 38th, 42nd and 63rd Bengal Native Infantry – with two experienced British regular regiments, Her Majesty's 40th and 41st Artillery, deployed in support. The latter, so crucial to winning victories against the Afghan enemy, also included one company of Bengal artillery (18-pounder guns), one 9-pounder field battery, one troop of the Shah's Horse Artillery and one troop of the Bombay European Horse Artillery. Cavalry support included the 3rd Bombay Light Cavalry and Haldane's and Christie's Horse. The force carried provisions for forty days but still required 10,000 public and private camels besides bullocks, asses, mules and *'tattoes'* (ponies). Camp-followers were estimated at double the number of the fighting men. Army Chaplain Isaac Allen vividly recalled the oppressive heat, dust and darkness of the first night's departure:

I got entangled amongst the baggage cattle, was nearly smothered in dust and lost a favourite terrier, which I never recovered. As daylight appeared and I got to the head of the column, the scene became very interesting; the ground was pretty undulated, and the waving line of red uniforms, the country, guns, and thousands of camels passing through it, was a striking contrast to the solitude around, and to the dark, rocky hills rising on each side.[68]

For the first three weeks, Nott's column progressed steadily, with little interruption. On 15 August 1842, sixteen miles from Teere-Un-Daz, the column passed the scene of Wyman's successful defensive action of May 1841, where a food convoy had been attacked by 3,000 Afghans, the spot 'marked by a small hill ... with three graves of the warriors in its immediate vicinity'. The column was soon joined by sepoy survivors of the earlier Ghazni surrender 'exceedingly thin and ragged' who, because of their caste were, nevertheless, to the horror of Padré Allen 'driven away as dogs' by higher-caste regiments. The recently demolished fences of Kalat were passed, a veritable 'heap of ruins', and soon Ghilzai raiders increased their attacks on stragglers notably 'two unfortunate camel-men, straying beyond their guard ... their throats cut by these wretches, who at the same time were bringing large quantities of grain and bhoosa into camp, professing friendship, attaining guards for the protection of their villages and quietly pocketing our rupees'.[69] Such behaviour could only excite further desires for revenge.

At Oba on Sunday 28 August 1842, an opportunity for vengeance presented itself as the British column launched a punitive drive against Ghilzai marauders who had murdered several grass-cutters. Unfortunately, the episode turned out to be an ambush, with the British cavalry, notably the 3rd Bombay Light Cavalry, being badly mauled by several hundred Afghan horse and foot concealed behind a hill. The losses were heavy with thirty-seven dead, including three captains. This mini-disaster seems to have triggered off a pattern of retribution which continued all the way to Kabul. A nearby fort was pinpointed for a punitive raid and, after a parley conducted by Nott himself, a volley of matchlock balls directed by the Afghan rebels at the British negotiating party decided its terrible fate. Contrary to Governor-General Ellenborough's directives, no male prisoners were taken in the ensuing assault and many of the defenders were apparently burnt alive. Wholesale plunder also took place, during which Nott and his senior officers, located, 'very near the walls apparently' did little to restrain. This 'painful spectacle' was observed and vividly recorded by a horrified Padré Allen:

Every door was forced, every man that could be found was slaughtered, they were pursued from yard to yard, from tower to tower and very few escaped. A crowd of wretched women and children were turned out and one or two wounded in the mêlée. I never saw more squalid and miserable objects. One door, which they refused to open upon summons, was blown in by a six-pounder and every soul bayoneted.... Destruction was going on in every form – dead bodies were lying here and there – sepoys and followers were dragging out sheep, goats, oxen and goods ... European and native soldiers were breaking open doors ... every now and again the discharge of a firelock proclaimed the discovery of a concealed victim, while the curling blue smoke and crackling sound from the buildings indicated that the fire was destined to devour what the sword had spared.[70]

This ferocious example of the British 'fire and sword' policy was curiously but perhaps significantly omitted from official accounts and dispatches. One Bengal officer merely referred to a fort 'which was surrounded and destroyed but only a few women and children were found inside'! By contrast, Padré Allen estimated that eighty to a hundred enemy were killed, whilst unknown numbers had 'perished in the flames'.

A greater reckoning was to be had a few days later on 30 August 1842, at Karabagh near Goyain, where an 'immense body' of 12,000 Afghan rebels confronted Nott's freshly blooded forces. As Nott's men attacked the fort, the enemy led by Shumshoodeen (the Ghilzai chief) boldly advanced, opening a galling fire from their two light guns and innumerable matchlocks. In response, the British artillery under Captain Anderson galloped to the front, checking their advance. One enemy gun was soon overrun and captured. On the sounding of the advance, the Light Infantry advanced at a brisk pace, clearing and crowning the heights, while the remaining infantry columns swept the valleys, completing the victory. The cavalry brutally mopped up, the Shah's Horse cutting down fifty enemy in the capture of the second gun. Major-General Nott particularly noted the 'admirably-served' enemy guns, which were turned on their owners. Amongst the enemy killed were some deserters of the British 27th Native Infantry from surrendered Ghazni, who predictably 'fought to the death' with 'peculiar ferocity' and whose skill in manning the captured British artillery trains undoubtedly accounted for the earlier accuracy and intensity of enemy fire. The British lost only one killed and twenty-seven wounded. It was a decisive victory; the enemy casualties probably reaching into the hundreds. Alongside the enemy guns were also found 4,000 rounds of the Honourable Company's ball cartridges which had been looted from the surrendered Ghazni garrison.

The aftermath witnessed yet more scenes of devastation which again proved 'melancholy and distressing' to Padré Allen. On this occasion, however, it was British sepoys, camp-followers and, in particular, Hazara auxiliaries, who perpetrated most of the excesses. From Makoor onwards Nott's force had been joined by thousands of vengeful Hazara tribesmen, sworn enemies of the Ghilzais and anxious to become new allies of the British. One Bengal officer reported their rampaging activities:

> On entering the valley of Makoor, the camp was joined by a large body of Hazarees, a tribe inhabiting the enjoining mountains. This singular race of people had always shown a friendly disposition towards us, claiming kindred with Europeans as descendants of Japheth. They marched as far as Ghuznee with General Nott, destroying numerous forts and villages on the route, having blood-feuds with the inhabitants.... They are a hardy and warlike people, strongly attached to their native hills which they never leave unless to punish aggression, which, on this occasion, was done effectually with fire and sword, a devastation which was unjustly attributed to our troops.[71]

What Nott's Hazara allies failed to plunder, the British sepoys and Indian followers soon made up for. When Goyain Fort was finally taken on 31 August 1842, more

> melancholy and distressing ... scenes of devastation were witnessed. Much spoil was taken in it; grain and forage and many articles ... captured at Ghuznee – officers' boots with brass spurs, camp bedsteads, swords etc. The sepoys and followers supplied themselves abundantly with firewood from the roofs and doors of this fort ... and the more distant ones were set on fire.[72]

The trail of destruction continued well beyond Goyain, the 'picturesque' scene of the significantly untouched friendly Hazara forts being starkly contrasted 'on the right' with 'the blazing and smoking forts of the Ghilgies'.[73] There were some attempts to limit Hazara depredations. One particularly rapacious Hazara band, summoned before 'political' Major Rawlinson for questioning, justified their attacks by the excessive taxes demanded by their former Ghilzai masters and claimed to be 'astonished that we had not anticipated them by dispersing our troops over the country for the same purpose'! The tension, the officer affirmed, 'was partly religious – Hazarees were predominantly Shias; and their hated Afghan enemies predominantly Sunni – and partly cultural, the Hazarees spoke Persian'.[74]

As Nott's force arrived before the 'far-famed' citadel of Ghazni, a stiff fight was anticipated. Much apprehension was expressed over the potential power and range of the enemy's famed 60-pounder gun, the 'Zubber Jung'.

Padré Allen recorded the terror inspired when only a few rounds from this gun landed near the 41st Foot's mess tent. Nearby, a large party of officers collected in front of the general's tent to view one unexploded shell, comprising an 'immense mass of hammered iron, weighing above fifty pounds'.[75] The Afghan gunners were, however, soon dispersed by the far more accurate reply of the two British 9-pounders in camp. As the British prepared for a full assault against a 'city full of men' and 'a range of mountains covered by heavy bodies of Cavalry and infantry', morale was lifted by the recovery of 327 sepoys of the 27th Native Infantry, 'some in a wretched state of destitution, fearfully emaciated and almost naked',[76] who had been sold into slavery and dispersed into villages thirty and forty miles around Ghazni after its surrender. Even more uplifting was the later realization that the city had, in fact, been largely evacuated; the enemy apparently taking fright at the sight of the erection of the British 18-pounder gun of 'C' Battery.

The scene was now set for the first great act of British retribution by Nott's 'Kandahar column'. Nott immediately gave orders for the complete destruction of the walls and citadels of Ghazni, an act duly executed by the placing of fourteen mines under the walls by an engineer's demolition party commanded by a Major E. Sanders. After two days of continuous explosions, he routinely reported, on 9 September 1842, 'The gateways of the town and citadel and the roofs of the principal buildings have been fired and are still burning.'[77] All the captured guns, including the famed Zubber Jung were 'burst'. The widespread burnings were an indiscriminate act, again carried out on the eve of an Afghan winter, but no doubt fuelled by the discovery of many poignant messages and relics left by the previously surrendered British garrison. Desperate messages, for instance, were found scrawled on the walls of the officer's room of incarceration, confirming both Afghan treachery and the subsequent torture of the garrison commander Colonel Palmer. Padré Allen was one of the many officers who personally surveyed the desolate scene, the treatment of Colonel Palmer and his men, 'marked by every species of insolence and oppression'. [78] Copies of the treaties so brutally betrayed by the Afghan rebels were even discovered secreted in a beam of the officer's prison.

The cycle of revenge continued relentlessly with both British troops and followers stripping local roofs for firewood – although further allegations of 'the destruction of orchards of fruit trees here and elsewhere' were, on this occasion denied by at least one observer on the basis that 'we had scarcely time and men for the destruction of military defences much less for the uprooting of hundreds of orchards, extending over miles of country',[79] but it is likely that, based on previous records of depredations, some destruction did occur, if only carried out by the many *badmashes* attached to the British column.

Brigadier-General Nott, this time on the direction of the Governor-General, also took the opportunity for a political and cultural humiliation of the enemy by removing, on an 18-pounder gun-carriage, the nearby prized gates of the sacred Hindu temple of Somnath. It was intended as a major 'cultural punishment'; 'political' Major Rawlinson recalled the deep distress of local fakirs or priests: 'These guardians of the tent, when they perceived our object, returned to the corner of the tent and wept bitterly; and, when the removal was effected, they again prostrated themselves before the shrine and uttered loud lamentations.'[80]

Leaving Ghazni a 'desolate ruin', the column slowly moved further towards Kabul passing, at Sidabad Fort, the melancholy scene of yet another 1841 defeat. Here Captain Woodburn and 150 sepoys had been betrayed and slaughtered after 'a promise of protection' and, amongst relics discovered in the fort, was Woodburn's will and even a complimentary letter from the equally doomed British Envoy, MacNaghten. The fort was duly destroyed and the usual cycle of destruction recommenced. There were now, however, worrying signs that this official (or, often unofficial) policy of relentless retribution was becoming politically counterproductive. Padré Allen observed: 'The enemy appear to be increasing in numbers ... this is not to be wondered at for the burning and destruction of their forts would of course drive them into the field, partly for necessity and partly to seek revenge.'[81]

For other Afghan groups, however, it was an appropriate time to pay homage to, or renew alliances with, the advancing, powerful, and vengeful British columns. Several-score pro-British Quizilbash chiefs and horsemen duly arrived to swear allegiance and 'from this we concluded that the successes of General Pollock's march from Gandamak were pretty certain'. Their previous record of opportunism during the Kabul crisis was, however, also duly noted by Padré Allen: 'Whenever the tide of prosperity turns they turn with it and they are very acute in distinguishing the marks of its ebb and flow.'[82]

Others, this time suspected rebel chiefs, also hurriedly petitioned for protection but were given short shrift. At Benir Badam on 13 September and at Maidan the following day, Nott faced his last serious challenges before entering Kabul. At these places Nott was confronted by an estimated 12,000 Afghan rebels, led principally by Shumshoodeen and Sultan Jan. They occupied a succession of strong mountain passes directly blocking his road. The British artillery, supported by the light infantry companies, soon 'dislodged them in gallant style' incurring only minor casualties[83]. In this action the 40th Foot under Captain Ferdinand White particularly distinguished themselves by securing the heights.

Between Maidan and Kabul, opportunities were taken to further despoil and dispossess the rural inhabitants. Again there was little evidence of direct orders to pillage, but some circumstantial evidence of a blind eye to such activities, which were on such a scale as to be scarcely unavoidable. Thus, at one 'sequestrated valley' lying in 'perfect stillness and beauty', some contingents of sepoys and camp-followers appeared to have again run amok. Padré Allen recalled:

> While I gaze the troops of various arms rushed down the steep, the fort was secured, the heights ... were carried by the light companies of the native infantry amidst the rattle of musketry and the roar of artillery; and, in the course of two or three hours, the crops on every side, ripe and unripe, were cut down; the villages wrapped in volumes of smoke and flame rising amidst and curling over the trees. The camp-followers on all sides were bringing in the spoil, timber from the houses for fuel and grass and forage for the cattle; and the growing prosperity of years was desolated in less than a day. Such are the horrors of war![84]

On 17 September 1842, Nott at last joined up with Major-General Pollock's column and halted and bivouacked his troops on a beautiful plain barely five miles west of Kabul. Only two priorities remained for the two avenging British columns, now united at Kabul. The first imperative was to secure the release of the British prisoners, particularly the women and children, taken during the retreat from Kabul. The second priority was to carry out one final and long-lasting act of revenge against the city of Kabul, commonly regarded as the centre of rebel activity.

The Fate of the Kabul Prisoners

After their initial ordeal in the snow-covered passes, the fate of the European prisoners taken into custody by Akbar Khan during the terrible retreat had significantly improved. Although accommodation was crowded and uncomfortable, the main threat emanated not from their Afghan captors but from legions of fleas which they amusingly called 'light cavalry', and lice, which they termed 'the infantry'!

The captors spent their first three months from January to March 1842 at the rebel stronghold of Badibad in the Lughman district, but only after further horrors had greeted them as they criss-crossed the scene of the disaster on the way to this winter prison. At one point 'they passed some 200 dead bodies, many of them European; the whole naked and covered with large naked wounds'.[85] Elsewhere they passed numerous doomed 'hindustani refugees sheltering in caves and stripped of all they possessed'. Most remained paralyzed with cold but a 'few crawled no more than a few yards being frost bitten in the feet'. Astonishingly, here also prisoner Lieutenant Johnson suddenly espied 'two of his servants; the one had his hands and feet frost bitten ... and a fearful cut across one hand and a musket ball in his stomach; the other had his right arm completely cut to the bone'. Both were 'utterly destitute of covering and had not tasted food for five days'.[86]

Nevertheless, these terrible journeys were made more bearable by acts of kindness by Akbar Khan, which throws doubt on the wholly malevolent image portrayed of him by so many vengeful commentators after the war. 'The chiefs gave us every assistance', Lady Sale reported. 'Mohammed Akbar Khan carried Mrs Wallah over behind him on his own horse.'[87]

The party of around fifty men, women and children (predominantly officers and their wives) were housed eventually in six spacious rooms with dull but adequate meals (invariably mutton stew prepared by Afghan cooks!). The captives were allowed to receive and send mail, including boxes from General Sale, although this privilege was put in jeopardy by one abortive attempt by Captain Messenger and Major Pottinger to send a 'private cossid' [courier]. Soon they were joined by survivors of the Gandamak final stand and Ghazni massacres, including Sergeant-Major Lissant, who was later to be released to Jalalabad to negotiate.

Nevertheless, the imprisonment was frequently marked by great blows to morale. News of the Gandamak massacre and false news of the fall of Jalalabad gravely depressed them, as did the death of disgraced General Elphinstone at Tezeen on 23 April 1842: 'A happy release for him ... from suffering of mind and body. Deeply he felt his humiliation and bitterly regretted the day when he resigned the home-borne pleasures of his native land, to hazard the reputation of his native land and of a proud name in a climate and station for which he was physically unfit.'[88]

Other much-lamented deaths followed, mainly from dysentery and typhus fever and, on 7 August, Captain John Connolly, brother of the celebrated Arthur Connolly (so tragically murdered in Bokhara) breathed his last. By happier contrast, several children were safely born into captivity, including two little girls to the recently widowed Mrs Trevor.

The morale of the ladies certainly suffered when they were systematically robbed of their jewels and medicines, although the stoic Lady Sale expressed the hope that the Afghan rebels might consume one particular perfume bottle which was filled with nitric acid and caustic soda![89] Such emotional strains appear to have cost at least one psychological breakdown and Lady Sale recorded how one European lady, Mrs Wade, wife of a British sergeant even 'changed her attire, threw off the European dress and adopted the costume of the Musselmans [and] ... consorted with the Nazir of our inveterate enemy, Mohammed Shah Khan, and gave information of some plans made by the men for their escape which nearly caused them to have their throats cut'.[90]

Just as the prisoners were at their lowest point, news of Pollock's and Nott's victories filtered in and, after an abortive attempt to transfer them to Bamian under a 400-strong Afghan escort, Major Pottinger was finally able to bribe their captor Salah Muhammed with 200,000 rupees to instigate negotiations for their release. On 25 August 1842 the captives were finally moved towards Kabul and freedom.

Back in the British cantonments in Kabul, a rescue party of 600 allied and, significantly, Qizilbash horsemen under Colonel Sir Richmond Shakespear had already been dispatched to meet and secure the captives, all 'received with one exception, with heartfelt pleasure'. The one exception was the ever-cantankerous Brigadier Shelton who was apparently furious with Shakespear for not addressing him first as the 'senior military man'![91]

When the prisoners arrived at the British camp at Kabul, 'great was the rejoicing as well may be conceived'.[92] However, their rescue was not achieved without some tension occurring between the two British Major-Generals. Both armies were exhausted by their respective marches and when in mid-September, Major-General Pollock, Nott's senior, directed Nott to send a brigade in support of Shakespear's cavalry expedition, he swiftly demurred. On 17 September, General Nott explained his cogent reasons, citing the exhausting 130-mile march to Kabul, a continuous march of six months, resulting in the loss of twenty-nine camels in one day. He was 'short of supplies ... had little or no money' and 'many sick and wounded'. Referring directly to Elphinstone's disastrous experience, Nott also strongly warned against 'the system of sending out detachments' for which 'disaster and ruin will follow'.[93]

Fortunately, his protest was accepted, Pollock generously leaving it 'entirely to your discretion to detach a brigade and as you seem to think it unadvisable it need not be done'.[94] In the event, Brigadier Sale's Brigade was sent instead in support of Shakespear's expedition. While a success, Nott's fears had starkly revealed the precarious nature of British power even at this triumphant juncture.

Final Retribution: the Sack of Kabul and Istalif

One overriding natural obstacle now precluded any delay in implementing the second objective of the expedition: the collective punishment of the Afghan rebels. The dreaded Afghan winter was rapidly closing in and Nott and Pollock now hurried to complete this far more controversial aspect of their mission. Two symbolic targets for wholesale destruction were quickly identified. One was the nearby fortress town of Istalif, which harboured one of the principal rebels, Aminullah Khan – but tragically also hundreds of frightened, innocent civilian refugees who had fled from Kabul in the wake of the British advance. The second principal target was the 'chouk' or Great Bazaar of Kabul, one of the architectural masterpieces of Central Asia, but one in which the heads and trunks of both MacNaghten and Burnes had been so outrageously displayed.

Major-General McCaskill's Brigade was accordingly readied for the punitive expedition against the alleged 'impregnable' fortress of Istalif. But, even before the operation started, British forces were systematically harassing and plundering local villages. A rare, translated written remonstrance delivered to General Pollock by local Afghan chiefs, including even Shureen Khan, the Qizilbash chief and ally of the British, which included angry complaints about the excesses of Nott's forces, is revealing. On 20 September, for instance, this document cited how the inhabitants of Aushar and Churdeh 'were plundered by the Candahar force and sustained loss of life and property: their women were not respected'. In another three villages, Deh Daun Causim, Zibar Timour Khan and Churdeh, several more inhabitants were allegedly murdered by British troops. On 21 September, local Afghan chiefs further protested about the destruction of Meer Hassin's fort, which 'also destroyed the property belonging to the people of the neighbourhood'. Furthermore, around a camp near Allahabad village, it was alleged that 'the force has already plundered our grain and fruit'. Calling for immediate 'redress' and for sirdars to be stationed at each village for its protection, the Qizilbash chiefs added tellingly: 'If your friends suffer this way what may your enemies expect?'[95]

Major-General Pollock invited General Nott to reply to these allegations. His response was again an emphatic denial, citing the murders of four unarmed Europeans in some of the villages and claiming that the population of the valley had left 'before my force arrived.... The troops', he asserted, 'had not behaved ill.'[96]

However, a closer examination of his written replies confirm his awareness of further depredations by his less-disciplined auxiliaries or camp-followers. He admitted to the 'exception of a few individuals' who behaved excessively in the valley operations, resulting in the 'severe punishment' of 'surwars and grass cutters' and he also admitted, in the same dispatch, that Brigadier-General Sale had 'ordered' a fort to be burnt ... but if he did I daresay he had good reasons'! Moreover, in an earlier dispatch to Pollock, Nott had already tacitly admitted to resorting to ruthless coercive measures in order to secure his supplies on arrival in Kabul: 'The people are not inclined to sell even at the high price offered. I cannot see my troops ... starve as long as supplies are in the country and I must therefore send parties out to seize what will be sufficient to take my army to Jelalabad.'[97] Nott's supply crisis was probably exacerbated by other factors. Pollock's army, which had arrived two days earlier, had already absorbed the vast amount of residual food and fodder in the region and the unexpected discovery of scores of crippled and starving sepoy survivors from the Elphinstone disaster, 'some of them in a pitiable state from having been frost bitten',[98] and the urgent need to feed them, undoubtedly greatly exacerbated his supply situation.

Worse was to follow. In late September 1842, the strong British force under Major-General Sir John McCaskill, comprising Captain Backhouse's Mountain Train, Captain Blood's 9-pounder battery, two 18-pounder guns and a large body of seasoned infantry (principally Her Majesty's 9th and 41st Foot and the 26th, 41st, 42nd and 43rd Native Infantry) and three squadrons of cavalry (principally Her Majesty's 3rd Light Dragoons, the 1st Light Cavalry and Captain Chicks' corps) left Kabul to strike at Istalif, identified as the main rebel stonghold in Kohistan. McCaskill's subsequent report noted the potentially severe practical difficulties of assaulting this allegedly 'impregnable' fortress. It consisted of

> masses of houses and forts ... built on the slopes of the mountain, in the rear of which are yet loftier eminences sitting in a defile which leads to Toorkistan and, in no way ... can this place of abode of 15,000 people be approached but by surmounting ranges of hills, separated by deep ravines, or traversed by narrow roads.[99]

Moreover, the British were, as ever, vastly outnumbered, with the whole of the mountainside and tops of houses bristling with fierce bodies of hostile 'Jezailchies'.

However, McCaskill soon found a way and, on 28 September 1842, two attack columns were formed, with one in reserve. With covering fire from skirmishers, both columns assailed and outflanked the key approach village of Ismillah: 'Their rapid and unhesitating advance soon left the enemy no resources but flight.'[100] It was a classic British infantry action with their superior discipline and mobility overwhelming an ill-organized enemy, and with Backhouse's mountain guns ascending the dizzy heights to skilfully disperse pockets of resistance below.

A complete victory with minimal losses to the British was now to be marred by more excessive behaviour, of which there are documented accounts. In accordance with the policy of retribution, McCaskill hurriedly directed 'the town to be set on fire in several places' and although the lives of hundreds of female and child refugees from Kabul were largely spared during the attack itself, they were callously left to their fate in the freezing weather. Historian Gleig recorded the furious 'work of vengeance ... they did not leave a house standing. Fire consumed both castle and cottage; and gardens, vineyards, orchards etc were cut down.'[101] Few of the male defenders were spared. One source alleged that: 'Every male past puberty was killed and many of the women raped. Tears, supplications, were no avail; fierce oaths were the only answer; the musket was deliberately raised, the trigger pulled and happy was he who fell dead.... In fact we are nothing but hired assassins.'[102] News of the atrocities aroused anger and comment both in the local Indian press and at home, and despite the denials of the local military authorities, an account of the action by Captain Mackenzie of the 41st Foot reveals the appalling extent of the Afghan civil and military losses, particularly as the civilian population was driven into the surrounding frozen mountains. Mackenzie confirmed the extreme weather prevailing during the attack: 'The night was bitter and intensely cold; it was scarcely possible to sleep and many of us were unprovided with either cloaks or posteens. The wind rose high and cutting about midnight; a sharp frost set in and continued throughout the following day and night.' After five hours of intense fighting, panic set in:

> When the terrified inhabitants became conscious ... that the city must be ours within the hour, they had poured forth in hundreds from the upper part of the town. Hundreds of women and children, enveloped in their long white boorkas, studded the side of the mountain as they plied their rapid and dangerous way towards the summit. Every moment their numbers became more dense, until ... the face of the hill appeared almost as if a wide and snow-like sheet had overspread it.[103]

The crisis was certainly magnified by the unexpectedly large numbers of these terrified refugees who had just arrived from Kabul. As Mackenzie explained:

The whole of the female population of Caubul and their families had been removed for greater safety to Istalif on the near approach of General Pollock's force, the impression obtaining that the 'Maiden City' ... was ... considered impregnable ... fatal mistake! It fell; and, throughout the bitter and inclement night, shrieks and wailings of perishing thousands were borne past by every icy gust which howled amid the ruins of the old castle, chanting, as it were, an unearthly requiem.[104]

It had been a cruel revenge, with scenes of acute human misery akin to the last days of the doomed Kabul force and, as the weather rapidly deteriorated, it was patently clear that the British had neither the inclination nor the logistical capacity to alleviate the huge scale of suffering which followed their victory. Mackenzie estimated that 'upwards of 4,000 men, women and children had perished from cold and hunger among the mountains'.[105]

Mackenzie's account also reaffirms that little quarter was given to the male defenders in the ferocious fighting. He observed that:

Superadded to the thousands which had succumbed to the extermination of cold and famishment among the hills, the purling and slender rivulets which careered adown her precipitous streets and declivities were deeply tinged with the blood of numbers of her defenders, whose lifeless and mutilated forms mingled in incongruous heaps with every imaginable description of merchandise, furniture, tents, brockades, velvets, satins and similar costly articles choked up every avenue which led to the citadel. The sufferings of these devastated people must have been terrific.[106]

The ultimate irony was that the absence of carriages and heavy transport amongst what was effectively an oversized British raiding party largely precluded the transfer of plunder back to the main camp at Kabul. Thus, to the dismay of British troops, vast amounts of spoil had to be abandoned as the force retired rapidly to Kabul to avoid the deteriorating weather. As Lieutenant Greenwood confirmed, the 'insufficient carriage even for accessories' led to 'all the valuable plunder' being burned alongside the smouldering ruins of the ransacked city.[107] Captain Mackenzie vividly recalled the final desperate scenes as the weary British troops trudged away in the snow:

On the morning of our departure from this scene of slaughter and devastation, even the fear of being shot down by the rear guard did not deter a number of famishing wretches from swarming different portions of the encamping ground ... and, gathering together every rag or piece of clothing they could find and every revolting particle of offal or bone that was likely to appease their ravenous hunger.[108]

Unfortunately, Captain Mackenzie appears to have been a lone critical voice. The few surviving accounts reveal that the expedition was generally seen as a wholly justifiable act of revenge for previous treacheries. Even Padré Allen was, on this occasion, more circumspect:

Much has been said both in Indian and English journals and in Parliament about the 'brutalities' and 'barbarities' committed on this expedition. I was not present and therefore cannot speak from my own personal knowledge nor am I at all disposed to maintain that it was free of the usual horrors accompanying warlike expeditions.... Nevertheless, I am satisfied that all means were used for the protection of women and children and that, and the absence of liquor, the usual incentive to every evil in a siege or storm were far less than in most of the military operations in the Peninsula and elsewhere.[109]

McCaskill's force had not quite finished their punitive operations. An equally ruthless act of revenge took place at Charikar, the scene of a gross betrayal of the British garrison in the previous autumn. The town was also completely sacked, although with a far lower loss of life than at Istalif.

It was now time for the final act of retribution – the complete destruction of the Great Bazaar of Kabul – although the eventual scale of destruction was to far exceed this area. Since the arrival of the British columns, the city had been ripe for the taking. Indeed, on General Pollock's arrival on 17 September, most of the city leaders, no doubt in the vain hope of avoiding punishment, had rushed to make their submission. As Ensign Stapylton recalled, 'on our old race ground at Cabul, we were met by the most influential of the inhabitants ... to tender their submissions'.[110] Moreover, it was an open city conspicuously devoid of defenders. As Captain Backhouse observed, 'The city of Kabool was almost entirely deserted as well as the villages in the vicinity.'[111] However, many were soon lured back as Pollock, desperate for supplies, issued several proclamations inviting the citizens to return and stating that their property would be protected. It was to prove to be a false promise.

Meanwhile, in the remaining days before its wholesale destruction, a few British officers had bravely ventured into the depopulated city to view its cultural areas. Their accounts provide a final fleeting glimpse of the Great

Bazaar, a cultural icon of Afghanistan. Passing by the site of MacNaghten's murder, 600 yards from the city of Kabul, Captain Backhouse, at great risk to his life,

> boldly made a shortcut by passing through the city itself having but one attendant orderly with me. I confess, however, that I became somewhat alarmed when I found myself in the middle of a splendid Arcade, 600 feet long with 2,000 shops all roofed over from end to end with glass; for I was perhaps the first European that had passed that way since the murder of our Envoy and other officers and the exposure of their bodies in this very place. What varieties of delicious fruit and other delicacies have met my gaze. How my mouth watered. But it was a mere tantalisation for I had not a penny in my pocket.[112]

Padré Allen also grabbed a last opportunity to explore the doomed city, even finding time to supervise services and conduct baptisms amongst the tiny pockets of Armenian Christians hiding in the city. He passed by the remains of the murdered Burnes' house: 'A melancholy spectacle, being now an utter ruin, the narrow street in which it stood, by the numerous scores of musket balls, bore indubitable evidence of the fury of the conflict which had raged about it.' The site of Burnes' garden, in his favourite residence 'overlooked by a ruined fort' proved equally distressing, especially as 'the very flowers he had planted, frail though they were ... had survived the hand that reared them'. Near the palace he even discovered 'in a small dark room' the remains of 'the poor old Shah Soojah ool Moolk, his body ... thinly covered with earth, forming a small mound; over this was a mat, which was again covered by a sort of palanquin when he was murdered; it was white and the blackened bloodstains were very evident upon it'.[113]

There was some prevarication before Major-General Pollock gave the final order for British demolition parties to enter Kabul, but it was the ominous signs of an Afghan winter which again proved decisive. As early as 26 September 'a great change of temperature' had already been observed with 'the first snow ... visible in the more distant hills'.[114] On Sunday 9 October 1842, the order for destruction was finally issued. The distress of the Kabul inhabitants was to be magnified as, during the three-week lull, many more of the initially terrified shop-owners had been lured back, if only to make handsome profit from the new army of occupation. Lieutenant Greenwood in particular vividly recalled the 'quantity of horses and fruits ... brought into our camp' by local Afghan traders. [115]

Four companies of the 31st Regiment and some detachments of the sepoy regiments were assigned to the onerous duties of destruction. While most official sources suggest that only the Great Bazaar was destroyed, Lieutenant Greenwood's eyewitness account vividly contradicts these, as these incursions degenerated into widespread scenes of burning and looting throughout Kabul:

> We proceeded ... and blew up the principal chokes and bazaar where Sir William MacNaghten's head and others had been exposed and set fire to the city in many places. The houses were of course gutted in very short time, and bales of cloth, muslins, fur cloaks, blankets and wearing apparel of every description were turned out and destroyed.[116]

The British demolition parties were undoubtedly further incensed by the discovery of 'the vast quantity of stores stolen from the Elphinstone's destroyed army ... quantities of English belts and pouches and a variety of other articles.... Some of the men found a number of English cases of hermetically-sealed grouse and other meats on which ... they had a fine feast.'[117]

From his observation point outside the city, key eyewitness Padré Allen was dismayed by the breakdown of discipline, which occurred even amongst some of the British regulars, soon after the first party of incendiaries were dispatched into the city. Their entry into the gates was, he observed, 'the signal for European soldiers, sepoys, followers, all who could get away from the camp, to commence plundering – a melancholy and disgraceful scene'.[118] By contrast, the historian, Gleig, argued that such rapacious acts were probably unavoidable:

> That the work of plunder could be wholly stopped, amid the confusion attendant on such proceedings was not to be expected. In spite of guards, camp followers and soldiers made their way into the burning town and loaded themselves with articles, scarcely one of which they were able, after the march began, to carry beyond the encampment. And here and there accidents occurred.[119]

Again, the scale of atrocities, or 'accidents' as Gleig chose to term them, strongly suggests that yet another Nelsonian blind eye was adopted by the senior commanders. Padré Allen remained neutral on this key issue: 'Whether it could or could not have been prevented by the proper exercise of decision and discipline on the part of the General by whom I am fully persuaded that it was not approved, becomes me not to say.'[120] Captain Neill was also an eyewitness to the chaos in the city, and his account throws further light on the situation. He noted how: 'The springing of the first mine was the signal for all the camp followers to rush into the town and commence the work of the most disgraceful plunder.' Although he also observed that: 'Guards ... were placed at the different gates to prevent anyone entering while the work of destruction was going on ... there were many points of ingress besides the gates and attempts to keep the followers out were futile.' Nevertheless, he concedes that some British regulars were involved. 'It is not to be denied that several of the soldiers contributed to the irregularities' but, he maintained, 'the misconduct of a few men does not incriminate the actions of an army'.[121]

Ironically, even amidst the frenzy of destruction, the British suffered some casualties. Lieutenant Greenwood confirmed that, in the process of blowing up the bazaars 'some of our officers and men received severe contusions from falling beams'.[122] Other buildings caught up in the indiscriminate destruction included the 'Feringhee mosque', recently constructed by Akbar Khan to celebrate his victory over Elphinstone's army. (The pro-British Qizilbash quarter was, however, significantly spared.)

The firestorm resulting from the destruction was undoubtedly helped by other factors outside British control. One eyewitness reported that, 'many houses were predominantly built of dry, light wood, and it would have been impossible to stop the ravaging element; the conflagration lasted the whole time we remained encamped ... and we still saw it when entering the Koord Cabul pass, on our return'. The work of destruction certainly left the demolition parties utterly exhausted. Lieutenant Greenwood recalled: 'many of our men looked just like chimney-sweepers from the fire and smoke'.[123]

However, nothing could excuse the incidents of rape and murder which occurred over the next three days. Padré Allen wrote that:

Every kind of disgraceful action was suffered to go in the town, the shops were broken open and rifled; every sort of plunder was displayed and offered for sale in the lines of both camps, which were like a fair ... and the utter disorganisation of the force appeared likely to ensue if this state of things were to continue.

Allen this time at least empathized with the many innocent Afghan merchants who were victims of injustice, noting: 'and this after a quiet halt of more than twenty days and when we had replenished the commissariat's supplies by the assistance of these poor people, who had returned to their shops upon an express proclamation of protection in the event of their doing so'.[124] The other, almost lone, military critic, Captain Mackenzie, freshly returned from the sacking of Istalif, agreed. Observing the destruction of the famed arched bazaars of Kabul left 'buried in a confused mass of blackened ruins', he continued:

> This has always appeared to me rather a wanton mode of exciting the hostility of harmless bunnists [shopkeepers] against us, for the insurrection and its concomitant disasters arose not amongst the mercantile community of Cabul, but amongst the warlike tribes. To punish the unfortunate house owners of the bazaars was not a dignified retaliation for our losses.[125]

There was even some dissent, if only for more tactical reasons, amongst the senior military, who remained less than happy with the turn of events. Major-General Nott, not normally known as a defender of Afghan rights, not only disapproved of the designated targets for destruction but also deprecated the long delay caused in face of the obvious signs of the approaching Afghan winter. Nott would have spared the city and the bazaar, deeming it 'cruel and unnecessary and unworthy of the British character to destroy the marts of the working population'.[126] From a military perspective he would have much preferred to have destroyed the great Afghan fortress of Bala Hissar. Indeed, Nott's deep and bitter frustration clearly emerges in private letters to his daughters, dated 26 September and 10 October 1842, which also revealed the extent of underlying friction existing between himself and his superior, Major-General Pollock:

> Why we are remaining here I know not. In fact I know nothing and am not admitted into the state secrets of a set of boys by whom General Pollock seems to be surrounded. I only know that my army marched thus far through the very heart of Afghanistan, *victorious* and had I not been superseded I would have blown up the Cabul Bala Hissar, asserted our national honour and the reputation of British arms, and, at this moment, should have been five marches on my road to Jalalabad.

He was fixated upon the deteriorating weather:

> This horrid delay is truly annoying. Fortunately the season as yet has been unusually mild or our men would have suffered greatly: but what man of sense would have run the risk for the sake of following at the heels and dancing attendance on a set of Affghans whose hands are still red with the blood of our murdered countrymen! Shame, shame![127]

In fact his more politically sensitive superior, Pollock, had decided to spare the Bala Hissar for the sake of the new 'British puppet', Prince Shapur, who had replaced the murdered Shah Shuja's successor Fath Jang on his recent, sudden abdication but who, in the words of historian Norris, 'lasted only as long as it took Akbar Khan to return to Cabul and gather together a few influential supporters'.[128]

At 11 a.m. on Wednesday 12 October 1842, after three days of chaotic looting, Pollock, now seriously alarmed by the snow falling on the surrounding hills, but undoubtedly equally anxious to prevent further ill-disciplined depredations in the still-burning city and conserve valuable supplies, led his armies away from Kabul. The army was split into three columns, and Pollock's forces actually reached Jalalabad without a single casualty. On the way, however, the column still had to confront logistical crises and experience again the psychological horrors of traversing the massacre sites. For instance, even crossing the first river outside Kabul led to chaos amongst the intermingled camel transports; all very reminiscent of Elphinstone's experiences, but this time without the lethal enemy and weather conditions. Indeed, it took six hours to march the first eight miles! At Bootkhak, part of Pollock's force also had to traverse the first campsite of Elphinstone's doomed forces. Here, Padré Allen observed 'the traces of their rowties and small tents' and 'many ghastly human remains ... the ground covered with tattered fragments of their clothing ... gloves and socks, sepoys' hair combs, broken china, all serve to remind us of the misery and humiliation of our troops'.[129] At the grim, already freezing, Khurd-Kabul Pass, scene of the greatest carnage experienced by Elphinstone's retreating forces, Pollock's forces had yet again to contend with the 'skeletons of the ill-fated troops' and 'large carrion-crows and vultures', the narrowest point 'literally choked with corpses of men, horses and camels'.[130]

At Jalalabad during a week's halt and under the direction of Major Broadfoot, the process of destruction of the town's defences now commenced and siege veteran Abbott at least felt 'sorry to see the old walls destroyed and our quarters burnt'.[131] On the journey to Peshawar the two rearguard columns clashed with local Afridi tribesmen, who took a heavy toll of baggage and stragglers. At the mouth of the Khyber Pass the commanding fortress of Ali Masjid was also partially demolished. Soon, the sight of the wide plains of the Punjab before them provoked a huge relief: 'At the sight of this the sepoys of the light companies ... set up a deafening cheer and most fully did we participate in their joy'.[132]

Many social and culinary delights awaited the weary columns as they crossed the Sutlej River into British India on 19 December 1842. Governor-

General Ellenborough had organized a stupendous welcome at Ferozepore. Here, surely, one of the grandest military displays of the Raj took place. The first to ford the river, across a bridge of boats festooned with streamers and ribbons reflecting the red, yellow and blue colours of India, was the remnant of the 'illustrious garrison, the Jalalabad brigade' headed by their gallant commander, 'Fighting Bob' Sale. Ellenborough personally welcomed the troops (awarding every man a medal), as did the huge 'army of reserve' comprising 40,000 men who formed up in a line extending two and a half miles. A salvo of nineteen guns was fired as numerous bands played, with the awaiting columns honouring the weary troops in review order. On 19 December, General Pollock first crossed the river, closely followed by the more cynical and decidedly less-impressed General Nott, reluctantly dragging behind him the great British trophy of the campaign, the revered Somnath Gates. According to Captain Abbott, these two recalcitrant generals were significantly 'not received with presented arms and salutes ... due to the orders of Lord Ellenborough'.[133] It was perhaps an ungracious act but one which graphically revealed the high degree of political friction still prevailing between the Governor-General and his feisty insubordinate Major-Generals.

It was a magnificent homecoming. Abbott recalled:

> We entered a long and glittering street formed of native cavalry, at the head of which were the Governor-General, the Commander-in-Chief and multitudes of aides-de-camp etc, composing their staff in every variety of uniform, and, ladies upon enormous elephants with havildars richly caparisoned; crimson and yellow were the prevailing colours, the latter distinguishing the numerous Sikh troops who were present.[134]

It was almost a Roman triumph, a procession marred only, in Padré Allen's view, by the Governor-General's pagan, childlike parade of the old gates of Somnath, which he conceived as both 'unwise and unbecoming of the representative of a Christian nation'.[135]

There followed days of frivolity and excess at the main reception area at Ferozepore. The troops enjoyed 'a saturnalia of banquets and balls' lasting a full week. The culmination of festivities, held on 26 December 1842, was the Governor-General's ball, to which all officers were invited. 'A suite of three enormous tents was lighted up and decorated with banners bearing scrolls and it had a very pretty effect',[136] wrote one participant. For the troops themselves it was a truly joyful commemoration of fours years of arduous campaigning and comradeship. For the veteran Her Majesty's 13th and 35th Native Infantry Regiments, between which unusually close bonds had been forged on the snowy ramparts of the Bala Hissar in the winter of 1839–40 and in the terrible 1841–2 siege of Jalalabad, old times were now finally celebrated with gigantic mutual banquets held in huge tents, in which racial and class differences were for once significantly ignored. After

> a most excellent traditional dinner of roast beef, pies, mutton, fowls and plum puddings, each man was provided with a bottle of beer ... the greatest treat of all, for they had not tasted it for years and an extra ration of rum; and for dessert sacks of oranges and almonds and raisins were provided and piled neatly on the tables.[137]

On 3 January 1843 the armies of retribution began to break up and it was left to Lord Ellenborough to pass his judgement on the three-year tumultuous 'Afghan affair'. In his proclamation, significantly signed on 1 October 1842 in the same room where Auckland's 'Simla Manifesto' of 15 October 1839 had been promulgated, Ellenborough officially confirmed the end of the war. He predictably dwelt on the restoration of British power rather than 'disasters unparalleled in their extent ... and by the treachery in which they were completed'. In one short campaign, he asserted, Britain had 'been avenged upon every scene of past misfortunes and the repeated victory in the field and the capture of the cities and citadels of Ghazni and Cabul have again attached the opinion of invincibility to the British arms'.[138]

His statement could not, however, disguise the overall failure of the British mission in Afghanistan. As General Napier so cynically observed in his journal: 'All Lord E's proclamations and decorations for Pollock's and Nott's affairs will not hinder the Affghans saying they destroyed one army and kicked two others out, and history will say the same.' Politically, Afghanistan, as Ellenborough himself admitted, had been left 'to create a government amidst the anarchy' which was 'the consequence of their crimes'. The British puppet, Shah Shuja, whose own 'fidelity' had even been brought into question, was dead by an assassin and, strategically, Britain had been forced to retreat to her 'starting position' or, as a chastened Ellenborough more prosaically put it, 'The rivers of the Punjab and Indus and the mountainous passes and the barbarous tribes of Afghanistan will be placed between the British army and an enemy approaching from the west – if indeed such an enemy there can be – and no longer between the army and its supplies.'[139] In his statement he also tacitly admitted to the logistical and military failures at the heart of the disasters as well as publicly repudiating the folly of his predecessor Lord Auckland's 'forward policy', which had cost the loyal British subjects of India dear, both in terms of development and taxation: 'The enormous expenditure required for the support of a large force at a distance from its own frontier and its resources will no longer arrest every measure for the improvement of the country and of the people.'[140]

It is important to reiterate here that, for Britain the First Anglo-Afghan War had indeed been a deeply traumatic experience. In terms of civilian-military relations, from the crossing of the Indus in 1839 to the final débâcle in Kabul, the strain had been immense. Auckland had committed an under-strength and ill-prepared military establishment to an immensely expensive campaign for which the *raison d'être* had already disappeared with the Russo-Persian withdrawal from Herat. From the outset also, the accompanying Company 'politicals', obsessed with social peace and building a future political base for their already discredited protégé, had restrained an angry and frustrated military from punitive action against murderous raiding tribes and turned a Nelsonian blind eye to the Shah's excesses, most notably the mass executions of prisoners outside Ghazni. During the occupation period both the overly ambitious MacNaghten and Burnes had run personal fiefdoms, neglecting or ignoring a deteriorating situation, falsifying reports home to Calcutta, whilst allowing the Shah's new regime to indulge in further corrupt practices which sowed the seeds of rebellion. Local critics, notably Nott and Roberts, had been either ignored or ruthlessly suppressed. Burnes' personal social excesses in Kabul itself had clearly and directly contributed to his horrible demise. When the storm inevitably broke, MacNaghten foolishly retreated into secret and allegedly duplicitous negotiations which blatantly excluded the military command cycle and even bungled relations with the Qizilbash, Britain's key local allies in Kabul. There was no 'comprehensive approach' here. It was left to an embattled Eldred Pottinger, the new Envoy after MacNaghten's brutal murder, a man who had warned of impending disaster over three months earlier, to reluctantly pick up the pieces of an irrevocably broken political jigsaw and negotiate a fatally flawed treaty with the insurgent leader Akbar Khan.

The military, also, were clearly not blameless. Poor intelligence and an incompetent Commissariat had greatly contributed to the terrible losses and it was ironically not them, but entrepreneurial Afghan traders and peasant farmers who 'rescued' the starving Army of the Indus at Kandahar in 1839 and who, in November/December 1841, after the incompetent loss of their winter stores, kept the Kabul garrison alive longer than might have been anticipated. It was left to Major-General Elphinstone to commit the ultimate blunder. His chronic physical infirmity and incompetent decision-making fatally emasculated a still-powerful over 5,000-strong army which, if better commanded and organized, could still have rescued the chronic political situation. Ultimately, of course, after the disaster, the military triumphed over their local political masters and the armies of retribution brutally demonstrated what an untrammelled military is capable of.

Nothing, of course, was said officially of the economic, social and political consequences for Afghanistan of over three years of war and occupation, not to mention the depredations of the two British armies of retribution which had destroyed two major cities, scores of villages, vast swathes of cultivation and left thousands of Afghans destitute or dead. While the war had provided great prosperity for some, especially Afghan peasant-farmers and traders located along the campaign routes and around British camps and garrisons (not to mention Indian Hindu traders attached to the British columns), the overall impact was deeply deleterious and this particular war, the first of three Anglo-Afghan Wars fought in the Raj period, is the one which, as Professor Dupree's extensive oral research in the 1960s and 1970s confirmed, still resonates most deeply in Afghan historical consciousness.[141]

Notes

1   NAM, 5910-152, Pearson, Diary, Jan–Feb, 1842.
2   T.H. Maddock, Secretary, Govt. of India, *Proclamation* (encl. in J.H. Stocqueler, *Memorials of Afghanistan* (repr. Saeed Jan Qureshi, Peshawar, 1983), p.180).
3   Greenwood, *Campaign*, pp.92–3.
4   J.H. Stocqueler, *Nott Memoirs*, vol 2, pp.426–7.
5   Neill, *Four Years Service*, (2 vols), p.191.
6   Napier, *Life of Sir Charles James Napier*, vol 2, p.174.
7   Seaton, *Cadet to Colonel*, pp.164–5.
8   See, notably, G.R. Gleig, *Sale's Brigade in Afghanistan* (John Murray, London, 1846), *passim*; N. Dupree, 'The Question of Jalalabad', Asian Affairs, vol. 62, parts 1 and 2, 1975; J. Lunt, 'The Illustrious Garrison; the Siege of Jalalabad', *History Today*, vol 16. No.7, 1966, p.494 and G.N. Molesworth, The Defence of Jalalabad,1840–1, JAHSR, vol xvi, p.146.
9   See for instance, Rev. W. Brock, *A Biographical Sketch of Sir Henry Havelock, KCB* (London, 1858), especially pp.63–4.
10 Seaton, *Cadet to Colonel*, p.165.
11 Gleig, *Sale's Brigade*, p.121.
12 C.R. Low (ed), *The Afghan War: Journal of Major General A. Abbott* (Richard Bentley and Son, London, 1879), p.235.

13   Seaton, *Cadet to Colonel*, p.168.

14   Low, *Abbott Journal*, p.286.

15   Low, *Abbot Journal*, p.260. See also, Seaton, *Cadet to Colonel*, p.183.

16   Low, *Abbot Journal*, p.263.

17   Seaton, *Cadet to Colonel*, p.182.

18   Gleig, *Sale's Brigade*, p.137.

19   Seaton, *Cadet to Colonel*, p.185.

20   Low, *Abbott Journal*, p.260.

21   Seaton, *Cadet to Colonel*, p.186.

22   Low, *Abbott Journal*, p.260.

23   Ibid, p.264.

24   Seaton, *Cadet to Colonel*, pp.192–3.

25   Gleig, *Sale's Brigade*, p.146.

26   Seaton, *Cadet to Colonel*, p.198.

27   Ibid, p.198.

28   Chetwynd Stapleton, Letters/Diary, 27 February 1842, p.16.

29   Seaton, *Cadet to Colonel*, p.211.

30   Napier, *Life of Napier*, p.170.

31   Seaton, *Cadet to Colonel*, pp.213–4.

32   J.S. Cumming, *A Six Year Diary* (Martin and Hood, London, 1847), p.170.

33   Greenwood, *Campaign in Afghanistan*, p.120.

34   Low, *Abbott Journal*, pp.306–7.

35   Ibid, p.315.

36   Pollock to Ellenborough, 2 April 1843, Kaye, *History*, vol 3, p.463.

37   Greenwood, *Campaign in Afghanistan*, pp.127–8.

38   Low, *Abbott Journal*, pp.316–8.

39   Ibid, pp.320 and 322.

40   Pollock to Maddock, 29 July 1842 (encl. in Stocqueler, *Memorials*, p.237).

41   Gleig, *Sale's Brigade*, pp.168–69.

42   NAM 6305/115, Backhouse Journal.

43   Ibid.

44   Seaton, *Cadet to Colonel*, p.218.

45   Greenwood , *Campaign*, p.135.

46   Pollock to Lumley (encl. in Stocqueler, *Memorials*, pp.246-7). As Captain Abbott reconfirmed: 'We destroyed all the vineyards, and cut deep rings around trees of two centuries growth. It is lamentable to see the mischief done but the example was quite necessary. We treated them well in November and they attacked our rear the moment we moved from Gandamuck.' (Low, *Abbott Journal*, p.330).

47   Seaton, *Cadet to Colonel*, p.220.

48 Ibid, p.220.
49 Ibid, p.221.
50 Greenwood, *Campaign*, p.221.
51 NAM 6305/115, Backhouse Journal.
52 Greenwood, *Campaign*, p.157.
53 Helsham Jones, *History and Geography*, pp.173–4.
54 Low, *Abbott Journal*, p.339.
55 Stocqueler, *Nott Memoirs*, vol 1, p.429.
56 *Recollections by a Bengal Officer* (Smith and Elder, London, 1845), p.56.
57 Stocqueler, *Memoirs*.
58 *Recollections by a Bengal Officer* (Smith and Elder, London, 1845).
59 Ibid.
60 Helsham Jones, *History and Geography*, p.167.
61 Napier, *Life and Opinions of Napier*, vol 2, p.223.
62 Ibid, p.169.
63 Kaye, *History*, vol 3, p.316.
64 Nott to Hammersley, 2 June 1842, Kaye, *Afghanistan*, vol 3, p.317.
65 PRO/30/12, Ellenborough Papers, Wellington to Ellenborough, 31 March 1842.
66 PRO/30/12, Ellenborough Papers, Ellenborough to Pollock, 23 July, 1842.
67 Kaye, *History of the War*.
68 I.N. Allen, *Diary of a March Through Sinde and Affghanistan* (London, 1843), 12 August 1842, pp.219–20.
69 Ibid, pp.224–7.
70 Ibid, p.241.
71 *Recollections of a Bengal Officer*, p.71.
72 Allen, *Diary*, 13 August 1842, p.257.
73 Ibid, p.258.
74 *Recollections of a Bengal Officer*, p.69.
75 Allen, *Diary*, p.267.
76 *Recollections of a Bengal Officer*, p.77.
77 Sanders to Nott (encl. in Stocqueler, *Nott*, vol 2, pp.129–30).
78 Allen, *Diary*, p.273.
79 Rawlinson Journal (encl. in Stocqueler, *Nott*, vol 2, pp.131–2).
80 Ibid.
81 Allen, *Diary*, p.285.
82 Ibid, pp.284–5.
83 Nott to Pollock, 16 Sept 1842 (encl. in Stocqueler, *Nott*, vol 2, pp.37–8).
84 Allen, *Diary*, p.202.
85 Sale, *Disasters*, p.279.
86 Ibid, p.280.

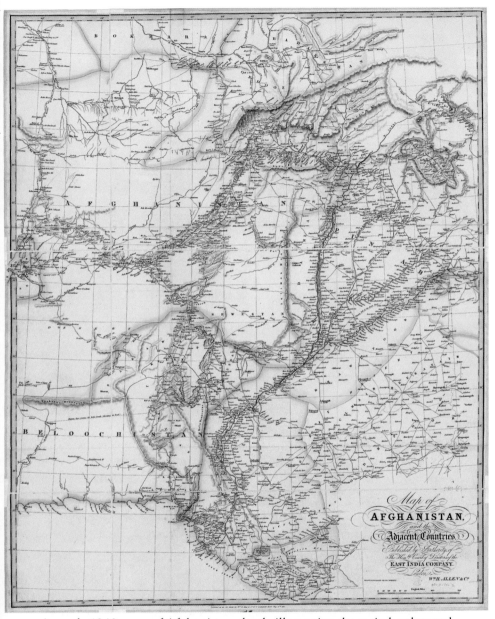

An early 1840s map of Afghanistan clearly illustrating the main borders and particularly the formidable passes of the Suleiman mountains, which always acted as a potential death-trap to invading armies.

A map *c.*1840 depicting Kandahar and Kabul. It gives a clear picture of the formidable terrain and communication difficulties confronting the British occupiers.

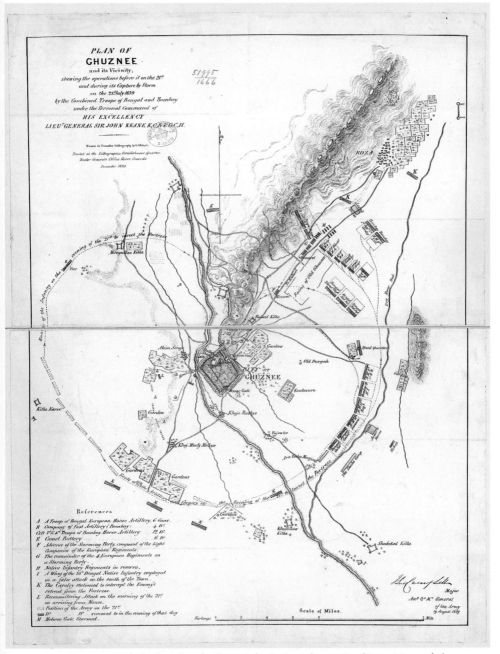

An 1839 map of the battle of Ghazni depicting the main disposition of the British forces during their major and successful assault of 23 July on this strategically important enemy stronghold. This was the first decisive victory for British troops in The First Anglo–Afghan War.

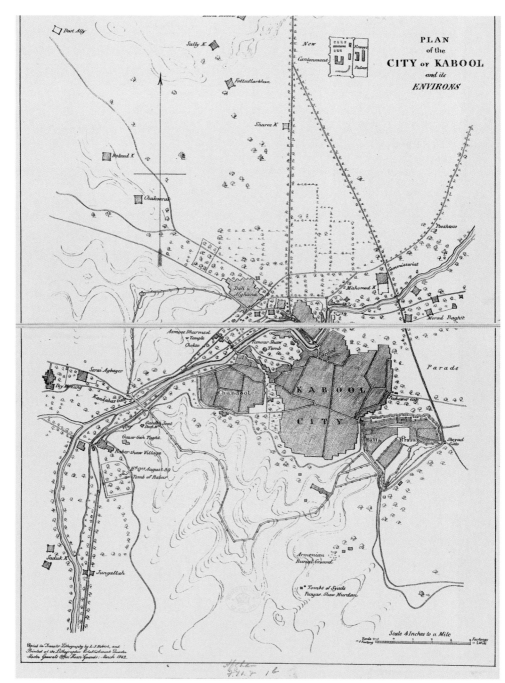

PLAN
of the
CITY OF KABOOL
and its
ENVIRONS

New
Cantonment

Envoys
Palace

Dost Ally

Sully K.

Futtoollarkhan

Sharee K.

Byland K.

Chukoora

Pooshteco

Commissariat

Deh i Afghana

Mahomed K.

Morad Baghet

Asmaee Dhurmsal
Temple
Choksa

Temour Shaw
Tomb

Nishat Dhurm

Parade

Serai Agbuger

Dey Mazung

Kandahar Gate

Chundool

KABOOL
CITY

Mahomed Gate

Guzar Gah Taght

Gardden Seat
Dost M.

Balla   Hissar

Sheyud
Gate

Raher shaw Village

H. Q. August 39
Tomb of Babur

Saduk K.

Jungallah

Armenian
Burial Ground

Tombs of Syude
Punyae Shaw Murdan

Scale 4 Inches to a Mile

Print in Transfer Lithography by L. J. Hebert, and
Printed at the Lithographic Establishment Quarter
Master General Office Horse Guards : March 1842.

An early 1840s plan of the occupied city of Kabul depicting key points in the
flawed British defences, notably the isolated and highly vulnerable British
cantonment and the neglected Balar Hissar fortress.

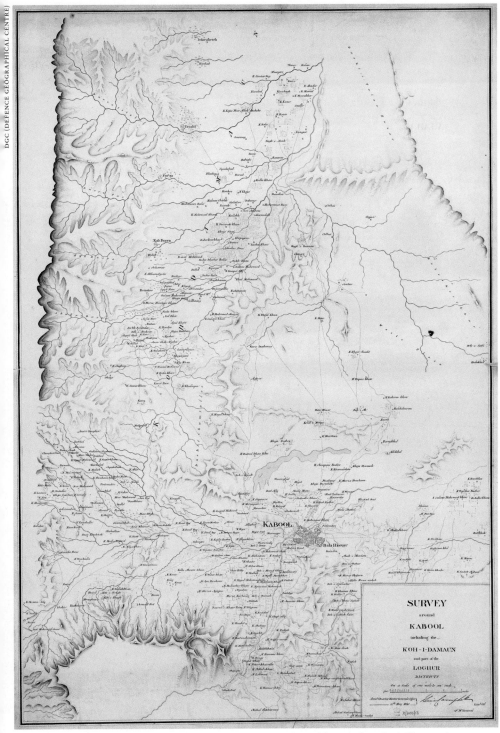

An early 1840s map of the provinces around and beyond Kabul illustrating the immense geopolitical difficulties confronting the British occupiers, which, by late 1841, had culminated in fatal overstretch.

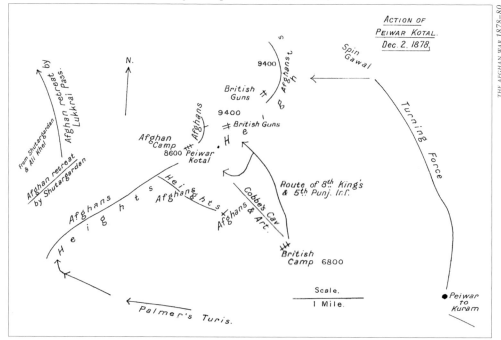

Sketch map of the retreat from Kabul, 6–13 January 1842, starkly revealing the formidable geopolitical obstacles confronting the grossly under-equipped 16,000 strong British Column. Especially problematic were the areas around the Khurd–Kabul and Jagdallak passes where vast numbers of British and Indian troops and their followers perished from the combined effects of exposure and the incessant attacks of Afghan marauders.

Sketch map of the battle of Peiwar Kotal, 2 December 1878, where British forces led by Major-General Frederick Roberts, VC., scored a major victory against a strongly defended Afghan mountain position during The Second Anglo–Afghan War (1878–80).

A map of what Kandahar and the surrounding area looked like *c.*1841, illustrating the tactical and strategic challenges confronting Major-General Nott's isolated and beleaguered British garrison before and after the destruction of Elphinstone's Kabul Brigade.

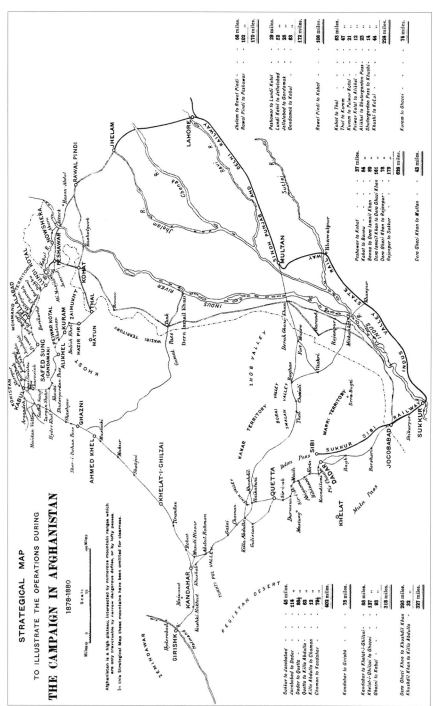

Strategic map of the 1878–80 Anglo–Afghan War, depicting the key battle sites of Peiwar Kotal, Ali Masjid, Ahmed Khel, Charasia (sometimes alternatively spelt Charasiab), Maiwand and Kandahar.

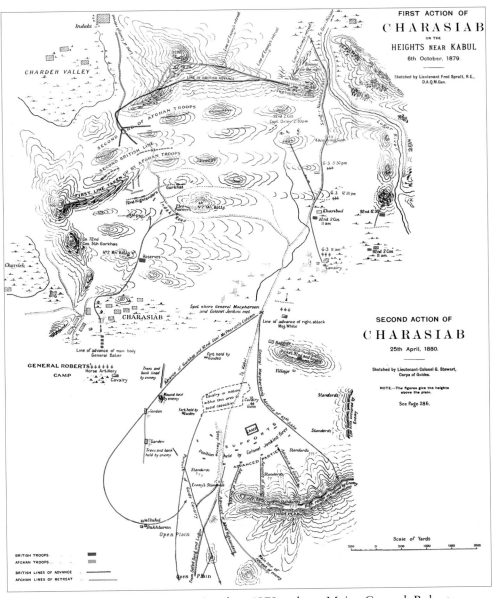

The Battle of Charasia, 6 October 1879, where Major-General Roberts achieved a decisive victory during the second 'revenge' campaign against Afghan rebel forces, which followed the earlier September 1879 massacre of Britain's Mission in Kabul.

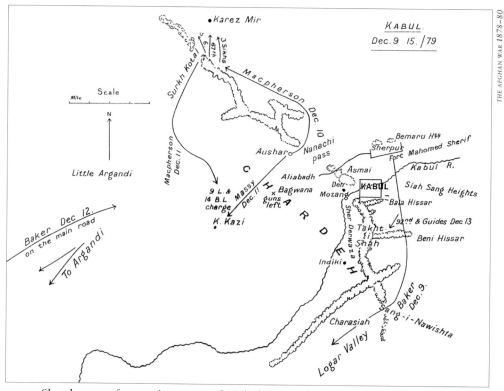

Sketch map of operations around Kabul, December 1879, depicting British defensive tactics including Brigadier-General Massy's cavalry disaster and Roberts' highly successful defence of the British fortified encampment at Sherpur.

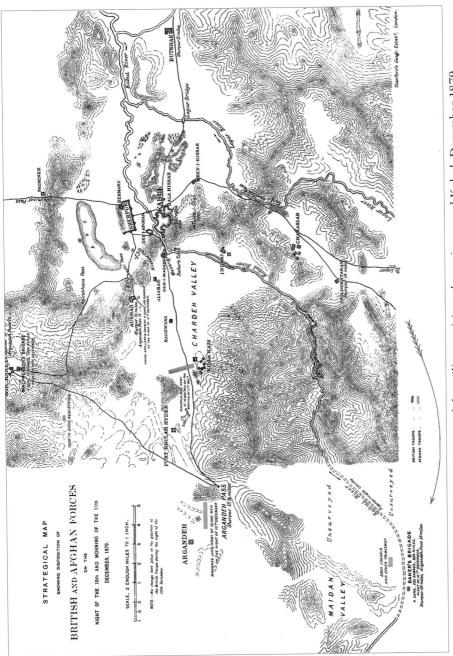

STRATEGICAL MAP

SHOWING DISPOSITION OF

BRITISH AND AFGHAN FORCES

ON THE

NIGHT OF THE 10th AND MORNING OF THE 11th
DECEMBER, 1879.

SCALE, 2 ENGLISH MILES TO 1 INCH.

NOTE:—No changes took place in the position of
the British Troops during the night of the
10th December.

Stanford's Geogl. Estabt. London.

A more detailed strategic map of the military crisis and terrain around Kabul, December 1879.

THE SECOND AFGHAN WAR 1878-79-80

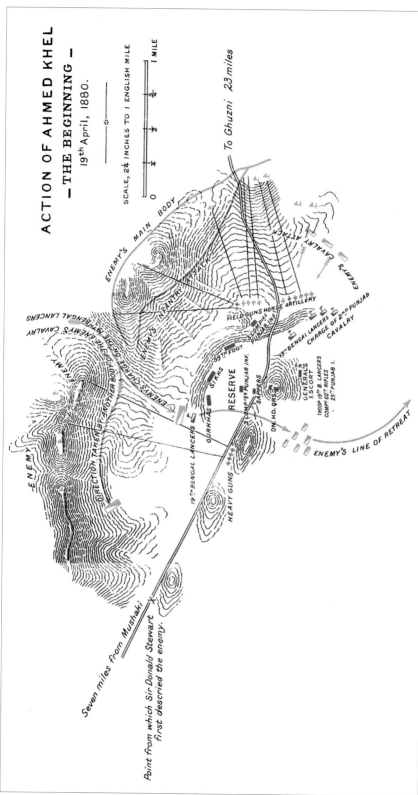

ACTION OF AHMED KHEL
— THE BEGINNING —
19th April, 1880.

SCALE, 2¼ INCHES TO 1 ENGLISH MILE

To Ghuzni 23 miles

ENEMY'S MAIN BODY

ENEMY'S INFANTRY ATTACK

ENEMY'S CAVALRY ATTACK

THE 19TH BENGAL LANCERS
ENEMY'S CAVALRY
THE CHARGE OF
ENEMY

DIRECTION TAKEN BY ANOTHER BODY OF THE
ENEMY'S CHARGE

FIELD GUNS HORSE ARTILLERY
3 COMP₉ 19TH PUNJAB N.I.
59TH FOOT
19TH BENGAL LANCERS
CHARGE OF 2ND PUNJAB CAVALRY

SIKHS
GURKHAS
RESERVE
SAPPERS
3 COMP₉ 19TH PUNJAB INF.

19TH BENGAL LANCERS
HEAVY GUNS
DN. HD. QRS.

GENERAL'S ESCORT
TROOP 19TH B. LANCERS
2 COMP₉ 60TH RIFLES
25TH PUNJAB I.

ENEMY'S LINE OF RETREAT

Seven miles from Mushaki

Point from which Sir Donald Stewart
first descried the enemy.

The battle of Ahmed Khel, 19 April 1880, where Major-General Sir Donald Stewart's vastly outnumbered force won an extremely narrow victory against an Afghan enemy force. This battle was notable for the deployment of unusually high numbers of fanatical *Ghazi* or religious warriors who nearly broke the British defensive lines.

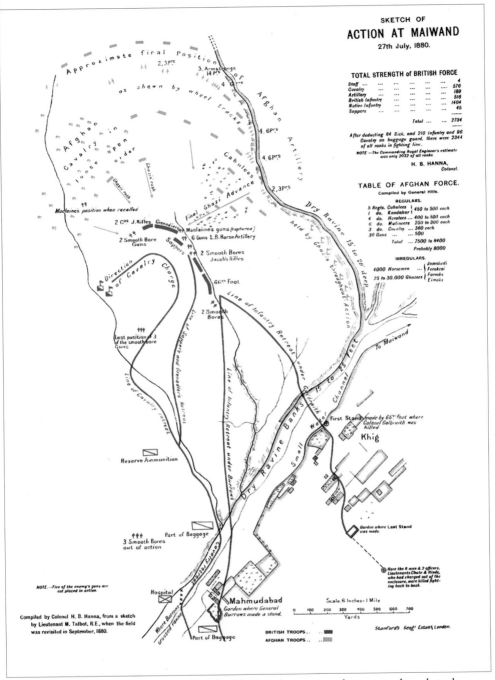

The battle of Maiwand, 27 July 1880, where a vastly outnumbered and under-equipped British brigade commanded by Brigadier-General Burrows was overwhelmed and virtually annihilated by Ayub Khan's forces, which again incorporated large numbers of formidable *Ghazi* warriors. This battle provided a rare instance of Afghan superiority over the British in the artillery sphere.

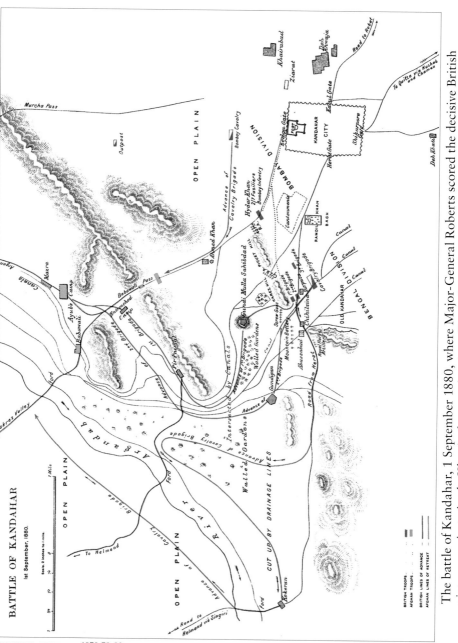

BATTLE OF KANDAHAR

1st September, 1880.

Scale 2 inches to 1 mile.

OPEN PLAIN

OPEN PLAIN

OPEN PLAIN

Murcha Pass

Outpost

Arghandab

Canal

Mazra

Ayub's Camp

Babawali

Ford

Shakrez Valley

Babawali Pass

1st Brigade

Karmuchud Camp

Pir-Paimal

Advance of
2nd Brigade

Gundigan

Intersected by Canals

Kokeran

Ford

River

Arghandab

Ford

To Helmand

Road to
Helmand via Singiri

Advance of
Cavalry Brigade

Advance of Cavalry Brigade

Walled Gardens

CUT UP BY DRAINAGE LINES

Walled Gardens

Ahmed Khan

Advance of
Cavalry Brigade

Bombay Cavalry

Hydar Khan
2/7 Fusiliers
Bombay Infantry

BOMBAY DIVISION

Gundi Mulla Sahibdad

Pir-Paimal Hill

Picquet Hill

Baba Wali Kotal

3rd Brigade
Mountain Battery

Cantonments

Bhoosabad

Screen Guns

Ahmed Khel

Cavalry Brigade

Trim Kariz

Road

BENGAL DIVISION

OLD KANDAHAR DIVISION

Canal

Canal

Canal

RANDUL
KHAN
BAGH

Khairabad

Ziarat

Deb Khwaja

Idgah Gate

KANDAHAR
CITY

Herat Gate

Kabul Gate

Shikarpore Gate

Road to Robat

To Quetta via Kushab
and Chaman

Deb Khak

BRITISH TROOPS

AFGHAN TROOPS

BRITISH LINES OF ADVANCE

AFGHAN LINES OF RETREAT

The battle of Kandahar, 1 September 1880, where Major-General Roberts scored the decisive British victory against Ayub Khan's forces, thereby effectively ending the Second Anglo–Afghan War (1878–80).

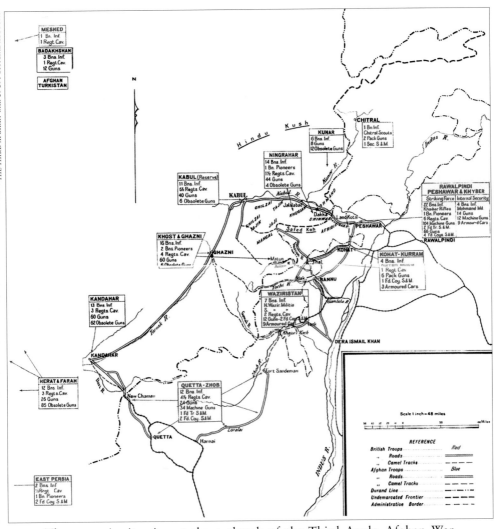

The strategic situation at the outbreak of the Third Anglo–Afghan War, 1919, depicting the main positions of the outnumbered British units and the invading regular Afghan army formations.

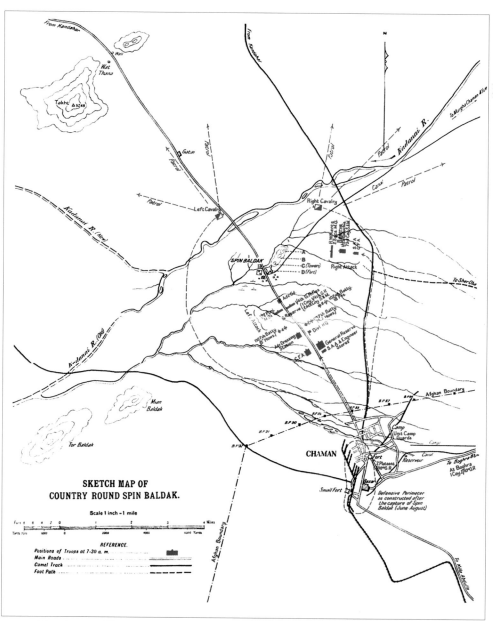

**SKETCH MAP OF
COUNTRY ROUND SPIN BALDAK.**

Scale 1 inch = 1 mile

REFERENCE.

Positions of Troops at 7-30 a. m. ....
Main Roads ....
Camel Track ....
Foot Path ....

Sketch map illustrating the successful British assault on the Afghan fortress
of Spin Baldak, 27 May 1919, which played a key role in bringing Amir
Amanullah's government to the negotiating table.

Shah Shuja (Sha Shuja-ul-Mulk), the Sadozai ruler of Afghanistan (1803–9) and effectively the British 'puppet' reinstalled on the throne of Afghanistan by force of arms in August 1839. His corrupt, unpopular regime came to an abrupt end following the disastrous British retreat of January 1842 and his brutal assassination in April the same year.

Sir Alexander Burnes (1806–41), the brilliant, charming, colourful but ultimately flawed British Deputy Envoy and Governor of Kabul, whose personal and political misjudgements significantly contributed to the British disaster there. He was murdered by an Afghan mob on 2 November 1841.

Dost Mohammed, the Barakzai ruler of Afghanistan. Deposed by the British in August 1839, he returned to power after the final British withdrawal in October 1842 and successfully ruled Afghanistan until his death in 1863.

Sir William Hay MacNaghten (1793–1841), British Envoy in Afghanistan, whose political misjudgements, culminating in his brutal, ignominious death at the hands of Dost Mohammed's son, Akbar Khan, was to signal a dramatic and tragic end to the first round of Britain's Central Asian 'Great Game'.

The famous Grand Bazaar of Kabul, *c.*1840, in which the dismembered bodies of Britain's two envoys, Sir William MacNaghten and Sir Alexander Burnes, were later publicly displayed. This iconic architectural masterpiece was later comprehensively destroyed by the combined 'Armies of Retribution' led by Major-Generals Nott and Pollock in the autumn of 1842.

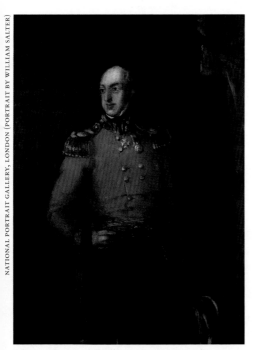

Major-General William George Keith Elphinstone (1781–1842), the elderly, chronically sick, ill-fated commander of the Kabul Garrison who, as overall military commander, was ultimately responsible for the disastrous British retreat in early 1842.

Mohammed Akbar Khan, the controversial son of deposed Dost Mohammed and the man who personally killed British Envoy Sir William MacNaghten. He was destined to oversee the wholesale destruction of Britain's main Afghan forces in January 1842. His triumph was short-lived and he died, possibly as a result of poisoning, at Jalalabad in 1847.

Retraite de Kabul; this dramatic watercolour, by a French artist and depicting a heroic, wounded Lady Florentia Sale as its centrepiece, vividly captures the brutal horrors of the British retreat through the dreaded Khurd-Kabul Pass where up to 3,000 perished.

A contemporary engraving depicting the British frontal assault on Ali Masjid on 22 November 1878 during the Second Anglo–Afghan War (1878–1880). Disaster was only narrowly averted.

A meeting between British Envoy Sir Louis Cavagnari and Amir Yakub Khan in Kabul, 1879, during the Second Anglo–Afghan War.

The execution of the Khotwal near the site of Cavagnari's murder, Kabul, 1879.

Last Stand of the 66th Foot at the battle of Maiwand, 27 July 1880.

A contemporary photograph of officers of the 66th Foot (Royal Berkshires), taken some time before the Maiwand disaster of July 1880.

A rare image of Afghan prisoners captured at the battle of Kandahar, 1 September 1879.

A British base/cavalry patrol on the Northwest Frontier at the time of the Third Anglo– Afghan War, 1919.

A platoon of the North Staffordshires on active Frontier service during the Third Anglo–Afghan War, 1919.

A British sentry posted high above the recaptured British outpost of Bagh Springs during the Third Anglo–Afghan War, 1919.

A British bi-plane on active service during the Third Anglo–Afghan War, 1919.

Captain Carruthers, his junior British officers and 2/11 Gurkha Rifles NCOs
pictured during a brief respite from active service on the Frontier, 1919.

A suspected Pathan sniper undergoing interrogation at a British base during the
Third Anglo–Afghan War, 1919. His fate was unknown.

Heady days of 2002; British paras attached to ISAF display a commemorative memorial to the disastrous 1842 retreat.

Royal Anglians, pictured in action near Nadi Ali, Helmand province, in 2009. Their regimental forbears included the 44th Foot (Essex Regiment) who, as we have seen, were virtually annihilated during the 1842 retreat from Kabul.

The Royal Anglians in action in Helmand during Herrick 11 where they faced relentless Taliban attacks and suffered increasing casualties from the widespread use of IEDs.

Brigadier Edward Butler, Commander of British Forces in Helmand, 2006. Provided with extremely limited resources, Butler was faced with the immensely complex and arduous task of stabilizing the most inhospitable, lawless and intractable province of Afghanistan.

British ISAF Commander David Richards and his escort halt on a road on the outskirts of Kabul, over-shadowed by the same brooding formidable mountains that witnessed the horrors of two previous occupations and the murder of two British envoys.

An otherwise politically beleaguered President Karzai finds time to pose with the British ISAF Close Protection team in the splendid surroundings of a Kabul official residence.

British HQ staff photographed in Kabul in 2006, soon after the appointment of General Richards as Commander of British Forces in Afghanistan.

A relaxed General Richards participates in one of countless media interviews in the aftermath of the controversial 2006 Helmand crisis.

A heavily protected General David Richards tours the Kabul streets circa 2007, soon after his arrival in Afghanistan.

A Royal Anglian British machine-gun post, littered with hundreds of expired GPMG rounds, symbolizes the intensity of conflict during the early desperate months of Helmand operations.

Afghan President Hamid Karzai tours British bases accompanied by overall British Commander General David Richards.

General David Richards escorts Tony Blair and Labour Defence Secretary Des Browne on an official visit to Kabul.

The occasionally fraught but immensely strong Anglo–American 'Special Relationship' in action: General Richards meets a senior American commander at a British base.

British troops in action at the time of the Panther's Claw offensive in 2009, when British forces took heavy casualties stabilizing Helmand ready for the Afghan elections.

As the threat from IEDs massively increased after 2006, the need for helicopters became a burning political and military issue.

As Britain finally declares a withdrawal date of 2014 for this long war, a British patrol wearily conducts yet another dawn mission in central Helmand.

87 Ibid, p.282.
88 Eyre, *Insurrection at Kabul*, p.302.
89 Sale, *Disasters*, p.319.
90 Ibid, pp.374–5.
91 Ibid, p.432.
92 Allen, Diary, p.295.
93 Nott to Pollock, 17 Sept 1842 (encl. in Stocqueler, *Nott*, vol 2, pp.142–3).
94 Pollock to Nott, 17 Sept 1842 (encl. in Stocqueler, *Nott*, vol 2, p.147).
95 Stocqueler, *Nott*, vol 2, p.148.
96 Nott to Pollock (encl. in Stocqueler, *Nott*, vol 2, p.149.
97 Ibid.
98 Ibid.
99 McCaskill Report (encl. in Stocqueler, *Nott*, vol 2, p.153.
100 Ibid.
101 Gleig, *Sale's Brigade*, p.180.
102 M. Edwardes, 'Defeat and Retribution', in *The British Empire,* (BBCTV Promotions, 1969), vol 2, p.525.
103 Mackenzie Journal (encl. in Stocqueler, *Nott*, vol 2, pp.158–9).
104 Ibid.
105 Ibid.
106 Ibid.
107 Greenwood, *Campaign*, p.163.
108 Mackenzie Journal, (encl. in Stocqueler, *Nott*, vol 2, pp.158–9).
109 Allen, *Diary*, pp.317–8.
110 Chetwynd-Stapylton, Stapylton Diary, 15 September 1842, p.28.
111 NAM 6305/115, Backhouse Journal.
112 Ibid.
113 Allen, *Diary*, p.303.
114 Ibid, p.310.
115 Greenwood, *Campaign*, pp.163-4.
116 Ibid.
117 Ibid.
118 Allen, *Diary*, p.321.
119 Gleig, *Sale's Brigade*, p.181.
120 Allen, *Diary*, p.321.
121 Stocqueler, *Nott*, vol 2, p.162.
122 Greenwood, *Campaign*, p.164.
123 Ibid.
124 Allen, *Diary*, p.321.
125 Stocqueler, *Nott*, vol 2, p.162.
126 Ibid, p.161.

127 Ibid, pp.163–4.
128 Norris, *First Afghan War*, p.416.
129 Allen, *Diary*, pp.325–6.
130 Allen, *Diary*, pp.328–9.
131 Abbott, *Journal*, p.342.
132 Allen, *Diary*, p.359.
133 Abbot, *Journal*, p.344.
134 Ibid.
135 Allen, *Diary*, p.444.
136 Chetwynd-Stapylton, Stapylton, Diary, p.37.
137 Seaton, *Cadet to Colonel*, p.234.
138 T.H. Maddock, 'A Proclamation made at Simla', 10 October 1842 (encl. in Norris, *First Afghan War*, pp.451–2).
139 Ibid.
140 Ibid.
141 L. Dupree, 'The First Anglo-Afghan War and the British Retreat of 1842: the functions of History and Folklore', *East and West*, Nos 3–4, Sept/Dec, 1976. See also P. Macrory, *Kabul Catastrophe* (Book Club Associates, London, 1966), pp.278–80. As eminent Victorian historian Kaye, remarked: 'The Afghans are an unforgiving race and everywhere from Candahar to Caubul and from Caubul to Peshawar were traces of the injuries we had inflicted upon the tribes.) (Kaye, *History of the War*, vol 3, p.399).

4. Lytton's Folly: the Second Afghan War 1878–80

Should a foreign power, such as Russia, ever seriously think of invading India from without ... our true policy, our strongest security, would be found to lie in previous abstinence from entanglement at either Kabul, Kandahar or any similar outpost.

Minute, Sir John Lawrence to Sir Henry Rawlinson (1869), encl. in A. Edwardes, *A History of India* (Thames and Hudson, London, 1967), p.276

It is evident that the Ameer has been trifling with us ... it must be made equally evident ... that we will not be trifled with any longer ... we have nothing further to say to the Ameer on any subject.

Viceroy Lord Lytton to Sir Richard Pollock, 3 April, 1877, BL, LP

When 'arf your bullets fly wide in the ditch,
Don't call your Martini a cross-eyed old bitch;
She's human as you are – you trust her as sich,
An' she'll fight for the young British soldier ...
When you're wounded and left on Afghanistan's plains,
And the women come to cut up what remains
Jest roll to your rifle and blow out your brains,
An' go to your Gawd like a soldier.

R. Kipling, 'The Young British Soldier', in *Barrack Room Ballads* (Methuen, London, 1903)

The First Anglo-Afghan War had indeed left a bitter legacy in Afghanistan. As the weary British Army slowly demobilized, 'all that they left behind of the work of the previous four years was the ruined bazaars, the skeletons piled high in the grim Khurd-Kabul Pass and a wound that rankled for fifty years ... more than fifty years. It has never quite been healed'.[1] The myth of British invincibility had been visibly punctured and the loss of British prestige undoubtedly had an impact on the outbreak of the great 1857 Indian Mutiny, barely fifteen years later. The human cost had been stupendous, with 15,000 officers and soldiers dead. Unknown numbers of camp-followers, certainly in their thousands, had perished. Fifty thousand camels were lost and around £20,000,000 of Indian revenue had been spent. Politically, little had been achieved, with Britain's arch enemy Dost Mohammed now firmly ensconced on the throne of Afghanistan.

'Phoney War': Anglo-Afghan Relations from 1843 to 1874

The next two decades of Anglo-Afghan relations was a period aptly termed by Governor-General Lord Dalhousie as 'sullen quiescence on either side, without offence but without goodwill or intercourse'.[2] There were several reasons for this ensuing 'phoney war'. Britain was soon diverted by two major conflicts between 1843 and 1849, first against the Sind Emirate and second, against the fractious Sikh Kingdom which, as widely feared, had largely disintegrated after strongman Ranjit Singh's death. In historian Fraser Tytler's words: 'The annexation of the Panjab was the inevitable outcome of the conditions bordering on anarchy which followed the death of Ranjit Singh.'[3] The restored Afghan ruler, Dost Mohammed, was similarly preoccupied with reconstructing his country, consolidating his borders and re-establishing overall political control. However, this did not deter him from provocatively and disastrously allowing hundreds of irregular Afghan Horse from assisting the Sikh cause at the battle of Goojerat. The decisive British victory there led to the rout and hot pursuit of his forces across the Indus River and back into Afghanistan.[4] It was a timely lesson and no major Afghan incursions occurred again until the outbreak of the Third Anglo-Afghan War in 1919.

Anglo-Afghan relations were briefly and tentatively revived in 1855 as Anglo-Russian relations plunged to a new low on the outbreak of the Crimean War (1854–6). With renewed fears of a Russian invasion of India, Britain needed an ally. The Amir, possibly not forgetting the earlier Goojerat debacle, was disposed to forget the past if the British would do the same. By the mid-1850s, he was prepared to ally himself with the British as a counter to both Russian pressure on himself and a recent Persian attempt to reassert their primacy over Afghanistan's western territories, notably Herat. Consequently, in March, 1855, the new British Governor of Sind, Sir Herbert Edwardes, met Dost Mohammed's envoy, his own son, Ghulam Haider, in Peshawar where a friendship treaty was signed. While doing little more than re-open Anglo-Afghan relations, the treaty gave assurances of British non-aggression and pledged the Amir to be 'the friend of the friends and enemy of the enemies of the Honourable East India Company'.[5]

Alleged Persian provocation and the actual seizure by them of Herat in October 1856, provided the *casus belli* for the British to intervene. Britain's resounding victory in the brief Anglo-Persian War reassured the Afghan Amir of his old enemy's fidelity. In 1856, the Amir accordingly signed a supplement to the 1855 treaty by which he was to receive one *lakh* of rupees (£10,000) in return for maintaining a sufficient body of troops to defend his possessions. Nevertheless, Dost Mohammed's bitter memories of the 1838–42 war still determined him to successfully veto renewed British proposals to place an envoy in Kabul to administer the subsidy. In January 1857, relations progressed further when Dost Mohammed personally visited Peshawar to sign a treaty of friendship. 'I have now made an alliance with the British government', he declared, 'and come what may I will keep it to death.'[6]

The outbreak of the Indian Mutiny in May 1857 presented a potentially severe test for Anglo-Afghan relations as initial British setbacks presented an unparalleled opportunity for the Afghan Government to intervene on the side of the mutineers and regain lost territory, notably Peshawar. In fact, Dost Mohammed kept his word and remained strictly neutral. Britain had successfully walked a diplomatic tightrope. In the wake of the horrific massacres of British troops and civilians at Meerut, Cawnpore and Delhi, one officer, a most relieved Major Lumsden, subsequently recorded in his diary on 2 July 1857:

We ought indeed to be grateful to Providence for having permitted our relations with Afghanistan to be so successfully arranged before the arrival of this crisis, for I am convinced that, had it not been that the minds of the Afghans were in a measure prepared for the Amir's non-interference, he could not have prevented a serial rush down the passes, which must have added gravely to our embarrassment at Peshawar and along the frontier.[7]

'Russophobia' Revived

The Russian 'bogey', however, remained and it was a new outbreak of 'Russophobia' in the mid/late 1860s which, after the death of Dost

Mohammed in 1863, introduced a far more fractious period in Anglo-Afghan relations. Despite the Crimean War, the 'long peace' between Britain and Russia in Central Asia had remarkably survived but, in 1864, Russian advances in the Middle and Near East and, more especially, towards the Pamirs mountain range of northern Afghanistan, suddenly resumed. In 1864 Russian authority was further extended to the borders of Khokand, Bokhara and Khiva. In 1865 Tashkent was occupied and, in 1867, the new province of Russian Turkestan was created and Bokhara became a subsidiary ally of the Tsar. Finally, in 1868, Samarkand, previously only temporarily occupied, was annexed by Russia.

This surge of Russian expansionism was politically and militarily justified in the famous 'Gorchakov Manifesto' issued by Prince Alexander, Mikhailovich Gorchakov, the Russian Foreign Minister, on 21 November 1864. He asserted that the Russian advance in Central Asia, was merely

> that of all civilised states which come into contact with half-savage wandering tribes possessing no fixed social organization. In order to cut short ... perpetual disorders we establish strong places in the midst of a hostile population.... But beyond this line there are other tribes which soon provoke the same dangers.... The state then finds itself in the horns of a dilemma. It must ... deliver its frontier over to disorder ... or it must plunge into the depths of savage countries.[8]

The manifesto represented a classic statement of the common imperial problem of 'turbulent frontiers'. Even more, Gorchakov claimed that it was simply an expression of 'manifest destiny' shared, he asserted, by other expanding or colonial powers such as the USA, under which 'all had been inevitably drawn into a course wherein ambition plays a smaller part than imperious necessity, and where the greatest difficulty is knowing where to stop'.[9]

Nevertheless, under such great political and military pressure the 'Great Game' was soon re-ignited. If the Russians were caught on the 'horns of a dilemma', internally, on the British side, an intense 'Great Game' had already emerged in terms of a furious debate about future policy towards Russian expansion in Central Asia. On the one side of this great debate in British imperial circles was the so called 'masterly inactivity' school, which included Lords Lawrence, Mayo and Northbrook. They tacitly accepted such Russian reassurances and advocated no further movement forward beyond the Indus River. On the other side were the 'forward policy' grouping, notably presented by Sir Bartle Frere and later by Lords Cranbrook and Lytton. They remained suspicious of Russian ambitions and strongly argued for a British advance to the Hindu Kush or even the Oxus River or, at the very least, some form of occupation or buffer zone which would include the British reoccupation of the Afghan cities of Herat and Kandahar.

The effective leader of the 'masterly inactivity' school was Sir John Lawrence, who had been Governor-General of India since 1864. The brutal lessons of the recent Indian Mutiny had convinced him of the need to limit British expansion and concentrate on winning Indian loyalty and thereby consolidate internal stability and progress. He even tacitly accepted Gorchakov's viewpoint when he actively promoted the desirability of entering direct negotiations with St Petersburg about the frontier question. He wrote: 'If an understanding ... were come to, the Government of India ... could look on without anxiety or apprehension at the proceedings of Russia on her southern frontier and moreover, welcome the civilising effect of her border government on the wild tribes of the Steppe.'[10]

In a nutshell, Lawrence's preferred strategy and that of his supporters was to defend India by improving the social conditions of the Indian peoples and ensuring a loyal population, rather than pursuing further costly military adventures across the frontier. Moreover, the views of the 'masterly inactivity' school found political support at home where Gladstone's first Liberal Government (1868–74) sought a diplomatic understanding with Russia; a position reinforced by Gorchakov's subsequent reassuring statement that Afghanistan lay completely outside the sphere upon which Russia might be called to exercise her influence.

The Road to War 1874–8

However, changes in British domestic politics and a new era of turbulence in Afghan politics following the death of Dost Mohammed in 1863, were to begin a fraught political journey towards a new crisis in Anglo-Afghan relations. In Britain the new, distinctly more imperialist-minded government led by Disraeli 'would not be content with a policy of masterly inactivity'. The situation, Disraeli believed, 'had changed ... Lawrence's policy was safe and economical only while there was no hostile power pressing upon the furthest frontier of Afghanistan ... the Russian advance in Central Asia made this no longer true'.[11]

Disraeli's Secretary of State for India, the Marquis of Salisbury, whilst more relaxed and less fearful of a direct Russian invasion than Disraeli, still felt the need to gather intelligence about Russian designs in the region. Rather than rely, as before, on occasional policy statements from St

Petersburg, or vague information filtering out from Kabul, he pressed for British agents to be stationed directly inside Afghanistan. He stressed the imperative need to watch and guide the new Amir, Sher Ali, 'for there is a double danger that he may play us false or, remaining true, may blunder into operations which will bring him into collision with Russia'.[12] The new Viceroy of India, Lord Northbrook, however, strongly disagreed and chose to resign, rather than force a British Resident on the Amir. On his departure, he accurately predicted that 'doing so would subject us to the risk of another unnecessary and costly war in Afghanistan before many years are over'.[13]

On Northbrook's resignation, in 1876, the more aggressive policies of his successor, Lord Lytton, left in no doubt Disraeli's view that 'masterly inactivity had ceased to be the official policy'.[14] It was a new, more confrontational, policy that was to lead ultimately to war with Afghanistan. Lytton's task was to persuade the already fearful and disillusioned Amir to receive a permanent British mission, but it was to make little progress over the next two years. Lytton's own personal character was admirably suited to fulfil Disraeli's new robust Afghanistan policy. As a confirmed member of the 'forward school' and armed with instructions for 'a more definite equilateral practical alliance with Afghanistan', he was a man in historian Edwardes' words: 'blinded with imperial illusions. His political concepts emerged from a poet's word: he was seduced by the grandeur of an imperial mission.' A brilliant and gifted writer, he set out 'to give his delusions reality with the utmost single-mindedness', a single-mindedness 'born out of intolerance of opposition and contemptuousness of those of inferior intellect'.[15] His military adviser, Colonel George Pomeroy Colley (later to meet a hero's death at the Battle of Majuba in the First Anglo-Boer War), was a typical gung-ho member of the Wolseley ring and, with his subsequent boast that a single British regiment armed with breech-loaders could conquer Afghanistan, proved to be an appropriate collaborator in the more aggressive policies to follow.

These aggressive policies were to be greatly facilitated by the Viceroy's political remoteness from the British Government in London. In 1858, imperial control had been theoretically reasserted as, in the wake of the disastrous Indian Mutiny, East India Company rule had been abruptly and forcibly ended. The Crown assumed all authority over India via a Secretary of State for India who sat in the Cabinet, with a local civilian Viceroy appointed to India and a Commander-in-Chief established to run the newly established British-led Indian Army. Nevertheless, the slowness of communication still gave the Viceroy, as the man-on-the-spot, significant scope for independent action comparable to the old Company Governor-Generals. In his war policies, Lytton was to exploit such a lacuna to the full.

Lytton's first major move towards breaking the political impasse was to secure British control over Kalat in Baluchistan. A mission led by the renowned, ambitious frontier agent from the Punjab, Captain Robert Sandeman, duly negotiated a treaty with the Khan of Kalat whereby a British agent was re-established at Kalat and later, one at Quetta, with a British garrison dispatched in support in 1876.

Events outside Afghanistan now hastened the journey along the road to war. Once again, as in the build-up to the First Anglo-Afghan War, it was events in the Balkans and the Near East which greatly influenced matters. In 1878, Britain refused to accept the Treaty of San Stefano which concluded the recent Russo-Turkish War and gave unacceptable dominance to Russia over Turkey. To further deter Russian expansion in Europe and the Near East, Disraeli's Government secured the occupation of the strategically placed island of Cyprus, and Indian troops were rushed to garrison this island as well as Malta. As historian Edwardes has succinctly observed: 'The obvious Russian reply was to rumble in the vastness of Central Asia and force the government of India to the logical conclusions of its frontier tactics, an expedition against Afghanistan.'[16] On 22 July 1878, a mission led by Russian agent, General Stolietov, duly arrived in Kabul in an attempt to arrange a treaty with the new, now highly anxious Amir, Sher Ali, third son of Dost Mohammed, who, in 1868 after a bitter power-struggle with his brother, Afzal Khan, had finally secured the Afghan throne.

Back in India, Lytton had steadily ratcheted up the pressure on Sher Ali to concede to a British presence in Afghanistan and thereby counter growing Russian influence. Lytton's negative attitude to the Amir and his subjects was further blighted by a high degree of personal and, indeed, racial animosity. As early as February 1877, he had already confided to a military colleague, Colonel Sir Lewis Pelly, that the Amir 'has been harbouring in silence a rambling resentment against us for years'.[17] He later warned Sir Louis Mallett that: 'You underrate his cunning and his hatred of us … the Afghan will certainly take any amount of money you like to give him but he will also take care to give you nothing in return.'[18] Lytton also confided to another colleague, Sir Henry Dawes, that the Indian Government had been: 'living in a profound and perilous ignorance and while, asleep in a fool's paradise, the Russian authorities have been most energetic and successful in working against us in Kabul'.[19] Later, in a dispatch to Pollock, he even more outrageously claimed that the Amir had been exciting British subjects in India to 'join' a 'holy war' against British rule.[20] At Simla in 1876 and Peshawar from January to February 1877, negotiations with the Amir's already mortally ill Afghan envoy, Nur Muhammed Ali, soon stalled yet again on the thorny issue of a permanent

British Resident in Afghanistan and, just before his death on 26 March, Nur Muhammed Ali bitterly accused the British Government of 'imposing upon the Afghan government a burden which we cannot bear'.[21]

The earlier arrival of the Russian envoy, Major-General Stolietov, in Kabul had given Lytton and the 'forward school' the opportunity to increase pressure on Amir Sher Ali. However, the signing of a treaty in Berlin in 1878 which settled the Russo-Turkish question, and the recall of the Stolietov soon after his arrival, nearly scuppered Lytton's erstwhile desire to force the issue. Despite backtracking by Disraeli and Salisbury after their 'diplomatic victory' in Berlin, Lytton persisted in his 'folly' by immediately, without prior permission, dispatching a mission under Sir Neville Chamberlain to proceed to Kabul. In historian Edwardes' view, 'The casus belli was carefully manufactured.' The firm but courteous refusal of an Afghan frontier official, Governor Faiz Muhammed, to allow the British Mission passage through the Khyber Pass was duly elevated by Lytton into a 'forcible repulse'.[22] The problem was probably exacerbated by the selection of personnel for the mission. Chamberlain was generally regarded as a 'hot-headed' personality and his main negotiator, the brilliant, highly experienced, half-French half-Italian, Sir Pierre Louis Cavagnari, was nevertheless described by one contemporary as 'a man of rash and restless disposition and overbearing temper'.[23]

In any event, the matter had now become a far more serious one of imperial prestige and even the reluctant of members of Disraeli's Cabinet felt obliged to accede to Lytton's demand for an apology by the Afghan Government. Nevertheless, the politically cornered Disraeli was simultaneously furious with Lytton, especially since, as he pointed out, Lytton had not only failed to await a Russian answer to a British deputation clarifying the issue of the Stolietov Mission, but had then pre-emptively and provocatively sent the Chamberlain Mission without authority from the India Office. It was an act, in his view, of double disobedience. Disraeli accordingly scolded the principal Cabinet 'hawk', Lord Cranbrook, Lytton's main supporter at home and a vociferous supporter of war: 'When viceroys and commander-in-chief's disobey orders, they ought to be sure of success in their mutiny ... Lytton by disobeying orders has only secured insult and failure.'[24]

The Outbreak of War

Nevertheless, the 'bullied' Disraeli and his Cabinet felt compelled to support Lytton on this all-important issue of imperial prestige, with all its implications for the control of the Raj and, after what Lytton termed an 'insolent reply' on 19 October 1878, the Cabinet agreed to an ultimatum to be sent on 2 November This required both an apology and the reception of a permanent British Mission in Kabul. The ultimatum was set to expire on 20 November 1878. The Amir, hopelessly boxed in between Russia and Britain and now forced to defend not only his country's sovereignty but also its honour, understandably failed to respond. On 21 November 1879, war was effectively declared when three British columns converged upon Afghanistan. In many senses it was again an unnecessary war for, as in 1838, the immediate *casus belli* had been already removed by the retreat of the Russian Mission. For both countries, the price to be paid was again to be high.

British forces were rapidly set in motion. The invading army was divided into three separate columns. The first column; the Peshawar Valley Field Force, was commanded by Lieutenant-General Sir Samuel Browne, whose previous claim to fame included the invention of the famous officer's belt. His second-in-command, leading the second of the two divisions attached to this force, was Lieutenant-General Frederick Francis Maude, an officer of the 3rd Buffs and a Victoria Cross holder from the Crimean War. On 6 October 1878 this force comprised 325 officers, 15,854 men and forty-eight guns. The Peshawar Valley Field Force was directed to take the 'Khyber route' from Peshawar, its primary directive being to capture the Ali Masjid Fort which dominated the Khyber Pass.

A second column, the Kandahar Field Force, was led by the more elderly Lieutenant-General Donald Stewart. His second division was commanded by his second-in-command, Major-General Michael Biddulph. This force comprised 265 officers, 12,600 men and seventy-eight guns and it represented by far the largest of the three columns. Stewart's force was directed to move towards Kandahar via the Bolan and Khojak passes. Its reserve force was commanded by Lieutenant-General Primrose and numbered 6,000 men.

The third column, the Kurram Valley Field Force, was led by the redoubtable Major-General Frederick Roberts. He had won a Victoria Cross in the 1857 Indian Mutiny and had participated in several minor African campaigns. Roberts was directed to proceed up the Kurram Valley from Kohat. Roberts' father, Brigadier Abraham Roberts had, as we have seen, commanded a brigade in the First Anglo-Afghan War and his son was destined to achieve enduring fame from this campaign as well as putting into practice valuable lessons learnt from his father's experience in that disastrous previous war. His force represented the smallest of the three columns, comprising 116 officers, 6,550 men and eighteen guns. The three columns together totalled over 700 officers, 35,000 men and 140 guns.

The initial campaign plans had been to deploy only two columns, one to be mobilized at Sukkur on the River Indus for an advance on Kandahar, the other at Kohat for operations in the Kurram Valley. However, by 9 October 1878 the decision was taken to deploy a third column, 'To make a demonstration in the direction of the Khaiber for the purpose of clearing the troops out of the pass.'[25]

It was Major-General Roberts' Kurram Valley Field Force which effectively comprised the central front and which was destined to face the severest military challenge of this first British campaign of the Second Afghan War. At the start of his operations, Roberts had already displayed serious misgivings about the immensity of his task, particularly in regard to logistics. Firstly, he lacked manpower to safeguard his rear, with the Kohat garrison reduced to a minimum on his departure. Secondly, he was acutely aware of the volatility and unpredictability of the various Afridi tribes confronting him, especially those residing in the vicinity of Kurram. Equally worrying was the loyalty and condition of some of his own Indian troops. His Muslim sepoy regiments were a 'cause of considerable anxiety', for Roberts 'was aware that they were not altogether happy at the prospect of taking part in a war against their co-religionist, the Ruler of Afghanistan, and that the mullahs were already urging them to desert our cause'.[26] Later, at the battle of Peiwar Kotal, Roberts' fears in regard to the loyalty of the Muslim 29th Native Infantry would, as we shall see, become starkly evident. Of greater concern, perhaps, was the poor health and fitness of his British regular troops, with echoes of the chronic situation in Kabul during the First Afghan War. His only British infantry regiment, the 2nd Battalion of the 8th Foot, 'was sickly to the degree' and 'in an unserviceable condition'. It was 'largely comprised of quite young, un-acclimatised soldiers, peculiarly susceptible to fever'. Indeed, when he rode out to meet the battalion on its way to Kohat, he 'was horrified to see the long line of doolies and ambulance-carts by which it was accompanied'.[27]

Compared to the previous war, the British forces in 1878 at least possessed superior firepower with which to combat their Afghan enemy. The old Brown Bess musket had long been superseded by the .450 single-shot breech-loading Martini-Henry service rifle, with a superior range of up to 1,500 yards and the formidable 21-inch long 'lunger' socket bayonet. Each soldier carried seventy rounds in his ammunition pouch. Scarlet coats were still worn as part of the 1871 valise pattern equipment, although khaki was now in service with many regiments such as the 66th Foot. Blue serge trousers complemented often poor-quality leather marching boots. More protection from the sun was provided by the white 'foreign service' helmet. Officers carried a variety of swords and revolvers, many preferring the rapid-firing Navy Colts. Artillery remained superior and formidable, especially the lighter mountain gun sections, although heavy artillery pieces were still transported by elephant!

Their Afghan enemy were of variable quality and mainly comprised, as in the First Anglo-Afghan War, tribal levies who were still predominantly armed with the long-range *jezail rifle*, *tulwars* and the dreaded Khyber knife. The most formidable fighters remained the fanatical *Ghazi*, who were to prove devastating 'shock troops' when deployed in close-quarter battles, such as Ahmed Khel and Maiwand. The Afghan regular formations were better armed but could be unreliable, especially if badly led or under-paid. Nevertheless, their trained gunners and some of their more modern artillery pieces could be very effective, as again witnessed at Maiwand.

As in the First Anglo-Afghan War, transport problems soon reared their ugly head for the assembling British Forces. Thousands of camels, mules and bullocks were purchased daily but only at exorbitant prices. Confusion reigned amongst the British Commissariats and few lessons had been learnt in this quarter. As Roberts confirmed: 'Not withstanding the difficult experiences in former campaigns from the same cause, the government had neglected to take any steps for the arrangement of a proper transport service while we were at peace.'[28]

While Roberts' logistical problems remained a continuous issue, the initial Afghan political response to his advance proved more positive than anticipated. As his under-strength column advanced into the Kurram, he received, on the 21 November, one letter from the 'Saidads of Kurram, 'enquiring when the force would arrive there as the people have been suffering much from the tyranny of the Amir'.[29] Proceeding along the 'bleak and deserted' sixty-mile long and three-to-ten-mile-wide Kurram Valley, Roberts further noted how 'the head men from different villages came out to welcome us and, on arriving at Hazir Pir, we found a plentiful repast awaiting us spread under the shade of some trees'.[30]

The Battle of Peiwar Kotal

Approaching the mountainous Peiwar Kotal, however, General Roberts faced his first serious military test of the campaign. This rocky, fir-crowned barrier, located at the western extremity of the Kurram Valley was, in the words of Roberts:

Indeed a formidable position, a great deal more formidable than I had expected; lying on the summit of a mountain rising abruptly 2,000 feet above us and only approachable by a narrow, steep, and rugged path, flanked on either side by precipitous spurs jutting out like huge bastions, from which an overwhelming fire could be brought to bear on the assailants.[31]

Occupying the heights and barring Roberts' advance was a hostile Afghan garrison led by Karim Khan, which comprised seven regular regiments with seventeen guns totalling over 7,000 men. The battle was nearly lost at the start. Receiving news of an apparent Afghan retreat, Roberts initially made some arguably rash deployments on 28 November which courted disaster. As historian Hanna succinctly observes, what Roberts called a 'reconnaissance in force' was 'misleading'. Probably lured by Turi spies in the pay of rebel Afghan Government agents, Roberts' gung-ho tactics in committing the bulk of his force against what appeared to be a retreating enemy constituted a huge risk. Both Brigadier-General Cobbe's Infantry Brigade and Brigadier-General Thelwall's Brigades were committed far too early against a still unknown enemy. It was contrary to all military precedent for a commander to, in the words of Hanna,

> make a reconnaissance with the whole of his force, including guns on elephants, and no general would direct his subordinates at the end of a twenty one mile march to attack, with hungry and exhausted men, an unknown enemy in a position of extraordinary natural strength, except in the hope of snatching a success by the very irregularity and temerity of his tactics.[32]

In fact, it was arguably only the ill-discipline of the Afghan artillery units, who opened fire too early, thereby revealing the hidden strength of their position, which redirected the British advance and thereby saved both Roberts' reputation and his force from a potential major defeat or, even, annihilation. As eyewitness Major Colquhoun, recalled:

> The eagerness of the Afghans to commence hostilities was the salvation of the force. If, knowing the range as they did, and being in an inaccessible position, they had been content to wait until the camp was pitched at Turai and had commenced to shell the camp with all their mountain guns after dark had set in, the consequence would have been most serious. Nothing could have been done except to withdraw from the camp, but, in all probability there would have been a stampede among the mules and their gunners and with the other camp-followers would have taken themselves well out of reach

of danger. The camp, with all the bedding and baggage might have been burned down and the Kurram Field Force have been rendered 'hors de combat' for some time.[33]

It had been a near-run thing.

In consequence, Roberts, now acutely aware of the immensity of the enemy challenge, proceeded to adopt far more sensible tactics. There was to be no frontal attack. Instead, three reconnoitring forces were dispatched. One returned with the crucial information that the enemy's left wing might be turned by a route over a ravine known as the Spingawi Kotal. Feigning a frontal attack by placing his gun batteries forward, Roberts' plan was now, by means of a night attack on the Spingawi Kotal, to throw his main body on the enemy's left, whilst the rest of his troops were to make a direct attack as soon as the turning movement could be developed. With Brigadier-General Thelwall as second-in-command, Roberts personally led the turning force. This consisted of the 29th Punjab Infantry, the 5th Gurkhas, the 72nd Highlanders, the 2nd Punjab Infantry, the 23rd Pioneers and eight guns, a grand total of 2,263 officers and men. At 10 p.m. on 1 December 1878, Roberts' force silently ascended the mountain and, at 6 a.m. on 2 December the column reached the foot of Spingawi Kotal. Here, Afghan sentries soon raised the alarm. Heavy fighting began and the 5th Gurkhas and the 72nd Highlanders fought ferociously as they carried stockade after stockade at the point of the bayonet, assisted by No. 1 Mountain Battery.

At 7.20 a.m. on 2 December, as the enemy's line was turned, Brigadier-General Cobbe, alerted by heliograph, duly opened fire upon the shaken enemy defences from the main British camp below. However, the battle on the heights did not proceed entirely smoothly and was checked at one precipitous gully where an isolated Major-General Roberts, losing touch with his Highlanders and Gurkhas, but displaying enormous sang-froid, only beat off the enemy with the help of the Sikhs and the less reliable 29th Punjab Native Infantry. By 1 p.m., reinforced by the 2nd Punjab Infantry, the crest of the hill was secured, enabling Brigadier-General Cobbe to move his guns forward and engage the Kotal batteries more closely.

The British infantry were now able to push forward and, by noon, were 1,400 yards from the top of the Kotal. Soon after 1 p.m. Cobbe's infantry had also gained a nearby hill, from which they fired at 800 yards upon the Kotal guns, driving off the Afghan gunners, a noted triumph for the volley fire of the Martini-Henry rifle. At about 2 p.m., to avoid the heavily armed Afghan flank, Roberts launched a second turning movement positioning him about a mile behind the Peiwar Kotal, thus completing the rout with

Cobbe's 8th King's Regiment advancing up the road to capture the Kotal, without further loss, at 2.30 p.m. The outflanked enemy fled, leaving eighteen guns and vast stores; the 12th Bengal Cavalry under Brigadier-General Gough engaging in hot pursuit. While the Afghan casualties ran into hundreds, the British only lost two officers and eighteen men killed and seventy-eight wounded.

Although later acclaimed as a significant victory, the battle of Peiwar Kotal had, in essence, been a high-risk enterprise. The British attack had suffered few casualties and great heroism and discipline had been displayed against a well-entrenched enemy. However, Roberts had nearly fallen into the enemy trap and some military historians, notably Hanna, considered even his subsequent turning movement dangerous: the turning force itself was isolated and lacked precise ground-level intelligence of the terrain and the Afghans, who fought bravely, could have overwhelmed Cobbe in the camp whilst Roberts was passing up the Spingawi Kotal *nullah* (ravine). Night movements are always risky, although Roberts was wise to attack at dawn. Overall, Colonel Hanna considered that Roberts' better plan might have been to contain the Afghans at the Peiwar, thus assisting the Khyber force, and then draw them from their positions (as Kitchener later drew the Dervish forces from Omdurman in 1898) and then finally to defeat them.[34] It was an initially flawed if, ultimately stunning, victory.

It remained for Roberts to mop up enemy remnants in the Kurram Valley and clear the Khost region. He launched what was essentially a punitive expedition, which revealed the ruthless side to Roberts' generalship. It was a ruthlessness first demonstrated by his treatment of a score of Muslim sepoy deserters, termed 'traitors', two of whom had fired shots during the night attack on Peiwar Kotal, allegedly in order to warn the enemy. Eighteen sepoys were duly given from one to fourteen years' transportation and one was executed. For Roberts, their mutinous behaviour had realized his worst initial fears. As he explained to the Adjutant-General: 'The serious misconduct of so many sepoys before the enemy, the recent desertions of trans-frontier men with their rifles from more than one regiment ... have all pointed for the necessity for a stern example.'[35]

While he expressed 'regret to have been obliged to adopt such stringent punitive measures', he remonstrated 'they will have a most salutary effect upon the minds of all Pathans or others whose sense of fidelity and ... duty may have been momentarily shaken by the appeals of their co-religionists'.[36]

Roberts' harshness was soon also evident in the punitive policies he adopted against those 'hostile' Khost villagers who had constantly harassed his weakly protected convoys in the rear. Roberts was still 'greatly hampered by limitations of transport' with 'very few supplies ... obtained in the vicinity of Kurram'.[37] His Commissary-General had further reported that provisions for only a few days remained in hand. Attacks by local tribesmen on his overstretched columns, again reminiscent of the First Anglo-Afghan War, had greatly exacerbated these supply difficulties. In January 1879 Roberts admitted that the 'apparent weakness of our force had attracted many from a distance in hopes of plunder and the preachings of the moollas had stirred up the well known fanatics of Khost'.[38] Earlier, in December 1878, his baggage train had suffered a major attack by 'a band of marauders belonging to the Mangals who live on the left bank of the Kurram River', the baggage only being saved by the 'steadiness of the 5th Goorkhas'. The Mangals had 'suffered severely' and 'the attack', he asserted, 'was quite unprovoked' and 'the tribe were probably induced to trouble by some refugees from the Amir's army'.[39]

Retribution, akin to that exacted by Major-Generals Pollock and Nott in 1842, was soon to follow as a vengeful Roberts approached a thirty-village complex near Matun. In January 1879, after the murder of twenty-two followers, four local Afghans were hanged and one flogged, all apparently caught 'red handed'. In a speech to the people of Khost at a 25 January *durba* (meeting), while claiming that there had not been a 'single incidence of a soldier entering your villages or molesting any of your people', Roberts, nevertheless, warned that those who opposed him would be 'severely punished'. After more heavy attacks on supply columns by an estimated 200-strong tribal raiding force, another British punitive column was dispatched toward several Khost villages. As Roberts himself put it, 'vigorous action was evidently necessary'.[40] On 7 January 1879 a largely cavalry force, consisting of mainly 10th Hussars and 5th Punjab Cavalry units, crushed an enemy attack on Roberts' camp and returned with 100 prisoners, 500 head of cattle and a large quantity of grain. At this point Roberts clearly overreacted, deciding that the tribesmen 'had not been sufficiently punished'. He therefore ordered a brutal collective punishment. As a deterrent, 'to prevent repetition of the attack', he 'ordered the destruction of the hamlets nearest us'.[41] A 'most unfortunate incident' then occurred. After the taking of over a hundred prisoners and hostages, who were to be released only after the payment of fifty rupees each by local Waziri headmen, six prisoners were killed and thirteen wounded after an attempted breakout.

Back in England, serious political repercussions soon followed these incidents and great capital was made by the anti-war party in parliament. One MP alleged that 'some ninety prisoners ... had been tied together with ropes' and that 'on their making some attempt to escape they were set upon and many of them slaughtered in their bonds [and] the dead, living, the dying and the wounded were left tied together and lying in one confused mass of bodies'.[42] Other allegations included reports that the punitive force of 7 January was ordered 'to give no quarter'. For the first time, Roberts had been exposed to the full fury of the British media, public opinion and parliament, to a degree never experienced by his First Afghan War antecedents. Whilst robustly defending the charges against him, an enraged Roberts opted for a relentless censorship policy towards the several news-paper correspondents accompanying his forces, although it was possible that military colleagues may have leaked the war crimes allegations. Thus war correspondent Mr MacPherson, Special Correspondent of the *London Standard*, was primarily singled out and sacked after a series of highly crit-ical reports, and from then on Roberts ensured he employed only those correspondents he deemed to be loyal, notably Howard Hensman. Thus, in April 1879, Roberts conveyed his thanks to Secretary Lyall for his warn-ings regarding another correspondent, Renwick, saying: 'I see his peculiarities and am aware he can't be trusted too far!' Roberts added: 'I have already forbidden him to send letters to Padshah Khan or anyone else in Kabul without my seeing them first.'[43] It was a control soon to be extended to the accompanying 'politicals', especially during the second 'revenge campaign' of 1879–80.

The Campaign of the Peshawar Valley Field Force

As Roberts controversially consolidated his political authority and stamped his authority over the Kurram and the Khost regions, the campaign of the second column under General Sam Browne had begun catastrophically. As with Roberts, the movements of the Peshawar Valley Field Force had been largely politically driven and deliberately planned to avoid clashes with key tribal groups. It was a lesson well-learnt from the costly 1839–42 campaign and other Frontier campaigns. For the attack on the great Afghan medieval fortress of Ali Masjid, which dominated the Khyber Pass, Browne's column left Peshawar, and occupied nearby Jamrud, on November 20th 1878. His two brigades under Brigadier-Generals MacPherson and Tytler initially planned their attack so as not to stir up local Afridi tribal groups. Accordingly both commanders worked their forces round to the extreme right and north of the fortress; the first, to attack on the flank, the second to take a wide detour to reach Kata Kushtai, two miles beyond Ali Masjid and thus command the defile by which the enemy could escape. It was, arguably, a high-risk manoeuvre in a country of such difficult and unknown terrain.

The timing of the attack was fixed for 1 p.m., 21 November 1878 and, on that day, Browne's central column marched up the Khyber and confronted the estimated 3,800-strong Afghan garrison led by Faiz Muhammed, whose force was supported by twenty-four guns. General Browne briefly halted to allow his own 40-pounder elephant batteries to catch up and then launched a ferocious assault. The Reverend Arthur Male witnessed the colourful scene:

> Presently, the bugle sounded the attack; and, as the last echo reverberated amongst the mountains, the 81st Regiment and the 14th Sikhs could be seen throwing forward a line of skirmishers to clear adjoining hill-sides while Manderson's Battery, ICRHA, came galloping around the bend of the hill and ... opened fire on the guns of the fort. In an instant the Afghan gunners returned the fire, and with good effect, for the range of the various points along the Pass had been carefully taken by them before the fighting opened. And now the crash of shells as they exploded and the constant rattle and roll of the rifle fire made valley and mountainside alive with deafening reverberation. The men pressed on with impetuous valour but the wild defenders of the fort and sungah [breastwork] were nothing daunted. Gun answered gun while crowds of Afghan warriors could be seen rushing out to man the outer entrenchments and even streaming over the hill-side. Suddenly, the welcome sound of the big forty pounders, a deep toned hoarse booming, could be heard behind. The elephant battery had at last arrived and taken up position and was now playing upon the same fortress to some tune. Gradually the enemy's fire was silenced, or more particularly slowed.[44]

Although the British now dominated the enemy artillery, their frontal infantry assault, which inexorably followed at 2.25 p.m., soon got into difficulty. Firstly, the British artillery began to run out of shells and secondly, General Browne had ordered the attack not only without knowing the precise position of his other two turning columns, but also on the 'political' advice of Sir Pierre Louis Cavagnari, who wished to impress the large numbers of Afghan tribal observers of the battle and deter them from joining in. With Brigadier-General F.E. Appleyard detached to the left as another 'turning force', Browne's forces slogged their way up, with severe losses sustained by the Sikh infantry regiments whilst bravely assaulting the well-defended enemy *sangars*.

The onset of night and the lack of news of MacPherson's and Tytler's progress, combined with the prospect of further heavy losses, decided

Browne to order what became a confused retreat to the valley. Fortunately for Major-General Browne, the morning revealed a total evacuation by the enemy of the Ali Masjid fortress positions, most fleeing westward to the right where Major-General Tytler, after a horrendous march literally scrambling through the rocks, was himself able to capture 260 of the fleeing Afghan troops. Tytler's particularly horrific night march and camp were vividly recalled by Captain R.J. Gordon Creed: 'There was no road or path.... The main body lost the advance guard.... It was bitterly cold all night; no fires were allowed to be lighted ... the ascent was exceedingly steep and, had the enemy been there, the summit could never have been reached without the loss of a great many lives'.[45]

Back in Calcutta, Lord Lytton was enraged by this pyrrhic victory, which nearly ended in disaster and even called for Browne's court martial. In fact Lytton's own last-minute order to advance on 21 November had given Browne little time to prepare. One military expert, Colonel Hanna, opines that Browne should have acted more prudently and, like Pollock in 1842, he should have declined to move until he had been reinforced.[46] However, General Browne, perhaps foolishly, had also allowed himself to be further divided in his military decision-making by the political counsels of the more aggressive and 'interfering' local 'political', Cavagnari, and had originally rushed his frontal attack without confirming the progress of his flanking columns. Such political interference again recalls the many incidents of the First Anglo-Afghan War where political advice undermined military operations.[47] Unlike Roberts, Browne lacked the ability, authority or wherewithal to control or to avoid excessive political interference in military operations.

From a purely military perspective, General Browne also lacked intelligence and suitable maps and, although his fellow commander, Roberts, achieved a brilliant night manoeuvre at Peiwar Kotal, such marches and turning movements in the dark, with separation of forces in difficult terrain, were always high-risk. Some tacticians have even suggested that Browne might have cut enemy communications with Dakka behind Ali Masjid by pushing part of his force past the fortress but this, again, would have involved superior co-ordination for a force distinctly lacking in intelligence and facing incredibly difficult terrain.[48]

Following this very narrow victory, General Browne moved on to secure Dakka, detaching Brigadier Appleyard with the 3rd Brigade to secure Landi Khana. At Dakka, however, there was no food and everything had to be carried from Peshawar in the face of numerous attacks by raiding Afridis. In the event, it took at least a brigade of troops to secure the line of communications. It took until 17 December 1878 before the discredited Major-General Browne's column finally reach Jalalabad.

As with Roberts in the Kurram, the Khyber campaign now deteriorated into a series of punitive raids mainly carried out by Browne's subordinate commander, Lieutenant-General Frederick Maude, whose 6,000-strong reserve force had earlier arrived at Peshawar. One of Maude's punitive expeditions was particularly ferocious. His expedition, comprising two columns, one launched from Dakka and the other from the now-occupied Ali Masjid, lasted from 19 to 22 December 1878. Numerous Afghan villages were burnt, looted of grain and firewood, and their protective towers razed to the ground. Northumberland Fusilier, Private Cooper, recalled the ferocity of one of these retribution raids launched from Jamrud against the Zakkha Khel Afridi tribal group in the Bazar Valley on 19 December. He reported how, after a stiff hand-to-hand skirmish involving the 5th Fusiliers and the 2nd Ghurkhas, a terrible fate befell the defenders of the village of Cheena: 'The enemy having been thoroughly beaten, they were all made prisoners, and, as after a short time some of them began to give trouble by attempting to escape from their captors, the whole of them were at once killed and their bodies 'reserved for the soup pot' in the evening.'[49]

By March 1879, frustration over the mounting number of murderous raids launched against British supply lines led Maude's commanders to resort to even more draconian measures. As the current system of punishment consisting of flogging and/or imprisonment for robbery 'was found to work very badly, it was determined that if any more prisoners were brought in they should be shot'. Thus, of five marauders captured by Lancers on March 11th four were accordingly shot, one 'ruffian' fortunately being spared after receiving fifty lashes and 'told to go to his tribe and tell them how he and his companions had been dealt with by the Kafirs'.[50] Worse was to follow. On 13 March 1879 the practice became official. Lieutenant-General Maude, accordingly: 'issued an order ... that all tribesmen caught in the act of robbery or murdering our followers, attacking any convoys, stealing camels, or even *attempting* to commit any of these or similar outrages, were not to be made prisoners but shot on the spot. This order seemed to have the desired effect.'[51]

Several contemporary critics deprecated these excesses, particularly the belligerent role of Browne's attached political officer and superior, Sir Pierre Louis Cavagnari, which was seen as counterproductive. 'The whole policy of punitive expeditions, urged on by Cavagnari, was foolish, and indeed Cavagnari should not have been there',[52] ventured one critic. Nevertheless, operations of this nature continued until April 1879. 'Severe punishment', was, for instance, awarded to the Shinwari villages near Pesh Bolak, an area already hit hard during the First Afghan War, with Major-General Tytler's Lancers charging and burning 'several villages'.[53]

By stark contrast to Roberts' controversial actions, many of these raids escaped public attention at home. However, military historian Colonel Hanna was particularly critical of the indiscriminate nature of such punitive expeditions. Cavagnari's first expedition was, he asserts, 'uncalled for and unwise', as 'for interfering in the domestic quarrels of the Mohmands, Cavagnari turned the whole tribe into enemies and compelled Sir Samuel Browne to waste the strength of his troops in exhausting and futile operations.' While accepting that there was 'good grounds' for the later expedition against the Shinwaris, Hanna argued that there was 'no excuse for burning down two of their villages and turning their women and children adrift in mid-winter'. He contended that the 'proper punishment' was fines or confiscation of arms or blowing up of towers as, 'these fall directly on the men of the tribes, and only indirectly affect its women and children'. During the Bazar Valley expedition, Hanna further pinpointed the old recurring problem of competing authorities in the field, or what he called 'the vexed question of the relationship between military commanders and political officers'.[54] Tytler's politically driven raids by small, vulnerable forces were, he asserted, arranged by Cavagnari and Sir Samuel Browne, 'but its real authors were the Viceroy and his government who kept the Second Division so weak that its commander had not sufficient troops to carry out single-handed the behests of the Political Officer to whom they had subordinated him'.[55] Similarly, General Maude, 'burdened with responsibility for the safety of communications of the whole Khyber Force' was 'compelled to take orders from men his inferior in age, standing and experience'. Regarding the roles of 'politicals' and military commanders, Hanna stated:

> Political Officers are useful and necessary to furnish the General to whose force they are attached with information and advice, supposing them to know the country in which war is being waged better than he does, and, to act as intermediaries between him and its inhabitants ... but ... when it comes to military measures, great or small, only he will be held accountable for their failure should they fail, and can justly be invested with the power to initiate, control and end them.

In a further indirect reference to Cavagnari's 'interfering role' and the failure to deploy local expert McNabb in the Bazar Valley campaigns, Hanna postulated: 'In the field, a Commander should be an autocrat; if a bad one the remedy is not to give him a civilian or, what is worse, a comparatively junior military officer as his master but to recall him and put a better man in his place.'[56]

Elements of Browne's column fought one more large-scale battle before the end of this first phase of the 1878–80 Anglo-Afghan War. On 2 April 1879, a column under Brigadier-General Gough clashed with 5,000 Afghans at Futtehabad, fifteen miles off the Jalalabad to Kabul road. Gough advanced his cavalry and, by gradually retiring, induced the enemy to leave their strong defensive position. The infantry then attacked them and, as they weakened, the cavalry completed the rout and, perhaps, the most decisive campaign action of the war.

The Campaign of the Kandahar Field Force

The third column, the Kandahar Field Force, led by Lieutenant-General Sir Donald Stewart, enjoyed a comparatively less eventful campaign than the other two, perhaps rather unjustifiably described by journalist and historian Archibald Forbes as a 'military promenade'. However, it was certainly forced to endure the worst marching conditions. The lead force under second-in-command Major-General Michael Biddulph, advanced at dawn on 21 November, crossing the Afghanistan frontier into the sandy wastes beyond. It was truly a 'wilderness campaign', most of the force traversing virtually the same extreme, arduous route as the 1839 invasion force through the deserts of Baluchistan, proceeding via the Bolan and Khojak Passes and thence to Quetta. Moreover, both Stewart's and Biddulph's columns suffered through a chronic lack of supplies, initially securing only seven days' rations since, 'no price, however high, could induce the people to part with their own winter-store'.[57] Many of the regular British detachments were, moreover, hopelessly ill-equipped for such a testing experience. Hanna described the 70th Foot (Royal Surreys) thus:

> No zeal or forethought, however, could compensate for the lack of articles of the first necessity, and they had to submit to the mortification and anxiety of seeing the 70th enter on its long march with no clothing save the cotton coats and trousers in which they had left Multan and of knowing that the camp followers were in still more pitiable case.[58]

Biddulph considered their situation as 'critical' and 'special arrangements had to be originated to ensure their comfort and security'.[59] At one stage around a hundred men of the 70th were unable even to walk. Their progress was seriously hampered by the huge amount of heavy artillery attached to the force, with huge delays incurred through negotiating the difficult gradients of the major passes. At Khojak Pass the column was even forced to re-use the old 'zigzag' route of 1839–42. Moving the guns through the sandy wastes around Rojan had been a particularly exhausting enterprise before the campaign even began, with the gun-carriage wheels cutting through the thin earth crusts and sinking into loose sand: 'Wagon after wagon stuck and was left behind.'[60]

As in the 1839–40 campaign, camels died in huge numbers and, even in the Pishin Valley, extreme temperatures took their toll: 'Day after day scores of famished camels were found of a morning, dead, frozen fast to the ground on which they had sunk down the previous evening.'[61] The column passed the Haikalzai, a place with ominous historical overtones, being the spot where General England's force had been repelled in 1842 and forced back to Quetta. Even the old Afghan *sangars* were still visible there.

Politically, the progress of Stewart's columns was at least easier than the other two, owing to the stupendous and skilful efforts of the experienced political agent for Baluchistan, Sir Robert Sandeman. He most skilfully negotiated successful terms with the Baluchi chiefs and secured hill camels, food and warm clothing supplies further along the route. By stark contrast to 1839, relations with the Khan of Kalat were firmly established: 'Our position on the plateau was very different now to what it had been in the former expeditions when the Khan and the people were wavering or hostile and when the want of food put our troops to the greatest straits and sacrifices.'[62] Tragically, as we shall see, Sandeman's valuable supportive role was to be a rare exception and his sterling efforts were soon negated by the nefarious activities of other political officers attached to, for instance, Major-Generals Browne's and Maude's columns.

Nevertheless, Baluchi aid was dearly bought at a rate of eight rupees for the conveyance of a camel-load, the whole cost reaching the grand total of £320! Once again, local merchants and traders had made huge profits from the progress of British columns. One bonus was that key Baluchi chiefs were successfully induced to join the column, and Biddulph confirmed that they exerted a highly beneficial influence over the border and around Kalat.[63]

After careful reconnaissance of the Rogani, Gwaja and Khojak Passes in early December 1879 the columns moved through without major incident, although Major-General Biddulph, arguably rather recklessly, detached himself from the main body to reconnoitre the hostile Kakar country. In Colonel Hanna's stern appraisal: 'The proper place of a commander moving in an enemy's country, especially if ignorant of that enemy's whereabouts and intention, is with his main body.'[64] On 15

December 1879 Biddulph's advance guard reached Chaman where his commander, General Stewart joined him via the Bolan Pass, and assumed overall control. For the rest of December 1878 Biddulph's column continued to stream into Chaman and his and Stewart's Divisions moved concentrically on Takht-i-Pul.

On 4 January 1879, Stewart's column had its first and only significant brush with the enemy in the Mel Valley. Elements of the 1st Punjab Cavalry and 15th Hussars charged a body of hostile Afghan cavalry. When they were within 200 yards the enemy's nerve failed. As they fled, the British cavalry halted, dismounted and opened a withering fire with their Martini-Henry carbines, emptying the saddles of their retreating enemy. It was an encouraging result. Biddulph wryly observed: 'This first encounter with the Afghan troops did not promise to us the sturdy resistance we had hoped for.'[65]

On 8 January 1879 the two British columns entered Kandahar, the city already evacuated by Afghan troops. Here, hopes of peace and fear of the impending hot weather led to orders from above directing Stewart to remain. In military terms, it had been a relatively bloodless campaign, but the poor healthcare and unsuitable equipment had resulted in rows between Generals Stewart and Biddulph, the former vilifying the latter for leaving disease-ridden camel corpses across his line of march at Quetta and along the Bolan Pass. In the words of one commentator:

> As far as the Baluchis were concerned Sir Robert Sandeman kept them quiet throughout the war and the real difficulty of the line east of Quetta arose from the insanitary conditions and from the congestion produced by the government's folly in sending along a siege train; perfectly useless unless Herat was to be besieged; west of Quetta ... the line was exposed.'[66]

Faced with this determined British aggression on three fronts, Amir Sher Ali predictably turned to his erstwhile Russian allies for support. None was to be forthcoming. On 30 November 1878 he had belatedly replied to the British ultimatum, offering to facilitate a temporary British Mission but refusing to apologize for the actions of Faiz Muhammed in the blocking of the Chamberlain Mission. The Amir's answer was swiftly rejected. As Sher Ali's armies crumbled after the Peiwar Kotal defeat, Russian General Kaufman finally and firmly rejected the Amir's desperate pleas for help, the Russian refusal being explained by the impossibility of sending Russian troops across the Hindu Kush passes in winter. On 22 December 1878, a now deeply depressed Sher Ali finally abandoned Kabul alongside the remaining members of the Russian Mission and took refuge in Russian territory. Weary and sick, he returned to Mazar-i-Sharif and, refusing food and medicine, died aged fifty-six on 21 February 1879. Before leaving Kabul, Sher Ali formally handed over control of his affairs to his son, Yakub Khan. As the British columns continued to triumph, negotiations for a settlement were opened and executed 'with ominous facility'[67] by the end of May 1879. The principal clauses of the Treaty of Gandamak of May 1879 required the new Amir to conduct his foreign relations in accordance with the advice and wishes of the British Government and to receive a permanent British representative at Kabul and elsewhere in Afghanistan as required. By the treaty the British were to retain control of the Khyber Pass and of the newly occupied districts of Pishin, Sibi and Kurram and to pay the new Amir an annual subsidy of £60,000.

Lord Lytton was overjoyed at the apparent success of his 'forward policies'. The Gandamak Treaty would avoid a costly British occupation, although he still considered the idea of dismembering Afghanistan. Many of his contemporaries, however, harboured secret doubts. As journalist and historian Archibald Forbes confirmed: 'There were many who distrusted the frivolity of the Treaty of Gundamuk.'[68] General Roberts was a major if covert critic, confining his pessimistic feelings to the Viceroy's military adviser, Colonel Colley and being, no doubt, anxious not to publicly upset his key patron, Lord Lytton. Later, in hindsight, Roberts again drew powerful parallels with the First Afghan War. In a letter which also deeply reflected his own racial stereotypes he wrote:

> I personally was not at all satisfied that the time had come for negotiation for I felt that the Afghans had not had the sense of defeat sufficiently driven into them to convince them of our strength and ability to punish breach of treaty.... The Afghan are an essentially arrogant and conceited people; they had not forgotten our disastrous retreat from Kabul, nor the annihilation of our army in the Khurd-Kabul and Jagdalak Passes in 1842, and believe themselves to be quite capable of resisting our advances on Kabul. No great battle had as yet been fought; although Ali Musjid and the Peiwar Kotal had been taken, a small force of the enemy had been beaten by Charles Gough's brigade near Jalalabad and a successful cavalry skirmish had occurred near Kandahar, the Afghans had nowhere sufficient serious loss, and it was not to be wondered at if the fighting men in distant villages and in and around Kabul Gahzni Herat Balkh and other places, still considered themselves undefeated and capable of defying us.[69]

However, this premature end to the conflict may also have equally reflected Roberts' own frustrated military ambitions. As he confided to Lyall, while 'to have Yakub Khan in a British camp is indeed a triumph ... It would have been very satisfactory to have taken my splendid division across the Shutargardan but I quite understand the necessity for ending the war as soon as possible.'[70] In fact, further military glory for Roberts was not to be long delayed. Many Afghans would not have forgotten recent British depredations, especially when it was announced that the ill-fated officer Sir Pierre Louis Cavagnari, a prime instigator of earlier collective punishment strategies, would be appointed as Britain's first Permanent Envoy to Kabul since the murdered MacNaghten.

The next tragic phase of British involvement in Afghanistan opened swiftly. The British Mission, with Cavagnari at its head, reached Kabul in July 1879. Major-General Roberts met him *en route* near the Shutargardan Pass but he was almost immediately filled with morbid apprehension. He wrote: 'After dinner I was asked to propose the health of Cavagnari and those with him, but somehow I did not feel equal to the task; I was so thoroughly depressed, and my mind was filled with such gloomy forebodings as to the fate of these fine fellows that I could not utter a word.' By stark contrast: 'Cavagnari ... showed no signs of sharing my forebodings; he spoke most hopefully of the future, talked of a tour he hoped to make with me in the cold weather along the northern and western frontiers of Afghanistan.'[71] It was not to be. Brave farewell hand-shakes were preceded by what Roberts considered one terrible portent of doom: 'As we ascended ... we came across a solitary magpie, which I should not have noticed had not Cavagnari pointed it out and begged me not to mention the fact of his having seen it to his wife, as she would be sure to consider it an unlucky omen.'[72] Perhaps Cavagnari privately shared Roberts' doubts. Indeed, when congratulated on his appointment by General Sir Frederick Haines, Commander-in-Chief, India, with the words, 'This is a great chance for you Cavagnari', Cavagnari had crypti-cally replied: 'Yes sir, it is a case of man or mouse.'[73]

After six weeks of uneasy quiet, Roberts' worst fears were realized. On 3 September 1879 the whole Mission was attacked and brutally massacred by large bodies of mutinous Afghan soldiers, supported by elements of the Kabul mobs. Cavagnari, three European colleagues, his escort of twenty-five Guides and fifty-two Gurkha infantry were overwhelmed. The story of their gallant resistance has been much recounted, reviving as it did the memories of the terrible fates of Envoys Burnes and MacNaghten in the winter of 1841. Officially, Cavagnari had remained cheerfully optimistic in the face of the oncoming storm, even telling the Viceroy on 30 July, 'I personally believe that Yakub Khan will turn out to be a very good ally and that we shall be able to keep him to his engagement.' His last telegram, dispatched to Lord Lytton the day before the massacre, ended with the fateful words: 'All well.'[74]

During these final days, like his murdered antecedent Alexander Burnes, Cavagnari also apparently received urgent warnings from friends and allies One warning, delivered by Nakhshband Khan, a local loyal Afghan-born sepoy home in Kabul on leave, led Cavagnari to riposte rather recklessly, 'Dogs that bark do not bite.' The sepoy allegedly replied in turn: 'But these dogs do bite and there is danger.' 'Well', Cavagnari concluded, 'they can only kill a handful of us here and our death will be well avenged.'[75]

The crisis apparently arose over pay arrears, leading to violent demonstrations by Afghan regular troops. However, friction had already arisen between Cavagnari's escort troops and Afghan soldiers in the bazaars during the preceding weeks. The mutineers were soon, either foolishly or maliciously, directed by one Afghan regular officer to the British Residency, ostensibly to collect their back pay from their new British paymasters. Stone-throwing soon broke out and Cavagnari, again rather like Burnes before him, was shouted down by the mob as he tried to placate them from the roof of the British Mission, which was located behind the Bala Hissar. As Cavagnari desperately tried to redirect the mob back to the Amir's palace or to the Treasury to collect their pay arrears, shots rang out and the desperate struggle began. It was a tactically hopeless situation as the Residency was easily dominated by the already looted Arsenal above them, and was also vulnerable to fire from above. With the mutineers now armed to the teeth, their ferocious assault was joined by local *badmashes*, eager for plunder. Cavagnari, after apparently shooting dead four mob leaders, was one of the first defenders to fall, shot in the forehead (one source claims from a ricochet), but his three fellow officers and civilian colleagues, Lieutenant Walter Hamilton VC, Surgeon-Major Dr A.H. Kelly and Mr William Jenkyns of the Bengal Civil Service, fought on with their Guides' escort, even bravely launching several desperate sallies against their attackers. One eyewitness, the same sepoy pensioner who had earlier warned Cavagnari, graphically recalled:

While the fighting was going on, I myself saw the four European officers charge out at the head of some twenty five of the garrison; they drove away a party holding some broken ground. When chased the Afghan soldiers ran like sheep before a wolf. Later, another sally was made by a detachment with but three officers at their head. Cavagnari was not with them this time. A third sally was made with only two officers leading, Hamilton and Jenkyns, and the last of the sallies was made by a Sikh Jemadar [native officer] bravely leading. No more sallies were made after this.[76]

Soon, by deploying escalading ladders, the attackers forced the defenders off the roof and into the interior of the building. The burden of the defence now fell upon a young subaltern, Lieutenant Walter Hamilton, whose final gallant exploits were to earn him a Victoria Cross and a place in the annals of Victorian heroism. Two big guns were then brought up by the mutineers and in another famous sortie Hamilton led the Guides in a brave if futile attempt to capture the guns. As the attackers bored loop-holes through the walls and the house caught fire, the situation became hopeless. Lieutenant Hamilton was finally killed on his third sally, after apparently killing three men with his pistol and cutting down two more with his sword! However, a further act of equal valour was carried out on a fourth and final sally by Jemadar Jeward Singh, a 'splendid Sikh officer of the Guides', who, after fiercely rejecting offers of surrender, led a doomed charge in which he personally accounted for eight more of the enemy.[77] The battle was finally over. Eighty-one defenders were killed but around them 'lay heaped six hundred dead'[78] Afghan attackers. The latter is possibly an exaggerated figure but, if accurate, it roughly equals the losses inflicted on the Zulu at the famous battle of Rorke's Drift in South Africa earlier that year; a victory achieved by a British force nearly twice the size of the Kabul Mission garrison but one for which eleven Victoria Crosses were awarded, as opposed to one at Kabul![79]

Conceivably, the defenders could have been saved. Frantic appeals for help were sent to the Amir, whose house lay only 250 yards away, and some attempts were made to stop the trouble, most notably by Daoud Shah, the Afghan Commander-in-Chief himself. However, after attempting to reason with the mob, he was stoned, unhorsed and trampled on by his own mutinous soldiers. Although none of the Amir's estimated 2,000 own soldiers initially 'joined the attacking party' some were allegedly later 'seen to do so at 2pm'[80]. Like Shah Shuja before him, the role of Yakub Khan in the massacre will remain controversial, although, as we shall see, many contemporary British military leaders, notably General Roberts and his Chief of Staff, Colonel MacGregor, remained deeply suspicious of a conspiracy led or shared by him. Historian Fraser-Tytler takes a more sanguine view. 'The fault', he asserted, did 'not lie with Yaqub but rather with the intractable nature of the problem itself in which he and Sir Louis Cavagnari were just another couple of pawns which had to be sacrificed.'[81]

As in 1842, reaction to this disaster was one of shock and disbelief followed by blood-curdling demands for revenge. At 2 a.m. on 5 September, Major-General Roberts, then based in Simla and serving on a commission for army reform, was abruptly awakened with the news by his wife and remained, 'paralysed for the moment'.[82] Colonel MacGregor, Roberts' future second-in-command, was similarly devastated by, 'the most terrible news from Kabul'.[83] For the rank and file, however, shock anger and disgust was matched yet again by prospects for action and glory. 'The massacre of Cavagnari and almost all his followers burst upon us like a thunderclap,' wrote Cavalry Major R.C.W. Mitford from the sleepy, hot and malaria-ridden Koorum garrison of the 14th Bengal Lancers. 'All were in the wildest state of excitement, not diminished when, two days later, came the order for our regiment to advance'.[84]

Again, as in 1842, bloody retribution was now to be sanctioned but, this time, directly by the highest political offices in India. At home it had been a crushing blow to Prime Minister Benjamin Disraeli, who telegraphed to Queen Victoria: 'I am quite overcome and was trying to write to my sovereign but I am unequal to it.'[85] A vengeful Queen reciprocated with vigour, telegraphing him from Balmoral on 6 September: 'We must act with great energy and, no hanging back or fear to be found fault with must deter us from strong and prompt measures.... Pray urge this on the Viceroy and assure him of our support and confidence.'[86] An angry and humiliated Lord Lytton was not a man to 'hang back'. In the florid words of historian Archibald Forbes, the policy of which he had been 'the figurehead has come down with a bloody crash and the "masterly activity" of wise John Lawrence stood vindicated in the eyes of Europe and of Asia'.[87]

Yet again the British had clearly failed to learn the lessons of the previous war. Both military and political leaders had committed excesses in a crude 'butcher and bolt' policy which, as in 1841–2, had ignored ethnic sensibilities and aroused a widespread resistance. There had been little civil-military co-ordination, with Sir Pierre Louis Cavagnari constantly and disastrously interfering with military operations. Only the gifted Sir Robert Sandeman had maintained a harmonious relationship with his military counterpart. As in 1839–42, intelligence and logistical blunders had further exacerbated the political situation. The British had sown the wind of resistance and were now to reap the whirlwind in the shape of a national religious war or *jihad*.

Notes

1   W.K. Fraser-Tytler, *Afghanistan*, p.120.
2   Lord Dalhousie, Minute, 14 March 1854 (encl. in Fraser-Tytler, *Afghanistan*, p.121).
3   Ibid, p.122.

4   For a good, if brief, modern study of the Sikh Wars see, for instance, E.R. Crawford, 'The Sikh Wars, 1845-49' in B. Bond, *Victorian Military Campaigns* (Hutchinson, London, 1967).

5   Fraser-Tytler, *Afghanistan*, p.123.

6   Bosworth Smith, *Life of Lord Lawrence*, vol 1, Chapter 15.

7   Major Lumsden, Kandahar Diary, 2 July 1857 (encl. in Fraser-Tytler, *Afghanistan*, p.125).

8   C. Miller, *Khyber* (Macdonald and Jane's, London, 1977), p.147.

9   Ibid.

10 C.U. Aitchinson, *Lord Lawrence and the Reconstruction of India under the Crown* (OUP, Oxford, 1897), pp.183–4.

11 R. Blake, *Disraeli* (Eyre and Spottiswode, London, 1966), p.659.

12 D. Dilks and R. Bridge, 'The Great Game', *The British Empire* (BBCTV/Times Life 1969), p.1320.

13 M. Edwards, *A History of India* (Thames and Hudson, London, 1961), p.303.

14 Blake, *Disraeli*, p.659.

15 M. Edwardes, *A History of India* (revised and enlarged edn, Thames and Hudson, London, 1967), p.277.

16 Ibid.

17 British Library (hereafter BL) MSS Eur E218/19, Lytton Papers (hereafter LP), Lytton to Sir Lewis Pelly, 12 February 1877.

18 Ibid, Lytton to Mallett, 14 March 1877.

19 Ibid, Lytton to Sir Henry Dawes, 2 April 1877.

20 Ibid, Lytton to Pollock, 3 April 1877.

21 M. Edwardes, *A History of India*, (revised edn, 1967) p.276.

22 Ibid, p.277.

23 Ibid.

24 Blake, *Disraeli*, p.602.

25 Field Marshal Sir F. Roberts, *Forty-one Years in India* (Richard Bentley and Sons, London, 1898), p.346.

26 Ibid, p.349.

27 Ibid, p.347.

28 Ibid, p.349.

29 F.G. Cardew, *The Second Afghan War*, (abridged official account, John Murray, London, 1908), p.99.

30 Roberts, *Forty-one Years*, p.353.

31 Ibid, p.355.

32 H.B. Hanna, *The Second Afghan War, 1878-79-80: Its Causes, Its Conduct and Its Consequences*, (3 vols) (Archibald Constable and Co., London, 1904), vol 2, p.67.

33 Major J.A.S. Colquhoun, *With the Kurram Field Force* (W.H. Allen, London, 1881), p.92.
34 Hanna, *The Second Afghan War*, vol 2, p.95.
35 National Army Museum (NAM), 880(581) 35162, Roberts to Adjutant-General, 24 December 1878.
36 Ibid.
37 Roberts, *Forty-one Years*, p.368.
38 Ibid, p.367.
39 NAM 7101-23-101-1, RP, Roberts to Lytton, 14 December 1878.
40 Roberts, *Forty-one Years*, p.371.
41 Ibid.
42 Ibid, p372.
43 NAM, 7101-23-101-1, RP, Roberts to Lyall, 8 April 1879.
44 A. Male, Revd., *Scenes Through the Battle Smoke* (reprint, Naval and Military Press, Uckfield, 2009), pp.7–8.
45 W. Trousdale, (ed), *The Gordon Creeds in Afghanistan* (BCAS, London, 1984), p.40.
46 Hanna, *Second Afghan War*, vol 2, p.23.
47 See, for instance, Chapter 1, pp.68–71 and p.75
48 J.H. Anderson, *The Afghan War* (RMAS Staff College, London, 1911), pp.13–4.
49 H. Cooper, *What the Fusiliers Did*, (reprint, Naval and Military Press, Uckfield, 2003), p.39.
50 Ibid.
51 Ibid, p.60.
52 Anderson, *Afghan War*, p.15.
53 Ibid, p.15. See also *The London Times*, 17 December 1878.
54 Hanna, *Second Afghan War*, vol 2, pp.185–8.
55 Ibid.
56 Ibid.
57 Ibid, p.110.
58 Hanna, *Second Afghan War*, vol 2, pp.124–5.
59 Biddulph, *March from the Indus to Helmand and Back, 1878, 1879* (RUSI, London 1880), p.21.
60 Ibid, p.22.
61 Hanna, *Second Afghan War*, vol 2, p.111.
62 Biddulph, *Indus to Helmand*, p.24.
63 Ibid, p.21.
64 Hanna, *Second Afghan War*, p.116.
65 Biddulph, *Indus to Helmand*, p.32.
66 Anderson, *The Afghan War 1878-80*, (RMAS Staff College, London,

1911), p.24.

67 Fraser-Tytler, *Afghanistan*, p.146.

68 A. Forbes, *The Afghan Wars,1839-42 and 1878-80* (Seely and Co. Ltd., London, 1892), p.182.

69 Roberts, *Forty-one Years*, p.380.

70 NAM, 7101-23-101-1, Roberts Paper, Roberts to Lyall, 12 May 1879.

71 Roberts, *Forty-one Years*, pp.380–1.

72 Ibid, p.381.

73 A.T. Heathcote, *The Afghan Wars*, (Osprey, London, 1980), p.114.

74 Roberts, *Forty-one Years*, pp.383.

75 Forbes, *Afghan Wars, 1839-42 and 1878-80*, p.184.

76 Ibid, pp.185–6.

77 G.J. Younghusband, *The Story of the Guides* (Macmillan, London, 1908), p.114.

78 Ibid, p.115.

79 See, especially E.J. Yorke, *Zulu: The Battle for Rorke's Drift* (Tempus, Stroud, 2005), p.172

80 Cardew, *Second Afghan War*, vol 1 pp.189–90.

81 Fraser-Tytler, *Afghanistan*, pp.146–7.

82 Roberts, *Forty-one Years*, p.383.

83 W. Trousdale (ed), *War in Afghanistan, 1879–1880; the personal diary of Major-General Sir Charles Metcalfe MacGregor* (Wayne State University Press, Detroit, 1985), p.75.

84 Major R.E.W. Mitford, *To Caubul with the Cavalry Brigade*, (reprint New Delhi, 2000), p.2.

85 W.F. Moneypenny and G.E. Buckle, *The Life of Benjamin Disraeli* (2 vols) (John Murray, London, 1929), vol 2, p.1350.

86 Ibid, p.1351.

87 Forbes, *Afghanistan*, p.186.

5. Roberts' Revenge

A scrimmage in a Border Station –
A canter down some dark defile –
Two thousand pounds of education
Drops to a ten-rupee jezail–
One sword-knot stolen from the camp
Will pay for all the school expenses
Of any Kurrum Valley scamp
Who knows no word or moods and tenses.
But, being blessed with perfect sight,
Picks off our messmates left and right.

R. Kipling, 'Arithmetic On The Frontier', *Departmental Ditties*
(M.F. Mansfield and Company, New York, 1886)

At a crisis War Council meeting held in Simla on 5 September 1879, the task facing Viceroy Lord Lytton, Commander-in-Chief Lieutenant-General Donald Stewart and Major-General Frederick Roberts in the aftermath of the Cavagnari massacre was, indeed, formidable. The north-west Indian frontier forces had already been reduced to a peacetime footing and their transport, for financial reasons, had also been severely cut. Sixty thousand camels had been lost in the first campaign and, as the bitter Afghan winter rapidly approached, the available troops for a strike on Kabul numbered no more than 6,500 men. Nevertheless, three skeletal British armies were still in being and maximum use was now to be made of these. Following the Simla War Council, the Indian Government promptly ordered Stewart to hold the line at Kandahar and the troops at Ali Khel were ordered to seize and hold the Shutargardan Pass ready for a move on Kabul. Roberts' Kurram column, now recognized as 'the only one in a position to reach Kabul quickly',[1] was ordered to march and all available resources were intensively focused upon support of this vanguard strike force. It was hoped that the Kabul force would be supplied through both the Kurram and the Khyber Passes, although the former would be closed in

258

winter. Roberts and his Chief of Staff Colonel Charles MacGregor commanded the Kabul Column comprising two infantry brigades and one cavalry brigade; this totalled 6,500 men in addition to 6,000 camp-followers and 3,500 baggage animals. At Shutargardan and Thal, Roberts' line of communications would be protected by 4,000 troops under Brigadier-General John Watson, with the Khyber Pass and Jalalabad line held by Major-General Bright and 4,600 men, the latter column already much weakened by disease. Bright would provide a mobile column to protect the road to Gandamak and to Kabul as well as holding Jagdalak. A reserve of 5,500 men under Major-General John Ross was stationed between Peshawar and Rawalpindi. Finally, the 9,000-strong Kandahar Force under General Stewart, echeloned between Kundi and Quetta, was directed to re-occupy Kalat-i-Ghilzai and threaten Ghazni. Meanwhile, General Stewart's 2,000-man reserve under General Robert Phayre would hold the line from Sukkur to Quetta.[2]

Roberts' political instructions from Lytton, contained within a famous dispatch of 9 September 1879, constituted one of the most draconian and indiscriminate sets of instructions ever delivered to a senior British military officer by his political superior. It provided a template for virtually total war against the Afghan people:

> You cannot stop to pick and choose ringleaders. Every soldier of the Herati regiments is ipse facto guilty and so is every civilian be he priest, or layman, mullah or peasant who joined the mob of assassins. To satisfy the conventions of English sentiment it will probably be necessary to inflict death only in execution of the verdict of some sort of judicial authority. But any such authority should be of the roughest and readiest kind such as a drumhead Court Martial. It is not justice in the ordinary sense, but retribution that you have to administer on reaching Kabul.... Your object should be to strike terror, and strike it swiftly and deeply; but to avoid a 'Reign of Terror'.

Lytton concluded with the ominous words: 'There are some things that a Viceroy can approve and defend when they have been done but which a Governor-General in Council cannot officially order to be done.'[3]

It was a *carte blanche* policy of punitive action to be studiously and controversially followed over the next few months by an equally vengeful Roberts and many of his junior commanders. As letters flooded in from the Amir, pleading his innocence of Cavagnari's murder ('My true friendship and honesty of purpose will be proved as clear as daylight', he pleaded), a disbelieving and distrustful Roberts could only coldly assure him that: 'The great British Nation would not rest satisfied unless a British Army marches to Kabul and there assisted Your Highness to inflict such punishment as so terrible and dastardly act deserves.'[4] Colonel MacGregor, his Chief of Staff, was more brutally forthcoming:

> Depend upon it there should be no turning back, we have got into a conflict with a race of tigers, and it is only by treating them with a rod of iron that they will ever give in.... They have killed Cavagnari ... if they see that their cowardly treachery and fanatical blood-thirstiness only makes us draw the yoke tighter they will give in sooner or later. Because they are curs at bottom.[5]

General Roberts soon made his punitive aims clear in several proclamations delivered to tribes *en route* to Kabul. At Camp Zergunshahr, while assuring the people of the Kabul region that 'the British Government does not make war on women and children' and that he would 'treat all classes with justice and respect', he promised 'full retribution for offenders'.[6] Equally significantly in his drive to Kabul, Roberts soon demonstrated his deep awareness of the military, social and logistical lessons of the 1842 disaster for his own troops. He was especially concerned about sexual malpractice. He urged general officers and officers commanding corps: 'to impress upon all officers under their command the necessity for constant vigilance in preventing irregularities likely to arouse the personal jealousies of the people of Kabul who are, of all races most susceptible in all that regards their women'. He went on to warn that 'the deep-seated animosity of the Afghan towards the English has been mainly ascribed to indiscretions committed during the first occupation of Kabul'. He reassured an anxious Lord Lytton that, having publicly warned 'officers to refrain from connection with Afghan women. I believe they will do so, not only for their own sakes but for mine.'[7]

On the military front, Roberts was equally aware of the logistical crisis of the 1841–2 campaign and the acute vulnerability of his lines of communications with such a diminutive force. From the outset, Roberts enforced an iron discipline upon both officers and men. In one telegram, for instance, dispatched to the allegedly over-cautious Brigadier-General Thomas Gordon, an angry Roberts expressed 'astonishment' at his 'alarming reports' from the rear lines of communication:

> I cannot believe your position to be in any way risky if only you adopt ordinary military precautions.... If you cannot I will beg you may be relieved of the Kurram command for the fate of my force

depends on my line of communications being held with a firm hand.... I am sorry to send this message ... but I cannot have constant alarms from the rear.[8]

To further speed up movement and relieve the enormous number of troops left guarding supplies, Roberts ordered strict controls over the size and weight of baggage. At least one commanding officer, Major Reginald Mitford, noted the beneficial impact of this at ground level:

A very short time suffices for the officers' preparations, few of us having any more than the authorised weight of kit consisting of a double-roofed tent, 7 ft square weighing 80 lbs; personal baggage restricted to the same weight (this required much consideration even to the possibility of taking an extra toothbrush!); 25 lbs of baggage for each follower and like amount for each charger. Little enough when it is considered that we are starting on a campaign of indefinite duration in an almost unknown country, but we were not long in finding out that our general had been quite right in thus restricting the amount of baggage.[9]

In fact the whole brigade marched out *on foot* with provisions for only five days – a stark contrast to the 1839 baggage extravaganza. Other senior officers were more sceptical of Roberts' haste, high-risk and over-ambitious approach, especially in the face of the ongoing transport crisis. Acknowledging that 'transport as usual is our greatest difficulty and what is there has been almost starved by the Commissariat', Chief of Staff Colonel MacGregor, although noted for his own overwhelming political ambition and suppressed rivalry with his Commander-in-Chief, later wrote from Kurram: 'Bobs knew perfectly well there was no carriage but he is in such a hurry. He is very jumpy and wants stabilising and when I get up I hope to be able to do it.... I scarcely think Bobs is much of a fellow and I believe a crisis will break him down.'[10] On 27 September 1879 Roberts left Kurram, 'leaving everything anyhow and no how'. It was a criticism to be levelled later in his career, specifically in regard to his logistic reorganization of the January/February 1900 offensive in the Second Anglo-Boer War.[11] Sir Mortimer Durand, his Political Secretary, was equally apprehensive. On 22 September 1879 he wrote: 'The state of affairs in Afghanistan generally is very serious. God grant we may escape any more national disasters. We need not fear the troops but the long communications and rough country are great difficulties, and our transport is very defective.'[12]

General Roberts certainly did not 'fear' the enemy or, indeed, the impending Afghan winter. 'When snow falls the people are nearly as helpless as we are for operations',[13] he asserted. In the midst of this logistical nightmare Roberts successfully crossed the Shutargardan Pass, having by now effectively denuded the Peshawar column of logistical supplies for his Kurram strike force. At Kushu on 24 September he had, to his embarrassment, already been joined by the still-recalcitrant Amir and innumerable 'Kabul loyalists' for whom he maintained deep distrust. 'I have little doubt', he confided to Lytton, 'but that the Amir and all with him were in the plot and knew what was going on.'[14]

The Battle of Charasia

Lack of transport forced Roberts to halt for one day at Zaidabad but, on 6 October 1879, he reached Charasia, where he faced his first great military test of this second campaign. Here, he confronted the Afghan *Sirdar* Nek-i-Muhammed who, with thirteen regiments of regular Afghan troops, blocked his advance to the key objective of Kabul, barely eleven miles away. Roberts' small force of 4,000 men was vastly outnumbered: they faced an estimated 8,000–10,000 Afghan troops. The Afghans had positioned their forces well, with their left wing and twelve guns straddling the pass of Sang-i-Nawishta and a detached hill to the south of the pass, with their right wing located on the heights above the Chardeh Valley (the 'Garden of Kabul'). Other bodies of the enemy occupied the hills on the other side of the Logar River, infesting also the road to the rear. Cavalry officer Major Mitford recalled the stunning sight as the battle unfolded:

> We had no sooner moved from under cover than the hills on both sides of the pass were seen swarming with the enemy, particularly those on the left front, in the Cabul direction. They had innumerable standards, red, white, dark-blue, green or yellow; these showed the different tribes or villages from which levees came. The Ghazis or religious fanatics, were all dressed in white and the Ameer's regular troops in dark brown with red facings. The tout ensemble was most picturesque.[15]

General Roberts' tactics were to be a virtual repeat of the earlier Peiwar Kotal battle. Politically, Roberts knew that it was imperative to attack immediately. In historian Hensman's words: 'Sir Frederick Roberts deemed it wise to attack without delay as to remain inactive before the mutinous regiments now facing him would probably encourage a general tribal uprising and, instead of 10,000, we should have 50,000 men to deal with.'[16] Roberts decided to hold the enemy left and turn their right. While Brigadier-General Thomas Baker with 2,000 men advanced to the left, a party under Major White of the 92nd Highlanders was ordered to threaten the pass and prevent the enemy occupying Charasia village. With his force Baker moved off to his left to confront the Afghan right. At around 2 p.m., after a 'hot and furious' struggle, the Afghan extreme right on the peak was carried by a frontal attack launched by a combination of the 5th Gurkhas and the 72nd Highlanders, with the 5th Punjab Infantry and 23rd Pioneers deployed in support. From there the advancing British troops were able to direct a cross-fire upon the 2,000 Afghans on the main ridge. The British advanced at the double and, by 3.45 p.m., the main ridge was carried, the 'turned' enemy fleeing towards Chardeh. Meanwhile Whites' two companies of the 92nd Highlanders had carried the other heights near the pass and, by 4.30 p.m., Brigadier-General Baker was able to shell the remnants of the fleeing enemy at the foot of the pass with his Mountain Batteries. Major Mitford vividly recalled the rare 'splendid sight' of a 'highland charge' by the 92nd:

> The dark green kilts went up the steep, rocky hillside at a fine rate, though one would occasionally drop and roll several feet down the slope, showing that the rattling fire kept up by the enemy was not all show ... still the kilts pressed on and up and it was altogether as pretty a piece of Light Infantry drill as could well be seen.[17]

It had been a resounding victory, clearing the way to Kabul with the 'wonderfully few'[18] British casualties totalling only eight killed and seventy wounded. The enemy had left an estimated 300 dead. The 72nd Highlanders had borne the brunt of the fighting, frequently crossing open ground, firing 20,000 rounds of the total 41,090 rounds expended, and taking thirty-six casualties. One of their number, Private McMahon, was subsequently awarded the Victoria Cross for an incredible lone charge up the heights.

The only discernible flaw in Roberts' battle plans was the absence of sufficient cavalry deployed with the turning force, thus precluding a complete rout whilst, on the logistical front, constantly jamming Gatling machine guns, used for the first time, proved a major disappointment. They were to be made 'little use of' in future fighting. On an equally technical front, and by stark contrast, the widespread use of the heliograph had proved crucial in facilitating tactical manoeuvres. The ever-uncharitable

Colonel MacGregor was loth to give credit to his rival Roberts, ungraciously recording in his diary: 'Altogether it has turned out most successful. But to Baker and White belong *all* the honour of the day. This is Bob's usual luck, he had absolutely nothing to do with it, but he would, of course, get all the credit.' It was a rather unfair judgement on a tactically brilliant victory.[19]

Arrival at Kabul

On 7 October 1879, with the route to Kabul now clear, Roberts' columns filed through the San-i-Nawishta Canal and, once again, the glittering prize of Kabul lay before British forces. On 9 October 1879 the British occupied the heights of Sihah Sang after Cavalry Commander, Major-General William Massy and Brigadier-General Baker had forced residual Afghan defending forces to evacuate the strategically vital Asmai Heights north-west of Kabul. Ninety-four pieces of abandoned Afghan artillery were captured here. On 13 October 1879, Roberts' victorious troops paraded through the city. An elated Roberts wrote: 'At last I was in Kabul, the place I had heard so much of from my boyhood and I had so often wished to see! The city lay beneath me with its near mud-coloured buildings and 50,000 inhabitants ... to the south east corner ... appeared the Balar Hissar, picturesquely perched on a saddle just beneath the Shar-i-Darwaza Heights.'[20]

Nevertheless, his father's experiences in 1840 and the 1841–2 disaster still haunted him. Roberts remained extremely wary of the city's sinister tragic politics and its potential as a death trap for British forces. 'Now I am really king of Kabul', he exclaimed to his wife, but 'it is not a kingdom I covet and I shall be right glad to get out of it.'[21]

As the British forces slowly enveloped the plain beneath Kabul there was, however, a brief loss of control as some vengeful elements of the British column began an orgy of looting. It was a scene reminiscent of the excesses of the old 'army of retribution' of September/October 1842. This time, however, stricter control was exercised and discipline quickly restored. Notwithstanding this, one officer, Major Mitford, was himself forced to intervene at gunpoint to stop some of the depredations. He vividly recalled the tense situation:

> Shortly after our arrival there was a tremendous row in neighbouring villages and some of the inhabitants came to complain they were being plundered. As the most stringent orders had been issued by Sir

Frederick Roberts prohibiting anything of that sort, I was at once sent to stop it. It was easy enough to turn out the soldiers but the camp followers, as usual, gave a good deal of trouble and I had to fire a couple of shots over their heads before I could induce them to leave the village.[22]

While the capture of Kabul had arguably been a 'risky feat', with Roberts only achieving it with a vulnerable, undermanned 'flying column' a manoeuvre which temporarily cut off his communications with the Shutargardan,[23] Roberts soon demonstrated his tactical and historical awareness in the overall skilful deployment of his troops throughout the city. Roberts was no Elphinstone. He chose to concentrate his forces in one spot, the expansive newly built Sherpur Barracks, recently vacated by the fleeing enemy forces, which offered superior protection to the semi-ruined Bala Hissar. Any open cantonment with scattered outposts and dispersed commissariat stores, such as that sustained by the doomed 1841 garrison, was studiously avoided. Sherpur's huge perimeter, however, still presented a tactical problem for Roberts in relation to his numerically small force. As he confirmed:

The draw back was that the great extent of its perimeter, more than four and a half miles, made it a very difficult place to defend; but, remembering the grievous results of General Elphinstone's force being scattered in 1841, I thought the advantage of being able to keep any troops together outweighed the disadvantage of having to defend so long a line.[24]

Over the next few weeks, as the Afghan winter closed in, frantic preparations for a possible siege began. Roberts, again conscious of Elphinstone's previous predicament, ruthlessly ensured that a full winter's supplies were secured for his garrison. Building materials were pillaged (often without compensation) from neighbouring villages. Grain stores were requisitioned directly from the nearby Bala Hissar, a cruel act against its Afghan residents but one which Roberts saw as the first act of 'retributive justice', it being the site 'in which the massacre had taken place and which was the symbol of the power of the Afghans'. Supplies, particularly grain, were allegedly paid for, but large quantities of 'khalsa' or state grain was predictably confiscated 'as our right'.[25]
Even before winter finally closed in, however, there were some ominous military setbacks. The British occupying force was stunned by two massive explosions which occurred on 16 October in the upper part of the Bala

Hissar, an area temporarily occupied by the 5th Gurkhas, with the 67th Foot camped in the garden below. Miraculously, the vast majority of British troops survived, with only Captain Shafto, Royal Artillery, and nineteen native soldiers killed. Tragically, however, several Afghan civilians were also killed at a distance of four hundred yards! The presumed accidental explosion had destroyed up to 400 tons of gunpowder and the doomed Captain Shafto had, only the day before, counted 800,000 rounds of English-made cartridges and, in one shed, 500,000 rounds of native make. Not surprisingly, the explosions and fires continued for hours and reconfirmed Roberts' decision not to occupy the ageing fortress permanently, especially as the lower reaches may have concealed further stores of powder.[26] Alarmists amongst the British forces had a field day, although one widely circulated rumour that the notoriously keen smoker Shafto had been seen entering the magazine with a lighted pipe in his mouth may have had some tragic credibility!

A far more serious and ominous setback, a cavalry disaster, occurred later in early December 1879, as large reconnaissance parties were dispatched into the local rebel-infested countryside to gather intelligence and supplies and secure command posts. On 11 December 1879 this disastrous action, involving the 9th Lancers, took place at Kila Kazi on the Ghazni road. To counteract the movements of insurgents in the vicinity of Kabul and prevent them combining, Roberts had earlier planned to send out two converging columns, one under Brigadier-General Herbert MacPherson, ordered to attack rebels in the north, and one under Brigadier-General Baker, ordered to occupy the line of retreat. Both were to combine in a pincer movement and to destroy the enemy. On 8 December MacPherson duly departed with a mixed force of 1,300 infantry, three cavalry squadrons and eight guns, heading for Aushar and aiming to drive Afghan leader Mohammed Jan's forces into Baker's trap. One day later, on 9 December, Baker deployed with a mixed force of 900 infantry and two and a half cavalry squadrons to begin dispersing the Logar Valley rebels and to intercept Mohammed Jan's forces. The two columns were, unfortunately, destined never to meet.

Brigadier-General MacPherson, after defeating 2,000 rebels at Karez Mir, called up reinforcements and Brigadier-General Massy's reserve force of four guns, two squadrons of 9th Lancers and one squadron of Bengal Lancers were ordered to advance in support by the Ghazni road but, crucially, ordered not to commit to any action. However, instead of confining himself to the main Ghazni road, Massy fatally took a short-cut via Killa Kazi. This caused him to go ahead of MacPherson's main force and thereby collide disastrously with Mohammed Jan's superior 7,500 main force.

General Massy then took a high-risk decision to attack and hold the enemy, expecting MacPherson to join him. However, vastly outnumbered, he was soon forced to retreat towards Deh Mozane Gorge in a desperate attempt to link up with an advancing rearguard unit the 72nd Highlanders. In the course of the retreat, the 9th Lancers, supported by the 14th Bengal Lancers, made two disastrous charges which culminated in the spiking of their supporting guns and their eventual retreat on foot. The 72nd Highlanders arrived, but far too late, and it was only frantic last-minute orders by Roberts himself, ordering MacPherson's whole column to advance in support, which saved part of Massy's struggling force. It was nearly a second 'Charge of the Light Brigade' and this reverse sent shock-waves through the British forces, as Massy's outflanked units had been the only forces between the insurgents and Kabul. Sir Mortimer Durand personally witnessed this serious setback for British arms in the Chardeh Valley as Massy's diminutive 400-strong cavalry force was overwhelmed by around 10,000 rebels:

Seeing that no impression could be made the guns retired and the enemy having advanced into open ground suited for the action of cavalry, the 9th and 14th were called up for a charge. It was an exciting moment. I saw them wheel into line, break into a trot, and disappear into a cloud of dust. A few seconds of anxiety followed and then I saw what I hope I may never see again. Our squadrons came out in a shapeless mass, the 9th on the right, the 14th on the left, utterly broken and galloping ventre à terre.[27]

Colonel MacGregor's view was significantly more damning. He scribbled in his diary: 'An awful day, the 9th Lancers did make a sort of charge but not a good one and then retired ... 9th Lancers quite out of hand, would not face them and went back and three guns had to be left.'[28]

The guns were, in fact, soon recaptured by MacPherson's forces but Mohammed Jan was able to occupy the Takht-i-Shah on the Sher Derwaza Heights, a key tactical position. The only fillip to British morale was the gallant action of Chaplain J.W. Adams, who physically rescued seven men of the 9th Lancers either wounded or trapped under their horses. He was later awarded the Victoria Cross. The loss was heavy; eighteen men and thirty-four horses were killed, with scores wounded and the 9th Lancer's commanding officer, Lieutenant-Colonel Cleland, was seriously wounded by shot and knife. General Roberts remained adamant that Massy's deviation from the planned route had been a primary cause in the setback: 'Had MacPherson marched at 7 a.m. instead of 8 a.m. and had Massy followed the route I had arranged for them to take, Mahomed Jan must have fallen into the trap I had prepared for him.'[29] Roberts never forgave Massy, subsequently informing Lytton: 'I have seen enough of him to be satisfied that he will never be a dashing or enterprising leader of cavalry.' In response, an angry and humiliated Massy led a protracted political campaign against Roberts, denying culpability for these alleged tactical errors.[30]

Retribution

If the military situation had reached a knife-edge by early December, 1879, Roberts' political conduct within the city of Kabul was to further inflame the situation as well as to excite further deep political controversy both in India and in faraway Britain. The execution of several-score alleged rebel leaders accused of murdering Cavagnari and his escort had proceeded to plan during the early weeks of occupation. Senior commanders on the spot and commentators at home, however, soon doubted the legality and mode of procedure. Cavagnari's body was never found but his head, like that of Burnes and MacNaghten, had allegedly been displayed in the Kabul Bazaar. There was little prima-facie evidence for the trials and the hangings that followed. Colonel Sir Charles MacGregor, appointed President of the hastily-assembled trial commission, thus scathingly recorded in his diary entry for 14 October 1879: 'I do not think that men who merely fought against us without having being concerned in Cavagnari's business should be killed but Bobs will kill them all. Anyway, I will not sentence such men to death, he may do as he likes.'[31]

Next day, as he prepared to examine Mohammed Aslam Khan, the *Kotwal* (chief magistrate) of Kabul and several other suspects, MacGregor further objected: 'I do not like this. Bobs has made up his mind to hang all five of these men but I will not find them guilty unless I am convinced of their guilt.' On 19 October MacGregor continued his invective against Roberts' mishandling of the trials: 'I think Bobs is the most bloodthirsty little beast I know. As a specimen of his way of doing business, he gave an order that the prisoners were to be tried and hung.' Such summary justice, often dispensed on the dubious evidence of local collaborators, notably one Afghan named as 'Hyat', was roundly condemned. On 21 October MacGregor further wrote: 'Find that men were being simply murdered under name of justice and only on the word of Hyat who himself is as big a scoundrel as exists.' On 22 October he even congratulated himself on having 'saved five men's lives today'.[32]

Roberts' determination to make an example was, however, unrelenting.

On 19 October he triumphantly reported to Lytton that: 'The Kotwal of the city, a denoted ruffian who carried Cavagnari's naked body through the streets of the city will be hanged tomorrow on gallows erected in the upper Bala Hissar on the spot just above the Residency over which fire was opened.'[33] Roberts was not alone in his quest for vengeance. Eyewitness Major Mitford, for instance like many British officers and men, shared Roberts' sentiments and he happily witnessed the first five executions, including that of the Kotwal:

> The Kotwal was dressed in a velvet skull-cap, a vest of green silk (the Mohammedan colour) and loose white trousers. He walked firmly up the ladder, and tried if the drop was secure before stepping on it. He was then blindfolded and pinioned which put a stop to the ceaseless telling of his beads which had continued up to that time. The rope was put around his neck, the Provost-Marshal (an officer of the 92nd) dropped his handkerchief and the wretch went to answer for his crimes before a higher tribunal.[34]

The scale and indiscriminate nature of Roberts' retribution policies were graphically revealed in his private letter to Lord Lytton, penned in late November 1879. Whilst admitting that 'all the men of note and position who were in any way implicated had fled from Kabul', Roberts declared, 'nearly one hundred men had been executed between the 12 October and 12 November; most of them were soldiers or city people; but with the exception of the Kotwal none of them were of any rank'.[35] What is crystal clear is that many more alleged rebels 'were executed in the surrounding villages'. Indeed, Roberts also admitted that one village, Indiki, 'from which our forces had been fired at on 5 October', had been 'heavily fined and all soldiers in it hanged'.[36] Other memoirs confirm the widespread and indiscriminate burning of villages and executions of rebel soldiers without trial. On 27 November 1879, for instance, Major Mitford recalled one punitive raid launched against a rebel chief in the Maidan Valley after which 'we destroyed all the Bahadur Khan's villages and left the valley full of smoking ruins and blazing stacks'.[37] Suspected mutineers were often hanged or shot on the spot and their fates left unrecorded officially. More alarming were the reports of torture (even burying alive) and murder of wanted enemy soldiers.[38] Roberts himself had to face allegations by a Doctor Bourke, a correspondent of the *Civil and Military Times of India*, accusing him of maltreatment and murder of enemy prisoners by his Gurkha contingents and by elements of the 72nd Highlanders. In his own defence the commanding officer of the

Gurkhas asserted that 'his men must have thought the Afghans were dead'.[39] However, his subsequent statement suggested that revenge killing, especially for the murder of British troops, was common practice. He admitted to 'the possibility of a dead Mahomedan being set fire to by his men as an act of retribution for the mutilation and indignities which their wounded and killed suffer when they fall into the hands of Mahomedans'.[40] Of course, today, such acts must be condemned but at the time many of the British military continued to be shocked and outraged by the murder and mutilation of their men. As Roberts himself later confirmed after the December cavalry disaster, many of the 'stripped and horribly mutilated' bodies of the 9th and 14th Bengal Lancers were left unrecognizable as a result of gratuitous mutilation by Afghan troops.[41] It was probably even worse for the more vulnerable and less mobile British infantry. One historian, J. Duke, recalled the 'dreadful death' of one 92nd Highlander, 'found in one of the villages' near Kabul:

> This man, who was sick, fell out, and was probably enticed towards the gate of the village by the offer of milk or water. His body was afterwards found inside, quite stripped and mutilated, his face and head being shattered and burnt. This had been cause by an explosion of powder forced into his mouth.... He was only recognised as belonging to the 92nd by some regimental checked socks which had been left on.[42]

The sight of a cold-blooded murder like this was calculated to excite, but not justify, feelings of horror and revenge against the perpetrators of such an outrage.[43]

Such retributive acts often led to increased friction between the military and their more sensitive political overseers, with one local 'political' contemptuously dismissed by one officer as 'one of these utterly super-fluous impediments'.[44] Indeed, at the highest level, extreme acts of revenge reminiscent of those by Major-Generals Pollock and Nott in the 1842 retri-bution campaign, were increasingly condemned by senior 'politicals' as counterproductive. After witnessing the destruction of 'two rebel villages' by General Roberts near Maidan, his political adviser, Sir Mortimer Durand, confided in his diary:

> I think this sort of thing is wrong and impolitic. It causes deep and lasting resentment and it will not quiet the country. These people have no cohesion or subordination, and though the well-to-do may be frightened by the example, they will never be wanting a few reckless

fellows, with little to lose, who will find the temptation to snipe at ... our men quite irresistible. It is only natural.[45]

Almost certainly, such indiscriminate acts of violence, ranging from the hanging of men by means of virtual kangaroo courts to the 'finishing off' of enemy wounded and prisoners and burning of villages, contributed to the ominous political situation which had escalated by the end of November 1879. It was veritable fuel for the Mullahs. At both a political and military level it was now quite clear that a storm was about to break around the diminutive British force in Kabul. Commander-in-Chief Roberts, however, like Envoys Burnes and McNaghton before him, initially exuded confidence – even complacency. In late October 1879 he had already baldy reassured Viceroy Lytton: 'as for troops I have enough to walk all over Afghanistan'.[46]

But it was a rapidly escalating crisis, already exemplified by the serious political vacuum in Kabul. There was a clear absence of any central Afghan political authority, particularly as Roberts and others remained hostile to and suspicious of the complicity of Yakub Khan in the massacre of the Cavagnari Mission, and not least because Lord Lytton and his advisers were still prevaricating over future plans for Afghanistan, ranging from partial British occupation to annexation. As early as 25 October, one of Roberts' senior political advisers, Sir Mortimer Durand, had already confided nervously in his diary:

> I am concerned about our want of hold on the country. We really get no information, and there is no government; nor do I believe that there will be until we have a definite scheme laid down. At present no one trusts us, our friends, if we have any, are afraid to come forward for seeing hard times hereafter if we leave the country. We have, so far as I can see, no means whatever of bringing influence to bear on Herat and the outlying provinces. Everyone knows that our outside margin before the winter is six weeks and that we shall not be able to do much mean-while.... Now that the Mustaufi and Vizier are in custody, there is not a man to be found of any real administrative experience or ability. The Barakzai Sirdars are seen as a useless, feeble set of people.... There is nothing to hold by, no men, no information; no great parties or interest ... I dread a condition of drift for the sake of the north and west. There is no saying what devilry may be brewing there.[47]

As we shall see, his deep concerns would be shared not only by other political advisers but also by MPs and media commentators at home and even lone senior military figures such as Colonel MacGregor. However, his and their views were to be initially brushed aside or ignored by Roberts and Lytton, both of whom were clearly intent on pursuing all-out revenge for the Cavagnari massacre.

Such dire political prognostications by his senior political adviser appear to have been frequently ignored by Roberts. In a letter to Lyall of January 1880, political adviser Sir Mortimer Durand further revealed the extent to which his advice and that of the senior adviser, Hastings, was being either overridden or ignored by Roberts and his senior commanders:

> Not long after joining my appointment I found that many of the views prevailing here were altogether out of accord with what I thought right ... and that I was likely, in some ways, to find the position a difficult one. Hastings was always in favour of moderate and careful measures, but he had no influence whatever with the General; and, after I had on two or three occasions given my opinion with his, I could see we were both looked upon as unsuited to the times. The General himself was almost always ready to let me have my say and hear me patiently; but on almost every point he thought me totally wrong and more than once, when I felt bound to persist, I found my doing so was by no means palatable. In fact, the views of the soldiers were absolutely predominant and other counsels had no chance. We were overruled about the treatment of Yakub Khan, about the arrest of the Ministry and numberless other things, until, finally, the most important matters came to be practically decided without our knowledge.[48]

Indeed, as Durand had earlier intimated, there was considerable 'devilry brewing'. Over the next few weeks the political vacuum outside Kabul was being rapidly filled by the 'fervent sermons of the venerated Mulla Mashk-i-Alra or 'Fragrance of the World', who denounced the 'infidels' in every mosque. By the end of November, Roberts was unknowingly facing a full-scale *jihad*, a phenomenon which destroyed his predecessor Major-General Elphinstone in the winter of 1841 and which, as we shall see, was proclaimed to launch the Third Anglo-Afghan War (and which, more recently, has been skilfully used by Al Qaeda and the Taliban in their protracted war against Britain and her Coalition allies).

It was only the reverse suffered by Massy's troops on 11 December which belatedly alerted a vastly outnumbered Roberts to the scale of the potential crisis facing him.

Brigadier-General Baker was the first to experience the 'December storm' as his frontal assault against the Tallh-i-Shah with 560 men proved to be an abject failure. Although the summit was subsequently secured by an assault by the 72nd and 92nd Highlanders and Gurkhas supported by eight guns (an action in which Sergeant John Yule of the 72nd Highlanders led the charge and won a Victoria Cross), success was, in the words of Roberts, 'shortlived [for] almost immediately I received a report from the city that the inhabitants had joined the tribesmen and that the cantonment was being threatened.'[49] Outflanked, General MacPherson was soon forced to evacuate Deh-i-Mozang and move to the Bala Hissar Heights, thus opening access to the city for, as an observer pointed out, 'Roberts wrongly thought that the western and southern efforts had been quite foiled.'[50]

On 14 December 1879 the 'Afghan chickens' finally came home to roost and the beleaguered British were shocked to be confronted by 8,000 hostiles gathered on the Asmai Heights, north-west of Kabul. General Baker's triumph in carrying these heights around noon in the face of the desperate courage of the *Ghazis* was, however, also short-lived. Enemy reinforcements, comprising an estimated 20,000 Afghan insurgents, counter-attacked and drove the small British forces back down the mountain with the loss of two mountain guns. General Roberts had clearly grossly underestimated his enemy and was now being seriously over-stretched: 'From that moment', he recalled, I realised what is hard for a British soldier, how much harder for a British commander, to realise that we were over-matched and that we could not hold our ground.'[51]

The Siege and Defence of Sherpur

All British garrisons were now rapidly withdrawn to the safety of the Sherpur entrenchments.[52] A surprisingly shaken Roberts immediately telegraphed to Calcutta notifying of the impending crisis. Gone was his earlier complacent tone and, in a panic-stricken message resonant with a sense of impending doom, he asserted:

'Our situation ... very serious; the combination is most extensive and will spread further, in fact it is a jehad ... nothing for it but to withdraw from all outposts.... We lost one position simply from overwhelming numbers ... we are in need of all the assistance you can send.'[53] It was a rare and clear failure of his judgement on this occasion; a situation eerily reminiscent of the November/December 1841 crisis when General Elphinstone's forces confronted overwhelming numbers of Afghan insurgents. As we shall see, it was again an astonishing example of political myopia, later to be matched or paralleled by the abject failure to see the impact of the build-up of a national *jihad* prior to the outbreak of the Third

Anglo-Afghan War and its global rise in the form of Al Qaeda prior to the outbreak of the current conflict. Sir Mortimer Durand recalled the dismal scenario of which he had forewarned barely two months earlier:

> The immense numbers and determined belligerence of the Afghans was such as to extort respect and the General finally resolved upon a measure which, a week before, he and all of us would have looked upon as impossible. Our men were withdrawn on all sides, the Bala Hissar abandoned and, by sunset, the whole force was concentrated in cantonments expecting an attack.[54]

The first few hours of the siege again conjured up parallels with the 1841–2 disaster, as even the walled garden, occupied by the 5th Punjab Cavalry and lying only 700 yards from the British perimeter was surrendered, with the loss of thousands of *maunds* of *bhoosa* (chopped straw, or chaff) and other stores. By 6 a.m. on 15 December 1879 the telegraph line had been cut, reinforcing a terrible sense of isolation for the British garrison. The inadequacy of such a large perimeter incorporating the whole of the Bemaru Ridge also became immediately apparent. Durand again recalled: 'Then we began to feel the inconvenience of having occupied this large and straggling position. It required all our force to defend it, and not a man could be spared for operations in the field. Indeed, the greatest fears were felt for the cantonment itself.'[55]

In his memoirs, however, Roberts stressed the importance of sustaining the long perimeter. He again cited the lessons of 1841: 'It was absolutely necessary to hold the Bemaru Ridge for its entire length; to have given up only part of it would have been to repeat the mistake which had proved so disastrous to Elphinstone's army in 1841.'[56] So began nine days of brutal siege conducted amidst the heavy snowfalls of an Afghan winter. But it was to be no repeat of the 1841–2 catastrophe. Unlike Elphinstone's beleaguered brigade and, indeed, by stark contrast, Roberts' Sherpur garrison had amassed (despite their early losses) sufficient food and forage for the winter and the men and officers were based in secure if overextended shelter with protection against the bitter cold. *En masse* they had superior weapons and firepower. Above all they benefited from a firm, united and capable – if not ruthless – leadership with the inspired, if occasionally impetuous, Roberts at their head. Nevertheless, in view of their small numbers it was to be 'a near run thing'.

Roberts' small garrison also benefited from one factor previously underestimated by military historians, namely the active support of key Afghan collaborators and allies, notably the Hazaras and the 'Kuzzilbashes'. From the arrival in Kabul of Roberts' force in October 1879, these groups had played a far more proactive role than in the 1841 crisis. Many acted as scouts and provided key local intelligence for Roberts' punitive raids. They fiercely defended their pro-British areas inside and outside of Kabul against the insurgents, and local 'Kuzzilbash' villagers provided significant military support and supplies to British forces. Thus, in pursuit of one enemy leader, the Loinab of Kohistan, for instance, Major Mitford was significantly accompanied by a leading chief 'Ibrahim Khan and another Kuzzilbash swell',[57] and it was a local 'Kuzzilbash' village which provided his cavalry unit and other British units with both hospitality and intelligence. Similarly, the Hazaras provided couriers and intelligence throughout the Sherpur siege. Correspondingly, journalist Hensman expressed his deep admiration for the 'very plucky Hazaras who go out willingly for a small reward ... we are now using ... them to carry letters and despatches'.[58]

Between 15 and 23 December the enemy build-up continued, reaching an estimated 50,000 men, and the skirmishes around the Sherpur defences intensified. Roberts now pinned his hopes on reinforcements from Brigadier-General Gough's 1,500-man garrison stationed at Gandamak. On 14 December 1879 he had accordingly telegraphed Gough: 'March to Kabul as soon as you can. Hold onto all posts that are strong enough to resist attack; others I would withdraw for it is very probable the Ghilzais will rise.'[59] By 16 December Roberts was even contemplating retaking the Bala Hissar, a reversal of his previous policy, although he would not risk it until Gough arrived with support. On 19 December, after Gough had pleaded that he had insufficient strength to support him, Roberts again revealed his ruthless side, asserting that he was 'at a loss to understand you are not strong enough to attempt an advance on Kabul ... it is impossible to overestimate the political importance of your early arrival here'. Roberts directed Gough 'to proceed without a single days delay.'[60] British survival remained on a knife-edge.

Inside the Sherpur garrison, Roberts remained suspicious of the loyalty of the Afghan *sirdars* sheltering with him and feared they might conspire with some of his Muslim Indian sepoy regiments, notably the Corps of Guides and the 5th Punjabis, both of whom, as we have seen, incorporated large numbers of 'Mohammedans' amongst them. Their position at the most vulnerable point of attack, the two extremities of the Bemaru Range, led him to covertly strengthen each post with two companies of Highlanders. Even Daud Shah, Yakub Khan's Commander-in-Chief, was treated with suspicion and placed under temporary arrest.

It was a horribly tense time. On 20 December Hensman recalled: 'Waiting for the attack has grown so terribly monotonous that we daily curse the tactics of Mahomed Jan, who only sends out 200–300 sharp-shooters to blaze away their ammunition at our sentries.'[61]

On the night of 21/22 December, Roberts received crucial information from local spies of a planned mass attack on the cantonment. As eyewitness Major Mitford revealed, it was again Qizilbash agents who provided the crucial information on this impending attack.[62] The signal was to be a lighted beacon on the Asmari Heights. Overnight, sentries in the King's Garden sector 'could distinctly hear the scaling-ladders being dragged along the crisp frozen snow'.[63] An hour before dawn the now fully alerted British troops fell silently under arms. At twilight the storm finally broke. Historian Hensman recalled the incredible scene; as at 5.30 a.m.:

> Every man's eyes were turned towards the east, watching for the predicted signal; yet when it came, so brilliant, so dazzling, was the light that ... men's hearts stood still with astonishment and awe ... never did soldiers gaze upon a more glorious, a more terrible spectacle ... every nook and corner of the vast enclosure, every defensive work, every group of defenders, clearly visible ... beyond, across the snow-clad valley, dotted with villages and forts, every seam and rock on the rugged, precipitous Asmari Height shone out as if traced by a pencil of fire.

Fed by oil and ghee, the brilliant glare lasted a full three minutes and then a 'continuous fire ... opened below the bastion on either side of the 72nd Gateway'. The firing, Mitford recalled, instantly coincided with the chilling sound of *jihad*; a terrifying 'dull wail of voices ... rose from the city. Above all could be distinguished from the continuous noise the "Ya Allah, Yah Allah, Ya Allah" of the priests and the monotonous rattle of countless war-drums beating to arms.... After the dead silence this had the most startling, magical ... theatrical effect.'[64]

Several observers recalled the first suicidal enemy frontal attacks from the direction of Bemaru, charges so cruelly exposed by star shells fired from Gough's mountain guns at a range of 1,000 yards. The 28th Punjab Infantry were amongst the first to open fire, and the Guides, 67th and 92nd in turn greeted 'by their volleys the Ghazis who approached close to the walls'.[65] Major Duke of the Bengal Medical Service observed:

> The enemy now opened a rapid fire from the King's garden and against nearly all the southern line and small bodies of men with huge ladders broke from the cover of the garden ... only one of the enemy's

ladders reached a broken wall about 400 yards in front of our lines. The fire of our carbines and of the Howitzers could not be faced.[66]

Ironically, many of the artillery pieces which relentlessly mowed them down originated from the Afghan artillery park earlier captured. Major Mitford recalled the horrible din of battle:

The under-current or bass was one ceaseless role of musketry, broken at frequent intervals by the roar of a heavy gun. Above this rose British cheers and Sikh war-cries answering the yells of the Moollahs and Ghazis, screams, shrieks, and noises of every hideous description. Added to this that the bullets were whistling about us, knocking up the stones, splintering the abattis and tearing down the empty tents.[67]

Roberts himself also vividly recalled the failure of repeated enemy attempts 'made to scale the south east wall' with 'heaps of dead marking the spots where these attacks had been most persistent'.[68]

The enemy plan of attack, to break through the space between the Native Field Hospital and Bemaru village was clearly failing. Although this appeared to be the weakest sector of the British Line, hardly more than a line of trees and a low barrier, it was, as historian Duke recalled, 'not so in reality'. The whole area was a trap for enfilading fire: 'The open space in front could be swept by a terribly hot flanking fire from the Bimaru village on one side and the Field Hospital on the other as did actually happen.'[69] It was here that the 500 or 600-man Afghan spearhead 'belonging to Koh Daman and Kohistan' had been 'told off' for the attack and experienced massive casualties. These poor Afghan tactics were nevertheless matched by individual acts of outstanding bravery. Major Mitford recalled them 'come on capitally', and how one brave Afghan leader, 'on a chestnut horse rode up in the coolest way right under the fire of our Infantry ... gave some orders ... and then rode off again as nonchalantly but not as safely as he came for 'before he had gone many yards' he threw up his arms and fell from his horse'.[70] Similarly, Duke recorded 'one huge standard ... borne bravely along for many yards, in spite of the heavy fire directed at the bearers that had all but gained the cover of a broken wall when it went down with the usual suddeness'.[71] At around 11 a.m. the Afghans renewed their assaults but, in historian Hanna's words, 'with less determination' – although Roberts felt that they were as 'hot as ever'.[72] At least four enemy Afghans reached the *abattis* under the field hospital but their courage was short-lived. 'One Afghan tried to flee but was shot down and the other three attempted to hide themselves in the brushwood where they were bayoneted by the Guides.'[73]

As the enemy's attacks peaked and faltered, General Roberts launched a cavalry attack to turn their flank. Lieutenant-Colonel Wilkinson of the 5th Punjab Cavalry was ordered out of the hollow in the Bemaru Range to break up the enemy massed around the village of Kurja Kila; the Afghans there wavered and broke. The battle now turned into a rout as the Afghan infantry broke and ran. A merciless pursuit ensued, led by Brigadier-General Massy's cavalry units, no doubt anxious for revenge after their recent defeat of 11 December. The 14th Bengal Lancers were sent to block the pass leading into the main rebel territory in Kohistan, while the Guides proceeded to guard the Buthak Road and the 5th Punjabi Cavalry and 9th Lancers were dispatched to hold the road leading to the city. It is clear from many contemporary accounts that few prisoners were taken. Historian Duke recalled the support afforded by the mobile British artillery gun detachments, who entered Bemaru village having 'killed all the Afghans they were able to lay their hands on'. The 5th Punjabis apparently 'distinguished' themselves leaving enemy corpses, which 'strewed the ground very fairly for onwards of half a mile or more on the line of retreat towards Kohistan'.[74] Likewise, journalist Hensman recalls crowds of Afghan enemy soldiers forced out of the village onto the plain only to be annihilated by the lances and carbines of the 9th Lancers and 5th Punjabis: 'All stragglers,' he observed, 'were hunted down in the nullhas in which they took shelter and then despatched'.[75] It was a curiously methodical killing ground: 'Two or three lancers or sowars were told off to each straggler and the men dismounting used their carbines when the unlucky Afghans had been hemmed in.'[76] It was a merciless rout which matched the brutal annihilation of King Cetschwayo's Zulus at the battle of Ulundi, South Africa, barely six months earlier.

The infantry and sappers who closely followed up the cavalry and gunners proved equally ruthless, with scores of forts blown up and villages burnt. Tragically, two British officers, Captain Dundas and Lieutenant Nugent of the Royal Engineers, were subsequently killed as a result of the misfire of captured Afghan time fuses. General Roberts calculated that the enemy finally exceeded 100,000 in number, with no less than 3,000 killed and wounded. One thousand enemy dead were counted on the battlefield itself. British losses were a mere eleven officers and men killed and forty-six wounded, with twenty-nine camp-followers killed or wounded.[77] Indeed, during the whole siege of Sherpur, British losses only totalled eighteen dead and sixty-eight wounded.

It had been a stunning victory, but owed more to poor Afghan tactics than to British ingenuity. General Roberts had clearly underestimated his enemy – although his eminent and wise use of defensive tactics, including the provision of supplies for several months – had, unlike his doomed predecessor General Elphinstone, undoubtedly secured his survival. The insurgent leaders had foolishly risked a mass frontal attack in daylight against a firmly entrenched British position with overwhelming firepower at their disposal. Had the Afghan commanders attacked earlier, before Roberts had consolidated his Sherpur defences, or used more long-term, subtle tactics of attrition or attacked at night, the result might have been less predictable or certain. The British Martini-Henry carbines and rifles had certainly proved their worth, the Afghans clearly surprised by the accuracy, weight and speed of delivery of these weapons, compared to the old Snider rifle, and, before it, the Brown Bess musket.[78] Historian Hanna further exposes the technical weaknesses of the Afghan enemy:

> Had Mahomed Jan commanded the services of a skilful military engineer he would have been able to capture Sherpur even after the completion of its defences; for with the unlimited labour at the disposal of the engineer, the place could quickly have been approached by parallels and zigzags, the walls mined and blown up at a number of points, and the whole length of the ramparts, on which unprotected as they were by traverses, enfiladed by a flanking fire from earthworks thrown up under cover of darkness within musketry range of the cantonment.[79]

With the battle over, Roberts remained proactive over the next few months, dispatching numerous follow-up punitive expeditions whilst stressing to his superior Lord Lytton that it was 'very necessary ... that we are not only to hold our own but to punish all those who have joined in the combination against us'.[80] Six weeks later he callously reminded a colleague, Major-General Dillon, 'Afghans require to be punished before they can be petted; they have received their punishment.'[81]

Nevertheless, while Roberts' battle for Sherpur had broken rebel concentrations in central and northern Afghanistan, the south remained highly vulnerable. Moreover, Roberts' colleague, Colonel MacGregor, like political adviser Durand before him, remained sceptical of the political impact of Roberts' ruthless retribution strategy, with still no sign of any victory over Afghan 'hearts and minds'. As Roberts continued to dispatch even more punitive expeditions under subordinates such as Major-Generals Gough and Baker, particularly aimed at punishing the leading rebel Kohistan chiefs, MacGregor noted:

He [Roberts] is sending Ross out with a squadron of his regiment, 4th Goorkhas, and some sappers to burn the village of Baghwana, a very appropriate name by the way, considering the way the 9th Lancers 'Baghoed' [rampaged] through it on the 11th.... How all this will end I do not know, there is no doubt a very strong feeling of hostility against us, which all this indiscriminate hanging and burning of villages intensifies; in fact we have not got a single friend in the country.[82]

This significant failure to win Afghan hearts and minds lay at the core of the earlier 1841 crisis and disaster and, as we shall see, was to present a major challenge to Britain's current war in Afghanistan, where war-fighting tactics were initially to predominate over Afghan welfare and development policies.

In barely more than six months the British were to discover that they, indeed, did not have 'a single friend in the country'. In the aftermath of the Cavagnari massacre and of the Sherpur victory which confirmed the collapse of Yakub Khan's Emirate, the British Government felt compelled to proceed with the dismemberment of Afghanistan. *Sirdar Wali* Muhammed was appointed Governor of Kabul while Shere Ali, whose father Mir Dil Khan, a brother of Dost Mohammed who had been driven out in 1839, was appointed as Governor of Kandahar in May 1880. The future of the third major city, Herat, remained, however, unresolved and politically volatile as Ayub Khan, brother of Yakub Khan and a powerful contender for the Afghan throne, now resided there with the remnant of the mutinous Afghan Army. Moreover, to add to the prevailing political confusion, after twelve long years in exile in Russia, Abdur Rahman, son of the earlier deposed contender, Mahommed Afzal, was about to rejuvenate his claim to the Afghan throne.[83]

As the political situation remained dangerously unresolved the Viceroy, Lord Lytton, himself under severe media and parliamentary pressure, and equally exercised by fears of the rapidly escalating cost of war, began to blame his generals for the overall lack of political and military progress. Lieutenant-General Samuel Browne, for instance, was castigated for his loss of 65,000 camels in the early stage of the campaign and even Roberts was thrust into the firing line over the alleged war crimes issue. Thus, in early January 1880, Roberts telegraphed the Private Secretary to the Viceroy in Calcutta to affirm that he was 'dismayed that the Viceroy should think that I would adopt unnecessary severe measures such as would embitter and prolong hostilities'.[84] The still-controversial Kabul proclamations and executions, the allegations of ill-treatment of prisoners of war and ordering unnecessary punitive expeditions, had combined to put Roberts' position under severe pressure. In a letter to Lord Lytton he further protested: 'I did not think that the "disturbances" were brought about by the proclamations of 12th October and 12th November or by the way in which our dealings with the people of Kabul had been carried on.'[85] In mitigation, it could be argued the Roberts was only following Lord Lytton's own draconian policy as outlined in his now infamous September 1879 dispatches.

As media and parliamentary pressure at home mounted further, Roberts felt it necessary to remind Lyall that there 'was not indiscriminate hanging as some of the newspapers would have people believe', claiming that, in direct reference to the brutal post-Mutiny revenge actions, the Afghans 'received much more consideration than was shown to the peoples of India in 1857–8'.[86] He reiterated his complaints to General Dillon: 'I am much distressed at being accused of mistreating the Afghans with unnecessary severity.'[87]

Other criticisms extended to Roberts' military performance, specifically to his management of the recent 11 December cavalry disaster. He conceded that:

> Matters were certainly not conducted as I could have wished but no blame is to be attributed to the troops. [Under] exceptional trying circumstances ... some officers who had never been under fire at all thought all was lost and perhaps gave the 'Times' and other corre-spondents reason to think there had been some kind of panic. There was nothing of the sort; nearly every officer of the 9th Lancers had been killed, wounded or dismounted and, for a few minutes, there was some confusion; but the men soon pulled themselves together and retired steadily enough as did the Squadron of 14th Bengal Lancers. It was not a pleasant sight for young soldiers; the plain was literally covered with the enemy who were rapidly outflanking us on both sides.[88]

In another letter to Lytton, Roberts drew direct parallels to the action of the 1842 'armies of retribution' as part of his defence:

> I find that in the last Kabul war very similar accusations were made against the troops under the command of Sir George Pollock.... There were no press correspondents in those days and if young officers wrote as much then as they do now, their letters took longer to reach England. There was the same outcry about burning villages, shooting

Afghans etc and both Generals Pollock and Nott had to defend themselves from attacks such as have been made on me.[89]

In the event, Massy became the ultimate scapegoat for the military setbacks but Colonel MacGregor at least exuded some sympathy. He opined: 'Massy is to go; "removed" from his appointment; he should never have been sent, but I do not see he was so very much to be blamed as it was Bobs who ordered the guns to be put where they were lost.[90]

In the event, for a distressed Roberts, it was a case of 'mud sticks' and the spring of 1880 saw major changes of command. As historian T.A. Heathcote succinctly observes: 'The dispatch to Kabul of an officer considered senior to Roberts was regarded in some quarters as a consequence of the allegations of British atrocities there.'[91] Lieutenant-General Sir Donald Stewart was his new military master and, with the defence of Kandahar handed over to the Bombay Army units commanded by Lieutenant-General J.M. Primrose, Stewart and his Bengal Army contingents assumed control of Kabul. A profoundly disillusioned General Roberts again complained to Lytton in June 1880 about how

irksome and uninteresting work is to me now.... The fact of General Stewart coming here is used by the newspapers to discredit me in the eyes of the public and I fear the longer I remain away from England the more opportunity General Massy and friends will have of abusing me and the less the dangers and difficulties of the occupation of Kabul will be remembered.[92]

As he advanced from Kandahar, Lieutenant-General Stewart himself faced fresh political difficulties as even the erstwhile Afghan allies of the British took advantage of the continuing political and military vacuum to spread disorder. The Hazaras, following Stewart's line of advance from Kandahar, started to loot and burn rival Ghilzai villages. Nevertheless, as the Hazaras had proved a key support to Stewart on this march from Kandahar to Kabul (one which, although less publicized, equalled in arduousness Roberts' later famous march from Kabul to Kandahar) he significantly declined to punish the offenders. Historian Hanna, however, considers this 'an impolitic omission for an act of justice, executed upon his "friends" in the interest of his enemies would have done much to disarm the hostility which, passive so far, was about to assume an active form'.[93] Arguably, Stewart, like Roberts before him, had missed an opportunity to win hearts and minds. The reality was that both Stewart and Roberts depended on the supply of intelligence and food by the Hazaras or 'barbarous cutthroats' as Stewart privately referred to them. The wider political consequences were, however, dire. Stewart's column was now encountering only deserted Pathan villages from which women, children and supplies had been already removed to escape Hazara depredations. This pre-emptive mass evacuation represented a sure sign of growing Pathan distrust of and hostility towards their British occupiers.

The Battle of Ahmed Khel

The region soon exploded and Stewart encountered the main body of hostile Ghilzais ensconced on a range of hills near a place called Ahmed Khel, twenty-three miles south of Ghazni. On 19 April 1880, Stewart's 7,000-strong Ghazni Field Force left Mushaki in the following order – first Brigadier-General C.H. Palliser, then Brigadier-General R.J. Hughes' 2nd Brigade and, last of all, Brigadier-General Barter's 1st Brigade. The order of march stretched six miles. With the batteries arranged in column along the route, General Hughes' infantry was advanced to the left in line with the leading battery. The cavalry was formed to the right of the guns in flat country; in reserve were the 19th Punjabi Native Infantry and Stewart's escort. At 7.45 a.m. General Barter was ordered to send up half his infantry and two cavalry squadrons. Thus the now-consolidated British column moved to about one and a half miles in front of the enemy's position, at which point the British guns came into action. The enemy, swarming over the hills for two miles, responded in a swift and devastating fashion. Historian Hensman described the terrifying scene as fanatical elements of an estimated 12,000–15,000 'Taraki, Aridari, Suleiman, Kheyls and Tokhis' tribesmen launched a suicidal attack. 'Having mustered their fighting men in obedience to the summons of the mullahs sent by Mushk-i-Alam', he recalled, 'a commotion was observed … the beating of tom-toms was redoubled and then, as if by magic, a wave of men, Ghazis of the most desperate type, poured down upon the plain.'[94] At the same time a large body of Afghan horsemen rode along the hills threatening the left flank and rear of the British position. Private J. Wall of the 59th Regiment, situated on the right British flank, remembered the terrifying scenes as his regiment halted at about 800 yards:

To tell you the Gods truth … I stood almost petrified … as far as you could see on either flanks of us were the enemy as thick as bees in a hive. They were in a horseshoe formation and, from one end to the other, reached at the very least two and a half miles and we were right in the centre of them. If there was one man there was 20,000. When I seen them all I said 'My God how is this handful of men going to scatter that horde'.[95]

As earlier at Kabul, on 11 December 1879, it was the British cavalry which took the initial shockwave as they briefly probed along two neighbouring ravines. The massed Afghan horse charged the still-trotting 19th Bengal Lancers who, lacking sufficient speed to meet them, fairly fell back in confusion. The concertina effect led to disorder among rear sections of the 3rd Gurkha Infantry. Meanwhile, the shock tactics of the Ghazi swordsmen created even more chaos. Hensman wrote:

The fanaticism of the 3,000 or 4,000 men who made this desperate charge has perhaps never been equalled; they had 500 or 600 yards to cover before they would come to close quarters with our infantry and yet they made nothing of the distance. They ... rushed forward in three lines; nearly all armed with tulwars, knives and pistols. Some carried rifles and matchlocks, while a few ... had simply pikes made of bayonets or pieces of sharpened iron fastened upon long sticks.[96]

The British infantry lines were left to absorb the first massive shockwave. 'Our regiment was preparing to advance', wrote Private Wall, 'but they never gave us the chance for before we had time to say "Jack Robinson" down poured from 4,000–5,000 Ghazis on our men and got to within eight or nine paces.... But they paid dearly for it for they fell by the hundreds.[97]

As the fanatical *Ghazis* closed in, the British gunners resorted to firing case and reversed shrapnel, 'but neither this, nor the heavy fire from the Martini Henry breech-loaders of the infantry could stop the rush of the Ghazis'.[98] Private Wall recalled the crucial moment. 'They even came within thirty paces of our artillery guns and they had to fire case-shot ... They must be pretty well pushed when they use case-shot.'[99] For a moment all was confusion as the *Ghazis* closed to hand-to-hand fighting and both gun batteries, now running out of case-shot, had to retire for 200 yards with the field battery shifted to the left centre. The infantry on the right were also pushed back, with all reserves called up. In the hurry and confusion some men apparently did not even fix bayonets. The desperate situation conjured up in Private Wall's mind memories of the terrible disaster at Isandlwana, South Africa where, over a year earlier, large elements of the 24th Foot had been wiped out by their Zulu attackers:

We were a bit funky that they would join our flanks and surround us but our cavalry did splendid work charging again and again to keep them back. I often wondered how the 24th Regiment had let the Zulus amongst them but I can quite understand it now, for none, only mad men, would attempt to advance under such a deadly fire.[100]

Some fanatical *Ghazis* actually penetrated to the rear, within twenty yards of the spot where the senior British commanders were observing the action and, 'so critical was the moment, that Sir Donald Stewart and every man of his staff drew their swords and prepared for self defence'.[101] Ammunition mules were stampeded and riderless horses of dead or wounded Lancers dashed around the headquarters' tents. But it was not to be an Isandlwana and it was, ultimately, the steadiness of the British infantry, their excellent discipline, leadership and superior firepower, which saved the day. After the initial confusion it was particularly the 'cool promptitude' and heroic actions of Colonel Lyster, VC, who quickly reformed his 3rd Gurkhas into company squares and whose sustained volley fire and those of the centre line, comprising the 2nd Sikhs and, on their right, the 59th Foot, which finally broke the back of the *Ghazi* charges. Thus checked by the deadly effect of the rifles, which mowed them down by the hundreds, the enemy slackened their attack and began to retire.[102]

The gunners had also held their new, hastily reformed line with well-directed shells fired from the 40-pounders of 6/11 Royal Artillery, which helped to check the hostile cavalry and to safeguard the baggage train. Private Wall recalled their devastating effect: 'Our reserve was drawing near and, with them, the 40 pounder batteries, who made some splendid practice on them at 4,000 yards sending men and horses flying in the air.'[103]

Cavalry honour was salvaged by repeated charges by the 2nd Punjab Cavalry which both relieved the broken squadron of the 19th Bengal Lancers and acted as fresh escort to the guns. By 9.45 a.m. the Afghan defeat became a rout and, at 10 a.m., the ceasefire was sounded. Unfortunately, no pursuit was possible as the cavalry was needed to protect the parks and baggage. The Afghan enemy sustained heavy losses, probably amounting to between 2,500 and 3,000 killed and wounded, with up to 1,000 corpses left prostrate in front of the British firing line. Private Wall was deeply shocked by the terrible carnage:

I had a walk over the field after the battle and I never seen such a sight in my life. Legs, arms, heads and bodies laying about in all directions as far as you could see. It was horrible but it served them right. They have admitted, since that day they lost 3,500 dead and wounded and that lot inside an hour ... it has given us satisfaction for all we have suffered.[104]

It is likely that few prisoners were taken on the battlefield as Britain's notoriously brutal Hazara irregular allies were let loose on their hated enemies, and journalist Hensman himself witnessed at least two captured recalcitrant *Ghazis* who 'had to be shot' by British troops, 'their lives ... taken as considerable experience has shown such fanatics always keep their word!'[105] Undoubtedly, as in the Zulu and Sudan wars, the continuing fanaticism of the defeated enemy did not encourage the taking of prisoners. Hensman again observed how, 'As our men passed along, Ghazis who had feigned death rose and fired at them and men, severely wounded, slashed at the legs of soldiers.'[106] Certainly, the horrific wounds sustained by many of the British casualties, notably Lieutenant Young of the 19th Bengal Lancers, whose horse unfortunately stampeded into the midst of the *Ghazis* and who was virtually slashed to ribbons, did not invoke empathy for captured *Ghazis* in particular.

It was a near-run but ultimately well-fought victory. The battle had displayed an interesting tactic of 'active defence', with the enemy allowed to attack and then to be broken by a strong counter-attack by the British. However, the inability of the cavalry to finish off the retreating Afghans meant that it was not decisive and, moreover, the gallant Afghan fighting spirit had nearly broken the British lines.

Notes

1   Roberts, *Forty-one Years*, p.384.
2   For further more precise details of the unit compositions of all these columns see, especially, Robson, *The Road to Kabul*, pp.287–97.
3   BL, LP, 518/4 Lytton to Roberts, 9 September 1879. See also Robson, *Road to Kabul*, p.140.
4   Roberts, *Forty-one Years*, p.388 and NAM 7101-3 (101), Roberts, Papers, Roberts to Amir, 25 September 1879.
5   Trousdale (ed), *War on Afghanistan 1879–80; The Personal Diary of Major General Sir Charles Metcalfe MacGregor* (Wayne State University Press, 1985), p.78.
6   NAM, 7101-23(101) RP, Roberts to Lyall, 18 September 1879 and Tel., Roberts to Gordon, 29 September 1879.
7   Ibid, Extract, Field Orders, encl. in Roberts to Lytton, 1 October 1879.
8   Ibid, Roberts to Gordon, 29 September 1879. As Pakenham significantly observes, by temperament and background, Roberts was not interested in

the dull grind of military administration, T. Pakenham, *The Boer War* (Faber & Faber, London, 1977).

9 R.C. Mitford, *To Caubul with the Cavalry Brigade* (repr. Bhavana Books, New Delhi, 2000), p.2.
10 Trousdale, *MacGregor Diary*, p.91.
11 Ibid, p.92.
12 Sir P. Sykes, *Sir Mortimer Durand* (Cassell, London, 1926), p.91.
13 NAM 7101-23(101) RP, Roberts to Lyall, 18 September 1879.
14 Ibid, Roberts to Lytton, 7 October 1879.
15 Mitford, *To Caubul*, p.26.
16 H. Hensman, *The Afghan War*, (W.H. Allen, London, 1882), p.29.
17 Mitford, *To Caubul*, p.26.
18 Roberts, *Forty-one Years*, p.406.
19 Trousdale, *MacGregor Diary*, p.100.
20 Roberts, *Forty-one Years*, p.410.
21 Heathcote, *Afghan Wars*, p.121.
22 Mitford, *To Caubul*, pp.36–7.
23 Anderson, *Afghan War*, p.29.
24 Roberts, *Forty-one Years*, p.419.
25 Ibid.
26 Sykes, *Durand*, p.98.
27 Ibid, pp.104–5.
28 Trousdale, *MacGregor Diary*, p.135.
29 Roberts, *Forty-one Years*, p.440.
30 NAM, 7101-23-101-1, RP, Roberts to Lytton.
31 Trousdale, *MacGregor Diary*, p.108.
32 Ibid, pp.111–4.
33 NAM, 7101-23-101-1, RP, Roberts to Lytton, 19 October 1879.
34 Mitford, *To Caubul*, p.104.
35 NAM, 7101-23-101-1, RP, Roberts to Lytton, 2 November 1879. This was probably an understatement and at least one Afghan general, Suffur-ood-Deen Khan, was also 'executed'; Mitford, *To Caubul*, pp.58–9.
36 NAM, 7101-23-101-1, RP, Roberts to Lytton, 2 November 1879.
37 Mitford, *To Caubul*, p.145.
38 Ibid, p.71.
39 NAM 7101-23-101-1, RP, Roberts to Military Secretary, 14 November 1879.
40 Ibid. An embarrassed and angry Roberts subsequently took personal revenge on Bourke by requesting from Lord Lytton that, 'he may not be allowed to return to Kabul', NAM 7101-23-101-1, RP, Roberts to Lytton, 22 November 1879.

41 Roberts, *Forty-one Years*, p.438. See also Mitford, *To Caubul*, p.155, who was unable to recover the corpses of many of his 14th Bengal Lancers as they were too 'hacked about' to load on to empty saddles.

42 J. Duke, *Recollections of the Kabul Campaign, 1879 and 1880*, (W.H. Allen, London, 1883), p.258.

43 For parallel issues in the context of the earlier 1879 Anglo-Zulu War, see E.J. Yorke, *Zulu*, pp.168–72.

44 Mitford, *To Caubul*, p.147.

45 Sykes, *Durand*, p.103.

46 NAM 7101-23-101-1, RP, Roberts to Lytton, 23 October 1879. It was a dangerous complacency shared, as in 1839–41, by many officers who as late as 3 December were indulging in similar leisurely pursuits such as 'sliding and snow-balling and all looked forward to a quiet and somewhat slow cold season', Mitford, *To Caubul*, p.148.

47 Sykes, *Durand*, pp.100–1.

48 Sykes, *Durand*, p.111.

49 Roberts, *Forty-one Years*, p.442.

50 Anderson, *Afghan War*, p.33.

51 Roberts, *Forty-one Years*, p.445.

52 The withdrawal effectively cut all mainland communications, notably from the key position of Lutta-land: Hensman, *Afghan War*, p.216.

53 NAM, 7101-23-(101) RP, Tel. Roberts to Lytton, 14 December 1879.

54 Sykes, *Durand*, p.106.

55 Ibid, pp.106–7

56 Roberts, *Forty-One Years*, p.449.

57 Mitford, *To Caubul*, pp.127 and 137.

58 Hensman, *Afghan War*, p.243.

59 NAM, 7101-23(101), RP, Tel. Roberts to Gough, 14 December 1879.

60 Ibid, Tels. Roberts to Gough, 16 December 1879 and Roberts to Gough, 19 December 1879.

61 Hensman, *Afghan War*, p.242.

62 Mitford, *To Caubul*, p.185.

63 Duke, *Recollections*, p.298.

64 Mitford, *To Caubul*, pp.185–6 and Hensman, *Afghan War*, p.252.

65 Roberts, *Forty-One Years*, p.453.

66 Duke, *Recollections*, p.299.

67 Mitford, *To Caubul*, p.187.

68 Roberts, *Forty-One Years*, p.453.

69 Duke, *Recollections*, pp.300–1.

70 Mitford, *To Caubul*, p.190.

71 Duke, *Recollections*. p.300.

72 Hanna, *Second Afghan War*, vol 3, p.245.

73 Duke, *Recollections*, p.302.

74 Ibid, pp.303–4.

75 Hensman, *Afghan War*, pp.254–5.

76 Ibid.

77 Roberts, *Forty-One Years*, pp.454–5. Mitford gives a figure of 60,000 Afghan besiegers; Mitford, *To Caubul*, p.193.

78 See Duke, *Recollections*, p.306.

79 Hanna, *Second Afghan War* vol 3, pp.250–1.

80 NAM 7101-23(101), RP Roberts to Lytton, 26 Deember 1879.

81 Ibid, Roberts to Dillon, 7 February 1880.

82 Trousdale, *MacGregor Diary*, p.142.

83 For details of the protracted negotiations between Abdur Rahman and the British leaders to his appointment as Emir, see, for instance, Heathcote, *Afghan Wars*, pp.142–6.

84 NAM 7101-23(101), RP, Tel. Roberts to Private Secretary, January 1880.

85 Ibid, Roberts to Lytton, 8 January 1880.

86 Ibid, Roberts to Lytton, 29 January 1880.

87 Ibid, Roberts to Dillon, 7 February 1880.

88 Ibid, Roberts to Major-General Dillon, 7 February 1880.

89 Ibid, Roberts to Lytton, 14 February 1880.

90 Trousdale, *MacGregor Diary*, pp.159–60 and 161.

91 Heathcote, *Afghan Wars*, p.137.

92 NAM 7101-23(101) RP, Roberts to Lytton, 5 June 1880.

93 Hanna, *Second Afghan War* vol 3, p.324.

94 Hensman, *Afghan War*, p.1393.

95 NAM 6904/3, Wall letters, Wall to Friend, April 1880.

96 Hensman, *Afghan War*, p.395.

97 NAM 6904/3, Wall to Friend, April 1880.

98 Cardew, *Official Account*, p.756. Captain Elias recalled the terriying spectacle confronting the British infantry lines: 'Most of them were big men, with long white robes flowing in the wind, right arms with swords or other weapons extended, and trying to guard their bodies (against Martini-Henry bullets!) with shields. Anyone with the semblance of a heart under his khaki jacket could not help feeling something like pity to see them thus advancing with their miserable weapons in the face of our guns and rifles, but their courage and numbers made them formidable.' (Captain Elias, *Journal of RUSI,* 24, No.117, pp.669–70).

99 NAM 6904/3, Wall to Friend, April 1880.

100 Ibid. An anonymous author later testified as to how shaky the British line had been as it absorbed the *Ghazi* shockwave: 'They had hardly finished

PLAYING THE GREAT GAME

deploying, many of them had omitted to fix bayonets and there was for a few seconds a tendency among some of them to waver and form into small groups. This, however, passed away as instantaneously as it arose, and during the rest of the action the men's steadiness left nothing to be desired.' (Anon, 'Sir Donald Stewart's March from Kandahar to Kabul', *Macmillan's Magazine*, May 1881, p.58.)

101 Hensman, *Afghan War*, p.396
102 Ibid, see also Hanna, *Second Afghan War*, vol 3, p.329.
103 NAM 6904/3, Wall to Friend.
104 Ibid. The British infantry losses were seventeen killed and 126 wounded but the total loss to the cavalry brigade was over one hundred, with the broken 19th Bengal Lancers suffering fifty-five casualties. Hensman, *Afghan War*, p.398.
105 Hensman, *Afghan War*, p.399.
106 Ibid.

6. From Defeat to Victory: Maiwand to Kandahar

Burrows was responsible for the tactics or lack of tactics which resulted in the defeat at Maiwand, but responsibility for the strategy which led up to that defeat, rests with his official superiors ... responsibility for the expedition to the Helmand as a whole, lies at the door of the Government of India.

> Colonel H.B. Hanna, *The Second Afghan War, 1878-79-80: Its Causes, Its Conduct, and Its Consequences* (Constable and Co., London, 1910), vol 3, pp.432–3

History has vindicated my father's action, and clearly shown the disastrous result of placing the political over the soldier in wartime.

> Lord Roberts, 'To whom should supreme control be entrusted in time of war – the Civilian or the Soldier?', Memo.4 May 1891, Simla. encl. in W. Murray Hogben, 'British Civil-Military Relations on the North West Frontier of India', A. Preston and P. Dennis (eds), *Swords and Covenants* (Croom Helm, London, 1976), p.129.

I am in great anxiety. Who is responsible for sending small detachments so far away from supports and how is the wont of knowledge of Ayub's force accounted for? ... the Queen herself thinks that a certain amount of discretion should be left to the Generals and that they should 4 be constantly interfered with for who can judge but those who are on the spot and who know the country.

> RA, India Correspondence, HM to Lord Ripon 3 and 5 August 1880 on receipt of the news of the Maiwand disaster.

Crisis in the South

The extremely narrow British victory at Ahmed Khel was a grave portent for the future and it was in the overstretched south that British authority now faced its most severe challenge. As Durand observed: 'The departure of Sir Donald Stewart's Division for Kabul in the spring of 1880 had much weakened the Kandahar garrison.'[1] Most significantly, as at Kabul in 1842, political charge was not invested in Lieutenant-General James Maurice Primrose as it had been in his predecessor, General Stewart. The resident 'political', Colonel Oliver St John, operated independently of the military commander. In official historian Cardew's view, 'this arrangement was probably a contributing cause to the subsequent disaster at Maiwand'.[2] Ayub Khan, rapidly building up his power in neglected Herat in the west of Afghanistan, soon spotted this lacuna in British power and, in May 1880, he commenced his advance on Kandahar from Herat. For several months the British military authorities in southern Afghanistan had been aware of rumours of his projected advance on Kandahar. On 1 June 1880 the British protégé, Ali Khan (the *Wali* or Governor who was designated to rule Kandahar if it came to be separated from Kabul), had been initially dispatched with 4,500 local Afghan troops and six guns to check any advance by Ayub's forces. When he eventually started from Herat on 15 June 1880, Ayub Khan had already gathered together 7,500 men and ten guns, the nucleus of an army which he correctly anticipated would be strongly reinforced *en route* by tribesmen, levies and *Ghazis*. On 21 June 1880 Colonel St John, the British political agent in Kandahar, officially raised the alarm by telegraph of Ayub Khan's advance and on, 4 July, a 2,300-strong brigade under Brigadier-General George Burrows duly detached itself from General Primrose's Kandahar garrison to reinforce Shere Ali and meet the burgeoning threat from Ayub Khan's army. However, by early July, Ayub Khan's army had swelled to 25,000. Burrows' orders were now not to cross the Helmand River, beyond which the *Wali's* forces would act alone. The reason was that Burrows' force was clearly under strength and the speed of Ayub Khan's advance meant that designated far-off reinforcements from India (from the Jacobadad, Hyderabad and Karachi garrisons) had no hope of arriving in time. Worse was to follow as, only two days after Burrows had arrived on the Helmand River on 11 July, the bulk of Shere Ali's troops suddenly deserted. It was a severe setback; Burrows was only able to recapture the gun battery but, perhaps fatally, not the *Wali's* stores or water supplies, or any of his skilled gunners. It was, indeed, a perilous situation and the scene was set for the battle of Maiwand, one of the greatest disasters to British arms of Queen Victoria's reign.

Burrow's logistical weaknesses were compounded as, having necessarily crossed the Helmand River in pursuit of the *Wali's* mutinous forces, he had entered a virtually waterless region which would inevitably restrict his movements. Moreover, as the Helmand River was low and fordable during that season, it also made it easier for Ayub Khan to cut off Burrows' retreat to Kandahar. As General Roberts subsequently observed: 'The first twenty five of the eighty five miles by which he was separated from Kandahar was a desert and no supplies were forthcoming owing to the hostile attitude of the people.'[3] Burrows was accordingly forced to divert and retire to Kushki-i-Nakhud on 16 July, halfway to Kandahar, where supplies of water were more plentiful and where he received fresh orders to watch Ayub Khan and prevent him moving on Ghazni. Near Kushki, he pitched camp and perhaps, as some writers suggest, unwisely stopped there for several days until 27 July. This delay certainly enabled Ayub Khan to reach the Helmand River crossing above Girishk with 4,000 cavalry, 4,000 infantry and 2,000 of the *Wali's* deserters, as well as numerous irregulars and thirty guns. Ayub Khan's fresh plans were to move north of Burrows' force, turn his position via the village of Maiwand (which is nearer to Kandahar than Kushki-i-Nakhud), gain the Argandab Valley and thus cut between Burrows and Kandahar or, alternatively, move directly on Ghazni.

On hearing of Ayub Khan's cavalry reaching Maiwand, and having received telegraphed messages from Calcutta on 21/22 July (reluctantly forwarded from Commander-in-Chief Sir Federick Haines) and from Primrose ordering him to intercept, Burrows decided to march rapidly to Maiwand with his depleted force, both to anticipate his enemy and, hope-fully, cut him in two. At 6.30 a.m. on 27 July 1880 – a dangerously late start for a summer's day march – Burrows 2,600-strong Brigade, which included only two gun batteries and 576 mounted men, marched for Maiwand. It was an offensive move, partly politically driven as, after further consultation with local 'political' Colonel St John, it was felt essen-tial to deal with the formidable *Ghazi* contingents before they linked up with Ayub Khan's main army. It was flawed advice: aside from being vastly outnumbered by over 10:1, Burrows' force was deeply compromised by being far from combat-ready. Indeed, his force may already have been doomed by fatally flawed intelligence as well as existing logistical short-comings as, initially, Burrows had no idea that he was confronting the *whole* of Ayub's army and, according to one source, even believed Ayub had no heavy guns![4]

Even before the imposing forces confronted each other at 10 a.m. on 27 July 1880, significant numbers of Burrows' troops were apparently suffering from shortages of food and/or water. Limber-Gunner Frances J. Naylor of the Royal Horse Artillery recalled, 'We had no breakfast nothing of any sort to eat.'[5] Moreover, the column was heavily fatigued, having spent most of a hot night packing up equipment. Burrows' force was further encumbered by immense baggage and numerous camp-followers who could not be left behind owing to insufficient manpower to guard them in this patently hostile region. Again, Gunner Naylor recalled:

> We marched on for several miles crawling cautiously … a long strag-
> gling body with not far short of 2,000 camels and many ponies,
> bullocks, donkeys, mules and horses and drivers and transport
> followers. To have only British troops, untrammelled would have
> been bad enough; to be burdened with these swathes of non-combat-
> ants and animals was disastrous.[6]

With the British being vastly outnumbered and overloaded, it was a situation reminiscent of the 1842 Kabul retreat, although this time the extreme summer heat of the Helmand plains substituted the icy winter cold of the north-east Afghan passes. General Burrows' position was further compromised by a stroke of bad luck; a deep summer heat-haze arose which soon concealed much of the enemy's movements. Captain Mayne of the 3rd (Queen's Own) Light Cavalry confirmed how the morning 'was peculiarly hazy and there was one of these mirages so common in these parts … it was impossible to see distinctly or to judge distances with any accuracy'.[7] Infantry officer Major Ready of the 66th Foot (Royal Berkshire Regiment) also observed 'a great deal of mirage and it was difficult to see clearly'.[8] Major Bray, attached to the rear baggage train, 'could not see our main body in front, owing to the dust'.[9]

The Battle of Maiwand

Indeed, it wasn't until as late as 10 a.m. that day that the existence of the mass of Ayub Khan's army, albeit still partly concealed by the thick haze (and only confirmed by a spy) became evident to a shocked Brigadier-General Burrows and his staff. Deciding it was too late to retreat and, critically, still unaware of Ayub Khan's full artillery strength, Burrows decided he had to make a stand. Worse was to follow. A reconnaissance, led by Major G.C. Hogg of the Cavalry Brigade, could only identify 600 to 800 enemy cavalry and he tragically failed to spot the infantry or guns owing to the 'configuration of the ground'. Brigadier-General Burrows accordingly ordered the advance to be sounded whilst the 'cavalry and artillery to the front' manoeuvre was executed in order to secure the apparently unoccupied village of Mandabad. Events subsequent to this remain confused and are still contested, but cavalry commander General Nuttall's and artillery commander Major Blackwell's units eventually crossed a ravine only to be suddenly confronted by 'countless numbers'.[10] The shock to these men must have been as great as when the British scouts first spotted the gigantic Zulu *impi* (army) which overwhelmed the British camp at Isandlwana on 22 January 1879, barely two years previously.

With one company of infantry diverted to baggage protection, Burrows could now bring only twelve guns, fifty British officers, 636 bayonets and 469 cavalry into battle against Ayub Khan's 15,000–25,000 infantry and cavalry with thirty guns (the latter including an Armstrong Battery of superior range!).

Before Burrows and his staff could react further, the arguably gung-ho actions of one junior commander, Lieutenant Hector Maclaine, Royal Horse Artillery, commanding a two-gun artillery section, forced Burrows' hand. Galloping 'further to the front and left flank than was considered advisable',[11] Maclaine's two guns and those of Lieutenant Fowell independently and precipitately engaged a group of Afghan horsemen at 1,800 yards' range before his belated urgent recall to the left flank on the cavalry line. As Ayub Khan's horsemen furiously reacted to Maclaine's opening shots and began to overlap Nuttall's cavalry on the left and rear, a full-scale action was 'rendered inevitable'. Moreover, Maclaine's aggressive actions had prematurely committed Burrows to changing his tactics, moving the British infantry to change front three-quarters left and advance to the edge of a distinctive *nulla* [dry river-bed].

Burrows' first line was deployed thus: the 66th Foot on the right, smooth-bore guns in the centre, 1st Bombay Grenadiers on the left, with Jacob's Rifles (30th Native Infantry) and sappers in support. Situated to the rear, outside the guns, with its left thrown back, was a troop of the 3rd Light Cavalry watching the Afghan horsemen approach. The British cavalry were, however, seriously compromised by the diversion of 146 sabres to the rear in order to guard the baggage train. The time was now around 11 a.m.

Recognizing the small numbers and narrow space now occupied by his British opponents, Ayub Khan issued orders to '*killaband*' or surround it. The Afghan cavalry acted as the vanguard, manoeuvring in circles and spreading out until they enveloped the British left and threatened the baggage train. For the British, defence of the baggage train was now to become a major distraction. Major Ready recalled the crippling diversion of manpower to the rear to combat

> hostile villagers who opened fire against the back of our line and [Lieutenant] Quarry had to detach half of his company to act against them. This half-company was engaged in near gardens the greater part of the day; while the other half-company under Quarry guarded

the baggage against the enemy's cavalry who hung in heavy clouds about our left flank.[12]

As Ayub Khan kept the mass of his force concentrated behind the rising ground, his fanatical *Ghazi* infantry wormed their way down the ravine towards Mahumdabad village in order to infiltrate the British from behind. Very soon the *Ghazis* fell upon the British right and the 66th were thrown back alongside the Jacob's Rifles (the only British reserve) and the sappers who had been called up into the front line between the four RHA guns and the 66th Foot. Two of the British smooth-bore guns were now moved from the centre to the right and Maclaine's two guns were retired on to the other four RHA guns and thrown back while two companies of Jacob's Rifles were placed on the extreme left. All the British fighting strength was now consolidated in line, with ten guns in the centre and two on the extreme right.

At around 12 noon the artillery duel, earlier commenced sporadically by the British Horse Artillery, reached far greater intensity as the enemy unmasked over thirty guns. It was, arguably, the decisive phase of the battle: it was British artillery which had often been crucial in winning battles with the Afghans over the previous forty years, but this time they were decisively outperformed in numbers, calibre and overall firepower. While the British infantry, already ordered to lie down by General Burrows, had successfully held back, by volley fire, the fanatical *Ghazi* attacks, hitherto pinning them down at 500 yards, nothing could be done to rectify the artillery deficiency. Limber-Gunner Naylor, RHA, was in the thick of the action and personally recalled the terrible inequalities of exchange as his battery endured the full might of Ayub's guns:

> It was just before noon when that final chapter of the great disaster happened. Instantly, as it seemed, the very ground rumbled and the air was filled with the flashes and thickened with the smoke of thirty two guns sweeping upon and into us and tearing into and through our huddled and disorganised masses. Picture if you can the horrors and consternation of an onslaught like that in a crowded space with a cruel enemy in overwhelming numbers surrounding us ... animals widely stampeding and transport followers and drivers thrown into panic and confusion. There were Krupp guns as well as smooth-bore guns and these weapons outnumbered us altogether.[13]

The *Wali's* guns, recaptured earlier, manned by men of the 66th and commanded by men of E Battery to the rear of Naylor's Battery 'did not', unfortunately, 'do much mischief'.[14]

Lieutenant Farrell recalled how the enemy took excellent advantage of the terrain, occupying the *nulla*

behind our position [and] also got guns on our flanks and enfiladed us.... Their artillery was extremely well served; their guns took ours in the flank as well as directly and their fire was concentrated. We were completely outmatched and although we continued to fire steadily, our guns seemed quite unable to silence theirs. Their six Armstrong guns threw heavier shell than ours and their smooth-bore guns had great range and accuracy and caused great damage especially among our horse and limbers which were totally without cover.[15]

Major Hogg summed up the resultant inferno:

We were exposed for three hours to the most horrific artillery fire ... any army ever had to stand in this country in as much as it was all concentrated from the front and flanks on a small surface not 200 yards long ... round shot after round shot, shell after shell and every conceivable missile, were hurled at us hour after hour from thirty guns, some of them Armstrong with admirable precision.[16]

After the battle the British were to discover that such 'admirable precision' was a direct consequence of the successful defection of the *Wali's* gunners prior to Maiwand.

But if the artillery were taking a drubbing, General Burrows' static and exposed cavalry units on the left wing were being ripped apart. As Captain Mayne of the 3rd Light Cavalry recalled, 'After more than half an hour's silence the enemy suddenly opened fire ... there was not a vestige of cover and the enemy had the advantage of the slopes; we were firing uphill, and my horses began to suffer.'[17] It can be left to Major Hogg to sum up the resultant terrible carnage:

I need hardly say that the Death Angel was soon at work. The infantry of course were tolerably safe lying down but the Cavalry and Artillery horses and men, especially the former, were falling in every direction ... horses shot poor brutes, with all their bowels hanging out with broken legs and broken backs, some spinning around, some trying to gallop away from the hellish scene, men with their legs shot off, torn by fragments of shell, struck by bullets here, there and everywhere – the dooly-wallahs in many cases bolting and wretched wounded men lying, imploring for help, unable to move, and, yet, not a man to spare to carry them off.[18]

Major Ready was far more critical of the situation and of the British leadership: 'All this time our cavalry was sitting idle, under a heavy artillery fire which was knocking over some men and many horses. In fact, they were given over to the enemy to be pounded into demoralisation.'[19] After noon, with the artillery and cavalry effectively nullified, it was left to the infantry to sustain the line. But, vastly outnumbered and outflanked, their position was also precarious. Early on, Captain Mayne noted their acute vulnerability as they 'marched up in line with no support that I could see and lay down close together; there was no extended firing line'.[20] Nevertheless, for at least two hours, the 66th Foot, the 30th Native Infantry and the Bombay Grenadiers blazed away. Indeed, for a while, the British line stabilized: 'Swarms of the white-coated Ghazis came on, followed by the regular regiments in red and blue and to meet them the whole of our infantry was allowed to open fire.'[21] The 66th took to firing volleys by companies despite Lieutenant-Colonel C.M. Griffiths later recalling that 'after a few rounds such was the din that words of command could not be heard and independent firing was carried on along the whole line.'[22] Major Ready vividly recalled how his colleague Lieutenant McMath was literally 'voiceless from shouting the word of command so he stood apart from his company and raised his sword as a signal when the volley was to be delivered'. Ready also noted that, in the early stages, the 'slaughter' of the *Ghazis* was horrific: 'In some places they would be seen to fall three deep and always those behind would quietly step over them and come on with their gleaming knives.'[23] Lieutenant-Colonel Anderson recalled the initial, hugely successful, fire of his Bombay Grenadiers who made it 'so hot' that three enemy regular regiments 'moved off'. Sadly, it may have been an opportunity missed as Anderson subsequently recalled how General Burrows hesitated when he remarked, 'They are off'. The General replied to him, 'Only a portion of them'. In Anderson's view: 'Had a general advance then been made I think the result of that day would have been different.'[24]

However, the vastly outnumbered British infantry could not survive in the long term without artillery and cavalry support and, somewhere between 1.30 and 2 p.m., the first cracks appeared in the British lines. Under cover of their superior artillery fire, the Afghan gunners were able to move a battery of guns forward and bring them to bear upon the British line at a distance of less than 500 yards. From then, 'Our losses became serious. The condition of both men and their rifles was also deteriorating with the sepoys in particular exhausted from want of food.'[25] Water was also in short supply. Technical problems added to the sense of crisis. Possibly around 2 p.m., in at least one section of the line, the Martini-Henry rifles and cartridges were seen to be overheating. Major Bray recalled:

> The rifles were now beginning to jam and one was continually trying to jerk out a jammed case from someone's weapon. The ordinary Martini clearing rod, without a jag, was too short to knock out the cartridge case. Had this cleaning rod not had a blob on the end that prevented it going down the barrel we would have used it effectually. Jags seemed at a premium ... what with firing and the sun the barrels had got so hot that men were wrapping cartridge packet paper around the barrels so as not to blister their fingers.

It was an equipment failure experienced a year earlier at the battle of Rorke's Drift during the Anglo-Zulu War and, possibly with fatal consequences, at the Isandlwana disaster. Unfortunately the problem had been ignored by the authorities, probably for budgetary or even technical reasons, and the same problem was to recur in the later Sudan campaigns of the 1880s before the rifle was eventually replaced with the technically superior Lee Metford and Lee Enfield rifles. Major Bray was eventually compelled to borrow a Snider cleaning rod from one of the Jacob's Rifles, 'and that cleaning rod worked hard'.[26] One can only speculate as to how far this problem undermined the efficiency of the volley firing in the later stages of the battle, but it could only have been an ominous development. Equally ominous, in the searing heat of the midday sun, was evidence of the growing shortage or lack of adequate distribution of food and water. We already know that some British regulars had missed breakfast earlier that morning and at least one source confirms that, 'the men were all gravely exhausted from want of food and the excessive heat of the day'.[27] All this combined with the incessant Afghan artillery bombardment, no prospect of reserve or reinforcement and, especially, the unrelenting nature of the fanatical *Ghazi* attacks, meant that a break in the line was inevitable.

Around 2 p.m. the break in the line finally occurred and virtually all sources agree that it was the hard-pressed Jacob's Rifles or 30th who broke. Major Hogg had already noticed, soon after 1 p.m., that 'nothing but a miracle could save us'.[28] In retrospect, it was surely a miracle that the final break took another hour to materialize. At 'just about 2', although the 66th Foot were still firing steadily, with still-bearable casualties, in the midst of a massive *Ghazi* charge, the crisis broke. While the *Ghazis* were still being 'literally mowed down in thousands',[29] Hogg thus recalled that, this time:

> It was of no avail, for there were thousands more to succeed them and as they swarmed sword in hand up to the infantry and were within one hundred yards of them, the 30th ... gave way and bolted, the 1st Grenadiers followed suit, running up against the 66th in their backward career and the 66th, seeing both the Native Infantry regiments retiring, followed suit and broke.[30]

It was, perhaps, an understandable collapse, as several sections of both the 30th (Jacob's Rifles) were not only short of food and water but were already, tactically, deeply compromised. As official historian Cardew succinctly observed, while 'the 66th, 30th Bombay Infantry and the sappers were all more or less covered by shallow depressions or rather folds in the ground ... the Bombay Grenadiers and the two detached companies of the 30th Bombay were much exposed and their loss was proportionally heavier'.[31] These latter regiments had also suffered a disproportionate loss of officers, with Lieutenant Cole, 'their only British officer' killed very early in the day and the only three native officers 'severely wounded'. Hanna confirms that command of 'the most important flank of the line had devolved upon a Jemadar'.[32] Major Ready further confirms that 'the crash' came when 'the only European officers with the two companies of the Jacobs Rifles between the guns and Peirse's company were shot down'.[33]

However, it was equally a further sudden, unexpected action by the already hard-pressed British artillery which perhaps proved the decisive blow to the morale of these units. By early afternoon the smooth guns had run out of ammunition and their rapid retirement to replenish their stocks apparently had a major deleterious impact upon infantry fighting spirit. Even the weary British regulars were shaken by the spectacle. One eyewitness recalled: 'I saw Captain Slade going out of action with some guns at a trot. I heard the men remarking to one another, "What is this, here are our guns going back." They seemed distracted by it and I said, "They are only going for more ammunition".'[34] If the British rank and file were 'distracted', the morale of the already struggling Indian regiments was decisively broken. Official historian Cardew confirms how the effect of the 'retirement' of the smooth-bore guns, though 'not evident at once', was nonetheless 'fatal'.[35]

Whatever the precise reason, the chaos in the ranks was both soon evident and catastrophic. General Burrows reported that 'the infantry gave way and, commencing on the left, rolled up on the 66th forming a helpless crowd of panic-stricken men'.[36] Major Ready noted that even the direction of their retreat had been fatal, running 'not straight back but behind the 66th, who were still standing firm, as if seeking safety there'.[37] A horrified Colonel Mainwaring directly witnessed the virtual dismemberment of his precious 30th Regiment and of the Grenadiers: 'The whole of the ground to the left of the 30th Native Infantry and between it and the Grenadiers was covered with swarms of Ghazis and banner men. The Ghazis were actually in the ranks of the Grenadiers, pulling the men out and hacking them with their swords.'[38]

One of the first of the 66th's companies to be cut to ribbons by the Afghan charge was Lieutenant Cullen's company, 'which was thrown back and broke its formation to pieces'. Gallant, if futile, efforts were still being made to reform the lines, with the 'rear rank of F and H companies 66th ... turned about by word of command and keeping up the fire on both sides'.[39] Even when 'about 2pm', according to Bray, 'from somewhere or other the retire was sounded', there was evidence that 'a portion at least of the regiment made a move, not *away from* but towards the enemy'.[40] Historian Cardew confirms that the 66th, despite being 'pressed by the Ghazis in front and by broken sepoys in the rear, retired to their right but still preserved cohesion, the men turning round to deliver their fire and keeping off the crowds at some twenty five yards'.[41]

The only hope in this crisis rested on a cavalry charge but, as noted earlier, Nuttall's cavalry units, subjected to over two hours of continuous Afghan artillery bombardment, were in no condition to fight. Nevertheless, General Burrows rode up to Brigadier Nuttall exclaiming: 'Nuttall, the infantry has given way; our only chance is a cavalry charge: do you think you could get the cavalry to charge the line of Ghazis in the rear of the infantry, and they might perhaps then be induced to re-form?'[42] As the orders to advance arrived, however, it was clear that the already much-depleted and deeply demoralized cavalry units (especially the Queen's Own Light Cavalry squadron, which was already reduced to a weak troop) were unwilling to move. Out of 460 horses, 149 had been lost.[43] Major Hogg witnessed the 3rd Sind Horse (about one hundred sabres) fatally 'hesitating ... they did not like the job'. Major Ready confirmed that 'the men could not be got to obey'.[44] Hogg's account continued the tragic story:

> Instead of going straight to their front and trying to smash through ... the Ghazis, they stopped short with a small band who were actually inside the Grenadier square cutting the men down and as soon as they had disposed of these, they wheeled to the right about and

returned without orders and in spite of their officers. As soon as we had got the men together again, a desperate attempt was made to get them to advance again but it was no use.

In an astonishing, surreal moment, in the midst of battle, the cavalry were seen steadily retreating 'at a walk' through Lieutenant Quarry's rear-guard line. In Hogg's words, 'The battle was of course then clean lost.'[45]

With no effective cavalry support, the retreating British infantry soon descended into a situation of utter chaos, and a desperate last order by Adjutant-Lieutenant C.W. Hinde to fix bayonets and form regimental squares only resulted in the companies being 'jammed together in an arrow-shaped mass', a virtual impasse in which neither bayonets could be used or shots fired. An 'appalling scene followed as the Ghazis rushed into the surging crowd ... dragged one after another into the open and hacked him to pieces with their swords'.[46] The retreat was greatly exacerbated by intermingling of retreating British soldiers and sepoys with their enemy pursuers. Cavalry commander Major Bray, whilst ordering his men to fire on 'any number of Afghans', discovered how, to his consternation, 'suddenly mixed up with them and drifting across our front, we saw the helmets and the red peaked caps the Grenadiers wore inside their turbans. So we had to stop firing.'[47] Moreover, as the infantry 'legged it ... there was no possible time, or means of assisting our wounded men who were hacked to pieces as they lay on the ground'.[48] The struggle to cross the *nullah* was particularly desperate: 'Into it they tumbled pell mell and, such was the rush, that McMath's colour-sergeant fell upon his own sword and was killed.'[49]

The main retreat from the village had commenced at 2.30 p.m. For the artillery survivors also it was now a case of *sauve qui peut*, although Lieutenant Maclaine, in a gallant but forlorn last effort, rushed off back to the front with his two guns firing both case-shot and shrapnel to 'terrible effect'. Soon, however, he and his guns were surrounded and he was captured to suffer, as we shall see, an appalling death in captivity. The last desperate moments of the Royal Horse Artillery group were graphically recorded by Limber-Gunner Naylor: 'There was no time even to spike the guns, they had to be abandoned. One of our men tumbled an Afghan over by thrusting at him with his rammer, and then managed to get away; another, cut through the stirrup-leather of one of the gunners and ran along with his horse and managed to escape'. The horses suffered terribly with nearly half killed and some 'shockingly wounded'. Naylor was haunted by the memory of their 'piteous' condition as they 'clung to us and followed us, one in particular who had his jaw shattered ... galloped on with us in our terrible retreat'.[50] Only Major Slade and his four guns managed to make the rear relatively intact.

The prospects of survival were now, in Hogg's words, more hideous than the horrors already gone through: 'We had marched that morning ten miles in the gruelling sun to fight a battle, we had fought hard for four and a half hours, the men were dying of thirst, there was no help near, the enemy's cavalry were in thousands and yet, Candahar, our only chance was fifty miles off.'[51]

For the largely helpless infantry involved in the rout, their previously disciplined formations now irrevocably broken, it was a veritable nightmare. As Major Ready observed: 'then the heavy losses began', with the 'Native Infantry an unresisting mass'. He further noted that, 'So utterly cowed were the men of Jacobs Rifles that when [Lieutenant] Peirse, standing with his cocked revolver at the rear entrance of one of the gardens, forbade them to leave it, they crouched down by the back wall until they were killed like a flock of unresisting sheep.'[52] More horrific scenes were witnessed:

> Among the Ghazis pressing on their heels one would sometimes be seen to stretch out his arm and drag a Grenadier from the ranks, then, with one hand, he would knock off the man's turban and with the other cut him down. The same game ... when tried on with our 66th men was a signal failure and in the retreat to the village garden the enemy kept such a respectful distance that our fellows had no need to use their bayonets. As each man retired he would be busy inserting a cartridge in his rifle and then he would turn round and fire and continue the retirement.[53]

Officer casualties were particularly heavy as they desperately tried to rally retreating regiments. Of the eighteen officers of the 66th who went into action, eleven were killed or wounded either before or shortly after entering the gardens.

There was, apparently a desperate, if futile struggle, to save the 66th's colours, originally carried by Lieutenants Oliver and Honey, both of whom clung to them after they were wounded. Lieutenant Barr and Sergeant-Major Cuppage, who next retrieved them, were 'killed almost at once', with the colonel himself last seen 'on his knees clinging to it.'[54]

During the retreat the one unrelenting memory for all the men was their incredible thirst. As Major Ready reiterated, 'no food or drink had passed the men's lips since they left camp in the early morning'.[55] With the *doolie*-bearers deserting *en masse* the abandoned wounded were particularly vulnerable, and those lucky few who were saved were hastily packed onto artillery carriages and carts and camels. Captain Mayne recalled how the limbers were 'crowded with wounded officers and men, others were helped onto baggage ponies, the loads being thrown away'. He continued: 'we were all suffering from thirst and not having drunk since the water we passed on the march in the morning'.[56] Even more desperate measures were soon undertaken. Gunner Naylor witnessed 'parched and swollen-tongued' sepoys smashing open medicine chests and frantically consuming the contents of the bottles, while a Staff Officer also observed how many 'foolish men' slaked their thirst from the Commissariat rum casks 'in too many cases, alas, paying the penalty of their folly with their lives'.[57] Naylor only eased his own thirst by drinking from a stagnant pool 'a horrible poisonous patch of water still and silent, thick with grass-green slime on top'. His enduring memory was seeing, in its reflection, his moustache, 'thick with the green slime'. At least one 'very badly wounded gunner' only got 'vinegar to drink; we had used up all our water'.[58] Many gave up the struggle and an officer observed how many of the 'fearfully thirsty men ... lay down exhausted and awaited the arrival of the savage Ghazis who followed them and cut them to pieces as they came across them'.[59] Scores more of the British fugitives were murdered by 'treacherous' villagers *en route*.

The water problem was apparently exacerbated by the haphazard direction of the retreat, with the 'bulk of the infantry dispersed over a very wide extent of country and in spite of every endeavour ... the further they went to the left, the further they went away from water'.[60] Many were undoubtedly lost forever, especially as night fell.

That the force was not completely annihilated was arguably down to four main factors. Firstly, the 66th Foot survivors managed at least three delaying stands, an initial one across the other side of the ravine commanded by Colonel Galbraith, a second, of approximately 150 men under General Burrows himself, on the outskirts of Mundabad Village, and a final stand inside the gardens of the village, protecting the colours. All helped to delay the enemy pursuit – especially the second stand under Burrows, which checked the enemy before he ordered their retirement. The final gallant, if disastrous, stand in the rear garden by about a hundred mixed troops, mainly 66th Regiment, and led by Colonel Galbraith, was witnessed by one of Ayub Khan's officers. 'He stated that these brave men were surrounded by the whole army and that, when all but eleven were killed, these made a desperate charge and perished fighting bravely to the last man.'[61] Sir Frederick Haines considered that this final 'stubborn defence may have delayed the pursuit as well as checked the desire to pursue'.[62] Overall, these last holding actions probably enabled at least two small collected bodies of the 66th to escape and proceed, 'one going ahead with Ready and Peirse and the other under baggage commander, Lieutenant Quarry, bringing up the rear.'[63]

Secondly, a significant element of the British cavalry remained cohesive after their early precipitate withdrawal from the battle, and were able to protect isolated bodies of British infantrymen during the retreat. Captain Mayne of the 3rd Light Cavalry escorted many stragglers and even dismounted his men 'to drive off some villagers who were firing at us from the opposite bank near Singiri'.[64] Elements of the other British cavalry units also protected the guns in the rear, 'the last gun was the last point protected and the men who failed to reach it were left behind'.[65]

Thirdly and, perhaps, equally importantly, the enemy were not only themselves exhausted but were understandably preoccupied with looting the British baggage train which had been abandoned by the terrified camel and transport drivers and rapidly overrun. As Major Ready confirmed: 'The prospect of plunder offered by the baggage stopped anything like a vigorous pursuit on the part of the enemy ... the enemy's infantry and Ghazis did not press the retreat far beyond the gardens.'[66] In fact the enemy pursuit petered out after eight to ten miles and consisted mainly of small marauding pockets of cavalry. A much more potent threat emanated from hostile bands of local villagers who tried to murder or plunder the retreating remnants of Burrows' army.

Fourthly, a very few isolated parties aside from Gunner Naylor's did secure some water in the later stages of retreat. Captain Mayne's mixed Sind and Light Cavalry for instance, were able to escort and locate 'abundant water' for General Burrows at Ata Karley, and Major Bray's unit latterly made 'a digression for water', whilst 'meeting a few other stragglers' and picking up 'other fugitives'.[67]

Also, the belated but otherwise valuable assistance from sections of the now-alerted Kandahar garrison (principally the 7th Fusiliers with artillery support) undoubtedly saved the lives of more men, particularly from the attacks by villagers during the final stages of the retreat. Major Ready thus recalled that, at Koheran, 'part of the Second Brigade ... drove off tribesmen who had collected to intercept them'.[68]

The Kandahar garrison had been alerted to the disaster as early as 1.30 a.m. on the next day, 28 July, although most of the survivors only staggered in during the late afternoon of that day. A horrified Lieutenant Fox, a Kandahar garrison officer, was one of the first to hear, woken at 1.45 a.m. with the inaccurate but staggering news that Burrows' force was 'cut to bits and that only twenty five Sind Horsemen who had just galloped in were alive to tell the tale'.[69] In the far north, General Roberts was equally appalled on hearing, as he rode to Sherpur with his new political and military superior, the 'lamentable story ... which almost took my breath away'.[70]

The question of who was to blame for this terrible calamity remains controversial today. Again, the 'politicals' must bear considerable responsibility for the failure. Clearly, Burrows had been sent out with an inadequate, under-strength force and the abject failure of intelligence by the Kandahar political officer, Colonel St John, indicated by his inability to assess the enemy size and build-up before Maiwand, had certainly contributed to the disaster. One appalled officer, Lieutenant Hamilton of the Queen's, based in Kandahar, tellingly commented:

> Such a disaster ... only shows how utterly bad our information was ... there will be a great uproar at home about this business ... I don't know who was to blame but just think of an army being in Kandahar nearly two years and no one taking the trouble to find out what was going on in Herat.[71]

Moreover, lacking essential intelligence, Burrows had been placed under intense, arguably unacceptable, *political* pressure to take the offensive after the collapse of the *Wali's* forces in order to forestall Ayub Khan from spreading political disaffection further north and west.

From the perspective of Burrows' own military performance there are, nevertheless, also some grounds for criticism. Burrows, and more specifically his Commissariat officers, had clearly failed to provide or ensure adequate logistical support, with many of his force clearly suffering from lack of food and water, not only before but during the march and the battle. His force had marched far too late for Afghan summer conditions. Ammunition supplies for the artillery were lacking and the latter's crisis undoubtedly contributed to the collapse of morale. Tactically, General Burrows had, after finally realizing the massive superiority of Ayub Khan's army, opted for a high-risk passive defence but then, instead of redeploying his infantry and cavalry, or even attacking decisively, had inexplicably allowed Ayub Khan to both deploy and probe his weaknesses over two hours, far too long a period of time. As this valuable time was squandered (even though Lieutenant Maclaine's actions had already arguably forced his hand), Burrows' decision to use the period to engage in a clearly futile and unequal artillery duel was, arguably, another fatal error, leaving his static cavalry force and several infantry and artillery sections to be severely depleted and their morale deeply compromised. His flanks should certainly have been protected and not left openly exposed; arguably he would have been better off *laagering* in the village behind him, where his lines/squares could be better consolidated and his baggage guarded more effectively and closely. The baggage train had diverted far too many able-bodied men: its escort had ultimately absorbed two and a half companies of the 66th Foot and over one hundred sabres.

With regard to the infantry and the more junior officers, little fault can be found. The collapse of the Jacob's Rifles was understandable if regrettable; they were poorly positioned and supplied, while the 66th excelled themselves even during the retreat, redeploying into several delaying stands which helped to slow the enemy's advance. The British cavalry had done their best under extremely trying circumstances. In the words of Captain Barttelot of the 7th Royal Fusiliers: 'The Scinde horse [were] refusing to charge; but when you come to think that they were under shellfire for four hours and that when the order came to charge the Ghazis were among them, it isn't likely they would.'[72] Significantly, Roberts and his Chief of Staff, Colonel MacGregor, reserved their scathing condemnations for the senior British political and military leaders. 'There seems to have been the most awful imbecility at Kandahar', MacGregor wrote, 'and Primrose, Burrows and St John should be recalled.'[73]

As Roberts and Stewart frantically prepared a response to this disaster, Roberts' existing anger over his enforced political subordination, possibly fuelled by the Maiwand disaster, resurfaced, with distinct echoes from the experience of his father, passed over for command in the First Anglo-Afghan War. In a bitter tirade addressed to Lyall, Secretary in the Indian Foreign Department, he recalled how his earlier command of the Kabul Field Force had made him initially 'supreme in political as well as military matters'. Since then, he complained, he had been politically 'superseded' by Sir Donald Stewart, 'By virtue of his superior rank and by the arrival of [senior political] Mr Griffin', an appointment which, in particular, had caused 'a division of authority which to my mind is most dangerous whilst an enemy's country is in military occupation'. Roberts warned 'that nothing should ever induce me again to accept a military command on service unless I was politically supreme'.[74] Roberts went on to demand personal military control of the crisis, arguing that 'the only means of affording speedy relief to the now besieged Kandahar garrison', was 'by sending a force from Kabul'.

The political authorities at Simla, however, objected and, 'looked to Quetta rather than Kabul' for a relief force.[75] As in 1842, however, the political authorities soon kowtowed to London and to wider imperial implications, no doubt acutely aware of how the Maiwand disaster had caused 'considerable excitement all along the border [and] throughout India ... a certain feeling of uneasiness' and at a time particularly 'anxious ... for those who remembered the days of the Mutiny'.[76] Once again, as in the 1842 military crisis, the local 'politicals' were compelled to take a backseat to their military counterparts. Indeed, it was a telegram sent directly to Roberts by the Foreign Secretary himself, Lord Ripon, which swiftly silenced his Simla critics, confirmed his authority and authorized the immediate departure of his force to relieve Kandahar.[77]

The Kabul to Kandahar Relief Force

To rescue Kandahar and avenge Maiwand, two British divisions were swiftly prepared. In addition to Roberts' own Field Force another division was dispatched from Quetta under General Phayre. Meanwhile, in the now-secure north, the rest of the Kabul garrison troops, under General Stewart, slowly retired by the Khyber route to India. Roberts' subsequent epic 325-mile march from Kabul to Kandahar, achieved in a remarkable twenty-two days, has achieved legendary status in the annals of British imperial history. A number of factors ensured its success. General Roberts, now freed from political interference, was given *carte blanche* assistance by his commander, Stewart. Secondly, Roberts was able to hand-pick his regiments and fighting men, although he wisely consulted the unit commanders before detailing the troops. In fact only three commanders declined their men on the ground that they were too fatigued and had already been too long away from home leave. After the Maiwand disaster Roberts avoided the Bombay regiments as he considered that 'but ... few are able to cope with the Afghans',[78] and he systematically weeded out, through rigorous health checks, 'every man not likely to stand the strains of prolonged forced marches'. Thirdly, Roberts had drawn a deep appreciation and awareness of the logistical problems of Stewart's earlier equally redoubtable if less publicized march from Kandahar to Kabul. Although supplies remained his 'greatest anxiety', especially as the primary objective was speed, he marched as light as possible, with no wheeled guns or transport and, initially, no camels Nevertheless, Roberts was still encumbered by over 8,000 followers and 2,300 horses and gunwheels on his epic march. Finally, at a local political level, Roberts would benefit greatly from the enthusiastic support of Abdur Rahman, the newly adopted British candidate for the Afghan throne, who loyally supplied officials and interpreters to facilitate the procurement of supplies along the projected route.

Major-General Roberts was given three brigades of infantry, one brigade of cavalry and three batteries of mountain artillery to conduct his daring march; a total of 2,562 British, 7,151 natives, 273 British officers and 18 (light mountain) guns. While the troops were probably the best to hand, including three strong British infantry regiments, the 72nd and 92nd Highlanders and the 60th Rifles (2nd Battalion) there were some doubts expressed over Roberts' leadership, possibly reflecting his previous gung-ho high-risk tactics. Once again Colonel MacGregor carped: 'Bobs more and more anxious to go, so I suppose there is no putting it off. I am not confident in Bobs generalship and should not be so sure he ... may ... not do something rash and rush at them without wanting to see how they were posted.'[79]

While, in military terms, the march proved to be an unqualified success, in personal and political terms it was not completely without cost. For the individual soldiers, many of whom, after two years' duty in Afghanistan, did not initially exhibit high morale, conditions were extremely tough. There were significant supply difficulties, particularly for wood for fuel, and water. The 'long stretches of desert had often to be traversed without a drop of water and ... troops had to march in the same clothes when the thermometer was nearly at freezing point as when it reached 110'.[80] There were constant sandstorms. As ever, the conditions for the followers and drivers were far worse. The slow-moving camp-followers, 'frequently on foot by 2.30 a.m. were too tired in the evening to cook their rations and just kept themselves alive on raw flour or Indian corn'.[81] Desertion represented an immediate problem, Roberts himself revealing that the 'Afghan drivers deserted to a man a march or two from Kabul and the Hazaras followed their example on reaching their own country'.[82] The arduous conditions led to serious outbreaks of sickness: 'Heat, thirst, improper food, irregular meals and ill-fitting boots', wrote the Surgeon-General, 'produced their natural results, dyspepsia, bilious vomiting, diarrhoea, sore feet – and as men and followers fell out the strain on the dhoolie bearers, always the weak part of an Indian Army's equipment, grew even greater.'[83]

Furthermore, the march was not as efficiently organized as many writers suggest. Colonel MacGregor noticed the constant confusion as baggage train and accompanying infantry units frequently concertinaed. On 26 August, the nineteenth day of the march, he duly recorded in his diary: 'We got along very slowly owing to the way the first brigade dawdled: the cavalry baggage as usual lapped around and surrounded us ... the march of the force is that of an organised rabble, an Afghan seeing it, said we were like an Afghan army, whereas Stewart's was like a European.'[84]

From Kandahar, the 'political' Colonel St John also worked to secure supplies along the projected march. For the local Afghan peasantry, as on previous campaigns, it was a time of mixed fortunes; for some a moment of great economic opportunity, for others a time of suffering. Although many supplies were paid for by Roberts' flying column, sources reveal that a significant degree of coercion was also often employed. Journalist Hensman noted the skilful opportunism of corn growers and vineyard owners in the Chinaz Valley, where a 'donkey-load made up of two large baskets, each weighing forty or fifty pounds cost us only three rupees (five shillings) ... although prices rose enormously as the day wore on'. Near Mukur, 'luxury' supplies of fowls, eggs and milk were abundant and purchased at 'reasonable rates'.[85] General Roberts purchased 5,000 sheep along the line of march and this must have been a source of lucrative profit for many Afghan herders.[86] Nevertheless, when supplies were not readily available – particularly after leaving Ghazni – Roberts' ruthless drive led to the not infrequent use of coercion to secure his needs. It was recorded, for instance, that, 'Roberts would not commit any trenching on his reserve of supplies, the flanking regiments had to go far and wide ... ransacking deserted villages in search of the people's carefully hidden stores of grain and, when unearthed, loading them on the three or four hundred animals by which they were accompanied.'[87] At Nani, Colonel MacGregor significantly recalled:

We had to turn off the road and unload and feed our animals by simply cutting down what fields we wanted; this is the only way to make war. No doubt it puts the people against you but I doubt if you would have much more trouble in the long run as, by our way of paying, they despise you.[88]

For converse political reasons, other Afghan ethnic groups also suffered. The Hazara people, hitherto loyal collaborators of the British, paid a heavy penalty in the aftermath of Maiwand. News of the British defeat encouraged a wholesale merciless attack on their villages by rival tribes and, specifically, by Ayub Khan's supporters. Their plight was witnessed during Roberts' relief march. Sir Montagu Gerard, stationed on 'flanking duty', graphically observed the terrible fate of several Hazara villages near Chardeh and in the Karabagh region: 'Never did I see such a scene of desolation and the devastation was apparently of very recent date. There was the mark of fire and sword everywhere, not a rooftop left to a homestead, not the trace of a living creature and even the fruit trees were barked or cut down.'[89] It certainly helped to explain the earlier mass desertion of Hazara drivers who had departed to defend their kinsfolk's villages.

Roberts' forces, in urgent need of transport, also clashed with elements of the Pashtun Powindah, the great Afghan trading tribe. The transport department insisted on purchasing 'fifty of their camels' and, after fruitless negotiations 'in the end' took them 'by force'.[90] These excesses contrasted starkly with Roberts' own somewhat egotistical and sanitized memoirs of the Afghan campaign and his statement that the 'persons and property of the Natives were respected and full compensation of supplies was everywhere given', certainly requires some qualification![91]

On 31 August 1880, Roberts' exhausted force struggled into Kandahar. This epic march, so ruthlessly directed by Roberts, had, indeed, taken a heavy toll. On arrival by the Shikapur Gate, a scene was witnessed: 'of the most indescribable confusion with the sick slowly driven in (I can use no other word) by the Baluchi Regiment closing the march of the Bengal Division. They certainly numbered five hundred wretched creatures and cripples mounted on refuse transport or in dandies or doolies, for whom it was difficult to find room'.[92] General Roberts himself could barely ride, significantly weakened by a fever he had contracted on the march. He confronted a 'demoralised' garrison of 4,000 British and Indian troops under Major-General Primrose, who 'seemed to consider themselves hopelessly defeated' and 'never even hoisted the Union Jack until the relieving force was close at hand'.[93]

The Battle of Deh Khoja

In fact the Kandahar garrison had been through several traumatic experiences, not only caused by the shock of the Maiwand defeat, but also by the subsequent reverse of 16 August, when General Primrose had, perhaps recklessly, ordered an ill-fated sortie by his garrison to force the besieging Ayub Khan to 'show his hand'. Primrose had earlier evacuated outlying cantonments as they were not defensible and had no water supply. The objective of the foray was the village of Deh Khoja, still occupied by Ayub Khan's forces and against which Primrose dispatched Major-General Henry Francis Brooke with 800 hundred rifles, a sapper detachment and 300 cavalry under Brigadier-General Thomas Nuttall. This force was a much smaller one than that suggested in the original plan submitted by the Commanding Engineer, Colonel Hills. The cavalry duly passed the Eedgah Gate and the infantry via the Kabul Gate, aided by fire from the city guns. The infantry promptly divided into three columns, with the centre and half of the right wing under Brooke and Lieutenant-Colonel A.G. Daubeny entering the south of the village under heavy fire. As the *Ghazis* tried to intercept from the south they were broken up by units of Nuttall's cavalry. It represented the only success of this ill-fated expedition.

The other half of the right column entered the gardens but Brooke's and Daubeny's one and a half columns, already ensconced in the village, met fierce resistance and the only hope was to gain time for the sappers to demolish the outer village wall facing the Kabul Gate. Outside, the left column, under Colonel Heathcote, gave what support it could to the south-west corner. Major-General Brooke, increasingly outnumbered and recognizing his extreme danger, reported it to Primrose and the latter precipitately ordered a retreat. Worst of all, it was an uncontrolled retreat. General Heathcote's left column, half the right and Nuttall's cavalry, rapidly fell back to the Kabul Gate but left Brooke's and Daubeny's centre and half the right column stranded and dangerously isolated. So fierce was the enemy's fire that Brooke's and Daubeny's columns at the north end of the village were then also fatally split, one section escaping from the north side, the other by the west side of Deh Khoja village. Major-General Brooke himself was shot and killed and only at 7 a.m. did firing cease as the victorious enemy also retired. Out of 1,556 British troops engaged, 226 were lost.[94]

This heavy skirmish was a serious British reverse, in effect a mini-Maiwand. It certainly reflected bad planning by Lieutenant-General Primrose and it was a serious blow to garrison morale. Although the timing of the attack at early dawn was wisely chosen, the initial use of artillery was an error, giving warning to the enemy and, moreover, the columns should never have been split into 'penny packet' detachments, especially when commanded from such a long distance. Above all, the aims of the foray were never made clear. General Roberts gave his own decidedly negative verdict: 'The objects and reasons for the sortie of the 16 August which was attended with such terrible loss of life ... are best known to General Primrose and was made without sufficient reason.'[95]

The Battle of Kandahar

The task for General Roberts was now greatly magnified; not only must he avenge Maiwand and restore British prestige over the whole of Afghanistan – and even northern India – but he now had to restore the collapsed morale of his front-line garrison. As he confirmed to Lyall: 'The Kandahar Garrison was quite demoralised from the senior officers, I'm afraid, downwards.'[96] Roberts was equally despairing of the capability of Major-General Robert Phayre's southern relief force, which had experienced horrendous marching conditions on its route from India: 'If Phayre's force had come into contact with Ayub's I do not think ... it would have been successful. The men, for the most part, looked worn and listless, better fitted for hospital than a campaign ... they had the appearance of troops retreating not advancing.'[97]

It was under such stringent political and military pressure that Roberts, still physically recovering from the march, and now assuming supreme command for all the British troops in southern Afghanistan, prepared his final showdown with Ayub Khan's forces outside Kandahar. The British troops in and around Kandahar totalled 3,800 British and 11,000 'Native' and were supported by thirty-six guns. They were outnumbered by Ayub Khan's forces, which were centred on the nearby villages of Baba *Wali* Kotal and Pir Paimal and extended overall between the Argandab River and Kandahar. General Roberts had initially halted his column for two hours outside the south wall of the city away from enemy fire. With temperatures reaching 105 °F his sick list had grown with 940 men hospitalized. Nevertheless, in his usual gung-ho style, he decided to strike early and, on 31 August 1880, he sent Brigadier-General Gough and his 3rd Bengal Cavalry and 3rd Sikhs and two guns to reconnoitre. Their intelligence revealed to him that 'any attempt to carry the Baba *Wali* Kotal by direct attack must result in very severe loss, and I determined to turn it'.[98] For the great battle the next day (1 September 1880), Robert had positioned his troops thus: the 1st Brigade under MacPherson on the right at Picquet Hill; the 2nd Brigade under Baker on the left at Chihilzina and the 3rd Brigade under MacGregor in reserve in front of Abasabad. The cavalry under General Gough were placed in the rear to threaten Ayub's potential line of retreat on Girishk. General Primrose's command of the (considered less reliable) Bombay troops was left to hold Kandahar city while Major-General Daubeny was to replace Roberts' troops after his advance. The remnants of Brigadier-General Burrows' force, equipped with four 40-pounder guns, were further deployed to fire on the Baba *Wali* Kotal entrenchments, while Nuttall, with his cavalry units, was briefed to watch the Kotal-i-Muncha Pass.

As Daubeny's Brigade began the feint attack at 7.30 a.m. on 1 September, followed by Brigadier-General Burrows' troops at 9 a.m., Captain Hardy's Royal Artillery Brigade opened fire on the Baba *Wali* Kotal. With, as planned, the enemy distracted by these attacks, Roberts ordered the 'real attack' with Major-General Ross's 1st and 2nd Brigades advancing against the village of Gundi Mulla Sahibadad. Roberts ordered Brigadier-General MacPherson to drive the enemy from the enclosures on Pir Paimal Hill and Brigadier-General Baker to advance to the west. The determined attack by the 1st Brigade on Gundi Mulla Sahibad was led by the 2nd Gurkhas and 92nd Highlanders. The two regiments carried the valley with 'splendid dash', the enemy 'sullenly and slowly withdrawing', although a 'good number of Ghazis remained to the very last to receive a bayonet charge of the 92nd'.[99] Some two hundred Afghan rebels were killed in the village alone, many of them again fanatical *Ghazis* who 'sold their lives dearly, many shutting themselves up in underground chambers and firing upon our men as they passed'.[100]

In the attack of Baker's 2nd Brigade, the 72nd Highlanders and the 2nd Sikhs 'bore the brunt of the fighting', taking positions by bayonet and incurring some severe losses, including Lieutenant-Colonel Brownlow, hero of Peiwar Kotal and the Asmai Heights. At 12 noon the 3rd Brigade, led by Colonel MacGregor, were sent forward.

With their position now untenable in the villages of Gundi Mullah and Gundigan, the enemy, reinforced by more fanatical *Ghazis*, fell back to the south-west of Baba *Wali* Kotal for what looked like a determined final stand. As the enemy guns were turned to enfilade the freshly taken Pir Paimal, it was the actions of a relatively junior officer which helped to clinch victory. Individual acts often turn a battle and it was Major White of the 92nd Highlanders, supported by the 2nd Gurkhas and part of the 23rd Pioneers, who took the initiative and they rushed forward and took the enemy gun entrenchments at the point of the bayonet. Jounalist Hensman graphically recorded White's famous gallant charge, apparently calling to his men sheltering in front of a water course, '"Highlanders, will you follow me if I give you a lead for those guns?" There was but one answer, a ringing cheer', which was followed by a rush across the open ground 'led by pipers playing the *Slogan* while Major White rode serenely on in front, drawing upon himself a terrific fire'.[101]

It was the final, fatal, blow to enemy morale and the battle turned into a rout as the enemy fled either towards Kokoran or to Ayub Khan's massive base camp at Mazra. At 3 p.m. the three infantry brigades found Ayub's camp empty, capturing thirty-two guns including the two British Horse Artillery guns captured previously at Maiwand.

One tragic event deeply blighted the celebration of victory. By a tent in the enemy camp lay the corpse of Lieutenant Hector Maclaine, the officer previously captured at Maiwand. Deputy Surgeon Hanbury dismounted and, on examining the body, 'found a clean incised wound on the neck, which all but severed the head from the body'.[102] Although Maclaine was probably murdered by his fanatical *Ghazi* guards, General Roberts was infuriated by the murder of a prisoner of war and personally blamed Ayub Khan for not ensuring his safety. Ayub Khan's camp had been left strangely intact: 'All the equipage of a half-barbarous army was left at our mercy, the meat and the cooking pots, the bread half-kneaded on the earthen vessels, the bazaar with its ghee-pots, dried fruits flour and corn, just as it had been deserted when the noise of battle rode up from Pir Paimal.'[103]

It was left to Gough's cavalry to pursue the fugitives and cut off the tail end of the retreating Afghans. But the great heat and subsequent exhaustion of the horses undermined his efforts and only a few scattered bands were overtaken and destroyed. Similarly, the Bengal Cavalry Brigade galloped along the Herat Road but *nullahs* and water courses prevented them overtaking the enemy at the Kokeran River ford.

British losses were recorded as three British officers, one native officer and thirty-six men killed and Roberts estimated that up to 1,200 enemy were left dead, with '600 bodies buried by us'[104] between Kandahar and Pir Paimal. Eyewitness Hensman estimated that the cavalry pursuit alone resulted in some 400 enemy dead. Hensman took time to examine the battlefield and expressed admiration for the fanatical, if futile, bravery of the white-clad *Ghazi* peasant infantry who comprised the majority of the dead and who had been deserted by Ayub's regulars at key stages of the battle. In their 'rude waist belts', he observed, 'not a single cartridge was left'. Enemy Martinis, Sniders or Enfields were 'taken by our soldiers as trophies, while matchlocks or Jhezails were broken to pieces and cast away'. Several relics of Maiwand were also discovered amongst the enemy dead. One dead enemy soldier was completely equipped in the uniform of the 66th Regiment and had with him a Martini rifle and bayonet',[105] while captured British tents of the 66th Foot were discovered throughout Ayub Khan's camp.

Despite the failure of the cavalry pursuit it had been a great victory, and Major White's plucky initiative had played a key role in the final stages of the battle. Roberts had successfully used his old turning manoeuvre to stunning effect. Although Roberts' other great victory at Charasia was militarily more decisive and glorious, Kandahar had been a prudent and, above all, a great 'political victory'. Ayub Khan's power, the main political obstacle to stability in Afghanistan, had been decisively broken and Maiwand had been fully avenged. In June 1880 Abdur Rahman, the newly arrived candidate for the Afghan throne, had already received the submission of the vast majority of Afghan warlords and was destined to be a loyal servant of the British for the next two decades.

Roberts' critics, however, saw it as an incomplete victory and pointed to his failure to provide an intercepting force to finish off Ayub Khan's army. But, as Hensman points out, there were not troops to spare for a full pursuit. General Roberts was, as ever, vastly outnumbered and to conduct a long chase might have exposed his main force to unnecessary danger. The use of the 4,000 'spare' Kandahar garrison troops was largely precluded by their poor state of fitness of morale: 'It would have been unwise … as much of the garrison still suffered from the shock of Maiwand and Deh Khoja.'[106] It is arguable, however, that the 1st and 2nd Brigade attacks could have been supported by a cavalry contingent; 500 sabres would have had a devastating impact in the open ground of the basin towards Mazra and the Argandab, which was swamped with enemy fugitives.

The battle of Kandahar marked the end of British military involvement in Afghanistan for another four decades, but the lively political debate concerning the best method to secure Afghanistan as a buffer state against Russian ambitions for the future was revived. However, with the advent that year of a Liberal Government whose leader, W.E. Gladstone had, his famous 1879 Midlothian speech, asserted to the British electorate that 'the sanctity of life in the villages of Afghanistan, among the winter snows is as inviolable in the eyes in Almighty God as can be your own',[107] a policy of complete withdrawal was highly probable. It was a classic and passionate 'hearts and minds' statement which, as we shall see, still underpins the avowed aims of the current British/ISAF mission in Afghanistan but one which, as today, has been consistently undermined by chronic policy failures such as political-military co-ordination at ground level and an overall profound lack of understanding of Afghan welfare and security needs. Moreover, with the new, apparently loyal, Amir Abdur Rahman promising to safeguard a British retirement and the *status quo* restored in the north, only the fate of Kandahar and the south was now seriously discussed.

General Roberts himself was in favour of retention of the southern provinces but other leading strategists, notably Lord Sir Lawrence and General Wolseley, stood firmly against occupation. The matter was finally settled by Gladstone and his Cabinet when, in January 1881, 'it was publicly announced that Kandahar would be evacuated, a decision sanctioned in the House of Commons by a winning majority of 120. Significantly and predictably, however, the evacuation was *censured* in the more reactionary Lords by 165 votes against 79'.[108] Nevertheless, the areas of Sibi, Pishin, Quetta, Boland and Zhob were retained in British hands. The new Amir of Afghanistan, Abdur Rahman, was effectively bribed with five *lakhs* of rupees and sufficient ammunition to take on the extra responsibility of Kandahar and, on 16 April 1881, the new *Sirdar* of Kandahar, Muhammed Hashim, arrived to take over the city on behalf of Abdur Rahman.

The Second Afghan War (1878–80), although by no means as disastrous as the first war and ending in a decisive military success, resulted effectively in a political and territorial stalemate. The British had secured stunning victories at Peiwar Kotal, Charasia, Sherpur, Ahmed Khel and Kandahar and a pro-British Amir was safely installed, but this must be balanced against the terrible disaster at Maiwand and the overall loss of up to 50,000 men killed, wounded and perished from disease, as well as the thousands of transport livestock lost. Historian T.A. Heathcote records that the animal transport resources of north-west India were literally 'destroyed' by this war.[109] Territorially, there had only been some minor gains which would, it was hoped, act as a useful springboard from India in the event of a future Russian advance or even invasion.

Nevertheless, the British had learnt some significant military lessons. General Roberts had conspicuously avoided the disastrous tactics of the First Afghan War, by assiduously protecting his supply lines, setting up well-defended supply bases and using speed and mobility of firepower to maximum effect. Indeed Roberts even physically carried with him the key history texts of the First Afghan War as a constant reminder of past follies. He understood, as never before, the importance of dominating the heights and guarding the passes with substantial logistical bases established along the key passes. Nevertheless, many of his operations were high-risk, notably the advance on Kabul in October 1879, where he was at serious risk of being cut off from both reinforcements and supplies, and where operations were conducted at an arguably unacceptable cost both to his own men and, in particular, local Afghan villages which, as we have seen, were the frequent victims of requisitions for food and of collective punishment. The Kabul trials and Kurram Valley punitive raids in particular were undoubtedly excessive actions. Nevertheless, as in all wars, there were winners as well as losers and, as in the First Afghan War, many Hindu merchants attached to the British forces, and local Afghan traders and peasants, benefited massively from the sale of fuel, livestock and agricultural produce to the numerous British columns criss-crossing Afghanistan.

Both the Hazara and Qizilbash groups had proved invaluable as allies and collaborators. As Roberts confided to Lytton: 'The Hazaras have aided us materially during the last few weeks and kept Mahomed Jan's party at Ghazni fully occupied.'[110]

As in the First Afghan War, it had also been a time of renewed and considerable friction between the 'politicals' and their military counterparts. While some, notably Sir Robert Sandeman and General Stewart, had discharged their mutual duties in a most harmonious manner, several, notably the ill-fated Sir Pierre Louis Cavagnari and his counterpart in Kandahar, Colonel St John, had clearly interfered in military operations, often to detrimental effect. Despite often publicly praising their work

General Roberts, in particular, had consistently only paid lip-service to or eschewed the advice of his political advisers and, particularly after the war crimes allegations, he had successfully kept at bay any form of what he considered intrusive journalism. He was indeed a most political general. His personal political advisers, Sir Mortimer Durand and Chief Political Officer Sir Lepel Griffin, had been either snubbed or kept at arm's length and Roberts only ever necessarily heeded the orders or advice of his key patron, Lord Lytton. The 1880 Maiwand crisis and the march from Kabul to Kandahar not only guaranteed him enduring fame but, finally, enabled him to break all local political bonds and assume total control of operations in southern Afghanistan.[111] Even General Stewart, his erstwhile overall political and military superior in Afghanistan, had clearly paid deference to Roberts' position during the final victorious stages of the war.

In terms of the Second Anglo-Afghan War as a whole, there were clearly still many lessons to be learnt, not least in the fraught area of political-military co-ordination. Many 'politicals' had again clearly exceeded their brief and directly interfered with military operations, often at great cost. Lord Lytton had flagrantly provoked a war without just cause when the military were logistically and operationally clearly ill-prepared. Conversely, several leading military commanders, notably Roberts himself, had clearly ignored political criticism and violated humanitarian principles by excessive punitive actions. Yet again, at the heart of the problem lay the paucity of resources afforded to them by the Indian and Home Governments to support such prolonged campaigns and this, in itself, had forced some commanders into hasty, indiscriminate and ill-judged actions, if only to defend their lines of communication. Many of these problems were to recur in the context of the Third and Fourth Anglo-Afghan conflicts. Moreover, the successful instalment of Abdur Rahman as a loyal servant on the back of a handsome British subsidy, suggests that such financial inducements could have occupied a far more prominent role in the securing of a loyal buffer state against supposed Russian ambitions, than such brutal and costly military operations. After all, it had been the withdrawal of key subsidies which, as we have seen, provoked the débâcle of the First Anglo-Afghan War.

Notes

1   Sykes, *Durand*, p.115.
2   Cardew, *Official Account*, p.468.
3   Roberts, *Forty-one Years*, p.469.

4   *The Royal Magazine*, 'Survivors' Tales of Great Events', vol 18, pp.368–74, 1960, Limber-Gunner Naylor's RHA Account, The Rifles' Museum Archives, Salisbury (hereafter RMA).

5   Ibid.

6   Ibid.

7   NAM, 8004-41, Mayne Report.

8   RMA, Ready Account.

9   Ibid, Bray Account.

10   Nuttall, Despatch, 3 August 1880 (encl. in Hanna, *Second Afghan War*, vol 3, p.406). Cavalry-Major Hogg later recalled the terrifying scene: 'From the village on our right faraway to the left up the Gurmas Valley they were drawn up in thousands and thousands, covering four or five miles of ground, and to be compared only to ants swarming out of their nests'. Royal Military Academy Sandhurst Archives (hereafter RMAS) Papers of Major C. Hogg, 1 August 1880.

11   Cardew, *Official Account*, p.505.

12   RMA, Ready Account.

13   RMA, *Royal Magazine*, Naylor Account.

14   Ibid.

15   RMA, Farrell Account.

16   RMAS, Hogg Papers.

17   NAM, 8004-41, Mayne Report.

18   RMAS, Hogg Papers.

19   RMA, Ready Account.

20   NAM 8004-41, Mayne Report.

21   Ibid.

22   Griffiths Account, encl. in Cardew, *Official Account*, p.511.

23   RMA, Ready Account.

24   Lt.-Colonel H. Anderson, 'An Historic Reverse in Afghanistan', Maiwand, 1880 RMA.

25   RMA, Bray Account.

26   Ibid. For a parallel perspective on the 1879 Anglo-Zulu War see Yorke, *Zulu The Battle for Rorke's Drift, 1879* (Tempus, Stroud, 2005), p.154.

27   Cardew, *Official Account*, p.513.

28   RMAS, Hogg Papers.

29   Ibid.

30   Ibid.

31   Cardew, *Official Account*, p.512.

32   Hanna, *Afghan War*, vol 3, p.412.

33   RMA Ready Account.

34   NAM, 8004-41, Mayne Account.

35 Cardew, *Official Account*, p.512.
36 Hanna, *Second Afghan War*, vol 3, p.514.
37 RMA, Ready Account.
38 RMA, Mainwaring Account.
39 RMA, Ready Account.
40 RMA, Bray Account.
41 Cardew, *Official Account*, p.517.
42 RMA, *Times of India*, 14 October 1880, Staff Officer Account. See also Cardew, *Official Account,* vol 2, p.517.
43 NAM, 8004-41, Mayne Report.
44 RMAS, Hogg Papers and RMA Ready Account.
45 Hogg Papers, RMA.
46 Hanna, *Second Afghan War*, vol 3, p.414.
47 RMA, Bray Account.
48 RMA *Times of India*, Staff Officer Account.
49 RMA, Ready Account.
50 RMA, *Royal Magazine*, Naylor Account.
51 RMAS, Hogg Papers.
52 RMA, Ready Account.
53 Ibid.
54 Ibid.
55 Ibid.
56 NAM, 8004-41, Mayne Report.
57 RMA, *Royal Magazine*, Staff Officer Account.
58 RMA, Royal Magazine, Naylor Account.
59 RMAS, Hogg Papers.
60 Ibid.
61 Cardew, *Official Account*, p.519.
62 Ibid, pp.519–20.
63 RMA, Ready Account.
64 NAM, 8004-41, Mayne Report.
65 Cardew, Official Account, p.522.
66 RMA, Ready Account.
67 NAM, 8004-41, Mayne Report and RMA, Bray Account.
68 RMA, Ready Account.
69 NAM, 8211-62, Fox Diary.
70 Roberts, *Forty-one Years*, p.471.
71 L.J. Rowley, *Afghanistan: The Three Wars*, p.37.
72 W.G. Barttelot, *The Life of Edmund Musgrave Barttelot*, (London, 1890), p.21.
73 Trousdale, *MacGregor Diary*, p.237.

74   NAM, 7101-23(101), RP, Roberts to Lyall, 6 August 1880.

75   Roberts, *Forty-one Years*, p.471.

76   Ibid, p.473.

77   Ibid.

78   NAM, 7101-23(101) RP, Roberts to Adjutant-General, 30 July 1880.

79   Trousdale, *MacGregor Diary*, p.222.

80   Cardew, *Official Account*, pp.560–1.

81   Hanna, *Second Afghan War*, vol 3, pp.473–4.

82   Roberts, *Forty-one Years*, p.474.

83   Special Report, Surgeon-Major-General, T. Crawford, encl. in Hanna, *Second Afghan War*, vol 3, p.474.

84   Trousdale, *MacGregor Diary*, p.236.

85   Hensman, *Afghan War*, pp.478–9 and 392. In Kabul Kizzilbash traders, as the primary economic collaborators with the British, made huge profits from sales of their produce. See, especially, Hensman, *Afghan War*, pp.407–15.

86   Anderson, *The Afghan War*, p.51.

87   Hanna, *Second Afghan War*, vol 3, p.478.

88   Trousdale, *MacGregor Diary*, p.230.

89   Sir Montagu Gerard, *Leaves from the Diary of a Soldier* (encl. in Hanna, *Second Afghan War*, vol 3), p.479.

90   Hanna, *Second Afghan War*, vol 3, p.479.

91   Roberts, *Forty-one Years*, p.495.

92   Hanna, *Second Afghan War*, vol 3, p.497. For a recent study of this epic march, see R. Atwood, *The March to Kandahar: Roberts in Afghanistan* (Pen and Sword, Barnsley, 2008), *passim*.

93   Roberts, *Forty-one Years*, p.484.

94   For an expanded account of this mini-disaster see Hanna, *Second Afghan War*, vol 3, pp.445–57 and Cardew, *Official Account*, pp.537–44. See also, account by Captain Barttelot, who recalled with pride that the Royal Fusiliers, 'was the only regiment which really got into the village and went right through it ... held it for about 15 minutes – but unaided, retreated.' Barttelot, *Life*, p.22

95   NAM, Roberts Papers, Roberts to Adjutant-General, 8 September 1880.

96   Ibid, Roberts to Lyall, 9 September 1880.

97   Ibid. For a detailed account of Phayre's equally desperate if less publicized march from Quetta see Hanna, *Second Afghan War*, vol 3, pp.483–92. His forces faced floods, extreme heat and ferocious attacks by rebellious Marri and Kakar tribesmen, all directly inspired by the British defeat at Maiwand.

98   Roberts, *Forty-one Years*, p.485.

99 Cardew, *Official Account*, p.475 and Roberts, *Forty-one Years*, p.489.

100 Hensman, *Afghan War*, p.514.

101 Ibid, p.518.

102 Hanna, *Second Afghan War*, vol 3, p.510.

103 Hensman, *Afghan War*, p.514.

104 Roberts, *Forty-One Years*, p.491.

105 Hensman, *Afghan War*, pp.527 and 522.

106 Ibid, pp.562–3.

107 R. Jenkins, *Gladstone* (Macmillan, London, 1995), p.425.

108 J. Morley, *The Life of Gladstone*, 3 vols (Macmillan, London, 1903), vol 3, p.10.

109 Heathcote, *Afghan Wars*, p.165.

110 NAM 7101–23 (101), RP, Roberts to Lytton, 11 February 1880.

111 Years after the 1878–80 campaign Roberts noted that the sole exception to the new rule of military dominance which he had personally so rigidly enforced 'was made on Sir Donald Stewart's departure from Kandahar, when political and military authority was temporarily separated. Whether this would have anything to say to the disaster at Maiwand it would be difficult to prove, but it is significant that the only failure should have occurred during the time when dual control was in force'. (Roberts, memo. 4 May 1891). 'To whom should supreme control be entrusted in time of war – the Civilian or the Soldier?' (Preston and Dennis, *Swords and Covenants*, pp.131–2).

7. 'Amanullah's War': the Third Afghan War

Civil officers should discharge diplomatic duties and military officers the conduct of war.

> Winston Churchill, *The Story of the Malakand Field Force*
> (repr. Mandarin, London, 1990), p.191

The ending of the Afghan War in such tame fashion merely stimulated the Waziristan tribes, the Wazirs and the Mahsuds, to become more offensive.

> Sir J. Smyth, *Milestones* (Sidgwick and Jackson, London, 1979), p.64

Almost four decades after the events of the previous chapter, in May 1919, the British were suddenly plunged into a wholly unexpected but, this time short-lived conflagration with Afghanistan. This was to be a far more 'political war', fought as much to sustain British prestige and control in the increasingly turbulent northern districts of India and to counter revolutionary (Bolshevist) Russian expansion, as to defeat Afghan aggression. Moreover, for a distinctly weakening Raj, it was to be a predominantly defensive war in which tensions between a government obsessed with local political control and financial economy, and military commanders, anxious to secure decisive victory, became even more prevalent than had previously been the case.

Simmering Peace: Anglo-Afghan Relations 1881–1919

Over the forty-odd years preceding this 1919 war, Afghanistan had seen some political stability, with only two changes of ruler. Amir Abdur Rahman Khan, with the aid of his £80,000 of British subsidy, had remained loyal and enjoyed an uninterrupted reign until his death in 1901. He was succeeded by his politically more mercurial, if less ruthless, son, Habibullah Khan (1901–19). During this period the British took the opportunity to consolidate their internal position in northern India west of the River Indus and to extend their 'forward policy' into the tribal areas south of the 1893 Durand Line.[1] British political control was slowly consolidated in the Khyber Pass and in the Kurram Valley, while Baluchistan, up to Chaman on the Afghan frontier and northwards to Fort Sandeman, was occupied, pacified and developed on the basis of a new tribal system. Communications, a key to political control, were significantly improved in 1887 by, for instance, the construction of a railway traversing the Bolan Pass and extending through Quetta to Chaman.

The Russian 'bogey' remained, penetrating eastwards through Turkestan and southwards across the Pamirs. After the seizure of Panjdeh in 1885, a compromise was reached in 1887. From the Indian side a Boundary Commission was established to define spheres of British and Afghan influence. The result was the famous 1895 'Durand Line', scrupulously demarcated by the British with boundary pillars but, locally, remaining largely unrecognized and seen as a direct challenge to their independence by both Abdur Rahman's Government and neighbouring Pashto-speaking tribes.[2] As we shall see, even today, the border area remains extremely volatile politically, and militarily intractable.

British military posts were extended north on the Samana Ridge overlooking Tirah from the south and, in 1895, a British post was also established at Miranshah in the Tochi valley of North Waziristan. Similarly, garrisons were placed in the most northerly tribal areas of the Malakand and Chitral. This 'forward policy' in the north-west tribal areas generated mixed results. In Baluchistan, the 'Sandeman Policy', named after the British agent to the Governor-General who initiated it in the 1870s, and aimed at settlement and improvement of tribal living conditions, had proved relatively successful. Law and order were maintained by the armed and unarmed police and by tribal 'levies'. A large British military garrison was maintained at Quetta for strategic purposes and a few small military posts were deployed in northern Baluchistan to support the police if required.

Further north, in the less controlled, more remote tribal areas of the Lower Mohmands and the Afridi of Tirah and Northern Waziristan, conditions were far 'more difficult, the tribes warlike, well-armed and truculent and jealous of their independence and tribal customs'.[3] A more coercive policy was required here in order to succeed in such notorious 'badlands' and this involved the raising of certain irregular corps such as the Mohmand Militia, the Khyber Rifles, the Kurram Militia, the Tochi

Scouts, the South Waziristan Scouts and, further north, the Chitral Scouts. As we shall see, because of stronger family or kinship loyalties, even some of these could never be relied upon fully in the event of a sustained tribal uprising. These tribal units, which manned the various British outposts, were controlled by the local British political officers, themselves placed under the direct orders of the Governor of the North West Frontier Province. From a military perspective they were also British-officered (seconded from the Army in India) and represented a sort of tribal police, supporting the Political Officer in the settlement of tribal differences and complaints and maintaining a rough kind of law and order in tribal territory. At times it was exceedingly 'rough' and in 1897, for instance, widespread tribal disorders necessitated full-scale British military action in the region.[4]

These irregular corps co-operated with another force, the Frontier Constabulary, which was located on the border of the Administered Districts and controlled by the local British civil authorities. The Frontier Constabulary, a 'very different armed police', tried to prevent tribal raiders penetrating their areas while their irregular Frontier Corps counterparts were in a position to intercept gangs when they returned to tribal areas. These elaborate policing networks, however, often made little or 'no impact on the basic troubles of ill-educated, predatory tribesmen who traditionally preyed on weaker groups to augment their economic needs'. As Molesworth has succinctly observed, there was an 'additional disability' in terms of civil military control which, as we shall see, would be greatly exacerbated by the 1919 conflict.[5] The problem arose from the fact that the irregular Frontier Corps were administered by the local political 'mandarin', the Chief Commissioner of the North West Province. They had their own Inspector-General and recruiting organization and obtained their officers' arms, clothing and ammunition on payment from army stocks. Thus neither senior army nor local commanders had any direct controls over them. Furthermore, as Molesworth points out, as the 'forward policy' expanded, those tribal areas in which the regular army might be called upon to fight tended to become a 'political closed shop' in which the local political officers, with their 'private political armies' resented any military interference. Molesworth aptly sums up the recurrent dilemma:

When any major disturbance took place the Frontier Corps, with their small numbers, lack of transport and armament only of rifles and a few post machine guns were quite incapable of dealing with it without military help. In such cases, the political authorities were very unwilling to admit the situation had passed out of their control until it was too late. Thus the military were confronted with situations necessitating action which might have been avoided by earlier notice.[6]

In times of all-out war in these turbulent frontier districts the situation could prove disastrous.

The Outbreak of War

The *raison d'être* for the 1919 Anglo-Afghan War still remains something of a mystery. Certainly, it was partly the result of a violent turn in internal Afghan politics. In February 1919, Britain's loyal ally, Amir Habibullah, was brutally murdered in his tent whilst engaged on a hunting expedition. Though initially a nationalist asserting Afghan independence Habibullah had, between 1905 and 1907, significantly moderated his political posture He signed a new treaty and, on visits to the Governor-General of India, Lord Curzon, he both confirmed his friendship and re-affirmed British control over Afghan foreign policy. In return, like his father, he gratefully accepted the newly enhanced traditional subsidy of 18 *lakhs* of rupees. While this never endeared him to the anti-British elements of his people, ever-incensed by past British violations or encroachments on their independent tribal territories, it was other political developments in Russia and the Near East which probably ensured his brutal demise and the rise of an xenophobic anti-British 'war party' in the government of Afghanistan.

Traditional 'Russophobia' had rapidly declined after the St Petersburg Convention of 1907, under which Britain and Imperial Russia finally agreed not to enter Tibet, that Iran should be divided into separate spheres of influence and that Britain would not expand its influence in Afghanistan The overturn of the Tsarist Government in 1917–18 by the Bolsheviks, however, raised new fears of more virulent and specifically anti-imperial revolutionary Soviet forces swooping onto the plains of British India. *The Times* reaffirmed such fears, frequently publishing evidence of Bolshevist links with Indian revolutionaries, the latter perceived as fomenting the widespread disturbances in the Punjab. In 1918, for instance, it was reported that Bolshevik representatives based in Stockholm had allegedly sent £25,000 to an anti-British Bombay revolutionary group.[7]

But it was a radical Islamic revival, sparked by Britain's First World War enemy, the Sultan of Turkey, the acknowledged spiritual leader of the Muslim world, which arguably played a far more significant role. In October 1915, a Turko-German Mission had arrived in Kabul and was joined by a number of notorious Indian revolutionary leaders. Although largely ignored by the still avowedly loyal and neutral Habibullah, the Mission established further firm links with the Afghan 'war party' and actively fomented trouble with Britain's recalcitrant 'Pathan' border tribes.

Even more sinister were the direct personal links that the Mission established with key conspirators in the Afghan Court, many closely related to Habibullah. These included his third son Amanullah Khan, the Amir's brother Nasrullah Khan and Nadir Khan, his Commander-in-Chief. Such was the threat perceived against him that Habibullah now took the unprecedented step of summoning a *jirga* or assembly of tribal leaders to Kabul, where he both explained his situation to them and obtained a declaration of loyalty and confidence. It proved to be a futile exercise. The nationalist 'war party' had already been incensed by Habibullah's failure to take advantage of British weaknesses in the First World War and thereby regain lost territory. In response to his loyal *jirga* the Afghan 'war party' simply went underground and promptly proclaimed an Islamic *jihad* against the British.

The subsequent widespread anti-British disturbances in Punjab Province of the Raj, culminating in the tragic massacre of Indian protesters at Amritsar in April 1919,[8] provided further opportunity for the Afghan 'war party' to contemplate war and gain freedom from British external control, or at least to gain plunder and territory by subverting this highly disaffected province of British India. *The Times* duly berated the post-war British Government for taking their eye off the 'Afghan ball'. The 'true cause' of the war, it asserted, 'lies outside the borders of Afghanistan altogether. Obsessive influences are at work throughout the Mohammedon world and all the secret wires run in the direction of Turkey. One of the mistakes of the Paris Conference is that in disposing of the Near East it has forgotten Islam.'[9] This British and Western 'political amnesia' in regard to the expansion of Islamic extremism in 1918–19 conjures up some striking early parallels to the post-Cold War neglect of the rise of Al Qaeda and the Taliban.

Further developments in internal Afghan politics provided the final spark for the Third Afghan War. The assassination of Amir Habibullah and the accession to power of Amanullah had by no means immediately or totally freed the new Amir from the murky waters of Afghan politics. As self-appointed Governor of Kabul and having arranged for tribal chiefs and notables to back him as Amir at a gathering held on 28 February 1919 (as well as the removable of rivals such as Nadir Khan from key posts), Amanullah nevertheless still had to confront powerful elements of the Afghan military, who remained loyal to the murdered Habibullah and who were actively seeking revenge. A counter-rebellion against Amanullah appeared imminent. A scapegoat was duly found and a probably innocent Afghan officer, Colonel Ali Raza, was duly 'tried' and hanged for the crime. To further encourage their loyalty, the pay of the regular Afghan Army was raised but, far more significantly for the British, Amanullah, in the words of *The Times*, now 'resolved on the perilous measure of distracting the attention of his people from the internal troubles by embarking on a war'.[10]

Accordingly, on 5 May 1919, following Amanullah's proclamation, calling for a *jihad* against Britain, Afghan regulars occupied the village of Bagh and attacked the British water pumping station at Tangi on the Khyber Pass. From here the Afghans could control the water supplies to the British garrison at Landi Kotal. Five innocent Indian workers were brutally murdered during the attack. War had begun. In fact, the seeds for war had already been sown by Amanullah's own agents. In the previous few weeks they had secretly stirred up tribal leaders on the British side of the Durand Line and actively fermented further violence in the Punjab to distract British forces as far as possible from a prospective 300-mile frontier war.

Strategically, the outbreak of war initially favoured Amanullah's forces. War had come at a most unfortunate time for both the Raj and a wider British Empire exhausted by four years of world war. Neither British nor Indian troops were up to strength. In 1914–16, most had been dispatched overseas to fight either on the Western Front or in Mesopotamia. A mere eight regular infantry battalions were deployed within India itself in 1919 and even these battalions had been ruthlessly plundered in order to supply officers and infantry reinforcements for the Mesopotamian campaign. Many absent experienced officers were replaced by young subalterns inexperienced in the skills of Indian frontier warfare. Indeed, British forces were arguably at their weakest in numerical terms since the great Indian Mutiny of 1857 and the resultant gaps in internal security duties were only plugged by territorial units and garrison battalions, the latter being static and composed largely of elderly men. During 1918–19 demobilization had thinned the ranks even further. As news of the Afghan incursions arrived, morale amongst the locally stationed war-weary British and Commonwealth troops slumped. It was in stark contrast to the jingoistic responses to war in 1839 and 1879. E. Holter of the 79th Battalion RFP, 16th Indian Division, recalled scenes of near mutiny as a 'nasty little rumour' of war on the Afghan frontier was confirmed:

> Everyone was up in arms about it and we had various meetings to try and get out of going. The Australians refused point blank to have anything to do with it and the powers-that-be soon found them a

boat and they were gone. Not so us ... the whole camp refused to parade and do any chores but it was to no avail and soon we were off on another adventure.[11]

Captain Price of the 2/76th Punjabis wrote to his mother in a mood of anger and despair: 'Everyone is fed up with this sort of thing as it may simply fizzle out and all this ... worry will be for nothing ... no one now wants a scrap. Most people have had enough already.[12]

British troops were barely mollified by government incentives such as two weeks' extra pay for serving in the North West Frontier war zone. Within the Indian Army, the recruiting barrel had been similarly scraped to the bottom and many units were full of raw and partially trained recruits. Brigadier Sir John Smyth VC, summed up the overall dire situation:

The British troops in India had only enlisted or been called up for the duration of the Great War and were clamouring for de-mobilisation and all my invaluable British signallers and clerks had to be weeded out and sent back. The resulting disorganisation and lack of efficiency made a difficult situation extremely trying. The force employed in these operations therefore had to be practically entirely Indian.[13]

The only consolation to the British was that, while their enemy was often numerically superior, the Afghan Army itself was chronically deficient in modern technology and lacking in experience, co-ordination and leadership. Afghan regular units totalled only 50,000. Commanded by Saleh Muhammed, they included personnel of stout fighting quality but they were, in the words of Molesworth, 'ill-trained, ill-led, ill-paid and probably under strength'. The cavalry, he asserted, was 'little better than indifferent infantry mounted on equally indifferent horses'.[14] The standard of Afghan firearms varied between modern German, Turkish and British types to obsolete Martinis and Snider rifles, the latter dating back to the Second Anglo-Afghan War. Few regular infantry units had bayonets, and artillery was reduced to only a few modern 10 cm Krupp howitzers and 75 mm Krupp mountain guns, supported by obsolete 7-pounders and Gardiner machine guns. Ammunition was in 'short supply' and ammunition workshops were based largely in the Kabul arsenal staffed by Sikh workers with limited skills. The Afghan Commissariat was, by European standards, rudimentary.

As in previous wars, Afghanistan's real strength lay in its vast numbers of irregular fighters, drawn especially from the Pashto-speaking border tribal groups and including the much-feared Mahsud and *Ghazi* fanatics.

Up to 130,000 of these were potentially available in the north-west border regions and they would present by far the greatest threat to the Anglo-Indian armies confronting them.

Nevertheless, if the British 'Tommy' felt demoralized, the British establishment and media remained ultimately confident of victory. *The Times* observed:

> The Afghan army has no experience of modern warfare and the development of our motor transport on the frontier and also that of the Air Force will prove very effective in the event of serious hostilities. The former gives extraordinary mobility to our troops and reduces the necessity of long marches ... a most important consideration in the hot weather. Aeroplanes are invaluable for reconnaissance in the hills and render it impossible for the enemy to concentrate large bodies of men in the narrow valleys without being discovered and, on discovery, being bombed with deadly effect. Wireless is also of great assistance.[15]

Important as these and other innovations, notably mortars, trench grenades and the most recent machine guns were, the British were still massively overstretched and fighting a war in the hottest season of the year against some of the best guerrilla fighters in the world. Moreover, as *The Times* later more realistically judged, ultimately: 'The situation really depends upon whether the tribes on our side of the political frontier remain quiet.'[16]

Initially, they did remain quiet but, as the British engaged their Afghan enemy on five distinct theatres, namely the Khyber (including Peshawar) and the Central, Northern, Southern (Baluchistan) and Chitral fronts, events were about to take a turn for the worse. In operational and chronological terms the British effort can be divided into three distinct phases. The first, predominantly defensive phase, which lasted from 6 to 25 May 1919, was to focus on holding the crucial Khyber Front and the containment of Afghan penetration. The second, an offensive and more decisive phase, was to last from 25 May to the signing of an armistice on 2 June, as Afghan Commander-in-Chief Nadir Khan invaded the central border region and inspired many Waziri tribal groups to revolt. While he managed to isolate Brigadier-General Eustace's British and Indian units at Thal he was defeated by Brigadier-General Dyer's relief force. The last phase, in which British forces were plunged into a full-blown politico-military crisis, constituted the post-armistice period and ran from 3 June until peace was finally signed on 8 August 1919.

As soon as war had broken out the local political authorities, fearful of internal disruption across the whole frontier region, had moved swiftly to assert their control over their military counterparts. In a letter to Lord Chelmsford, the Viceroy at Simla, Sir George Roos-Keppel, the experienced, highly energetic and forceful Chief Commissioner of the North West Frontier Province (1908–19), starkly spelt out to him the acute *political* dangers arising from this conflict and the imperative need for him to be made supreme in all political and military affairs. Noting that the 'Satyagrah agitation and resentment at the repressive measures in the Punjab have united all in hatred to British rule', he warned that, 'if the people help the Afghans our position here will be very difficult but I think that if I am to be of use to you I must have wide powers to take sharp and decisive action'. He urgently requested to be appointed: 'Military Governor of the Frontier Province with power to proclaim Martial Law at any time and, given the temporary rank of Lieutenant-General to make me senior to all the general officers on the frontier and put me in a position to issue orders instead of asking favours'. Further claiming that he did 'not wish to interfere in ordinary military matters' and that he was 'not making this suggestion with any idea of self-aggrandisement', Roos-Keppel further stressed, 'I feel that my position is weak and that in a crisis like this I would be more value to you were my hand strengthened.'[17]

His wishes were readily granted by a Simla Government, deeply aware of the impact of both the recent, widely unpopular Rowlatt Act, which had given new powers of internment without trial and non-jury trial, and the horrific massacre at Amritsar in April 1919, where Lieutenant-General Dyer's forces had opened fire on Indian demonstrators resulting in over three hundred dead. The general commanding the North West Frontier was accordingly telegraphed three days later:

> Chief desires you to ensure that all measures in neutral or friendly tribal country within our sphere are carried out in close consultation with Sir George Roos-Keppel whose advice will, of course, guide your actions in the political aspects of operations. As regards to the Political Officers on your staff for dealing with Afghans and tribes outside our sphere we should like the joint recommendation of Sir Roos-Keppel and ourself.[18]

In view of the internal political crisis of the Punjab, the Viceroy himself was understandably hesitant and anxious for a quick and cheap war and an early peace. Never a 'forward policy' man, the war had come as a 'bolt out of the blue' for Chelmsford. He had even soft-pedalled the initial

British response to Amanullah's aggression in order both to give the Amir a way out and in the forlorn hope of forcing an Afghan withdrawal without collision. Within hours, however, when it was clear that war was inevitable and that he would now need to act decisively to impress the local tribes, he quickly, 'laid stress on overwhelming force as we cannot afford an insurrection'.[19]

It was the Khyber Front that was perceived as being the most precarious and, with the political and military interface firmly delineated in favour of the 'politicals', measures for the relief and reinforcement of the tiny, belea-guered British garrison at Landi Kotal were rapidly instigated. The restoration of British political prestige was now of the highest priority. For the military it had all come as an unwelcome shock. In early May 1919, British troops at the main depot in Peshawar had remained in blissful igno-rance of the gathering storm. Their complacency was exemplified when, even on 5 May, the first day of the war, one small, weakly protected motor-ized column had been sent to embattled Landi Kotal, fortunately without incident. Nevertheless, even this small opening manoeuvre provoked some initial politico-military friction, as the Chief Commissioner insisted that the military commander of the column should be *junior* to Major Campbell, the 'political officer' commanding the Khyber Rifles.[20]

On 6 May, as news finally broke of serious fighting in the northern Khyber, major reinforcements consisting of the second battalion, the Somersets (a veteran regiment of the Afghan Wars and already renowned for their defence of Jalalabad in 1841–2), one section of No. 8 Mountain Battery and several Sikh and Gurkha battalions were rapidly dispatched up the Khyber Pass.

As in previous campaigns, logistical crises soon arose which, at times, reached a farcical level. Insufficient lorry transport led to the abandonment of one platoon and when three lorries were eventually filched from a depot they were found on arrival at Landi Kotal to contain only casks of beer! Only one day's worth of rations were initially taken and, with 'no local supplies available' over the next few weeks, the Khyber column had to rely on the garrison's own meagre supplies of canned corned beef and weevil-ridden biscuits. It was an inauspicious start to the campaign, although Molesworth recalled that the early use of hooded, infantry-laden lorries had at least proved to be unexpectedly successful 'Trojan horses' as the local tribesmen, believing them to contain merely routine replacement stores, thankfully left them unmolested.[21]

At least the many important tactical lessons derived from mountain warfare in previous Anglo-Afghan and North West Frontier conflicts had been well absorbed. Captain John Parry of the Green Howards recalled the use of a new, highly skilful mix of both permanent and rotating pickets in the Khyber, who represented 'a thorn in the side' to the 'bands of lawless Mohmands.... As the pickets advanced up the hill they choose a ridge of high ground where they are continuously in sight of a covering party who protect their advance to the summit.' The summit, he recalled, was always the point of 'greatest danger' owing to the cleverly concealed Pathan enemy and it was 'the practice to hold a section to give covering fire for the final advance'. Often permanent pickets overlooking extremely narrow passes were established, consisting of a stone *sangar* or miniature fort built of stones, boulders or even sandbagged, loop-holed and protected by barbed wire. Pickets were also deployed early as a means to surround rogue Pathan villages prior to encirclement and punishment.[22]

With the Landi Kotal garrison reinforced, the scene was now set for a British offensive. The First Battle of Bagh was to be as much a battle for British prestige as a military operation. On 7 May 1919 the sudden desertion of scores of men of the Khyber Rifles had highlighted the need for a quick victory, both to deter further desertions and, far worse, full-scale tribal uprisings along the Khyber. The British confronted five Afghan infantry battalions and six guns. At this crucial juncture, however, further British reinforcements for Landi Kotal had to be suddenly diverted to suppress political disturbances in the key frontier city of Peshawar. Once again political exigencies had overridden military imperatives. The situation there had certainly deteriorated. On 7 May information had been received by the Criminal Investigation Department (CID) that the Afghan Postmaster in Peshawar and the Indian Revolutionary Committee based there had planned to collect a mob of 7,000 men in order to burn the cantonments and civil lines, damage the railway and destroy the mobilization stores. This 'rabble', according to the Official·History, 'consisted of Afghan subjects, trans-border bad characters and bazaar loafers'. A translated letter from the Postmaster to the Amir of Afghanistan was intercepted on the same day, apparently ordering 'armed resistance ... against the British government' as part of a 'Holy war in Peshawar city'. Eight thousand Peshawaris, 'both Hindus and Muslims' and '2,000 villagers from outside', had apparently 'offered their assistance'.[23]

The British response was swift and uncompromising. From the 2nd Divison, the 6th Brigade was detached and moved up from Rawalpindi during the night of 7/8 May 1919. On the afternoon of 9 May, the 1st King's Dragoon Guards, the 2nd North Staffs and the 2/11th Gurkhas surrounded the city. They closed all the gates and effectively overawed the inhabitants. Equally significantly, the water supply was cut off. As historian Fraser-Tytler succinctly observed: 'No city of the plains of India can last for more than a few hours in May without water and the rebellion was nipped in the bud.'[24] The Afghan Postmaster and twenty-two other revolutionary leaders were surrounded, arrested and brought out before sunset. Not a shot was fired. It had been a brilliant pre-emptive operation. Roos-Keppel was ecstatic, praising the British General, Sir Arthur Barrett for the 'remarkable promptitude and skill with which the operation was effected ... I do not think we shall have any more trouble there'.[25] But it had been a near-run affair. Ten days later, Roos-Keppel confided to J.L. Maffey, Private Secretary to the Viceroy: 'I ran it rather too fine about the Peshawar city. I knew of the intended rising but I also knew of the delays in the Afghan plan of campaign and the rising was to be simultaneous with the Afghan advance. On the morning of the 8th I came to the conclusion that the city would go off prematurely.' He had to act, otherwise 'we would have had a mob of 8,000–10,000 men to smash up everything'.[26]

As it was, their diversion of resources to Peshawar and the subsequent delays, with the troops exhausted by forced marches from the Peshawar operations, was to have significant political and military consequences for the Bagh operational area. The British tactics for the First Battle of Bagh focused on recovering the lost territory by launching offensives by the Somersets and Gurkhas against the surrounding heights of 'Suffolk Hill' and 'Bright's Hill'. This would allow a mixed Sikh and Gurkha force to retake the pumping station. This force would then bear left to attack the main Afghan positions located around the village of Bagh. Despite the capture of Bright's Hill, the surprise attack, launched at 4.45 a.m., had petered out by 9 a.m. as the undermanned and exposed forces faced stiff resistance from the Afghan defenders and artillery, and as the British infantry became pinned down in difficult terrain.

This patently unsuccessful and indecisive first battle of the Third Afghan War was subsequently heavily criticized. For political reasons it had been a rushed operation; there was insufficient reconnoitring of the 'Basin' to enable British machine gun and artillery units to give covering fire to the exposed infantry on the ridges.[27] Moreover, reinforcements had been delayed or had arrived exhausted as a consequence of the Peshawar crisis. The situation was also compromised by fears of an attack from the north of Landi Kotal, which led the British Commander to divert some of his force to protective duties. The overall political implications were dire. Another picket of the Khyber Rifles had already deserted with their rifles from their positions near Landi Kotal and 'it was fully realised that if another unsuccessful attack was made large bands of Afridis would join the Afghans and that our communications with Peshawar would be endangered'.[28] It was now, more than ever, a war of prestige and even Roos-Keppel was briefly panic-stricken.

On 9 May 1919 Major-General Fowler, Commander of the 1st Division, rushed to Landi Kotal to take command. He was dismayed to discover that the 'Afghans were still holding onto their positions with great confidence and the Afridis were showing signs of restlessness'.[29] It was a highly ominous situation, particularly as the high hills to the south were covered with large bodies of armed men who were watching the course of events around Bagh.

Fortunately for the British, the Second Battle of Bagh proved to be much more decisive. More reinforcements were sent up the Khyber Pass from Jamrud and were, perhaps predictably, attacked by tribesmen. Significantly, the attacks were launched from the line of pickets held by the now-unreliable Khyber Rifles. A worried Fowler decided on immediate action, 'otherwise the whole of the Khyber tribes would flare into revolt'.[30] Accordingly, the main attack on 11 May was carried out by elements of the 2nd Infantry Brigade including the 2nd North Staffordshires, 2/11thGurkhas and 2/123 Outram's Rifles They advanced from below Michni Kandau post. Simultaneously, the 2nd Somersets and a section of 263 Machine Gun Company moved south of Suffolk Hill to a rocky spur on Tangi Nala in order to bring enfilading fire upon the Afghan positions.

This time, by sharp contrast to the First Battle of Bagh, the British attack went like clockwork. The greater and more accurate artillery support (especially howitzers) and the use of machine guns enabled the Somersets, despite relentless sniping, to reach their objective. Meanwhile the North Staffordshires successfully assaulted the hill up to the Afghan breastworks, stopping only once in the severe heat merely to gain breath. They reached a position 'so close to the bursting shells that the men of the leading platoons were stained yellow and many of them even vomited through inhaling the lydite fumes'.[31] The regulars of the Somersets duly watched the progress of the North Staffordshires with morbid fascination: 'We could see them coming up to each "sangar" in turn and lobbing hand grenades into them. Some Afridis jumped out and ran for it along the ridge but none got very far.'[32] Many were bayoneted and some, fleeing south and west, were caught by the Somersets' enfilading fire. The 2/11th Gurkhas then burst through the Afghan centre so swiftly that most of the Afghan gunners were bayoneted on the spot and were unable to remove their artillery pieces. By 2 p.m. the 2nd Infantry Brigade, led by the Gurkhas, were bivouacked in Bagh village. The RAF completed the rout, bombing and machine-gunning the Afghan fugitives. The Afghans lost one hundred killed and three hundred wounded, with sixty bodies burnt by the British the next day. The British force lost only eight dead and thirty-nine wounded. It had been a very skilfully conducted operation, this time with the efficient co-operation of all arms and significantly better artillery support. The deployment of fresher and more enthusiastic troops, especially the 2/123rd Outram Rifles, some of whom even abandoned their sick beds to join the action, epitomized the high fighting spirit displayed that day.

For Roos-Keppel and his 'politicals', the victory had come not a moment too soon. On 13 May he had sent a stark dispatch to Viceroy Lord Chelmsford. While downgrading the threat from the Afghan regulars as 'not ... a very serious danger', he nonetheless conceded that they had 'fought better than I expected ... with great bravery and tenacity'. He ultimately concluded, however, that with 'no organised commissariat or transport' they were 'incapable of conducting a campaign on a large scale'.[33] A far 'greater danger', Roos-Keppel warned, 'than the Afghan is the tribes: that they have not risen against us is extraordinary as we have always counted on the almost certainty of their rising should the Amir declare war'. But for him, still, the 'greatest danger' was the political state of Northern India. He warned:

> The agitation of the last month was so skilfully conducted ... that the whole country is poisoned and, although the people are not at all anxious for an Afghan invasion by which they would of course lose heavily, a large number hate us with such bitterness that they would welcome even invasion if they saw a chance of getting rid of us.[34]

Roos-Keppel had already used his new executive powers to take extraordinary internal measures to 'cleanse his region of potential dissidents'. Earlier, he had exhorted General Barrett to pacify some of the villages near disaffected Peshawar, notably the 7,000 inhabitants of the town of Charsadda, who had exhibited 'a good deal of dangerous talk ... and are inclined to help the Afghans if they get a chance'. Barrett was asked to 'surround the village ... before dawn ... arrest the leading agitators and about 100 of the leading men'. On a broader front, Roos-Keppel announced to the Viceroy a policy of 'ethnic cleansing' on the British side of the border: 'I shall go on steadily purging the province of Afghan subjects but as we cannot afford troops or police for internment camps and as these unarmed Afghans will be of no use to Afghanistan, being *bouches inutiles*, I shall steadily deport them to their own country.'[35]

In order for the British authorities to sustain political prestige it was seen as imperative to retain the military initiative. It was now decided to take advantage of the recent demoralization of the Afghan Army on the Khyber

Front and seize Dakka, which afforded facilities for the concentration of troops for a possible advance upon Jalalabad and Kabul. There was ample space there for camping grounds, an air-strip and an unlimited supply of water. And it was here that the RAF played their first significant role by bombing the exposed Afghan troop concentrations in the town and forcing them to evacuate.

As British troops occupied Dakka, however, there were already serious signs of overstretch both on land and in the air. As we have already seen, some tribal militias, notably the Khyber Rifles, had become extremely unreliable. Roos-Keppel had been personally appalled by their earlier mutinous behaviour at Landi Kotal, where they had 'behaved very badly', and he was particularly distressed as he was their honorary Colonel. British outposts were now to be handed over to the regulars and the whole unit was to be disbanded, 'the end of what was a fine corps'.[36] Unfortunately, for other operational reasons, the 'green' regular British-officered Indian infantry were no better off. Riding with the commanding officer of the 1/35th Sikhs, 'down the Khaibar', to Dakka, Molesworth ominously recorded the grave problems arising from their combat inexperience: 'In the course of conversation he said to me, "I hope we are not going to have any more serious scraps as all my lads are raw recruits and I don't know what may happen."' Molesworth added ominously: 'The same remark might have been made by commanding officers of other Indian units and reflected what many of us knew.'[37]

For technical reasons the RAF was in little better shape, as it was mainly supplied with a few obsolete and worn-out BE2Cs 'Camels', 'so underengined and decrepit that they could not make height to cross the main Khaibar massif and had to fly up the valleys'. Consequently, the pilots 'experienced the novel conditions of being fired down on by tribesmen on the hills above them'![38] Nevertheless, their bombing raids on Jalalabad on 17, 20 and 24 May and on Kabul on 24 May were to have a major psychological impact on the Afghan political and military establishments later in the war.

The acknowledged inexperience of both cavalry and infantry units, especially officers, probably played a key role in the British reverses subsequently experienced around Dakka. Despite continuing logistical problems, the British had established a vast tented camp there, but one sited in an extremely vulnerable position. It was a tactical nightmare, overlooked by high ground and consequently exposed to Afghan snipers and artillery. Worse was to follow. A mixed cavalry and infantry reconnaissance force, comprising mainly the 1st King's Dragoon Guards and the 1/15th Sikhs under Colonel Macmullen, unexpectedly ran into a large body of Afghan reinforcements heading for Dakka. They were badly mauled near the village of Girdi and forced to retire. Moreover, in the fighting retreat to Dakka camp, the Dragoons, having launched one of the last cavalry charges in British history, took significant casualties in a gallant rearguard action. The political consequences were dire. As The Official History observed: 'As is always the case in frontier warfare the retrograde movement was a sign for increased activity on the part of the enemy.'[39]

The astonishing lack of outer defences for the Dakka camp now forced the British to renew their offensive and clear the surrounding heights, principally the main position of Sikh Hill and another hill feature called 'Stonehenge'. The camp itself was now facing daily shelling and sniping, which frequently stampeded the vast number of transport animals herded within the perimeter. However, some of the crude Afghan shells fired from a 'pony-drawn battery of very ancient pieces' did at least stimulate some British amusement. As they 'bounced along the ground before exploding like a child's firework ... one cricketer clubbed his rifle in the hope he might hit one for six, but he was not successful'! Moreover, poor fusing meant that many of the enemy's Krupp shells misfired, with one shell, luckily unexploded, landing under the operating table of the Cavalry Field Ambulance station.[40]

The offensive to secure 'Stonehenge' was led at dawn on 16 May 1919 by the 1/35th Sikhs and the 1/9th Gurkha Rifles. However, the leading platoon of Sikhs was pinned down, with heavy casualties, a hundred yards short of the crest and forced to retire rapidly through the Gurkha lines. The assault on Sikh Hill had also come to a standstill by 10 a.m. as three companies of the 1/15th Sikhs were also pinned down three hundred yards from the summit. Logistical problems added to the chaos as the British artillery promptly ran out of ammunition.

The situation was saved by the arrival of Major-General Skeen's reinforcements from Landi Kotal, which included the 1st Battalion Yorkshire Regiment (Green Howards), the 2/1st Gurkha Rifles and, most significantly, a howitzer section of No.6 Mountain Battery and three lorry-loads of ammunition. Meanwhile, the Somersets, held in reserve until now, launched a successful re-offensive with the 1/9th Gurkhas against 'Stonehenge'. They were ably supported by high explosive rounds fired from the howitzers below, which had devastating effects upon the top of the ridges. By 1 p.m., after this incessant cannonade, the Afghans were forced into full retreat. 'Stonehenge', subsequently renamed 'Somerset Hill' in honour of the assaulting British regiment, was secured by 1.35 p.m. It had been an arduous battle and during the last one hundred feet many Somersets had been forced to 'sling their rifles and climb hand and foot'.

Tragically, on this final precipitous climb, Colonel Molesworth recalled how his units came across the deeply demoralized remnants of the 1/35th Sikhs and the 1/9th Gurkhas still clinging to the lower ridge. With their British officers missing, dead or wounded, his appeals to them to advance were of no avail. He observed: 'These Indian rankers had had a bad time for many hours and I could not get any of them to move. In addition they were all young and inexperienced men. So we had to go on without them.' Certainly, the wounds inflicted by the Afghan Snider rifles loaded with clay-filled expanding bullets had added to their misery and demoralization. 'One dead Sikh', Molesworth recalled, 'had only been hit in the back of the knee but that leg was nearly severed.'[41] Meanwhile, the 1/15th Sikhs had successfully taken 'Sikh Hill', despite tragically losing two British officers, one Indian officer and seven privates to 'blue-on-blue' fire by the supporting Yorkshire Regiment, who had misunderstood their orders and joined the attack rather than staying in reserve.

Of an estimated 3,000 men, the Afghan force had lost 200 killed and 400 wounded, and also lost five of their seven Krupp guns. British casualties were twenty-two dead and 157 wounded. British discipline and superior artillery (especially the use of howitzers) had yet again triumphed over indifferent Afghan leadership and training, and poor equipment and maintenance. Nevertheless, the attack would not have been necessary had the picketing of the heights around Dakk, a cardinal principle of North West Frontier warfare, not been so foolishly disregarded. Moreover the attack had exposed the rawness of British and Indian troops, particularly junior officers, unexpectedly thrown into a full-scale frontier war.

The *Official Account* of this action by the 1st (Peshawar) Division described the Sikh Hill and Somerset ('Stonehenge') Hill actions as 'one of the hardest fought fights which have taken place on the North West Frontier.... After this action the enemy dispersed in utter rout and the Afghan forces in this area never attempted any further aggression'.[42] For Chief Commissioner Roos-Keppel, obsessed with this highly political war, these victories on the Khyber Front had been of vital importance. He informed Massey:

I am quite certain that nothing but our taking the offensive at Bagh and Dakka saved us from a simultaneous rising of Afghans supported by the tribes who must have joined them when they got into tribal territory and abetted by many of the inhabitants of Northern India. Our offensive has destroyed many Afghan delusions and ... upset their plan of campaign.[43]

The Central Front

The campaign was a long way from being finished. During May, other theatres, notably the Central Front, remained on a knife-edge. On 13 May 1919 Roos-Keppel confided to the Viceroy: Things in Tirah are looking ugly but the leading men of the tribe ... are still on our side but are afraid that they may be committed by their young men in which case they may say that it is as well to be hung for a sheep as a lamb.'⁴⁴ At the outbreak of war on 6 May the only signs of enemy activity on the Central Front had been the building of *sangers* on the Peiwar Kotal. Seventeen days later, however, the advance of senior Afghan General Nadir Khan from Matun finally released the tribal 'dogs of war' in the region. Roos-Keppel's fears were not misplaced, as the Central Front encompassed some of the most formidable tribes of the North West Frontier region. The area ran roughly from the Safed Koh Range in the north and included much of the Kohat District, all of the Kurram River valley, the Tochi River valley in the centre and the South Waziristan Scouts' posts in Southern Waziristan, bordering Northern Baluchistan. To the north-east lay the hills of Afridi Tirah and bordering the Kohat District and the Kurram Valley were the Orakzei, Chamkanni and Wazir tribes, all well armed and of good fighting value, as well as the Jajis and Mangals of the Afghan Khost lying to the south-west. Further south were the Wazir clans of the Tochi Valley and, south again, the various Mahsud clans.

British overstretch was soon apparent as, initially, with only seven battalions of infantry, they remained seriously outnumbered by the sixteen battalions of infantry, four regiments of cavalry and sixty guns controlled by Afghan General Nadir Khan. Faced with further widespread desertions by militiamen, notably at Miranshah, the only prospect was a staged withdrawal of outposts and General Eustace, apparently without informing his political counterparts, commenced the abandonment of several key positions in the tribal territories. Escorted by two squadrons of the 31st Lancers, the British garrisons at Spinwam and Shewa were accordingly evacuated to Idak. These were soon followed by the abandonment of British posts in the upper Tochi and South Waziristan, including Wana and Gomal. One group of over a thousand deserters had seized 1,190 rifles and over 700,000 rounds of ammunition! If tactically prudent, this was regarded as a catastrophe by the local political authorities and sparked off the first of several politico-military clashes of the war. A furious Roos-Keppel demanded the punishment of the military commanders responsible but, in reply, Viceroy Chelmsford, whilst 'sympathising with you over the

Tochi affair', refused to act. He explained: 'Disappointing as it is I think we should hear the views of the man who gave the order for the withdrawal before we assume that he exercised his discretion wrongly. Everybody is not a Roos-Keppel.'[45]

The political results were dire. Hundreds more Waziri tribesmen joined Nadir Khan and, equally ominously, scores of North and South Waziristan Militia men defected to the enemy or deserted. On 26 May mutinous Waziri and Afridi militia actually seized Wana Fort, even as the evacuation was actually in progress. This forced Major Russell, the British commanding officer, to conduct a running retreat across the Gamel River into Baluchistan. It was a retreat which, as we shall see, had a concertina effect on other fronts and directly sparked off troubles on the neighbouring Baluchistan front.

By 27 May 1919, Nazir Khan's invading Afghan columns had appeared before the key British fort at Thal and the bombardment and siege of that post began. Thal consisted of a large village with a 'Beau Geste' fort and was located at the eastern end of the Kurram Valley. Despite reinforcements, the garrison, commanded by General Eustace, was outnumbered and remained on the defensive. His inexperienced troops, comprising four battalions of infantry, one squadron of cavalry and four mountain guns, confronted an Afghan army of 3,000 regulars and up to 4,000 tribal allies. The Afghan artillery included two 100 mm Krupp howitzers and seven 75 mm mounting guns.

On 28 May 1919, the Afghan bombardment of Thal, principally conducted by their 100 mm howitzers, greatly intensified. It destroyed the British wireless station and set fire to fuel and fodder stores. The Official History significantly recorded that 'this was the only occasion during the campaign when we were definitely inferior to the Afghans in artillery'.[46] The intense bombardment caused the irregular Frontier Constabulary to desert overnight and allowed the vital water pumping station to fall into Afghan hands.

On news of this setback, panic broke out at the British North West Frontier Headquarters at Peshawar and reinforcements were called up to Kohat from Indian garrisons as far away as Lahore, Agra, Ferozepore and Ambala. But, as Molesworth points out, these were of no immediate use as 'they had little experience of frontier warfare or conditions and they had to be brought a considerable distance'.[47]

The day was fortunately saved by a relief force dispatched under the leadership of the now-notorious Brigadier-General Reginald Dyer, perpetrator of the earlier Amritsar massacre of April 1919. He rushed his 45th Infantry Brigade of one British and three Indian battalions and fourteen 15-pounder static guns by railway and lorry to Togh via Hangu. The 'Thal Relief Force' included the 2/6th West Sussex, 1/25th London and 1/5th Hampshire regiments as well as several Gurkha, Dogra, Punjabi and Baluchistani units. In a brilliant feint on 2 June, Dyer attacked and successfully split two '*lashkars*' or tribal gatherings to the north and north-east under their leader Malk Babrak, both of which had dominated the heights outside Thal. To give the false impression that both groups were to be attacked simultaneously, British artillery fire was opened on Thal villages and the heights overlooking Mohammedzi held by both Waziri and Khostwal 'Pathan' tribesmen. The British ruse worked, with Dyer's main strength launched at Bubrak's command post. The result was a headlong Afghan retreat. By 4 p.m. that day the 1/69th Punjabis had seized the heights with the 'trifling loss of only four wounded'. One section of the 89th Battery RFA then trotted forward to Thal where they silenced the enemy guns at Khapianga.

As Dyer prepared to annihilate the Afghan forces in the hills to the west, and to proceed to Matun, he was halted by dramatic news on the political front. A flag of truce which arrived from Nadir Khan's headquarters, brought news of the Amir's request for an armistice on 31 May. However, while awaiting official confirmation, the indomitable Dyer merely responded with the words that 'his guns would give an immediate reply'.[48] He continued mopping-up operations by sending a column to destroy the large Wazir village of Biland Khel as a punishment for supporting Nadir Khan. The British were, however, cheated of the opportunity to finally plunder Nadir Khan's main camp at Yusuf Khel on 3 June, as a column of 37th Lancers and 1/25th Regiment sent from Thal found it already looted overnight by local tribesmen!

Afghan overtures for peace had, in fact, been proceeding for the previous two weeks, particularly as Afghan territorial and manpower losses mounted after the British victory at the Second Battle of Bagh. But it was probably the more decisive British successes on the southern and northern fronts, and particularly the psychological impact of British air-power, which prompted the Afghan Amir to sue for peace.

The Southern (Baluchistan) Front

On the Southern Front in Baluchistan, the British had, by the end of May 1919, triumphed emphatically over the Afghan regulars and their tribal allies. In many respects the outbreak of war in this region presented fewer difficulties for the British. The 106,000-square mile Baluchistan had, for many years, been a more settled Administered District.

Parts of it were 'on lease' from the Khan of Khelat and the government was conducted mainly through British Political Officers. While its western borders were defended by irregular levies and militia with 'very little serious work to do', its borders with Afghanistan encompassed no independent, heavily armed fighting tribes as were encountered elsewhere on the North West Frontier. The more fragmented tribal groups, comprising Afridis, Ghilzais, and various Baluchi clans such as the Kakars, Achaki and Sherannis, were normally peaceful except for occasional minor raiding parties and crime. Militarily, the British enjoyed another distinct advantage. Amir Amanullah had deployed his main offensive further north on the Central and Khyber Fronts. By concentrating his best troops there he had little left either in quality or quantity for any offensive action in the south. The British were therefore in a good position to launch a local offensive, despite a lack of transport and artillery, and greatly aided by the railway line built from Quetta to their main base at New Chaman.

The British Commander, Lieutenant-General Richard Wapshare, believed that a pre-emptive strike would forestall any Afghan attempt to stir up the tribes on the border. The target for the British 'Baluchistan Force' was the major Afghan fort at Spin Baldak, which was situated on a plain some six miles north-west of New Chaman. Reported to be the strongest Afghan fort, it was also constructed in a 'Beau Geste' style, with a bastion at each corner and complemented by a massive gatehouse and a moat. The walls were loop-holed for musketry and the fort was some 250 yards square, with walls twenty-five to thirty feet high. On paper it was formidable, even a veritable 'death trap' for infantry, but it was now to be severely challenged by the modern First World War tactics and equipment deployed by the British forces.

Wapshare decided to deploy two columns of cavalry to form a cordon to the north-west and south in order to prevent the Afghan infantry from escaping whilst two infantry columns (including several Indian units and the 1/4th Royal West Kent and 1st Duke of Wellington Regiments), covered by artillery fire, were directed to storm the ridge and fort. On 27 May 1919 battle commenced. Captain Brearly of the 21st Brigade RFA recalled the opening salvos soon after the initial negotiations for surrender or parley broke down:

> Major Jackson and myself acting as RO went with a small party and a white flag but when we got within rifle range ... they opened fire on us from every loophole. I went back to the main body ... and went into action opening fire on the main fort with 5" Howitzers while the 4.5" Howitzers fired on the towers.[49]

This 'creeping barrage', launched at 8 a.m., was followed by sustained infantry attacks at 8.30 a.m. The Royal West Kents, supported by the 1/129th Baluchis on the right, made slow progress through sand dunes, only to be checked for two hours by Afghan *sangars*. The left column of 1/4th Gurkha Rifles and 1/22nd Punjabis enjoyed better, if mixed, success. The Gurkhas reached their objective by 8.45 a.m. but the 1/22nd Punjabis were held up by a fifteen-foot wall which proved immune to both bayonets and entrenching tools.

As the 1/22nd Punjabis called for scaling ladders another major setback occurred, when RAF planes mistakenly bombed their position, killing three British officers, one subedar and eleven men. It was an apposite example of the technical limitations of air-power, notwithstanding its undoubted major psychological impact on the Afghan enemy.

The situation was ultimately saved by sustained artillery fire and a major attack on the flank of the Afghan positions by British reserves, led by men of the Duke of Wellington's Regiment and 270 Company Machine Gun Corps. This relieved the pressure on the British right and left columns. At 9.50 a.m. the constant artillery fire resulted in breaches of the walls, and a concerted breakout by two hundred Afghan regulars signified the blow to their morale by this bombardment. By 12 noon the 1/22nd Punjabis, aided by the 1/4th Gurkha Rifles, had penetrated through a breach in the wall just as the three main towers fell to assaulting parties of the 1st Duke of Wellington's and 1/4th Royal West Kent Regiments. The buildings were then mopped up and all Afghans who refused to surrender were bayoneted and killed. By 1.45 p.m. the fighting was over, the Afghan garrison losing 170 men killed and 186 taken prisoner. The British Force lost fifty-seven dead and wounded. Tragically, around 60 per cent of British officer mortality and 25 per cent of other ranks had been caused by British air-power!

Although by no means a perfect military operation, the bulk of British troops had performed well. Aside from the RAF bombing error, the howitzers had lacked a sufficient calibre to be immediately decisive and a cavalry mix-up had allowed a sizable portion of the Afghan garrison to escape. Nevertheless, it represented a clear defeat for the Afghan high command and the political gains overrode such military shortcomings.

The Northern (Chitral) Front

On the Northern Front around Chitral the British enjoyed further successes. Chitral, an area of predominantly bare, upland country, was ruled over by a loyal supporter of the British, the 40-year-old Mehtar (provincial ruler), Shuja-ul-Mulk. From the city of Chitral, his control stretched in the south to the Malakand, Dir and Swat and, to the north, his domain extended a vast distance to the Pamirs, bordering both Soviet Russia and China. The Mehtar was supported by a British Resident and a garrison of Anglo-Indian regular and irregular troops, principally a company of the 1/11th Rajputs (450 rifles) and around 1,000 rifles of the Chitral Scouts.

After war broke out, the British Resident mobilized the Chitral Scouts over four days between 5 and 8 May 1919. Kala Drosh, the other major town on this front, was similarly placed in a state of defence. On 12 May the Afghans invaded, seizing a small post at Dokalim opposite their main base across the border at Birkot. The British vigorously counter-attacked and a small expedition, comprising mainly two companies of Chitral Scouts and led by Major Reilly, dashed forward and defeated the Afghans in a significant, small but bloodless victory which cost the enemy thirty dead and forty wounded.

The British now took the initiative, advancing in four columns (including one mobile) which incorporated the 1/4th Rajputs, Chitral Scouts and elements of the Mehtar's bodyguard and sections of Mountain Battery sappers and miners. With no indication of any threat from the north, and with local tribesmen remaining loyal in the south-west, the commanding officer of the 1/11th Rajputs decided to advance from Kala Drosh, take Arnawai, and thereby drive the Afghans out of Chitral State. On 21 May the British right column seized the Istrogotz Bridge over the River Istor while the left gained the Kanttham Pass on the same day without opposition. The 1/11th Rajputs, marching in the British centre, forced the Afghans to evacuate Arnawai after securing the Doklim Ridge at 4.10 a.m. While the attack was in progress the right and left columns linked up and seized Birkot. Whilst camp was being set up on the night of 23/24 May, however, a party of *Ghazis*, hiding in a nearby cornfield, made one last futile attempt to undermine the British victory. They attacked the 1/11th Rajputs' headquarters, wounding the commander and two orderlies before they were all bayoneted to death.

Overall, this was an extremely successful operation with the British incurring only sixty-five casualties, of whom only sixteen were killed, compared to an estimated 250 Afghan casualties and fifty-five taken prisoner. Four enemy guns were captured. For Roos-Keppel it was a major psychological and political victory: 'Reilly's bitter fight in Chitral has bucked up the Chitralis wonderfully', he enthused in a dispatch to the Viceroy. Moreover, he noted the Mehtar's promise that Chitral was 'determined not to remain on the defensive but will harry the Afghans in

Badakstan'! The ever pugnacious Roos-Keppel additionally noted: 'Reilly's system of raising the Kafirs of the Hindu Kush against the Afghans is interesting and if we could do it we should pay the Afghans out in their own coin!' But, in view of Britain's existing resource crisis, even he acknowledged that 'it is a large order to dispose of the Hindu Kush at this early stage in the proceedings'.[50]

So far, the British civil and military authorities had operated in relative harmony, enabling the British both to survive the pressures of the Central and Khyber Fronts and secure decisive victories on the Northern and Southern fronts. The agreement to an armistice on 3 June 1919, however, was to cause unprecedented friction between the 'politicals' and their military counterparts.

Post-Armistice: a Political Débâcle

The Anglo-Afghan Armistice, strictly imposed by the Simla Government and the local British political authorities, immediately banned all offensive action by British military commanders but was predictably not adhered to by most of their Afghan counterparts. Consequently, on most operational fronts, British military commanders were suddenly placed in a dangerously defensive position. With their hands tied they would face two more months of bitter fighting until peace negotiations were finally concluded at Rawalpindi on 23 August 1919. It represented a truly disastrous 'period of inaction' which the Commander-in-Chief of India, Sir Charles Monro, roundly condemned and which resulted, in his words in, 'great hardship' as 'Afghan officials were everywhere inciting the tribesmen to rise' and British columns 'were sniped, convoys ambushed, militia incited to mutiny and massacre their officers while ... protracted negotiations were proceeding'.[51]

The British Government had plausible reasons for their prolonged passive posture. The Afghan conflict had become politically risky and extremely expensive in terms of men and material. It was clear to them by late May 1919 that the frontier defence organization in Waziristan and Zhob was in virtual collapse and that it would take time and money to repair. Equally, on a broader strategic front, in the words of one historian: 'The British government had no desire whatever to add to their commitments by continuing a fight which would in all probability lead to the disintegration of Afghanistan and the disappearance of the buffer between India and Russia.'[52]

It was a highly cautious policy to be immediately and rigidly enforced by both London and Simla, even against their own senior political agents on the frontier. The aggressive forward policies of Chief Commissioner Roos-Keppel were swiftly suppressed. In late May he had already confidently informed Sir John Maffey, Private Secretary to the Viceroy, that:

> We shall be forced to go to Cabul and I am not sorry as the last Afghan war is forgotten and its effect has gone. In the forty years which have elapsed myths have grown up about the Afghan fighting strength and these were firmly believed by the people of India. If we got to Cabul we shall dispel them ... we ought to take Jalalabad and make the Loi-Shilman railway to it. Cabul could never offend again and we should have many advantages including tapping the unlimited timber supply of the Hindu Kush and Chitral. We should also get behind the Afridis and Mohmands and should never have any trouble with them again.[53]

His gung-ho views were immediately suppressed by the London and Simla authorities. In a handwritten and highly unsupportive, terse memo, Sir Hamilton Grant, Foreign Secretary to the Government of India, made their opposition clear. 'The Secretary of State', he reported, was 'greatly alarmed at what has happened'. He 'evidently wants us to get out of the business as soon as possible, and [was] equally anxious to close down the war at the earliest possible moment compatible with honour and due guarantees for the future'.[54]

There was another more sinister reason for the anxiety of the British Government to close down the war. They had been deeply unnerved by the continuing crisis of morale affecting British troops, particularly the restless Territorial battalions who were anxious to be repatriated now the main war was over. For instance, at Hassan Abdal, a major demobilization camp situated on the railway east of Rawalpindi, some 2,000 mutinous British troops were put under canvas and refused to do anything except draw their rations. Whilst orderly they refused to go westwards and, from the name of their Brigadier, they soon became notorious as 'O'Dowda's Bolshie Brigade'.[55] Further south, at Poona, large numbers of discontented British clerical staff handling demobilization records had 'downed pens' and were hardly restrained from more violent action.[56] As we have already seen, many senior officers had expressed alarm that raw British and Indian troops and British officers (particularly subalterns) unversed in frontier warfare skills, had often been thrust into challenging military situations, sometimes with disastrous results. Even the non-combatant transport units were showing dissent. British personnel of the Heavy Motor Transport

Companies, in huge demand for this highly mobile war, showed their discontent by refusing to serve beyond Dakka. They claimed that they had, 'joined up to fight the Germans but if India was ... to conduct a new war against Afghanistan it was none of their business and beyond what they had contracted for'.[57]

The problem was compounded by a blatant government deception of many of these men. In one letter home, an infuriated Captain Price, recently transferred from the Somerset regiment to 2/76th Punjabis angrily 'spilt the beans':

> You probably do not know that the soldiers at Deolali demobilization camp, who were stated in the papers to have been asked to volunteer out here, were, in reality, ordered to stay here. Oh the government is cunning. They the soldiers were asked to volunteer and, two hours later, were *ordered* off to different stations. Then people at home were told they volunteered ... what can employers at home think when they read that the men whose jobs they are keeping open ... voluntarily stay in India. It's most misleading.... There were four hundred of them, officers and men here and they were fed up.[58]

Another serving Somerset officer recalled the policy as a 'most grievous blunder, quite untrue and it had an immediate effect'.[59]

The British Government's policies, whilst understandable for these broader strategic and financial reasons, proved militarily disastrous. At ground level, in the words of one contemporary observer, the ban on offensive action after the armistice: 'imposed an almost intolerable strain on commanders and troops alike ... failure to retaliate against hostile action has always been interpreted as a sign of weakness, leading to further hostile action'.[60] This, in itself, poses the question as to whether the *raison d'être* of the previous wars, so clearly started by the British, was as ultimately justifiable as the Third and Fourth Anglo-Afghan conflicts which, as we shall see, were provoked by Afghan and Taliban aggression.

In desperation some local military commanders took measures to thwart the new, stricter controls exerted by their political masters. On 10 June 1919, for instance, a mixed patrol of the Somerset Regiment and various Indian regular units captured two tribesmen strongly suspected of sniping and 'hiding in a nulla, complete with their rifles which had, obviously been recently fired. They were handed over to the political authorities. When we asked what had been done about them we were told that they were "friendly shepherds" and had been released. As a result we never took any more prisoners.'[61] The consequences were predictably dire for many captured Pathan insurgents. At Dakka camp, for instance, 'Three enemy snipers were rounded up by the Green Howards and shot, their equipment, arms and ammunition being brought in'.[62]

Elsewhere, the enforced British defensiveness in the post-armistice period had even more dire consequences On the Southern Front in Baluchistan (including Zhob) the earlier British success at the Battle of Spin Baldak was soon undermined by the new political freeze on offensive operations. As elsewhere, Afghan commanders, ignoring or possibly even not aware of the armistice agreement, aggressively massed their forces at Dabrai, north-west of Chaman. British plans to attack this force pre-emptively at dawn on 3 June were, however, 'vetoed by higher authority' and local commanders were informed that 'no further offensive action could be taken by British forces'![63] On 12 June, when the leading British squadron of the 25th and 45th Cavalry, sent out to investigate the cutting of Spin Baldak's water supplies, discovered 3,000 Afghan regulars and tribesmen occupying nearby villages, they were, nevertheless, told to retire 'since hostilities had been forbidden'. The whole force was subsequently withdrawn some two miles, at which point negotiations were started with the Afghan commander. While the Afghan regulars halted, their tribal allies, ignoring the ceasefire, soon outflanked the British force and opened fire. The Afghan commander subsequently agreed to re-open the water supply but, by 3 p.m., with no sign of water in the duct, the cavalry force had no option but to retire to New Chaman, 'an enforced withdrawal which did much to encourage tribal hostility'.[64]

During July also, despite the armistice, opposing Afghan forces were blatantly strengthened to four cavalry regiments, ten infantry battalions, thirty-eight guns and 6,000 tribesmen. When the Baluchistan Force headquarters again asked for permission to attack this enemy concentration their request was abruptly refused, 'unless the military security of your force is threatened'.[65]

In north Baluchistan and the Zhob valley also, British security was severely undermined as local military commanders found their hands similarly tied. As Ian Colvin confirmed, the British Commander, General Wapshare, was forced 'to wait in miserable inaction while, in spite of the terms of the armistice, the enemy continued to encroach near the British border'.[66] Around Fort Sanderson, five days after the armistice had been signed, local tribesmen launched a series of ferocious attacks on the nights of 8, 9 and 10 June. They looted and burnt the native bazaar and fired on the British pickets. Several convoys in the area were subsequently ambushed between Lakaband and Fort Sandeman. This culminated in one full-scale disaster on 14/15 July 1919, when a British convoy of 225 men of the 1st Gurkha Rifles and seventy-five of the Zhob Militia, with a section of mountain guns, was suddenly attacked by between 800 and 900 mostly Waziri tribesmen. Panic broke out amongst the British force, a situation greatly exacerbated by the premature actions of one young and inexperienced British subaltern who, with 'forty rifles, abandoned the nearby post at Dewar'. The gallant convoy commander, Captain Goulden, was himself subsequently killed as the retreat became a *sauve qui peut*.

Forced to resort to defensive measures, under-resourced and hampered by inexperienced troops and officers, the Baluchistan Field Force was thus left to resort to largely ineffectual punitive raids conducted around Kapip and Mandkhel, Hindu Bagh. In an example of further desperate measures, Kakar villages were indiscriminately burnt down. These extreme half-measures only served to further inflame the tribes and several more British outposts had to be abandoned, notably those of Kapip, Azozai and Zarozai. Military historian Molesworth aptly summarized the politico-military debacle occurring on this front: 'It must be said for both military and political leaders in Baluchistan and for the forces they controlled ... this rigid policy that was forced upon them was a source for annoyance frustration and despair which was exceedingly bad for morale.'[67]

On the crucial Khyber Front, the gateway to British India, British commanders were also incensed by 'treacherous ambushes', principally by Afridi *lashkars* (tribal war parties) and continued attacks from snipers, long after the armistice had been agreed. In some areas, military units again openly side-stepped political controls, resorting to ever-more brutal reprisals and even major counter-ambushes. Whole villages were subject to collective punishment, often taking the form of brutal reprisals. One officer recalled the ferocious response of his men to one horrible discovery. Whilst on patrol near Girdi in the infamous 'Khurd Khaibar' defile they found the decomposing and horribly mutilated bodies of some troopers of the King's Dragoon Guards, who had been cut off and killed during the earlier action there on 16 May. This sight, he recalled 'infuriated the troops'. Anger mounted as 'a small party had the nauseating task of collecting and burying the remains and a chaplain was hastily summoned up from the camp to read the burial service'. 'Poor man', Molesworth vividly recalled, 'he had to stop twice to be sick'. Revenge was soon forthcoming. On return to the area ten days later, at a time of 'intense heat' and constant sniping and with the troops still 'very bitter over the mutilations' a brutal reprisal was concocted. The officer recalled the details:

> We decided to lay some booby traps in Girdi village to which the inhabitants returned when we withdrew. We kept this plan secret for

fear it might be stopped by political officers. Accordingly we planted some well-contrived traps with Mills grenades and very thin wire. Next time we visited Girdi we found ample evidence they had all been exploded successfully.[68]

Revenge was achieved in more conventional ways under the guise of 'defensive operations'. In the same area near Girdi on 20 June, 'one of the biggest ambushes on the North West Frontier' was conducted by the 33rd Cavalry, 1/9th Gurkha Rifles and 1/15th Sikhs. As the 33rd conducted a feigned retreat, culminating in a 'realistic bolt' to the Kabul riverfront, hundreds of tribesmen lured into the pursuit were cut down by the rapid fire of the concealed British artillery and machine guns.[69]

Along the Khyber Pass itself the military situation was equally tough and frustrating. During June for instance, British garrisons at Ali Masjid, deployed to protect key supply routes to the 1st Peshawar Division and Landi Kotal, were subjected to sustained Afridi attacks. These mainly emanated from Chora Fort where the principal tribal rebel, Yar Mohammed had, in defiance of the armistice, been provocatively building up his forces. Once again tied to the defensive, British units such as the Punjabis and Gurkhas, the 1st Royal Sussex, the 1st South Lancashires and various Indian regular units were left to fend off savage tribal attacks conducted against key positions such as 'Barley Hill' and 'Orange Patch Ridge'. The problem for the British was further complicated by the appearance amongst enemy ranks of scores of the recently deserted or demobilized (and still khaki-clad!) Khyber Rifles, and also other formerly British irregular units. As the British were unable to respond, the attacks by these tribal groups became bolder. On 17 July 1919 the Khyber Pass was even temporarily closed as several thousand tribesmen gathered in the Bazar Valley, an aggressive movement no doubt encouraged by the continuing passivity of the British military. For those attached to the frequently attacked motorized convoys which transported urgent supplies to the British camps at Ali Masjid and Landi Kotal, the experience was terrifying This was especially true when the fighting spilled over from the mountains onto the road itself. One British driver, Corporal B.G.L. Rendall, vividly recalled one such incident from which he narrowly escaped:

Once we were caught out on the road with four or five Afghans, me and my second driver. The Khyber was a damned dangerous place after dark and a fool sergeant kept us hanging about too long. It was really dusking down before he let us off back to Jamrud. He should have known better. We were lucky that it was only a small party that caught us, the second driver had two with his revolver and I clobbered one with my rifle more in fright than anything else ... he dropped his jezail on the ground and I retrieved the bullet.[70]

Ever-more ruthless tactics of suppressing the tribes were adopted. Even the use of chemical weapons was considered. On 31 July the Green Howards war diary duly recorded a visit by Brigadier-General Foulkes CB, who arrived with his staff officer to make 'investigations regarding the use of poison gas on this kind of terrain'. His staff officer was of the opinion that the 'use of gas shells would produce good and satisfactory results'.[71] Fortunately this tactic was never resorted to. In the event more tried, tested and orthodox tactics were extended, including the use of machine guns to suppress tribal snipers and even mobile artillery units traversing the tortuous Khyber route. Corporal Rendall witnessed one successful artillery response on the Khyber road where 'we couldn't reach them with our rifles' Instead 'four guns firing shrapnel shells' were deployed which 'caught a load of tribesmen coming down the hillside. There were forty or fifty of them ... there was a blasted row, bloody smoke.... The smoke drifted away in the mountain heat and we could see the bodies ... strewn there like dead flowers.'[72]

Indeed, during these fraught months of June and July before the peace treaty was finally signed, only on the Northern Front near Chitral and the Central Front around Kurram were the British forces allowed any respite from attacks by Afghan forces or local tribes. In the Kurram area, Shia and Sunni religious divisions and ongoing tribal feuds amongst the local Waziris (principally between the Turikhel and Bangash clans) successfully diverted animosities away from the British. Moreover, the local people there generally resented any border incursions by the alien Afghans. In Chitral, the Mehtar remained loyal and the Chitral Scouts, like the Kurram militias, also remained loyal as they were also fighting for their homes and families against their traditional Afghan border enemies.

Not surprisingly, the conclusion of peace negotiations with Afghan envoys on 8 August 1919 was greeted with profound relief by most British units along the frontier. These last two months of the war had become even more desperate owing to mounting failures in the supply of medical supplies and other essential equipment. The British Field Ambulance units, for instance, remained chronically short of drinking water, ice for heatstroke and disinfectant for wounds. They were also confronted by the growing problem of disease caused by the insanitary conditions prevailing at the huge new camps constructed at Ali Musjid and Dakka. In the former camp as late as 20 May, the Brigade there were reported to be still using trench latrines 'as no latrine tents yet available'. On 3 June the latrines of the 2/54th Sikhs and 1/33rd Punjabis were further reported to be 'filled with faeces and the sweepers on duty ... asleep'.[73] The inevitable result was a widespread outbreak of disease. This included an epidemic of cholera, which particularly flourished in the Khyber camps. The epidemic was focused on Kohat, Jamrud and Ali Masjid. It reached 1,663 cases with 566 deaths, with 'the vast majority occurring amongst followers such as camel, bullock and labour corps' who were 'without sanitary establishment and medical officers'.[74] Many British officers were appalled by such chronic serving conditions. Some laid the blame squarely on the shoulders of the Simla administration. One officer, citing the searingly hot temperatures of 127 °F experienced at Jacobabad and 117 °F recorded at Peshawar, duly lambasted 'an exquisitely bad and incompetent Government' with 'disease (six British officers have died from cholera), which cannot be coped with owing to the lack of proper medical arrangements.' He further claimed that '2,500 cases for medical treatment ... have been evacuated owing to heat and disease and those numbers for a comparatively small force.... People are fed up ... Simla is patting itself on the back and has created itself a war area so as to lose no opportunities of getting decorations.'[75]

In another letter penned at the close of hostilities by the same officer, he further castigated the authorities for poor training and equipment: 'The Afghans know full well that the government is unprepared and that the new British soldiers arriving out here are absolutely untrained to mountain warfare and that the old regular man is rotten with fever.' Despite acknowledging the undoubted beneficial psychological impact of the RAF, whose bombing of Kabul and Jalalabad had broken Afghan fighting spirit, the officer nevertheless recalled that most of these planes had become 'death traps' for their pilots. He continued:

When even the aeroplanes are dud ones the Afghans have the laugh of us still more ... only three aeroplanes are safe to use, the others are useless.... The Indian government has got something to answer for. You at home do not hear of the airmen who have come to grief on the Afghan side of the frontier and it isn't because they are shot down.... At the outset of this show people thought the Indian government were going to do things well but they have seen by events that the government is still asleep, criminally incapable and most culpably unready.[76]

It was a bitter epitaph to a war in which the military had been severely undermined by political imperatives. It had, indeed, been a war latterly aimed at peace at all costs rather than military victory. The price of British passivity on several fronts, especially Waziristan, was now to be paid for by the sacrifice of many more British and Indian lives as Amanullah's war 'left the tribes of the north west frontier in a state of endemic unrest'.[77] The Official History bluntly summarized the problems caused by the post-armistice overstretch and such a dangerously defensive posture. While the 'susceptibility' of the Afghans to a vigorous offensive had been:

> clearly demonstrated by the ... action of Bagh, on the 11 May, by the fight at Dakka on the 17th May and General Dyer's operations during the relief of Thal ... the inaction at Dakka, in the Khyber, in the Korram, in Waziristan and at Chaman, brought in all the tribesmen against us from the borders of Chitral to Baluchistan.

It further noted that despite the steadfastness of the Chitral Scouts, the Mohmand and Kurram Militias, the much-vaunted system of 'employing the frontier militias as a covering force behind which the Field Army could concentrate proved a failure in the Khyber and Waziristan'.[78] Frontier veteran Major-General Elliot summarized the extremely dire political consequences for future border control, as Amanullah won the propaganda war not only by claiming victory but by impressing influential Mohmand and Wazir maliks (tribal elders) invited to Kabul that hostilities would be resumed. In Elliot's words:

> Never in the long history of the frontier have the dice been so heavily loaded in favour of the tribesmen ... the country was in a ferment; Mahsud and Wazir were united as they had never been before, the ranks of the lashkars were reinforced by the large numbers of military deserters whose military training and knowledge of our tactics was an asset of very great consequence. On the material side they had ... acquired something like 2,000 government rifles and about a million rounds of ammunition.[79]

In military terms such huge losses provided the essential fuel for continual fighting on the North West Frontier which was to last until the end of the Raj in 1947.

In terms of civil-military relations the war had proved nearly as disastrous as the First Anglo-Afghan War. During the armistice period, many British military commanders on at least two fronts had covertly and clearly defied their political masters and conducted widespread punitive actions against their Afghan and tribal attackers. Elsewhere, there had been, as we have seen, widespread military disillusionment over the political conduct of the war and the resultant loss of blood, treasure and overall British prestige.

If politically enforced military passivity had encouraged the crisis, the political concessions conceded under the treaty of Rawalpindi of 8 August 1919 could only help perpetuate it. Roos-Keppel, now seen as a dangerous 'Afghanphobe', was deliberately sidelined by the nervous London and Simla Governments obsessed with a desire for speedy peace. Despite the objections of Sir Edwin Montagu, Secretary of State for India, the British Government, for the first time, abandoned the key principle of external control over Afghan foreign policy. Sir Hamilton Grant, Foreign Secretary to the Government of India, accordingly confirmed that the war had 'cancelled all previous treaties'. It had been a frustrating conclusion to a hard-fought war but, for historian Fraser Tytler, it probably reflected tacit British acceptance of a profound decline of British power and prestige after the high watermark of the mid-nineteenth century. Crippled by the First World War and facing troubles in India and the Near East it was, he asserted, probably a 'realistic option in a changed world'.[80] But, internally, it further condemned Britain to another quarter century of bitter north-west campaigns, principally focused on Waziristan, and culminated in a messy Indian partition, which left the tribal badlands of newly independent Pakistan still fiercely recalcitrant, essentially lawless and deeply loyal to a fundamentalist Islamic faith. Half a century on, many of these peoples would again, under the joint banners of Al Qaeda and the Taliban, and aided by a hard-pressed and divided government in Pakistan, rise again to challenge Britain and her Western allies.

Notes

1   For detailed discussions of British policies and wars on the North and North West Indian Frontier during this and previous Anglo-Afghan Wars, see, especially, G. Alder, *British India's Northern Frontier* (Longman's, London, 1963), H.L. Nevill, *Campaigns in the North West Frontier*, (London, 1912), G.J. Younghusband, *Indian Frontier Warfare* (Kegan Paul Trench, Trubner and Co., London, 1898) and W. Churchill, *The Malakand Field Force* (London, 1898, repr. Mandarin, 1990), Major-General J.G. Elliott, *The Frontier 1834–1947* (Cassell, London, 1968), T.R. Moreman, *The Army in India and the Development of Frontier Warfare, 1849 to 1947* (Palgrave, Basingstoke, 1998) and A. Swinson, *North West Frontier*, (Hutchinson, London, 1967).

2　For details of the Panjdeh incident and the establishment of the 'Durand Line' see, principally, C. Miller, *Afghanistan: The Story of the North-West Frontier* (Macdonald and Jane's, London, 1977), pp.240–1 and Fraser-Tytler, *Afghanistan*, pp.164–7 and 188–9.

3　Lt.-General G.N. Molesworth, *Afghanistan 1919: An Account of Operations in the Third Afghan War* (Asia Publishing House, London, 1962), p.18.

4　For a detailed study of the 1897–8 campaigns see Nevill, *Campaigns*, pp.209–306, and Churchill, *Malakand Field Force*, *passim* and, more recently, K. Surridge, 'The Ambiguous Amir: Britain, Afghanstan and the 1897 North-West Frontier Uprising', *Journal of Imperial and Commonwealth History*, 36, 3, Sept. 2008, pp.417–34.

5　Molesworth, *Afghanistan*, p.19.

6　Ibid.

7　*The Times*, 23 April 1919.

8　For a detailed narrative and discussion of the 'Amritsar Massacre', see, especially, A. Draper, *The Amritsar Massacre; Twilight of the Raj* (Ashford, Buchan and Enright, London, 1981) and R. Furneaux, *Massacre at Amritsar* (Allen and Unwin, London, 1963).

9　*The Times*, 8 May 1919.

10　*The Times*, 16 May 1919.

11　Imperial War Museum (hereafter IWM) 81/9/1, Holter Papers.

12　IWM Misc 23/419, Price Letters, Price to Mother, 8 May 1919.

13　Sir J. Smyth, *Milestones*, p.106.

14　Molesworth, *Afghanistan*, p.25. For a detailed assessment of Afghan fighting strength, equipment and deployment see, *The Afghan War 1919; Official Account* (Calcutta, 1926), pp.22–5.

15　*The Times*, 19 May 1919.

16　Ibid.

17　BL MSS Eur. D 163/3, Roos-Keppel to Chelmsford, 5 May 1919.

18　BL MSS Eur, Tel. Chief General Staff, India, to General Barrett, 8 May 1919.

19　BL MSS Eur. D 163/3, Chelmsford to Roos-Keppel, 6 May 1919.

20　BL MSS Eur. D 163/3, Roos-Keppel to Barratt, 7 May 1919.

21　Molesworth, *Afghanistan*, p.39.

22　Green Howards Museum (hereafter GHM), Article by J. Parry *Green Howards Regimental News* No. 104, Sept 2002. For a detailed discussion of frontier tactics see, especially, Moreman, *Army in India*.

23　General Staff Branch, Army HQ India, *The Third Afghan War 1919: Official Account* (Calcutta, 1926), p.29.

24　Fraser-Tytler, *Afghanistan*, p.196.

25 BL MSS Eur, RKP, Roos-Keppel to Barrett, 10 May 1919.

26 BL MSS Eur, RKP, Roos-Keppel to Maffey, 17 May 1919.

27 *Official Account*, pp.28–9.

28 *Official Account*, p.31.

29 Ibid.

30 Molesworth, *Afghanistan*, p.49.

31 *Official Account*, p.31.

32 Molesworth, *Afghanistan*, p.33.

33 BL MSS Eur, RKP, Roos-Keppel to Chelmsford, 13 May 1919.

34 Ibid.

35 BL MSS Eur, RKP, Roos-Keppel to Chelmsford, 17 May 1919.

36 BL MSS Eur RKP, Roos-Keppel to Chelmsford, 17 May 1919.

37 Molesworth, *Afghanistan*, p.58.

38 Ibid, p.34. For a comprehensive treatment of the use of air-power in colo-
    nial wars, including the 1919 Afghan War see D. Omissi, *Air Power and
    Colonial Control* (MUP, Manchester, 1991).

39 *Official Account*, p.39.

40 Molesworth, *Afghanistan*, p.61.

41 Ibid, pp.67–9.

42 Ibid, p.69.

43 BL MSS Eur, RKP, Roos-Keppel to Maffey, 17 May 1919.

44 BL MSS Eur, RKP, Roos-Keppel to Chelmsford, 13 May 1919.

45 BL MSS Eur, RKP, Chelmsford to Roos-Keppel, 31 May 1919.

46 *Official Account*, p.57.

47 Molesworth, *Afghanistan*, p.117.

48 I. Colvin, *The Life of General Dyer*, (William Blackwood, London, 1929),
    p.223.

49 IWM, 87/45/1 Brearley Papers.

50 BL MSS Eur, RKP, Roos-Keppel to Chelmsford, 17 May 1919.

51 Sir Charles Monro, encl. in *Official Account*, pp.50–1.

52 Fraser-Tytler, *Afghanistan*, p.196.

53 BL MSS Eur, RKP, Roos-Keppel to Maffey, 17 May 1919.

54 BL MSS Eur, RKP, Sir Hamilton Grant to Roos-Keppel, 25 May 1919.

55 Molesworth, *Afghanistan*, p.87.

56 Ibid.

57 Ibid, p.80.

58 IWM, Misc. 23/419, Price Letters, Price to Mother, 22 May 1919.

59 Molesworth, *Afghanistan*, p.87.

60 Ibid, p.154.

61 Ibid, p.84.

62 GHM Green Howards War Diary, 18 May 1919.

63 Molesworth, *Afghanistan*, p.152.
64 Ibid, p.153.
65 *Official Account*, p.108.
66 Colvin, *The Life of General Dyer*.
67 Molesworth, *Afghanistan*, p.154.
68 Ibid, pp.77–8.
69 Ibid, pp.84–5.
70 B.G.C. Rendell, enc. in C. P. Mills (ed), *A Strange War; Burma, India and Afghanistan, 1914–1919*, (Alan Sutton, Gloucester 1988) p.116.
71 GHM, Green Howards War Diary, 30 July 1919. For a detailed discussion of the use of chemical weapons on the North West Indian Frontier, see Professor E.C. Spiers, 'Gas on the North West Frontier', *Journal of Strategic Studies*, 4, No. 6, pp.94–112.
72 Mills, *Strange War*, p.118.
73 IWM p.272. Major-General Gill RAMC, War Diary, 1 June 1919.
74 *Official Account*, p.128.
75 IWM, Misc.23/419, Price letters, Price to Mother 8 August 1919. See also several letters printed in *The Times*, 7 July 1919, also protesting about the issue of medals to 'comfortable' Simla-based officials rather than the 'real fighting troops'. Conversely, for a defence of the Simla Government see Letter to the Editor, *The Times*, 12 July 1919.
76 IWM, Misc.23/419, Price to Mother 8 August 1919.
77 Molesworth, *Afghanistan*, p.173. For a recent comprehensive treatment of the Waziristan Campaign of 1919–20 see, especially, B. Robson, *Crisis on the Frontier: The Third Afghan War and the Campaign in Waziristan 1919–20* (Spellmount, Staplehurst, 2004), *passim*.
78 *Official Account*, p.132.
79 Elliott, *Frontier*, p.249.
80 Fraser-Tytler, *Afghanistan*, pp.196–8.

8. Chasing the Taliban: the Fourth Afghan War

For us, Afghanistan is destroyed ... it is turning to poison.... If you are a terrorist you can have shelter here no matter who you are. Day by day there is the increase of drugs. Maybe one day they will have to send hundreds of thousands of troops to deal with that. And if they step in they will be stuck. We have a British grave in Afghanistan. We have a Soviet grave. And then we will have an American grave.

Abdul Haq (Mujahideen leader) *New York Times*, March 1994

We will be very happy if we leave Helmand without a shot being fired.

Dr John Reid, Secretary of State for Defence, January 2006

The theatre of operations must also be understood as a broader concept than the spatial one of industrial war ... in the Afghanistan theatre ... war amongst the people is conducted best as an intelligence and information operation, not as one of manoeuvre and attrition in the manner of war.

Major-General Rupert Smith, *The Utility of Force*
(Penguin Books, London, 2005), p.390

In October 2001, for the first time in over eighty years, British regular troops again set foot on the dusty plains and formidable mountains of Afghanistan. The Raj had long gone and this Fourth Anglo-Afghan conflict is being fought neither in its name nor in defence of a far-flung empire. This conflict reflects a distinctly different one from the territorially driven 'Great Game', its *raison d'être* an ostensibly globalized and theocratically inspired struggle between traditional Islam and Christianity but one which is essentially, at least in former British Prime Minister Anthony Blair's view, one of competing 'values' and clashing political ideologies. On the one hand stands the liberal democratic tenets of the British and their Coalition allies; on the other an essentially radical and inherently autocratic branch of Islam which openly seeks to destroy the very roots of Western civilization. Moreover, it is a conflict being fought by Britain and her Coalition allies with sophisticated weaponry and revolutionary technology far in advance of previous Anglo-Afghan conflicts. Equally importantly, it is a campaign being conducted by a Britain further diminished in power following the Second World War and numerous economic recessions. Thankfully, however, it is a campaign not being fought in 'splendid isolation' but with the help of powerful allies, notably the USA, the world's only superpower, and one which includes several other leading NATO powers. Nonetheless, it is a war in which tensions between the British military and the political authorities are again starkly evident, especially as it is a war markedly unlike previous 'imperial' wars in which the winning of Afghan hearts and minds is equal (if not paramount) to military imperatives, and one in which the spectre of resource constraints under the pressure of two concurrent wars is again seriously undermining military imperatives.

The trigger for this conflict was, of course, the infamous devastating strike launched by Al Qaeda operatives against the 'Twin Towers' in New York on 9 September 2001 (commonly referred to as '9/11'). This resulted in the deaths of over 3,000 people, with British subjects suffering the second-highest mortality rate. Nearly one hundred Britons perished in this first major attack on American soil since Pearl Harbor in 1941, although it has subsequently become clear that this was only the culmination of several attacks on Western interests conducted in the early 1990s. These included the bombing of the New York Trade Centre in 1992 and the African Embassy bombings of the late 1990s. Moreover, it was direct attack on American and Western interests, directly inspired and facilitated by the decisive victories achieved by Mujahideen resistance forces over the Soviet Armies in Afghanistan in the 1980s. And it was the failed state of Afghanistan, so tragically neglected by Western powers, happily basking in the fruits of post-Cold War victory, which provided Al Qaeda leader Bin Laden and his adherents with both a fertile training ground and the main base for future conflict against the 'infidel' West.

After the fall of Kabul and the brutal takeover of power by the radical Islamist Taliban faction in 1996, plus the arrival of Bin Laden, scores of training camps were established for global operations against the West. Consequently Afghanistan was to be the logical primary target for any post 9/11 counter-offensive or indeed 'revenge attacks' by the USA and her 'coalition of the willing'. As Prime Minister Anthony Blair rapidly made clear, British troops were to be an integral part of this operation and the slow build-up of British forces which began in the autumn of

2001 had culminated in the deployment of over 9,000 troops by the autumn of 2009.

In order to analyze the complex security environment and the challenges confronting the British and their Coalition partners in Afghanistan, so clearly indicated by General Rupert Smith in the opening quotation to this final chapter, it is possible to structure the fluctuations in the British experience in this conflict in three key phases. Firstly, I will consider an initial phase of incomplete or 'hollow victory', an embryonic period when 'industrial war' decisively triumphed over the regular Taliban enemy but when many of the key tenets or principles for achieving long-term social peace and stability or state-building were, arguably, tragically neglected. Secondly, I will identify a distinct phase of 'quagmire', lasting around four years from 2002–6 in which, it will be argued, a continued fallacious emphasis upon fighting a war frequently compromised efforts at peace-building and reconstruction, and resulted in a steady resurgence of Taliban military activity. This predominantly 'war-fighting' phase culminated in the still-controversial 'Herrick 1' campaign in Helmand of 2006. Finally, I will focus upon and analyze a continuing post-2006 and distinctly less ambitious and reformist phase of long-term 'reconstruction, stabilization and containment', in which British policy-makers have eschewed any concept of all-out victory (as widely predicted in the heady days of 2001–2). This phase has culminated in a watershed or 'tipping point' in which Britain, while achieving limited military and political gains in some of her operational areas, remains in a position of what former British Foreign Secretary David Miliband has described as 'strategic stalemate'. Within the umbrella of these three phases of what is an ongoing crisis, strong parallels will again be drawn with the three previous Anglo-Afghan Wars, especially in terms of continuing civil-military tensions, intelligence failures and resource starvation.

Before embarking upon this analysis, however, it is important to briefly assess the formidable enemy which has confronted Britain and her NATO/Coalition allies in Afghanistan in recent years. In many respects, the Taliban enemy of the twenty-first century possesses indigenous characteristics similar to the tribal enemy long-confronted by Britain during her three previous conflicts in the area, and so accurately depicted in this extract from the 1908 *Imperial Gazette*: 'Their step is full of resolution, their bearing proud and apt to be rough – inured to bloodshed from childhood they are familiar with death, audacious in attack but easily discouraged by failure. They are much under the influence of the mullahs.'[1]

These intrinsic national characteristics of resilience and toughness have barely changed, especially in the more remote rural areas. However, old skills honed against the British, ranging from mountain ambushes to hit and run attacks on patrols and convoys, have been perfected by the more recent experiences gleaned from the prolonged, bitter war against the Soviets in the 1980s. Then, thousands of Soviet troops were killed or wounded in skilful roadside ambushes, helped by the importation of huge numbers of more modern weapons such as RPG7s and AK47s, as well as more sophisticated ones – notably the American-supplied anti-helicopter 'Stinger' missiles. In the aftermath of the end of the Cold War and Soviet withdrawal in 1989, these guerrilla fighting skills were further honed in the notorious Taliban military training camps which flourished throughout the late 1990s.

However, the term 'Taliban', so often used to denote the enemy confronting Britain and her allies in Afghanistan, must be carefully qualified. Indeed, in many ways it is a misnomer. The original Taliban grouping emerged in the mid-1990s as a fundamentalist Islamic backlash against the chaos, lawlessness and horrors of the bloody civil war which followed the Soviet retreat. Their original avowed intention was to purge Afghanistan of all those Mujahideen 'who have become killers, thieves and drug traffickers in the name of Islam'.[2] Led by the elusive Mullah Mohammed Omar and drawing support and core fighters from the countryside *madrassa* (Koranic schools and study centres) or 'Taliban' located both within Afghanistan but mainly across the border in Pakistan, they successfully courted popularity from a war-weary, demoralized Afghan peasantry by providing economic relief and social order strictly regulated by the revered Koran. In the words of one Taliban leader, 'We were fighting against Muslims who had gone wrong.' It was an irresistible force for national redemption. In the words of Michael Griffin, the 'establishment of a pure Islamic State was an unarguable proposition for a people reared upon the irreducible truth of the Koran'.[3]

By 1996, following the capture of Kabul by Taliban forces, the new Taliban Government was ripe for alliance with the new, virulently anti-western Al Qaeda movement led by Osama Bin Laden, who had arrived in Afghanistan that same year. Since 2001, however, the original 'Taliban', so deeply fragmented if undefeated by 'Enduring Freedom' (the massive offensive by the allies of 2001–2), has come to represent a much broader, looser alliance of anti-government groups, including not only Taliban purists, Al Qaeda or foreign *jihadists* but, perhaps most significantly of all, disaffected warlord factions and disparate tribal groups, fighting more in defence of local political and economic interests (notably opium growing) than as any new political or socio-religious order. In the words of the key international think-tank, the Security and Development Policy Group's (SENLIS) Report in February 2007: 'More generally, anti-government elements have been recruited from the growing number of discontented, jobless locals who are increasingly fighting alongside the Taliban, even though they may not share their fundamentalist values and principles.'[4]

For Britain and her Coalition allies, therefore, the term 'Taliban' has come to reflect a complex, often 'unholy alliance' of vastly differing interest groups. Indeed, their only common denominators might be their predominantly ethnic origins in the Pashtun tribal belt which straddles the southern border of Afghanistan and north-west Pakistan and their centuries-old traditional dislike of the *feringhee* alien invaders. Religion is by no means the dominant catalyst and, as we shall see, despite the best efforts of Taliban propagandists, it is the Western Coalition's and the Karzai Government's policies of drug-eradication which have acted as a greater stimulus to resistance and hostility in this region than any fears of Christian or 'infidel' intrusion into this overwhelmingly Muslim country. Aside from these complexities, the willingness of many, especially Taliban/Al Qaeda extremists, to die for their cause and their ability to merge into the civilian populations of the area has made them, militarily, an elusive and highly dangerous foe.

Phase 1: Hollow Victory 2001–2

So this was the formidable, intangible and ruthless enemy that confronted Britain and her Coalition allies as, under the banner of 'Operation' Enduring Freedom', they poured troops into Afghanistan in the autumn of 2001. Almost immediately Britain was subjected to several key restraints not present in previous Anglo-Afghan conflicts. Militarily, unlike the days of the Raj, she was clearly no longer in full control of her own destiny, albeit as still the second most powerful nation of a Western/ NATO coalition overwhelmingly dominated by her 'special' superpower ally the USA. As a regional or medium power, as distinct from a global military power, she was potentially overstretched by her participation not only in a NATO-led ISAF peace-keeping force located round Kabul, but by her much wider major regional support for American forces. After April 2003 this overstretch was to be significantly increased by the still-controversial decision to open up a second front in Iraq. Also, her 'special' political dependence on the USA and her more obvious operational dependency, especially in the areas of air transport, logistics, intelligence and rapid-reaction air support, meant that any future independent political or military strategy to solve the crisis could be severely compromised.

In the short term at least, these political and military constraints were less evident. In 2001–2, after the rejection of an ultimatum to surrender Bin Laden, Britain and her NATO and Coalition allies proceeded to systematically crush the regular forces of the Taliban. It was very much an 'industrial war' in which the Americans in particular have always excelled. The massive deployment of sophisticated American technology and weaponry, especially air-power, soon overwhelmed any organized Taliban resistance.

'Operation Enduring Freedom' began on 7 October 2001, barely a month after 9/11. The British were quick to support their American allies militarily, supplying both valuable expertise in the form of up to a hundred special forces personnel and high technology in the form of submarine-launched Tomahawk cruise missiles and RAF reconnaissance, although the British Government only publicly admitted to the presence of British special forces over a month into the conflict. Their initial role, in the words of defence expert Mike Yardley, was threefold: 'The first is gathering intelligence on the Taliban and presumably also looking for Osama Bin Laden. The second is acting as forward observation officers to target in laser guided weapons and pass on communications. The third is to act as some sort of snatch destroy or killer group to attack Bin Laden or his lieutenants in their lairs'.[5] A key role for the British special forces was also to provide support for the anti-Taliban Northern Alliance comprising a motley formation of ethnic groups notably Uzbeks, Tajiks and Hazaras (the latter traditional allies of the British) hitherto marginalized or persecuted under Taliban rule. These armed groups, in concert with anti-Taliban Pashtun forces in the south and backed mainly by unrelenting American air-power, soon defeated and ejected Taliban forces from the key cities of Kabul, Kandahar, Mazar-i-Sharif and Kunduz. The speed of victory certainly astounded the British Government, with Defence Secretary Geoffrey Hoon announcing that 'the speed of collapse of the Taliban in the north had come as a surprise' and asserting that 'the Taliban frontlines … had taken a 'terrible pounding'.[6] It was, arguably, the start of an unfortunate trend of underestimating the enemy, culminating in the then Defence Secretary Dr Reid's now-notorious 2006 statement about achieving success in Afghanistan 'without firing a single shot'.

Nevertheless, for the first British soldiers to arrive in support of ISAF and wider operations it was initially, as in previous campaigns, a time of optimism – even exuberance. New experiences, including promotion and the prospect of medals and awards, seemed to beckon in this still largely unknown, faraway, enigmatic country (known to some only through the 'Flashman' novels!). Captain Jed Stone of 13 AASR RLC exclaimed: 'High morale. We were excited by knowing we were some of the first to theatre.'[7]

Captain William Downham of the RSME was a little more cautious. He felt good, excited but wary of the local population 'and acutely aware of a country with a very poor infrastructure that, as an engineer, I felt I could only do so much to help. The place would need to develop over such a long future period'. Most challenging for him was 'the imminent threat of being easily surrounded, disarmed by warring militia local to sites'.[8] Like their military forbears, those deployed to Kabul were struck by the picturesque if now sadly polluted scenes. Major Andrew Banks of the RMP observed: 'Very mountainous, warm, very poor air quality in Kabul', but he was also 'keen to get on with the job'. He was even involved in embryonic attempts to win 'hearts and minds' and, with a comment strikingly reminiscent of the heady days of the earlier British occupation of 1839–41 recalled: 'Worked closely with the Afghanistan Cricket Federation and was made a "development officer" after I got them kit and equipment.'[9] Despite acute homesickness even some Christmas traditions harked back to merry old times in previous wars. For Royal Engineer Captain Nick Colvin, like the officers and men of the 13th Foot and the 35th in 1839, his highest point of morale was: 'Christmas Day – alcohol was procured for the evening and after opening presents we had brought with us and made the phone call home we made our own entertainment. We had sports, inter-rank tug-of-war, secret Santa and horse racing and a damn good piss-up. The hangover next day was horrendous.'[10]

On the higher political front, optimism during this initial phase also remained high. Compared to the later Iraq campaign of 2003, the war in Afghanistan had all the prospects of being a 'good' war, with a high level of international legitimacy. It was also a conflict firmly in line with Blair's much-trumpeted 1997 pronouncement of an 'ethical dimension' to Labour foreign policy. The Afghanistan conflict enjoyed the support of major UN resolutions, notably UNSCR 1386 which, along with the Bonn Agreement of December 2001, established the Afghan Interim Authority (AIA) and the nineteen-nation NATO-led ISAF security force.

On the socio-economic front prospects also seemed good. At the 2001 Tokyo Donor Meeting a substantial sum of $5.2 billion was promised by international donors for post-war reconstruction purposes. At this time of politico-military triumph however, the complex 'politics of ethnicity' in the region were already beginning to befuddle British politicians. The occupation of Kabul by anti-Taliban forces in November 2001 had only served to spark off old tensions between rival ethnic groups jockeying for power, as some 3,000 Hazara fighters, those old allies of Britain, suddenly threatened to occupy the city on the basis that the Northern Alliance leadership had 'broken its promise not to enter the city'. This prompted a somewhat naïve British response in which Foreign Secretary Jack Straw declared that 'there was a relatively strong, stable Afghan state for forty years up to 1973 so we have a fair idea what works',[11] a statement which only served to ignore the fact that Afghanistan as a country had never enjoyed any strong tradition of central government and, moreover, failed to add that it had spent the last thirty-odd years in a state of war and civil anarchy. With no attempt to broker power between these groups and with no attempt to incorporate the loyal Pashtun warlords and their followers in the south, who now understandably felt even more marginalized because of their assumed support for the Taliban, future political prospects were not good.

The situation was exacerbated by the profound lack of constructive British and American strategic thinking about the longer-term future of Afghanistan. As ISAF peace-keeping operations commenced in the north, centred on and around Kabul, and as Britain deployed a contingent of peace-keeping forces there, principally of Royal Marines, US Defence Secretary, Donald Rumsfeld bluntly stated that it was 'highly unlikely' that American troops would join any peace-keeping force. It was soon clear that the overriding and principal aim of US policy-makers was war-fighting designed to achieve the essential military goals of finishing off Taliban regular forces, securing Northern Alliance domination but, above all, capturing the hated Osama Bin Laden, the principal architect of 9/11. Issues of peace-keeping and humanitarian relief were very low on the policy agenda of the Bush administration in these early days in Afghanistan.

By Christmas 2001, in the aftermath of apparent victory, as British military planners based at Northwood, London, already honed in the political complexities of Northern Ireland, the Balkans and Sierra Leone, sought to avoid 'mission creep' and establish troop tasks, rules of engagement and a finite period of involvement, her dominant political and military partner, the USA, was slowly and almost subconsciously drawing her into a more politically insensitive prolonged war of attrition. As Mats Berdal, Director of Studies at The International Institute of Strategic Studies confirmed, there was then an imperative need for 'a balance to be struck between military efficiency and meeting local sensitivities'[12] or, in General Sir Rupert Smith's terms, avoiding substituting an industrial war for a 'people's war' and for achieving a force level that 'gives an impression of being reasonably serious but ... not an occupying force'.[13] The United States, however, had, in Berdal's words, only 'one goal and will not think about anything else until that goal has been achieved'. The United States' unwillingness to contribute troops for the security force, he postulated, reflected a broader disinclination to see its armed force involved in 'constabulary' duties and 'nation building'. It was a scepticism born not solely out of seeking revenge for 9/11 but a reflection of recent humiliating experiences in Somalia, a lingering 'body-bag syndrome' dating back to Vietnam and specifically 'a concern that as the proven military superpower its troops would become choice targets'.[14] It was a narrow 'war-lite' (to give it a US spelling) policy, which began with only 1,800 American troops deployed in October 2001 and left Afghanistan 80 per cent unsecured by the end of that year.

In terms of British military strategy, her post-Second World War counter-insurgency campaigns had evolved from the operational art of the 1920s and 1930s to a full military doctrine by the late 1950s and 1960s. The chief pioneers of British COIN (counter-insurgency) had been Sir Robert Thompson and, to a lesser extent, Frank Kitson.[15] Both had devised a strategy based on several basic principles. These included clear political aims of establishing and maintaining a free, independent and united country with political and economic viability; respect for the rule of law and prevention of excesses by either side; an integrated civil and military intelligence and a police strategy aimed primarily at defeating political subversion as the cause of insurgency (rather than the insurgents them-selves) and to include development and reconstruction; and, finally, the security of bases essential for any long drawn-out campaign.

Critically dependent upon or dominated by United States military support and war aims, such tried and tested British COIN models were to be diluted, violated or simply sidelined over the next four years, and plans for a larger peace-keeping force scaled down. But it was an imbalanced strategy which was by no means solely American driven. As *The Economist* confirmed, it was a policy partly dictated by strategic fears in London as well as in Washington where 'a similar note of caution has been struck by his [Rumsfeld's] political counterpart, Geoffrey Hoon who is hearing muffled cries of protest from the military. The generals fear that a muddled mission in Kabul could spoil an unfinished war and cost British lives'.[16] Moreover, Tory opposition leader, Ian Duncan Smith, also shared 'deep misgivings about the idea of a British-led peacekeeping effort being under-taken at a time when "search and destroy" missions by American soldiers, with some participation by British forces, was still in progress'. *The Economist* concluded: 'In practice the peacekeeping mission would not be undertaken unless American concerns are allayed. We believe that if the expedition succeeds in its limited tasks it may mark the end of a chapter in British defence policy'.[17] For a while at least peace-keeping and peace-building needs were to be sacrificed on the altar of an initial US obsession with war-fighting and a mixture of British internal policy confusion and compliancy with its superpower ally. The political analysts, Hodes and Sedra, summed up the resultant dangerously imbalanced strategy: 'The allied intervention in 2001 was ... to overthrow the Taliban ... not to transform the state or consolidate a certain type of peace. As a result, the state-building process was critically under-resourced.... The USA and its allies were trying to carry out major strategic change on the cheap.[18]

In the spring of 2002 the 'political chickens' came home to roost, as American forces with mainly British, Australian, New Zealand and Canadian troops in support, launched large-scale operations against Taliban and Al Qaeda remnants. It signified the start of a distinctive second phase of nearly four years of continuous fighting in which policies of reconstruction remained of secondary importance. 'Operation Anaconda', of which the British sector was called 'Operation Jakala', represented the biggest British deployment of conventional operations since the First Gulf War, eleven years earlier. The British contingent, spearheaded by 45 Royal Marine Commando, was specifically requested by the Americans for its expertise in mountain warfare. While the Coalition forces killed an estimated 500 insurgents in this purely war-fighting exercise, several critics doubted such high figures in a costly campaign, in which eight American soldiers were killed and in which one American 10th Mountain Division soldier astonishingly confessed, 'We don't do mountains'![19]

Meanwhile, Osama Bin Laden remained at large. In London some politicians were already belated realizing that Afghanistan was militarily 'not a quick fix ... there are pockets of Taliban and Al Qaeda building up all over Afghanistan ... they are quite well disciplined. They are committed to their task. They have a range of small arms, some anti-tank weapons, some anti-aircraft weapons and they are proving themselves pretty agile at tactical and manoeuvre operations'.[20] Even the Allied Coalition commander, American General Tommy Franks, conceded that more battles lay ahead as the militants tried to regroup. In 2002 also, a five-man United Nations monitoring group had already observed that many of the estimated 30,000 to 50,000 'defeated' Taliban regular troops had merely 'disappeared into the countryside and that the Taliban are now 'likely to remain a threat for some time to come'. Consequently, the group ominously concluded: 'The possibility cannot be ignored that the Taliban and their supporters still possess the means to stage an uprising.'[21]

The follow-up operations in April and May 2002 underlined the relative futility of 'seek and destroy operations' in which local political needs and fundamental COIN principles were being largely ignored. On 28 April 2002 'Operation Snipe'[22] involving 1,000 British Royal Marine Commandos, the first major mission for British troops in Afghanistan since

1919, began with an unfortunate statement by their somewhat gung-ho commander, Royal Marines Brigadier Lane. Speaking at Bagram military base he announced on 8 May: 'We believe the fight against Al Qaeda and the Taliban in Afghanistan is all but won.'[23] It was the first evidence from a senior British officer of a gross underestimation of the enemy.

As British troops disengaged, the British media added to growing public scepticism by exposing not only this exaggerated military hype but the overall folly of a flawed military strategy often dominated by the Americans. As Lieutenant-General Reith, Chief of Joint Operations, sought to reduce both the Government's and Brigadier Lane's discomfort by explaining that the latter 'may not have got it right in media handling',[24] far more damning media reports flooded in, highlighting frequent mis-targeting by United States planes which resulted in the destruction of Afghan villages and soaring numbers of civilian deaths. Veteran reporter John Swain recorded one such incident, this time involving Australian troops, and one of many which was bound to inflame the local Pashtun tribal groups. This tragic incident began 'when a group of Afghan farmers stumbled across a team of Australian SAS. Their fate was sealed when they raised their weapons. On instruction the Australians opened fire.' Later, the press were misleadingly briefed that coalition ground forces had shot two Al Qaeda terrorists![25] One despairing Afghan border villager summed up the dangerous, if not farcical, situation as well as inadvertently exposing the shortfalls in Anglo-American tactics at this time: 'There are not and never have been any Arabs in this village. The English are wasting their time. But they are welcome because once they have verified there are none the Americans will not bomb our villages.'[26]

Such chronic intelligence failures led at times to almost comical situations on the ground as British officers and troops were constantly bewildered by their elusive enemy. As reporter Mark Turner revealed: 'They faced airborne goats, amorous Afghan men, opium sellers and hordes of fleas, in fact about the only thing the British marine commandos did not encounter in their week long sweep through south east Afghanistan was a clear-cut enemy.'[27] Major Phil Joyce of Whisky Company confirmed: 'This is a COIN operation and it is very difficult to identify the enemy. It is not a clear-cut enemy.' Noting a 'bewildering mosaic of warring factions ... many fear could drag the coalition into a confusing war with no clear strategy'. Joyce continued: 'There's a huge power struggle ... there were a lot of warring factions ... one village will say the village across the valley is Al Qaeda but that village will say the same thing; the Afghans jump from one side to the other.'[28] Royal Marines Lieutenant-Colonel Tim Chicken was even more circumspect: 'The enemy has been here but he has scarpered!'[29]

Both 'Anaconda' and 'Snipe' (and the later 'Condor') operations revealed the first serious signs of military stalemate and of political failure in the British and US strategies in Afghanistan. In *The Guardian's* words, 'Mr Hoon will find it difficult ... to portray the performance of the marines as a triumph of British and American military planning. The troops are coming home. But Al Qaeda is still out there.'[30]

The MOD ingeniously tried to salvage the débâcle by claiming success from, 'the lack of a visible enemy.... The fact that we did not come across large numbers of Al Qaeda or Taliban could indicate the effectiveness of past operations. We are not measuring the success by the number of dead.'[31] Even hawkish US Secretary of State for Defence, Donald Rumsfeld, took a rare reality check: 'There are still Taliban and Al Qaeda in the country and neighbouring countries.... We have no intention of announcing an end date or anything of that type.'[32]

The warning signs were there. It was a campaign watershed and from mid-2002 to autumn 2006 the British and her Coalition allies entered a distinct second phase of political and military quagmire as they struggled to devise a campaign to both break Taliban and Al Qaeda power, but more importantly, fill the growing political vacuum and win the all-important battle for Afghan hearts and minds.

Phase 2: Quagmire

One clear political and military problem emerging was not only the frightening lack of ground-level intelligence, an essential prerequisite for any successful COIN operation, but the imperative strategic need to control the southern border with Pakistan where many Taliban and Al Qaeda groups were actively reforming. As Julian Manion strikingly revealed in a series of sometimes farcical interviews, these early operations were devoid of any clear information of Taliban tactics or the ethnic make-up of operational areas, particularly in the Pashtun belt. After Brigadier Lane himself had later conceded that intelligence before 'Operation Snipe' had 'fluctuated wildly', Manion sought clarification from one of the Brigadier's advisers, 'a man well trained in Whitehall mandarin speak'. The adviser opined: 'Some of the local tribesmen have been a bit naughty, they've been denouncing their rivals as Taliban or Al Qaeda.' 'But,' Manion asked, wasn't "wildly fluctuating" some sort of criticism of the intelligence operation?' The reply was: 'No, it doesn't mean anyone is to blame it just means it is very difficult'! As Manion correctly surmised, the 'politics of the border', so inextricably tied up with the sovereignty of Pakistan, lay at the heart of an emerging British political and military divide: 'What is clear is that military opinion strongly favours some sort of action against what are seen as Al Qaeda bases in the tribal areas across the Pakistani border; essential is a word I've heard. It is also clear that such action could risk the collapse of the Mushariff regime.'[33] Moreover, as we have seen, the border remained a truly phantom one, demarcated along the infamous 1893 Durand Line but still ignored by the Pashtun clans located in the area. In fact the border problem had been obvious from the start of the campaign, with the failure to capture Bin Laden and his key lieutenants mainly caused by the lack of any Allied blocking force on the border. Furthermore, the border crisis could be seen as an unwelcome return of Britain's 'imperial migraine' of 1919–47; the vast mountainous, lawless and intractable wastes of Waziristan, the graveyard of so many British soldiers during the countless North West Frontier campaigns, were now to provide a suitable haven for her new Taliban and Al Qaeda foes and their ruthless leadership.

Military frustration over their inability to conduct hot pursuit in this bandit country – the 'South Armagh' of Afghanistan – was compounded by the particularly chronic intelligence vacuum. Unlike in previous wars, the shortage of competent political and military officers with local ethnic knowledge and linguistic skills (such as Sir Robert Sandeman and Major Molesworth) had, as we have seen, represented a distinct lacuna in political policy to the region. As *The Times* observed, the problem persisted until as late as May 2006: 'The Foreign Office has only despatched one political officer who does not speak Pashto to Helmand. It is a far cry from the time when political agents, who worked the Afghan frontier during the Raj, spoke local languages and immersed themselves in local lore.'[34]

Long gone were the days when, as retired Field Marshal and ex-Gurkha officer Sir John Chapple recalled, every British regiment traditionally incorporated several officers fluent in Pashto, whose invaluable local knowledge and intimate personal links with several generations of tribal leaders or elders did much to forestall or avoid problems on this notoriously turbulent imperial frontier.[35] Indeed the British Government's abject failure to fully tap the huge reservoir of corporate knowledge held by surviving veterans of these campaigns, or even to consult North West Frontier/Afghan historians or specialists such as Professor Malcolm Yapp, Dr T.R. Moreman or Dr Garry Alder,[36] remains a glaring indictment of British policy during the early years of this new form of ideologically driven 'Great Game'. This is not to say that plans for a Malayan-style solution (as applied during Britain's major COIN operation in Malaya against communist insurgents in 1948–62), including 'ink-spot' development zones protected by military units were not then advanced but, as we shall see, the manpower, material resources and suitable organization to achieve this aim were not present in the theatre at this time. Moreover, the Afghan terrain and the complex mosaic of ethnic groupings were arguably unsuited to a Malayan solution, especially as Afghanistan, unlike Malaya, was never a permanent colony of Britain and lacked any existing colonial infrastructure. It was, of course, a problem shared by Britain's Coalition allies, but with far less excuse in view of the immense British historical experience in this area. Despite more recent strenuous efforts by Defence Intelligence, MI6 and other institutions to close the intelligence gap, it remains the 'Achilles' heel' of British and Coalition strategy today.

Externally, the problems of this 'second phase' of British operations in Afghanistan were greatly magnified by a major political diversion: the Blair Government's decision to invade Iraq in 2003 and the commencement of a draining two-front war. It was a major distraction at a crucial time for Afghanistan and arguably another still-controversial example of a slavish tendency to follow American leadership. *The Times* journalist and experienced Afghanistan commentator Christina Lamb certainly saw it as a deadly blow to the Coalition war effort in Afghanistan: 'If there is one factor most responsible for the Taliban resurgence it is the war in Iraq which distracted the attention of London and Washington at a critical time. While United States marines were toppling statues of Saddam Hussein and then finding themselves fighting a bloody insurgency, the Taliban regrouped and retrained in Pakistan'.[37]

As the Taliban duly exploited this politico-military vacuum and conducted fresh large-scale offensives after 2003, the impact of this still-controversial decision to attack Iraq was having an inevitable impact upon British logistical resources, especially in terms of manpower or 'boots on the ground'. In October 2005 Defence Secretary Dr John Reid, while announcing the dispatch of 4,000 more British troops to Afghanistan to counter this resurgence, nevertheless claimed that this huge new commitment 'would not affect other commitments or overstretch the armed forces. Anything I need for Afghanistan is independent of the requirements to draw resources in Iraq'.[38] However, as hundreds of British troops poured into Helmand Province in 2006, his view was not reflected in the reports of many military commanders at ground level, or those of outside observers. One serving infantry officer, Major Charles Heyman, duly observed: 'It's quite obvious that there aren't enough boots on the ground to maintain security. It makes you gasp when you realise what they are being asked to do.'[39] His view was echoed by the British Lieutenant-General David Richards, the new NATO/ISAF commander in Kabul in

2006. He worryingly asserted that 'Every general would like more troops because then I could do things quicker. But I will just have to construct a campaign that reflects what we have got. If we were trying win a war we'd have a problem'![40]

These problems were compounded by serious deficiencies in, or short-ages of, equipment, especially helicopters and armoured vehicles, as insurgents increasingly switched to deadly roadside IEDs (improvised explosive devices) to kill British and Coalition troops. A *Daily Telegraph* editorial protested: 'There are glaring and dangerous gaps in equipment being delivered ... roadside bombs are becoming one of the frontline weapons of the enemy ... this is no time for British troops to be making unnecessary road trips ... this is no time to run out of helicopters.[41]

In fairness, it was not entirely a British problem: it was also a problem generated by the widely varying commitments of her NATO allies. While British, American, Canadian and Danish forces were, for instance, fighting costly and bitter battles in the south, a clear discrepancy in the size of contributions by other NATO allies had emerged by 2006–7. As *The Times* succinctly put it:

> A clearly defined mission: troop strengths and structures composed to fit the task: consolidated public will: the generation of mass and precise execution of force: these are some of the principles of war stated as necessary for victory by the greatest military thinkers.... They all seem dangerously absent in Afghanistan where General Daniel McNeill commands a disparate force of 40,000 NATO troops drawn from 38 nations, each with a varying preparedness to fight.[42]

But solving the problems of domineering or reluctant allies, intelligence failures, porous borders and resource overstretch constitute only one half of the equation for achieving stability in the complex political and security environment of Afghanistan. As we have seen accepted COIN strategies, principally forged in Malaya (1948–62) and Northern Ireland (1969–97), required success not only in separating the insurgents from the people but in winning the latter's hearts and minds. And it was the support of the Pashtun, this formidable people occupying the strategically important southern border, already politically dispossessed by the victories of the Northern Alliance back in 2001–2, that was most vital. This Pashtun region was crucial for one other reason. The south, especially Helmand Province, was the source of a substantial proportion of the four-fifths of the world's heroin supplied from Afghanistan. In addition to constituting a threat to Western societies themselves, the Afghan heroin trade was a potent local security problem for Britain and her allies. The vast profits from drug sales were clearly being used not only to fuel the insurgency itself but also to sustain high levels of corruption at government level.

On the vitally important internal political front, under which the joint problems of drugs proliferation and widespread corruption needed to be tackled, Britain, the USA and their Coalition allies had early favoured a top-to-bottom approach. In December 2001, Western solutions had prevailed with the appointment of President Karzai to lead an interim government. The obvious political advantages accruing from his Pashtun origins, however, were soon compromised by the appointment of rival ethnic groups (notably the Tajiks) and members of his own Alokozai Pashtun clan to key security positions. This further alienated other rival southern Pashtun clans or communities such as the Ishaqzai. Moreover, his middle-class origins and heavy reliance upon corrupt warlords, many of whom held seats in the Afghan parliamentary assembly, did not endear him to the mass of heavily exploited Pashtun peasantry. The democratic elections of 2005, heralded as a triumph in the West, did little to alter the still-negative perception of isolated Pashtun rural communities, particularly as corruption at local government level still flourished under local governors and police commanders appointed from a distant and increasingly discredited Kabul administration. Furthermore, many of the promised economic and social reforms so vital to winning Afghan 'hearts and minds' (notably new bridges, roads, schools, health centres, etc.) were, because of corruption, misplaced security strategy or maladministration, simply not materializing during these first three or four years.

The Coalition's other security sector reform policies, launched in 2001, were optimistically designed to provide reliable, uncorrupted soldiers and policemen to carry out the Karzai Government's reform policies, notably drug eradication and the rebuilding of infrastructure. It was upon the efficiency and success of these policies that (as in Iraq) the Coalition's exit strategy ultimately depended, but they were fraught with difficulties.[43] The training of the Afghan National Army (ANA), launched in December 2001 and 50,000-strong by 2006, was still encountering problems in the key area of leadership training, with low pay and poor living conditions resulting in ill-discipline and high rates of desertion. More significantly, the Coalition had, from the start, failed to address issues of ethnic balance, with 40 per cent of initial recruits being of Tajik origin, although they represented only 20 per cent of the national population. The force was initially only 30 per cent Pashtun, undoubtedly reinforcing their existing sense of disenfranchisement after the Northern Alliance victory of 2001–2. It again constituted a glaring lacuna in British and coalition intelligence, revealing a complete failure to understand ethnic sensitivities in this complex society.

The training of the Afghan National Police (ANP), equally essential to the future political credibility of the Karzai Government, was also fraught with difficulty. Established in 2003 and reaching 45,000 in number by 2006, the training programme soon revealed even deeper problems than those encountered with the ANA. Not only was there a huge difficulty in securing suitable recruits, but the force was plagued by high levels of illiteracy and corruption, especially amongst the low-paid highway police. As late as 2006 an estimated 80 per cent of the ANP were directly involved in the drug trade.

In this administrative lacuna the targeting of the poppy-fields, the key to the survival of the vast majority of Pashtun farmers, could only engender further hostility. With initially little or late compensation for the destruction of their opium crops and little evidence of reconstruction, villagers became easy targets for Taliban propaganda and willing recipients of Taliban aid and/or wages to pay their 'angry young men' to fight British and Western Coalition forces. As a SENLIS report stressed: 'The United States and the United Kingdom-led failed counter-narcotics policies have led directly to the return of the Taliban by creating security and hunger crises in southern Afghanistan.'[44]

The 2006 offensive in Helmand Province, the area of massive deployment by 3,300 fresh British troops, typified virtually all of these ongoing problems in British and Coalition strategy. It was the culmination of this second phase of 'quagmire' or political and military decline and it was to lead to massive criticism from the British media regarding the *raison d'être* of the British presence in Afghanistan. The province of Helmand presented a mighty challenge to the British. Four times the size of Wales, it produced 20 per cent of the world's opium and 42 per cent of Afghanistan's total output in 2006. It was, in the words of reporter Stephen Grey, 'the largest and most lawless province in Afghanistan',[45] an area in which the Karzai Government writ barely ran and where there had been a minimal military presence.

Already, by February 2006, 165 schools in Helmand had been closed as a result of Taliban threats. Along the nearly one hundred miles of border with the 'badlands' of Waziristan in north-west Pakistan, there was not a single trained border policeman. Above all, Kandahar, the chief city of Helmand Province, represented the spiritual home of the Taliban and would invariably attract some of its most fanatical fighters to drive out the hated British *feringhee*. The province had significantly been the last to fall when the Taliban Government was overthrown in 2001.

It was an area of deep historical resonance for the British. In the First Anglo-Afghan War, as we have seen, it had been a notorious problem area for the thinly spread British troops struggling to uphold the unpopular government of Shah Shuja. Even then it was characterized by low tax yields and frequent direct defiance of Central Government authority in Kabul. It was the scene of a major tax revolt by the Durrani tribal confederacy in 1841, which arguably represented the start of the collapse of British authority in the region. During the Second Anglo-Afghan War it had been the scene of the major British disaster at Maiwand in July 1880 (a rare Afghan victory which is still embedded in local Afghan memory today),[46] and which was only remedied by General Roberts' famous desperate relief march from Kabul to Kandahar and the decisive battle of Kandahar in September 1880. Equally ominously, and in direct relation to current operations, the British had already been unfavourably associated with the hated Americans, whose bombing raids in the earlier 2001–2 offensive had caused major civilian casualties in the area. As one Taliban spokesman put it:

Bush and Blair are like the twin ears of the horse. They are the same. We don't care if we win or lose. Our only goal is to do jihad. If you look at history you will see we have defeated the British three times despite their equipment being thirty times stronger. If we tolerate some losses we will be able to beat them again.[47]

Ironically, neither the British military nor even British politicians had any illusions about the difficulties awaiting them in Helmand. In the House of Commons even Defence Secretary Reid, in one of his more considered moments, forecast many 'risks and difficulties'. Described by one correspondent as 'the Faluja of Afghanistan only bigger', one officer of the Royal Green Jackets readily admitted that: 'Coming to a province where there has been no military presence at all and with so many problems we are bound to draw fire. It really is like poking a stick in the hornet's nest.'[48]

In socio-economic terms, Helmand Province had represented a virtual no-go area for development and reconstruction. With over a thousand aid agencies established in Kabul by 2006, only five were active in Helmand because they and the UN considered the area unsafe. There had been no international relief force there until a US-led provincial reconstruction team (PRT) was established in 2005 in Lashkargar, the provincial capital.

The British mission mandate for tackling this neglected region, overrun with corrupt warlords and hardened Taliban fighters, initially abrogated any further focus on war-fighting. In January 2006, Defence Secretary Reid reassured the House of Commons that the British force would no longer be there to 'wage war' or carry out the 'seek and destroy' operations the Americans had mounted. Instead the British mission was defined as one of denying terrorists 'an ungoverned space in which they can ferment and export terrorism, building up the Afghan state and security forces and supporting anti-narcotic efforts'.[49] Brigadier Ed Butler, commander of the British task force, confirmed that the initial British plan was 'very simple ... build up forces increasingly and start to expand our operations ... in conjunction with the Foreign Office aims and objectives and the development and reconstruction aims of DfiD, that was the thinking'.[50] At ground level, support troops worked frantically to prepare for this great 'British invasion'. Engineer Captain Nick Colvin recalled: 'Our focus was to prepare for 16 Air Assault Brigade's first foray and the emphasis was getting everything ready for them. The war seemed to be waiting for the "Maroon Machine" to arrive.'[51]

Within weeks of this (in hindsight) grossly over-optimistic political mandate, the newly arrived British troops, drawn principally from the 3rd Battalion Parachute Regiment (3 Para), 13 Air Assault Group and 27 Squadron RAF, and based in the three main towns of Lashkargar, Kandahar and Girishk, were plunged into some of the most bitter and intense fighting since the Korean War. It reflected a sudden relapse to a predominantly war-fighting strategy in which reconstruction and development policies were again relegated to the lowest priority. For weeks on end, under the still-controversial and infamous 'platoon house strategy' (where troops were spread so thinly they termed them 'platoon houses'), British units were dispatched to defend often indefensible remote local government centres. By September 2006 this costly strategy had resulted in fifteen British dead and many wounded.

How did this strategic volte-face happen? In fact the crisis stemmed directly from British obligations to the increasingly discredited Karzai Government and in 2006 it was that body's fears of a total loss of control of this lawless southern region which sucked Whitehall and local British military commanders (virtually devoid of local intelligence and estimating only 1,000 Taliban fighters) into this still-controversial and costly military campaign. In early 2006 the *Sunday Times* revealed that, in response to the British offensive, Taliban fighters had overrun the Karzai Government's major district centre at Baghan and, by mid-May 2006, were launching probing attacks upon other key government centres at Musa Qala, Nawzad and Sangin.[52] Brigadier Ed Butler, the commander of the British of southern Afghanistan (principally 16 Air Assault Brigade), who, in line with his political masters had initially and optimistically announced that 'we are not going out to look for trouble', was soon sucked into this local political crisis as the Karzai Government 'put pressure on the British to act'.[53] Moreover, it was a pressure reflecting a more sinister motivation as it reflected also President Karzai's personal desire to protect his own loyal Alokazai Pashtun clan domiciled in the area of conflict As British troops were forced to adapt to the highly controversial tactic of defending these remote outposts, described by one British soldier as 'murderous hell holes', and propping up and protecting often corrupt government officials, Butler later outlined the impossible dilemma he had been confronted with: 'If the leader of a pro-western Islamic state that has adopted democratic government and principles asked for your support you are in quite an awkward position to say no.' The local Helmand Governor, Mohammed Daoud, had been particularly blunt with him: 'If you don't go in and do as we ask what is the point of you being here ... you might as well go home',[54] although Daoud later claimed it was a consensual decision with Brigadier Butler.

The British political authorities had been misled by their own ally. As Michael Semple, Deputy Head of the EU Mission 2005–7, duly observed, local people were 'infuriated' when it became clear that 'the same people were in place' and 'the British were seen as tricked.' But, if it was largely a politically led débâcle it was also arguably a significant *military* blunder if some elements of the British media can be believed. As *The Times* reported in January 2006, '*Service chiefs* made it clear that the Armed Forces could cope with running two significant operations at the same time,'[55] a comment which possibly also reflected a military desire to compensate for or divert attention away from Britain's clearly and rapidly declining fortunes and reputation in the Iraq theatre at this time.

While agreeing that the presence of platoon houses had acted as a 'magnet for Taliban forces', Brigadier Butler, in his defence, also pointed out that, tactically, the strategy had not been without some benefits. Butler correctly stressed that the British 'never lost a platoon house' and that if his troops had not gone north, the Taliban front line would have run along the main road from Kandahar thus 'cutting the province in two'. 'We would', he asserted, 'have had the enemy on our doorstep'. Moreover, the platoon houses had acted as a 'breakwater' for the Taliban, who had 'thrown themselves against them repeatedly and been overwhelmingly beaten'.[56] In his operational planning, Butler was also deeply compromised by problems of command and control as he was bombarded by competing action plans by other Coalition commanders. Again, NATO politics and competing national caveats had resulting in 'plenty of ambiguity as to which plan everybody was working to'.[57] As British ISAF commander

General Richards later confirmed: 'it wasn't helpful that Ed Butler ... did not have command of his own brigade as far as the Americans and NATO commanders were concerned'.[58]

It was a brave defence of what was essentially, for Butler and other British ground-level commanders, an impossible political dilemma in which the British were the military 'fall guys'. They had been inadvertently sucked into the quagmire of local ethnic politics. In retrospect, despite Butler's sound military perceptions, the blood-price paid was still probably too high and the political ramifications outweighed any military imperatives. For British troops of 16 Air Assault Brigade, including the crack 3rd Parachute Regiment, so brutally dumped 'on the doorstep' of this battle, the experience was traumatic, if not horrendous. One British major of 3 Para revealed, for example, how his isolated platoon house based in Sangin, a strategically vital post located at the entrance to the Bagram Valley, had been attacked thirty times in thirty-four days.[59] The intense, relentless nature of the fighting had often involved close-quarter combat and left his men forced to sleep in their body armour, with weapons permanently by their sides and sweltering in temperatures reaching as high as 60 °C/140 °F! Again, equipment shortages and lack of training for the limited stocks of new equipment were the major focus of complaints. On 28 April, Major Will Pike wrote: 'Bit of an issue over ballistic protection for the vehicles, not enough to go round, manufacturer cannot make them fast enough, all of which comes back to the delayed announcement of the deployment and thus no activation of budgets – and no kit.... Feel that we are badly let down.' Two days later he observed: 'A day marked by comms. [communications] difficulties. We have Bowman Secure HF and Tascat, however both are relatively new to the blokes and so we are not yet skilled in their use. Added to which the HF is not at its best in arid conditions and the Tascat needs to be pointed in the right bearing and elevation.' On 16 April he reiterated: 'Comms system is woeful. It is staggering that with all the problems over Iraq we still cannot get this right.'[60]

Criticisms were even levelled at the impotence or 'utter uselessness' of RAF support, but it was soon made clear that they, also, were unprepared and under-resourced for these sudden politically driven and unexpected new tasks. One 3 Para officer was more empathetic with the RAF dilemma, writing: 'The light levels were such that the aircraft couldn't really fly at night – there was not enough ambient light for their Night Vision Goggles to work. There was also the risk to crew and air frame to be considered.'[61] One officer of the Royal Regiment of Fusiliers further reflected on the anger and frustration felt by many British officers and troops over this costly strategy: 'The scale of casualties has not been properly reported and shows no sign of reducing. Political and not military imperatives are being followed in this campaign.'[62] Under incessant Taliban attack another officer lambasted the failure, as late as the end of June 2006, to adjust Rules of Engagement (ROE) to what had become all-out war-fighting. He wrote home: 'We remain constrained by self defence ROE – essentially, we must wait for them to fire first – although there is talk of putting us onto Measure 429 – in essence, war fighting ROE.'[63] At least two British officers later resigned their commissions in disgust over the conduct and equipping of this operation.

Equally damning was the continuing chronic lack of intelligence and logistical support, the latter leading to serious overstretch. Few lessons had apparently been learnt from the previous five years. One officer of the Scots Guards, for instance, on entering 'bloody Sangin' in May 2006, was 'horrified' to discover that his unit had so little intelligence they did not even know the location of the district chiefs' headquarters: 'We fought our way into town and then were literally asking people where the building was', he recalled. 'Our intelligence was zero. Absolute, f— zero.'[64]

There was also a chronic lack of manpower to support these and other outposts, such as Nawzad and Kajaki, with the defending British troops 'often running out of food because of the dangers of re-supply' and even 'forced to drink canal water'. Unable to take the offensive, 'men were also left fighting hand to hand or reliant on bombing from the likes of A10 tank busters'.[65] As one senior MOD official admitted in June 2006: 'Every single location where we have troops is now coming under attack every single day.'[66]

As in the previous Afghan wars, at the back of every British soldier's mind was the fear of being captured alive by such a ruthless and fanatical foe who took no prisoners: 'Had I been captured the mind boggles, there is no way I would have survived but it is more the manner of one's death that frightens, and the aftermath – perhaps strung up in the bazaar!... Certainly I would have fired every last round.... But would I leave a round for myself and would I have been able to do it?'[67]

With such intense fire-fights there were frequent shortages of ammunition, with some garrisons forced to borrow ammunition from their Canadian allies. By early September 2006, British forces had already expended over 400,000 rounds of ammunition. All this contributed to a sense of abandonment by the Government: 'The initial strain of our stay in Sangin', wrote on officer, 'came from this slight feeling of "abandonment" in a barely viable location with lots of enemy about. Dien Bien Phu came to mind on occasion.'[68] As reporter Stephen Grey observed: 'Some senior officers felt that they had been betrayed by the politicians.'[69]

Certainly, at the root of the problem lay the initially poor intelligence and both political and military strategic planning resulting in budgetary and equipment shortfalls. Major Will Pike, 3 Para Company Commander again opined:

> This has been the most extraordinary and in many respects saddening build up to a deployment. At its core the problem seems to have stemmed at the strategic level. First, the UK waited till January to formally declare that we would commit even though it was clear a year ago that there was no credible alternative to committal. Hence the rush at the operational level. Second once the decision was made and the plans developed, those at PJHQ and higher have resolutely refused to allow the plans to be altered despite events on the ground suggesting they should be. The impact of this higher level ignorance of sound military principles has evidence in morale and physical areas – huge uncertainty and constant changes of plan, so ... the soldiers feel f.cked about and think that much less of the chain of command.[70]

This watershed year of 2006 exemplified other problems for a new British policy, which had aimed at minimal military activity and a new focus on winning Afghan hearts and minds, thereby achieving longer-term social peace and stability. In this unexpected and destructive war of attrition, in which British forces, rather than containing their Taliban enemy, had been drawn into almost continual war-fighting, the much-vaunted 'ink-spot strategy', which envisaged social and economic development slowly spreading outwards from designated secure zones, was being deeply undermined. As one British Captain, Leo Docherty, succinctly observed, social peace was unattainable with such aggressive tactics.

> We had all these study days before deploying, looking at how we dealt with the Malayan insurgency of the 1950s and how we were going to use the same strategy of first creating the secure zones or ink-spots around the main locations of Lashkar Gah and Gereshk and then move out. The whole focus was supposed to be not high intensity but construction of a nation state. Instead we've deviated spectacularly from the plan and scattered in a meaningless way across northern towns of Helmand. To withdraw from these now would be seen as defeat and the only way to survive is to increase the level of violence.[71]

The focus on *destruction* rather than *construction* and the lack of any developmental input was staggering. In early May, one officer wrote home: Because DfID and NGO's obsess about separation, they become easier targets for the insurgents, who then wreck their work, thus they stop working and no development takes place – whereas if they would only embrace a civil-military concept ... then they could work within a security blanket that the insurgent would find hard to penetrate, and thus tangible benefits would come to the people.... What is so frustrating is that it is so obvious and simple that this must be the way. It is this approach and not military activity alone that will finally finish off the Taliban.[72]

The executive director of the SENLIS Council identified the 'trap' or political and military quagmire the British and, by proxy, her Coalition allies were now in:

We're adding violence to violence ... each time we kill so-called Taliban we are creating new enemies. Not only is there no hearts and minds happening in the south; it's the exact opposite. The international community needs to realise that the whole nature of the insurgency has changed. You are no longer fighting a group of trouble makers but a civil war where you're perceived as having taken one side.[73]

It was a comment which elicits striking parallels to the previous 'jihad crises' which confronted the British authorities in the summer of 1841 prior to the Kabul insurrection, and Viceroy Lytton and Major-General Roberts immediately prior to the Battle of Sherpur in December 1879.

The political situation was exacerbated by the increasing incidences of 'unfriendly fire'. Over 15,000 Afghan civilians had been killed between January 2006 and June 2007, many from American bombing. As tribal elders curtly informed American liaison officers at Khogiani in June 2007, 'You apologise but you keep making mistakes'.[74] The political damage caused to the Karzai Government by this excessive behaviour by their Western allies was also becoming ominously more evident. On a rare visit outside Kabul to the village of Shiband, a frustrated and embarrassed President Karzai struggled to explain Coalition excesses to tribal elders at one *shura* (meeting) who had bitterly complained of scores of casualties caused by Allied bombing, including many women and children. 'Foreign troops, he asserted 'are like painful drugs that cure a disease but have powerful side effects as well.'[75]

The dislocation of thousands of Afghan civilians as a result of the intense fighting of 2006, combined with the comparatively small funds spent on development by the autumn of 2006, could only reinforce negative Afghan perceptions of the British presence. One source tellingly pointed out that, in 2006 that while $822.5 billion (£44.2 billion) had been spent on military operations since 2002, only $7.3 billion had been expended on development! The British, as leaders of opium eradication in Helmand Province and by their extreme level of military activity, had understandably dealt a further blow to local Afghan confidence with 'a pervasive belief that the British forces are only in Helmand to eradicate the poppy'. As one senior officer admitted: 'The Taliban have won the information war ... everyone is convinced we are there to destroy the poppy and thus their livelihood. We're not providing any information to farmers so why should they think different.'[76] *The Times* correspondent Camilla Cavendish put it in a nutshell: 'Afghans faced with overwhelming poverty caused by the West's obliteration of their poppy crops are switching allegiance to the Taliban and other insurgents. You cannot attack poppies and insurgents at the same time. Attacks on one breed the other.'[77]

Colonel Charles Knaggs summed up the terrible dilemma confronting British policy-makers and the rural peoples of Helmand:

People here have a pretty stark choice, either they want the government or the Taliban. They are in a pretty nasty situation. They're held hostage by the poppy and the drug lords on the one side and also held hostage by the Taliban. They can see very little viable alternative. Our *challenge* is to convince people and win them over and a lot of that is providing a secure environment so that the Afghan government and NGOs can then come in with development work.'[78]

Helmand Governor Mohammed Daoud bluntly agreed: 'This is the real challenge.... In fighting terrorism we are fighting Al Qaeda and Taliban but in fighting against drugs we are not fighting them but also our own people.'[79] His preferred solution was to target the middle-men, the drug smugglers, and to close the borders.

This raised other problems in the Security Reform Sector, with a growing emasculation of government police and army contingents in Helmand Province. As the ANP lay largely paralyzed by the intense war-fighting of 2006, the ANA were frequently ambushed and still required British and Coalition support. ANA morale was low and the men were generally unfit for combat. On 26 June Major Pike described the dire situation at FOB (Forward Operation Base) Robinson, some four miles south of hard-pressed Sangin: 'There are about 200 ANA soldiers there but all they do is sit in their sangars. They do not patrol.'[80] Of these two crucial security props of Afghan Government credibility, the deeply demoralized ANP had suffered most. One British officer accordingly described Helmand as a place where police 'don't seem to be able to keep their bodies connected to their heads'.[81] In October 2005, only a few months before the British deployment, one police convoy had lost sixty-five men in a Taliban attack; this in a province with just 540 police and a narcotics squad only thirty strong![82]

Criminality and corruption were rife, further tainting the image of their British allies. At Sangin on 18 June Major Pike reported that the ex-Chief of Police 'had raped a girl in the town. Taliban and the locals were in uproar and he, the current Chief of Police, and thirty ANP/Militia were holed up in the compound to the south of the bazaar'. One day later he wrote that, 'apparently up to forty policemen have been killed and some dragged through the streets'.[83] Worse still, many ANP, already steeped in the drugs trade, were regarded as Taliban sympathizers. In beleaguered Sangin Major Pike's 'worse-case scenario … saw the police (in league with the Taliban) acting as a sort of Trojan Horse followed by a rushed assault by Taliban'. He later added devastatingly: 'We are also sure, by our own observations and EW intercepts, that the police may as well be Taliban. It is immensely disquieting to have such an enemy within.'[84]

For some local British Army commanders, the 2006 Helmand crisis was directly attributable to a failure of British Government policy. COIN strategies had been fatally undermined, not only by a failure of intelligence, but by a total lack of policy co-ordination which had left the army to pick up the pieces. As one officer, Captain Docherty observed:

> We had a two week window where we could have done something and shown local people this is why we're here. But the military is just one side of the triangle and there was no representation by any of the other players (the Foreign Office or Department for International Development). DfID should have been there saying this is the plan, we're going to sink these wells, pave the bazaar, build this bridge. But they would not come because to them it's insecure so they left us unable to offer anything.[85]

For Captain Ben Reid of 45 Royal Marine Commando, the enduring memory was predominantly the 'lack of joined up civil and military co-ordination – many, many agencies all trying to help and do their bit, however all focused on their own area'.[86] Major Will Pike readily concurred:

> The strategic direction of UK operations ... in Afghanistan seems ad hoc, poorly coordinated, and not very well thought through. There seems to be rival strands – military, FCO, DfID and so forth all with their own lines of management, agendas and processes. None seems to be fused very well at the strategic level so that direction downwards is equally incoherent.... There does not seem to be a UK plan for Afghanistan or Helmand.[87]

Such a divide was as much a problem of competing cultures as of planning. As in the earlier Anglo-Afghan Wars, the primary emphasis by the 'politicals' on maintaining political stability and, towards the end of the Empire, upholding human rights, has always been at loggerheads with the traditional 'military mindset' invariably more focused upon quick and efficient victories at minimum loss.

Even General Richards concurred, claiming that the British didn't know enough about Helmand and that the place was undeniably dominated by the drugs lords of one kind or another, It was, he said, 'very difficult to determine just how things would pan out'.[88] Brigadier Butler identified over-cautious officials in London with a 'perception in Whitehall' that, 'all of Helmand was on fire' and that it was 'too risky or too dangerous to do their side of the plan, i.e. reconstruction'.[89]

American General Dan McNeill recalled more localized civil-military friction with a 'constant struggle' between Commander Helmand Task Force and the British Embassy, both 'very important' but 'less effective if not properly coordinated and supportive of one another'.[90]

For some in the military, including a frustrated Colonel Worsley of the Royal Green Jackets, development strategy, particularly drug eradication, was perhaps understandably not even perceived as part of the British Army agenda. 'Counter narcotics is the FO's responsibility. We certainly won't be marching into fields and stripping poor farmers of their crops or taking them away at gun point or searching vehicles for drug barons.'[91]

Liam Fox, the British Shadow Defence Secretary, concurred. In May 2006 he also lambasted the fact that there 'appears to be complete confusion about British objectives which included reconstruction, military training, assistance with poppy eradication and COIN'.[92]

For some, perhaps more cynical observers, the new British offensive in Helmand represented merely a further example of her damaging deferential position in regard to her superpower ally, the USA, who it was argued, remained obsessed with Iraq and the capture of Bin Laden. In the view of

Simon Jenkins:

> Britain is being set up by the Americans in Afghanistan. Donald
> Rumsfeld, the US Defence Secretary, regards that country as past
> history, a forward base for terrorist-hunting and 'interrogation'. Some
> 10,000 troops are still combing the mountains seeking Osama Bin
> Laden with bounties and disregard for law or international bound-
> aries. Anyone can be killed anywhere; anyone bombed. As for 'nation
> building', Washington is not interested. It has installed Hamid Karzai
> in Kabul and protects him. That is enough.[93]

American pressure for the already overstretched British to be even more
proactive was felt at ground level. Noting in mid-April 2006 how US ODA
activity had already been 'deeply unhelpful and irresponsible', Major Will
Pike cynically observed: 'US pressure building for a series of ambitious
offensive options towards mid/end May. Talking about defeating the
Taliban insurgency – cloud cuckoo land – with what is a two week, temporary offensive with no lasting effect. Too many parallels with the books I
am reading on Indo-China!'[94]

If the Helmand crisis was a problem exacerbated by our closest ally it
was, once again, equally exacerbated by the policies of other Coalition
partners, particularly those in NATO. The Dutch, for instance had, by late
2006, already shown a reluctance to commit more combat troops to
Helmand. In the north also, the French and Germans had shown no signs
of willingness to increase their troop contributions. On the southern
border, British commanders and diplomats were further 'horrified' by the
proposal of their key regional ally, Pakistan, to withdraw its troops from
the border province of North Waziristan where over 700 Pakistani regulars
had already been killed, a decision which would obviously provide an even
greater safe haven for Al Qaeda and Taliban operatives.

Above all, the Helmand campaign of 2006 revealed as never before the
wider strategic overstretch of British forces lacking both the full support of
her NATO allies and struggling to meet the accelerating demands of a two-
front war in Iraq and Afghanistan. Even the enemy recognized the
unfolding crisis. As a spokesman for the reclusive Taliban leader, Mullah
Omar, dramatically put it: 'The British don't have the capacity to fight us
face to face. We are here to destroy the British. We will hunt and kill them.
We will not let them go back to England and say that they have defeated
the Afghans.'[95] One *Jane's Defence Weekly* reporter identified a serious
operational overstretch in Helmand as early as July 2006, particularly in
terms of the vital support helicopter fleet whose commanders 'did not
envisage UK armed forces involved long term in two current medium scale

operations as they are now in Afghanistan and Iraq'.[96] On 29 June 2006 a big 'military beast', retired Field Marshal Lord Inge, former Chief of the Defence Staff, entered the political fray. He spoke in a House of Lords' defence debate in which he angrily accused the British Government of 'breaking the basic rules of military tactical and operational level planning'. UK forces, he asserted, were in danger of being stretched too thin, with no adequate reserve in theatre 'ready and available' in Helmand Province or for General David Richards, the new commander of the Allied Rapid Reaction Corps. 'Where is the main effort?' Lord Inge asked. 'Is it Iraq or is it Afghanistan? I sense there is lack of European political will and European military capability to support both theatres of operation adequately.... I hope we are not making the mistake of trying to be strong everywhere and ending up being strong nowhere.'[97]

Further evidence of crisis was provided by the SENLIS report, 'Afghanistan Five Years Later: The Return of the Taliban'. Published in the summer of 2006, this damning report concluded that the situation in Afghanistan was far worse than in 2001, with the Taliban holding 'a strong grip on the southern half of the country and with international military coalition forces failing to secure their 2001 objectives to "guarantee a secure and stable Afghanistan"'. Instead the country was on the 'verge of collapse'. The report noted that the 'militarised failed counter-narcotics strategies have destroyed many Afghans livelihoods'. These policies had, in turn, 'eroded confidence in the Afghan government and international community' and, it asserted, the Taliban was sweeping into power over the back of rural communities frustrated and disappointed. The report gave three main recommendations; firstly that international security forces 'must stop killing civilians, secondly they must counter Taliban propaganda 'ideally through sequenced viable alternative development projects that would enable Afghan farmers to survive on crops other than the poppy' and, finally it was necessary to 'enable the development of emergency poverty relief ... in particular, international military forces could play a pivotal role in delivering food aid and necessary healthcare to insurgent areas'.[98]

This official perception was reinforced by perceptions at ground level where the British were seen as inextricably linked to the corrupt Karzai administration At a *shura* of about sixty local tribal leaders, conducted at Sangin on 22 June 2006, Major Pike scribbled in his diary:

The main theme seems to be that they would rather we went away, since our presence would guarantee a fight with the Taliban, which would affect business in the bazaar. They would rather live under the coercive terror of the Taliban than actively help us, or the Afghan Government. I stated that we had no intention of leaving and that our presence was the first indication of the Afghan Government commitment to reconstruction in the area. This didn't seem to convince them, with some justification, since the Afghan Government has done basically nothing for these people in four years and is seen to be largely corrupt. The lesson is clear – we must demonstrate a tangible benefit of Afghan governance to the people.[99]

A second SENLIS Council report, issued in June 2006 and entitled 'Helmand at War' reiterated many of their previous recommendations, but further insisted that 'all opium eradication operations must stop' and more clarification of rules of engagement 'must be given'. It added two recommendations specific to Helmand Province. One, regarding border control, stressed the urgent need to develop a more assertive strategy to tackle the problem of insurgent safe havens in Pakistan by greater co-operation with Pakistan and by 'acknowledging the democratisation of Pakistan as a key to the security of Afghanistan' and, perhaps, most significantly, giving 'cross border Pashtun tribes ... the opportunity to participate in the development of stabilisation efforts in the region'. The fourth recommendation focused specifically on British policies in Helmand. This stressed the need for *balance*. 'British troops in Helmand should adopt a new stabilisation doctrine to reverse the negative legacy of the OEF operations in Helmand and break the vicious circle of violence'. The report concluded that the troops: 'must balance a robust and well targeted use of force with a far reaching development effort. A peaceful and sustainable outcome in Helmand and in Afghanistan at large cannot be determined only by military means – comprehensive and long term developmental efforts must be instigated which take into account the needs of the local population.'[100]

By early September 2006 the cost of the Helmand campaign in men and material was proving unacceptable for some senior military commanders The tragic loss on 2 September of a Nimrod aircraft with all fourteen crew killed allegedly owing to a combination of equipment failure and MOD neglect apparently 'triggered thoughts of retreat'. According to Brigadier Butler, the ensuing heated debate he was drawn into involved 'six or seven opinions', some advocating that 'we must withdraw' and others, including General Richards and the Afghan Government, demanding that 'on no account must you withdraw ... because of the effect on the prestige of the British army and the effect on the Taliban' who would 'claim they had defeated us'.[101]

Sir Jock Stirrup was among those who initially 'wanted to pull out' querying, 'Was there any reconstruction going on?' and 'Was there any plan to deliver governance ... the answer was patently "No".'[102] Richards vetoed a pullout 'which ... would have been a defeat of British arms ... a very difficult thing to contemplate', whilst conceding that: 'Half a year into the British entry into Helmand reconstruction had turned into war ... neither side was winning.'[103] In the event a compromise was found, with the British reaching a negotiated deal with local representatives to pull out of Musa Qala in return for promises to keep the Taliban out. Unfortunately, the deal only lasted three days before Taliban forces again infiltrated the vacated town.

This apparent setback horrified Britain's most powerful ally. Many American commanders saw it as a British defeat and as setting a 'dangerous precedent' for the future. A horrified General Dan McNeill opined that British commanders should 'never negotiate unless you can do so from a position of strength', noting that forces 'were far too thin in the south'. He likened the situation to a 'chess game ... jumping here, jumping there and trying to get something in check ... it's challenging when you are under-resourced' with 'no fixed lines' and 'no really safe places where development work could take place'.[104] Arguably this event triggered off a growing crisis of confidence within American leadership circles regarding British tactics and their overall ability to hold Helmand. For a somewhat defensive General Richards, however, it was by no means a tactical error but 'based on Petraeus's Iraq approach ... an early experiment in giving the tribal elders influence'.[105]

In the wake of these reports and the withdrawal from Musa Qala, in themselves scathing indictments of the failure of its COIN strategy, the British Labour Government also faced a torrent of criticism directed both from both the Opposition parties and the British media in the early autumn of 2006. On the back of two major critical articles published in *The Times*, stressing 'military and developmental anarchy'[106] and biting criticism from David Cameron, Leader of the Conservative opposition (who, in broader terms, had deprecated Britain's 'slavish' bonds with the USA), the Government faced a particularly bitter attack by veteran war correspondent Sir Max Hastings. In September 2006, in a damning indictment of the Government's Afghanistan policies, he observed that: 'Not a man here has forgotten John Reid's declaration that the Army was not going into Helmand to fight terrorists ... the minister said in one of many grossly misleading government statements, our troops would be able to go home having done their job of helping Afghan reconstruction "without a shot being fired".' Asserting that 3 Para had alone experienced '320 contacts' with the Taliban since May 2006, with '300,000 rounds of rifle and machine gun ammunition and 2,500 mortar rounds expended and the loss of eleven men dead and thirty-five wounded', Hastings observed that, 'While the original British plan may have made political sense ... it was military nonsense. It simply provided the Taliban with fixed targets which they have exploited to the full.' He continued: 'Back in 2002 and 2003 if the Americans and their allies had got down seriously to the business of sorting out this country instead of rushing off to invade Iraq it might have been a relatively easy and cheap task to sort it out'. In a comment which conjured up powerful historical memories of the First Anglo-Afghan War, when Shah Shuja's increasingly paralyzed government was propped up by British bayonets, he noted that: 'In the intervening four years, though elections had been held and a president installed, his writ runs little further than local warlords will allow and by a stunning consequence of Western neglect Afghanistan has become the largest narco-economy in the world, growing more than one billion pounds worth of opium poppies a year'. Hastings concluded: 'This country may well be solvable. But if we want to assist with the attempt the government must start telling the truth about what the rescue operation will cost in terms of the lives of our soldiers.'[107]

Two weeks after this article was published the Government became more 'economical with the truth'. In a major speech delivered to the Royal United Service Institute, the then Labour Defence Secretary, Des Browne, finally admitted that the Government had grossly underestimated the enemy. 'The Taliban tenacity in the face of massive losses', he confessed, 'has been a surprise, absorbing more of our effort than predicted and consequently slowing progress on reconstruction.' Revealing that there had been 'little progress' on building up public institutions and infrastructure in southern Afghanistan and with security 'some way off', Browne worryingly concluded: 'Success won't be what we understand by security and prosperity and proper governance, but it will be progress and it will be massively worth achieving.'[108]

It was left to another major SENLIS international think-tank report, aptly entitled 'Countering the Insurgency in Afghanistan: Losing friends and making enemies', to both sum up and confirm the débâcle in Coalition and particularly British COIN strategies after the first five years of the Afghan conflict:

The practice of counter-insurgency in Afghanistan has so far predominantly focused on military instruments to fight against the insurgency. By doing this it has wrongfully left out all the non-military elements that form part of counter-insurgency theory: for example humanitarian aid, economic development, establishing health care and developing the educational system ... what Afghans in the south see in their daily lives from the international community are mere negative policy instruments. They see military bombing campaigns, where bombs do not distinguish between innocent civilians and insurgents. The policy of poppy eradication reinforces poverty and fuels anger both towards the government and the international community, while it also provides the insurgency with an easy recruitment base.[109]

The result was a substantial rethink of policy in the late autumn of 2006 and spring of 2007. It represented a discernible change in British political and military policies towards Afghanistan. It heralded what I would contend was a distinct third phase in Britain's Afghanistan policies; an emergence from a distinct political and military quagmire to a new phase of slow internal military containment and stabilization, increased reconstruction and development and a political regionalization of the Afghanistan crisis.

Phase 3: Containment, Stabilization, Dialogue and Regional Peace

The 'politicals' led the way. Following Des Browne's 'confession' in September 2006 of major shortfalls in British strategy, Prime Minister Blair, on a November 2006 visit to Afghanistan, launched a new political initiative. He renewed British long-term political and military commitments to the Afghanistan campaign. 'Here in this extraordinary piece of desert is where the future of the world's security in the early 21st century is going to be played out',[110] he told 600 service men and women in a high-security visit to Camp Bastion, the British main base in Helmand. This was widely seen as an attempt to refocus international attention away from Iraq and into Al Qaeda's heartland. Prime Minister Blair followed through with a major attack on Iran for allegedly arming the Taliban in order to stir 'chaos and inflict more casualties on British and other Western troops'.[111] In January 2007 Blair followed up his 'war zone' speech by placing a renewed emphasis upon the crucial importance of the hitherto neglected socio-economic side of Britain's COIN strategies: 'In truth this is a hearts and minds battle as much as a military one. Reconstruction and reconciliation, development and governance are every bit as crucial ... in Afghanistan as military might. Indeed the might is only effective as a means of making possible the political progress. We do this better than most countries, perhaps better than any.'[112]

It was a belated official recognition of a deeply imbalanced policy in which essential internal Afghan reconstruction and development had been afforded a dangerously low priority. Blair's successor, Prime Minister Gordon Brown, heavily reinforced Blair's initiatives. In December 2007 he also reiterated Britain's commitment to a long haul in order to 'isolate and eradicate' the Taliban, with full support pledged to President Karzai 'over the next few years'. Even more significantly, while emphasizing that there would be 'no negotiations' with the 'senior Taliban leaders', he confirmed a new emphasis on dialogue with key tribal groups. Britain, he asserted, would support efforts by the Afghanistan Government to negotiate with tribal fighters now supporting the Taliban, 'but only if they support democracy'. He talked of giving Afghanistan a new economic stake in the future with 'high impact projects designed to show the rewards to be had from beating the Taliban'. More military support was promised, notably 150 additional patrol vehicles and a further £450 million in development aid, scheduled to run from 2009 to 2012.[113]

The political results of this regeneration of Britain's Afghan strategy were soon seen at several levels. In 2007, at one level, the British diplomatic presence in Afghanistan was massively boosted by news of the appointment of a new dynamic ambassador, Sir Sherard Cowper-Coles and the arrival of thirty-five extra staff at the British Embassy in Kabul. This highly significant diplomatic upgrade was complemented by a firm public commitment by Cowper-Coles to a long-term British presence in Afghanistan. It was, Cowper-Coles asserted, 'a marathon rather than a sprint'. As John Simpson, the veteran BBC World Affairs Correspondent confirmed, it was a 'huge commitment' of up to thirty years, as envisaged by this new enthusiastic diplomatic 'big hitter'. Cowper-Coles stressed a fresh commitment to long-term confidence-building and stabilization: 'Their worry isn't about us staying, it's about us going, about us not taking the job of standing up for the police, standing up for the security forces, standing up for the judicial system, putting schools and hospitals in place.'[114]

At ground level, Britain unilaterally began secret talks with tribal leaders and Taliban 'moderates' in Helmand (or 'mullah lites' as they were irreverently called), a policy which, while controversial, had already borne fruit in Northern Ireland in the late 1980s and 1990s and more recently in peace talks with Shia insurgent leaders in Basra, Iraq. The British secret and intelligence services were heavily involved in a policy of 'divide and rule'. *The Times* outlined the new strategy:

British intelligence services had divided the Taliban into three tiers: the hardcore leaders that reject any kind of reconciliation and has strong links with Al Qaeda; a middle layer that is committed to the cause but is not necessarily beyond redemption, and the massed ranks of tier three who comprise young, out-of-work Afghans or hard-up farmers who fight for the Taliban for £5–10 a day. Officials believe that there is scope for persuasion with the middle and lower tiers.[115]

It was a high-risk policy and not without initial short-term setbacks. Earlier, for instance, the overrunning of the key strategic town of Musa Qala by Taliban forces had effectively destroyed one British negotiated truce drawn up in the autumn of the previous year. Similarly, the brutal murder of eight moderate Waziri tribal leaders at Wana (an old British outpost) in north Waziristan in the border badlands, on the orders of the key Taliban leader, Baitullah Mehsud, only emphasized how risky and long-term any policy of engagement might have to be.[116] Nevertheless, it was an enduring policy implemented with the full support of the then Defence Secretary Des Browne who, whilst acknowledging in March 2008 that the situation in Afghanistan remained 'on a knife edge', stressed that Afghanistan was 'a playground for terrorists. If we don't deal with these people there then they will come to us.' Britain, he reaffirmed, should be talking to extremist groups: 'What you need to do in conflict resolution is to bring the people who believe that the answer to their political ambitions will be achieved through violence into a frame of mind that they accept that their political ambitions will be delivered by politics.'[117]

The British efforts to talk to their enemy in Helmand, initially a unilateral and clandestine policy which was probably partly designed to avoid too close an association with the increasingly discredited Karzai Government, has predictably led to some friction with the latter. Thus two UN-sponsored officials, Mervyn Pattison and Michael Semple, were expelled by President Karzai for setting up talks with Taliban leaders. As *The Times* observed: 'The duo's trip to Helmand, which was made with British military assistance, was to an area where links with the Taliban are essential to survive and was made at a time when the British military is attempting to peel off enemy fighters from the insurgency by persuading them to defect.'[118] It was seen by many as a somewhat hypocritical intervention by a Kabul Government desperately seeking credibility. As Semple himself revealed, he had contacted around 200 Taliban commanders with 'the approval of both governments' and 'the idea that it was covert is patent nonsense', with 'no basis in reality'. He had even 'presented his plans 'on PowerPoint … to Helmand officials and senior officials in Kabul'. His talks, Semple concluded, were mistakenly seen as 'weakening Karzai's hold on power'.[119] As even a Taliban spokesperson observed: 'This is a drama by Karzai's administration trying to show off that they are independent. We're amazed why Karzai would show sensitivity to the fact that they had met with the Taliban while he himself publicly says he is ready to meet the Taliban.'[120]

The British military were not slow to respond to these new political initiatives. In early September 2006 ISAF commander, Lieutenant-General David Richards, had even predicted that the military tide was slowly turning. Whilst tacitly admitting to the failure of the 'platoon house strategy' – 'The platoon houses were occupied before I took control ... I am not going to be critical, but they are only one tactic. They have some bene-fits'– he revealed stunning success in the ongoing 'Operation Medusa' where 500 insurgents had already died. Designed to drive the Taliban away from the crucial city of Kandahar, 'Operation Medusa' had caused signifi-cant losses to the estimated 7,000 full and part-time Taliban fighters. Later, American General James Jones estimated that 1,000 Taliban fighters were killed in this operation with only six NATO fatalities.[121]

By October 2006 the switch from failing 'ink-spots' to Afghanistan Development Zones (ADZs) had also commenced. One of the first desig-nated areas stretched from Gereshk to the provincial capital of Lashkar Gah, an area some twenty-five miles long by twelve miles wide. It was the embryonic start of a new policy appraisal, particularly by the British mili-tary which, it was admitted, had hitherto been 'slanted more to war fighting than to reconstruction'.[122] From 2007, British troops, notably 42 Royal Marines Commando, were focused specifically on protecting key development projects such as the Kajaki Dam where, for instance, the contract firm, Louis Berger, demanded a six-kilometre buffer zone, free from Taliban attack before getting to work. As Britain's most senior officer in Helmand, Brigadier Mark Carleton-Smith confirmed eighteen months later, it was now his 'main job ... not to go after Taliban insur-gents but to use his soldiers to win the hearts and minds of the Afghan people'. He summed up the new, more balanced, British COIN strategy:

The Taliban military effort is on the back foot so we want to isolate and marginalize the Taliban and then set the conditions to ensure that Afghan government and rule of law can proceed in the province ... while 2006 was enemycentric, its now about the Afghan people and the flavour for 2008 will be about securing the civilian population.[123]

It represented a decisive tactical switch from 'clear' to 'clear, hold and build' and was a response welcomed by General Dannatt, the then head of the British Army, who, while emphasizing that Britain faced a long-term commitment 'on the edge of a new and deadly Great Game in Afghanistan' and confronting a 'strident Islamist shadow', extolled the 'significant achievement in Afghanistan as a short-term objective for the army'.[124]

Within this security umbrella, Special Forces contingents have maintained an aggressive policy of assassination of those key Taliban and Al Qaeda leaders considered to be irreconcilable. For instance, up to seventy-five were killed in 2006 and, in May 2007, a British fifty-man Special Boat Service squadron successfully eliminated Mullah Dadullah, identified as 'the highest profile leader to be killed since the US-led invasion of Afghanistan in 2001'. In the previous two years Dadullah had emerged as the 'brutal linchpin of the resurgent Taliban' and his elimination was widely portrayed as a significant military and intelligence success.[125] Nevertheless, some observers have seen this policy as counterproductive, allowing new, younger and often more radical leaders to emerge, who may be less willing to negotiate.

On the border, a more co-ordinated British politico-military strategy was exemplified by the retaking of the key strategic town of Musa Qala in December 2007. This not only symbolized the slow restoration of British military fortunes but represented a noted triumph for both Britain and her NATO allies and for their security sector reform policies within Afghanistan. In early December, after a ten-day build-up, Britain launched one of her largest military operations since the invasion of Iraq in 2003. She joined a mixed American (primarily 82nd Airborne Division) and ANA force in retaking this vital town, ably supported by RAF and USAF A-10 and Apaches and helicopter gun-ships, notably Chinooks and Blackhawks. A big brigade-sized ANA column, supported by US and British Special Forces, led the advance with 'the emphasis being to persuade Taliban leaders to flee Musa Qala or defect to the government'.[126] It was a new-style military campaign, politically orientated and designed to capitalize on a known Taliban split. One Taliban leader, Mullah Abdul Salaam, had already indicated his wish to defect with one-third of the defenders of Musa Qala.

Up to 3,000 British troops were involved in operation Mar Kardad – nearly half the entire British force in Afghanistan. The force included large units of Royal Marines and the Household Brigade, with about 200 'trainers' (mentors to the Afghan troops) from the 2nd Battalion Yorkshire Regiment fighting alongside the ANA. Defence Secretary Des Browne recognized the prize as one of 'iconic importance' and, as diplomatic correspondent Bronwen Maddox of *The Times* observed, the triumph was not only one of strategic value, 'but even more because the town has become a symbol of the Taliban's ability to resist NATO and Afghan forces'. It was, she asserted, 'the only town in Afghanistan undeniably under the control of Islamists'.[127] It was a triumph not only for Britain and her NATO allies but for the ANA. As the British commander of forces in Afghanistan, Brigadier Andrew MacKay readily confirmed, 'we kicked the door in and they went through it'.[128] However, one journalist critic, embedded with the attacking forces, disagreed. 'What I saw', Stephen Grey asserted, 'was the British and Americans doing most of the fighting and the Afghans raising the flag'.[129] For Brigadier MacKay, however, the importance lay more in political symbolism for the future: 'We wanted the Afghan army ... hoisting the flag'.[130]

In 2008 in the aftermath of the Musa Qala success, the British military position in Afghanistan was massively bolstered by the arrival of up to 35,000 American troops. The deployment of sizeable contingents of the Marine Expeditionary Force in April 2008, designed in the words of American General Dan McNeill to 'stir things up in the remote southern districts', helped to heal the growing friction between the two nations in relation to American political policy in Afghanistan. America's previous, allegedly over-robust force doctrines, leading to mounting incidents of unfriendly fire in which the bombing of Afghan civilian targets had, in the view of some British commentators, deeply undermined Britain's attempts to win hearts and minds in the area. As one British officer scathingly put it in July 2007: 'The Americans will lose the war for us. They have no idea about COIN and they have no idea about winning hearts and minds.' Friction had reached higher policy levels in the wake of 2007, with Britain even accusing her 'special friend' of being fixated with Iraq at the expense of Afghanistan where Britain was 'winning the battles but losing the war'.[131] Another source asserted: 'The Americans see a bit of military success in Afghanistan and think it's all fine. They are blinkered by Iraq and this is becoming symptomatic of a lack of serious engagement on policy across the piste.'[132] Conversely, US officials suspected Prime Minister Brown's Labour Government of sliding out of the 'bad war' in Iraq by concentrating on the 'good war' in Afghanistan and had accused their British military counterparts of mismanaging the Taliban threat in 2006 and underestimating their enemy.[133]

In fact this American 'mini surge', directly inspired by the success of General Petraeus's massive surge in Iraq, produced some distinctly beneficial results. These have included, for instance, a fresh and successful offensive against Garmsir, a major staging post for drug traffickers and Taliban operatives. Conversely, some observers have seen the American reinforcements as a tacit admission that Britain has failed to 'dim the insurgency'.

From a purely military perspective, there were certainly some individual successes from greater Anglo-American co-operation. The combined operations of 200 soldiers of the 2nd Battalion Royal Scots and 1,200 American marines (24 MEU), for instance, were significant successes, with US troops guided by British troops on night-time operations along the southern drug routes. There has also undoubtedly been some underestimation by the British of American progress in their COIN operations in neighbouring provinces. For instance, despite occasional setbacks in Kunar Province, the Americans had supplied, by May 2008, some 2,095 tonnes of aid and built 124 miles of road, nine bridges, twenty clinics and sixteen schools. 'If the daily rate for a fighter is $5 a day then I will pay $5.50 for someone to work on a construction site', asserted American Commander Dan Dwyer, leader of this major reconstruction project in Kunar Province. Overall, in east Afghanistan, American military-led aid PRT efforts have successfully integrated a $280 million (£140 million) reconstruction project.[134]

Moreover, American COIN tactics have considerably improved from the clearly war-fighting dominated strategy of the first three or four years of the current Afghan conflict. Their 're-education' has arguably been significantly underestimated by their British partners. As military historian Dan Marston observes:

> Much of this re-focus in the basics of counter insurgency came about as a result of personnel changes within the command structure of Combined Forces Command/Afghanistan (CFC-A) in 2004 where General David Barro, 'recognized that the focus of the effort should now be on the "Afghan" people and not the hunting down and killing of Al Qaeda and the Taliban'.

With the 'people as the centre of gravity', American military commanders have also recognized that 'a viable army and national police force ... were critical to establishing a stable and secure civil administration'.[135]

Britain's top military commander, the former Chief of the Defence Staff, has gone further, reinforcing an American view that some British officers were arrogant and 'complacent' about their Taliban enemy when first deployed to Helmand in 2006. Echoing the accusations made by Robert Gates, the US Defence Secretary and a number of senior American officers, who claimed that their British counterparts spent too much time boasting about their previous COIN experiences, Sir Jock Stirrup commented: 'I think that we were a bit too complacent about our experiences in Northern Ireland and certainly, on occasion, we were a bit too smug about those experiences.'[136] Indeed, the early fruits of Anglo-American security-sector reform co-operation have been shown not only operationally, through successful battles such as Musa Qala, but also in relation to the major American re-equipping of the ANA. Hundreds of rusty old Russian AK47s have been replaced by the lighter and more adaptable, if less robust, M16 rifle.[137] On a diplomatic level, the Americans have more recently used their great diplomatic clout to pressurize the German Government, in particular, to send more troops to Afghanistan to support those few NATO members who have sent substantial contingents so far (notably Britain, USA, Canada and the Netherlands).

Equally important for Britain were signs of a volte-face in French military policy towards Afghanistan. In March 2008, President Sarkozy boosted French commitment to NATO by dispatching up to 1,000 French troops to the area. As he put it, in suitably Churchillian rhetoric, 'We cannot afford to lose Afghanistan.... We cannot afford to see the Taliban and Al Qaeda returning to Kabul. Whatever the costs, however difficult the victory, we cannot afford it. We must win.'[138]

Nevertheless, the turbulent and porous southern region bordering northwest Pakistan remains the enduring problem, despite several encouraging initiatives by Britain's deeply troubled ally, Pakistan, to the area. It was a problem recognized by several British officers at ground level both during and after the 2006 Helmand crisis as the Taliban drew recruits and supplies from the badlands south of the Helmand border. Thus, on his 2006/7 tour, Royal Marine Captain Ben Reid deeply lamented the 'complete lack of focus on Pakistan' with a 'very narrow focus' in COIN operations on 'the result rather than the source'.[139]

Since 2004 the Government of Pakistan has conducted extensive military operations against Al Qaeda and Taliban groups within its territory and, more recently, have themselves resorted to controversial talks with key tribal leaders. After finally and publicly admitting, in September 2006, that Al Qaeda and Taliban groups were actively using territory in Pakistan to carry out cross-border attacks, but also denying, with significantly less credibility, the widely held belief that extreme Muslim elements in his regime (notably the powerful Inter-Services Intelligence Agency) had been secretly supporting the Taliban, former President Mushariff made serious political and military efforts to counter their activities. However, several offensives by up to 80,000 regular Pakistani troops in the recalcitrant tribal areas of Northern Waziristan in the summer of 2007, aimed at eliminating an estimated 8,000 gunmen, proved to be indecisive and risked the prospect of civil war inside Pakistan. The problem was not helped by the continuing war of words between former President Mushariff and his Afghan counterpart President Karzai. President Karzai has bluntly criticized Mushariff's earlier deals with tribal groups, while Pakistani officials have understandably retorted that they must avoid unnecessarily inflaming internal Muslim opinion and risking civil war. Furthermore, the Pakistani Government has protested that they have been given no credit for the loss of over 700 Pakistani troops in border fighting, or for the successful capture of senior Taliban and Al Qaeda figures. More ominously, in recent times Taliban fighters have extended their grip on this 'wild west' region, even setting up quasi-independent mini-Islamic republics in the north-west tribal districts of Pakistan (principally in Bunar), reportedly threatening the very outskirts of the key border town of Peshawar.

On the socio-economic front there has been, as we have seen, limited but significant progress, not only in some of the American-controlled eastern provinces but, more recently, in small pockets of British-controlled Helmand. Despite pungent criticisms of the effectiveness of Britain's development mission, Mike Foster, Parliamentary Under Secretary of State for the Department for International Development, has pointed out how, by 2009, British aid had 'made a significant difference to millions of ordinary Afghans. In Helmand in 2001 one in four children died before the age of five but, today, thanks to clinics supported by DfID this has been reduced to less than one in five'. He also asserted that, in Helmand: 'We have built 2,000 wells to provide clean water and sanitation for 300, 000 people.'[140]

In terms of development, British political will remains strong. A most striking example occurred in the summer of 2008 when up to 5,000 British troops carried out one of the largest logistical operations of the Afghan conflict and one of the most daring since the Second World War, when they successfully escorted a vital huge turbine to the heavily guarded Kajaki Dam across one hundred miles of heavily mined land. In a complex operation, using classic deception tactics, an estimated two hundred insurgents were killed and, once the turbine is installed, up to two million people in Helmand and Kandahar Provinces will start to receive electricity (although, as critics point out, this is still dependent on the erection of secure power lines and, at the time of writing, the turbines themselves have yet to be fitted to the dam complex). Across Afghanistan five million Afghan children have returned to school and three and a half million refugees have returned home since 2001.

However, the most insidious problem, the drug problem remains. Afghanistan still produces over 90 per cent of the world's heroin and there continues to be considerable NATO disarray over drug eradication policies, particularly between Britain and the USA. The Americans, who currently constitute over two-thirds of NATO's military strength in Afghanistan, have been angered by the British refusal to countenance air-spraying of opium crops in Helmand. Britain, rather than alienating local opinion, has opted for the longer-term policy of training Afghan anti-narcotic teams and persuading farmers to plant alternative crops, notably wheat. By stark contrast, in American-controlled Nangarahr Province, the Americans pushed strongly for eradication, with the local governor arresting growers and destroying crops. While many Afghan farmers reportedly switched to wheat, the long-term impact of such American policies on hearts and minds remains questionable from the British perspective. While PRTs continue important reconstruction work, the proper co-ordination between these nationally run agencies continues to hamper progress.

The Labour Government's policy in Afghanistan, however, did not escape the attention of powerful critics. Leading Afghanistan expert, Professor Rory Stuart, for instance, argued powerfully that not only is there no military solution to the Afghan problem, but that the continuing policy of 'clear, hold and build', which has so far worked in Iraq, is not applicable to the a more decentralized Afghanistan where 'the Kabul Government lacks political depth or legitimacy' and 'the Taliban is elusive'. He advocated reducing the size of the huge and costly Coalition 'military footprint' and using Special Forces and intelligence operations to exclude Al Qaeda whilst continuing to provide long-term financial support to the Afghan Government and its military forces. In this way, he claimed, the Coalition would 'develop a lighter, more affordable and ultimately sustainable relationship with Afghanistan'.[141]

Heavy casualties resulting from Britain's 2009 offensive, 'Operation Panther's Claw', in which Britain lost eight soldiers in twenty-four hours, including Lieutenant-Colonel Rupert Thorniloe, the highest-ranking officer killed since the Falklands War, reignited the debate over both Britain's war aims and the insufficiency of resources allocated to her ever-expanding military tasks in Helmand. The Labour Government of the time, and specifically former PM Gordon Brown, were again directly targeted over a failure to provide appropriate equipment to the troops, and the row led to a major breakdown in civil-military relations. For the first time, there were also signs of a breakdown in the traditional political consensus over the war. General Sir Richard Dannatt, the former Chief of the General Staff (and probably the best-loved British senior officer since Field Marshall Slim), again led the crusade. His assertion that there were too few troops and helicopters in the Afghan war zone to win and hold ground put him at serious odds with the official government line, which contended that the number of troops at the time (around 9,000) were 'sufficient to cope with the offensive'. Furthermore, figures in the Labour Government accused Dannatt of 'playing politics', with one Labour politician scathingly adding: 'General

Dannatt has crossed an important line. He is playing a high-risk game.' Further revelations in leading newspapers alleged, however, that when 'Operation Panther's Claw' was being planned in March 2009, and when the service chiefs supported an option of sending 2,000 additional troops to Afghanistan, the Prime Minister 'chose the cheapest option', opting to send 'only a 700-strong battalion for a limited period'.[142] General Dannatt himself advocated that a total force of 10,000 troops was the minimal requirement. More recently, Dannatt skilfully used the media to step up the pressure for more British helicopters. On a tour of Helmand in mid-July 2009 he used an American Black Hawk helicopter explaining: 'If I moved in an American helicopter it's because I haven't got a British helicopter.'[143] When challenged by the then opposition leader, David Cameron, on 15 July 2009 over the helicopter shortages and high death-toll issues Brown replied: 'I think that we should look at this particular Operation Panther's Claw and be absolutely clear that it is not an absence of helicopters that has cost the loss of lives.' The Prime Minister further stated that helicopter numbers had risen by 60 per cent over the past two years with 84 per cent more lift time.[144] But Cameron's and Dannatt's views were supported by other leading military figures. General Sir Mike Jackson, a former head of the army, told the BBC: 'If a commander wanted to make a manoeuvre by air and ... because there weren't available helicopters and he was forced therefore to do it on the ground against his own judgement, then yes that would arguably be the case.'[145]

Former Chief of the Defence Staff General Guthrie was an even more damning critic of the Government revealing that, as early as 2004, Gordon Brown as Chancellor of the Exchequer cut the helicopter budget from £4.5 billion to £3 billion (which David Cameron later described as a 'bad mistake'). Guthrie claimed that, when Gordon Brown was Chancellor of the Exchequer, the Treasury had spent 'the minimum they could get away with on defence' and that it was 'disingenuous of the government to say British forces had enough helicopters in Afghanistan ... fewer British soldiers would have died if they had had more helicopters.'[146] Guthrie's comments were underlined by the revelation by Colonel Stuart Tootal, former commander of 3 Para, who had earlier resigned over the alleged lack of logistical support for his troops. He recalled how, after MOD stonewalling, he had even appealed to Prince Charles to request more helicopters for the Helmand mission in 2006. His comments received the support of retired Brigadier Ed Butler.[147]

The row deeply threatened the previously strong domestic party consensus regarding the conduct of the Afghan War. Whilst Leader of the Opposition, David Cameron stated that the failure to provide helicopters was 'a scandal'[148] and the Liberal Democrats' leader Nick Clegg denigrated the government policy in similar terms. Liam Fox, as Shadow Defence Secretary, staunchly reinforced his leaders' view: 'No amount of evasion and creative accounting can disguise the fact that our troops are being let down. Gordon Brown was never willing fully to fund Tony Blair's wars and our troops are paying.'[149]

More devastating was the criticism emanating from within the Government's own ranks. These included a searing attack launched by former Defence Secretary John Hutton who, it was revealed, had earlier supported the Service Chiefs' call for 2,000 more troops in March 2009. In his first public statement on the war since he left the Cabinet in June 2009, Hutton made a stunning statement on the collapse of politico-military relations, demanding that the army should be given the extra troops and equipment it needed to beat the Taliban: 'When it comes to the numbers and equipment it is absolutely essential politicians listen to advice from the military. Politicians must not become armchair generals. They must make decisions based on clear military advice.'[150] It was a statement which resonated deeply with the failures of British politicians during the first three wars to supply sufficient troops and equipment to their armies in Afghanistan.

Other comments from leading Labour ministers added to the Government's discomfort over this issue. In July 2009 Lord Malloch-Brown, then Foreign Office Minister responsible for Afghanistan, asserted 'we definitely do not have enough helicopters' but, adding to the obvious confusion in Government policy, he later claimed that he had been, 'making the point ... that while there are without doubt sufficient resources in place for current operations, we should always do what we can to make more available on the front line'.[151]

It is probable that, on this occasion, the military triumphed over the 'politicals'. General Dannatt followed up his criticisms by submitting a £500 million 'shopping list' to the Prime Minister to help the troops, and the *Independent* opined on 23 July 2009: 'The government is expected to arrange reinforcements for British troops in Afghanistan within a month, in a victory for military commanders over politicians in Westminster.'[152]

The Government's military critics received strong support from the Commons Defence Committee led by its robust chairman, James Arbuthnot. Whilst not directly attributing army deaths to the shortage of suitable equipment, a hard-hitting cross-party report warned that the problem could get worse as a result of the MOD's procurement plans, which envisaged a significant reduction in medium and heavy lift helicop-

ters: 'We are convinced that the lack of helicopters is having adverse consequences for operations ... and, in the longer term, will severely impede the
ability of the UK armed forces to deploy ... we are concerned that operational commanders in the field are unable to undertake potentially valuable
operations because of the lack of helicopters.'[153]

The British deficiency in equipment was highlighted by statistics
published in *The Times*. These revealed that, in July 2009, Britain was
deploying only twenty-five helicopters in Afghanistan with sixteen on the
way compared to 120 Blackhawk helicopters operated by the US Marine
Corps in Helmand alone. Whilst the Government had ordered 248
Mastiff armoured vehicles, so far at that stage the US military in
Afghanistan had, by stark contrast, deployed over 3,000 MRAPs (Multi-
Role Armoured Personnel Carriers).[154] Public opinion appeared to be
moving in support of the military. A YouGov opinion poll for the *Sunday
Times* on 19 July 2009 revealed that 60 per cent of voters believed that
Prime Minister Brown was trying to fight the war 'on the cheap' and only
20 per cent believed that he was doing his best to provide the necessary
equipment.[155]

The Foreign Affairs Select Committee report of July 2009 added to
the growing army of critics by arguing that the Government ran a
'serious risk' of losing public support for the Afghan mission unless it
better explained why British soldiers were fighting there. Citing severe
overstretch, Chairman Mike Gapes questioned why Britain had the lead
role in fighting the drugs trade when it lacked the resources to do the
job. The report confirmed that Britain had moved from an initial goal in
2001 of supporting the United States in fighting international terrorism
into the realms of counter-insurgency, counter-narcotics, protection of
human rights and state-building. Echoing the fears of British strategic
planners in late 2001 the Committee asserted: 'We conclude that there
has been significant "mission creep" in the British deployment to
Afghanistan.... We recommend that in the immediate future the
Government should refocus its efforts to concentrate its limited
resources on one priority, namely security.'[156] It was eerily reminiscent of
a re-run of the first two Anglo-Afghan Wars, in which British forces had
been sucked into extended operations in order, apparently, to restore
security and which, on at least one occasion, had resulted in major
disaster, as at Maiwand in 1880.

The financial and human burden was highlighted when it was revealed
that the cost of military operations in Helmand had more than trebled from
£750 million in 2006–7 to £2.6 billion in 2008–9 and with Britain
suffering its bloodiest month of the conflict in July 2009 with twenty-two

soldiers killed. Above all, the poor co-ordination between the Ministry of Defence, the Foreign and Commonwealth Office and the Department for International Development was again criticized.[157] The Government response was predictably robust, with Armed Forces Minister Bill Rammell accusing the Committee of 'wildly exaggerating' the resource problem, but also notably acknowledging that 'the scale of the challenge in Helmand is greater than we expected'.[158]

Indeed, it had been the growing military challenge offered by the Taliban/Al Qaeda alliance which had accentuated the problem of insufficient resources. Their increasingly skilful use of deadly radio-controlled or pressure-based IEDs against the overstretched British troops was proving devastating in the short term and, ironically, their use as a widespread and favoured tactic may have reflected the harsh lessons learnt from the 2006 campaigns, when they incurred great losses from frontal attacks against 'platoon house' garrisons, and in the follow-up 'Operation Medusa'. This is not to say such tactics can be politically or militarily decisive. As Professor Michael Clarke succinctly observed:

> The loss of more troops in Afghanistan shocks the nation but not the soldiers. They are on the offensive and know that such operations are a dangerous business.... The military equation does not bother the NATO troops too much.... Taliban commanders have made Helmand their key objective and new recruits flow in from Pakistan but they are not well-trained or led. Unless they get very lucky Taliban forces cannot overwhelm any unit of NATO Troops who are so much better equipped and backed by air power. Hence they resort to improvised explosive devices. IEDs can be devastatingly effective even against the most heavily armoured vehicles but they are the technique of the terrorist; not decisive and not the weapon that will win the campaign.[159]

But the row had wider implications for Britain's Coalition partners and especially for her relationship with her vital US ally. Senior NATO sources reported that: 'The Americans are concerned about the public mood in Britain following the high number of recent deaths.' The new NATO commander, American General Stanley McChrystal, however, empathized with the shortage of 'boots on the ground', with the British Army unable to secure the south of Helmand as 'it was given tasks wider than its numbers allowed it to do'.[160] Conversely, Seth Jones, a counter-insurgency expert at the Rand Corporation, an American think-tank, pinpointed the need for greater British adaptation to defeat the insurgency and 'not just in the area of technology.... This fight is increasingly not about equipment but about how much they can use local leverage'. Noting that in the Iraqi Sunni Triangle, American lives were saved by armour and by co-opting locals who then informed on where and when the roadside bombs were being laid, Jones continued: 'The British have talked about dialogue but they haven't taken enough advantage of the tribes in Helmand who are not supportive of the Taliban.'[161] In fact, British General Michael Rose had already pointed to the possibility of 'forming irregular tribal militias' to help establish security and facilitate civil reconstruction, a strategy, he asserts, successfully pursued in the Oman Campaign of 1964–76.[162] It was a solution once favoured by the British in the Second and Third Anglo-Afghan Wars, where Hazara and Quizilbash irregulars and later regular tribal militias had been widely used to bolster British security in Afghanistan and on the North West Frontier of India.

However, the British experience in the 1919 Third Afghan War, when several key tribal militias either deserted or defected to the enemy, is a salutary reminder of the potential pitfalls in such tactics in a region in which ties of kith and kin and tribal loyalties are so strong. In any event, concern over the resources controversy and recent British losses had been serious enough to elicit a rare public declaration of support from the American President himself. On Sky News on 11 July 2009, President Barack Obama openly praised the British role in Afghanistan: 'My heart goes out to those British soldiers. Great Britain has played an extraordinary role in this coalition.... The contribution of the British is critical ... the likelihood of a terrorist attack on London is just as high if not higher than it is in the US.'[163]

Despite the pungent criticisms of the British Government over 'resource starvation', most critics reaffirmed their support for the central aim of fighting the main war in Afghanistan in order to prevent the scourge of terrorism from expanding into Western democracies. Indeed, the dire political and strategic implications of not sustaining the war in Afghanistan were succinctly underlined by General Dannatt himself: 'Things are much clearer if you flip the coin and look at the other side and ask yourself the question; what if we were to pull out unilaterally, what if we were to come out of this mission? Frankly, the consequences of that are appalling. So we will succeed. We must succeed.'[164] His statement was echoed in a robust speech delivered at Chatham House by the retiring NATO Secretary-General, Jaap de Hoop Scheffer on 20 July 2009:

We can debate the right numbers of helicopters to have in

Afghanistan and we should.... But to me there can be no serious debate about the necessity or the legitimacy of this mission. If we were to walk away, Afghanistan would fall to the Taliban, with devastating effect for the people there – women in particular ... will suffer the consequences, with all that implies for international security. Central Asia would see extremism spread. Al Qaeda would have a free run again and their terrorist ambitions are global.[165]

Eternal Quagmire? – Conclusions and Future Prospects

In conclusion, Britain's experience in Afghanistan over the past one and three-quarter centuries has been predominantly one of political and military quagmire. The First Anglo-Afghan War, based on misplaced or exaggerated 'Russophobia', the mordant fear of Russian expansionism, ended in political and military catastrophe with the return to power of Britain's arch enemy Dost Mohammed. For the British it was a highly unsatisfactory political settlement and one in which her honour and pride were only partially salvaged by the ruthless and, by today's standards, morally dubious campaign of retribution conducted by two avenging armies under Major-Generals Nott and Pollock. It was a war and occupation characterized by political complacency and resultant military paralysis, in which the final collapse of British power was arguably caused as much by violations of Muslim social and religious principles as by acute military and financial over-stretch. The Second Anglo-Afghan conflict, also driven, as it turned out, by misplaced 'Russophobia', ended in military victory but not without a major defeat at Maiwand and with continuing political and strategic tensions with Russia. These culminated in the 1885 Panjdeh border incident and the drawing up of the still locally unrecognized Durand boundary line. The Third Anglo-Afghan War, primarily the product of internal Afghan power struggles, ended in political armistice, but was notable for the surrender of Britain's long-held principle of external control over Afghan foreign affairs. Militarily, it was also essentially a pyrrhic victory as government restraints on military action and resources seriously weakened British control over the North West Frontier, notably Waziristan; the area remained a running sore in British control until the end of the Raj in 1947. It was a dangerous British legacy, reluctantly inherited by the new Government of Pakistan and today, as we have seen, the Taliban strongholds in the Federally Administered Tribal Area (FATA) continue to engender serious control problems on the southern

Helmand border.

If 'Russophobia' dominated the minds of British policy-makers during the first two Anglo-Afghan Wars, the potent threat from radical Islam was never far away. Both wars sparked off *jihads* and, indeed, Afghan aggression in the Third Afghan War was launched directly under the banner of another and even wider-based *jihad*, inspired by the Turkish Caliphate, and which ostensibly aimed to liberate Muslim India. Indeed, in retrospect, it might conceivably be argued that excessive paranoia over both these threats and the resultant heavy cost to Britain of meeting them in four protracted wars, might, one day, be compared to the equally costly American-driven Cold War obsession with the domino effect of communism and that such problems, some might argue, if not better managed, should even have been left well alone.

The Fourth Anglo-Afghan conflict, which commenced in 2001, when a deadly, newly emerged post-Cold War radical Islamic threat replaced old 'Russophobic' obsessions, remains highly problematical but not, it has been contended, unsolvable. The lost opportunities and initial strategic and tactical mistakes made by Britain and her principal Coalition partners, when 'industrial' war-fighting tactics clearly predominated over more balanced COIN and nation-building strategies, and when the 2003 Iraq campaign diverted vital military and political resources, culminated for Britain in the Helmand crisis of 2006. It was initially a flawed, indeed barren, politico-military strategy, conducted by an American-dominated Coalition pursuing a war-fighting strategy in which Britain was assigned a not insignificant but essentially junior role. It reflected some basic misunderstandings of the economic and political dynamics of Afghan society and a clear underestimation of the enemy, something for which Britain shares a special culpability in view of her huge historical experience in this region.

All four wars have reflected, to varying degrees, significant and often damaging friction between the military establishment and the 'politicals'. In the First Anglo-Afghan War the military were plunged into a war in which the primary threat, the Russian-backed Persian attack on Herat, had already visibly evaporated. After arriving they were virtually halved in numbers and were then progressively and fatally starved of administrative funds by an economy-conscious Calcutta and Home Government. This led directly to a 'crisis of collaboration' in which all key communications to India were cut by the subsidy-starved eastern Ghilzai, and other border tribes and the weakened British garrisons were rapidly surrounded. The result was the virtual annihilation of the main British force at Kabul and other smaller garrisons such as Charikar and Ghazni. It was a war in which local political interference in military operations frequently demoralized if not undermined British military commanders and largely precipitated the belated and disastrous retreat from Kabul in 1842. In the subsequent inquiry it was the local military commanders, notably the deceased Major-General Elphinstone and in particular the unfortunate Brigadier Shelton who bore the blunt of the blame, rather than their political counterparts, Sir Alexander Burnes and Sir William McNaghten. Shelton was, however cleared and the Government's position proved ultimately hypocritical when, in an unprecedented move on the eve of the 1842 'retribution campaign', they moved swiftly, if belatedly, to subordinate all local political authority to their avenging generals. It represented a tacit admission of Government failure in this disastrous enterprise.

In the Second Anglo-Afghan War, again largely the product of provocative and over-aggressive policies pursued by local political supremo, Viceroy Lord Lytton, the leading military commander, the talented if ruthless and egotistical Major-General Roberts, quickly learnt the lessons of his father and successfully, if not always productively, distanced himself from both his local political advisers and 'interfering media' in his ruthless pursuit of victory. It was a war which was also characterized by a blatant and often ill-advised interference in military operations by prominent 'politicals', notably the ill-fated Sir Pierre Louis Cavagnari, Britain's doomed Envoy to Kabul, and Colonel St John, his political counterpart in Kandahar. This is not to deny the fact that, on occasions, great civil-military harmony was achieved. Sir Robert Sandeman, for instance, played a key role in securing logistical supplies for Commander-in-Chief General Stewart's Kandahar Field Force, and political advisers Sir Mortimer Durand and Sir Lepel Griffin played vital roles in securing an overall political settlement. Invariably, at the heart of civil-military friction, there have always been the issues of too few troops and general resource starvation so evident in the prosecution all the three past Anglo-Afghan Wars.

What is striking about this study of the earlier British experience in Afghanistan – and arguably a by-product of persistent Government 'resource starvation' – is the heavy, at times crucial, reliance upon Afghan political and economic collaborators. Even amidst the often brutal policies of 'butcher and bolt', which particularly characterized the first two wars, the 'Afghan voice' was never silenced. While thousands perished as a result of British depredations, hundreds of other Afghans, notably Hazara and Qizilbash tribesmen, acted as intelligence agents, messengers and scouts as well as fighting auxiliaries for the British forces. Indeed it could be argued that it was ultimately the British (specifically MacNaghten's) failure to harness the loyalty of the Kabul Qizilbash community which doomed the

Kabul Brigade during the 1841–2 crisis.

Conversely, during the 1878–80 campaign, Hazara and Qizilbash support, as even Roberts acknowledged, played a crucial role in securing the survival of Roberts' forces firstly at Sherpur and secondly when his military reputation was at stake during the famous Kabul to Kandahar march following the Maiwand disaster of July 1880. Hundreds more Afghan peasant farmers and traders, notably nomadic Pindari merchants, paralleling their Hindu Indian counterparts to the south, supplied the British columns with food and transport during the first three Anglo-Afghan Wars. As we have seen, Qizilbash traders and merchants profited massively through sales of goods to British forces in Kabul during the Second Anglo-Afghan War. Indeed, the British (and their Coalition allies) have frequently been lacking in their use of local collaborators and in their creation of allies, as their initial mistakes in the creation of the ANA and ANP in the current conflict ably demonstrate.

In the most recent campaign the armed forces have, according to some observers, suffered severely from Government failures, if not outright betrayal. The Labour Government's decision to open a second front in 2003 in Iraq at a critical time for the Afghanistan campaign has been cited by several commentators as a serious political and strategic error and Labour Ministers have, as we have seen, frequently admitted to a significant underestimation of the enemy. Above all the British military has clearly been, until recently, starved of key resources in both manpower and equipment – particularly counter-IED experts and apparatus, helicopters and suitably armoured vehicles, which are considered crucial to avoid mounting casualties from IED-based attacks on road convoys. The IED remains the principal killer of British soldiers in Helmand and the toll on morale of this invisible weapon has been high for many of the British troops who have served in Afghanistan since 2001.

This military deficiency might, again, be considered a deleterious by-product of the Iraq campaign. The British Government has tried to rectify these problems by, for instance, the supply of better-armoured 'Mastiff 2' vehicles and more funding and manpower but this has invariably been seen by many critics as plaster-sticking or 'too little, too late'. More manpower is clearly essential if troops are to hold ground and avoid merely 'mowing the lawn'. The scandal over the seven-year mothballing of several 'Chinook' helicopters, considered vital for safe troop transport in Afghanistan, exemplified the impression of Government incompetence in these key areas, and such situations have certainly had a negative impact on troop morale. With, for instance, barely 4,000 troops initially sent to police Helmand (an area four times the size of Wales), ground-level military commanders were, from the start, arguably short-changed by a Government already financially and logistically overstretched by a two-front war. As the distinguished journalist William Rees-Mogg asserted:

> The indictment would be that the government failed to back the troops with adequate funding.... It was the Prime Minister who decided the policy; it was the Chancellor who controlled the funding. If there has been a mismatch between commitments and funding they must take the responsibility.... The army is seriously overstretched.... This has done serious strategic damage to its morale and future capacity.[166]

Britain's Afghan campaign losses, deeply depressing and tragic as they are, still compare favourably with other lengthy conflicts such as Korea 1950–3 (over 600 dead) and Malaya 1948–62 (400 dead). Nevertheless, the overall failure to consistently provide more troops and suitable equipment remains a serious indictment against the British Government and has caused an ongoing crisis in civil-military relations which is comparable to any of the three previous Anglo-Afghan conflicts. This is not to deny military culpability in the current campaign. Senior service chiefs in the MOD almost certainly played a role in the 2006 débâcle by their underestimation of military resources, not to mention their 'gung-ho' attitudes which prevailed among some of the local commanders of front-line troops.

The crux of the extraordinary levels of civil-military friction which have materialized over Afghanistan reflects the fact that British politicians and governments have never, unlike other parts of the imperial nexus, perceived this intractable country as a *colony*. The constant aim of the 'politicals' has been to secure and sustain Afghanistan as a strong, friendly but *independent* state intended to deter foreign intrigue and aggression against India. This aim was promoted sometimes by invasion, but primarily by donations of money and arms. In short, Afghanistan has acted solely as a *buffer state*, initially against Russian and French ambitions and, more recently, as an area of containment against the spread of radical Islamist groups. The often terrible consequence for the military establishment has been an overriding tendency for successive British governments to try to run their Afghan wars 'on the cheap' and such chronic under-investment has inevitably invoked the wrath of the military and, in more recent wars, even a dangerous backlash against individual military commanders.

It has not been simply a problem of funding but equally one of *co-ordi-*

nation of government policies, both within and between the government departments and their ground-level agencies. The military are but one strand of policy and, as British General Freeland famously pointed out in 1969 in relation to British deployment during the Northern Ireland 'troubles', the military can only hold the line for a limited period and it is for the politicians to find a solution.[167]

In terms of development and reconstruction, Britain's record remains patchy and her efforts have been somewhat diminished by the political dysfunction which has occurred, particularly between the three key ministries; the Ministry of Defence, the Foreign Office and the Department for International Development. As one editorial in *The Times* succinctly observed: 'This is a division that works less well in practice than it might in theory. Civil Departments, notably the DfID remain much happier at organising aid schemes in Africa than in dovetailing with the military in what is in essence a war zone.'

Afghanistan remains the running sore in Britain's much-vaunted 2005 'Comprehensive Approach' aimed at 'joining up the dots' of the strategic arms of policy-making. In the telling words of Dr Tim Bird, in direct reference to the 2006 Helmand debacle:

> The absence of timely and coordinated economic aid and diplomatic initiatives to accompany, underpin and follow military operations is a source of concern and irritation among sections of the chain of command.... The effects of this are played out in Afghanistan.... For example, all DfID representation was pulled out of Helmand province on the orders and sole initiative of the departmental civil service hierarchy. No-one, least of all the military, were consulted over the decision.... A coherent approach to military intervention in the era of fourth generation warfare is not here yet.[168]

Above all, internally and at ground level, it is the target clients of British and Coalition COIN strategies in Afghanistan – the critical, strategically placed Pashtun peasantry, straddling the turbulent southern borders of Afghanistan – who require even more focus. Social peace in this area can only be achieved by solving the drug problem which largely fuels the insurgency and simultaneously striving to separate the hardcore insurgents from the more moderate 'tiers'. There is still much potential political capital to be exploited here. As at least one observer has pointed out, the Pashtun Taliban are not natural friends of the Arab-based Al Qaeda despite Bin Laden being initially afforded sanctuary by their leader, Mullah Omar. Journalist Simon Jenkins opines: 'The Taliban objective is not world domination but a share of power in Afghanistan. While they cannot defeat western troops they can defeat NATO's war aim by continuing to build on their marriage of convenience with Al Qaeda which supplies them with a devastating arsenal of suicide bombers.'[169] At the same time the Pashtun rural communities need more incentive to cease poppy growing other than destruction by force, which can only be counterproductive in terms of hearts and minds. Radical solutions may be needed In the opinion of *The Times'* leading commentator, Anatole Kaletsky: 'Only by accepting that farmers in Afghanistan are entitled to grow opium as the farmers of Turkey or Virginia are to grow tobacco, and by making arrangements to buy up their crops at higher prices than the opium traders can afford, will the western coalition make any headway in winning Afghan hearts and minds.'[170] This, of course, not only raises questions of morality but would require much more money as well as manpower. Britain's NATO allies, excluding the USA, must provide more of both.

Externally, the security of the southern border, inextricably connected to the drug eradication problem, clearly remains an open sore in British and Western Coalition policies towards Afghanistan. The political solution lies not solely in Brussels, London or Washington, but is clearly local. Without the support of the key regional players, notably Pakistan (albeit still in political turmoil), the battle in Afghanistan will be unwinnable. As David Miliband said when British Foreign Secretary: 'Pakistan and Afghanistan are part of the same problem.'[171] Pakistani sovereignty clearly precludes or at least complicates cross-border military intervention by Britain and her Coalition allies (especially as it has long been known that her approach to the problem has been consistently compromised or undermined by the pro-Taliban sympathies of the ISI, her key intelligence arm). Nevertheless the long-term solution still clearly lies in regional co-operation in which not only Pakistan but other key players, notably India and Iran (and even Russia and China) would have to be consulted in order to squeeze out Al Qaeda and Taliban influence. This would not be easy in view of continuing friction between the Pakistani and Afghanistan Governments and between the Pakistani and American military over American hot-pursuit strategies across the border, and also in view of Anglo-American accusations of Iranian complicity in insurgent attacks. It will require massive diplomatic action and resources.

The situation is made more precarious as India and Pakistan remain fierce regional rivals over Afghanistan, and India, as a staunch ally of the Karzai Government, remains a primary target for Islamist terrorist groups. In recent years, the bombing of the Indian embassy in Kabul and the 2008 massacre in Mumbai, allegedly perpetrated by Islamist terrorist groups based in Pakistan, underline the wider political and strategic problems of the Afghan quagmire. Nevertheless, the diplomatic offensive launched by the American administration of President Barack Obama, including the offer of a 'hand of friendship' to Iran, augers well for the future and for British fortunes in Afghanistan.

More importantly, massive American diplomatic pressure on Pakistan, constituting virtually an ultimatum to 'get their house in order', accompanied by substantial military aid, has resulted in an unprecedented, continuing massive offensive by the Pakistani Army against Taliban militants in the Swat valley. These operations have extended right up to the Helmand border. In the words of Pakistani President Asif Ali Zardari: 'We're going into Waziristan, all these regions ... Swat is just the start. It's a larger war to fight.'[172] This, in turn, has enabled a crude pincer movement in tandem with British and American forces on the other side of the Helmand border, which could finally eliminate Al Qaeda and Taliban strongholds in an area which President Obama has described as 'the most dangerous place in the world.'

But there is along way to go. A nuclear-armed Pakistan borders on the verge of being a failed state and the creation of over two million refugees and displaced persons as a consequence of these offensives (the largest movement of people since the 1947 British partition) could lead to even greater social unrest, terrorist bombings and support for radical Islamic groups in the region.

Within Afghanistan, Britain herself has made small but significant strides since the 2006 political military impasse. Security sector reforms in terms of the ANA are showing some signs of improvement and, in co-operation with her all-powerful ally, the USA, there have recently been significant military successes inside southern Helmand. Such a combination of British diplomacy and American might should be productive in the long term, and the major surge of 300 British and around 35,000 American troops into northern Helmand, along the lines of those conducted in Iraq by General David Petraeus, has injected fresh hope in this current situation of strategic stalemate. These massive American reinforcements have, however, also renewed press speculation of continuing Anglo-American friction, namely that Britain is being sidelined by her American ally and that America sees Britain as 'failing' in the province (one unfortunate joke which apparently went the rounds in American Headquarters ridiculed specifically British efforts by redefining ISAF as 'I saw Americans fighting'!). However as CDS Sir Jock Stirrup has pointed out Britain will retain 'the key lead in the centre of Helmand with its provincial reconstruction team and with the partnership it has with the provincial governor and with local governance.'[173] Furthermore, observers have stressed the recent improvements in Anglo-American command relations, with former Sandhurst War Studies Senior Lecturer and US defence expert Dr Daniel Marston commenting: 'Things (are) getting better because the British are recognising that they made mistakes and they were arrogant.'[174]

General David Petraeus, formerly head of US Central Command and currently Commander of NATO forces in Afghanistan, has played a central role in healing any existing friction, notably by appointing one of Britain's leading generals, formerly retired Lieutenant-General Sir Graeme Lamb (and a former Director Special Forces), to mastermind a programme of reconciliation with members of the Taliban. Stressing how 'our soldiers have shed blood side by side', General Petraeus would not predict how long he expected British and other NATO troops to be engaged in fighting the Taliban, but said that the alliance needed to maintain a 'sustained and substantial commitment'. He continued: 'I wouldn't hazard the number of years this will take but the coalition was facing an industrial-strength insurgency.... We can pursue local reconciliation; this has already been done, but we have to kill, capture or run off the irreconcilables [the top tier of Taliban leaders].

Petraeus described the main threat as a 'syndicate of extremist insurgent elements in Afghanistan and Pakistan which had a loose affiliation with al-Qaeda headquarters in FATA [the Federally Administered Tribal Area in Pakistan].[175] Echoing British General Dannatt and NATO Secretary-General Jan de Hoop Scheffers, Petraeus also took the opportunity to restate the vital nature of the Coalition's mission in Afghanistan: 'Let us not forget why we are in Afghanistan. It's because we want to ensure that this country cannot become once again a sanctuary for al-Qaeda and the other transnational extremists to carry out more attacks in the US and Britain and elsewhere.'[176]

In fact, if the American political and military surge led by Generals David Petraeus and Stanley McChrystal reflects anything it is not British tactical failures but the ongoing crisis in British manpower (a proposed British 'surge' was reduced from 3,000 to 300!) In her counter-narcotics operations in southern Afghanistan, Britain has also made significant, if still embryonic, advances in her attempts to eradicate or at least control the growing of opium. However, this and any solution to the cross-border security problem will clearly be long term and will require not only patience but far greater international resources, particularly from some of Britain's European NATO allies. As the former British Defence Secretary John

Hutton observed: 'I think we'll know it when we get there and when the Afghans are able to take responsibility for law and order in Afghanistan. It is going to take time. COIN campaigns are not the traditional state on state war-fighting campaigns ... this going to be by its very nature a long-term commitment.'[177] The controversial statement by General Sir David Richards, the new head of the British Army, who envisaged that British troops could be in Afghanistan 'for the next thirty to forty years',[178] exceeding even the prognostication of Ambassador Sherpur-Coles in 2007, is salutary. Certainly, the results of the Afghan Presidential Elections in August 2009, which pointed to widespread fraud and intimidation, particularly by President Karzai's supporters, whilst also revealing that the turnout in Helmand was as low as 8 per cent (with barely 150 out of a voter's roll of 80,000 casting ballots in the district where British forces launched 'Operation Panther's Claw') indicates clearly the immensity of the task that still lies ahead.[179]

What is certain is that there has never been and never will be a purely external military solution to the Afghanistan problem. In this clearly unfinished 'long war', conducted in such a complex security environment as Afghanistan, British strategic aims must be (and are now) focused not on any concept of 'victory' but on one of 'holding the line'; of a long-term military containment, stabilization and development, conducted in the hope of both an internal and a regionally based political solution, and one in which vastly expanded indigenous security forces will ultimately shoulder the security burden. Indeed, in tandem with regional co-operation a successful British and Coalition exit strategy does crucially depend on the creation of a loyal and viable indigenous Afghan security force. This task alone will take several more years. But, in the light of the announcement by the incoming Coalition Government of a withdrawal date for British *combat* troops by 2014, it may be that British public opinion, clearly aghast at the scale of the recent losses, has proved to be the final arbiter of Britain's sustainability of this current Afghan campaign.[180]

The lessons for Britain of the four Anglo-Afghan Wars are clear and unequivocal and, perhaps, are best summed up through the medium of the new and much-heralded ten principles of British counter-insurgency. While there must ultimately be (1) *primacy of political purpose*, incorporating the upholding of key humanitarian and democratic principles, there must also be (2) *unity of effort or a 'comprehensive approach'* between all government departments and associated agencies and the military establishment. (3) *Understanding of the human terrain*, (4) *integrating intelligence* and (5) *securing the population* by (6) *neutralizing the insurgent* (so often neglected in the wars up to and including the 2006 Helmand campaign), must be strictly adhered to in order to win hearts and minds and to (7) *gain and maintain popular support.* The Afghan people remain the prize in securing victory in such 'hybrid wars', incorporating such conventional and diverse non-conventional challenges, ranging from security sector reform to combating narco-crime. (8) *Operating in accordance with the law* and thereby dominating the moral high ground is arguably the most vital concomitant of all such principles, and excesses against the local Afghan civilian population, a feature of all four campaigns, must be avoided at all costs. Britain must always be willing to (9) *learn and adapt* and, unlike in some previous campaigns, to (10) *prepare for the long term.* It is essential not to underestimate the crucial importance of the stated principles of sustaining corporate intelligence, and of learning from the past. In the chastened words of the 3 Para Post-Operational Report for Herrick 4, issued in 2007: 'Many of the lessons learnt from the British government's resulting experiences ... in Helmand Province ... are not new.... The key lesson is that we ignore previous experiences of campaigns and those of our allies at our peril.'[181]

Moreover, the Afghans themselves are, as we have clearly seen, notorious for their inability to act as long-term hosts for alien invaders and, in the most recent and protracted round of this new, far more ideologically driven version of the 'Great Game', one should, perhaps, conclude with the wise words of Sir Olaf Caroe, the departing Governor of Britain's North West Province of India during the last days of the Raj: 'Unlike other wars, Afghan wars only become serious when they are over.'[182]

Notes

1   BNL *Imperial Gazette* (London, 1908).
2   M. Griffin, *Reaping the Whirlwind: the Taliban Movement in Afghanistan* (Pluto Press, London, 2001), p.38. For other key sources see, Kamal Matinuddin, *The Taliban Phenomenon: Afghanistan 1994–1997* (OUP, Oxford, 2001).
3   Griffin, *Reaping the Whirlwind*, p38.
4   SENLIS Afghanistan, 'Countering the Insurgency – Losing Friends and Making Enemies', (SENLIS, London, February 2007), p.27.
5   Terry Judd, 'British Special Forces on the ground, advising Alliance', *The Independent*, 12 November 2001. See also 'SAS used knives in hand to hand fight for caves', *Sunday Times*, 9 December 2001.
6   Kim Sengupta, 'UK Troops go in amidst fears of tribal war', *The Times*, 16 November 2001.

7   Interview, Captain Jed Stone, 2008.
8   Interview, Captain William Downham, 2008.
9   Interview, Major Andrew Banks, 2008.
10 Interview, Captain Nick Colvin, 2008.
11 Sengupta and Rice, 'UK Troops, go in amid fear of tribal war'.
12 M. Berdal, quoted in White, David, 'UK led force keen to avoid mission creep', *Financial Times*, 19 December 2001.
13 Major General R. Smith, *The Utility of Force* (Penguin Books, London, 2005), p.390.
14 White, 'UK led force keen to avoid mission creep'.
15 See Sir R. Thompson, *Defeating Communist Insurgency* (Chatto and Windus, London, 1966) and Sir F. Kitson, *Bunch of Fives* (London, Weidenfeld and Nicolson, 1979), *passim*.
16 'Just the Job for us', *The Economist*, 22 December 2001.
17 Ibid.
18 Cyrus Hodes and Mark Sedra, *The Search for Security in post-Taliban Afghanistan*, Adelphi Paper 391, (ISS, London, 2007).
19 Kim Sengupta, 'Royal Marines hunt remnants of the Taliban in Afghanistan mountains', *The Independent*, 17 April 2002.
20 Ibid.
21 James Bone, 'British Peacekeepers face chemical weapons threat', *The Times*, 24 January 2002.
22 For the aims and objectives of 'Operation Snipe' see, for instance, Kim Sengupta, 'Marines launch high-risk attack on Al-Qaida in biggest combat mission since Gulf war', *The Independent*, 2 May 2002.
23 Kim Sengupta, 'British commander says war against Al-Qaida is all but won', *The Independent*, 9 May 2002.
24 R. Norton-Taylor and J. Steele, 'Mission unaccomplished: how 3000 crack British troops failed to find the enemy', *The Guardian*, 20 June 2002.
25 J. Swain, 'Marines losing war with thin air', *Sunday Times*, 12 May 2002. See also Dr D. Marston, 'Lessons in COIN in Afghanistan 2001-7' in *Counter-insurgency in Modern Warfare* (Osprey, Oxford, 2008), pp.226-7.
26 Ibid.
27 M. Turner, 'Under unusual fire during six days of the Condor', *Financial Times*, 25/26 May 2002.
28 Ibid.
29 J. Clark, 'Marines go to "hell" in search of the enemy', *Sunday Times*, 18 April 2002. See also Norton-Taylor and Steele, 'Mission unaccomplished'.
30 Clark, 'Marines go to "hell" in search of the enemy', *Sunday Times*, 18 April 2002.

31 Alex Spilliers, 'Commando Sweeps find arms but no Taliban', *Daily Telegraph*, 10 May 2002. See also Mark Turner, 'How Coalition struggled to pass the intelligence test', *Financial Times*, 11 June 2002.

32 Spilliers, 'Commando Sweeps'.

33 Julian Manion, 'Snipe and Spin', *The Spectator*, 11 May 2002.

34 Isambard Wilkinson, *The Times*, 30 May 2006.

35 Author's conversation with Field Marshal Sir John Chapple, National Army Museum, 29 January 2009.

36 See especially, G. Alder, *British India's Northern Frontier, 1865–1895* (Longman, London, 1963) and T.R. Moreman, *The British Army in India and the Development of Frontier Warfare 1849–1947* (Palgrave, Basingstoke, 2001).

37 Christina Lamb, *The Times*, July 2006.

38 Defence Secretary, *Daily Telegraph*, 1 October 2005.

39 *The Times*, 18 June 2006.

40 Ibid.

41 Editorial, *Daily Telegraph*, 16 June 2007.

42 Anthony Lloyd, 'Some won't fight: Some can't fight in snow', *The Times*, 25 October 2007. For further discussion of NATO's principal problems in Afghanistan see J. Medcalf, *Going Global or Going Nowhere?; NATO's role in Contemporary International Security*, (Peter Lang, Bern 2008), especially Chapter 6. See also 'Afghan Dilemma', *The Times*, 18 January 2006 and M. Evans and N. Parkes, 'NATO must play greater part in war on Taleban', *The Times*, 5 September 2006.

43 For the long-term problems of constructing the ANA and ANP see especially, Ali A. Jalali, 'Rebuilding Afghanistan's National Army', *Parameters*, Autumn, 2002, vol 32, 3; Mark Sedra, 'New Beginning or Return to Arms', Bonn International Centre for Conversion (BICC) workshop, 30 May–1 June 2003; and Dr Antonio Giustozzi, 'Rebuilding the Afghan army', LSE Development Research Centre, 17 January 2004.

44 'Return of the Taliban', SENLIS Report (London 2007).

45 Stephen Grey, Channel 4, *Dispatches*, 'Afghanistan – Mission Impossible?', 6 April 2009.

46 See, for instance, T. Coghlan, 'British head for Afghan land of hate', *The Times*, 26 Oct. 2005.

47 *Sunday Times*, 24 May 2006.

48 Christina Lamb, 'The bandits wait for the British?', *Sunday Times*, 29 January 2006.

49 T. Harding, 'Task Force to tackle Afghan drug barons', *Daily Telegraph*, 27 January 2006.

50 Interview, Brigadier Ed Butler (retd), 'Afghanistan: Mission Impossible',

Channel 4, 6 April 2009.

51 Interview, Captain Colvin, 2008.
52 Christina Lamb, 'Karzai blamed for hellhole strategy', *Sunday Times*, 17 September 2006.
53 Interview, Brigadier Butler, 'Mission Impossible?'
54 Ibid.
55 Interview, Michael Semple, 'Mission Impossible?' and M. Evans, '3,300 British troops head into Taleban territory for first time', *The Times*, 17 January 2006.
56 Interview, Brigadier Butler, 'Mission Impossible?'
57 Ibid.
58 Interview, General Richards, 'Mission Impossible?'
59 M. Evans, 'Major who called RAF useless tells of Taliban attacks', *The Times*, 25 September 2006.
60 Lt-General Sir Hew Pike (ed), *From the Front Line: Family Letters and Diaries 1900 to the Falklands and Afghanistan* (Pen and Sword, Barnsley, 2008), p.173.
61 Ibid, p193.
62 Evans, 'Major who called RAF useless tells of Taliban attacks', *The Times*, 25 September 2006.
63 Pike, *From the Front Line*, p.199. For a stirring account of 3 Para's ferocious war in Helmand in 2006 see P. Bishop, *3 Para: Afghanistan Summer 2006*, (Harper Press, London, 2007), *passim*.
64 Christina Lamb, 'What a bloody hopeless war', *Sunday Times*, 28 May 2006.
65 Ibid.
66 *The Times*, 25 September 2007.
67 Pike, *From the Front Line*, p.202.
68 Ibid, p.193.
69 Grey, 'Mission Impossible'.
70 Pike, *From the Front Line*, pp.170–2.
71 *Sunday Times*, 10 September 2006.
72 Pike, *From the Front Line*, pp.179–80.
73 SENLIS Report: 'Return of the Taliban' (London 2001).
74 Anthony Lloyd, 'Afghans blame NATO the invited peacekeepers for civilian deaths', *The Economist*, June 2007.
75 Ibid.
76 Christina Lamb, 'British target lair of opium lords', *Sunday Times*, 5 February 2006.
77 Camilla Cavendish, 'The War on Drugs is not the War on Terror', *The Times*, 8 June 2006.
78 *Sunday Times*, 26 June 2006.

79 Ibid.

80 Pike, *From the Front Line*, p.198.

81 Lamb 'British target lair of opium lords', *Sunday Times*, 5 February 2006.

82 Ibid.

83 Pike, *From the Front Line*, p.190.

84 Ibid, pp.196–7.

85 Christina Lamb, 'Counter narcotics is the FCO's responsibility', *Sunday Times*, 29 January 2006.

86 Interview, Captain Ben Reid, 2008.

87 Pike, *From the Front Line*, p.210.

88 Interview, General Richards, 'Afghanistan: Mission Impossible'.

89 Interview, Brigadier Butler, 'Afghanistan: Mission Impossible'.

90 Interview, General Dan McNeill, 'Afghanistan: Mission Impossible'.

91 Lamb, 'The Bandits wait'.

92 T. Albone and N. Parker, 'British Troops are caught in deadly trap as trouble grows on two fronts', *The Times*, 19 May 2006.

93 Simon Jenkins, 'By Jingo our brave boys are off to tame the Afghans. And they'll fail', *Sunday Times*, 29 January 2006.

94 Pike, *From the Front Line*, p.173.

95 T. Albone, 'Hunters may become the hunted in Taleban's venomous heartland', *The Times*, 19 May 2006.

96 Tony Skinner, 'Stretched too thin?', *Jane's Defence Weekly*, 19 July 2006, p.48. See also, M. Evans, 'The drain on men and machines, *The Times*, 4 September 2006 and *Times* editorial, 'A dangerous but necessary mission that must be properly equipped', 4 September 2006.

97 Field Marshal Inge, speech, *Hansard*, 29 June 2006.

98 SENLIS Report, 'Afghanistan Five Years Later: the Return of the Taliban', (London, Spring/Summer 2006).

99 Pike, *From the Front Line*, pp.194–5.

100 SENLIS Report, 'Helmand at War', (London, June 2006).

101 Interview, Brigadier Butler, 'Afghanistan: Mission Impossible'.

102 Interview, Sir Jock Stirrup, ibid.

103 Interview, General Richards, ibid.

104 Interview, General Dan McNeill, ibid.

105 Interview, General Richards, ibid.

106 See especially Christina Lamb, 'Death Trap', *The Times*, 9 July 2006; 'What a Bloody Hopeless War', *The Times*, 10 September 2006. See also Matthew Paris, 'Let's admit it. As a country we're impotent', *The Times*, 27 October 2006, in which he noted that Britain was at loggerheads with the Americans about nation building, was hopelessly under-resourced and that 'counter-narcotics has been an unmitigated disaster'.

107 Sir Max Hastings, 'Tell the Truth, Mr Blair', *Daily Mail*, 5 September 2006.

108 Richard Norton-Taylor, 'Labour admits: we made mistakes on Afghanistan', *The Guardian*, 19 September 2006.

109 SENLIS Report, 'Countering the Insurgency in Afghanistan: Losing Friends and Making Enemies' (London, February 2007).

110 Benedict Brogan, 'Blair tries to rally', *Daily Mail*, 21 November 2006.

111 David Blair, 'Iran arms the Taliban against the West', *Daily Telegraph*, 2 June 2007.

112 Speech by Prime Minister Blair, 'Our Nation's Future', 12 January 2007.

113 Thomas Hardy, 'Army needs to recruit for ten years in Afghanistan and David Blair, 'Our Allies talk to the Taliban. We should admit it', *Daily Telegraph*, 13 December 2007.

114 Interview, Sir Sherard Cowper-Coles, BBC Radio 4, 20 June 2007.

115 T. Harding, 'Army held talks with terrorists to end attacks', *Daily Telegraph*, 12 December 2007.

116 T. Coghlan, 'Taliban seize towns and destroy landmark truce', *Daily Telegraph*, 3 February 2007.

117 D. Browne, 'We should talk to the men of violence says Browne', *Daily Telegraph*, 29 March 2008.

118 Nick Meo, 'Karzai "praised" for UN expulsions', *The Times*, 28 Deember 2007, and T. Harding and T. Coghlan, 'Britain in secret talks with the Taliban', *Daily Telegraph*, 26 December 2007.

119 Interview, M. Semple, 'Mission Impossible'.

120 Meo, 'Karzia "praised"'.

121 Patrick Bishop, 'We're on the way to defeating the Taliban', *Sunday Times*, 12 September 2006 and Declan Walsh 'After the fighting a battle for hope', *The Guardian*, 25 September 2006. Ironically, the impact of 'Medusa' may have encouraged the Taliban to switch to more deadly tactics, notably the use of IEDs and suicide bombers. See Christina Lamb, 'Taliban switch tactics to hit cities with suicide bombers', *Sunday Times*, 22 October 2006.

122 Anthony Lloyd, 'Troops turn away from "ink spots" for control', *The Economist*, September 2001.

123 M. Evans, 'Britain's biggest force takes aim at hearts and minds but the guns are muted', *The Times*, 19 April 2008.

124 M. Evans, 'Army Chief predicts a "generation of conflict"', *The Times*, 28 August 2007.

125 R. Morarjee, 'Coalition kills top Taliban Commander', *Financial Times*, 14 May 2007, and 'SBS behind Taliban leader's death', *Sunday Times*, 27 May 2007.

126 Stephen Grey, 'Terror on road to Taliban stronghold', *Sunday Times*, 9 December 2007, and T. Coghlan, 'British forces in push to capitalise on

Taliban "split"?', *Daily Telegraph*, 13 November 2007.

127 Bronwen Maddox, 'Success in Musa Qala matters more for symbolic worth than strategic value', *The Times*, 10 December 2007.

128 M. Evans, 'Brigadier strides into battle against Taliban', *The Times*, 17 December 2007.

129 Stephen Grey, 'Mission Impossible'.

130 Evans, 'Brigadier strides'.

131 Tim Albone and M. Evans, 'Two British soldiers die in clashes with Afghan rebels', *The Times*, 2 July 2007.

132 Tom Baldwin, 'Britain tells US: we're winning Afghanistan battles but not the war', *The Times*, 7 September 2007.

133 Ibid. As Brigadier Mark Carleton-Smith, Commander of Task Force Helmand observed: 'This operation has severely dislocated Taliban control of an area in which they have traditionally enjoyed considerable authority', Evans, ' US Marines on raids to disrupt main Taliban supply routes', *The Times*, 12 May 2008.

134 Richard Beeston, 'Now Americans take up the Great Game', *The Times*, 5 May 2008, and Beeston, 'US Marines to "stir things up" with 3,500 extra troops', *The Times*, 29 April 2008.

135 D. Marston, 'Lessons in 21st Century Counterinsurgency: Afghanistan 2001–7' in *Counter-Insurgency in Modern Warfare* (Osprey, London, 2008), p.231.

136 Beeston, 'US Marines to "stir things up"... *The Times*, 29 April 2008.

137 M. Evans, 'Afghan troops told to lay down their rusty AK47s', *The Times*, 15 April 2008.

138 C. Bremner and M. Evans, 'Sarkozy will lay out plan to put troops in Afghanistan as NATO struggles for victory', *The Times*, 31 March 2008.

139 Interview, Captain Ben Reid, 2008.

140 Interview, M. Foster, 'Mission Impossible'.

141 Rory Stewart, 'What worked in Iraq won't help Afghans', *The Times*, 17 March 2009.

142 M. Evans and Philip Webster, 'Army chiefs asked for 2,000 more men: Brown sent 700', *The Times*, 14 July 2009.

143 Rosa Prince, 'Army chief left to hitch US flight', *Daily Telegraph*, 16 July 2009.

144 'Helicopter shortages puts lives at risk', *The Guardian*, 16 July 2009.

145 Ibid.

146 Jonathan Oliver and Michael Smith, 'Labour clashes with Army as Afghan death toll mounts', *Sunday Times*, 12 July 2009.

147 Margarette Driscoll, 'My secret helicopter mission with Prince Charles',

Sunday Times, 19 July 2009.

148 Oliver and Smith, 'Labour clashes with Army'.

149 Richard Norton-Taylor, 'Helicopter shortages undermine British operations and risk soldiers' lives', *The Guardian*, 17 July 2009.

150 J. Oliver, 'Hutton breaks silence to fight for the generals', *Sunday Times*, 19 July 2009.

151 Ken Sengupta and Andrew Grice, 'Reinforcements for Afghanistan "within a month"', *The Independent*, 23 July 2009.

152 Ibid.

153 R. Norton-Taylor, 'Helicopter shortages risks soldiers' lives', *The Guardian*, 17 July 2009.

154 M. Evans, 'Black Hawks frowned upon but army was left with little choice', *The Times*, 16 July 2009.

155 Oliver, 'Hutton breaks silence'.

156 Deborah Haynes, 'Tell the public why we're in Afghanistan', *The Times*, 3 August 2009.

157 Ibid.

158 Ibid.

159 M. Clarke, 'What the soldiers want most is reinforcements', *Sunday Times*, 12 July 2009. Contrast, Christina Lamb, 'The Taliban will never be defeated', *Sunday Times*, 17 June 2009.

160 M. Evans and T. Coghlan, 'Rethink on troops needed if we want to succeed', *The Times*, 15 July 2009.

161 T. Coghlan and Catherine Philip, 'Tribal intelligence is the key to victory', *The Times*, 16 July 2009. See also, 'US pins its hopes on "Dad's Army" to turn tide in fight for local loyalties, *The Times*, 27 April 2009.

162 General Michael Rose, 'Afghanistan: Some recent observations', *RUSI Journal*, October 2008.

163 Oliver and Smith, 'Labour Clashes'.

164 Evans and Coghlan, 'Rethink on troops needed', *The Times*, 15 July 2009.

165 Jan de Hoop Scheffer, Transcript of Speech at Chatham House, 20 July 2009.

166 William Rees-Mogg, 'The deadly price of the Blair-Brown War', The Times, 12 March 2007.

167 General Freeland, ITV documentary, 'The Troubles', 1971.

168 Dr Tim Bird, 'Implications and Conclusions: A Comprehensive Approach', International Studies Association Conference, Chicago, 2007. For a highly critical ground-level analysis of the breakdown of civil-military strategy in Helmand by an intelligence officer, see Major M. C. Miller, 'A Comprehensive Failure: British Civil-military strategy in Helmand Province', *The British Army Review*, No. 146, spring 2009. See also,

'Joined-up Thinking', editorial, *The Times*, 29 April 2008 and Major-General Anthony Stone, 'Joining the dots in Afghanistan', Letters to the Editor, *The Times*, 2 May, 2008.

169 Simon Jenkins, 'Stop killing the Taliban – they offer the best hope of beating Al Qaeda', *The Times*, 12 June 2008.

170 Anatole Kaletsky, 'Just don't do it: a sound motto for the year ahead', *The Times*, 3 January 2008. 'As Sir Winston Churchill noted in his unedited notes as War Correspondent for the *Daily Telegraph* in 1897, future Afghan wars would be "won by silver and not by bullets. Give money to Afghans growing poppies", he recommended, "and let them set up legitimate businesses",' Major Alan Taylor-Smith (retd.), letter to the Editor, *Daily Telegraph*, 12 February 2010. An article in *The Times* revealed that military action in Helmand has, according to the UNODC, resulted in a 33 per cent cut in opium production there this year with 12,000 farming households switching to cultivating government-distributed wheat seed. Michael Evans, 'Military action and a new crop bring big cut in opium growing', *The Times*, 2 September 2009.

171 D. Miliband.

172 President Asif Ali Zardari.

173 Interview, Sir Jock Stirrup, 'Mission Impossible'.

174 Marston, 'Lessons in COIN', *Counterinsurgency in Modern Warfare*, p.235.

175 M. Evans, 'Briton leaves retirement to befriend the enemy', *The Times*, 21 August 2009.

176 Ibid.

177 Interview, Secretary of State for Defence.

178 *Sunday Times*, 9 August, 2009.

179 Jeremy Page, T. Coghlan, Julius Cavendish, 'Flawed poll: fraud and intimidation mar election as the voters stay away', *The Times*, 21 August 2009. But see also, Rosemary Righter, 'Don't sneer at Afghanistan's wind of change'. She argues that, even with a second round to decide a winner, 'the power vacuum will be little more than has long existed in Karzai-ruled Kabul. A refreshing wind of change is blowing through Afghan politics. It must be allowed to take its course whether you want to call that democracy or not.'

180 See especially Nad Ali, 'And the soldier came home from the hill', *The Economist*, 18 July 2009, and Deborah Haynes, 'Tell the public why we're in Afghanistan', *The Times*, 3 August 2009. See also BBC2 TV *Newsnight*, 'Why are we in Afghanistan?', London, 13 July 2009.

181 3 Para Post Operations Report, Operation Herrick IV, 2007. For an extended version and explanation of the ten new COIN principles see, British Army Field Manual, vol 1, Part 10, Countering Insurgency (HMSO,

October 2009).

182 Sir Olaf Caroe, *The Pathans* (source kindly supplied by *Times* journalist Christina Lamb.) 'As Sir Winston Churchill famously warned half a century before in his final unedited notes as *Daily Telegraph* War Correspondent in Afghanistan in 1897: "Never return to fight in Afghanistan again. If we do, the whole Muslim world will turn against the British".' Major Alan Taylor-Smith (retd.), letter to the Editor, *Daily Telegraph*, 12 February 2010 (source kindly supplied by Lt.-Colonel Ian Bennett).

Select Bibliography
and References

Secondary Sources

The First Anglo-Afghan War

A Bengal Officer, *Recollections of the First Campaign West of the Indus and of the Subsequent Operations of the Candahar Force under Major-General Sir W Nott* (London, Smith Elder, 1845).

Allen, I.N., *Diary of a March Through Sinde and Affghanistan* (John Murray, London, 1843).

Atkinson, J., *The Expedition into Affghanistan* (reprint, Naval and Military Press, Uckfield, 2004).

Barr, W., *Journal of a March from Delhi to Peshawur and From thence to Cabul* (reprint, Delhi, 2003).

Boulger, D.C., *Lord William Bentinck* (Clarendon Press, Oxford, 1892).

Buist, G., *Outline of the Operations of the British Troops in Scinde and Afghanistan betwixt Nov. 1838 and Nov. 1841* (*The Times*, Bombay, 1843).

Burnes, Sir A., *Travels into Bokhara*, 3 vols (John Murray, London, 1834).

— *Travels into Bokhara, being the account of a journey from India to Cabool, Tartary and Persia*, 3 vols (John Murray, London, 1842).

Carter, T., *Historical record of the forty-fourth or the East Essex Regiment* (reprint, Naval and Military Press, Sussex, 2003).

Chetwynd-Stapylton, G.R.(ed), *The First Afghan War: An Ensign's Account* (Worthy Down, 2007).

Connolly, A., *Overland Journey to the North of India* (John Murray, London, 1829).

Cumming, J.S., *A Six Years Diary* (Martin and Hood, London, 1847).

Dennie, W.H., *Personal Narrative of the Campaigns in Afghanistan* (William Curry, Jim and Company, Dublin, 1843).

Durand, Sir H., *The First Afghan War and its Causes* (reprint, Bhavana Prints, New Delhi, 2000).

Eden, E., *Up the Country: Letters written to her sister*, 2 vols (Bentley, London, 1846).

Elphinstone, M., *An Account of the Kingdom of Caubul* (reprint, Munshiram Manoharlal, New Delhi, 1998).

Evans, George de Lacy, *On the Practicability of an Invasion of India* (Richardson, London, 1829).

Eyre, Major-General Sir Vincent, *The Kabul Insurrection of 1841–2* (revised ed, W.H. Allen, London, 1879).

— *The Military Operations at Cabul, Which Ended in the Retreat and Destruction of the British Army* (John Murray, London, 1843).

Ferrier, J.P., *The Afghans* (John Murray, London, 1858).

Gleig, The Reverend G.R., *Sale's Brigade in Afghanistan* (John Murray, London, 1846).

Greenwood, J., *The Campaign in Afghanistan* (reprint, Nonsuch, Gloucestershire, 2005).

Haigh, W., *A Review of the Operations of the British Force at Cabool* (Calcutta, 1849).

Holdsworth, A.H., *Campaign of the Indus*, (Private Print, 1840).

Hough, W., *Narrative of the March and Operations of the Army of the Indus in the Expedition to Afghanistan in the Years 1838–39* (W.H. Allen, London, 1841).

Ingram, E., *The Beginning of the Great Game in Asia, 1828–1834* (OUP, Oxford, 1979).

Kaye, J.W., *History of the War in Afghanistan*, 3 vols (reprint, Elibron Classics, London, 2003).

Lal, Mohan, *Life of Dost Mohammed Khan of Kabul* (reprint, Asian Educational Services, New Delhi, 2004).

Low, C.R., *The Afghan War, 1838–1842 from the Journal and Correspondence of the late Major-General Augustus Abbott* (Richard Bentley and Son, London, 1879).

Lunt, J. (ed), *From Sepoy to Subedar* (Routledge and Kegan Paul, London, 1970).

Macintyre. B., *Josiah the Great: The True Story of the Man who would be King* (Harper Collins, London, 2004).

Mackenzie, Lt.-General C., *Storms and Sunshine*, 2 vols (David Douglas, Edinburgh, 1884).

McNeill, J., *The Progress and Position of Russia in the East* (Bentley, London, 1836).

Macrory, P., *Kabul Catastrophe* (OUP, Oxford, 1986).

Moorcroft, W. and G.T., *Travels in the Himalayan Provinces of Hindustan and the Punjab from 1819 to 1825* (reprint, OUP, Oxford, 1979).

Kennedy, R.H., *Narrative of the Campaign of the Army of the Indus in Sind and Kaubool 1838–39,* 2 vols (Richard Bentley, London, 1840).

Masson, C., *Narrative of Various Journeys in Balochistan, Afghanistan and the Panjab,* 3 vols (reprint, Munshiram Manoharlal, New Delhi, 1997).

Mohan Lal, *Travel in the Punjab, Afghanistan and Turkestan* (John Allen, London, 1846).

— *Life of the Amir Dost Mohammed Khan of Kabul,* 2 vols (Longman, London, 1846).

Napier, Lt.-General Sir W., *The Life and Opinions of General Sir Charles James Napier,* 4 vols (John Murray, London, 1857).

Neill, J.M.D., *Four Years Service in the East with H M Fortieth Regiment* (S & J Bentley, Wilson and Fley, London, 1845).

Norris, J.A., *The First Afghan War 1838–42* (CUP, Cambridge, 1967).

Outram, J., *Rough Notes of the Campaign in Scinde and Afghanistan in 1838–9* (reprint, Naval and Military Press, Uckfield, 2003).

Pottinger, G. and Macrory, P., *The Ten-Rupee Jezail: Figures in the First Afghan War,* 1838–1843 (Michael Russell, Norwich, 1991).

Pottinger, H., *Travels in Beloochistan and Sind* (Longman, London, 1816).

Sale, Lady F., *Journal of the Disasters in Affghanistan, 1841–2* (John Murray, London, 1843).

Sale, General Sir R., *The Defence of Jellalabad* (John Murray, London, 1843).

Seaton, T., *From Cadet to Colonel* (Routledge & Son, London, 1866).

Stavey, Colonel L.R., *Narrative of Services in Beloochistan and Afghanistan, 1840–2* (W. H. Allen, London, 1848).

Stewart, J., *Crimson Snow: Britain's First Disaster in Afghanistan* (History Press, Stroud, 2008).

Stocqueler, J.H. (ed), *Memorials of Afghanistan* (Calcutta, 1843).

— *Memorials of Afghanistan* (reprint, Saeed Jan Qureshi, Peshawar, 1983).

— *Memoirs and Correspondence of Sir William Nott,* 2 vols, (London, Hurst and Blackett, 1854).

Trotter, Capt. L.J., *Rulers of India: Lord Auckland* (Clarendon Press, Oxford, 1893).

Yorke, E.J., *The Fall of Kabul 1841–2* (History Press, 2012).

The Second Anglo-Afghan War

Aitchinson, C.U., *Lord Lawrence and the Reconstruction of India Under the Crown* (OUP, Oxford, 1897).

Allen, I.N., Diary of a March Through Sinde and Affghanistan (London, 1843).

Anderson, F.H., The Afghan War 1878–80 (RMAS Staff College, London, 1911).

Atwood, R., The March to Kandahar, Roberts in Afghanistan (Pen and Sword, Barnsley, 2008).

Balfour, Lady Betty, Lord Lytton's Indian Administration (Longman's Green & Co, London, 1899).

Bartelott, W.G., The Life of Edmund Musgrave Bartelott (London, 1890).

Biddulph, Major-General Sir Michael A., The March from the Indus to Helmund and Back, 1878, 1879 (RUSI, London, 1880).

Blacker, L.V.S., On Secret Patrol in High Asia (John Murray, London, 1922).

Blake, R., Disraeli, (Eyre and Spottiswode, London, 1966).

Bosworth Smith, Life of Lord Lawrence 2 vols (Smith, Elder, London, 1883).

Cardew, F.G., The Second Afghan War (abridged official account, John Murray, London, 1908).

Colquhoun, Major J.A.S., With the Kurram Field Force 1878-9 (W.H. Allen, London, 1881).

Cooper, H., What the Fusiliers Did (reprint, Naval and Military Press, Uckfield, 2003).

Duke, J., Recollections of the Cabul Campaign 1879 and 1880 (W.H. Allen, London, 1883).

Hanna, H.B., The Second Afghan War 1878-79-80; Its Causes, Its Conduct and Its Consequences, 3 vols (Archibald Constable & Co, London, 1904).

Hannah, W.H., Bobs: Kipling's General (Leo Cooper, London, 1972).

Helsham Jones, H., The History and Geography of Afghanistan and the Afghan Campaign of 1838-9 and 1842 (RMAS Staff College, London, 1878).

Hensman, H., The Afghan War, (W.H. Allen, London, 1882).

Jenkins, R., Gladstone (Macmillan, London, 1995).

Le Mesurier, A., Kandahar in 1879 (W.H. Allen, London, 1880).

Male, Reverend A., Scenes Through the Battle Smoke (reprint, Naval and Military Press, Uckfield, 2009).

Maxwell, L., My God Maiwand: Operations of the South Afghanistan Field Force 1878–80 (London, Leo Cooper, 1979).

Moneypenny, W.F., and Buckle, G.E., The Life of Benjamin Disraeli, 2 vols (John Murray, London, 1929).

Morley, The Life of Gladstone, 3 vols (Macmillan, London, 1903).

Mitford, Major R.C.W., *To Caubul with the Cavalry Brigade* (reprint Bhavana Books, New Delhi, 2000).

Rahman, Abdur, *The Life of Abdur Rahman, Amir of Afghanistan* (John Murray, London, 1900).

Ridley, J., *Lord Palmerston* (Constable/Panther, London, 1972).

Roberts, Field Marshall Sir Frederick, *Forty-one Years in India* (Richard Bentley and Son, London, 1898).

Robson, B., *The Road to Kabul* (Spellmount, Staplehurst, 2003).

Shadbolt, S.H., *The Afghan Campaign of 1878–80* 2 vols (Blackwell, London, 1882).

Sykes, Sir P., *Sir Mortimer Durand* (Cassell, London, 1926).

Swinson, A., *North West Frontier: people and events, 1839–1947* (Hutchinson, London, 1967).

Thornton, T.H., *Colonel Sir Robert Sandeman: His Life and Work on our Indian Frontier* (John Murray, London, 1895).

Trousdale, W. (ed), *War in Afghanistan 1879–80; the Personal Diary of Major-General Sir Charles Metcalfe McGregor* (Wayne State University Press, Detroit, 1985).

Trousdale, W. (ed), *The Gordon Creeds in Afghanistan* (BACSA, London, 1984).

Warburton, Colonel Sir Robert, *Eighteen Years in the Khyber, 1879–1898* (reprint, OUP, Oxford, 1970).

Wylly, Colonel H.C., *The Military Memoirs of Lieutenant-General Sir Joseph Thackwell* (John Murray, London, 1908).

Younghusband, G.J., *The Story of the Guides* (Macmillan, London, 1908).

Yorke, E.J., *Battle Story: Maiwand, 1880* (History Press, 2012).

The Third Anglo-Afghan War

Churchill, W., *The Malakand Field Force* (reprint Mandarin, London, 1990).

Colvin, I., *The Life of General Dyer* (William Blackwood, London, 1929).

Draper, A., *The Amritsar Massacre: Twilight of the Raj*, 2nd edn (Buchan and Enright, London, 1985).

General Staff Branch, Army HQ, India, *The Third Afghan War 1919: Official Account* (General Staff Branch, Army HQ, Calcutta, 1926).

Mills, C.P., *A Strange War* (Alan Sutton, Gloucester, 1988).

Molesworth, Lt.-General G.N., *Afghanistan 1919: An Account of Operations in the Third Afghan War* (Asia Publishing House, London, 1962).

Omissi, D., *Air Power and Colonial Control* (MUP, Manchester, 1991).

Robson, B., *Crisis on the Frontier: The Third Afghan War and the Campaign in Waziristan 1919–20* (Spellmount, Staplehurst, 2004).

Smyth, General Sir J., *Milestones: A Memoir* (Sidgwick and Jackson, London, 1979).

The Fourth Afghan Conflict (2001–)

Bishop, P., *3 Para: Afghanistan Summer 2006* (Harper Press, London, 2007).

Fergusson, J., *A Million Bullets: The real story of the British Army in Afghanistan* (Bantam Press, London, 2008).

Giustozzi, A., *Koran, Klashnikov and Laptop – the Neo-Taliban Insurgency in Afghanistan* (Hirst, London, 2007).

Hodes, C. and Sedra, M., *The Search for Security in Post-Taliban Afghanistan* (Institute of Strategic Studies, London, 2007).

General Works

Alder, G.A., *British India's Northern Frontier, 1865–1895* (Longman, London, 1963).

Allen, C., *Soldier Sahibs* (John Murray, London, 2000).

Barthorp, M., *Afghan Wars and the North-West Frontier* (Cassell, London, 1982).

Beckett , I. , *The Victorians at War* (Hambledon, London, 2003).

Callwell, Capt. C.E., *Small Wars: Their Principles and Practice* (HMSO, London, 1899).

Caroe, O., *The Pathans: 550 BC to AD 1957* (Macmillan, London, 1958).

Crowley, Lt.-Colonel, P.T., *Afghanistan: The Three Wars* (Prince of Wales' Royal Regiment, 2002).

David, S., *The Indian Mutiny* (Penguin, London, 2002).

— *Victoria's Wars* (Penguin, London, 2007).

Dupree, L., *A History of Afghanistan* (Princeton University Press, Princeton, 1980).

Edwardes, M., *A History of India* (Thames and Hudson, London, 1967).

— *Playing the Great Game; A Victorian Cold War* (Hamish Hamilton, London, 1975).

Elliott, Major-General J.G., *The Frontier 1839–1947* (Cassell, London, 1968).

Evans, M., *Afghanistan: A New History* (Curzon Press, Richmond, Surrey, 2001).

Conflict in Afghanistan: Studies in Asymmetrical Warfare (Routledge, Abingdon, 2005).

Ferguson, N., *Empire: How Britain Made The Modern World* (Penguin, London, 2004).

Forbes, A., *The Afghan Wars 1839–1842 and 1878–80* (Seely and Co. Ltd, London, 1892).

Fortescue, H.J.W., *History of The British Army*, 6 vols (Macmillan, London, 1915).

Fraser-Tytler, W.K., *Afghanistan: A Study of Political Developments in Central Asia* (OUP, Oxford, 1950).

Fremont-Barnes, G., *The Anglo-Afghan Wars, 1839–1919* (Osprey, Oxford, 2009).

Griffin, M., *Reaping the Whirlwind: the Taliban Movement in Afghanistan* (Pluto Press, London, 2001).

Gwynn, Major-General Sir Charles W., *Imperial Policing* (Macmillan, London, 1934).

Hamilton, A., *Afghanistan* (London, Heinemann, 1906).

Heathcote, T.A., *The Afghan Wars* (Osprey, London, 1980).

— *The Military in British India* (MUP, Manchester, 1995).

Hopkirk, P., *The Great Game: On Secret Service in High Asia* (OUP, Oxford, 2001).

James, L., *Raj: The Making and Unmaking of British India* (Little, Brown & Company, London, 1997).

— *The Rise and Fall of the British Empire* (Abacus, London, 2000).

Ingram, E., *In Defence of British India* (Cassell, London, 1984).

Kitson, F., *Bunch of Fives* (Faber & Faber, London, 1977).

Lamb, C., *The Sewing Circle of Herat: My Afghan Years* (Harper Collins, London, 2002).

Lovett, Major A. and MacMann, Major G.F., *The Armies of India* (Adam and Charles Black, London, 1911).

Loyn, D., *Butcher and Bolt: Two Hundred Years of Foreign Engagement in Afghanistan* (Hutchinson, London, 2008).

MacMunn, Lt.-General Sir George, *Afghanistan: From Darius to Amanullah* (Jarrolds, London, 1929).

Maley, W., *The Afghanistan Wars* (Palgrave, Basingstoke, 2002).

Marston, D. and Malkasign, C. (eds), *Counterinsurgency in Modern Warfare* (Osprey, Oxford, 2008).

Mason, P., *A Matter of Honour* (Jonathan Cape, London, 1974).

Masters, J., *Bugles and a Tiger* (Michael Joseph, London, 1956).

Matinuddin, K., *The Taliban Phenomenon: Afghanistan 1994–1997* (OUP, Oxford, 1999).

Medcalf, J., *Going Global or Going Nowhere: NATO's role in Contemporary International Security* (Peter Lang, Bern, 2008).

Miller, C., *Khyber: The Story of the North West Frontier* (Macdonald and Jane's, London, 1977).

Moreman, T.R., *The Army in India and the Development of Frontier Warfare 1849–1947* (Palgrave, Basingstoke, 1998).

MacMunn, Lt.-General Sir George, *The Lure of the Indus* (Jarrolds, London, 1934).

Nevill, H.L., *Campaigns on the North-West Frontier* (John Murray, London, 1912).

O'Ballance, E., *Afghan Wars: 1839–1992* (Brasseys, London, 1993).

Omissi, D., *The Sepoy and the Raj* (Macmillan, Basingstoke, 1994).

Preston, A. and Dennis, P. (eds), *Swords and Covenants* (Croom Helm, London, 1976).

Pakenham, T., *The Boer War* (Weidenfeld and Nicolson, London, 1979).

Pike, Lt.-General Sir Hew (ed), *From the Front Line: Family Letters and Diaries, 1990 to the Falklands and Afghanistan* (Pen and Sword, Barnsley, 2008).

Roberts, A., *A History of the English Speaking Peoples since 1990* (Weidenfeld and Nicolson, London, 2006).

Smith, General Sir Rupert, *The Utility of Force* (Penguin Books, London, 2005).

Smith, V., *Oxford History of India* (OUP, Oxford, 1981).

Spear, P., *The Oxford History of India* (OUP, Oxford, 1958).

Spiers, E.M., *The Late Victorian Army, 1868–1902* (MUP, Manchester, 1992).

Strachan, H., *The Politics of the British Army* (OUP, Oxford, 1997).

— *From Waterloo to Balaclava: Tactics, Technology and the British Army, 1815–54* (CUP, Cambridge, 1985).

Stewart, Rory, *The Places In Between* (Picador, London, 2004).

Stokes, E., *A Peasant Armed* (Clarendon Press, Oxford, 1986).

Tanner, S.I., *Afghanistan: A Military History from Alexander the Great to the Fall of the Taliban* (Da Capo Press, New York, 2002).

Thompson, R., *Defeating Communist Insurgency* (Chatto and Windus, London, 1966).

Trotter, L.J., *Rulers of India* (Clarendon Press, Oxford, 1893).

Warburton, Colonel Sir R., *Eighteen Years in the Khyber 1879–1898* (reprint, OUP, Lahore, 1970).

Yapp, M.E., *British Strategies in India: Britain, Iran and Afghanistan, 1798–1850* (Clarendon Press, Oxford, 1980).

Yorke, E.J., *Zulu: The Battle for Rorke's Drift* (Tempus, Stroud, 2005).
Younghusband, G.J., *Indian Frontier Warfare* (Kegan Paul, Trench Trubner & Co, London, 1898).

Primary/Manuscript Sources

Records

1. **Public Record Office, Kew (PRO) (now National Archives)**
   PRO 30.12. Ellenborough Papers
   FO 539: Private and Confidential Correspondence relating to Persia and Afghanistan

2. **British Library, Oriental and India Office Collections, London (BL)**
   Roos – Keppel Papers
   MSS Eur. E218: Lytton Papers
   516: Letters from Secretary of State
   517: Letters from England
   518: Letters dispatched
   519: Correspondence in India
   521: Miscellaneous papers on Afghanistan

3. **National Army Museum, Chelsea, London (NAM)**
   (i) Roberts Papers
       7101-23-101-1: Correspondence with India and England
       7101-23-147: Miscellaneous letters and telegrams
       7101-23-148: Confidential Reports on officers of the Kurram Force
       7101-24-92-18: Diary for 1878
       7101-24-92-19: Diary for 1879
       781255 MFN Nicholls (Sir Jasper) Papers

   (ii) Miscellaneous diaries / papers – especially:
       Backhouse Papers
       Gaisford Papers
       Shelton Court Martial Notes
       Mayne Journal/Diary

4. **Royal Military Academy Sandhurst (RMAS)**
   Hogg Papers

5. Reading University Library Collection (RULC)
   Miscellaneous papers (compiled by Dr G. Alder – Afghanistan/India 1800–1845)

6. Imperial War Museum, Lambeth, London (IWM)
   Brearly Papers
   Gill War Diary
   Price letters
   Holter papers

7. The Gurkha Museum, Winchester, Hants
   Afghan Campaign: Gurkha regimental War Diaries and Miscellaneous items

8. The Green Howards Regimental Museum, Richmond, Yorkshire (GHM)
   Green Howards Regiment (1st Yorks) War Diaries 1919

9. Essex Regimental Museum, Chelmsford, Essex (ERM)
   Miscellaneous correspondence, First Anglo-Afghan War (44th Foot)

10. The Rifles' Museum Archives, Salisbury, Wiltshire (RMA)
    Naylor Account
    Ready Account
    Bray Account
    Farrell Account
    Griffiths Account
    Mainwaring Account

The Royal Archives, Windsor Castle (RA), by kind permission of HM the Queen
Queen Victoria's Journal (QVA) 1839–42, 1878–80

Unpublished Theses

Chavda, V.K., 'India, Britain and Russia, 1838–78' (PhD, Leeds 1962).

Jeffery, K., 'The Military Defence of the British Empire, 1918–22' (PhD, Cambridge, 1978).

Kapadia, E.R., 'The Diplomatic Career of Sir Claude Wade' (MA, SOAS).

Majumdar, A., 'Lord Minto's Administration in India (1807–13) with special reference to his Foreign Policy' (D.Phil., Oxford, 1962–3).

Stanwood, F.J., 'Britain in Central Asia 1917–19, A Study of the Empire's Response to Nationalism, Bolshevism and Idealism' (PhD, University of California, 1971)

Yorke ,E.J., 'A Crisis of Colonial Control: War and Authority in Northern Rhodesia 1914-18' (PhD, University of Cambridge, 1984).

Key Articles

Alder, G.J., 'The "Garbled" Blue Books of 1839 – Myth or Reality?', *Historical Journal*, 15, 2 (1972).

Biddulph, S., 'Afghanistan and the Future of Warfare: Implications for Army and Defence Policy', US Army War College Paper, November 2002.

Dupree, L., 'The First Anglo Afghan War and the British Retreat of 1842: The Functions of History and Folklore, *East and West*, 26, Nos. 3–4, Sept/Dec, 1976.

Hawkins, S.R., 'What not to Learn from Afghanistan', *Parameters*, Summer, 2002.

Giustozzi, Dr A., 'Re-building the Afghan Army', Crisis States Programme, Development Research Centre, LSE, April 2004.

— 'Respectable Warlords?: The Politics of State Building in Post Taliban Afghanistan', Crisis State Programme, Development Research Centre, LSE, 2004.

Jalali, A.A., 'Afghanistan: Regaining Momentum', *Parameters*, Winter, 2007–8.

Maloney, S.M., 'Afghanistan: From Here to Eternity?', *Parameters*, 30, 4, No.1, Spring, 2004.

— 'Afghanistan Four Years On: An Assessment', *Parameters*, 30, No. 3, Autumn, 2005.

McNerney, M.J., 'Stabilisation and Reconstruction in Afghanistan: Are PRT's a Model or a Muddle?', *Parameters*, 25, No. 4, Winter, 2005–6.

Sedra, M., 'New Beginning or Return to Arms?: The Disarmament, Demobilisation and Reintegration Process in Afghanistan'.

— Workshop Paper, 'State Reconstruction and International Engagement in Afghanistan', Bonn, May–June, 2003.

Newspapers and Journals

British Army Review
Daily Mail (2005)

Daily Telegraph (2001–9)
Foreign Affairs (2001–9)
International Affairs (2001–9)
Journal of the Society for Army Historical Research (JSAHR) (various dates)
Parameters (2001–9)
Punch (1840–2, 1878–81)
Sunday Times (2001–9)
Royal Magazine
Royal United Services Journal (RUSJ)
Small Wars and Insurgencies
Soldiers of the Queen: The Journal of the Victorian Military Society (various dates)
The Economist (2001–9)
The Graphic (1878–81)
The Guardian (2001–9)
The Illustrated London News (1840–2, 1878–81, 1919)
The Independent (2001–9)
The Journal of Imperial and Commonwealth History
The Times (principally 1839–42, 1878–81, 1919, 2001–9)

Index